GRAMMAR

FOR THE WELL-TRAINED MIND

RED WORKBOOK

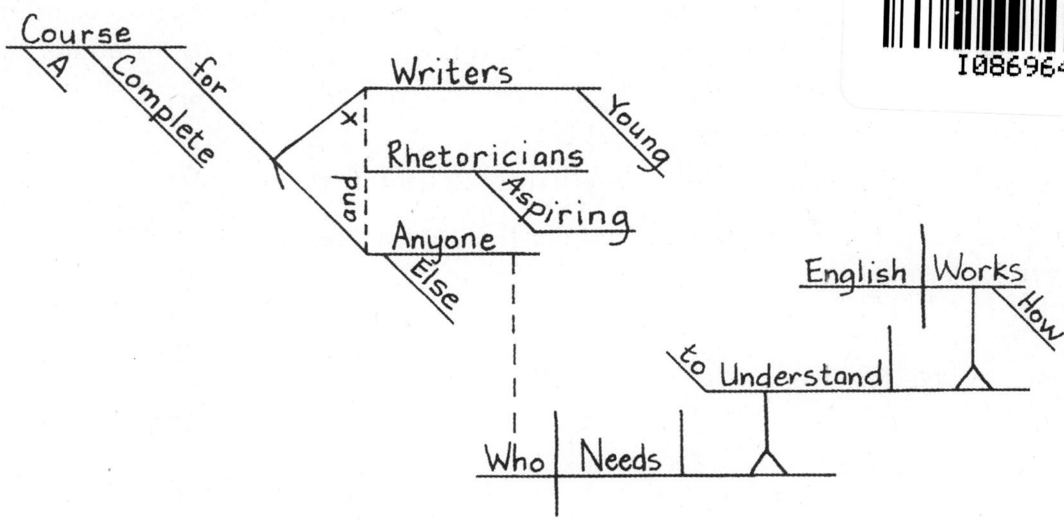

By Susan Wise Bauer

with Amanda Saxon Dean and Audrey Anderson,

Diagrams by Patty Rebne

For a list of corrections, please visit **www.welltrainedmind.com/corrections**.

Table of Contents

FOREWORD

Welcome to *Grammar for the Well-Trained Mind*!

This innovative grammar program will take you from basic definitions ("A noun is the name of a person, place, thing, or idea") all the way through detailed analysis of complex sentence structure. Once you complete it, you'll have all the skills needed for the study of advanced rhetoric—persuasive speech and sophisticated writing.

WHAT MAKES UP THE FULL PROGRAM

Grammar for the Well-Trained Mind is a four-year program. Once you've finished it, you will have a thorough grasp of the English language. No further grammar studies will be necessary.

The nonconsumable *Core Instructor Text* is used for each of the four years of the program. It contains scripted dialogue for the instructor, all rules and examples, and teaching notes that thoroughly explain ambiguities and difficulties.

There are four *Workbooks* with accompanying *Keys*. Each consumable workbook provides one full year of exercises and assignments. Each corresponding key gives complete, thoroughly explained answers. You should aim to complete one workbook during each of the four years of study.

All rules and definitions, with accompanying examples, have been assembled into a handy reference book, *The Grammar Guidebook. The Diagramming Dictionary* organizes every diagramming skill covered in *Grammar for the Well-Trained Mind* into categories for easy reference -- from basic subject/predicate layout through advanced sentence structure and analysis. Beautifully designed diagrams and color-coded examples walk you through how to place each and every part of the English sentence on the traditional diagramming framework. These handbooks will serve you for all four years of study—and will continue to be useful as you move through advanced high school writing, into college composition, and beyond.

HOW THE PROGRAM WORKS

Language learning has three elements.

First: You have to understand and memorize rules. We call this "prescriptive learning"—grasping the explicit principles that govern the English language and committing them to memory. *Grammar for the Well-Trained Mind* presents, explains, and drills all of the essential rules of the English language. Each year, you will review and repeat these rules.

Second: You need examples of every rule and principle ("descriptive learning"). Without examples, rules remain abstract. When you memorize the rule "Subjunctive verbs express situations that are unreal, wished for, or uncertain," you also need to memorize the example "I would not say such things if I were you!" Each year, you will review and repeat the same examples to illustrate each rule.

Third: You need *practice*. Although the four workbooks repeat the same rules and examples, each contains a completely new set of exercises and writing assignments, along with a *Key* providing complete answers.

The combination of *repetition* (the same rules and examples each year) and *innovation* (brand-new practice materials in every workbook) will lead you to complete mastery of the English language.

HOW TO USE GRAMMAR FOR THE WELL-TRAINED MIND

When you first use the program, begin with the *Core Instructor Text* and any one of the *Workbooks* with its accompanying *Key* (*Purple*, *Red*, *Blue* or *Yellow*). Keep *The Grammar Guidebook* and *The Diagramming Dictionary* on hand for reference.

During this first year, you won't necessarily grasp every principle thoroughly. Simply go through the dialogue with your instructor, complete the exercises, check the answers, and discuss any mistakes.

You may need more than one year to complete your first *Workbook*; the exercises increase in complexity and difficulty from Week 20 on. That's absolutely fine. Feel free to take as much time as necessary to finish this workbook.

When your first *Workbook* is completed, you and your instructor will go back to the beginning of the *Core Instructor Text* and start over, this time using a *Workbook/Key* combination of a different color. You'll go over the same dialogue, the same rules, and the same examples—with an entirely fresh set of exercises. This combination of repeated information along with new and challenging exercises will truly begin to build your competence in the English language.

Follow this same procedure for the third and fourth years of study, using workbooks of the remaining two colors, along with their matching keys.

Regular reviews are built into the program. Every three weeks, take some extra time to do the exercises reviewing what was covered in the three weeks before. After Week 27, the reviews double in scope: twelve exercises review the material all the way back to the beginning of the course. These reviews, beginning with Review 9, become one week's work each. During review weeks, try to do three exercises per day, and then go back and review the rules and principles of any exercise in which you miss two or more sentences/examples.

WHICH WORKBOOK?

Because each workbook makes use of the same rules and examples, you may use any one of the four workbooks during your first year in the program. It is highly recommended, however, that you then go back and finish the earlier workbooks as well. The program is designed to take *at least* four years, no matter where you begin.

IMPORTANT PRINCIPLES OF LEARNING

As you study, keep the following in mind.

- Language is a rich, complicated tapestry. It is occasionally logical, and sometimes irrational. Mastering its complexities takes time and patience. Don't expect to master—or even completely understand—every principle the first time through. Repetition and practice will eventually bring clarity. Be diligent—don't abandon the curriculum because of frustration! But accept occasional confusion as a natural part of learning. If you don't understand subjunctives the first time through, for example, accept it, move on, and then repeat the following year. Eventually, the concepts will come into focus.
- Always ask for help if you need it. This isn't a test. It's a learning process.
- From Week 19 (halfway through the course) on, you are encouraged to read sentences out loud. Reading out loud is an important part of evaluating your own writing. Follow the directions—don't ignore them and read silently.
- Take as long as you need to finish each lesson. As noted above, it's perfectly acceptable to take more than one year to finish a workbook (particularly the first time through). The earlier lessons are shorter and simpler; they increase in both complexity and length as the book goes on. But especially in the later lessons, don't worry if you need to divide a lesson over two days, or take more than one week to complete a week's worth of lessons. In subsequent years, you'll go much more quickly through the earlier lessons, giving you time to stop and concentrate on areas of challenge later on.

ABOUT DIAGRAMMING

Grammar for the Well-Trained Mind uses diagramming exercises throughout.

Diagramming is a learning process. Think of the diagrams as experimental projects, not tests. Attempt the diagram, look at the answer, and then try to figure out why any differences exist. Expect these assignments—particularly in the second half of the book—to be challenging. Ask for help when you need it. Always diagram with a pencil (or on a whiteboard or blackboard), and expect to erase and redo constantly.

Also remember that diagramming is not an exact science! If you can explain clearly why you've made a particular choice, the diagram might be correct even if the key differs. To quote a 1914 grammar text: "Many constructions are peculiar, idiomatic, and do not lend themselves readily to any arrangement of lines" (Alma Blount and Clark S. Northup, *An English Grammar for Use in High and Normal Schools and in Colleges*).

WEEK 1

Introduction to Nouns and Adjectives

— LESSON 1 —

Introduction to Nouns
Concrete and Abstract Nouns

A noun names a person, place, thing, or idea.
Concrete nouns can be observed with our senses. Abstract nouns cannot.

Exercise 1A: Abstract and Concrete Nouns

Decide whether the underlined nouns are abstract or concrete. Above each noun, write *A* for abstract or *C* for concrete. If you have difficulty, ask yourself: Can this noun be touched or seen, or experienced with another one of the senses? If so, it is a concrete noun. If not, it is abstract.

Our adventure began with a tattered map.

Seeing the chocolates, the little girl's face lit up with delight.

The orchestra will be performing my favorite symphony.

My curiosity led me to peek at the gift before my birthday.

Charlotte's favorite book is a mystery about a lost princess.

Distracted by the loud noise, Bradley forgot to finish combing his hair.

Mrs. Kim was filled with pride as her daughter sang her solo.

A shadow passed by the window and gave us all a fright.

The baby let out what was clearly a cry of exhaustion.

Exercise 1B: Abstract Nouns

Each row contains two abstract nouns and one concrete noun. Find the concrete noun and cross it out.

amazement	wonder	fireworks
notebook	neatness	ideas
discovery	interest	gold
danger	cliff	peril
conceit	mirror	arrogance
stomach	appetite	satiety

— LESSON 2 —

Introduction to Adjectives
Descriptive Adjectives, Abstract Nouns
Formation of Abstract Nouns from Descriptive Adjectives

An adjective modifies a noun or pronoun.
Adjectives tell what kind, which one, how many, and whose.
Descriptive adjectives tell what kind.
A descriptive adjective becomes an abstract noun when you add -*ness* to it.

cheerful	cheerfulness
grumpy	grumpiness

Exercise 2A: Descriptive Adjectives, Concrete Nouns, and Abstract Nouns

Decide whether the underlined words are concrete nouns, abstract nouns, or descriptive adjectives. Above each, write *DA* for descriptive adjective, *CN* for concrete noun, or *AN* for abstract noun.

The sentences below were taken from *Alice's Adventures in Wonderland*, by Lewis Carroll. Some have been slightly adapted.

By this time she had found her way into a tidy little room with a table in the window.

Luckily for Alice, the little magic bottle had now had its full effect.

Alice noticed that the pebbles were all turning into little cakes as they lay on the floor,

and a bright idea came into her head.

An enormous puppy was looking down at her with large round eyes.

She had just succeeded in curving her neck down into a graceful zigzag, when a sharp hiss made her draw back in a hurry.

The Fish-Footman began by producing from under his arm a great letter, nearly as large as himself.

Exercise 2B: Turning Descriptive Adjectives into Abstract Nouns

Change each descriptive adjective to an abstract noun by adding the suffix *-ness*. Write the abstract noun in the blank beside the descriptive adjective. Remember this rule: When you add the suffix *-ness* to a word ending in *-y*, the *-y* changes to *-i*. (For example, *grumpy* becomes *grumpiness*.)

smart ______________________________

fretful ______________________________

friendly ______________________________

marvelous ______________________________

vicious ______________________________

merry ______________________________

rich ______________________________

decisive ______________________________

Exercise 2C: Color Names

Underline all the color words in the following paragraph. Then write *A* for adjective or *N* for noun above each underlined color word. If you are not sure, ask yourself, "[Color name] *what?*" If you can answer that question, you have found a noun that the color describes. That means the color is an adjective.

Keiko closed her eyes and considered different shades of green. She wanted the green grass in her painting to look like the golden sunlight was shining down on it through the trees. She chose two green paints to mix together and began to paint. Green was her favorite color, she thought—or was it red? Then again, she loved the purple flowers she'd painted below one of the trees. And the blue sky had been fun to do as well. She even liked brown or gray when one of those was the right color for the job. "Actually," she said to herself, "there isn't a single color I don't like!"

— LESSON 3 —

Common and Proper Nouns
Capitalization and Punctuation of Proper Nouns

A common noun is a name common to many persons, places, things, or ideas.
A proper noun is the special, particular name for a person, place, thing, or idea.
Proper nouns always begin with capital letters.

Capitalization Rules

1. Capitalize the proper names of persons, places, things, and animals.

boy	Peter
store	Baskin-Robbins
book	*Little Women*
horse	Black Beauty

2. Capitalize the names of holidays.

Memorial Day
Christmas
Independence Day
Day of the Dead

3. Capitalize the names of deities.

Minerva (ancient Rome)
Hwanin (ancient Korea)
God (Christianity and Judaism)
Allah (Islam)
Gitche Manitou or Great Spirit (Native American—Algonquin)

4. Capitalize the days of the week and the months of the year, but not the seasons.

Monday	January	winter
Tuesday	April	spring
Friday	August	summer
Sunday	October	fall

5. Capitalize the first, last, and other important words in titles of books, magazines, newspapers, movies, television series, stories, poems, and songs.

book	*Alice's Adventures in Wonderland*
magazine	*National Geographic*
newspaper	*The Chicago Tribune*
movie	*A River Runs Through It*
television series	*The Waltons*
television show	"The Chicken Thief"
story	"The Visit of the Magi"
poem	"The Night Before Christmas"
song	"Joy to the World"
chapter in a book	"The End of the Story"

6. Capitalize and italicize the names of ships, trains, and planes.

ship	*Titanic*
train	*The Orient Express*
plane	*The Spirit of St. Louis*

Exercise 3A: Capitalizing Proper Nouns

Write a proper noun for each of the following common nouns. Don't forget to capitalize all of the important words of the proper noun. Underline the name of the magazine you choose, to show that it should be in italics if it were typed. Use quotation marks around the title of the song you choose.

Common Noun	**Proper Noun**
singer	______________________________
restaurant	______________________________
country	______________________________
park	______________________________
magazine	______________________________
song	______________________________

Exercise 3B: Proper Names and Titles

On your own paper, rewrite the following sentences properly. Capitalize and punctuate all names and titles correctly. If you are using a word processing program, italicize where needed; if you are writing by hand, underline in order to show italics.

The song the star-spangled banner is the national anthem for the united states.

himno nacional mexicano is thought by many to be one of the most beautiful national anthems.

germany sank the lusitania in may 1915.

michael and phyllis recited william makepeace thackeray's poem a tragic story.

In the book charlotte's web, wilbur is a pig who was born in the spring.

keith's favorite show was star trek; he especially loved the episode the trouble with tribbles

Exercise 3C: Proofreading for Proper Nouns

In the following sentences, indicate which proper nouns should be capitalized by underlining the first letter of the noun three times. This is the proper proofreading mark for *capitalize*. The first noun is done for you.

justinian was an emperor in byzantium, and his wife, theodora, was politically helpful to him.

The cathedral in constantinople known as the hagia sophia was built while justinian ruled.

justinian's general, belisarius, successfully conquered the barbarians living in the northern part of africa and proceeded into italy to retake rome from the ostrogoths.

The court historian, procopius, wrote a book called *the secret history*, which portrayed justinian in a very negative light.

— LESSON 4 —

Proper Adjectives
Compound Adjectives (Adjective-Noun Combinations)

1. Capitalize the proper names of persons, places, things, and animals.
2. Capitalize the names of holidays.
3. Capitalize the names of deities.
4. Capitalize the days of the week and the months of the year, but not the seasons.
5. Capitalize the first, last, and other important words in titles of books, magazines, newspapers, movies, television series, stories, poems, and songs.
6. Capitalize and italicize the names of ships, trains, and planes.

A proper adjective is formed from a proper name. Proper adjectives are capitalized.

	Proper Noun	Proper Adjective
Person	Aristotle	the Aristotelian philosophy
Place	Spain	a Spanish city
Holiday	Valentine's Day	some Valentine candy
Month	March	March madness

Shakespeare wrote a number of sonnets.
I was reading some Shakespearean sonnets yesterday.

Mars is the fourth planet from the sun.
The Martian atmosphere is mostly carbon dioxide.

On Monday, I felt a little down.
I had the Monday blues.

The English enjoy a good cup of tea and a muffin.
Gerald enjoys a good English muffin.

The German-speaking tourists were lost in Central Park.
The archaeologist unearthed some pre-Columbian remains.

Words that are not usually capitalized remain lowercase even when they are attached to a proper adjective.

A compound adjective combines two words into a single adjective with a single meaning.

When the mine collapsed, it sent a plume of dust sky high.
I just had a thirty-minute study session.

N ADJ
sky high

ADJ N
thirty minute

N ADJ
user friendly

ADJ N
high speed

The sky-high plume of dust could be seen for miles.
My study session was thirty minutes.

Those directions are not user friendly!
I prefer user-friendly directions.

The connection was high speed.
He needed a high-speed connection.

Exercise 4A: Forming Proper Adjectives from Proper Nouns

Form adjectives from the following proper nouns. (Some will change form and others will not.) Write each adjective into the correct blank below. If you are not familiar with the proper nouns, you may look them up online at Encyclopaedia Britannica, Wikipedia, or some other source (this will help you complete the sentences as well). This exercise might challenge your general knowledge! (But you can always ask your instructor for help.)

Newton	Kentucky	Korea	China	Boston
June	America	Georgia	Germany	Monday
Gregory	Easter	Sherlock Holmes		

My favorite ______________________ dish is sauerbraten, though nothing beats streuselkuchen when it comes to desserts!

The ______________________ New Year begins sometime in January or February of the ______________________ calendar year.

Thoroughbred horses race each May in Louisville at the ________________ Derby.

The largest aquarium in the Western Hemisphere is the ______________________ Aquarium, located near the World of Coca-Cola in Atlanta.

Nina will go far as a detective, with her ______________________ deductive and observational skills.

______________________ calligraphy had long used characters from China's writing system, but in the twentieth century calligraphers began using the *hangul* alphabet in response to nationalist feelings among the people.

Computer programmers will sometimes hide special features or messages in their work; these little ______________________ eggs can be fun to find.

They say that ______________________ brides are the most common, but my wedding was in December.

It's nice to have a long weekend, but a ______________________ holiday always throws me off for the rest of the week—I can't remember which day it is!

Non-______________________ fluids have many interesting properties; for example, it's possible to run on top of oobleck!

The ______________________ Massacre, in which five colonists were killed by the British, was a key event leading to the ______________________ Revolution.

Exercise 4B: Capitalization of Proper Adjectives

In the following sentences:

- Correct each lowercase letter that should be capitalized by underlining it three times.
- Then, circle each proper adjective.
- Finally, put a check mark above each proper adjective that has not changed its form from the proper noun.

rube goldberg machines, which involve complicated ways of completing simple tasks, were named for an american cartoonist and inventor.

An associated press article by edward van winkle jones in 1950 marked the first mention of mysterious disappearances in the bermuda triangle.

The pythagorean theorem is only true for euclidean geometry.

thomas jefferson, who was a philosopher, a musician, and an architect in addition to being a united states president, is an example of a renaissance man.

The first olympic games in modern times were held in 1896 in the greek city of athens.

In the southeastern asian kingdom of ayutthaya, the king trailokanat died; his two sons, ramathibodi II and boromarachathirat III, inherited his crown and divided the siamese territories between them.

Exercise 4C: Hyphenating Attributive Compound Adjectives

Hyphens prevent misunderstanding! Explain to your instructor the differences between each pair of phrases. The first is done for you. If you're confused, ask your instructor for help.

the ten-gallon containers of soap *are multiple containers that each hold ten gallons*
the ten gallon containers of soap *are ten containers that each hold one gallon*

a private-eye company
a private eye company

an assisted-living facility
an assisted living facility

the well-trained mind
the well trained mind

the second-place runner
the second place runner

WEEK 2

Introduction to Personal Pronouns and Verbs

— LESSON 5 —

Noun Gender
Introduction to Personal Pronouns

Exercise 5A: Introduction to Noun Gender

How well do you know your animals? Fill in the blanks with the correct name (and don't worry too much if you don't know the answers . . . this is mostly for fun).

Animal	Male	Female	Baby	Group of Animals
leopard	______	______	______	leap OR prowl of leopards
kangaroo	buck/boomer/jack	______	______	______ OR ______
donkey	jack	______	______	herd OR drove of donkeys
alligator	bull	______	______	______
hamster	______	doe	______	______
hedgehog	boar	______	______	______
turkey	______	______	______	rafter of turkeys
jellyfish	______	______	planula	______ OR ______
squid	______	______	chick	______

Nouns have gender.
Nouns can be masculine, feminine, or neuter.
We use *neuter* for nouns that have no gender, and for nouns whose gender is unknown.

Subha Datta set off for the forest, intending to come back the same evening. He began to cut down a tree, but he suddenly had a feeling that he was no longer alone. As it crashed to the ground, he looked up and saw a beautiful girl dancing around and around in a little clearing nearby. Subha Datta was astonished, and let the axe fall. The noise startled the dancer, and she stood still.

Subha Datta thought he was dreaming.

Although she did not yet know it, the fairy had not convinced Subha Datta.

A pronoun takes the place of a noun.
The antecedent is the noun that is replaced by the pronoun.
Personal pronouns replace specific nouns.

I	we
you	you (plural)
he, she, it	they

Exercise 5B: Nouns and Pronouns

Write the correct pronoun above the underlined word(s). The first one is done for you.

James Watson and Francis Crick discovered the structure of DNA in 1953. James Watson and Francis Crick (They) built on the work of Rosalind Franklin.

Rosalind Franklin had done work on X-ray images of DNA. Rosalind Franklin might have received Nobel Prizes for her work later on, but Rosalind Franklin died at the age of 37.

Scientists all over the world worked on the Human Genome Project. The Human Genome Project was an effort to determine what every single gene in the human body does.

When scientists mapped all the genes in the human body, scientists declared the Human Genome Project complete in 2003.

Omar told his mother, "Mother can get the ingredients ready, and Omar can help mix them together!"

As soon as Ezra arrived home, Ezra called out with excitement, "Ezra and his family won the competition!"

The teacher pulled Roxanne and Anita aside after class. "Roxanne and Anita are going to represent our class at the assembly," the teacher told them.

Exercise 5C: Replacing Nouns with Pronouns

Does the passage below sound awkward? It should, because it's not what the author Heather Vogel Frederick wrote in her novel *The Voyage of Patience Goodspeed*. Cross out the proper nouns (and any accompanying adjectives or modifying words such as *the*) that can be replaced by pronouns, and write the appropriate pronoun from the list at the beginning of this lesson over each crossed-out noun.

The narrator is Patience Goodspeed. The story is told from her viewpoint, in the first person—which means she refers to herself with the pronoun *I* when she's acting alone, and *we* when she's in a group with others.

Finally, the day came when Patience Goodspeed and Papa and Tad were packed and ready. Patience Goodspeed and Papa and Tad made the rounds of friends and neighbors to say our farewells, Papa accepting their wishes of "greasy luck" — our Nantucket way of bidding whale-men a profitable voyage, with many barrels of oil — with all the dignity of a departing monarch. Which in a sense Papa was, as were all whaling captains on the tiny kingdom that was our island...

On the evening prior to our departure, Papa took his leave in order to make the final arrangements aboard the *Morning Star.* After Papa left, Patience Goodspeed tossed and turned all night, my thoughts a jumble. Oh, why didn't Patience Goodspeed have the courage to defy Papa! But what was the use? Even if Patience Goodspeed were to run away and hide, Papa would find me. And besides, my little brother needed me. It was me my little brother had looked to since Mama's death, not Papa, who was still a stranger to him. Patience Goodspeed couldn't desert Tad now.

Martha awoke us at dawn, and Tad and Patience Goodspeed tumbled groggily out of bed.

"Come along now, Tad," Martha said, wrestling my sleepy and protesting brother into the small ell off the kitchen. "Won't do for the captain's son to step aboard looking like an orphan." Tad emerged a few minutes later, unnaturally clean.

Exercise 5D: Pronouns and Antecedents

Circle the personal pronouns in the following sentences, and draw an arrow from each pronoun to its antecedent. If the noun and pronoun are masculine, write *m* in the margin. If they are feminine, write *f*; if neuter, write *n*. Look carefully: Some sentences may have more than one personal pronoun, and some personal pronouns may share an antecedent!

The sentences below were taken from C. S. Lewis's *The Voyage of the Dawn Treader*. Some have been adapted or condensed. The first one is done for you.

Eustace made the following diary entry: "*September 3*. The first day for ages when (I) have been able to write." m

If Caspian had been as experienced then as he became later on in this voyage he would not have made this suggestion; but at the moment it seemed an excellent one.

Eustace was surprised at the size of his own tears as they splashed on to the treasure in front of him.

"Please, Aslan," said Lucy, "what do you call *soon*?" "I call all times soon," said Aslan; and instantly he was vanished away and Lucy was alone with the Magician.

The Duffers are visible now. But they are probably all asleep still; they always take a rest in the middle of the day.

Eustace now did the first brave thing he had ever done.

"How beautifully clear the water is!" said Lucy, as she leaned over the port side early in the afternoon of the second day. And it was.

— LESSON 6 —

Review Definitions
Introduction to Verbs
Action Verbs, State-of-Being Verbs
Parts of Speech

A noun names a person, place, thing, or idea.
A common noun is a name common to many persons, places, things, or ideas.
Concrete nouns can be observed with our senses. Abstract nouns cannot.
An adjective modifies a noun or pronoun.
Adjectives tell what kind, which one, how many, and whose.
Descriptive adjectives tell what kind.
A descriptive adjective becomes an abstract noun when you add *-ness* to it.

A verb shows an action, shows a state of being, links two words together, or helps another verb.

Part of speech is a term that explains what a word does.

State-of-Being Verbs

am	were
is	be
are	being
was	been

Exercise 6A: Identifying Verbs

Mark each underlined verb *A* for action verb or *B* for state-of-being verb.

The submarine, having accomplished her work, backs off to a safe distance, explodes these torpedoes by means of a galvanic battery, and up goes the enemy, in more pieces than one can well count. If a vessel under sail or steam is to be assaulted, the submarine dives down and lies hidden right under the track of her foe; then at the exact moment loosens a torpedo furnished with a percussion apparatus; the enemy strikes this, explodes it, and up she goes past all hope of redemption.

"We had quite a sad accident yesterday," he wrote in a letter home. "A 'machine' we had here and which carried eight or ten men, by some mismanagement filled with water and sank, drowning five men, one belonging to our vessel, and the others to the *Chicora*. They were all volunteers for the expedition and fine men too, the best we had."

"I am part owner of the torpedo boat the *Hunley*," he began, and "have been interested in building this description of boat since the beginning of the war, and furnished the means entirely of building the predecessor of this boat, which was lost in an attempt to blow up a Federal vessel off Fort Morgan in Mobile Harbor. I feel therefore a deep interest in its success."

The incoming rounds brought with them a new sense of urgency. With the city now under the very guns of the Union Army, something had to be done to drive the invaders away. The city's forts and batteries, while plentiful and powerful, were necessarily restricted to defensive action. Charleston's small flotilla of ironclads and warships was not the answer either, for they were unable to effectively take the offensive against the Federal warships steaming outside the bar. The situation facing Charleston was growing increasingly more desperate, and Battery Wagner on Morris Island was under daily threat of collapse. Thus the hopes of many now rested on the submarine *Hunley*.

Many in the Victorian Age considered inventions such as submarine boats and underwater mines to be "infernal machines," inhuman in their method of attack. If they were treated as war criminals or on the order of spies, they could be hung for their service. In an attempt to legitimize their endeavor—at least in the eyes of the Federals—Hunley placed an order with Charleston's quartermaster on August 21 for "nine grey jackets, three to be trimmed in gold braid." Feeling the need to justify his request, he added that "the men for whom they are ordered are on special secret service and that it is necessary that they be clothed in the Confederate Army uniform."

—From Mark K. Ragan, *Submarine Warfare in the Civil War*

Exercise 6B: Choosing Verbs

Provide an appropriate action and state-of-being verb for each of the following nouns or pronouns. The first one is done for you.

	State-of-Being	Action
Example: The camel	was (or is)	drank
A printer	______	______
The professors	______	______
Puppies	______	______
We	______	______
The flight	______	______
The grass	______	______
Friends	______	______
They	______	______
Robert Louis Stevenson	______	______

Exercise 6C: Using Vivid Verbs

Good writers use descriptive and vivid verbs. First underline the action verbs in the following sentences. Then rewrite a different, vivid verb in the space provided. The first one is done for you. You may use a thesaurus if necessary.

Example: The sudden noise scared the little girl.	startled
I looked at the man across the restaurant, trying to determine whether I knew him.	______
When presented with the evidence, Lars finally said that he was the one who had stolen the money.	______
The thunder sounded from across the lake.	______
As she awaited the announcement of her scores, the figure skater shook with nervous energy.	______
Alexis saw a flaw in the plan.	______

The old woman walked down the street, carrying several heavy bags. ______________________

Marcus made a new system to increase the group's efficiency. ______________________

After running the race, Oscar wanted some water. ______________________

I ran to the finish line. ______________________

— LESSON 7 —

Helping Verbs

Part of speech is a term that explains what a word does.

Exercise 7A: Introduction to Helping Verbs

In each sentence below, underline the action verb once. Seven of the sentences also include helping verbs; underline each helping verb twice.

These sentences are from O. Henry's short story "After Twenty Years." Some have been slightly adapted or condensed.

The policeman on the beat moved up the avenue impressively.

Chilly gusts of wind with a taste of rain in them had well nigh depeopled the streets.

Now and then you might see the lights of a cigar store or of an all-night lunch counter.

The light showed a pale, square-jawed face with keen eyes, and a little white scar near his right eyebrow.

Twenty years ago to-night, I dined here at "Big Joe" Brady's with Jimmy Wells, my best chum, and the finest chap in the world.

He and I were raised here in New York, just like two brothers, together.

The policeman twirled his club and took a step or two.

Are you going to call time on him sharp?

I will give him half an hour at least.

The wind had risen from its uncertain puffs into a steady blow.

You may read it here at the window.

Helping Verbs

am, is, are, was, were
be, being, been
have, has, had
do, does, did
shall, will, should, would, may, might, must
can, could

Exercise 7B: Providing Missing Helping Verbs

Fill in each blank with a helping verb. Sometimes, more than one helping verb might be appropriate.

This excerpt is adapted from Washington Irving's "Rip Van Winkle."

Whoever ________________ made a voyage up the Hudson ________________ remember the Kaatskill Mountains. They are a dismembered branch of the great Appalachian family, and ______________ seen away to the west of the river, swelling up to a noble height and lording it over the surrounding country. Every change of season, every change of weather, indeed, every hour of the day produces some change in the magical hues and shapes of these mountains, and they ______________ regarded by all the good wives, far and near, as perfect barometers. When the weather is fair and settled, they ___________ clothed in blue and purple, and print their bold outlines on the clear evening sky; but, sometimes, when the rest of the landscape is cloudless, they ________________ gather a hood of gray vapors about their summits, which, in the last rays of the setting sun, ______________ glow and light up like a crown of glory.

At the foot of these fairy mountains, the voyager ________________ ______________ described the light smoke curling up from a village, whose shingle roofs gleam among the trees, just where the blue tints of the upland melt away into the fresh green of the nearer landscape. It is a little village of great antiquity, having ________________ founded by some of the Dutch colonists in the early times of the province.

Certain it is that Rip Van Winkle was a great favorite among all the good wives of the village. The children of the village, too, _______________ shout with joy whenever he approached. Not a dog _______________ bark at him throughout the neighborhood.

The great error in Rip's composition was an insuperable aversion to all kinds of profitable labor. It ___________ not be from the want of assiduity or perseverance, for he ___________ sit on a wet rock, with a rod as long and heavy as a Tartar's lance, and fish all day without a murmur, even though he ___________ not be encouraged by a single nibble. He ___________ never refuse to assist a neighbor even in the roughest toil. But as to doing family duty and keeping his farm in order, he found it impossible.

In fact, he declared it was of no use to work on his farm; it was the most pestilent little piece of ground in the whole country; everything about it went wrong, and ____________ go wrong, in spite of him. His fences ____________ continually falling to pieces; his cow _____________ either go astray or get among the cabbages; weeds were sure to grow quicker in his fields than anywhere else. Though his patrimonial estate ______________ dwindled away under his management, acre by acre, until there was little more left than a mere patch of Indian corn and potatoes, yet it was the worst-conditioned farm in the neighborhood.

— LESSON 8 —

Personal Pronouns

First, Second, and Third Person

Capitalizing the Pronoun *I*

Personal Pronouns

	Singular	**Plural**
First person	I	we
Second person	you	you
Third person	he, she, it	they

Although they are not very hungry, I certainly am.

ich i I

As the German-built plane rose into the air, I experienced a strange loneliness.

Exercise 8A: Capitalization and Punctuation Practice

Correct the following sentences. Mark through any incorrect small letters and write the correct capitals above them. Insert quotation marks if needed. Use underlining to indicate any italics.

Note: The name of a radio program should be treated like that of a television program.

the first month of the year is january. january was named after the roman god janus, who is the god of transitions, because this month marks the transition to a new year. numa pompilius added this month to the roman calendar around the year 700 bc.

when the mercury theatre on the air broadcast an adaptation of h. g. wells's novel the war of the worlds on october 30, 1938, many people thought an alien invasion was actually happening. the radio program became a sudden huge hit, and campbell soup decided to sponsor it. the program was renamed the campbell playhouse.

in 1862, a dutch ophthalmologist named herman snellen developed the snellen chart, which has a large E at the top and several more rows of letters, to measure visual acuity.

the first published crossword puzzle appeared in the sunday edition of the new york world on december 21, 1913. the puzzle was written by arthur wynne, who was born in liverpool, england, and its original title was word-cross puzzle.

the summy company, which was later acquired by warner/chappell music, claimed for years that it owned the copyright to the song happy birthday to you. on september 22, 2015, judge george h. king ruled that this claim was invalid, and the song is now considered to be in the public domain.

after much debate over prime minister lester b. pearson's proposal for a new flag, canada adopted its current flag with the image of a maple leaf on february 15, 1965. in 1996, february 15 became known in that country as national flag of canada day.

in 1948, eleanor abbott made a game for children called candy land. the game was published by milton bradley beginning the next year, and it quickly became a bestseller. children have enjoyed playing candy land for decades, and it was inducted into the national toy hall of fame in 2005.

according to guinness world records (a reference book previously known as the guinness book of world records), robert wadlow was the tallest man in medical history. wadlow was born in alton, illinois, on february 22, 1918. when he was measured on june 27, 1940, he was found to be 8 feet, 11.1 inches tall.

Exercise 8B: Person, Number, and Gender

Label each personal pronoun in the following selection with its person (1, 2, or 3) and number (*s* or *pl*). For third person singular pronouns only, indicate gender (*m, f,* or *n*).

The first is done for you.

Ermengarde began to laugh.

3sf

"Oh, Sara!" she said. "You *are* queer—but you are nice."

"I know I am queer," admitted Sara, cheerfully; "and I *try* to be nice." She rubbed her forehead with her little brown paw, and a puzzled, tender look came into her face. "Papa always laughed at me," she said; "but I liked it. He thought I was queer, but he liked me to make up things. I—I can't help making up things. If I didn't, I don't believe I could live." She paused and glanced around the attic. "I'm sure I couldn't live here," she added in a low voice.

Ermengarde was interested, as she always was. "When you talk about things," she said, "they seem as if they grew real. You talk about Melchisedec as if he was a person."

"He *is* a person," said Sara. "He gets hungry and frightened, just as we do; and he is married and has children. How do we know he doesn't think things, just as we do? His eyes look as if he was a person. That was why I gave him a name."

— From *A Little Princess*, by Frances Hodgson Burnett

WEEK 3

Introduction to the Sentence

— LESSON 9 —

The Sentence
Parts of Speech and Parts of Sentences
Subjects and Predicates

A sentence is a group of words that contains a subject and predicate.

part of speech — noun verb

The cat sits on the mat.

part of the sentence — subject predicate

The subject of the sentence is the main word or term that the sentence is about.
Part of speech is a term that explains what a word does.
Part of the sentence is a term that explains how a word functions in a sentence.
The predicate of the sentence tells something about the subject.

part of speech ________ ________

The *Tyrannosaurus rex* crashes through the trees.

part of the sentence ________ ________

Exercise 9A: Parts of Speech vs. Parts of the Sentence

Label each underlined word with the correct part of speech AND the correct part of the sentence.

part of speech ________ ________

We saw the huge tree.

part of the sentence ________ ________

part of speech ________ ________

The leaves were red.

part of the sentence ________ ________

part of speech ________ ________

A squirrel scampered up the trunk.

part of the sentence ________ ________

part of speech ________ ________

It jumped to the next tree.

part of the sentence ________ ________

Exercise 9B: Parts of Speech: Nouns, Adjectives, Pronouns, and Verbs

Label each underlined word with the correct part of speech. Use *N* for noun, *A* for adjective, *P* for pronoun, and *V* for verb.

The first night, then, I went to sleep on the sand, a thousand miles from any human habitation. I was more isolated than a shipwrecked sailor on a raft in the middle of the ocean. Thus you can imagine my amazement, at sunrise, when I was awakened by an odd little voice. It said:

"If you please—draw me a sheep!"

"What!"

"Draw me a sheep!"

I jumped to my feet, completely thunderstruck. I blinked my eyes hard. I looked carefully all around me. And I saw a most extraordinary small person, who stood there examining me with great seriousness.

— From *The Little Prince*, by Antoine de Saint-Exupéry

Exercise 9C: Parts of the Sentence: Subjects and Predicates

In each of the following sentences, underline the subject once and the predicate twice. Find the subject by asking, "Who or what is this sentence about?" Find the predicate by saying, "Subject what?"

Example: Flamingos make nests out of mud.

> *Who or what is this sentence about?* Flamingos.
> *Flamingos what?* Flamingos make.

Flamingos eat brine shrimp or algae.

Their food contains carotenoids.

The carotenoids turn the flamingos' feathers pink.

Baby flamingos have white or gray feathers.

Lake Natron, in Tanzania, is the birthplace for over half the world's lesser flamingos.

Caribbean flamingos are the only flamingo species native to North America.

South America is home to Chilean, Andean, James's, and Caribbean flamingos.

Greater flamingos live in Europe, Africa, and Asia.

— LESSON 10 —

Subjects and Predicates
Diagramming Subjects and Predicates
Sentence Capitalization and Punctuation
Sentence Fragments

A sentence is a group of words that contains a subject and predicate.
The subject of the sentence is the main word or term that the sentence is about.
The predicate of the sentence tells something about the subject.

He does.
They can.
It is.

Hurricanes form over warm tropical waters.

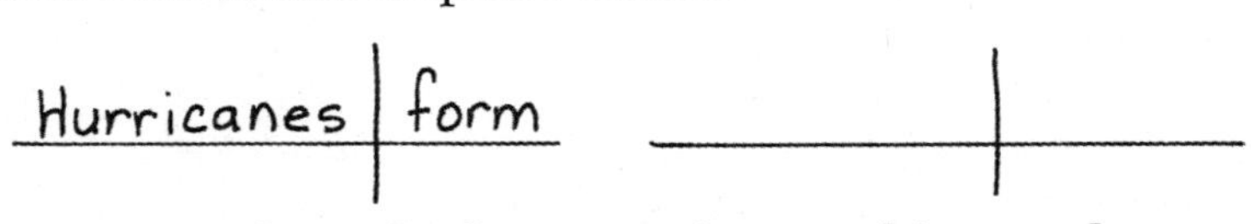

A sentence is a group of words that contains a subject and a predicate.
A sentence begins with a capital letter and ends with a punctuation mark.

No running in the kitchen.

Can we measure intelligence without understanding it? Possibly so; physicists measured gravity and magnetism long before they understood them theoretically. Maybe psychologists can do the same with intelligence.

Or maybe not.

—James W. Kalat, *Introduction to Psychology* (Cengage Learning, 2007)

Because he couldn't go.
Since I thought so.

A sentence is a group of words that usually contains a subject and a predicate.
A sentence begins with a capital letter and ends with a punctuation mark.
A sentence contains a complete thought.

Exercise 10A: Sentences and Fragments

If a group of words expresses a complete thought, write *S* for sentence in the blank. If not, write *F* for fragment.

while jumping up and down ________

the girl saw a train approaching ________

made of popsicle sticks ________

the delectable meal set before us ________

the window was slightly ajar ________

three tall men in brown suits approached ________

because the elevator was broken ________

Exercise 10B: Proofreading for Capitalization and Punctuation

Add the correct capitalization and punctuation to the following sentences. In this exercise you will use proofreader's marks. Indicate letters which should be capitalized by underlining three times. Indicate ending punctuation by using the proofreader's mark for inserting a period: ⊙ Indicate words which should be italicized by underlining them and writing *ital* in the margin.

The first is done for you.

the name texas comes from a caddo word that means friends⊙

the state of pennsylvania gets its name from its founder, william penn, and the latin word for woods

a spanish novel, las sergas de esplandián, described a fictional place called california; this is the likely source of the us state name

the french king louis xiv was honored in the name louisiana

florida's name, chosen by juan ponce de león, came from the spanish phrase "pascua florida," meaning "feast of flowers" and referring to the easter season

michigan is the ojibwa word for "large lake" changed to a french form

Note: Look carefully at the next part! There are three separate sentences here, so you will need to insert three periods.

during the civil war, the confederates took an old union ship, the merrimack, covered it with iron plates, and renamed it the virginia the virginia battled against another ironclad ship, the monitor this first battle between two ironclad ships ended in a draw

Exercise 10C: Diagramming

Find the subjects and predicates in the following sentences. Diagram each subject and predicate on your own paper. You should capitalize on the diagram any words that are capitalized in the sentence, but do not put punctuation marks on the diagram. If a proper name is the subject, all parts of the proper name go on the subject line of the diagram.

Example: Joseph jumped jubilantly.

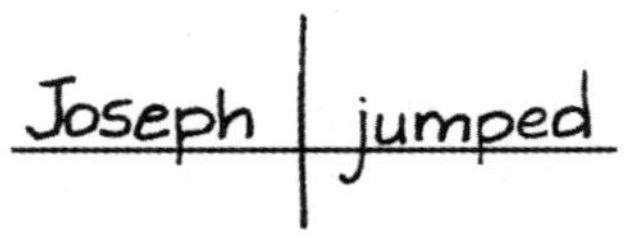

The enormous elephant entered the elevator.
My big brother borrowed Ben's book.
Six sleeping snails sat on the sill.
We watched Waldo's walrus on Wednesday.
Clara clandestinely climbed the cliff.
Isabella Ingalls itched in the igloo.
The floral fabric from Finland flatters Fiona's face.

— LESSON 11 —

Types of Sentences

A sentence is a group of words that usually contains a subject and a predicate.
A sentence begins with a capital letter and ends with a punctuation mark.
A sentence contains a complete thought.

A purple penguin is playing ping-pong.

A statement gives information. A statement always ends with a period.
Statements are declarative sentences.

An exclamation shows sudden or strong feeling.
An exclamation always ends with an exclamation point.
Exclamations are exclamatory sentences.

A command gives an order or makes a request.
A command ends with either a period or an exclamation point.
Commands are imperative sentences.

Sit!
Stand!
Learn!

The subject of a command is understood to be you.

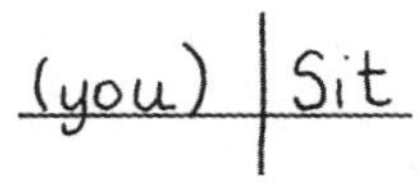

A question asks something.
A question always ends with a question mark.
Questions are known as interrogative sentences.

He is late.
Is he late?

Exercise 11A: Types of Sentences: Statements, Exclamations, Commands, and Questions

Identify the following sentences as *S* for statement, *E* for exclamation, *C* for command, or *Q* for question. Add the appropriate punctuation to the end of each sentence.

	Sentence Type
Do you like to play basketball	________
Please dust the furniture	________

	Sentence Type
I want to change clothes before going to the party	________
Will you give me some advice	________
I love square dancing	________
Don't get into any trouble	________
What a huge volcano	________
Daniel wanted a sandwich with strawberry jam	________
Take off your hat	________
How long would it take to hike to the top of that mountain	________

Exercise 11B: Proofreading for Capitalization and Punctuation

Proofread the following sentences. If a small letter should be capitalized, draw three lines underneath it. Add any missing punctuation.

what is your decision

tell me the price of this game

i want to start my own fashion design company

the dog likes chasing his own tail

pass me your plate

that baby was cute as a button

may we open the box now

Exercise 11C: Diagramming Subjects and Predicates

On your own paper, diagram the subjects and predicates of the following sentences. Remember that the understood subject of a command is "you," and that the predicate may come before the subject in a question.

We enjoyed lunch.
Were you happy?
Eat your vegetables!
The tiger is beautiful.
Please get your toys.
Harriet ambled into the store.
Are the geese by the lake?
I see a mouse!

— LESSON 12 —

Subjects and Predicates
Helping Verbs
Simple and Complete Subjects and Predicates

The subject of the sentence is the main word or term that the sentence is about.
The simple subject of the sentence is *just* the main word or term that the sentence is about.

Its fleece was white as snow.

The complete subject of the sentence is the simple subject and all the words that belong to it.

The predicate of the sentence tells something about the subject.
The simple predicate of the sentence is the main verb along with any helping verbs.
The complete predicate of the sentence is the simple predicate and all the words that belong to it.

Complete Subject	**Complete Predicate**
Lambs born in the spring	must remain with their mothers until July.
Plentiful turnips	should be provided for them.

Exercise 12A: Complete Subjects and Complete Predicates

Match the complete subjects and complete predicates by drawing lines between them.

The three children	pulled into the driveway.
Grandfather	was growing crystals on a string in a glass.
Last year, he	waited excitedly for their grandfather's arrival.
All that summer, they	smiled and hugged each of them.
Their favorite experiment	wondered what Grandfather would bring this time.
As they waited, the children	showed the children their new gift: a gardening kit!
Finally, Grandfather's car	always brought gifts when he came to visit.
With cries of delight, the children	had come with a chemistry kit that they could all use.
The elderly man	performed experiments and made discoveries with the kit.
Reaching into the car, Grandfather	opened the door and ran out to greet him.

Exercise 12B: Simple and Complete Subjects and Predicates

In the following sentences, underline the simple subject once and the simple predicate twice. Then, draw a vertical line between the complete subject and the complete predicate. The first is done for you.

These sentences are adapted from the Zulu story "The Day Baboon Outwitted Leopard," as told by Nick Greaves in *When Hippo Was Hairy: And Other Tales from Africa.*

Leopard | called her friend Baboon.

After a while, Baboon dozed off.

Now an angry, hungry leopard is not a very reassuring sight.

Despite their past friendship, she opened her jaws for a bite.

Quick as a flash, Baboon climbed up into the safety of the thickest thorns at the top.

Other animals were gathering around.

Leopard's pride could not stand it.

To this day, the leopard hunts the baboon in preference to all other food.

Exercise 12C: Diagramming Simple Subjects and Simple Predicates

On your own paper, diagram the simple subjects and simple predicates from Exercise 12B.

— REVIEW 1 —

Weeks 1-3

Topics
Concrete/Abstract Nouns
Descriptive Adjectives
Common/Proper Nouns
Capitalization of Proper Nouns and First Words in Sentences
Noun Gender
Pronouns and Antecedents
Action Verbs/State-of-Being Verbs
Helping Verbs
Subjects and Predicates
Complete Sentences
Types of Sentences

Review 1A: Types of Nouns

Fill in the blanks with the correct description of each noun. The first is done for you.

	Concrete / Abstract	Common / Proper	Gender (M, F, N)
cherry	C	C	N
Times Square	______	______	______
decision	______	______	______
Johnny Cash	______	______	______
hour	______	______	______
Cleopatra	______	______	______
sister	______	______	______
zipper	______	______	______
ram	______	______	______
Suwannee River	______	______	______

Review 1B: Types of Verbs

Underline the complete verbs in the following sentences. Identify any helping verbs as *HV*. Identify the main verb as *AV* for action verb or *BV* for state-of-being verb.

Bones are both flexible and strong.

Collagen, a type of protein, gives bones their flexibility.

The strength of bones comes from minerals like calcium.

Have you ever broken a bone?

Bones may break with too much pressure.

A fracture can be open or closed.

With an open fracture, bone has come through the skin.

Closed fractures do not pierce the skin.

Doctors must consider many factors for treatment of broken bones.

The smallest bone in the human body is the stapes, a stirrup-shaped bone in the middle ear.

Review 1C: Subjects and Predicates

Draw one line under the simple subject and two lines under the simple predicate in the following sentences. Remember that the predicate may be a verb phrase with more than one verb in it.

Simon will visit the Rocky Mountains next month.

Natalie did not multiply the numbers correctly.

Throughout the show, the actors appreciated the audience's laughter.

The man with the untidy appearance was actually an undercover police officer.

Besides milk and stamps, I should add fruit to my shopping list.

The sad little girl wished for a friend.

An ominous knock sounded at the door.

Today may be the most exciting day of your life!

The storm had delayed our flight by three hours.

Review 1D: Parts of Speech

Identify the underlined words as *N* for noun, *P* for pronoun, *A* for adjective, *AV* for action verb, *HV* for helping verb, or *BV* for state-of-being verb.

The following excerpt is from Scott O'Dell's *Island of the Blue Dolphins.*

After Kimki had been gone one moon, we began to watch for his return. Every day someone went to the cliff to scan the sea. Even on stormy days we went, and on days when fog shrouded the island. During the day there was always a watcher on the cliff and each night as we sat around our fires we wondered if the next sun would bring him home.

But the spring came and left and the sea was empty. Kimki did not return!

There were few storms that winter and rain was light and ended early. This meant that we would need to be careful of water. In the old days the springs sometimes ran low and no one worried, but now everything seemed to cause alarm. Many were afraid that we would die of thirst.

Review 1E: Capitalization and Punctuation

Use proofreader's marks to indicate correct capitalization and punctuation in the following sentences. The first has been done for you.

did enough students sign up for the september trip to new york city ?

in the twentieth century, the year 1935 had more solar eclipses than any other year; they occurred on january 5, february 3, june 30, july 30, and december 25

the saturday evening post magazine featured artwork by norman rockwell for forty-seven years

what an amazing sunset

have you ever seen george p. burdell at a georgia tech football game

a canadian newspaper editor, joseph coyle, invented egg cartons in 1911 when inflation is taken into account, the highest-grossing film of all time is gone with the wind, starring clark gable and vivien leigh

annabel lee was the last poem edgar allan poe wrote

fred and i loved the performance of the phantom of the opera

Review 1F: Types of Sentences

Identify the following sentences as *S* for statement, *C* for command, *E* for exclamation, or *Q* for question. If the sentence is incomplete, write *I*.

The following sentences are from *The Adventures of Tom Sawyer*, by Mark Twain. Some have been slightly adapted.

	Sentence Type
"I can."	________
"Can't!"	________
"What's your name?"	________
"You're a liar!"	________
"Take a walk!"	________
"Why don't you do it?"	________
"It's because you're afraid."	________
"Get away from here!"	________
"I'll tell my big brother on you."	________
"I've got a brother that's bigger than he is."	________
Both brothers were imaginary.	________
"Don't you crowd me now."	________
"You said you'd do it!"	________
At last the enemy's mother appeared and ordered Tom away.	________

WEEK 4

Verb Tenses

— LESSON 13 —

Nouns, Pronouns, and Verbs
Sentences
Simple Present, Simple Past, and Simple Future Tenses

A noun names a person, place, thing, or idea.
A pronoun takes the place of a noun.
A verb shows an action, shows a state of being, links two words together, or helps another verb.

State-of-Being Verbs

am	were
is	be
are	being
was	been

Helping Verbs
am, is, are, was, were
be, being, been
have, has, had
do, does, did
shall, will, should, would, may, might, must
can, could

A sentence is a group of words that usually contains a subject and a predicate. A sentence begins with a capital letter and ends with a punctuation mark. A sentence contains a complete thought.

A verb in the present tense tells about something that happens in the present.
A verb in the past tense tells about something that happened in the past.
A verb in the future tense tells about something that will happen in the future.

Exercise 13A: Simple Tenses

	Simple Past	Simple Present	Simple Future
I			will paint
You	snored		
She		climbs	
We	conquered		
They		bounce	

Form the simple future by adding the helping verb *will* in front of the simple present.
A suffix is one or more letters added to the end of a word to change its meaning.

Forming the Simple Past
To form the past tense, add *–ed* to the basic verb.

sharpen–sharpened
utter–uttered

If the basic verb ends in -e already, only add *–d*.

rumble–rumbled
shade–shaded

If the verb ends in a short vowel sound and a consonant, double the consonant and add *–ed*.

scam–scammed
thud–thudded

If the verb ends in *-y* following a consonant, change the *y* to *i* and add *-ed*.

cry–cried
try–tried

Exercise 13B: Using Consistent Tense

When you write, you should use consistent tense—if you begin a sentence in one tense, you should continue to use that same tense for any other verbs in the same sentence. The following sentences use two verb tenses. Cross out the second verb and rewrite it so that the tense of the second verb matches the tense of the first one.

The first sentence is done for you.

will play
After the rain, we will go outside and the children ~~played~~ in the puddles.

I love the smell of the air after the rain, so I closed my eyes to enjoy it.

Frances saw two little frogs hopping and will take a picture of them.

The clouds will clear soon and the sky is bright blue.

Philip squealed when Kira splashes him with water from a puddle.

An earthworm wriggles on the ground, and a robin looked at it hungrily.

Tomorrow it will be sunny and we went to the beach.

Exercise 13C: Forming the Simple Past Tense

Using the rules for forming the simple past, put each one of the verbs in parentheses into the simple past. Write the simple past form in the blank. Be sure to spell the past forms of regular verbs correctly, and to use the correct forms of irregular verbs.

These passages are condensed from *Five Children and It*, by E. Nesbit.

Then the postman was heard blowing his horn, and Robert ________________ (rush) out in the rain to stop his cart and give him the letters. And that ___________ (is) how it ________________ (happen) that, though all the children _______________ (mean) to tell their mother about the Sand-fairy, somehow or other she never ___________ (get) to know.

The next day Uncle Richard ______________ (come) and ______________ (take) them all to Maidstone in a wagonette—all except the Lamb. Uncle Richard __________ (is) the very best kind of uncle. He ______________ (buy) them toys at Maidstone. He ______________ (take) them into a shop and ______________ (let) them all choose exactly what they wanted, without any restrictions about price, and no nonsense about things being instructive. Robert ______________ (choose), at the last moment, and in a great hurry, a box with pictures on it of winged bulls with men's heads and winged men with eagles' heads. He ________________ (think) there would be animals inside, the same as on the box. When he ____________ (get) home it was a Sunday puzzle about ancient Nineveh! The others ______________ (choose) in haste, and ___________ (is) happy at leisure.

Then Uncle Richard ______________ (take) them on the beautiful Medway in a boat, and then they all ______________ (have) tea at a beautiful confectioner's and when they ________________ (reach) home it ___________ (is) far too late to have any wishes that day. . . .

Anthea ______________ (wake) at five. At the very moment when she ______________ (open) her eyes she ________________ (hear) the black-and-gold clock down in the dining-room strike eleven. So she _______________ (know) it _____________ (is) three minutes to five. The black-and-gold clock always _______________ (strike) wrong, but it _________ (is) all right when you ______________ (know) what it ______________ (mean). She ___________ (is) very sleepy, but she ___________________ (jump) out of bed and _____________ (put) her face and hands into a basin of cold water. This is a fairy charm that prevents your wanting to get back into bed again. Then she ________________ (dress), and ________________ (fold) up her night dress.

Then she ______________ (take) her shoes in her hand and ________________ (creep) softly down the stairs. She __________________ (open) the dining-room window and __________________ (climb) out. It would have been just as easy to go out by the door, but the window ___________ (is) more romantic, and less likely to be noticed by Martha.

— LESSON 14 —

Simple Present, Simple Past, and Simple Future Tenses
Progressive Present, Progressive Past, and Progressive Future Tenses

A verb in the present tense tells about something that happens in the present.
A verb in the future tense tells about something that will happen in the future.
A verb in the past tense tells about something that happened in the past.

study   will study   studied

Forming the Simple Past:
To form the past tense, add *–ed* to the basic verb.
If the basic verb ends in *e* already, only add *–d.*
If the verb ends in a short vowel sound and a consonant, double the consonant and add *–ed.*
If the verb ends in *-y* following a consonant, change the *y* to *i* and add *-ed.*

Exercise 14A: Forming the Simple Past and Simple Future Tenses

Form the simple past and simple future of the following regular verbs.

Past	Present	Future
	wander	
	exercise	
	search	
	delay	
	chop	
	confuse	
	step	
	carry	
	tame	

Yesterday, I cried. I was crying for a long time.
Today, I learn. I am learning my grammar.
Tomorrow, I will celebrate. I will be celebrating all afternoon.

A progressive verb describes an ongoing or continuous action.

Exercise 14B: Progressive Tenses

Circle the ending of each verb. Underline the helping verbs.

will be confessing

was preventing

were mourning

am tasting

will be drumming

are shivering

was decorating

is juggling

The progressive past tense uses the helping verbs *was* and *were.*
The progressive present tense uses the helping verbs *am, is,* and *are.*
The progressive future tense uses the helping verb *will be.*

Spelling Rules for Adding *-ing*
If the verb ends in a short vowel sound and a consonant, double the consonant and add *–ing.*

skip–skipping
drum–drumming

If the verb ends in a long vowel sound plus a consonant and an -e, drop the e and add *–ing.*

smile–smiling
trade–trading

Exercise 14C: Forming the Past, Present, and Progressive Future Tenses

Complete the following chart. Be sure to use the spelling rules above.

	Progressive Past	Progressive Present	Progressive Future
I chew	I was chewing	I am chewing	I will be chewing
I gather			
I encourage			

	Progressive Past	Progressive Present	Progressive Future
I yawn			
You invent	You were inventing	You are inventing	You will be inventing
You breathe			
You shrug			
You sail			
We remind	We were reminding	We are reminding	We will be reminding
We love			
We spot			
We copy			

Exercise 14D: Simple and Progressive Tenses

Fill in the blanks with the correct form of the verb in parentheses.

Leonhard Euler, a Swiss mathematician, ______________________ (simple past of *become*) nearly blind in his right eye in 1738, and in 1766, he ____________ (simple past of *go*) blind in his left eye as well.

When he ______________ (simple past of *lose*) the use of his right eye, Euler ____________ (simple past of *say*), "Now I ___________________ (simple future of *have*) less distraction."

Despite his almost total blindness, Euler ________________ (progressive past of *produce*) about one mathematical paper per week in 1775; his students ________________ (simple past of *help*) him develop and record his ideas.

Students of mathematics today ________________ (progressive present of *learn*) many concepts Euler ______________________ (simple past of *develop*).

Euler ______________________ (simple past of *introduce*) or ______________________ (simple past of *standardize*) much mathematical notation that people ________________ (progressive present of *use*) today, such as the symbol π for the ratio of a circle's circumference to its diameter.

When you ________________ (progressive present of *study*) algebra in high school, one thing you ________________ (progressive future of *learn*) about is a special number named after Euler.

Euler said that "in the theory of numbers, observations ______________ (simple future of *lead*) us continually to new properties which we ______________________ (simple future of *endeavor*) to prove afterwards."

— LESSON 15 —

Simple Present, Simple Past, and Simple Future Tenses
Progressive Present, Progressive Past, and Progressive Future Tenses
Perfect Present, Perfect Past, and Perfect Future Tenses

A progressive verb describes an ongoing or continuous action.

Yesterday, I was studying tenses.
Today, I am studying tenses.
Tomorrow, I will be studying something else!

NEWS BULLETIN!
A diamond theft occurred at the National Museum yesterday. The thief had already fled the scene when a security guard discovered that the diamond was missing.

A perfect verb describes an action which has been completed before another action takes place.

I practiced my piano.
I was practicing my piano all day yesterday.
I had practiced my piano before I went to bed.

Perfect Past	Perfect Present	Perfect Future
I had practiced yesterday.	I have practiced.	I will have practiced tomorrow.
I had eaten before bed.	I have eaten already.	I will have eaten by bedtime tomorrow.
I had seen the movie a week ago.	I have seen the movie once.	I will have seen the movie before it leaves the theater.

Perfect past verbs describe an action that was finished in the past before another action began.

Helping verb: had

Perfect present verbs describe an action that was completed before the present moment.

Helping verbs: have, has

Perfect future verbs describe an action that will be finished in the future before another action begins.

Helping verb: will have

Exercise 15A: Perfect Tenses

Fill in the blanks with the missing forms.

Simple Past	Perfect Past	Perfect Present	Perfect Future
I planted	I had planted	I have planted	I will have planted
I ignored			

Simple Past	Perfect Past	Perfect Present	Perfect Future
I glared			
I flipped			
We pined	We had pined	We have pined	We will have pined
We objected			
We refrained			
We napped			
He pondered	He had pondered	He has pondered	He will have pondered
He escaped			
He contributed			
He jogged			

Exercise 15B: Identifying Perfect Tenses

Identify the underlined verbs as perfect past, perfect present, or perfect future. The first one is done for you.

perfect present
I have decided to make a quilt.

I have purchased fabric and thread.

I had practiced sewing straight lines before I decided to try a quilt.

The quilt will be the same size as my brother's baby blanket; I have measured it carefully.

Yesterday I was reading a book about quilting after I had watched some videos showing how to quilt.

My grandmother has shown me several quilts she made.

I have learned about the different steps in making a quilt.

When I finish, I will have pieced nine blocks for my quilt.

Exercise 15C: Perfect, Progressive, and Simple Tenses

Each underlined verb phrase has been labeled as past, present, or future. Add the label *perfect, progressive,* or *simple* to each one. The first one has been done for you.

progressive progressive
FUTURE PRESENT
Maria will be turning thirteen soon. She is planning her birthday party.

PAST PAST
Maria had gone to the bakery with her father to look for a cake, but she decided to order cupcakes instead.

FUTURE FUTURE
The baker will decorate the cupcakes so that each one will have a frosting soccer ball.

PRESENT PRESENT
Maria loves to play soccer. She has played since the age of four.

FUTURE PRESENT
Maria will invite all her teammates to her party. While music plays, everyone

FUTURE
will be enjoying the soccer ball cupcakes!

PAST
"I was hoping we could have the party on Saturday afternoon," said Maria, "but the coach

PAST
scheduled practice for that time."

— LESSON 16 —

Simple Present, Simple Past, and Simple Future Tenses
Progressive Present, Progressive Past, and Progressive Future Tenses
Perfect Present, Perfect Past, and Perfect Future Tenses
Irregular Verbs

go	run	are	know	make
go-ed	run-ned	ar-ed	know-ed	mak-ed
went	ran	were	knew	made

Exercise 16A: Irregular Verb Forms: Simple Present, Simple Past, and Simple Future

Fill in the chart with the missing verb forms.

	Simple Past	Simple Present	Simple Future
I			will lead
You			will build
She	meant		
We		grow	
They		understand	
I	spread		
You		fight	
He			will drink
We		freeze	

	Simple Past	Simple Present	Simple Future
They		sleep	
I			will lose
You	caught		
It		sets	
We	gave		
They			will fall
I		seek	
You	sent		
We		come	
They		hide	

	Simple Past	Simple Present	Simple Future	Progressive Past	Progressive Present	Progressive Future	Perfect Past	Perfect Present	Perfect Future
go	went	go	will go	was going	am going	will be going	had gone	have gone	will have gone
eat	ate	eat	will eat	was eating	am eating	will be eating	had eaten	have eaten	will have eaten

Exercise 16B: Irregular Verbs, Progressive and Perfect Tenses

Fill in the remaining blanks. The first row is done for you.

Simple Present	Progressive Past	Progressive Present	Progressive Future	Perfect Past	Perfect Present	Perfect Future
send	was sending	is sending	will be sending	had sent	has sent	will have sent
grow						
spread						
build						
understand						
hide						
mean						
drink						
sleep						
catch						
lead						

Simple Present	Progressive Past	Progressive Present	Progressive Future	Perfect Past	Perfect Present	Perfect Future
fall						
set						
lose						
freeze						
give						
seek						
come						
fight						

WEEK 5

More About Verbs

— LESSON 17 —

Simple, Progressive, and Perfect Tenses
Subjects and Predicates
Parts of Speech and Parts of Sentences
Verb Phrases

I yawn today. Yesterday, I yawned. Tomorrow, I will yawn.
I am yawning today. Yesterday, I was yawning. Tomorrow, I will be yawning.

A progressive verb describes an ongoing or continuous action.

I have yawned today already.
Yesterday, I had yawned before I had my dinner.
Tomorrow, I will have yawned by the time the sun goes down.

A perfect verb describes an action which has been completed before another action takes place.

Exercise 17A: Simple, Progressive, and Perfect Tenses

All of the bolded verbs are in the past tense. Label each bolded verb as *S* for simple, *PROG* for progressive, or *PERF* for perfect.

This passage has been adapted from *Oliver Twist*, by Charles Dickens.

It **chanced** one morning, while Oliver's affairs **were** in this auspicious and comfortable state, that Mr. Gamfield, chimney-sweeper, **was wending** his way adown the High-street, and was deeply **cogitating** in his mind, his ways and means of paying certain arrears of rent, for which his landlord **had become** rather pressing. Mr. Gamfield's most sanguine calculation of funds could not raise them within full five pounds of the desired amount; and in a species of arithmetical desperation, he **was** alternately **cudgelling** his brains and his donkey, when, passing the workhouse, his eyes **encountered** the bill on the gate.

"Woo!" **said** Mr. Gamfield to the donkey.

The donkey **was** in a state of profound abstraction—wondering, probably, whether he was destined to be regaled with a cabbage-stalk or two, when he **had disposed** of the two sacks of soot with which the little cart was laden; so, without noticing the word of command, he **jogged** onwards.

Mr. Gamfield **growled** a fierce imprecation on the donkey generally, but more particularly on his eyes. After he **had given** the donkey a reminder that he **was** not his own master, Mr. Gamfield **walked** to the gate to read the bill. The gentleman with the white waistcoat **was standing** at the gate with his hands behind him, and he **smiled** joyously when Mr. Gamfield **came** up to read the bill.

had rejoiced
will have rejoiced

A phrase is a group of words serving a single grammatical function.

have greatly rejoiced
They will have all rejoiced

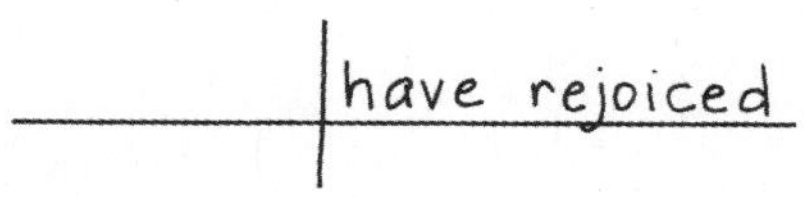

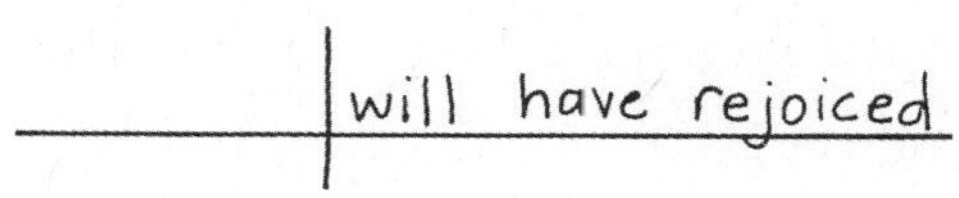

The subject of the sentence is the main word or term that the sentence is about.

The simple subject of the sentence is *just* the main word or term that the sentence is about.

The predicate of the sentence tells something about the subject.

The simple predicate of the sentence is the main verb along with any helping verbs.

Part of speech is a term that explains what a word does.

A noun names a person, place, thing, or idea.

A pronoun takes the place of a noun.

Part of the sentence is a term that explains how a word functions in a sentence.

A verb shows an action, shows a state of being, links two words together, or helps another verb.

Exercise 17B: Identifying and Diagramming Subjects and Predicates, Identifying Verb Tenses

Underline the subject once and the predicate twice in each sentence. Be sure to include both the main verb and any helping verbs when you underline the predicate. Identify the tense of each verb or verb phrase (*simple past*, *present*, or *future*; *progressive past*, *present*, or *future*; *perfect past*, *present*, or *future*) in the blank. Then, diagram each subject and predicate on your own paper.

These sentences are adapted from *Oliver Twist*, by Charles Dickens.

The two boys had scoured with great rapidity through a most intricate maze of narrow streets and courts. ____________________

The Dodger made no reply. ____________________

Will you speak? ____________________

The dog coiled himself up in a corner very quietly without uttering a sound. ____________________

The old gentleman's eyes were vacantly staring on the opposite wall. ____________________

Miss Nancy arrived in perfect safety shortly afterwards. ____________________

Mr. Brownlow's abrupt exclamation had thrown Oliver into a fainting-fit. ____________________

Oliver had never had a new suit before. ____________________

Oliver was talking to Mrs. Bedwin one evening. ____________________

I will talk to you without any reserve. ____________________

I feel strongly on this subject, sir. ____________________

He is deceiving you, my dear friend. ____________________

I know a great number of persons in both situations at this moment. ____________________

— LESSON 18 —

Verb Phrases
Person of the Verb
Conjugations

	Progressive Past	Progressive Present	Progressive Future
I run	I was running	I am running	I will be running
You call	You were calling	You are calling	You will be calling
He jogs	He was jogging	He is jogging	He will be jogging
We fix	We were fixing	We are fixing	We will be fixing
They call	They were calling	They are calling	They will be calling

PERSONS OF THE VERB

	Singular	Plural
First person	I	we
Second person	you	you
Third person	he, she, it	they

Simple Tenses

REGULAR VERB, SIMPLE PRESENT

	Singular	Plural
First person	I pretend	we pretend
Second person	you pretend	you pretend
Third person	he, she, it pretends	they pretend
First person	I wander	we wander
Second person	you wander	you wander
Third person	he, she, it wanders	they wander

REGULAR VERB, SIMPLE PAST

	Singular	Plural
First person	I wandered	we wandered
Second person	you wandered	you wandered
Third person	he, she, it wandered	they wandered

REGULAR VERB, SIMPLE FUTURE

	Singular	Plural
First person	I will wander	we will wander
Second person	you will wander	you will wander
Third person	he, she, it will wander	they will wander

Perfect Tenses

REGULAR VERB, PERFECT PRESENT

	Singular	Plural
First person	I have wandered	we have wandered
Second person	you have wandered	you have wandered
Third person	he, she, it has wandered	they have wandered

REGULAR VERB, PERFECT PAST

	Singular	Plural
First person	I had wandered	we had wandered
Second person	you had wandered	you had wandered
Third person	he, she, it had wandered	they had wandered

REGULAR VERB, PERFECT FUTURE

	Singular	Plural
First person	I will wander	we will wander
Second person	you will wander	you will wander
Third person	he, she, it will wander	they will wander

Exercise 18A: Third Person Singular Verbs

In the simple present conjugation, the third person singular verb changes by adding an *-s*. Read the following rules and examples for adding *-s* to verbs in order to form the third person singular. Then, fill in the blanks with the third person singular forms of each verb.

The first of each is done for you.

Usually, add *-s* to form the third person singular verb.

First Person Verb	Third Person Singular Verb
I treat	he treats
I fold	she ________
I divide	it ________

Add *-es* to verbs ending in *-s*, *-sh*, *-ch*, *-x*, or *-z*.

First Person Verb	Third Person Singular Verb	
we punish	she	punishes
we embarrass	it	______
we relax	he	______

If a verb ends in *-y* after a consonant, change the *y* to *i* and add *-es*.

First Person Verb	Third Person Singular Verb	
I supply	it	supplies
I hurry	he	______
I identify	she	______

If a verb ends in *-y* after a vowel, just add *-s*.

First Person Verb	Third Person Singular Verb	
we stay	he	stays
we employ	she	______
we obey	it	______

If a verb ends in *-o* after a consonant, form the plural by adding *-es*.

First Person Verb	Third Person Singular Verb	
I outdo	she	outdoes
I undergo	it	______
I solo	he	______

Exercise 18B: Simple Present Tenses

Choose the correct form of the simple present verb in parentheses, based on the person. Cross out the incorrect form.

Zayan (love/loves) to play board games.

He (invite/invites) his friends over to play games whenever he can.

Sometimes, Zayan and his friends (play/plays) a game Zayan (own/owns). Other times, his friends (bring/brings) their games.

"I (want/wants) to play your newest game!" Zayan's friend Derek (announce/announces). "It really (sound/sounds) like a lot of fun!"

Zayan's brother Rehan (speak/speaks) up. "It is! I (enjoy/enjoys) playing it."

The other two friends (agree/agrees) to try out the new game.

Zayan (pick/picks) up the red player token, and Derek (choose/chooses) the yellow one. The others (select/selects) their player tokens as well, and they all (play/plays) for a while.

Then Zayan (bring/brings) out some snacks, and all the players (take/takes) a break from the game.

Exercise 18C: Perfect Present Tenses

Write the correct form of the perfect present verb in the blank.

These sentences are taken or adapted from *Redwall*, by Brian Jacques.

"Humph! After all the help and assistance that I ____________________ [give], countless hours of study and valuable time. Really!"

"At least I hope I ____________________ [solve] it."

The hare beckoned Sam. "C'm'ere, you dreadful little rogue! I ____________________ [get] the very thing for you."

"Now that my son ____________________ [bring] my new ingredients I can certainly give you medicine to make you sleep, sir."

"Look, Jess ____________________ [make] it over the gutter! She's on the roof."

"It is all here, but as I ____________________ [say] before, I will not concern myself with the fighting of a war."

— LESSON 19 —

Person of the Verb
Conjugations
State-of-Being Verbs

English	Latin		
conjugate	*conjugare*	*con*	+ *jugare*
to join a verb to each person in turn	to join together	with	+ to yoke

REGULAR VERB, SIMPLE PRESENT

	Singular	Plural
First person	I conjugate	we conjugate
Second person	you conjugate	you conjugate
Third person	he, she, it conjugates	they conjugate

REGULAR VERB, SIMPLE PAST

conjugated

REGULAR VERB, SIMPLE FUTURE

will conjugate

REGULAR VERB, PERFECT PRESENT

	Singular	Plural
First person	I have conjugated	we have conjugated
Second person	you have conjugated	you have conjugated
Third person	he, she, it has conjugated	they have conjugated

REGULAR VERB, PERFECT PAST

had conjugated

REGULAR VERB, PERFECT FUTURE

will have conjugated

REGULAR VERB, PROGRESSIVE PRESENT

am conjugating

STATE-OF-BEING VERB, SIMPLE PRESENT

	Singular	Plural
First person	I am	we are
Second person	you are	you are
Third person	he, she, it is	they are

Exercise 19A: Forming Progressive Present Tenses

Fill in the blanks with the correct helping verbs.

Regular Verb, Progressive Present

	Singular	Plural
First person	I ______________ scribbling	we ______________ scribbling
Second person	you ______________ scribbling	you ______________ scribbling
Third person	he, she, it ______________ scribbling	they ______________ scribbling

STATE-OF-BEING VERB, SIMPLE PRESENT

	Singular	Plural
First person	I am	we are
Second person	you are	you are
Third person	he, she, it is	they are

STATE-OF-BEING VERB, SIMPLE PAST

	Singular	Plural
First person	I was	we were
Second person	you were	you were
Third person	he, she, it was	they were

STATE-OF-BEING VERB, SIMPLE FUTURE

	Singular	Plural
First person	I will be	we will be
Second person	you will be	you will be
Third person	he, she, it will be	they will be

STATE-OF-BEING VERB, PERFECT PRESENT

	Singular	Plural
First person	I have been	we have been
Second person	you have been	you have been
Third person	he, she, it has been	they have been

STATE-OF-BEING VERB, PERFECT PAST

	Singular	Plural
First person	I had been	we had been
Second person	you had been	you had been
Third person	he, she, it had been	they had been

STATE-OF-BEING VERB, PERFECT FUTURE

	Singular	Plural
First person	I will have been	we will have been
Second person	you will have been	you will have been
Third person	he, she, it will have been	they will have been

STATE-OF-BEING VERB, PROGRESSIVE PRESENT

	Singular	Plural
First person	I am being	we are being
Second person	you are being	you are being
Third person	he, she, it is being	they are being

STATE-OF-BEING VERB, PROGRESSIVE PAST

	Singular	Plural
First person	I was being	we were being
Second person	you were being	you were being
Third person	he, she, it was being	they were being

STATE-OF-BEING VERB, PROGRESSIVE FUTURE

	Singular	Plural
First person	I will be being	we will be being
Second person	you will be being	you will be being
Third person	he, she, it will be being	they will be being

Exercise 19B: Forming Progressive Present, Past, and Future Tenses

Regular Verb, Progressive Past

	Singular		Plural	
First person	I ____________	learning	we ____________	learning
Second person	you ____________	learning	you ____________	learning
Third person	he, she, it ____________	learning	they ____________	learning

Regular Verb, Progressive Future

	Singular		Plural	
First person	I ____________	rejoicing	we ____________	rejoicing
Second person	you ____________	rejoicing	you ____________	rejoicing
Third person	he, she, it ____________	rejoicing	they ____________	rejoicing

— LESSON 20 —

Irregular State-of-Being Verbs
Helping Verbs

Forms of the State-of-Being Verb *Am*

SIMPLE PRESENT

	Singular	Plural
First person	I am	we are
Second person	you are	you are
Third person	He, she, it is	they are

SIMPLE PAST

	Singular	Plural
First person	I was	we were
Second person	you were	you were
Third person	he, she, it was	they were

SIMPLE FUTURE

	Singular	Plural
First person	I will be	we will be
Second person	you will be	you will be
Third person	he, she, it will be	they will be

PERFECT PRESENT

	Singular	Plural
First person	I have been	we have been
Second person	you have been	you have been
Third person	he, she, it has been	they have been

PERFECT PAST

	Singular	Plural
First person	I had been	we had been
Second person	you had been	you had been
Third person	he, she, it had been	they had been

PERFECT FUTURE

	Singular	Plural
First person	I will have been	we will have been
Second person	you will have been	you will have been
Third person	he, she, it will have been	they will have been

PROGRESSIVE PRESENT

	Singular	Plural
First person	I am being	we are being
Second person	you are being	you are being
Third person	he, she, it is being	they are being

PROGRESSIVE PAST

	Singular	Plural
First person	I was being	we were being
Second person	You were being	you were being
Third person	he, she, it was being	they were being

PROGRESSIVE FUTURE

	Singular	Plural
First person	I will be being	we will be being
Second person	you will be being	you will be being
Third person	he, she, it will be being	they will be being

Exercise 20A: Simple Tenses of the Verb *Have*

Try to fill in the missing blanks in the chart below, using your own sense of what sounds correct as well as the hints you may have picked up from the conjugations already covered. Be sure to use pencil so that any incorrect answers can be erased and corrected!

Simple Present

	Singular	Plural
First person	I have	we ______
Second person	you ______	you ______
Third person	he, she, it ______	they ______

Simple Past

	Singular	Plural
First person	I ______	we ______
Second person	you ______	you ______
Third person	he, she, it ______	they ______

Simple Future

	Singular	Plural
First person	I will ______	we ______
Second person	you ______	you ______
Third person	he, she, it ______	they ______

Exercise 20B: Simple Tenses of the Verb *Do*

Try to fill in the missing blanks in the chart below, using your own sense of what sounds correct as well as the hints you may have picked up from the conjugations already covered. Be sure to use pencil so that any incorrect answers can be erased and corrected!

Simple Present

	Singular	Plural
First person	I do	we ______
Second person	you ______	you ______
Third person	he, she, it ______	they ______

Simple Past

	Singular	**Plural**
First person	I ______________	we ______________
Second person	you ______________	you ______________
Third person	he, she, it ______________	they ______________

Simple Future

	Singular	**Plural**
First person	I will ______________	we ______________
Second person	you ______________	you ______________
Third person	he, she, it ______________	they ______________

I will be	I shall be	I shall be!
You will run	You will run	You shall run!
He, she, it will sing	He, she, it will sing	He, she, it shall sing!
We will eat	We shall eat	We shall eat!
You will shout	You will shout	You shall shout!
They will cavort	They will cavort	They shall cavort!

I **will** go to bed early.
When I was young, I **would** always go to bed early.

I **would** like to go to bed early.
I **should** probably go to bed now.

I **would** eat the chocolate caramel truffle.
I **should** eat the chocolate caramel truffle.
I **may** eat the chocolate caramel truffle.
I **might** eat the chocolate caramel truffle.
I **must** eat the chocolate caramel truffle.
I **can** eat the chocolate caramel truffle.
I **could** eat the chocolate caramel truffle.

Am, is, are, was, were, be, being, and *been* are forms of the verb *am.*
Have, has, and *had* are forms of the verb *has.*
Do, does, and *did* are forms of the verb *do.*
Shall and *will* are different forms of the same verb.
Should, would, may, might, must, can, and *could* express hypothetical situations.

WEEK 6

Nouns and Verbs in Sentences

— LESSON 21 —

Person of the Verb
Conjugations
Noun-Verb/Subject-Predicate Agreement

SIMPLE PRESENT

	Singular	Plural
First person	I enjoy	we enjoy
Second person	you enjoy	you enjoy
Third person	he, she, it enjoys	they enjoy

PERFECT PAST

	Singular	Plural
First person	I had been	we had been
Second person	you had been	you had been
Third person	he, she, it had been	they had been

PROGRESSIVE FUTURE

	Singular	Plural
First person	I will be running	we will be running
Second person	you will be running	you will be running
Third person	he, she, it will be running	they will be running

Complete Conjugation of a Regular Verb

SIMPLE PRESENT

	Singular	Plural
First person	I grab	we grab
Second person	you grab	you grab
Third person	he, she, it <u>grabs</u>	they grab

SIMPLE PAST

I grabbed, etc.

SIMPLE FUTURE

I will grab, etc.

PERFECT PRESENT

	Singular	Plural
First person	I have grabbed	we have grabbed
Second person	you have grabbed	you have grabbed
Third person	he, she, it has grabbed	they have grabbed

PERFECT PAST

I had grabbed, etc.

PERFECT FUTURE

I will have grabbed, etc.

PROGRESSIVE PRESENT

	Singular	Plural
First person	I am grabbing	we are grabbing
Second person	you are grabbing	you are grabbing
Third person	he, she, it is grabbing	they are grabbing

PROGRESSIVE PAST

	Singular	Plural
First person	I was grabbing	we were grabbing
Second person	you were grabbing	you were grabbing
Third person	he, she, it was grabbing	they were grabbing

PROGRESSIVE FUTURE

I will be grabbing, etc.

Exercise 21A: Person and Number of Pronouns

Identify the person and number of the underlined pronouns. Cross out the incorrect verb in parentheses. The first one is done for you.

These sentences are adapted from *The Story of Doctor Dolittle*, by Hugh Lofting.

	Person	**Singular/Plural**
He (~~talk~~/talks) every language—and Greek.	third	singular
I (am/is/are) never quite sure of my age.	______	______
They (has/have) to stay at the Doctor's house for a week.	______	______
John Dolittle was a strong man, though he (was/were) not very tall.	______	______
It (am/is/are) a nasty thing to find under the bed.	______	______
They (has/have) heard of you, and (beg/begs) you to come to Africa to stop the sickness.	______	______
You (go/goes) and (ring/rings) it every half-hour.	______	______
We (see/sees) the shores of Africa.	______	______

SIMPLE PRESENT

	Singular	**Plural**
Third person	He, she, it grabs	They grab
	The man grabs	The men grab
	The woman grabs	The women grab
	The eagle grabs	The eagles grab

PERFECT PRESENT

	Singular	**Plural**
Third person	He, she, it has grabbed	They have grabbed
	The boy has grabbed	The boys have grabbed
	The girl has grabbed	The girls have grabbed
	The bear has grabbed	The bears have grabbed

PROGRESSIVE PRESENT

	Singular	Plural
Third person	He, she, it is grabbing	They are grabbing
	The father is grabbing	The fathers are grabbing
	The mother is grabbing	The mothers are grabbing
	The baby is grabbing	The babies are grabbing

PROGRESSIVE PAST

	Singular	Plural
Third person	He, she, it was grabbing	They were grabbing
	The king was grabbing	The kings were grabbing
	The queen was grabbing	The queens were grabbing
	The dragon was grabbing	The dragons were grabbing

Exercise 21B: Identifying Subjects and Predicates

Draw two lines underneath each simple predicate and one line underneath each simple subject in the following sentences. If a phrase comes between the subject and the predicate, put parentheses around it to show that it does not affect the subject-predicate agreement.

Okapis live in central Africa.

Giraffes are in the same family as okapis.

The two animals, though very different in appearance, have similar long, sticky tongues.

With their tongues, they can reach their eyes and ears.

They also walk with both legs on one side of the body, then both legs on the other side of the body.

Many other animals, such as deer, alternate sides of the body instead.

The okapi's striped legs camouflage it in the rainforest.

Exercise 21C: Subject-Verb Agreement

Cross out the incorrect verb in parentheses so that subject and predicate agree in number and person. Look out for any confusing phrases between the subject and predicate.

Yunseo (get/gets) a balloon, a funnel, and an empty bottle.

Ella (bring/brings) some vinegar and baking soda.

The girls carefully (work/works) together to add baking soda to the balloon with the funnel.

The other students in the lab (prepare/prepares) their balloons the same way.

Next, Yunseo (hold/holds) the bottle still while Ella (pour/pours) vinegar into it.

Ella then (wrap/wraps) the balloon's opening over the bottle.

Yunseo, a smile on her face, (shake/shakes) the baking soda from the balloon into the bottle.

All the students in the room eagerly (watch/watches) their balloons as the two materials in the bottles (react/reacts).

— LESSON 22 —

Formation of Plural Nouns
Collective Nouns

A collective noun names a group of people, animals, or things.

Exercise 22A: Collective Nouns

Write the collective noun for each description. Then fill in an appropriate singular verb for each sentence. (Use the simple present tense!) The first one is done for you.

Description		Collective Noun	Verb	
a large number of books	The	library	has	my favorite book.
people singing together	The	______	______	the piece.
flowers arranged together and held	The	______	______	lovely.
many grapes together	This	______	______	sour.
many airplanes	The	______	______	for battle.
a number of arrows all in the same place	The	______	______	full.
many cookies made at the same time	This	______	______	great.

Exercise 22B: Plural Noun Forms

Read each rule and the example out loud. Then rewrite the singular nouns as plural nouns in the spaces provided.

Usually, add *-s* to a noun to form the plural.

Singular Noun	Plural Noun
carpenter	carpenters
nut	____________
queen	____________
basketball	____________

Add *-es* to nouns ending in *-s*, *-sh*, *-ch*, *-x*, or *-z*.

Singular Noun	Plural Noun
business	businesses
bush	____________
peach	____________
wax	____________
waltz	____________

If a noun ends in *-y* after a consonant, change the *y* to *i* and add *-es*.

Singular Noun	Plural Noun
library	libraries
harmony	____________
industry	____________
party	____________

If a noun ends in *-y* after a vowel, just add *-s*.

Singular Noun	Plural Noun
way	ways
alley	____________
turkey	____________
essay	____________

Some words that end in *-f or -fe* form their plurals differently. You must change the *f* or *fe* to *v* and add *-es*.

Singular Noun	Plural Noun
knife	knives
life	____________
self	____________
sheaf	____________

Words that end in *-ff* form their plurals by simply adding *-s*.

Singular Noun	Plural Noun
cuff	cuffs
mastiff	________________
earmuff	________________

Some words that end in a single *-f* can form their plurals either way.

Singular Noun	Plural Noun
dwarf	dwarfs/dwarves
handkerchief	________________

If a noun ends in *-o* after a vowel, just add *-s*.

Singular Noun	Plural Noun
studio	studios
kangaroo	________________
scenario	________________
cameo	________________

If a noun ends in *-o* after a consonant, form the plural by adding *-es*.

Singular Noun	Plural Noun
tomato	tomatoes
embargo	________________
torpedo	________________
veto	________________

To form the plural of foreign words ending in *-o*, just add *-s*.

Singular Noun	Plural Noun
alto	altos
tango	________________
casino	________________
canto	________________
libretto	________________

Irregular plurals don't follow any of these rules!

Singular Noun	Irregular Plural Noun
ox	oxen
louse	lice
emphasis	emphases

Singular Noun	Irregular Plural Noun
crisis	________________
phenomenon	phenomena
nucleus	nuclei
moose	moose
sheep	________________
elk	elk

Exercise 22C: Plural Nouns

Complete the following excerpt by filling in the plural form of each noun in parentheses.

The following is slightly condensed from L. M. Montgomery's *The Story Girl.*

Outside of the orchard the grass was only beginning to grow green; but here, sheltered by the spruce (hedge) ________________ from uncertain (wind) ________________ and sloping to southern (sun) ________________, it was already like a wonderful velvet carpet; the (leaf) ________________ on the (tree) ________________ were beginning to come out in woolly, grayish (cluster) ________________; and there were purple-pencilled white (violet) ________________ at the base of the Pulpit Stone.

"It's all just as father described it," said Felix with a blissful sigh, "and there's the well with the Chinese roof."

We hurried over to it, treading on the (spear) ________________ of mint that were beginning to shoot up about it. It was a very deep well, and the curb was of rough, undressed (stone) ________________. Over it, the queer, pagoda-like roof, built by Uncle Stephen on his return from a voyage to China, was covered with yet leafless (vine) ________________.

"It's so pretty, when the (vine) ________________ leaf out and hang down in long (festoon)________________," said the Story Girl. "The (bird) ________________ build their (nest) ________________ in it. A pair of wild (canary) ________________ come here every summer. And (fern) ________________ grow out between the (stone) ________________ of the well as far down as you can see. The water is lovely."

We then went to find our birthday (tree) ________________. We were rather disappointed to find them quite large, sturdy ones. It seemed to us that they should still be in the sapling stage corresponding to our boyhood.

"Your (apple) ________________ are lovely to eat," the Story Girl said to me, "but Felix's are only good for (pie) ________________. Those two big (tree) ________________ behind them are the twins' (tree) ________________—my mother and Uncle Felix, you know. The (apple) ________________ are so dead sweet that nobody but us (child) ________________ and the French (boy) ________________ can eat them. And that tall, slender tree over there, with the (branch) ________________ all growing straight up, is a seedling that came up of itself, and NOBODY can eat its (apple) ________________, they are so sour and bitter. Even the (pig) ________________ won't eat them. Aunt Janet tried to make (pie) ____________ of them once, because she said she hated to see them going to waste. But she never tried again. She said it was better to waste (apple) ________________ alone than (apple) ________________ and sugar too. And then she tried giving them away to the French hired (man) ________________, but they wouldn't even carry them home."

The Story Girl's (word) ______________ fell on the morning air like (pearl) ___________ and (diamond) ________________. Even her (preposition) ________________ and (conjunction) ____________________ had untold charm, hinting at mystery and laughter and magic bound up in everything she mentioned. Apple (pie) ________________ and sour (seedling) ________________ and (pig) ________________ became straightway invested with a glamour of romance.

— LESSON 23 —

Plural Nouns
Descriptive Adjectives
Possessive Adjectives
Contractions

An apostrophe is a punctuation mark that shows possession. It turns a noun into an adjective that tells whose.

Possessive adjectives tell whose.

An adjective modifies a noun or pronoun.
Adjectives tell what kind, which one, how many, and whose.
Descriptive adjectives tell what kind.
A descriptive adjective becomes an abstract noun when you add *-ness* to it.

Form the possessive of a singular noun by adding an apostrophe and the letter *-s*.

Exercise 23A: Introduction to Possessive Adjectives

Read the following nouns. Choose a person that you know to possess each of the items. Write the person's name in the first column. Then, in the second column, write the person's name, an apostrophe, and an *s* to form a possessive adjective.

Example: Clara	Clara's	stuffed animal
________	________	finger puppets
________	________	instrument
________	________	bedside table
________	________	bunny slippers
________	________	handwriting

Form the possessive of a plural noun ending in -*s* by adding an apostrophe only.

Form the possessive of a plural noun that does not end in -*s* as if it were a singular noun.

Exercise 23B: Singular and Plural Possessive Adjective Forms

Fill in the chart with the correct forms. The first row is done for you. Both regular and irregular nouns are included.

Noun	Singular Possessive	Plural	Plural Possessive
sidewalk	sidewalk's	sidewalks	sidewalks'
lunch			
bucket			
deer			
woman			
kitten			
hospital			
army			
creature			
foot			
stranger			

	SINGULAR		PLURAL	
	Pronoun(s)	**Possessive Adjective**	**Pronoun(s)**	**Possessive Adjective**
First person	I	my	we	our
Second person	you	your	you	your
Third person	he, she, it	his, her, its	they	their

INCORRECT	CORRECT
I's book	my book
you's candy	your candy
he's hat	his hat
she's necklace	her necklace
it's nest	its nest
we's lesson	our lesson
they's problem	their problem

Contraction	**Meaning**
he's	he is
she's	she is
it's	it is
you're	you are
they're	they are

A contraction is a combination of two words with some of the letters dropped out.

Exercise 23C: Common Contractions

Drop the letters in grey print and write the contraction in the blank. The first one is done for you.

Full Form	**Common Contraction**	**Full Form**	**Common Contraction**
are not	aren't	she is	__________
we had	__________	I have	__________
who is	__________	was not	__________
you will	__________	I would	__________
has not	__________	he would	__________
she had	__________	we will	__________
did not	__________	he has	__________
where is	__________	we have	__________

— LESSON 24 —

Possessive Adjectives
Contractions
Compound Nouns

A contraction is a combination of two words with some of the letters dropped out.

Contraction	Meaning	Not the Same as
he's	he is	his
she's	she is	her
it's	it is	its
you're	you are	your
they're	they are	their

It's hard for a hippopotamus to see its feet.
It is *hard for a hippopotamus to see its feet.*
It's hard for a hippopotamus to see ***it is*** *feet.*

You're fond of your giraffe.
You are *fond of your giraffe.*
You're fond of ***you are*** *giraffe.*

They're searching for their zebra.
They are *searching for their zebra.*
They're searching for ***they are*** *zebra.*

Exercise 24A: Using Possessive Adjectives Correctly

Cross out the incorrect word in parentheses.

(Your/You're) standing too close to the experiment—(your/you're) hair could catch fire!

My lunch is over there. (Its/It's) the one in the superhero bag.

(His/He's) flight has arrived, but (his/he's) still waiting for his luggage.

The employees will call out (your/you're) number when (their/they're) ready for you.

(Hers/She's) going to be very surprised when she learns that the award is (hers/she's).

(Its/It's) time for the computer to download (its/it's) update.

Where are (your/you're) scissors? (Your/You're) going to need them for this project.

Did you hear about the lion that escaped from (its/it's) cage? (Its/It's) on the front page of today's newspaper.

(Your/You're) coach will not be pleased if (your/you're) late for practice.

(Its/It's) supposed to rain tomorrow. Will you bring (your/you're) umbrella, or should my sister bring (hers/she's)?

A compound noun is a single noun composed of two or more words.

One word	shipwreck, haircut, chalkboard
Hyphenated word	self-confidence, check-in, pinch-hitter
Two or more words	air conditioning, North Dakota, *The Prince and the Pauper*

Exercise 24B: Compound Nouns

Underline each simple subject once and each simple predicate (verb) twice. Circle each compound noun.

The dishwasher will finish soon.

Li Na saw an inchworm on the windowsill.

My new keyboard has a green cover.

The babysitter played hide-and-seek with the five-year-old.

Jenna's high school prepared an excellent yearbook.

Rita's young granddaughter made a mess with her mother's makeup.

Fireflies lit the pathway.

In *A Charlie Brown Christmas*, Lucy van Pelt wishes for real estate.

If a compound noun is made up of one noun along with another word or words, pluralize the noun.

passerby passersby passerbys

If a compound noun ends in *-ful*, pluralize by putting an *-s* at the end of the entire word.

truckful trucksful truckfuls

If neither element of the compound noun is a noun, pluralize the entire word.

grown-up　　grown**s**-up　　grown-up**s**

If the compound noun includes more than one noun, choose the most important to pluralize.

attorney at law　　attorney**s** at law　　attorney at law**s**

Exercise 24C: Plurals of Compound Nouns

Write the plural of each singular compound noun in parentheses in the blanks to complete the sentences.

Did you bring extra (baseball) ________________ so we can play at the park?

It doesn't matter which of the (playground) ____________________ I take them to; the (six-year-old) ________________________ I watch on Saturdays always want to play on (merry-go-round) ________________________.

Both of my (sister-in-law) ____________________ live on the other side of the country.

We ate lots of (hotdog) ______________ when we went to see the (firework) ______________.

The (police officer) ____________________ were chasing the (redhead) ________________.

My mother brought home (bucketful) _________________ of (blueberry) ________________ from the farm.

When we were serving as interns, my brother and I acted as (go-between) _______________ for the two arguing (Congressman) ________________________.

The celebrity made a fuss about the paparazzi, but in reality he loved having so many (hanger-on) ________________________.

— REVIEW 2 —

Weeks 4-6

Topics
Simple, Progressive, and Perfect Tenses
Conjugations
Irregular Verbs
Subject/Verb Agreement
Possessives
Compound Nouns
Contractions

Review 2A: Verb Tenses

Write the tense of each underlined verb or verb phrase on the line to the right: simple past, present, or future; progressive past, present, or future; or perfect past, present, or future. The first one is done for you. Watch out for words that interrupt verb phrases but are not helping verbs (such as *not*).

These sentences are taken or adapted from Robert Louis Stevenson's *Treasure Island.*

	Verb Tense
Now, to tell you the truth, from the very first mention of Long John in Squire Trelawney's letter, I had taken a fear	perfect past
in my mind that he might prove to be the very one-legged sailor whom I had watched for so long at the old "Benbow."	______________
Another pause, and then, not a quarter of a mile in front of me, I beheld the Union Jack flutter in the air above a wood.	______________
"Tom, my man," said I,	______________
"you're going home."	______________
"They'll be glad to be packing in the schooner."	______________
"These poor lads have chosen me cap'n, after your desertion, sir."	______________
He was whistling to himself, "Come, Lasses and Lads."	______________
I had already deserted my eastern loophole.	______________

But he stuck to it like a man, in silence. ____________

Gray and I were sitting together at the far end of the ____________
blockhouse; and Gray took his pipe out of his mouth and ____________
fairly forgot to put it back again, so thunderstruck he was ____________
at this occurrence.

"If I am right, ____________
he's going now to see Ben Gunn." ____________

"I'll tell you one thing," ____________
says I: ____________
"I'm not going back to Captain Kidd's anchorage." ____________

I began to fear that ____________
something had gone wrong. ____________

"I dare you to thank me!" ____________
cried the squire. ____________

"And I'll be taking this to square the count." ____________

Review 2B: Verb Formations

Fill in the charts with the correct conjugations of the missing verbs. Identify the person of each group of verbs.

PERSON: ____________

	Past	Present	Future
SIMPLE	she	she	she will discover
PROGRESSIVE	she	she is discovering	she
PERFECT	she	she	she

PERSON: ____________

	Past	Present	Future
SIMPLE	I	I	I
PROGRESSIVE	I	I	I will be following
PERFECT	I had followed	I	I

PERSON: ____________

	Past	Present	Future
SIMPLE	you answered	you	you
PROGRESSIVE	you	you	you
PERFECT	you	you	you will have answered

PERSON: ____________

	Past	Present	Future
SIMPLE	they	they	they will yell
PROGRESSIVE	they	they	they
PERFECT	they had yelled	they	they

Review 2C: Person and Subject/Verb Agreement

Cross out the incorrect verb in parentheses.

The following sentences are taken from the Malaya story "The Deceitful Pelican" in *Folk Tales and Fables of Asia and Australia*, by Robert Ingpen and Barbara Hayes.

Ruan (was/were) not clever. Few fish (is/are).

When he (was/were) not eating Ruan lay in the cool water at the bottom of the pool and tried to look like a mottled brown stone.

The great pouch under the pelican's large beak (was/were) empty.

The pelican tossed his head and said, "The creatures of this pool (lives/live) in times of dreadful danger. How I (admires/admire) their courage."

"I (has/have) a young family to consider."

"I (has/have) traveled the world," said the pelican. "I (knows/know) many things."

"You (has/have) found a new home of exquisite beauty for me and my wife and little ones."

His wife and young ones (was/were) confused at this startling news.

The baby fish pressed eagerly forward and showed that they (was/were) true children of their father.

Review 2D: Possessives and Compound Nouns

Complete the chart below, writing the singular possessive, plural, and plural possessive of each singular pronoun or compound noun. The first one has been done for you.

Noun	Possessive	Plural	Plural Possessive
notebook	notebook's	notebooks	notebooks'
I	__________	__________	__________
hallway	__________	__________	__________
it	__________	__________	__________
butterfly	__________	__________	__________
chairwoman	__________	__________	__________
he	__________	__________	__________
president-elect	__________	__________	__________
you	__________	__________	__________
ladybug	__________	__________	__________
spokesperson	__________	__________	__________
she	__________	__________	__________
jellyfish	__________	__________	__________
toothpick	__________	__________	__________

Review 2E: Plurals and Possessives

In the following sentences, provide the possessive, the plural, or the plural possessive for each noun in parentheses as indicated.

These sentences are from *Pollyanna*, by Eleanor H. Porter.

To Mrs. Snow's unbounded amazement, Pollyanna sprang to her (foot, plural) __________ and clapped her (hand, plural) __________.

"I like old (folk, plural) __________ just as well, maybe better, sometimes—being used to the (Lady, plural possessive) __________ Aid, so."

(Nancy, possessive) __________ (lip, plural) __________ parted abruptly, as if there were angry (word, plural) __________ all ready to come; but her (eye, plural) __________, resting on (Pollyanna, possessive) __________ jubilantly trustful face, saw something that prevented the (word, plural) __________ being spoken.

She told me afterwards she reckoned she'd have gone raving crazy if it hadn't been for (Mr. White, possessive) ____________________ (sister, possessive) ____________________ (ear, plural) ____________________.

Your aunt telephoned down to the (Harlow, plural possessive) ____________________ place across the way.

"I know it, poor little thing," crooned Pollyanna, tenderly, looking into the little (creature, possessive) ____________________ frightened (eye, plural) ____________________.

"Yes; and I'd tell it better this time," hurried on Pollyanna, quick to see the (sign, plural) ____________________ of relenting in the (boy, possessive) ____________________ face.

Review 2F: Contractions

Finish the following excerpt by forming contractions from the words in parentheses.

In the following transcript (which has been abridged), "LBJ" stands for Lyndon Baines Johnson, and "MLK" stands for Martin Luther King Jr. This conversation between them happened a few days after Johnson was inaugurated as President of the United States following the assassination of John F. Kennedy.

LBJ: . . . and a good many people told me that they heard about your statement. ____________ (I have) been locked up in this office, and I ____________ (have not) seen it. But I want to tell you how grateful I am, and how worthy ____________ (I am) going to try to be of all your hopes.

MLK: Well, thank you very much. ____________ (I am) so happy to hear that, and I knew that you had just that great spirit, and you know you have our support and backing, because we know what a difficult period this is.

LBJ: ____________ (It is) just an impossible period. ____________ (We have) got a budget coming up ____________ (that is)— ____________ (we have) got nothing to do with it; ____________ (it is) practically already made. And ____________ (we have) got a civil rights bill that ____________ (had not) even passed the House, and ____________ (it is) November, and Hubert Humphrey told me yesterday everybody wanted to go home. ______________ (We have) got a tax bill that they ____________ (have not) touched. We just got to let up—not let up on any of them and keep going and—

MLK: Yes.

LBJ: —I guess ____________ (they will) say that ____________ (I am) repudiated. But ____________ (I am) going to ask the Congress Wednesday to just stay there until they pass them all. They ____________ (will not) do it. But ____________ (we will) just keep them there next year until they do, and we just ____________ (will not) give up an inch.

MLK: Uh-uh. Well this is mighty fine. I think ____________ (it is) so imperative. I think one of the great tributes that we can pay in memory of President Kennedy is to try to enact some of the great, progressive policies that he sought to initiate.

LBJ: Well, ____________ (I am) going to support them all, and you can count on that. And ____________ (I am) going to do my best to get other men to do likewise, and ____________ (I will) have to have y'all's help.

MLK: Well, you know you have it, and just feel free to call on us for anything.

WEEK 7

Compounds and Conjunctions

— LESSON 25 —

Contractions
Compound Nouns
Diagramming Compound Nouns
Compound Adjectives
Diagramming Adjectives
Articles

A contraction is a combination of two words with some of the letters dropped out.

Exercise 25A: Contractions Review

Write the two words that form each contraction on the blanks to the right. Some contractions have more than one correct answer. The first is done for you.

Contraction	Helping Verb	Other Word
she's	is (or has)	she
who's	________	________
aren't	________	________
I'd	________	________
we've	________	________
shouldn't	________	________
can't	________	________
you'll	________	________
hasn't	________	________

Our air conditioning is working!

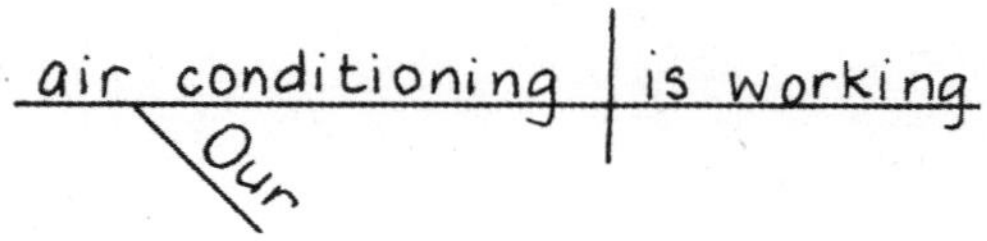

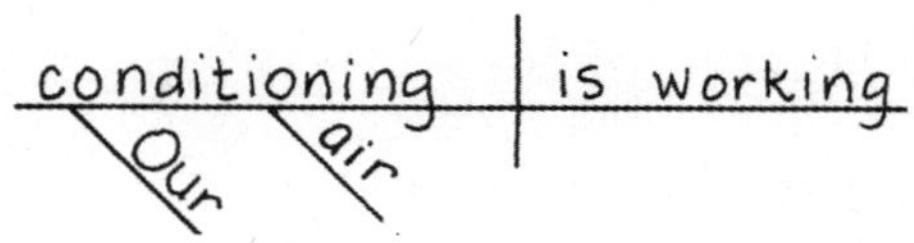

Exercise 25B: Diagramming Adjectives and Compound Nouns

On your own paper, diagram every word of the following sentences.

Kristi's ice cream melted.
Our post office closed.
Humpty Dumpty has fallen.
Marie Curie researched.

The large-headed monster had twenty-seven teeth.

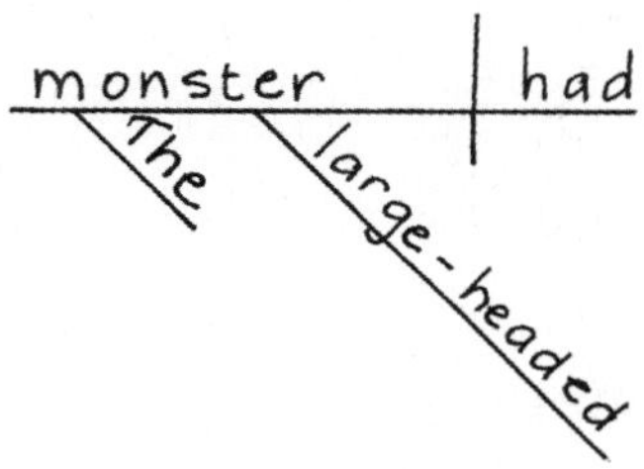

The articles are *a, an*, and *the*.

Exercise 25C: Compound Nouns

Draw a line to match each word in Column A with the correct word in Column B to form a single-word compound noun. Then rewrite the new compound noun on the space provided. The first is done for you.

Column A	Column B	New Compound Noun
base	book	baseball
key	crow	______________
note	ball	______________
grape	worm	______________
scare	fruit	______________
earth	cake	______________
pan	board	______________

Exercise 25D: Compound Adjectives

Correctly place hyphens in the following phrases.

forty seven full length novels
a part time job
time saving devices
the long distance runner
three fourths cup of sugar
a twelve story building
twenty four three year old children

Exercise 25E: Diagramming Adjectives, Compound Nouns, and Compound Adjectives

On your own paper, diagram every word in the following sentences. These are adapted from *The Secret Garden*, by Frances Hodgson Burnett.

The long-lasting rainstorm had ended.
The rabbits' tremulous noses were sniffing.
A laurel-hedged walk curved.
Pink-cheeked Mary Lennox was running.
Fair fresh rosebuds uncurled.

— LESSON 26 —

Compound Subjects
The Conjunction *And*
Compound Predicates
Compound Subject-Predicate Agreement

The fireman hurries.
The policeman hurries.
The fireman and the policeman hurry.

SIMPLE PRESENT

	Singular	**Plural**
First person	I hurry	we hurry
Second person	you hurry	you hurry
Third person	he, she, it hurries	they hurry

Compound subjects joined by *and* are plural in number and take plural verbs.
A conjunction joins words or groups of words together.

The farmer plants.
The farmer harvests.
The farmer plants and harvests.

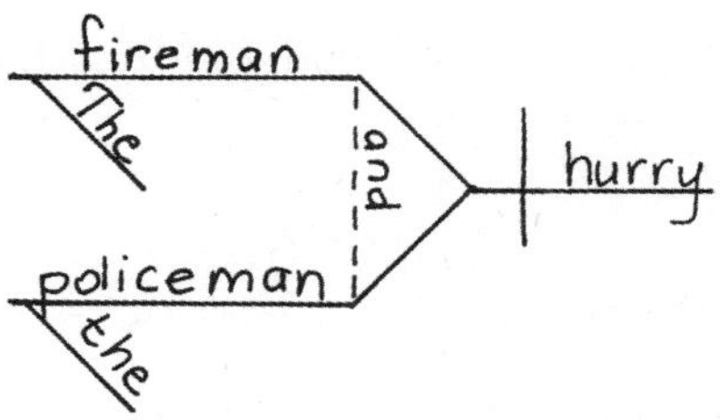

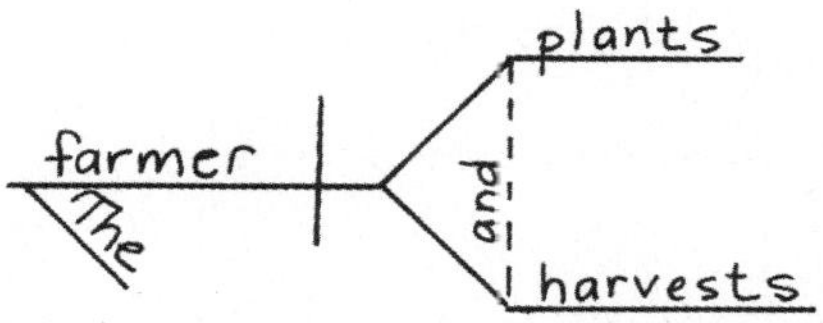

Exercise 26A: Identifying Subjects, Predicates, and Conjunctions

Underline the subject(s) once and the predicate(s) twice in each sentence. Circle the conjunctions that join them. The first one is done for you.

These sentences are adapted from E. L. Konigsburg's *From the Mixed-Up Files of Mrs. Basil E. Frankweiler.*

So she lay there in the great quiet of the museum next to the warm quiet of her brother and enjoyed the soft stillness around them: a comforter of quiet.

He felt its cool roundness and splashed his way over to Claudia.

Michelangelo, Angel, and the entire Italian Renaissance waited for them until morning.

We'll get our mailbox number, write it in, and take it to the museum office.

Jamie paid the rent, signed a form under the name Angelo Michaels and gave his address as Marblehead, Massachusetts.

They stood in line and got tickets for a tour.

Four Americans, two Englishmen, and one German have thus far examined the statue.

Exercise 26B: Diagramming Compound Subjects and Predicates

Underline the subject(s) once and the predicate(s) twice in the following sentences. Circle any conjunctions.

When you are finished, diagram the subjects (and any articles modifying the subjects), predicates, and conjunctions (ONLY) of each sentence on your own paper.

Alexandra and Raphael play tic-tac-toe together.

Bats and balls flew into the air and landed on the grass.

Megan calculated the answer and corrected her sister's work.

The puppy and the piglet study each other through the fence.

The vase on the nightstand teetered and fell.

The newborn lambs and the curious rabbits delighted and amused the children during their visit to the petting zoo.

Exercise 26C: Forming Compound Subjects and Verbs

Combine each of these sets of simple sentences into one sentence with a compound subject and/or a compound predicate joined by *and*. Use your own paper.

Bimala parks the car.
Bimala locks the car.

The fern needs watering.
The geranium needs watering.

The hurricane has caused horrific damage to the town.
The tornado has caused horrific damage to the town.

The red kangaroo clucks.
The red kangaroo hops.
The golden-mantled kangaroo hops.
The golden-mantled kangaroo clucks.
The wallaroo hops.
The wallaroo clucks.

Exercise 26D: Subject-Verb Agreement with Compound Subjects

Choose the correct verb in parentheses to agree with the subject. Cross out the incorrect verb.

The visitor (approach/approaches) the door and (knock/knocks) softly.

Louisa and Peter (run/runs) to open the door.

Louisa (ask/asks) if Mrs. Kim would like to see the new baby.

Mrs. Kim (smile/smiles) and (nod/nods).

Mother and Father (come/comes) into the room and (greet/greets) Mrs. Kim.

The tiny new baby (study/studies) the guest with wide eyes.

— LESSON 27 —

Coordinating Conjunctions
Complications in Subject-Predicate Agreement

A conjunction joins words or groups of words together.
A coordinating conjunction joins similar or equal words or groups of words together.

and, or, nor, for, so, but, yet

Indonesia and Greater Antilles are groups of islands.
I will nap or go running.
They will not help me, nor you.
I ran after them, for I needed help.
I stubbed my toe, so now my foot hurts.
I was exhausted, but my sister was still full of energy.
He was laughing, yet he seemed sad.

Exercise 27A: Using Conjunctions

Fill the blanks in the sentences below with the appropriate conjunctions. You must use each conjunction at least once. (There is more than one possible answer for many of the blanks.)

These sentences are adapted from *A Wrinkle in Time*, by Madeleine L'Engle.

She has doctors' degrees in both biology ____________________ bacteriology.

Calvin held her hand strongly in his, ____________________ she felt neither strength ____________________ reassurance in his touch.

Not only is there no need to fight me, ____________________ you will not have the slightest desire to do so. ____________________ why should you wish to fight someone who is here only to save you pain ____________________ trouble?

Charles Wallace slid down from his chair ____________________ trotted over to the refrigerator, his pajamaed feet padding softly as a kitten's.

On the dais lay—what? Meg could not tell, ____________________ she knew that it was from this that the rhythm came.

We could feel her heart, very faintly, the beats very far apart. ____________________ then it got stronger. ____________________ all we have to do is wait.

With a good deal of difficulty I can usually decipher Meg's handwriting, ________________ I doubt very much if her teachers can, ____________________ are willing to take the time.

You could learn it, Charles. ____________________ there isn't time. We can only stay here long enough to rest up ____________________ make a few preparations.

It had the slimness and lightness of a bicycle, ____________________ as the foot pedals turned they seemed to generate an unseen source of power, ____________________ the boy could pedal very slowly ____________________ move along the street quite swiftly.

Charles Wallace continued his slow walk forward, ____________________ she knew that he had not heard her.

Compound subjects joined by *and* are plural in number and take plural verbs.

I am friendly.
George and I are friends.

The policeman or the fireman hurries.

The dog and the cat are sleeping on the sofa.
The dog or the cat is sleeping on the sofa.
The dogs or the cat is sleeping on the sofa.

When compound subjects are joined by *or*, the verb agrees with the number of the nearest subject.

The pies were scrumptious.
The pies on the table were scrumptious.
The box of pencils is on the top shelf.

A can of red beans sits on the table.

The young man at all of the meetings was bored.

Fractions are singular if used to indicate a single thing.
Fractions are plural if used to indicate more than one thing.

Three-fourths of the pie was missing.
Three-fourths of the socks were missing.

Expressions of money, time, and quantity (weight, units, and distance) are singular when used as a whole, but plural when used as numerous single units.

Thirty dollars is too much to pay for that shirt.
Thirty dollars are spread across the table.

Seven years is a long time to wait.
The minutes tick by.

A thousand pounds is far too heavy for that truck.
Fifty gallons of water are divided among the refugees.
Four miles is too far to walk.

Collective nouns are usually singular. Collective nouns can be plural if the members of the group are acting as independent individuals.

The herd of cattle was grazing quietly.
The herd of cattle were scattered throughout the plains.

Exercise 27B: Subject-Predicate Agreement: Troublesome Subjects

Choose the correct verb in parentheses to agree with the subject noun or pronoun in number. Cross out the incorrect verb.

The invention of light bulbs (have/has) had a significant influence on society.

Now that pictures (have/has) been taken, the soccer team (have/has) returned to their classes.

Either this book or that poem (are/is) the most difficult thing I've studied this year.

The company of actors (take/takes) their places on the stage.

One hundred ten degrees (are/is) just too hot to play outside!

Seven days (have/has) passed since I made the decision to run for office.

The board (have/has) decided to enact the new rule.

The pie or the cupcakes (seem/seems) like a good choice for dessert.

The jury (wait/waits) for the judge to read the verdict.

The oranges on the tree (are/is) nearly ripe!

Sixteen dollars (are/is) a great deal for that coat!

The birds in the trees (are/is) chirping merrily.

About half of the attendees (were/was) planning to leave the conference after lunch.

Every Tuesday, Justine and Annika (sit/sits) on a bench in the park and (tell/tells) each other stories.

When I wake up in the morning, my mother or my father (have/has) made breakfast.

One-fourth of the money (were/was) intended for charity.

A band of outlaws (were/was) waiting for the stagecoach.

My brother, my sister, or I (take/takes) the trash out every week.

Exercise 27C: Fill in the Verb

Choose a verb in the present tense that makes sense to complete each sentence. Be sure the verb agrees in number with its subject!

The fog in the streets ________________ driving dangerous.

The books with the author's signature ________________ more.

The bevy of admirers ________________ the rock star.

Your impudence ________________ me to eject you from this classroom!

Nine dollars ________________ not a large amount.

Green, red, and purple ________________ my favorite colors.

The mice in the cage ________________ with fright as the cat ________________ near.

I listen as either the old man or the clumsy child ________________ up the stairs.

Two-thirds of the children ________________ as soon as they get to the playground.

— LESSON 28 —

Further Complications in Subject-Predicate Agreement

Many nouns can be plural in form but singular in use: measles, mumps, rickets, politics, mathematics, economics, news.

Mathematics is my favorite subject.

Singular literary works, works of art, newspapers, countries, and organizations can be plural in form but are still singular in use.

Little Women was written by Louisa May Alcott.
The United States is south of Canada.

Many nouns are plural in form and use but singular in meaning: pants, scissors, pliers, glasses.

Pants are too hot in the summertime.

In sentences beginning with *There is* or *There are*, the subject is found after the verb.

There is a skunk in the brush.
There are three skunks in the brush.

***Each* and *every* always indicate a singular subject.**

In Masai villages, each woman cares for her own cattle.
In Masai villages, each of the women cares for her own cattle.
In Masai villages, each cares for her own cattle.

In Masai villages, women care for their own cattle.

Every man needs friends.
Men need friends.

Compound nouns that are plural in form but singular in meaning take a singular verb.

Fish and chips is my favorite British dish.

Compound subjects joined by *and* take a singular verb when they name the same thing.

The owner and manager of the ice cream shop is also working behind the counter.

Nouns with Latin and Greek origins take the singular verb when singular in form and the plural verb when plural in form.

The data suggest otherwise.

Singular	**Plural**
medium	media
datum	data
criterion	criteria
phenomenon	phenomena
focus	foci
appendix	appendices

Exercise 28A: Subject-Verb Agreement: More Troublesome Subjects

Choose the correct verb in parentheses and cross out the incorrect verb.

Mathematics (is/are) one of my favorite things to study.

Every ant in the colony (has/have) a job.

There (is/are) a little ice cream shop downtown near the park.

The criteria for the project (was/were) not made clear to the students.

The pianist and organist (is/are) also performing a trumpet solo.

Ham and cheese (is/are) my favorite kind of sandwich.

There (is/are) three children in the yard.

Each child (wants/want) a popsicle.

Each of the children (prefers/prefer) a particular flavor.

The Lion, the Witch, and the Wardrobe (was/were) the first book C. S. Lewis wrote in the Chronicles of Narnia.

My pants (is/are) too short!

Linguistics (is/are) a fascinating field of study.

The foci of an ellipse (determines/determine) what the ellipse will look like.

Romeo and Juliet (is/are) one of Shakespeare's tragedies.

Ginevra's left-handed scissors (has/have) green handles.

Spaghetti and meatballs (sounds/sound) like a great idea for dinner.

"Here (is/are) an interesting phenomenon in the skies," said the astronomy professor.

Each of the runners (was/were) determined to win the race.

The United Arab Emirates (is/are) a country on the Arabian Peninsula.

Every koala (loves/love) eucalyptus leaves.

Exercise 28B: Correct Verb Tense and Number

Complete each of these sentences by writing the correct number and tense of the verb indicated. When you are finished, read each sentence aloud to your instructor (don't read the bracketed instructions, though!).

These sentences are adapted from Lewis Carroll's *Through the Looking-Glass.*

"There [simple present of am] _______________ the effect of living backwards," the Queen [simple past of say] _______________ kindly.

The Messenger, to Alice's great amusement, [progressive past of open] _______________ a bag that hung round his neck.

The words of the old song [progressive past of play] _______________ in Alice's mind.

There [simple past of am] _______________ elephants that looked like bees.

The beautiful brown eyes of the Fawn [progressive present of fill] _______________ with alarm.

The Knight with the odd inventions [simple past of am] _______________ not a good rider.

Alice [simple past of think] _______________ to herself, "Thirty times three [simple present of make] _______________ ninety. I wonder if anyone [progressive present of count] _______________?

The egg on the shelf [progressive past of become] _______________ larger and larger, and more and more human.

There [simple past of am] _______________ a pause in the fight just then, and the Lion and the Unicorn [progressive past of pant] _______________ while the King [simple past of call] _______________ out "Ten minutes allowed for refreshments!"

Bread-and-butter [simple present of am] _______________ what you get when you divide a loaf with a knife.

WEEK 8

Introduction to Objects

— LESSON 29 —

Action Verbs
Direct Objects

A direct object receives the action of the verb.

Cara built a bonfire.
We roasted marshmallows over the bonfire.
Tom ate the delicious cookie.
Julia, hot and thirsty, drank the fresh-squeezed lemonade.
She visited her grandfather.
He had forgotten her name.
She found peace.

We roasted marshmallows.

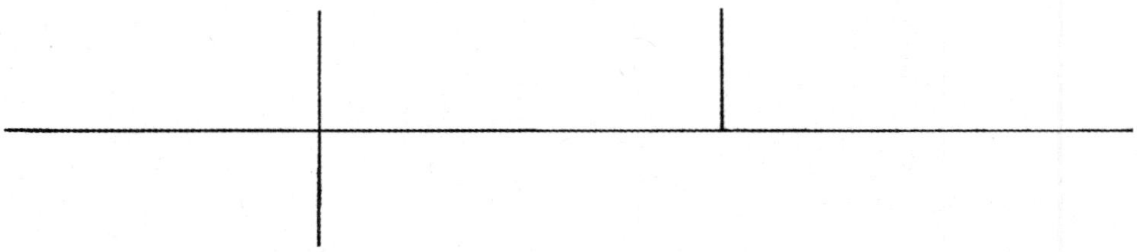

We roasted soft marshmallows and beefy hot dogs.

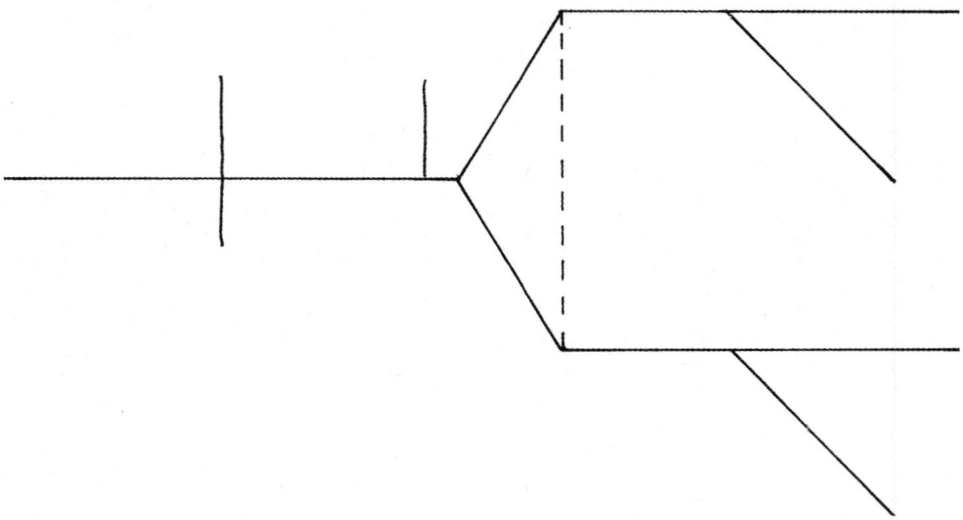

My friend and I rode roller coasters and ate popcorn and cotton candy.

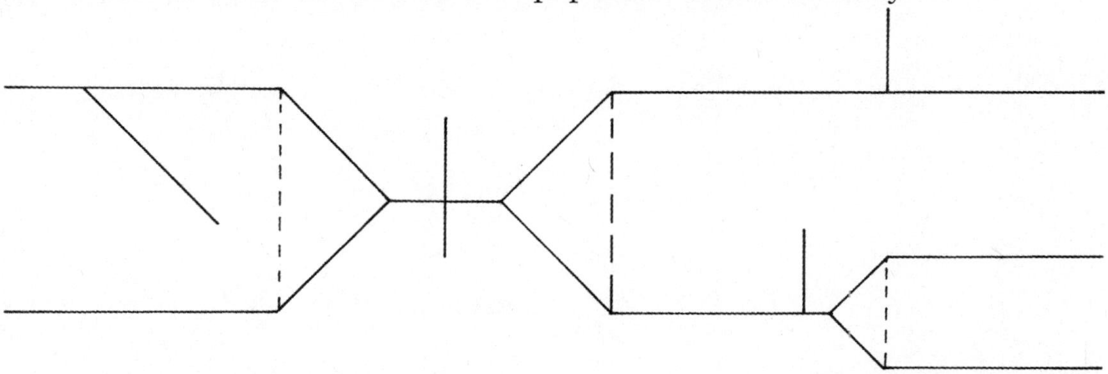

Exercise 29A: Direct Objects

In the following sentences, underline the subjects once and the predicates twice. Circle each direct object.

If the sentence is a command, write the understood subject in parentheses and underline it once.

Nate dragged the sled to the top of the hill.

The excited young girl shook the present too hard.

Would you pour the tea for us?

Place the candles on the cake.

Victoria and Max will play the game.

The officers at the event direct traffic and answer questions.

After their performance in the ice skating competition, Yaroslav and Maria quenched their thirst and awaited their scores.

My new camera takes great pictures and videos.

Asami discarded the twos, threes, and fours, and dealt the rest of the cards.

The eccentric old man wore a fedora, a corsage, and a bright green apron.

In the bakery, I see and smell my favorite things.

Anya and Matthias popped their balloon and extracted the next clue for the game.

Camila, Tomás, and Maite crossed the bridge and waited.

Stamp and deliver this important letter!

The angry boy slammed the door and hid.

Exercise 29B: Diagramming Direct Objects

On your own paper, diagram the subjects, verbs, and direct objects in the sentences from Exercise 29A.

— LESSON 30 —

Direct Objects
Prepositions

I broke my breakfast plate!
The pottery plate broke into pieces.

A preposition shows the relationship of a noun or pronoun to another word in the sentence.

Prepositions
aboard, about, above, across
after, against, along, among, around, at

before, behind, below, beneath
beside, between, beyond, by

down, during, except, for, from
in, inside, into, like

near, of, off, on, over
past, since, through, throughout

to, toward, under, underneath
until, up, upon
with, within, without

Exercise 30A: Identifying Prepositions

In the following sentences (adapted from J. R. R. Tolkien's *The Hobbit*), find and circle each preposition. Be careful: One word on the preposition list is also on the list of conjunctions you learned in Lesson 27. Only circle it when it functions as a preposition!

It had a perfectly round door like a porthole, painted green, with a shiny yellow brass knob in the exact middle. The door opened to a tube-shaped hall like a tunnel: a very comfortable tunnel without smoke, with paneled walls, and floors tiled and carpeted, provided with polished chairs, and lots of pegs for hats and coats—the hobbit was fond of visitors. The best rooms were all on the left-hand side, for these were the only ones with windows, deep-set round windows looking over his garden, and meadows sloping to the river.

Exercise 30B: Word Relationships

The following sentences all contain action verbs. Underline each subject once and each action verb twice. If the sentence has an action verb followed by a direct object, write *DO* above the direct object. If the sentence contains a preposition, circle the preposition and draw a line to connect the two words that the preposition shows a relationship between. The first two are done for you.

The clothes hung on the line.

DO

Genevieve remembered her grandmother's instructions.

The man charmed the snake.

Mrs. Wójcik teaches in the science lab.

The plumber with the green hat jumps very high.

The fidgety dog accidentally pressed the round purple button.

Jerome snapped his fingers.

The mighty ship with seven passenger decks rocked violently.

Enormous stones rolled down the hill.

A large black bear waited near the cave entrance.

My sister devoured her dinner.

The purple flowers by the curb were growing wildly.

Kiara reluctantly swallowed her pride.

I study at the library every Tuesday.

Exercise 30C: Diagramming Direct Objects

On your own paper, diagram the subjects, predicates, and direct objects only from the sentences above. If a sentence does not have a direct object, do not diagram it.

— LESSON 31 —

Definitions Review

Prepositional Phrases

Object of the Preposition

A noun names a person, place, thing, or idea.
An adjective modifies a noun or pronoun.

A pronoun takes the place of a noun.
A verb shows an action, shows a state of being, links two words together, or helps another verb.
A conjunction joins words or groups of words together.
A coordinating conjunction joins similar or equal words or groups of words together.
A phrase is a group of words serving a single grammatical function.
A preposition shows the relationship of a noun or pronoun to another word in the sentence.

Prepositions
aboard, about, above, across
after, against, along, among, around, at
before, behind, below, beneath
beside, between, beyond, by
down, during, except, for, from
in, inside, into, like
near, of, off, on, over
past, since, through, throughout
to, toward, under, underneath
until, up, upon
with, within, without

A brook sluggishly flows (through) low ground.

Dark draperies hung (upon) the walls.

The tunnel wound (into) the green hill.

A prepositional phrase begins with a preposition and ends with a noun or pronoun. That noun or pronoun is the object of the preposition.

Put your hand beneath your workbook.

Calvin ran across the floor.

I baked a pie for my mother.

Exercise 31A: Objects of Prepositional Phrases

Fill in the blanks with a noun as the object of the preposition to complete the prepositional phrases.

Liliana placed her backpack near the ________________.

The mouse scurried past the ________________.

Beyond the ________________ lies an ancient ruin.

The toddler's favorite toy was finally found beneath the _______________.

With great _______________, Mae climbed aboard the _______________.

Charles inched toward the _______________.

Exercise 31B: Identifying Prepositizonal Phrases

Can you find all eleven of the prepositional phrases in the following excerpt from J. R. R. Tolkien's *The Hobbit*? (Beware words that can be prepositions but can also function as other parts of speech!) Underline the complete prepositional phrases. Circle each preposition. Label each object of the preposition with *OP*.

In a great hall with pillars hewn from the living stone sat the Elvenking on a chair of carven wood. On his head was a crown of berries and red leaves, for the autumn was come again. In the spring he wore a crown of woodland flowers. In his hand he held a carven staff of oak.

Exercise 31C: Remembering Prepositions

Can you remember all 46 prepositions without looking back at your list? On your own paper, write them down in alphabetical order. The first letter of each preposition and the number of prepositions that begin with that letter are found below, as a memory aid.

A	B	D	E	F	I	L
aboard	________	________	________	________	________	________
________	________	________		________	________	
________	________				________	
________	________					
________	________					
________	________					
________	________					
________	________					
________						
________						

N	O	P	S	T	U	W
________	________	________	________	________	________	________
	________			________	________	________
	________			________	________	________
	________			________	________	
					________	

— LESSON 32 —

Subjects, Predicates, and Direct Objects
Prepositions
Object of the Preposition
Prepositional Phrases

The subject of the sentence is the main word or term that the sentence is about.
The simple subject of the sentence is *just* the main word or term that the sentence is about.
The complete subject of the sentence is the simple subject and all the words that belong to it.

The warrior saw on the opposite mountain two great globes of glowing fire.

The predicate of the sentence tells something about the subject.
The simple predicate of the sentence is the main verb along with any helping verbs.
The complete predicate of the sentence is the simple predicate and all the words that belong to it.
A direct object receives the action of the verb.
A preposition shows the relationship of a noun or pronoun to another word in the sentence.

Prepositions
aboard, about, above, across
after, against, along, among, around, at
before, behind, below, beneath
beside, between, beyond, by
down, during, except, for, from
in, inside, into, like
near, of, off, on, over
past, since, through, throughout
to, toward, under, underneath
until, up, upon
with, within, without

A prepositional phrase begins with a preposition and ends with a noun or pronoun. That noun or pronoun is the object of the preposition.

DO

The warrior | saw on the opposite mountain two great globes of glowing fire.

The warrior saw two great globes.

The Dragon King with his retainers accompanied the warrior to the end of the bridge, and took leave of him with many bows and good wishes.

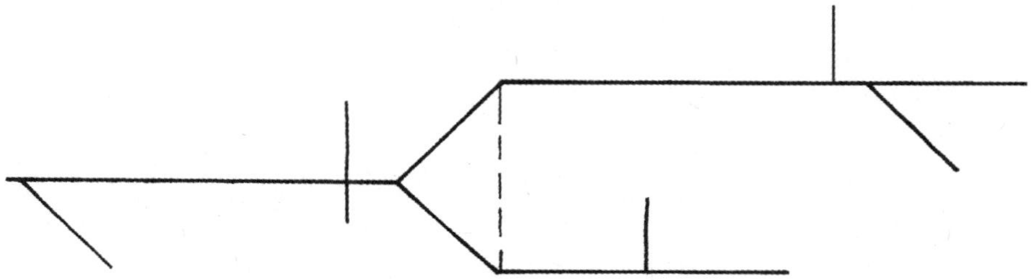

Exercise 32A: Identifying Prepositional Phrases and Parts of Sentences

In the following sentences from L. M. Montgomery's *Anne of Green Gables*, circle each prepositional phrase. Once you have identified the prepositional phrases, underline subjects once, underline predicates twice, and label direct objects with *DO*.

By the end of the term Anne and Gilbert were promoted into the fifth class.

In geometry Anne met her Waterloo.

For Anne the real excitement began with the dismissal of school.

After the tea at the manse Diana Barry gave a party.

I bought the dye from him.

I shut the door and looked at his things on the step.

In the evening Miss Barry took them to a concert in the Academy of Music.

She went into her big house with a sigh.

The Avonlea hills beyond them appeared against the saffron sky.

A professional elocutionist in a wonderful gown of shimmering gray stuff like woven moonbeams was staying at the hotel.

The stout lady in pink silk turned her head and surveyed Anne through her eyeglasses.

Exercise 32B: Diagramming

On your own paper, diagram all of the uncircled parts of the sentences from Exercise 32A.

WEEK 9

Adverbs

— LESSON 33 —

Adverbs That Tell How

A sneaky squirrel stole my sock slowly.
A sneaky squirrel stole my sock sleepily.
A sneaky squirrel stole my sock cheerfully.
A sneaky squirrel stole my sock rapidly.

An adverb describes a verb, an adjective, or another adverb.

An **exceptionally** sneaky squirrel stole my sock slowly.
A sneaky squirrel stole my sock **very** rapidly.

Adverbs tell how, when, where, how often, and to what extent.

Adjective	**Adverb**
serious	seriously
fierce	________
thorough	________
crazy	crazily
scary	________
cheery	________

He left hurriedly.
Hurriedly, he left.
He hurriedly left.

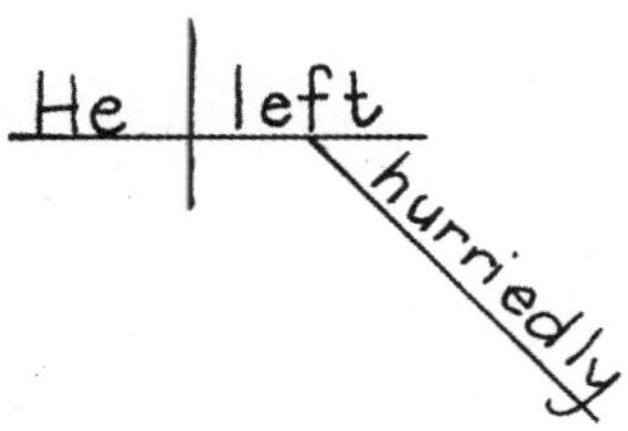

Exercise 33A: Identifying Adverbs That Tell How

Underline every adverb telling how in the following sentences, and draw arrows to the verbs that they modify.

These sentences are slightly adapted from *Imprudent King: A New Life of Philip II*, by Geoffrey Parker.

Ferdinand's obstinacy led Charles to exclaim angrily, "We need to establish who is emperor: you or me."

The ambassador dutifully informed his master.

Philip again complained selfishly.

He concluded briskly, "And so I am confident that you will gladly shoulder your part of the burden."

Philip scribbled grumpily, "If I were God and knew everyone's inner nature, this would be easy; but we are men, not gods."

Philip replied wearily that things were not nearly so bad.

He rode majestically through the streets of Genoa.

The prince spoke little and so softly that few could hear his words.

Some flatly refused to accept the posts that Philip offered them.

The condemned man unwisely appealed to the council again, and they recommended further clemency to the king.

The king sentenced him to be secretly strangled in his cell.

Exercise 33B: Forming Adverbs from Adjectives

Turn the following adjectives into adverbs.

Adjective	Adverb	Adjective	Adverb
useless	______________	unnecessary	______________
courageous	______________	lazy	______________
natural	______________	owlish	______________
stern	______________	dainty	______________
limp	______________		

Exercise 33C: Diagramming Adverbs

On your own paper, diagram the following sentences.

The tired woman stared vacantly.

The new band enthusiastically plays songs.

My old flashlight dimly lit the narrow passageway.

Adeline answered the question truthfully.

Sleepily, Travis answered the red phone.

The furious bull snorted menacingly.

— LESSON 34 —

Adverbs That Tell When, Where, and How Often

Exercise 34A: Telling When

Calvin dropped his recipe cards for banana bread. Help him get organized by numbering the following sentences from 1 to 5 so he can make the bread.

_______ Later, combine the wet ingredients with the dry ingredients.

_______ First, mash the bananas in a bowl.

_______ Second, add the egg, sugar, and cooking oil to the bananas.

_______ Finally, cook for 50 to 55 minutes in a 350° oven.

_______ Next, mix flour, baking powder, baking soda, cinnamon, and salt in a separate bowl.

An adverb describes a verb, an adjective, or another adverb.
Adverbs tell how, when, where, how often, and to what extent.

Yesterday I washed my dog outside.

The dog ran away.

Then the dog lay down.

Now my dog is sleeping there.

My glasses are lying there.

My red book is sitting here.

There are my glasses.

Here is my red book.

Now my dog is sleeping there.

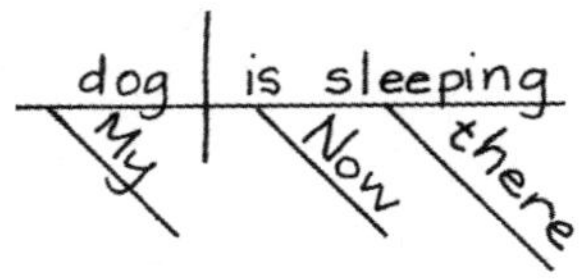

There are my glasses.

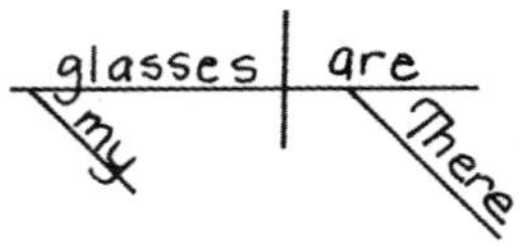

Here is my red book.

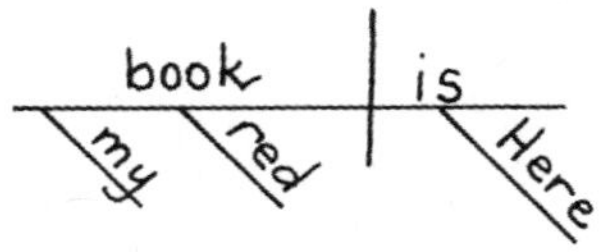

***Here* and *there* are adverbs that tell where.**

I wash my dog weekly.
Richie is always looking for adventure.
I will often be eating.

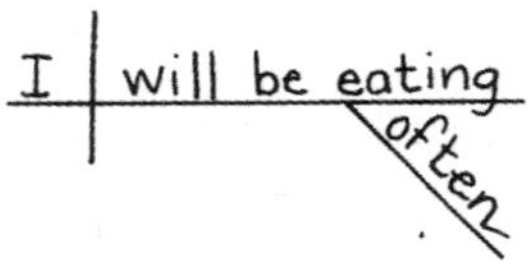

When will you arrive?
Where is my hat?
How are you doing?

you will arrive When.

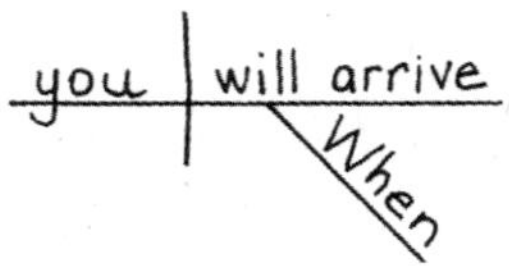

my hat is Where.

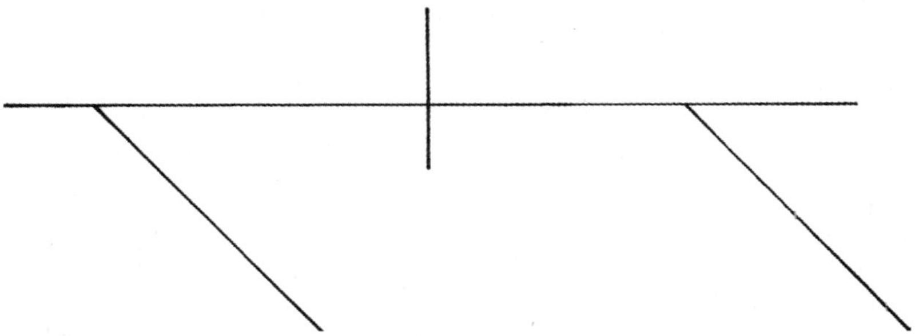

Exercise 34B: Distinguishing among Different Types of Adverbs

Put each of the following adverbs in the correct category according to the question it answers.

poorly	upstairs	sometimes	yesterday
fourth	regularly	sweetly	frequently
later	here	everywhere	happily

When	**Where**	**How**	**How Often**
____________	____________	____________	____________
____________	____________	____________	____________
____________	____________	____________	____________

Exercise 34C: Identifying Adverbs of Different Types

Underline the adverbs in the following sentences that tell when, where, or how often.

I will complete my homework later.

That stray cat often stays near the restaurant.

The coyote never catches the roadrunner.

Get your jacket now.

Quincy occasionally forgets a line, but he usually recovers from his mistakes.

Prairie dogs tunnel constantly.

The turtle was on that rock yesterday.

Tia is always changing her mind.

Antonio searched everywhere in the house for his keys.

I left my bag inside.

Exercise 34D: Diagramming Different Types of Adverbs

On your own paper, diagram the following sentences.

I was sneezing constantly yesterday!

Tomorrow, greet the new student warmly.

Cautiously, the timid girl stepped outside.

Bonnie and Reginald settled their differences yesterday.

Our neighbors were playing baseball earlier and accidentally broke Mr. Larson's window.

My dedicated instructor prepares lessons daily.

— LESSON 35 —

Adverbs That Tell To What Extent

An adverb describes a verb, an adjective, or another adverb.
Adverbs tell how, when, where, how often, and to what extent.

The extremely humid day was unpleasant.
Sharon runs quite quickly.
Larry shrieked especially loudly.

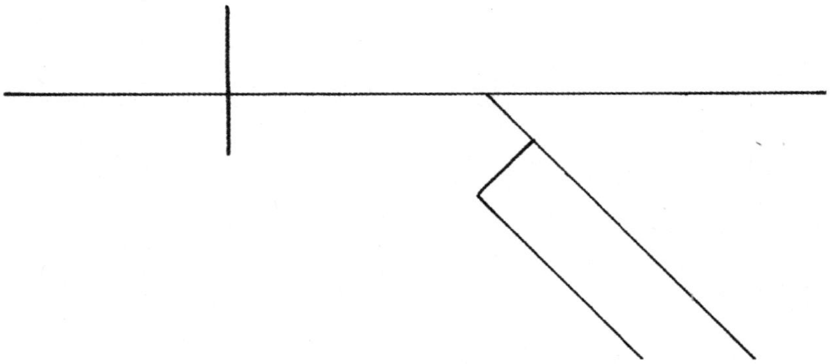

Extremely skittish Larry ran away.

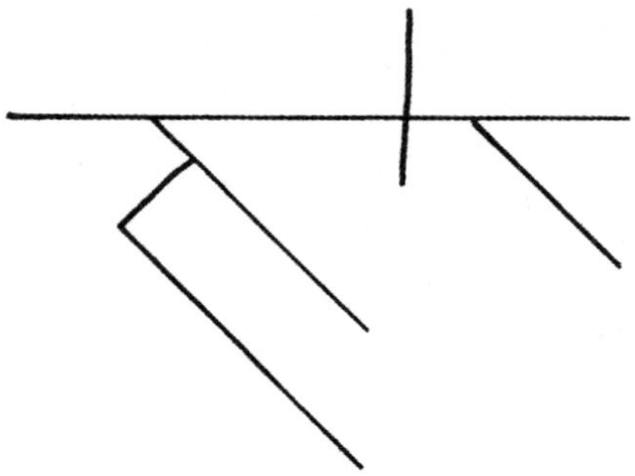

Exercise 35A: Identifying the Words Modified by Adverbs

Draw an arrow from each underlined adverb to the word it modifies.

These sentences are slightly adapted from Stephen Jay Gould's *The Flamingo's Smile: Reflections in Natural History.*

He was barely able to reconstruct the story later from his sadly inadequate record.

No other theme so well displays the human side of science.

Mottled shells are equally inconspicuous (indeed remarkably camouflaged) when dappled sunlight filters through the vegetation.

I shall then summarize the three major arguments from modern biology for the surprisingly small extent of human racial differences.

What cause could yield a periodicity so regular, yet so widely spaced?

The chain of being had always vexed biologists because, in some objective sense, it doesn't seem to describe nature very well.

We know, in retrospect, that England and most of northern Europe were, quite recently, covered several times by massive continental ice sheets.

One question has always predominated in this case—individuality.

Many of these plants contain psychoactive agents, avoided by mammals today as a result of their bitter taste.

The alkaloids simply don't taste good (they are bitter); in any case, mammals have livers happily supplied with the capacity to detoxify them.

As an animal, or any object, grows (provided its shape doesn't change), surface areas must increase more slowly than volumes—since surfaces get larger as length squared, while volumes increase much more rapidly, as length cubed.

A master in the art of teaching, he exercised an almost irresistible influence over his students.

He never married, socialized little, and published less.

Exercise 35B: Diagramming Different Types of Adverbs

On your own paper, diagram every word of the following sentences.

The extremely old chair wobbled threateningly.

Angie and Brian presented a completely workable solution.

Somewhere, this very untidy room contains my completely finished project.

Kick the ball much more forcefully.

Sophia retrieved the next clue quite easily.

Where are you going so hurriedly?

— LESSON 36 —

Adjectives and Adverbs
The Adverb *Not*
Diagramming Contractions
Diagramming Compound Adjectives and Compound Adverbs

An adjective modifies a noun or pronoun.
Adjectives tell what kind, which one, how many, and whose.

An adverb describes a verb, an adjective, or another adverb.
Adverbs tell how, when, where, how often, and to what extent.

It matters naught.

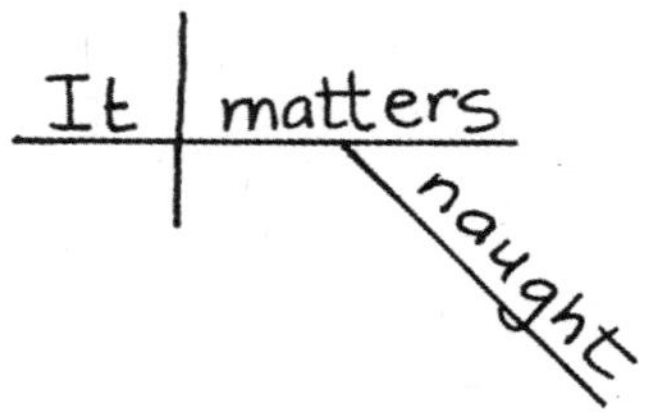

It does not matter.

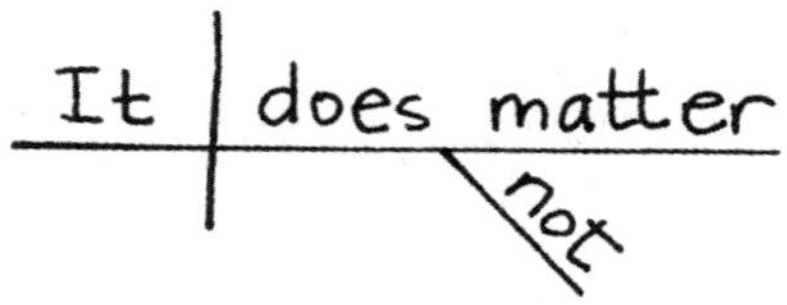

A contraction is a combination of two words with some of the letters dropped out.

It doesn't matter.

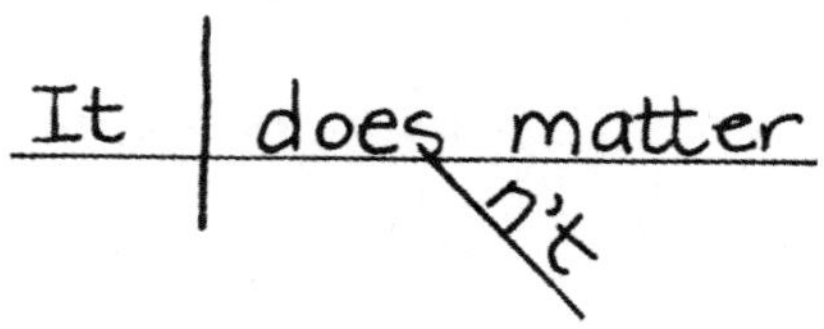

It's not there.

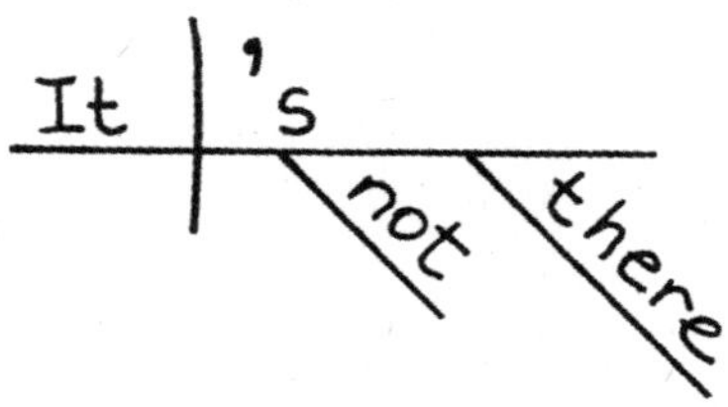

Tall and wide arches weren't often built.

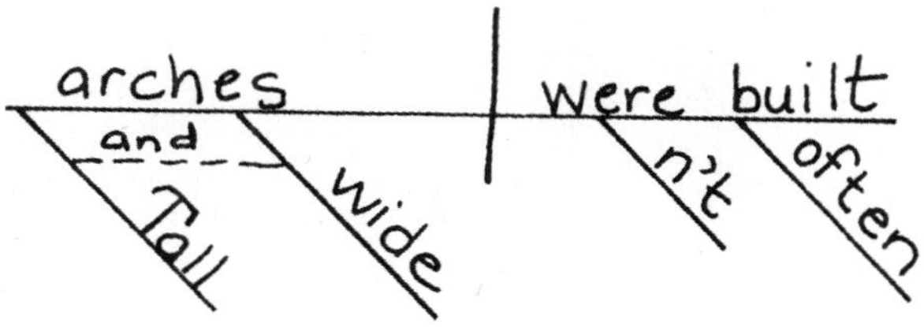

The idea was deeply and widely held.

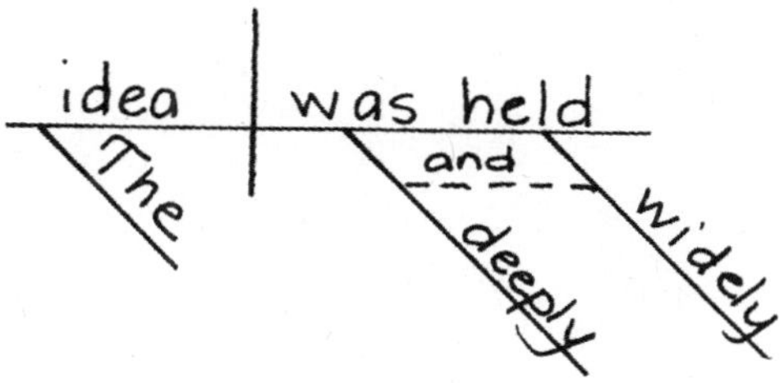

Exercise 36A: Practice in Diagramming

On your own paper, diagram every word of the following sentences.

These sentences are adapted from *Rebecca of Sunnybrook Farm*, by Kate Douglas Wiggin.

I've almost broken my neck.

She extended her dress still farther.

The thought gradually permeated Mr. Jeremiah Cobb's slow-moving mind.

Mother always keeps her promises.

We don't use the front stairs.

She fell down and wept very loudly.

Miss Dearborn heard many admiring remarks.

She did not tread the solid ground.

She smoothed it carefully and pinched up the white ruffle.

I didn't make a bad guess.

— REVIEW 3 —

Weeks 7-9

Topics
Parts of Speech
Compound Parts of Sentences
Prepositions
Prepositional Phrases
Objects of Prepositions
Subjects and Predicates
Subject-Verb Agreement
Verbs and Direct Objects

Review 3A: Parts of Speech

In the passage below, from Jules Verne's *Journey to the Center to the Earth*, identify the underlined words as *N* for noun, *ADJ* for adjective, *ADV* for adverb, *PREP* for preposition, or *CONJ* for conjunction. The first is done for you.

My uncle (N) said nothing. He was too busy examining his papers, among which of course was the famous parchment, and some letters of introduction from the Danish consul, which were to pave the way to an introduction to the Governor of Iceland. My only amusement was looking out of the window. But as we passed through a flat though fertile country, this occupation was slightly monotonous. In three hours we reached Kiel, and our baggage was at once transferred to the steamer.

We had now a day before us, a delay of about ten hours, which fact put my uncle in a towering passion. We had nothing to do but to walk about the pretty town and bay. At length, however, we went on board, and at half past ten were steaming down the Great Belt. It was a dark night, with a strong breeze and a rough sea, nothing being visible but the occasional fires on shore, with here and there a lighthouse. At seven in the morning we left Korsör, a little town on the western side of Seeland.

Review 3B: Recognizing Prepositions

Circle the 46 prepositions from your list in the following bank of words. Try to complete the exercise without looking back at your list of prepositions.

since against there during of before by small

after inside you past aboard went most

under in until now upon above ours pony

over behind near with he eat between

know beside like around and underneath grew about

from through beyond when sick oops their

toward among to off where without for but

up mine throughout they below been at

or within on hers beneath across down our

note along into star front except more

Review 3C: Subjects and Predicates

Draw one line under the simple subject and two lines under the simple predicate. These lines are from the poem "Wynken, Blynken, and Nod," by Eugene Field. Watch out for compound subjects and predicates!

Also, remember that in poetry, sometimes the order of words is different than in normal speech—once you have found the verb, ask "who or what?" before it to find the subject.

Wynken, Blynken, and Nod one night sailed off in a wooden shoe.

Where are you going?

And what do you wish?

The old moon asked the three.

The old moon laughed and sang a song.

The little stars were the herring fish.

Now cast your nets.

All night long their nets they threw to the stars in the twinkling foam.

Then down from the skies came the wooden shoe.

Wynken and Blynken are two little eyes.

And Nod is a little head.

And you shall see the beautiful things.

Review 3D: Complicated Subject-Verb Agreement

Cross out the incorrect verb form in parentheses.

The economics quizzes (is/are) challenging.

Linguistics (is/are) my favorite class.

There (is/are) four beverage options; Sally (wants/want) lemonade.

There (is/are) a man with yellow glasses near the statues.

A one-eyed dragon or a seven-headed dog (lies/lie) behind that door!

The quarterback and captain of the team (is/are) inviting everyone to his house after the game.

My pants (is/are) on backwards!

The faculty (is/are) waiting in the auditorium for the principal's announcement.

The faculty (has/have) different theories about what the principal might say.

Every book in those three sections (has/have) been checked out.

Grandmothers and grandfathers (is/are) seated near the front for the performance.

Songs or poems (makes/make) memorization easier for many people.

Each criterion (has/have) been met.

Each of the buttons in the quilt (represents/represent) a different place the quilter visited.

Review 3E: Objects and Prepositions

Identify the underlined words as *DO* for direct object or *OP* for object of preposition. For each direct object, find and underline twice the action verb that affects it. For each object of the preposition, find and circle the preposition to which it belongs.

These sentences are adapted from Andrew Peterson's *On the Edge of the Dark Sea of Darkness.*

He lifted a ring of keys from the wall, opened the barred door, and shoved the children into a cell.

People were walking, pushing carts, driving carriages, leading sheep, and loading wagons with fish.

Podo's weak voice echoed from the carriage again.

Immediately, Janner sensed a smell in the air, or some subtle sound on the wind.

He enjoyed the food and the fine filth of the place.

Brimney Stupe strolled through the corridors of the mansion at night with a candle above his head.

Peet fished a leather pouch from a small box beside him and sprinkled some of its contents into the pot.

Tink wiped his brow and shook his head.

Leeli hugged Mr. Reteep around his sizable waist.

WEEK 10

Completing the Sentence

— LESSON 37 —

Direct Objects
Indirect Objects

She gave **Odysseus** bread and sweet wine and sent him forth.

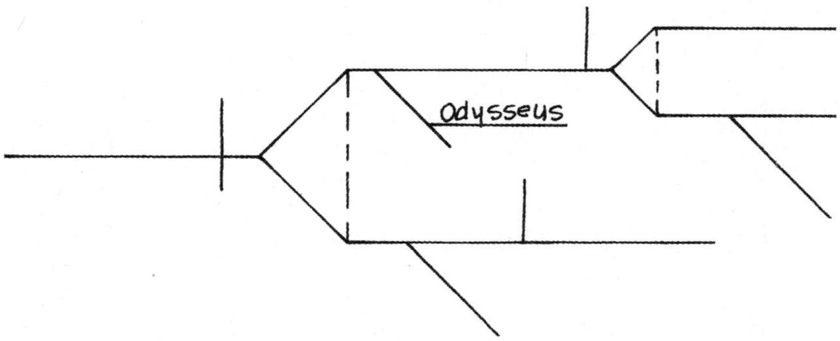

A direct object receives the action of the verb.
An indirect object is the noun or pronoun for whom or to whom an action is done.
An indirect object comes between the action verb and the direct object.

Odysseus asked the stranger a question.
Brandon sent his cousin and uncle an email.

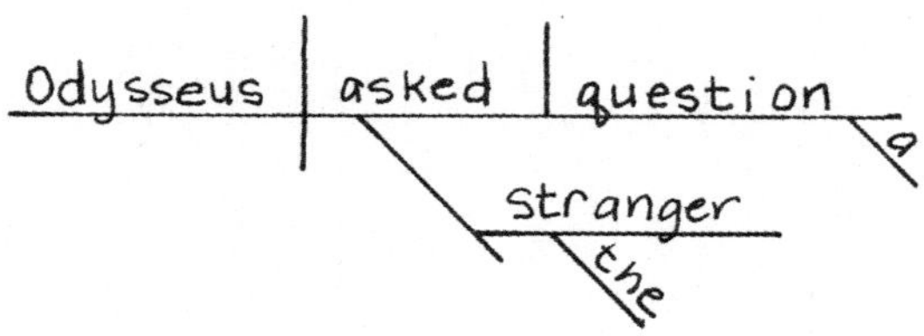

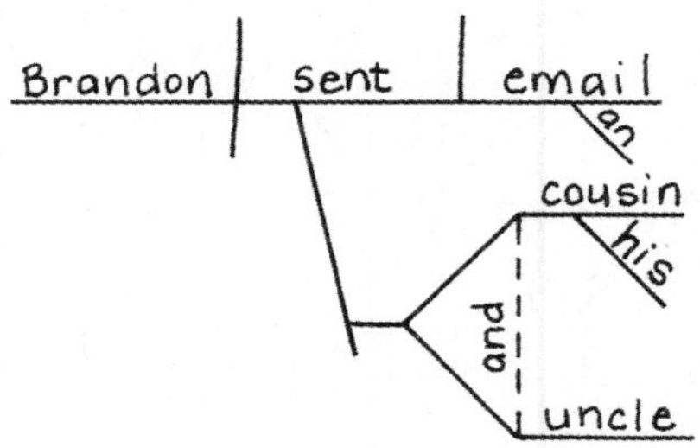

Exercise 37A: Identifying Direct Objects

Underline the action verbs (and any accompanying helping verbs) and circle the direct objects in these sentences. Remember that you can always eliminate prepositional phrases first if that makes the task easier.

The sentences are adapted from the Aztec folktale "The Earth Giants," as told by Robert Ingpen and Barbara Hayes in *Folktales and Fables of the Americas and the Pacific.*

And can you not lift it?

Zipacna lifted the huge tree onto his shoulder.

I will take the tree there.

Zipacna pulled several hairs from his head and gave them to some ants.

They built a great house over the ditch.

The heavenly twins made a model of a large, delicious-looking crab and put it in the river at the foot of the mountain.

He rubbed his hand across his eyes.

Exercise 37B: Identifying Direct Objects, Indirect Objects, and Objects of Prepositions

Underline every object in the following sentences. Label each one: *DO* for direct object, *IO* for indirect object, or *OP* for object of the preposition.

Cornelius cut Ryan an enormous slice of cake.

Jacques baked an enormous pie for his grandmother.

I cannot guarantee you a role in the play.

The first baseman lackadaisically tossed the pitcher the ball.

Mr. Cruz assigned us forty math problems yesterday!

Has someone actually sent me a present in the mail?

Rosa handed Corrie a pink backpack and a yellow pencil.

Noora had a new idea and asked us for our opinions about it.

Exercise 37C: Diagramming Direct Objects and Indirect Objects

On your own paper, diagram the following sentences.

Lend me your ears!
The teenager stood and offered the elderly lady his seat.
The mother gave her baby a toy and sang him a song.
Will you read me a story?
Gwendolen showed Rachna and Ethan the secret passage.
The artist sold him a unique painting.
Ms. Fitzpatrick will bring us the leftover cake tomorrow.

— LESSON 38 —

State-of-Being Verbs
Linking Verbs
Predicate Adjectives

The tiny, jewel-colored hummingbird is strong and frantically energetic.

A verb shows an action, shows a state of being, links two words together, or helps another verb.

A linking verb connects the subject to a noun, pronoun, or adjective in the complete predicate.

A predicate adjective describes the subject and is found in the complete predicate.

The subject of the sentence is the main word or term that the sentence is about.
The simple subject of the sentence is *just* the main word or term that the sentence is about.
The complete subject of the sentence is the simple subject and all the words that belong to it.

The predicate of the sentence tells something about the subject.
The simple predicate of the sentence is the main verb along with any helping verbs.
The complete predicate of the sentence is the simple predicate and all the words that belong to it.

State-of-Being Verbs
am were
is be
are being
was been

I am.

I am hungry.

They are being.

They are being loud.

The sunset was.

The sunset was spectacular.

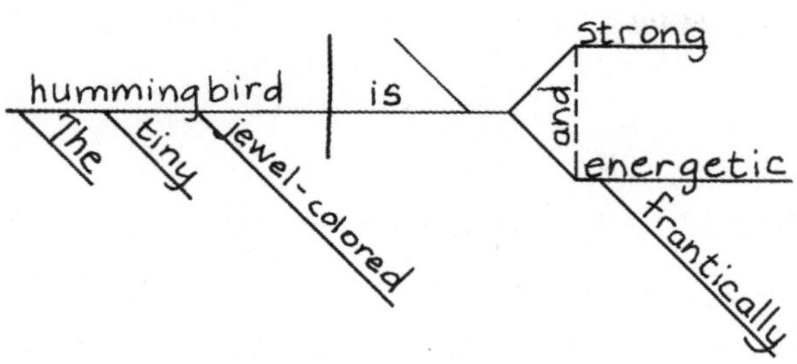

LV PA
Hummingbirds are tiny.

AV DO
Tiny hummingbirds sipped sweet nectar.

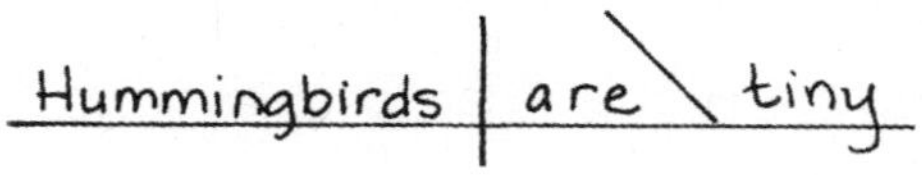

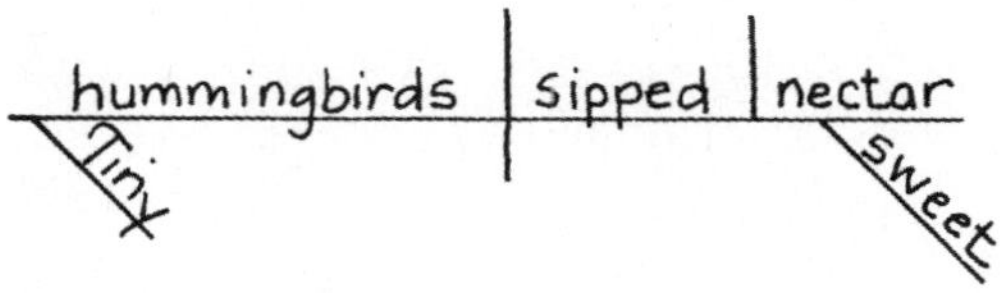

Exercise 38A: Action Verbs and Linking Verbs

In the following sentences, adapted from a letter Christopher Columbus wrote describing his first voyage, underline the simple subjects once and the simple predicates twice. If the verb is a linking verb, write *LV* over it, circle the predicate adjective, and label it *PA*. If the verb is an action verb, write *AV* over it, circle the direct object, and label it *DO*. If the sentence also includes an indirect object, circle it and label it *IO*. The first is done for you.

LV PV
The harbors are incredibly fine.

I found very many islands with large populations and took possession of them for their Highnesses.

The land is high and has many ranges of hills.

The trees, fruits, and plants are very different from those of Cuba.

They are amazingly timid.

All these islands are extremely fertile.

I gave them a thousand pretty things.

They gave me a good reception everywhere.

These men soon understood us.

Their hair is straight.

I will bring back a large cargo.

All was conjectural, without ocular evidence.

They should hold great celebrations.

Exercise 38B: Diagramming Direct Objects and Predicate Adjectives

On your own paper, diagram *only* the words you labeled (simple subjects, simple predicates, predicate adjectives, direct objects, and indirect objects), along with any conjunctions used to connect compounds, from the sentences in Exercise 38A.

— LESSON 39 —

Linking Verbs
Predicate Adjectives
Predicate Nominatives

I am unpopular.
I am a flower.
I am a berry.

A predicate adjective describes the subject and is found in the complete predicate.
A predicate nominative renames the subject and is found in the complete predicate.

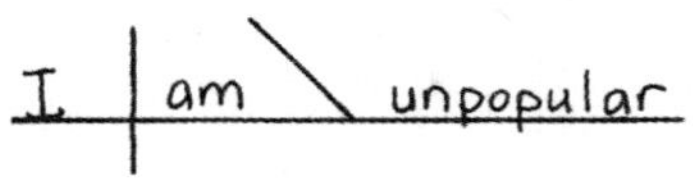

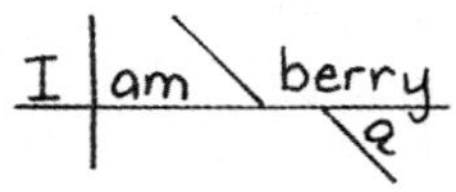

Iguanas are reptiles.
Iguanas = reptiles (predicate nominative)

Iguanas are scaly.
scaly iguanas (predicate adjective)

reptiles iguanas not a predicate adjective
iguanas ≠ scaly not a predicate nominative

Exercise 39A: Identifying Predicate Nominatives and Adjectives

In the following sentences, underline the simple subjects once and the simple predicates twice. Circle the predicate nominatives or adjectives and label each one *PN* for predicate nominative or *PA* for predicate adjective. Draw a line from the predicate nominative or adjective to the subject that it describes. There may be more than one of each.

The octopus, the squid, and the cuttlefish are cephalopods.

Cephalopods are very intelligent.

Salt water is home to cephalopods.

The blue-ringed octopus is poisonous and very dangerous.

The colors on the blue-ringed octopus are a warning to predators.

The striped pyjama squid is actually a cuttlefish.

It is active at night.

A cephalopod's ink is a defense.

Exercise 39B: Writing Predicate Nominatives and Adjectives

Finish each sentence in two ways: with a predicate nominative and with a predicate adjective. If you need to use more than one word in a blank to complete your sentence, circle the word that is the predicate nominative or predicate adjective. The first is done for you.

Curling is ______ my favorite (sport) ______. (predicate nominative)
Curling is ______ entertaining ______. (predicate adjective)

The ice cream was ______________________. (predicate nominative)
The ice cream was ______________________. (predicate adjective)

My aunt's dog is ______________________. (predicate nominative)
My aunt's dog is ______________________. (predicate adjective)

The boy in the blue shirt is ______________________. (predicate nominative)
The boy in the blue shirt is ______________________. (predicate adjective)

The white fence is ______________________. (predicate nominative)
The white fence is ______________________. (predicate adjective)

The final clue was ______________________. (predicate nominative)
The final clue was ______________________. (predicate adjective)

Exercise 39C: Diagramming

On your own paper, diagram every word of the following sentences.

Kittens are adorable.
A crib is a baby's bed.
The bouquet was strikingly beautiful.
Diligent students check their work.
Tomatoes and pumpkins are fruits.
Be a good sport!
Thunder and lightning began.
Will you be late?
Forgetful Tim burned our breakfast.

— LESSON 40 —

Predicate Adjectives and Predicate Nominatives
Pronouns as Predicate Nominatives
Object Complements

A linking verb connects the subject to a noun, pronoun, or adjective in the complete predicate.

A pronoun takes the place of a noun.
The antecedent is the noun that is replaced by the pronoun.

I	we
you	you (plural)
he, she, it	they

It is I.
The winner is you.
My best friend is she.

It = I
winner = you
friend =she

(plural noun) ______________________________ are we.

(singular noun) ______________________________ has been you.

(plural noun) ______________________________ were they.

We elected Marissa leader.
The explorers found the camp abandoned.
He painted the fence white.

An object complement follows the direct object and renames or describes it.

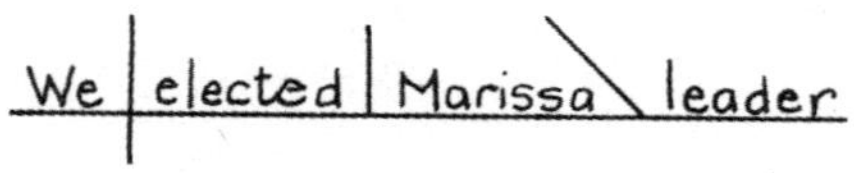

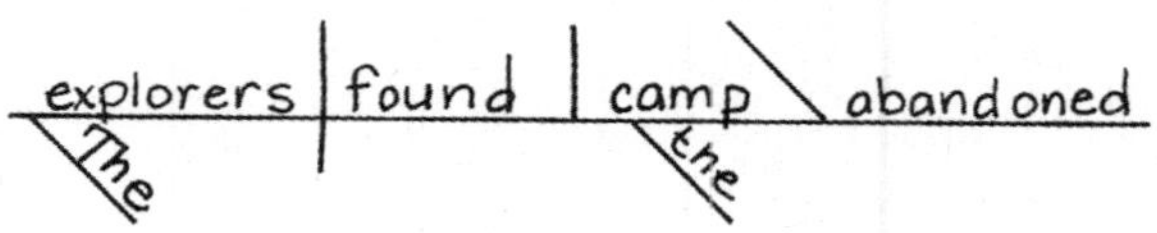

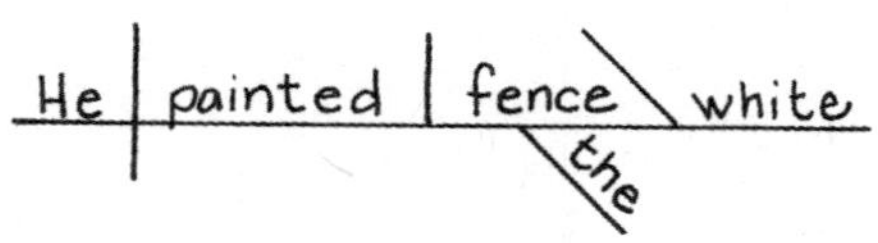

An adjective that comes right before the noun it modifies is in the *attributive position*.

They are user-friendly directions.

An adjective that follows the noun is in the *predicative position.*

Those directions are user friendly.

My friend dyed his hair purple.
My friend dyed his purple hair.
My friend dyed his purple hair orange.

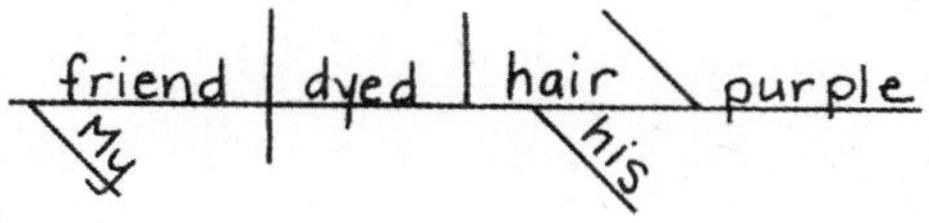

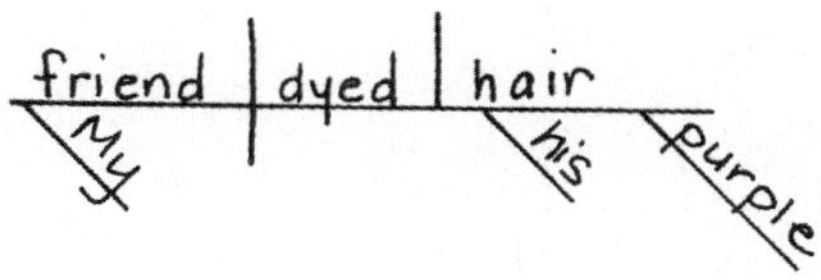

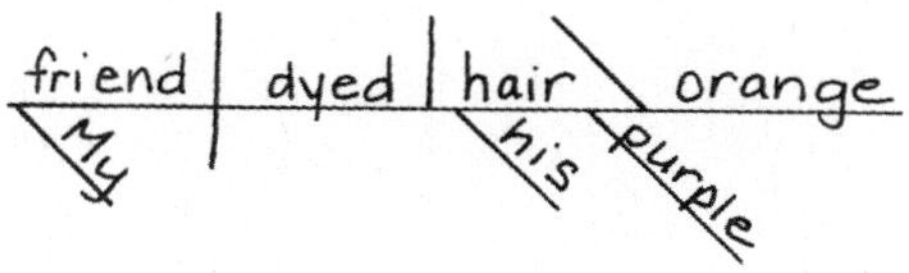

Exercise 40A: Reviewing Objects and Predicate Adjectives and Nominatives

Identify the underlined words as *DO* for direct object, *IO* for indirect object, *OP* for object of preposition, *PN* for predicate nominative, or *PA* for predicate adjective.

- For each direct object (or direct object/indirect object combination), find and underline twice the action verb that affects it. Include helping verbs!
- For each object of the preposition, find and circle the preposition to which it belongs.
- For each predicate nominative and predicate adjective, find and draw a box around the linking verb that it follows. Include helping verbs!
- When you are finished, answer the questions at the end of the selection.

The following passage is from L. M. Montgomery's *Anne of Green Gables.*

"But they shouldn't call that lovely place the Avenue. There is no meaning in a name like that. They should call it—let me see—the White Way of Delight. Isn't that a nice imaginative name? When I don't like the name of a place or a person I always imagine a new one and always think of them so. There was a girl at the asylum whose name was Hepzibah Jenkins, but I always imagined her as Rosalia DeVere. Other people may call that place The Avenue, but I shall always call it the White Way of Delight. Have we really only another mile to go before we get home? I'm glad and I'm sorry. I'm sorry because this drive has been so pleasant and I'm always sorry when pleasant things end. Something still pleasanter may come after, but you can never be sure. And it's so often the case that it isn't pleasanter. That has been my experience anyhow. But I'm glad to think of getting home. You see, I've never had a real home since I can remember. It gives me that pleasant ache again just to think of coming to a really truly home. Oh, isn't that pretty!"

They had driven over the crest of a hill. Below them was a pond, looking almost like a river so long and winding was it. A bridge spanned it midway and from there to its lower end, where an amber-hued belt of sand-hills shut it in from the dark blue gulf beyond, the water was a glory of many shifting hues—the most spiritual shadings of crocus and rose and ethereal green, with other elusive tintings for which no name has ever been found. Above the bridge the pond ran up into fringing groves of fir and maple and lay all darkly translucent in their wavering shadows. Here and there a wild plum leaned out from the bank like a white-clad girl tiptoeing to her own reflection. From the marsh at the head of the pond came the clear, mournfully-sweet chorus of the frogs. There was a little gray house peering around a white apple orchard on a slope beyond and, although it was not yet quite dark, a light was shining from one of its windows.

Find the compound adjective in this passage. Write it in the blank below and cross out the incorrect choice.

_______________________________ is in the (attributive/predicative) position.

Find the object complement in the first sentence. Write it in the blank below and cross out the incorrect choices.

_______________________ is (an adjective/a noun) that (describes/renames) the direct object.

Find the other object complement in the first paragraph! (It's a different name.) Write it in the blank below.

____

Exercise 40B: Parts of the Sentence

Label the following in each sentence: *S* (subject), *LV* (linking verb), *AV* (action verb), *DO* (direct object), *OC-A* (object complement-adjective), *OC-N* (object complement-noun), *IO* (indirect object), or *PN* (predicate nominative).

The instructor found the students quickly.

The instructor found the students intelligent.

The instructor declared Marisa his apprentice.

The instructor gave Marisa an apprenticeship.

The circus made the children happy.

My sister named her puppy Aminga.

Can you keep the jewelry safe?

Can you keep the dog outside?

The president will be you.

The group elected you president.

The girl dyed her hair green yesterday.

Exercise 40C: Diagramming

Diagram the sentences from Exercise 40B on your own paper.

WEEK 11

More About Prepositions

— LESSON 41 —

Prepositions and Prepositional Phrases
Adjective Phrases

Prepositions
aboard, about, above, across
after, against, along, among, around, at
before, behind, below, beneath
beside, between, beyond, by
down, during, except, for, from
in, inside, into, like
near, of, off, on, over
past, since, through, throughout
to, toward, under, underneath
until, up, upon
with, within, without

A preposition shows the relationship of a noun or pronoun to another word in the sentence.
A prepositional phrase begins with a preposition and ends with a noun or pronoun.
That noun or pronoun is the object of the preposition.
A phrase is a group of words serving a single grammatical function.

I could have been running away.

Speed of Sound

Ring of Fire

Bridge Over Troubled Water

Time of Your Life

The Sound of Silence

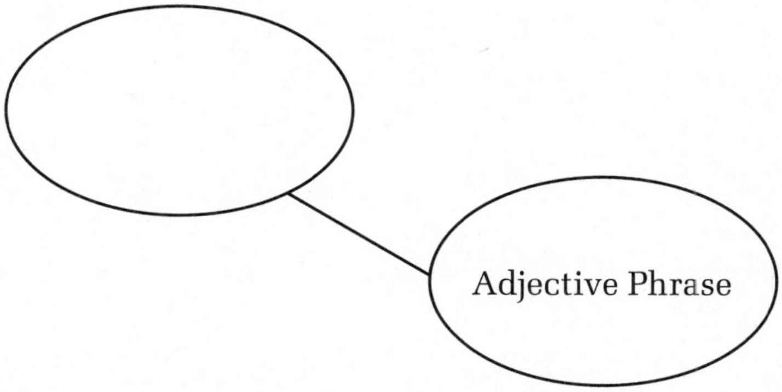

Prepositional phrases that act as adjectives are also called adjective phrases.

The boy with the freckles was whistling.
The old man on the bench hummed a tune.
Arthur borrowed a book of mine.

Adjective phrases usually come directly after the words they modify.

Caleb climbed a tree with thick branches.

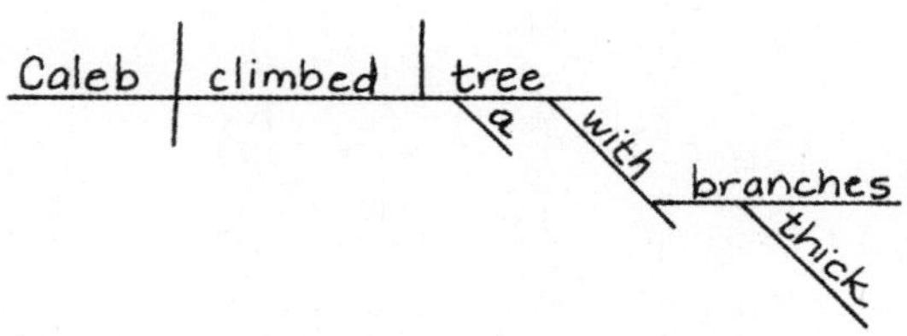

The children in the house were sleeping.

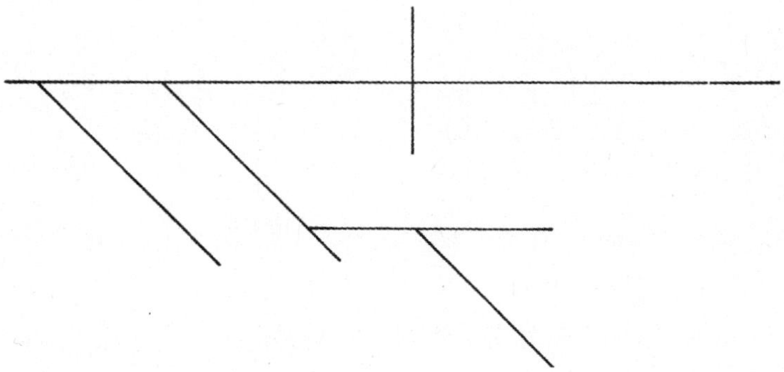

Exercise 41A: Identifying Adjective Phrases

Underline the adjective phrases in the following sentences. Draw an arrow from each phrase to the word it modifies. The first is done for you.

These sentences are adapted from *The Histories* by Herodotus, the fifth-century BC Greek historian (translation by Aubrey de Sélincourt).

The people of Samos did not want liberty.

Persians of the highest rank then placed chairs of state there.

I will keep the priesthood of Zeus.

The birds fly down and carry away the joints of meat.

Another tribe to the east is nomadic.

You have personal experience of the effect.

He destroys the structure of ancient tradition and law.

The anniversary of this day is now a red-letter day in the Persian calendar.

This was a further indication of the truth.

You are the son of Hystaspes.

Exercise 41B: Diagramming Adjective Phrases/Review

Diagram each sentence from Exercise 41A on your own paper. Follow this procedure, and ask yourself the suggested questions if necessary.

1. Find the subject and predicate and diagram them first.
   What is the verb?
   Who or what [verb]?

2. Ask yourself: Is the verb an action verb? If so, look for a direct object.
   Who or what receives the action of the verb?

   If there is a direct object, check for an indirect object.
   To whom or for whom is the action done?

   Remember that there may be no direct object or no indirect object—but you can't have an indirect object without a direct object. If there is an indirect object, it will always come between the verb and the direct object.

3. Ask yourself: Is the verb a state-of-being verb? If so, look for a predicate nominative or predicate adjective.
   Is there a word after the verb that renames or describes the subject?

4. Find all prepositional phrases. Ask yourself: Whom or what do they describe?

5. Place all other adjectives and adverbs on the diagram.

If you have trouble, ask for help.

— LESSON 42 —

Adjective Phrases
Adverb Phrases

Prepositional phrases that act as adverbs are also called adverb phrases.
An adverb describes a verb, an adjective, or another adverb.
Adverbs tell how, when, where, how often, and to what extent.

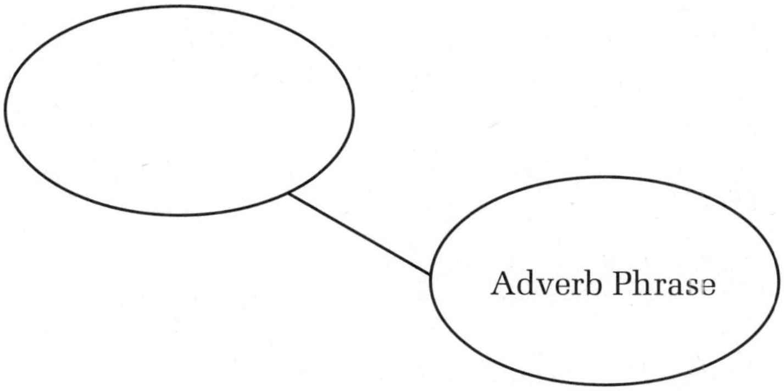

Fly Me to the Moon

I Fall to Pieces

Wake Me at Sunset

Sitting on the Dock of the Bay

Cameron scuba-dives in Hawaii.
At 6:00 a.m., Cameron wakes.

Adverb phrases can be anywhere in a sentence.

With great confidence, Hank Aaron swung the bat through the air.

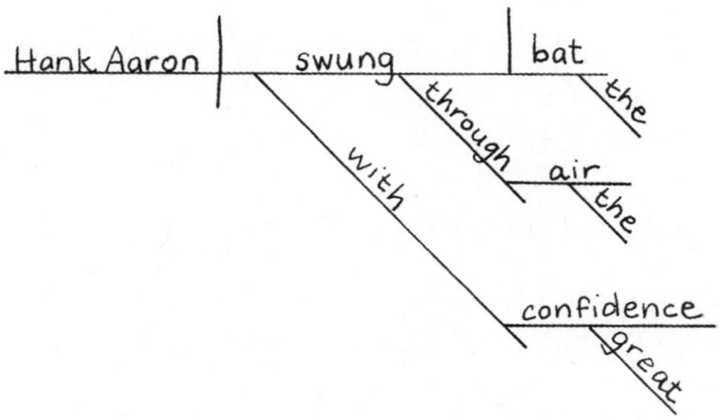

In summer, the car was hot beyond belief.

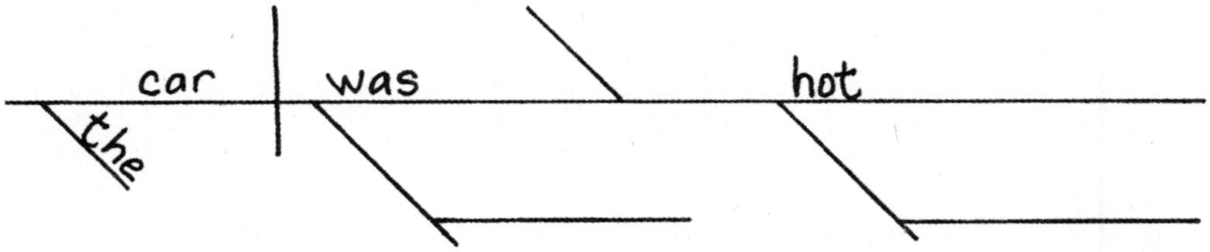

Exercise 42A: Identifying Adverb Phrases

Underline the adverb phrases in the following sentences and circle the preposition that begins each phrase. Draw an arrow from the phrase to the word it modifies. The first is done for you.

In the morning, we will walk over the hill.

Mrs. Puri encouraged the nervous performers with a smile.

The audience stared curiously at the first scene.

The race will begin in the Guru Nanak Stadium at noon.

Amanjit hid the gift with haste.

With reluctance, Jothi walked onto the stage and began her speech.

The tour guide described in great detail the building's history.

Please hang your umbrella on this hook.

The crowd quickly formed a line in an orderly fashion.

Sani yawned frequently during class.

You spilled lassi on my shirt!

In unison, the students nodded their heads.

Exercise 42B: Diagramming Adverb Phrases

On your own paper, diagram the following sentences, slightly adapted from the nineteenth-century botanical handbook *Punjab Plants.*

The purple fruit is found in the extreme northwest of the Punjab.
The seed is spread by birds on the tops of buildings.
The European olive had been introduced into the Calcutta Botanical Gardens in 1800.

In Kashmir, a proportion of the fiber is mixed with the material for paper-making.
The fruit is commonly eaten without bad effects.
The tree is found below the Niti Pass.

— LESSON 43 —

Definitions Review
Adjective and Adverb Phrases
Misplaced Modifiers

An adjective modifies ______________________________.

Adjectives tell ______________________________.

A preposition shows ______________________________
word in the sentence.

A prepositional phrase ______________________________
______________ **or pronoun.**

______________________________ **object of the preposition.**

A phrase is ______________________________ **function.**

Prepositional phrases that ______________________________
adjective phrases.

Adjective phrases usually ______________________________.

An adverb describes ______________________________.

Adverbs tell ______________________________ **extent.**

____ are also called adverb phrases.

Prepositions

A ________________, a ________________, a ________________, a ________________.

A __________, a __________, a __________, a __________, a __________, a __________.

B ________________, b ________________, b ________________, b ________________.

B ________________, b ________________, b ________________, b ________________.

D ____________, d ____________, e ____________, f ____________, f ____________.

I ________________, i ________________, i ________________, l ________________.

N ____________, o ____________, o ____________, o ____________, o ____________.

P ________________, s ________________, t ________________, t ________________.

T ________________, t ________________, u ________________, u ________________.

U ________________, u ________________, u ________________.

W ________________, w ________________, w ________________.

The cat scratched Brock's sister with the striped tail.

A misplaced modifier is an adjective phrase in the wrong place.

The beautiful girl was dancing with the handsome man in the red dress.

On the pizza, Molly ate the mushrooms.

I cut my finger while I was cooking badly.

I saw that the toast was burned with a glance.

I spotted the dog chewing on the sofa leg from the stairs.

Exercise 43A: Distinguishing between Adjective and Adverb Phrases

Underline all the prepositional phrases in the following sentences. Write *ADJ* above the adjective phrases and *ADV* above the adverb phrases.

These sentences are adapted from *The Princess and the Goblin*, by George MacDonald.

In the morning he had laid some bread in a damp hole in the rock.

The growl continued in a low bass for a good while.

The goblins had a special evil design in their heads.

That place is swarming with wild beasts of every description.

At every moment he was nibbling with his fingers at the edges of the hole.

In a moment the troop disappeared at a turn of the way.

At length, he had almost rushed into the middle of the goblin family.

The nurse left her with the housekeeper for a while.

She emptied the contents of an old cabinet upon the table.

Through the passages she softly sped.

A large oval bed stood in the middle.

Exercise 43B: Correcting Misplaced Modifiers

Circle the misplaced adjective and adverb phrases in the following sentences. Draw an arrow to the place where the phrase should be. The first is done for you.

The red book is on the shelf with the worn cover.

The dragons breathed fire with green tails.

The young boy on the baseball regarded the player's signature with awe.

Four squirrels are hiding nuts with bushy tails in the back yard.

Inside the nest, Gilbert saw three eggs.

Theodore showed a goldfish to his father in a tank.

The adorable kitty drank the milk with the long whiskers.

The clowns juggled the balls in the funny hats.

Mr. Dunlap under the sofa discovered the missing books.

My mother told me about how she learned at bedtime to ride a bicycle.

Our teacher with chocolate loves to eat pretzels.

— LESSON 44 —

Adjective and Adverb Phrases

Prepositional Phrases Acting as Other Parts of Speech

The ship went down into the Gulf of Guinea and, with many stops on the way, approached the mouth of the Congo.

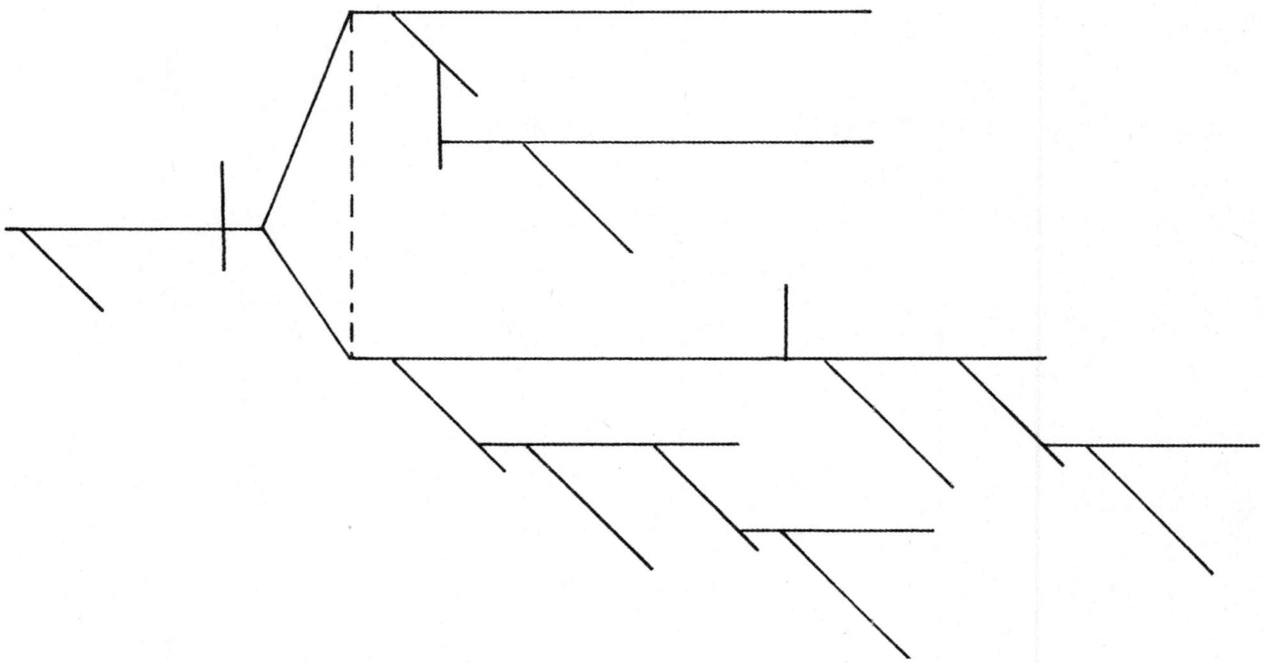

A swamp is not a safe place.

Under the bridge is not a safe place.

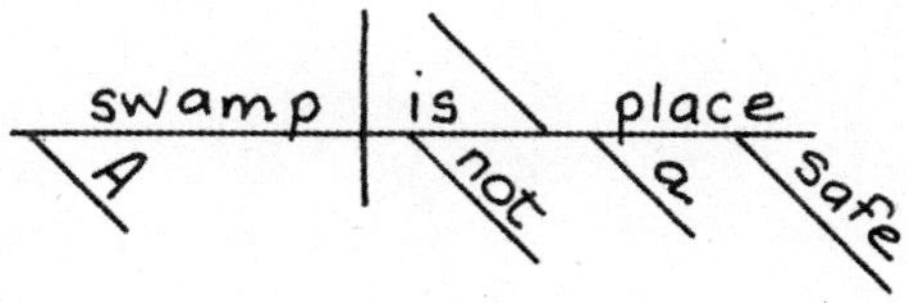

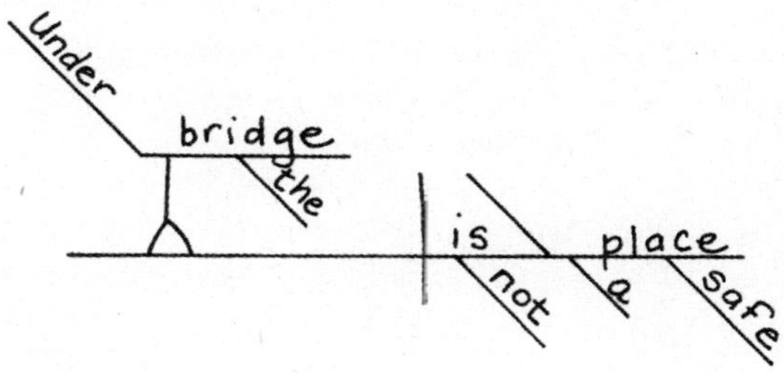

The best place for the treasure is my closet.

The best place for the treasure is under the bed.

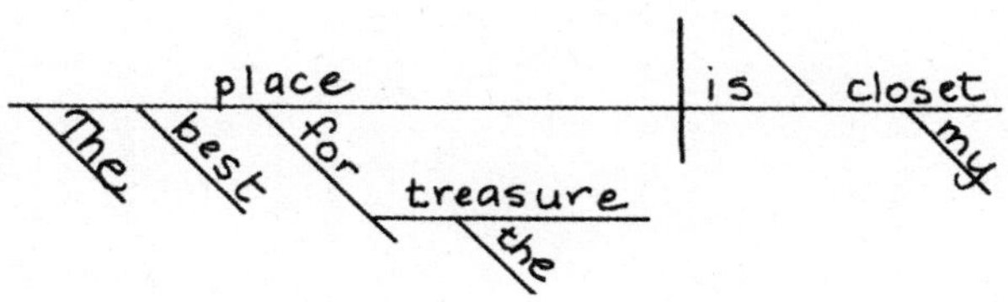

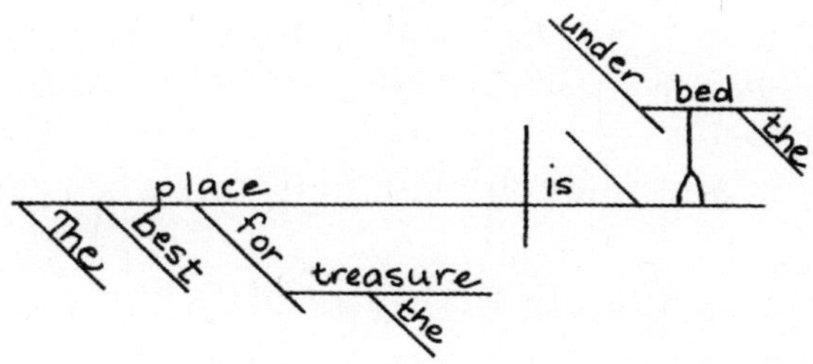

He stepped from the dark.

He stepped from behind the tree.

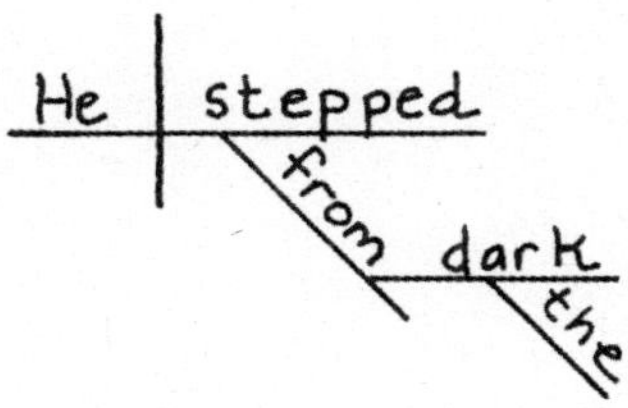

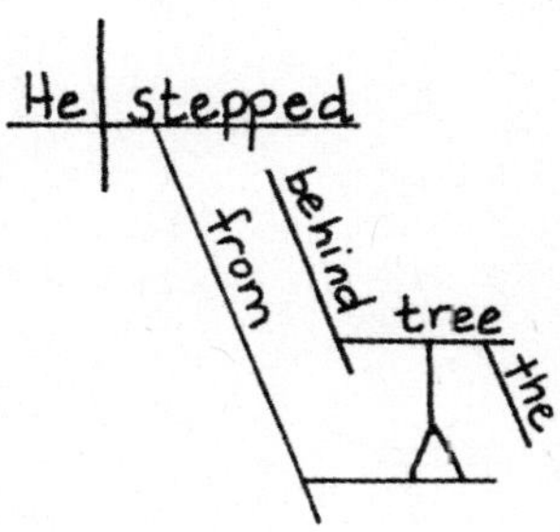

The man is happy.

The man is in love.

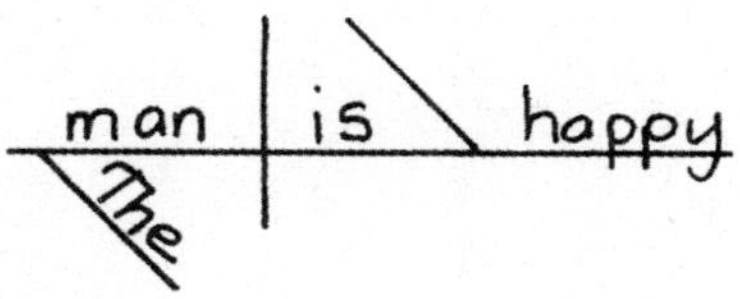

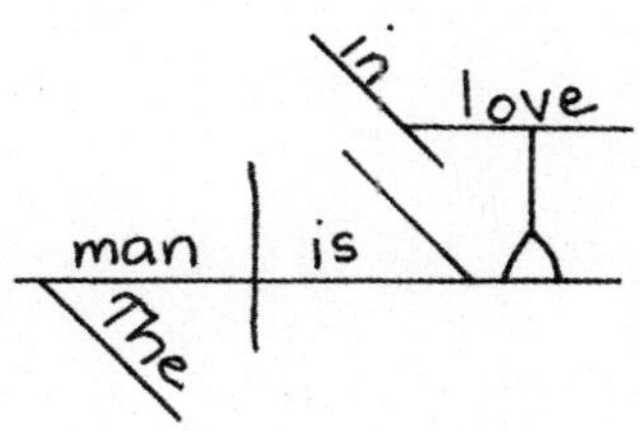

Exercise 44A: Prepositional Phrases Acting as Other Parts of Speech

In each sentence below, circle any prepositional phrases. Underline the subject of the sentence once and the predicate twice. Then label the prepositional phrases as *ADJ* (adjective phrase), *ADV* (adverb phrase), *S* (subject), *PA* (predicate adjective), *PN* (predicate nominative), or *OP* (object of a preposition).

Our flight is on time.

The argument between the candidates was on the news.

Beneath that tree is my favorite spot.

My favorite spot is beneath that tree.

We crawled through the tunnel and jumped across the stream.

Our father telephoned us from across the country.

The group's meetings are at the library.

In the sun is too hot today!

The house upon the hill was full of mystery.

Exercise 44B: Diagramming

On your own paper, diagram the sentences from 44A.

WEEK 12

Advanced Verbs

— LESSON 45 —

Linking Verbs
Linking/Action Verbs

State of Being/Linking Verbs
am, is, are, was, were
be, being, been

Additional Linking Verbs
taste, feel, smell, sound, look
prove, grow,
remain, appear, stay
become, seem

I tasted the candy.

The candy tasted delicious.

The fried chicken tasted crispy.

The chicken tasted the birdseed.

Thomas felt the baby chick.
Thomas felt sad.

ACTION	**LINKING**
He proved the theory.	He proved unreliable.
The farmer grew wheat.	The farmer grew tired.
The dog remained on the porch.	The dog remained wary.
The cloud appeared in the sky.	The cloud appeared threatening.
We stayed home.	We stayed happy with our home.

The student became confused.
The grammar seemed difficult.

Exercise 45A: Distinguishing between Action Verbs and Linking Verbs

Underline the verbs in the following sentences. Identify them as *AV* for action verb or *LV* for linking verb. If the verb is followed by a direct object (*DO*), predicate adjective (*PA*), or predicate nominative (*PN*), label it.

Remember that a verb with *no* direct object, predicate adjective, or predicate nominative will be an action verb, unless it is a state-of-being verb. Also remember that direct objects, predicate adjectives, and predicate nominatives are never found within prepositional phrases.

Herman suspiciously tasted the new food.

The food tasted wonderful!

Herman ate everything on his plate.

Please stay alert during the flight attendant's instructions.

Stay in your seat during takeoff.

Ana felt the edge of the platform with her foot.

She felt somewhat nervous.

She grew less nervous throughout the dance.

Her mother and father looked at her.

They looked proud.

Ana proved a capable dancer.

The mathematician proved her idea.

It seemed reasonable.

She became a renowned professor.

Exercise 45B: Distinguishing Different Kinds of Nouns

Underline all of the nouns in the following sentences. Identify them as *S* for subject, *OP* for object of a preposition, *IO* for indirect object, *DO* for direct object, or *PN* for predicate nominative.

Clara Lazen discovered a new kind of molecule.

She was a fifth-grade student.

Her teacher was using ball-and-stick models for molecules.

She combined oxygen, nitrogen, and carbon into a new formation.

Was her design a real molecule?

Her teacher sent a scientist a picture of it.

The scientist told her teacher the good news.

Clara's design became tetranitratoxycarbon.

Scientists have not yet synthesized this new molecule.

Exercise 45C: Diagramming Action Verbs and Linking Verbs

On your own paper, diagram the following sentences.

Pumpkins become ripe.
Jackson told me the truth.
This smells funny.
Bobcats are predators.
Bobcats hunt rabbits.
Bobcats are solitary.

— LESSON 46 —

Conjugations
Irregular Verbs
Principal Parts of Verbs

Verbs in the simple past, simple present, and simple future describe actions that simply happen.
Verbs in the progressive past, progressive present, and progressive future describe actions that go on for a while.
Verbs in the perfect past, perfect present, and perfect future describe actions which have been completed before another action takes place.

Exercise 46A: Forming Simple, Perfect, and Progressive Tenses

Fill in the missing blanks in the chart below.

Simple Present

	Singular	**Plural**
First person	I zoom	We ____________
Second person	You ____________	You zoom
Third person	He, she, it ____________	They zoom

Simple Past

	Singular	Plural
First person	I ________	We ________
Second person	You ________	You ________
Third person	He, she, it ________	They zoomed

Simple Future

	Singular	Plural
First person	I ________	We ________
Second person	You will zoom	You ________
Third person	He, she, it ________	They ________

Perfect Present

	Singular	Plural
First person	I ________	We ________
Second person	You ________	You ________
Third person	He, she, it has zoomed	They ________

Perfect Past

	Singular	Plural
First person	I ________	We ________
Second person	You ________	You had zoomed
Third person	He, she, it ________	They ________

Perfect Future

	Singular	Plural
First person	I will have zoomed	We ________
Second person	You ________	You ________
Third person	He, she, it ________	They ________

Progressive Present

	Singular	Plural
First person	I ________	We are zooming
Second person	You ________	You ________
Third person	He, she, it ________	They ________

Progressive Past

	Singular	Plural
First person	I ______________	We ______________
Second person	You were zooming	You ______________
Third person	He, she, it ______________	They ______________ zooming

Progressive Future

	Singular	Plural
First person	I will be zooming	We ______________
Second person	You ______________	You ______________
Third person	He, she, it ______________	They ______________

Simple Present	Simple Past	Simple Future
build	built	will build
buy	bought	will buy
choose	chose	will choose
sell	sold	will sell

Exercise 46B: French and English Words

Draw lines to match the English word with its French equivalent. Because English and French have similar backgrounds, you should be able to complete this exercise easily, even if you've never learned any French!

English	French
insert	A. fleur
family	B. insérer
negotiate	C. palais
history	D. famille
stomach	E. limon
lemon	F. négocier
flower	G. estomac
perfume	H. histoire
magnificent	I. parfum
palace	J. magnifique

English verbs have three principal parts.

First Principal Part: The Simple Present (Present)

(I) conjugate *(I)* _______________

Second Principal Part: The Simple Past (Past)

(I) conjugated *(I)* _______________

Third Principal Part: The Perfect Past, Minus Helping Verbs (Past Participle)

(I have) conjugated *(I have)* _______________

Exercise 46C: Principal Parts of Verbs

Fill in the chart with the missing forms.

	First Principal Part Present	Second Principal Part Past	Third Principal Part Past Participle
I	delay	delayed	delayed
I	embarrass		embarrassed
I			tumbled
I	visit		
I		reminded	
I			copied
I	borrow		
I		skipped	
I	whistle		
I			counted

Exercise 46D: Distinguishing between First and Second Principal Parts

Identify each underlined verb as *1* for first principal part or *2* for second principal part.

These sentences are from Carol Berkin's *A Brilliant Solution: Inventing the American Constitution.*

The Virginia resolutions provided a governmental skeleton, a structural blueprint for the new Constitution.

Sensibly, Madison turned his days in Philadelphia to good use.

"I confess there are several parts of this constitution which I do not at present approve."

John Mercer, the young, opinionated delegate from Maryland, arrived in late July.

"I agree to this Constitution with all its faults, if they are such."

— LESSON 47 —

Linking Verbs
Principal Parts
Irregular Verbs

Linking Verbs
am, is, are, was, were
be, being, been
taste, feel, smell, sound, look
prove, grow,
remain, appear, stay
become, seem

Present	**Past**	**Past Participle**
(I) taste	(I) tasted	(I have) tasted
(I) become	(I) became	(I have) become
(I) feel	(I) felt	(I have) felt

COMMON IRREGULAR VERBS

Present	Past	Past Participle				
SAME PRESENT, PAST & PAST PARTICIPLE:						
beat	beat	beat	(OR	beat	beat	beaten)
burst	burst	burst				
cost	cost	cost				
cut	cut	cut				
fit	fit	fit				
let	let	let				
put	put	put				
quit	quit	quit				
hit	hit	hit				
hurt	hurt	hurt				
set	set	set				
shut	shut	shut				
SAME PAST & PAST PARTICIPLE:						
bend	bent	bent				
send	sent	sent				
lend	lent	lent				
bleed	bled	bled				
feed	fed	fed				
feel	felt	felt				
keep	kept	kept				
lead	led	led				
leave	left	left				
meet	met	met				
read	read	read				
sleep	slept	slept				
bring	brought	brought				
buy	bought	bought				
catch	caught	caught				
fight	fought	fought				
seek	sought	sought				
teach	taught	taught				
think	thought	thought				
lay	laid	laid				
pay	paid	paid				
say	said	said				
sell	sold	sold				

tell	told	told
lose	lost	lost
shoot	shot	shot
find	found	found
wind	wound	wound
dig	dug	dug
sit	sat	sat
win	won	won
stand	stood	stood
understand	understood	understood
hear	heard	heard
make	made	made
build	built	built

DIFFERENT PAST AND PAST PARTICIPLE:

awake	awoke	awoken
bite	bit	bitten
break	broke	broken
choose	chose	chosen
forget	forgot	forgotten
freeze	froze	frozen
get	got	gotten
give	gave	given
drive	drove	driven
eat	ate	eaten
fall	fell	fallen
hide	hid	hidden
rise	rose	risen
shake	shook	shaken
speak	spoke	spoken
steal	stole	stolen
take	took	taken
write	wrote	written
ride	rode	ridden
become	became	become
begin	began	begun
come	came	come
run	ran	run

drink	drank	drunk
shrink	shrank	shrunk
ring	rang	rung
sing	sang	sung
swim	swam	swum
draw	drew	drawn
fly	flew	flown
grow	grew	grown
know	knew	known
tear	tore	torn
wear	wore	worn
do	did	done
go	went	gone
lie	lay	lain
see	saw	seen

— LESSON 48 —

Linking Verbs
Principal Parts
Irregular Verbs

Linking Verbs
am, is, are, was, were
be, being, been
taste, feel, smell, sound, look
prove, grow,
remain, appear, stay
become, seem

Verbs in the simple past, simple present, and simple future describe actions that simply happen.
Verbs in the progressive past, progressive present, and progressive future describe actions that go on for a while.
Verbs in the perfect past, perfect present, and perfect future describes actions which have been completed before another action takes place.

PRINCIPAL PARTS
present, past, past participle

Exercise 48A: Principal Parts

Fill in the blanks in the following chart of verbs.

Present	Past	Past Participle
fight		
cut		
	drove	
		fed
	grew	
sell		
		quit
freeze		
		taught
	tore	
		paid
bleed		
buy		
		jumped
		burst
	brought	
		flown
draw		
	slept	
	made	
		sent
cost		
awake		
		stood
	broke	
set		

Present	Past	Past Participle
______	______	risen
______	______	thought
tear	______	______
build	______	______
______	______	gotten
______	______	hit
hear	______	______
______	sniffed	______
______	______	shaken
______	______	brought
______	said	______
______	______	found
shoot	______	______
fall	______	______
______	forgot	______
______	______	kept

Exercise 48B: Forming Correct Past Participles

Write the correct third principal part (past participle) in each blank. The first principal part is provided for you in parentheses. The first is done for you.

Kristin had ___set___ (set) her bag near the stairs.

The dog has ______________ (dig) a new hole under the fence.

I had long ______________ (seek) the ancient treasure, and now I have ___________ (find) it!

The announcer said Timothy had ___________ (win) the award.

Timothy will get his award later; he was not feeling well and has already __________ (leave) the ceremony.

I have not ______________ (ride) a horse since I was five years old.

Ouch! A mosquito has ______________ (bite) me!

Asa has ____________ (wear) his favorite shirt three times this week.

Exercise 48C: Forming Correct Past Tenses

Write the correct second principal part (past) in each blank. The first principal part is provided for you in parentheses. The first is done for you.

Priscilla ___spoke___ (speak) to me about the event.

This shirt is on sale today; yesterday it ______________ (cost) thirty dollars!

Last year we ______________ (grow) zucchini in our garden.

Marcus ______________ (read) the book before class.

Unhurriedly, my father ______________ (drive) through the mountain village and ____________ (let) us see the lovely foliage.

On our vacation, I __________ (catch) one fish, but my sister __________ (throw) it back.

The alarm clock ____________ (ring) at least five times before I ____________ (awake).

Exercise 48D: Proofreading for Irregular Verb Usage

In the passage below, adapted from Frances Hodgson Burnett's *A Little Princess*, you will find seven errors in irregular verb usage. Cross out the incorrect forms and write the correct ones above them.

He thinked that her eyes looked hungry because she had perhaps had nothing to eat for a long time. He did not know that they looked so because she beed hungry for the warm, merry life his home holded and his rosy face speaked of, and that she had a hungry wish to snatch him in her arms and kiss him. He only knowed that she had big eyes and a thin face and a common basket and poor clothes. So he putted his hand in his pocket and finded his sixpence and walked up to her benignly.

Exercise 48E: Diagramming

On your own paper, diagram the following four sentences.

Who painted the sign on the lawn blue?

Ron tasted the ice cream and nodded his head approvingly.

The time for questions is before the exam.

Outside the house, I felt very cold.

— REVIEW 4 —

Weeks 10-12

Topics:
Direct and Indirect Objects
Linking Verbs
Predicate Adjectives
Predicate Nominatives
Articles
Adjective Phrases
Adverb Phrases
Action vs. Linking Verbs
Irregular Verbs
Principal Parts (Present, Past, Past Participle)

Review 4A: Action vs. Linking Verbs

Identify the underlined verbs as *A* for action or *L* for linking.

Margaret smelled the mystery container from the refrigerator.

The contents smelled suspiciously strange, so Margaret emptied the container into the trash.

Something else would probably taste better.

Sound the alarm! This sale sounds like the biggest sale of the year!

These deals seem fabulous.

With our new products, you look great and feel wonderful!

Come to our store today and try these amazing products for yourself!

You'll become the envy of all your friends!

Review 4B: Predicate Adjectives and Predicate Nominatives

Underline the linking verb in each of the following sentences. If the sentence concludes with a predicate nominative or predicate adjective, circle each and write *PA* for predicate adjective or *PN* for predicate nominative above it.

The geese in the sky were ridiculously loud.

Your cousin is a famous actress in our city.

Latin class seemed extremely long today.

The rabbits under the deck look skittish.

The fresh bread at the bakery smelled delectable.

Jacques, Ricky, and Razak became a team.

For several hours, the human statue remained motionless.

Stephanie's locket was a keepsake from her grandmother.

Review 4C: Adjective and Adverb Phrases

In the following excerpt from Andrew Peterson's *North! Or Be Eaten*, identify each underlined prepositional phrase as *ADJ* for adjective phrase or *ADV* for adverb phrase.

Podo thought it would be funny to strike the tent with Oskar still sleeping in it, so after a quick breakfast of dried fruit, Janner and Tink helped Podo pull the stakes and lift the center stick that held the canvas aloft. They laughed and whispered to one another as they raised it like a giant umbrella and exposed Oskar to the sunlight, and still he snored. When the tent was rolled and lashed to Podo's pack, there was nothing left to do but rouse Mister Reteep. Leeli nudged his shoulder, and his only response was a slight shift in the tone of his snore. Nia joined Leeli and prodded Oskar on the other side. Soon they were rocking him back and forth so hard that Podo, Tink, and Janner doubled over with laughter. Oskar snored and scratched at his belly.

Review 4D: Forming Principal Parts

Complete the following excerpt (from J. R. R. Tolkien's *The Two Towers*) by writing the correct principal part of the verb in parentheses (*1stPP*, *2ndPP*, or *3rdPP*).

"Good! Good!" ____________ (*say*, 2nd PP) Treebeard. "But I ____________ (*speak*, 2nd PP) hastily. We must not ____________ (*be*, 1st PP) hasty. I have ____________ (*become*, 3rd PP) too hot. I must ____________ (*cool*, 1st PP) myself and ____________ (*think*, 1st PP); for it is easier to shout *stop!* than to do it."

He __________ (*stride*, 2nd PP) to the archway and __________ (*stand*, 2nd PP) for some time under the falling rain of the spring. Then he __________ (*laugh*, 2nd PP) and __________ (*shake*, 2nd PP) himself, and wherever the drops of water __________ (*fall*, 2nd PP) glittering from him to the ground they __________ (*glint*, 2nd PP) like red and green sparks. He __________ (*come*, 2nd PP) back and __________ (*lay*, 2nd PP) himself on the bed again and was silent.

Review 4E: Irregular Verbs

Find and correct the FIVE errors in irregular verb usage in the following excerpt from *The Wonderful Wizard of Oz*, by L. Frank Baum. Cross out each incorrect form and write the correct form above it.

There beed few birds in this part of the forest, for birds love the open country where there is plenty of sunshine; but now and then there comed a deep growl from some wild animal hidden among the trees. These sounds maked the little girl's heart beat fast, for she did not know what maked them; but Toto knowed, and he walked close to Dorothy's side, and did not even bark in return.

Review 4F: Misplaced Modifiers

Circle the misplaced adjective and adverb phrases in the following sentences. Draw an arrow to the place where each phrase should be.

Our trip was a comedy of errors to California.

In the soda, Grandpa told me that there were 140 calories.

People are learning to swim across the country.

The lady cuts my hair with seven dogs.

The owner in his pocket of the restaurant has twenty dollars.

The quilt keeps the sick child with green and purple squares warm.

In the trash can, the worried woman searched frantically for her wallet.

The monster frightened the boy with two heads.

Review 4G: Diagramming

On your own paper, diagram the following sentences.

The moon appears largest near the horizon.
At that point, the moon's image is actually farther away.
This optical illusion has given observers a puzzle for many centuries.
Aristotle and others declared the atmosphere responsible for the illusion.
The atmosphere only changes our perception of the moon's colors.
Smaller objects near the horizon might influence our ideas about the size of the moon.
Have you looked at the moon lately?
It may look different at different times of night!

WEEK 13

Advanced Pronouns

— LESSON 49 —

Personal Pronouns
Antecedents
Possessive Pronouns

Lindsay woke up when Lindsay heard Lindsay's mother call Lindsay. Lindsay ate Lindsay's breakfast and brushed Lindsay's teeth and got ready for Lindsay's day.

A pronoun takes the place of a noun.
The antecedent is the noun that is replaced by the pronoun.

Personal Pronouns

	Singular	**Plural**
First person	I	we
Second person	you	you (plural)
Third person	he, she, it	they

Exercise 49A: Personal Pronouns and Antecedents

Circle the personal pronouns in the following sentences, adapted from Margery Sharp's *The Rescuers*. Draw an arrow from each pronoun to the antecedent. In the margin, write the gender (*F*, *M*, or *N*) and number (*S* or *PL*) of each pronoun.

Miss Bianca recognized the model speedboat at once. It was the Boy's, a gift from the American Naval Attaché.

Albert was Miss Bianca's favorite. (He had a very noble, serene expression. Miss Bianca was convinced, she told Bernard, that Albert hadn't exactly come down in the world, but had renounced the world.)

Miss Bianca threw Bernard a grateful look. But she was very anxious there should be no bickering.

For a moment Miss Bianca, Bernard, and Nils all thought about The Barrens. Then they all thought about the prisoner, and courage was renewed.

Personal Pronouns (Full List)

I, me, my, mine

you, your, yours

he, she, him, her, it

his, hers, its

we, us, our, ours

they, them, their, theirs

Possessive Adjectives (same as Possessive Pronouns)

my	our
your	your
his, her, its	their

Peter's sword	__________ sword
The Pevensie children's wardrobe	__________ wardrobe
The tree's silver leaves	__________ leaves
Lucy's cordial	__________ cordial

The tree's silver leaves glistened.
Its silver leaves glistened.

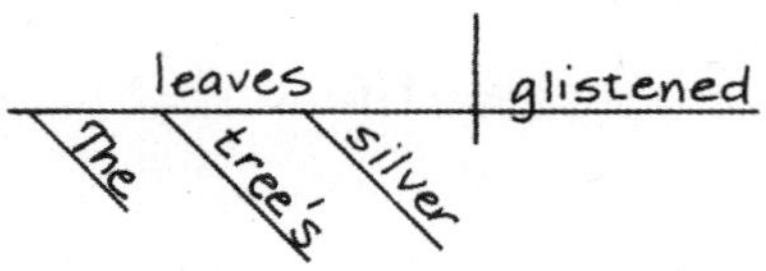

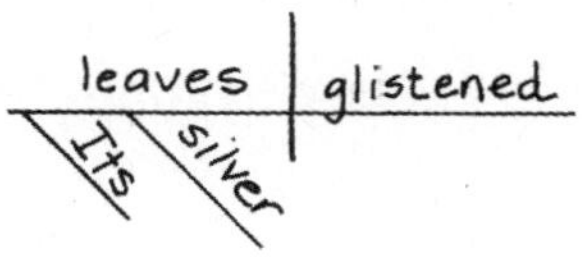

Lucy's cordial healed Edmund.

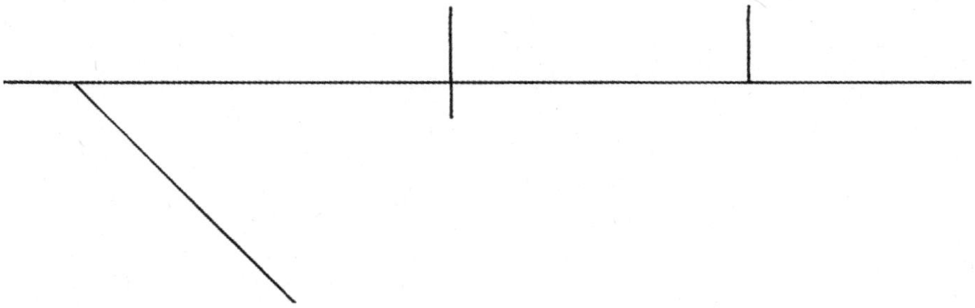

Her cordial healed Edmund.

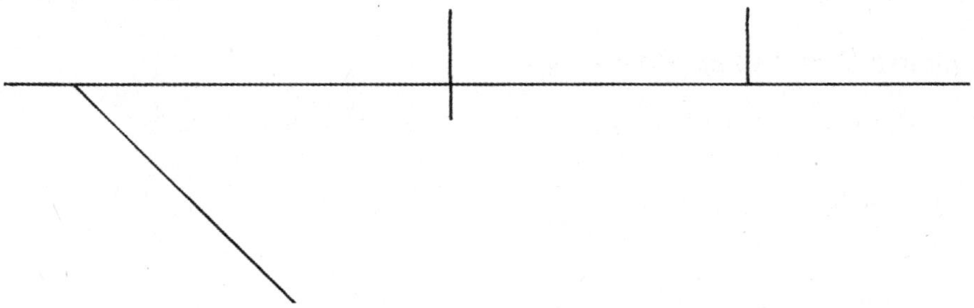

The chocolate is my candy.
The chocolate is mine candy.
The chocolate is mine!

He is your baby brother.
He is yours baby brother.
The baby brother is yours!

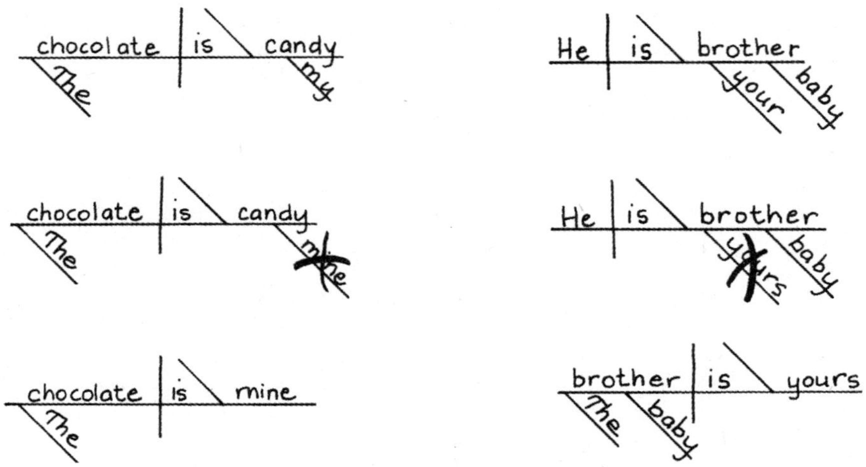

Exercise 49B: Identifying Possessive Pronouns

Underline the possessive pronouns in the following sentences from Thomas Streissguth's *The Transcontinental Railroad*. Each possessive pronoun is acting as an adjective. Draw an arrow from the pronoun to the noun it modifies. There may be other pronouns in these sentences as well; ONLY underline the possessive ones!

To cross California, however, his line would have to rise from Sacramento, at 50 feet above sea level, and cross the steep Sierra Nevada, where the lowest passes lay more than a mile higher.

The scheme gave the company a much-needed boost in its bank accounts in very lean times.

I remember very well, Mr. Lincoln looked at the map and said, "I have got a quarter-section of land right across there, and if I fix it there, they will say that I have done it to benefit my land."

The directors of the Union Pacific had to build their road as quickly as possible.

Exercise 49C: Using Possessive Pronouns

Write the correct possessive pronoun above the underlined word(s).

The little wren perched on the bird feeder and shook <u>the wren's</u> tail.

Stacy and Nila worked diligently on <u>Stacy's and Nila's</u> project.

I met Oscar because we had identical luggage; I had picked up Oscar's suitcase, and he had grabbed my suitcase.

Krista called out to Aziz, "Hey! You forgot Aziz's jacket!"

On Luisa's birthday, Luisa finally got the thing she'd been wanting for months.

Janet said, "My sister and I like to imagine what my sister's and my future jobs will be."

Becoming an ornithologist is Janet's plan; becoming a translator is my sister's.

Saul's phone battery was drained of all the battery's power.

Nate's father shook Nate's father's head. "No," he answered, "we cannot add five puppies to Nate's and Nate's father's household, no matter how cute they are."

Exercise 49D: Diagramming Pronouns

On your own paper, diagram every word in the following sentences. These sentences are adapted from Thomas Streissguth's *The Transcontinental Railroad.*

In 1865, twelve-year-old Robert Gifford walked the four miles from his home in Dutch Flat to Gold Run.

Theodore Judah had several bitter confrontations with his directors.

The workers of the Central Pacific were now compensating for their years of slow, heavy labor in the mountains.

— LESSON 50 —

Pronoun Case

Personal Pronouns (Full List)
I, me, my, mine
you, your, yours
he, she, him, her, it
his, hers, its
we, us, our, ours
they, them, their, theirs

My crown, I am; but still my griefs are mine.
—William Shakespeare, *Richard II*

Object pronouns are used as objects in sentences.
me, you, him, her, it, us, them

Mark each bolded pronoun as *DO, IO,* or *OP.*

> For **me**, my lords, I love **him** not, nor fear **him.**
> —William Shakespeare, *Henry VIII*

> Give **us** notice of his inclination.
> —William Shakespeare, *Richard III*

> A virtuous and a Christian-like conclusion,/To pray for **them** that have done scathe to **us**.
> —William Shakespeare, *Richard III*

Subject pronouns are used as subjects and predicate nominatives in sentences.
I, you, he, she, it, we, they

Mark each bolded pronoun as *S* or *PN.*

> **I** am **he**.
> —William Shakespeare, *Richard III*

> Stand **we** in good array; for **they** no doubt,/Will issue out again and bid us battle.
> —William Shakespeare, *Henry VI*

> **I** blame her not, **she** could say little less;/**She** had the wrong. But what said Henry's queen?
> —William Shakespeare, *Henry VI, Part III*

You need to learn grammar. I will teach you.

I met her at the park. She was wearing her jacket.

It is not very hard. I will learn it.

CORRECT	***INCORRECT***
I am he.	I am him.
The students are we.	The students are us.
The teachers are they.	The teachers are them.

The kitten licked Jim. The kitten licked __________.

The winners were Judy and Diane. The winners were __________.

OP OP
Give the prize to Madison and him. NOT: Give the prize to *he.*

S S
Dad and I made brownies. NOT: *Me* made brownies.

Exercise 50A: Subject and Object Pronouns

Underline all the personal pronouns in the following selections from *The Great Revolt of 1381*, by Charles Oman. Identify each personal pronoun as *S* for subject, *O* for object, or *P* for possessive.

Wraw's gang pillaged his manor, and not finding his plate and other precious goods in the house, went to seek them in the church. They broke open its doors and distributed the silver, but did no further damage to the sacred edifice.

Then they (the rebels) asked them if they had any traitors among them, and the townsfolk said that there were three, and named their names. These three the commons dragged out of their houses and cut off their heads.

It would have puzzled a much more capable set of men than those who now served as the ministers and councillors of his grandson to draw England out of the slough into which she had sunk. Her present misfortunes were due to her own fault.

When the king heard of their doings he sent his messengers to them, on Tuesday after Trinity Sunday, asking why they were behaving in this fashion, and for what cause they were making insurrection in his land. And they sent back by his messengers the answer that they had risen to deliver him, and to destroy traitors to him and his kingdom.

Exercise 50B: Using Personal Pronouns Correctly

Choose the correct word(s) in parentheses and cross out the incorrect word. Be sure to select the grammatically correct choice for writing, which may not necessarily be the one that sounds best to your ear.

The person you are looking for is (I/me).
For Pearl and (I/me), the choice was clear.
Do you think Mr. Evans will help (we/us) with the painting?
Near the lake at the edge of the property, (we/us) found a large group of turtles.
Early this morning (he/him) went for a run.
We thought we saw (he/him), but the runner we saw was not (he/him).
(Martin and she/Martin and her) measured the room carefully.

Exercise 50C: Diagramming Personal Pronouns

On your own paper, diagram the following sentences. Personal pronouns are diagrammed exactly like the nouns or adjectives they replace.

The mayor is she.
We sent her a letter.
They read it.
He wrote us a response.
It was brief.
We appreciated it.
She understands us.

— LESSON 51 —

Indefinite Pronouns

Gollum wanted the ring. He longed for it.
Everyone hoped that Frodo would succeed.

Indefinite pronouns are pronouns without antecedents.

Indefinite Pronouns
Singular

anybody	anyone	anything
everybody	everyone	everything
nobody	no one	nothing
somebody	someone	something
another	other	one
either	neither	each

Plural
both, few, many, several

Singular or Plural
all, any, most, none, some

All of the cake was eaten.

All of the pieces were eaten.

Most of the people . . .

None of the water . . .

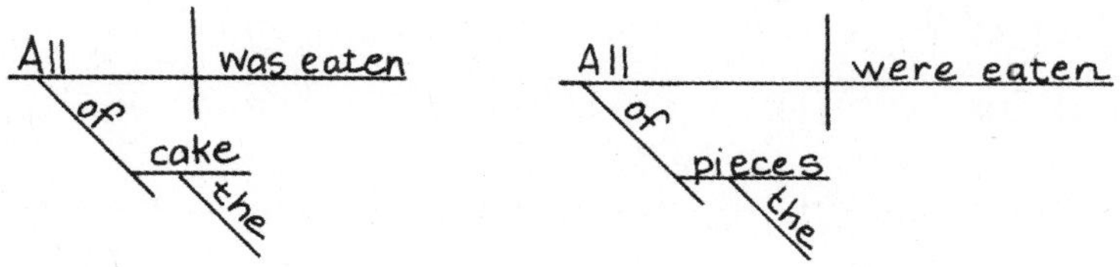

Many of the guests arrived early.

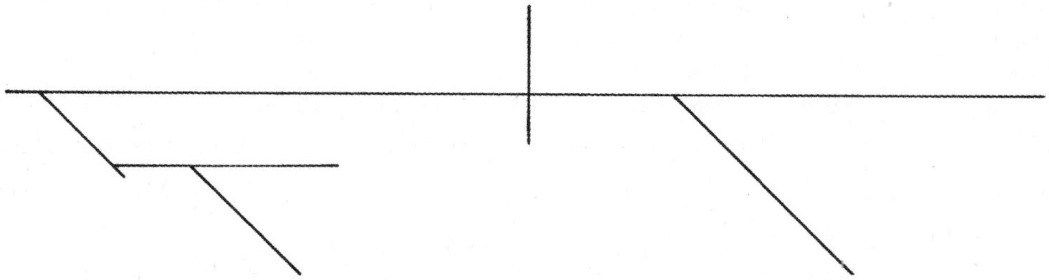

Many guests arrived early.

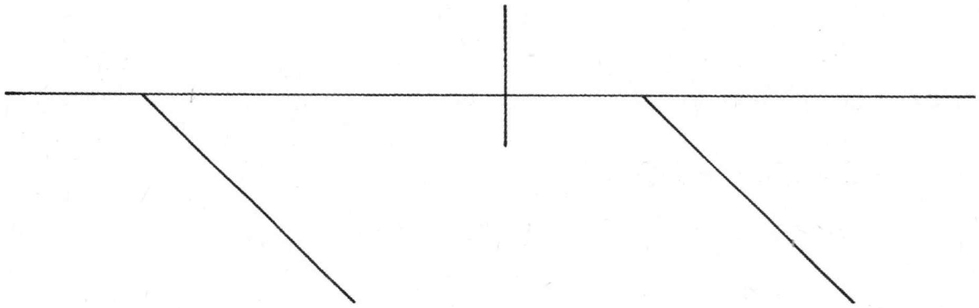

Exercise 51A: Identifying Indefinite Pronouns

Underline all the indefinite pronouns in the following sentences. Each sentence may contain more than one pronoun. The sentences are adapted from Richard Peck's *The Ghost Belonged to Me.*

Inside, everything looked regular, and I was thinking seriously about checking around upstairs, though I could see from the cobwebs that nobody had been up there in quite some time.

I was not sure I followed Lucille's reasoning, since people have been known to attend a party out of nothing but curiosity. But I supposed she had all of it worked out in her own mind.

But if somebody will just tell me what all of the fuss is about, I'll be gone. You know I never rest till I know everything.

We neither of us had come all this way to be led around like children.

She'd have been a lot more pleased with the both of us if she could have gotten me to knuckle down and apply myself to scholarship.

Exercise 51B: Subject-Verb Agreement: Indefinite Pronouns

Choose the correct verb in parentheses. Cross out the incorrect verb.

Some of the choir members (is/are) preparing a surprise for the director.

Everyone (loves/love) her, and someone (has/have) learned that her birthday is today.

Both of the assistant directors (is/are) in on the surprise, and one of them (is/are) going to pick up the flowers.

Nobody (knows/know) the director's favorite kind of flower, but a few of us (remembers/remember) her saying white and yellow are her favorite colors, so all of the flowers (is/are) white and yellow.

Each of us (has/have) been asked to sign a birthday card for her.

Some of the rehearsal time (is/are) wasted because everyone (is/are) excited about the surprise.

One of the assistant directors (appears/appear) with the card and flowers, and all of us (shouts/shout), "Happy birthday!"

Exercise 51C: Diagramming Indefinite Pronouns

On your own paper, diagram the following sentences, adapted from Mary Norton's *The Borrowers.*

All of its feathers fell off.
No one will ever believe me.
Something did happen.
Someone saw one of them.
Your father's got nothing now.

— LESSON 52 —

Personal Pronouns
Indefinite Pronouns

Personal Pronouns
I, me, my, mine
you, your, yours
he, she, him, her, it
his, hers, its
we, us, our, ours
they, them, their, theirs

Subject pronouns: ____

____

______________________ am delighted to be doing grammar.

______________________ are delighted to be doing grammar.

______________________ is delighted to be doing grammar.

Object pronouns: ____

____

The walrus splattered water all over ______________________.

The rain drenched Kim and ______________________.

Possessive pronouns/possessive adjectives in attributive position: ______________________

____

I grabbed ______________________ umbrella.

The cloud began dropping ______________________ moisture.

The soaked tourists ran for ______________________ cars.

Possessive pronouns/possessive adjectives in predicate position: ______________________

____

That raincoat is ______________________.

Those waterproof ponchos are ______________________.

Indefinite pronouns are pronouns without antecedents.

Singular Indefinite Pronouns

anybody	anyone	anything
everybody	everyone	everything
nobody	no one	nothing
somebody	someone	something
another	other	one
either	neither	each

Everyone __________ in the kitchen.

Nobody __________ in the dining room.

Neither of them __________ in the garden.

Plural Indefinite Pronouns
both, few, many, several

Both __________ cooking eggplants.

A few of the crowd __________ objecting to eggplant.

Several __________ quite happy with the prospect of eggplant.

Singular or Plural Indefinite Pronouns
all, any, most, none, some

All of the fire engines __________ there.

All of the mansion __________ destroyed in the fire.

Is everyone coming to get __________ Christmas present?

____

Are they all coming to get their Christmas presents?

Exercise 52A: Subject and Object Pronouns

In the following sentences from Mary Norton's *The Borrowers*, cross out the incorrect pronouns.

(She/Her) had been lying under her knitted coverlet staring up at the ceiling.

"Oh," (he/him) said again and picked up two petals of cherry blossom which (he/him) folded together like a sandwich and ate slowly.

"(He/Him) means," said Pod, "that Lupy must have set off to come here and that (she/her) never arrived."

Pod held (she/her) tightly by the ankle. It was not easy to control (she/her) as (he/him) was lying on his back.

(She/Her) dragged (he/him) roughly across the hall.

(I/Me) showed (he/him) where it was.

(She/Her) lay back among the stalks of the primroses and (they/them) made a coolness between (she/her) and the sun.

(I/Me) led (he/him) into that one too!

(I/Me) will bring you some supper.

(They/Them) were making a bed-quilt.

It was Mrs. May who first told (I/me) about (they/them).

(They/Them) never asked anyone up there and (I/me), for one, never wanted to go.

Oh, (we/us) did have some lovely things!

(She/Her) shrieked and felt behind (she/her) for a chair. (She/Her) clambered on to it and it wobbled beneath (she/her) and (she/her) climbed, still shrieking, from the chair to the table.

(She/Her) brushed past (he/him).

Didn't (he/him) see (they/them) come out?

Exercise 52B: Possessive and Indefinite Pronouns

In these sentences adapted from Anna Sewell's *Black Beauty*, cross out the incorrect word in each set of parentheses.

It was all quite still except the clatter of my feet on the stones; everybody (was/were) asleep.

"We'll just go home by Farmer Bushby's, Beauty; and then if anybody (wants/want) to know, you and I can tell (him/them)."

Nobody (likes/like) to come too near his fist.

"O Harry! there never (was/were) anything so beautiful; Mrs. Fowler says we are all to go and live near her."

No one (was/were) ever kind to her, and why should she not bite?

Some of the sights (makes/make) me sad even now to think of.

Everybody (was/were) sorry; but the master began directly to make arrangements for breaking up his establishment and leaving England. We used to hear it talked about in our stable; indeed, nothing else (was/were) talked about.

Some of the men (was/were) standing together talking; some (was/were) sitting on their boxes reading the newspaper; and one (was/were) feeding (his/their) horse with bits of hay and a drink of water.

None of the other young colts (cares/care) for me, and I care for none of them.

Flies tease her more; anything wrong in the harness (frets/fret) her more.

"Of course I could not be warranted free from vice, so nothing (was/were) said about that."

"If anybody (has/have) been saying that about James, I don't believe it."

Several of the men (was/were) applauding this, till Jerry said, "That may sound well enough, but it won't do; everyone must look after (his/their) own soul."

As Smith's death had been so sudden, and no one (was/were) there to see it, there was an inquest held.

Exercise 52C: Writing Sentences from Diagrams

Use the diagrams below to reconstruct these sentences. Write the sentence on the blanks below each diagram. Pay careful attention to each part of speech! Punctuate each sentence properly.

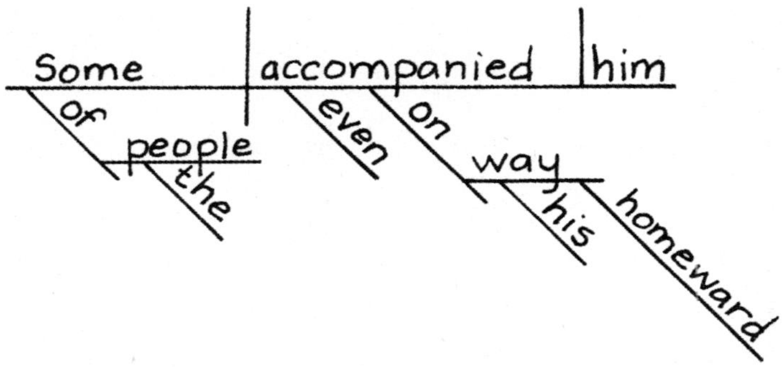

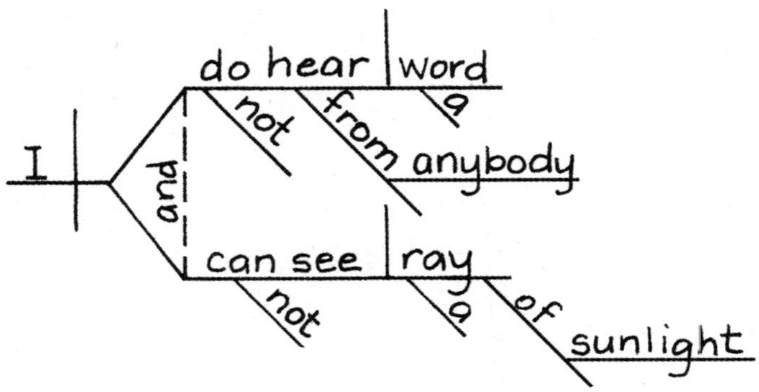

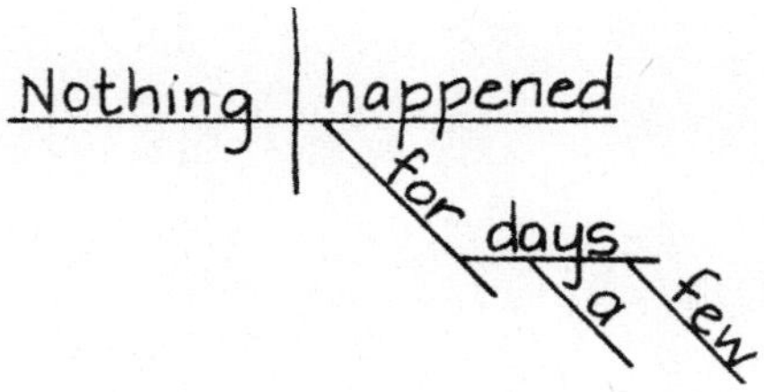
Nothing
happened
for
days
a
few

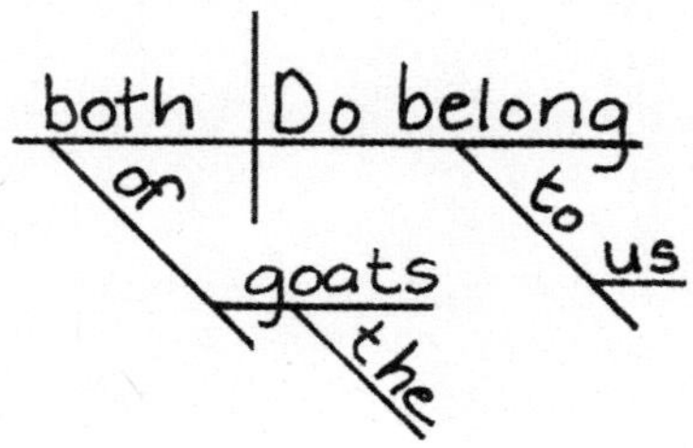
both
Do belong
of
goats
the
to
us

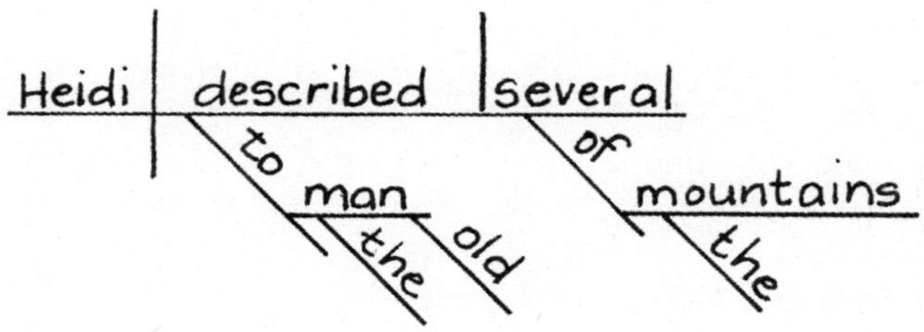
Heidi
described
several
to
man
the
old
of
mountains
the

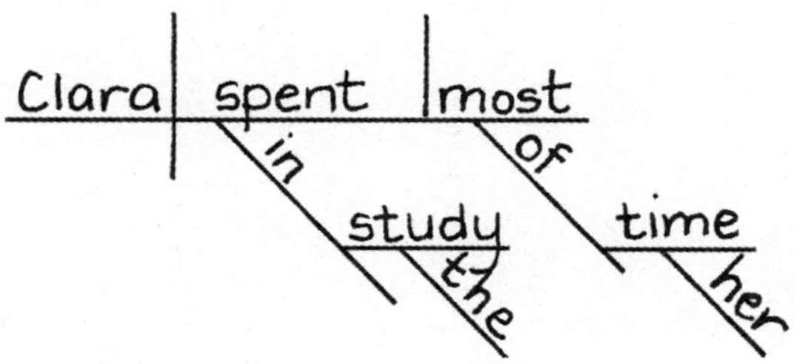
Clara
spent
most
in
study
the
of
time
her

WEEK 14

Active and Passive Voice

— LESSON 53 —

Principal Parts
Troublesome Verbs

She set the set of sorted stuff
Beside the seat where she had sat.

English verbs have three principal parts.
The first principal part is the simple present.
The second principal part is the simple past.
The third principal part of a verb is found by dropping the helping verb from the perfect past.

Exercise 53A: Principal Parts of Verbs

Fill in the chart with the missing forms.

	First Principal Part Present	Second Principal Part Past	Third Principal Part Past Participle
I	perform		
I		ate	
I			won
I		cost	
I			snored
I	bear		
I		bit	
I		felt	

Troublesome Irregular Verbs

Verb	Principal Parts	Definition
sit	(sit, sat, sat)	to rest or be seated
set	(set, set, set)	to put or place something
lie	(lie, lay, lain)	to rest or recline
lay	(lay, laid, laid)	to put or place something
rise	(rise, rose, risen)	to get up or go up
raise	(raise, raised, raised)	to cause something to go up or grow up
let	(let, let, let)	to allow
leave	(leave, left, left)	to go away from or allow to remain

Exercise 53B: Using Correct Verbs

Choose the correct verb in parentheses. Cross out the incorrect verb.

The dancer (rose/raised) her arms gracefully above her head.

Don't (sit/set) down yet! I need you to (sit/set) these flowers on the table.

Before we (let/left) the stadium, the team members (let/left) us pose for pictures with them.

When Gabriella arrived home, she (lay/laid) her purse on the table and immediately fell asleep on the couch.

She has (laid/lain) there all afternoon.

I want to (rise/raise) money for my favorite charity. Will you (let/leave) me wash your car to earn some money?

Yesterday, Jasper (sat/set) near the back of the room, but today he has (sat/set) his things on a desk near the front.

Exercise 53C: Correct Forms of Troublesome Verbs

Fill in the blanks with the correct form of the indicated verb. The sentences below are from *The Wonderful Wizard of Oz*, by L. Frank Baum.

The house whirled around two or three times and ___________ slowly through the air. (rise)

They had taken the sparkle from her eyes and ___________ them a sober gray. (leave)

Indeed, the old Witch never touched water, nor ever ___________ water touch her in any way. (let)

The cyclone had ___________ the house down, very gently—for a cyclone—in the midst of a country of marvelous beauty. (set)

The Scarecrow ___________ in the big throne and the others stood respectfully before him. (sit)

At last she crawled over the swaying floor to her bed, and ____________ down upon it; and Toto followed and ____________ down beside her. (lie)

It was some time before the Cowardly Lion awakened, for he had ____________ among the poppies a long while, breathing in their deadly fragrance; but when he did open his eyes and roll off the truck he was very glad to find himself still alive. (lie)

They carried the sleeping girl to a pretty spot beside the river, far enough from the poppy field to prevent her breathing any more of the poison of the flowers, and here they ________ her gently on the soft grass and waited for the fresh breeze to waken her. (lay)

On the feet were some old boots with blue tops, such as every man wore in this country, and the figure was ____________ above the stalks of corn by means of the pole stuck up its back. (raise)

Exercise 53D: Proofreading for Correct Verb Usage

Find and correct SEVEN errors in verb usage by crossing out the incorrect verbs and writing the correct ones above them.

As the sun raised in the eastern sky, I laid in my bed and thought about my day. I knew it would be very busy. My father had let me in charge of the family store while he went to a conference. I had done all the jobs before, but today I would be raising to a new level of responsibility, because my father would not be right there with me. I got dressed—I had lain out my clothes the night before—and had some breakfast, then walked over to the store. As soon as I sat out the "OPEN" sign, one of our regular customers came in. "Leave me help you with that," I said with confidence. I knew my father would be proud of me upon his return.

— LESSON 54 —

Verb Tense

Active and Passive Voice

present	simple
past	progressive
future	perfect

A simple verb simply tells whether an action takes place in the past, present, or future.
A progressive verb describes an ongoing or continuous action.
A perfect verb describes an action which has been completed before another action takes place.

Exercise 54A: Reviewing Tenses

Write the tense of each underlined verb above it. These sentences are from *The Lost World*, by Arthur Conan Doyle. The first is done for you.

simple future
If it will support the weight of one and let him gently down, it will have done all that is required of it.

Oh, it was rank nonsense about some queer animals he had discovered. I believe he has retracted since.

I had been hopelessly in the wrong before, but this man's menaces were putting me in the right.

It was a fearsome walk, and one which will be with me so long as memory holds.

Flinging away my useless gun, I set myself to do such a half-mile as I have never done before or since.

The door had been fastened upon the inner side, and the windows were blocked by old-fashioned shutters with broad iron bars.

He fastened the door upon the inner side.

In a sentence with an active verb, the subject performs the action.
In a sentence with a passive verb, the subject receives the action.

I punched you.
You were punched by me.

The Egyptians constructed pyramids.
Pyramids were constructed.
Pyramids were constructed by the Egyptians.

Active Verb	Passive Verb
Present Freddy tricks the alligator.	**is/are + past participle** The alligator is tricked by Freddy.
Past Freddy tricked the alligator.	**was/were + past participle** The alligator was tricked by Freddy.
Future Freddy will trick the alligator.	**will be + past participle** The alligator will be tricked by Freddy.

Progressive Present Freddy is tricking the alligator.	**is/are being + past participle** The alligator is being tricked by Freddy.
Progressive Past Freddy was tricking the alligator.	**was/were being + past participle** The alligator was being tricked by Freddy.
***Progressive Future** Freddy will be tricking the alligator.	***will be being + past participle** The alligator will be being tricked by Freddy.
Perfect Present Freddy has tricked the alligator.	**has/have been + past participle** The alligator has been tricked by Freddy.
Perfect Past Freddy had tricked the alligator.	**had been + past participle** The alligator had been tricked by Freddy.
Perfect Future Freddy will have tricked the alligator.	**will have been + past participle** The alligator will have been tricked by Freddy.

*The passive form of progressive future verbs is awkward and not often used.

State-of-being verbs do not have voice.

Exercise 54B: Distinguishing between the Active and Passive Voice

Identify the following sentences from William Makepeace Thackeray's *The Rose and the Ring* as *A* for active or *P* for passive. If you're not sure, ask yourself: Is the subject *doing* the verb, or is the verb *happening to* the subject?

She toddled down the great staircase into the hall. ________

He was pinned to the door. ________

He was turned into metal! ________

The painters dabbed him over the mouth and eyes. ________

She capered away on her one shoe. ________

Betsinda was not puffed up by these praises. ________

She thought her cousin very handsome, brave, and good-natured. ________

She was walking through the court of the Palace on her way to their Majesties. ________

Here a very pretty game may be played by all the children. ________

He was making fun of Prince Bulbo. ________

He made himself very comfortable in the straw. ________

The market-place was filled with soldiers. ________

She declined his invitation in her usual polite gentle manner. ________

His Majesty's agitation was not appeased by the news. ________

He sat down and began writing an adieu to Angelica. ________

He was treated with the greatest distinction by everybody. ________

Exercise 54C: Forming the Active and Passive Voice

Fill in the chart below, rewriting each sentence so that it appears in both the active and the passive voice. Be sure to keep the tense the same.

These sentences are adapted from Walter Farley's *The Black Stallion*. The first one is done for you.

ACTIVE	PASSIVE
Alec picked up the pail and cloths.	The pail and cloths were picked up by Alec.
They watched the falling snow.	
	The people's curiosity was aroused by his articles on the mystery horse.
	I was attacked by this horse!
	A long, slender staff was cut from a tree by Alec.
A line of policemen kept the eager spectators away.	

— LESSON 55 —

Parts of the Sentence
Active and Passive Voice

(These sentences are adapted from Walter Farley's *The Black Stallion*.)

Alec was lifted from his feet.

Then the sound of a police siren reached Alec's ears.

Alec and Henry climbed into the front seat.

Both of them were going to Chicago.

The horse was awakened in the middle of the night.

— LESSON 56 —

Active and Passive Voice

Transitive and Intransitive Verbs

Active Voice	Passive Voice
Present	**am/is/are + past participle**
The farmer grows wheat.	Wheat is grown by the farmer.
Past	**was/were + past participle**
I made a cake.	The cake was made by me.
Future	**will be + past participle**
The princess will keep the key.	The key will be kept by the princess.
Progressive Present	**is/are being + past participle**
The farmer is growing wheat.	Wheat is being grown by the farmer.
Progressive Past	**was/were being + past participle**
I was making a cake.	The cake was being made by me.
Progressive Future	**will be being + past participle**
The princess will be keeping the key.	The key will be being kept by the princess.
Perfect Present	**has/have been + past participle**
The farmer has grown wheat.	Wheat has been grown by the farmer.
Perfect Past	**had been + past participle**
I had made a cake.	The cake had been made by me.
Perfect Future	**will have been + past participle**
The princess will have kept the key.	The key will have been kept by the princess.

I laugh out loud.
The baby slept soundly.
The queen will sit in the front row.
He died.

transire (Latin for "to pass over")

Transitive verbs express action that is received by some person or thing.
Intransitive verbs express action that is not received by any person or thing.

Common Intransitive Verbs

cough	go	arrive
sit	lie	rise
shine	sneeze	am, is, are, was, were

Common Transitive Verbs

love	eat	help
set	lay	raise
cut	hug	save

I am sitting on the front porch.
I lay down on the grass.
I will have risen early in the morning.

I am setting the heavy box down.
I laid my weary head on my arms.
I will have raised my hand at least once by the end of class.

Verbs That Can Be Used as Transitive or Intransitive

turn	break	speak
fly	run	spread
taste	eat	sing

The cook turns the meat on the spit.

I will spread gochujang mayonnaise on the burger bun.

He is singing a difficult aria.

The captain turned towards the sunset.

The mist spread across the river's surface.

He's singing in the shower.

The cook turns the meat on the spit.

___

I will spread gochujang mayonnaise on the burger bun.

___

He is singing a difficult aria.

___

Exercise 56A: Transitive and Intransitive Verbs

Underline each verb in the following sentences twice. Write *T* above each transitive verb and *IT* above each intransitive verb. Circle the direct object of each transitive verb.

These sentences are adapted from *Drought*, by Christopher Lampton.

The many farms in the Great Plains states provide food for people around the country.

In the 1930s, drought arrived in the Great Plains.

The Sahel region borders on the Saharan desert.

In the middle of a high-pressure system, you can expect fair weather with no rain.

Water also has a solid form.

In the 1980s, a mass famine in Africa lasted for much of the decade and took thousands of lives.

All living things need water for survival.

Plagues of grasshoppers and other insects descended on the Great Plains.

The dust storms blew across the plains and down the streets of cities.

They covered automobiles, homes, and people with thick layers of dust.

In Southeast Asia, monsoons provide rains after the dry winters.

Normally, the monsoon winds blow from south to north.

Every ring on the exposed surface of a tree stump represents one year in the tree's growth.

After a few days a high-pressure system usually moves on.

With a stalled high-pressure system, the area underneath can go for long periods without rain.

Water in the ocean can take the form of water vapor and enter the air.

Eventually, the droplets of water in the cloud will clump together into larger droplets.

Finally, water rationing began.

Exercise 56B: Active and Passive Verbs

In the blanks below, change each sentence from active to passive or from passive to active.

These sentences are adapted from *South Africa at the Crossroads*, by Jacqueline Drobis Meisel.

The Dutch were greatly disrupting the Khoikhoi way of life.

____

The German colony of South West Africa was defeated by South African forces.

____

From the very beginning, some groups opposed the policy of apartheid.

____

In 1960, the Pan-African Congress organized a campaign of peaceful protest.

____

Police and army vehicles patrolled the troubled township streets.

____

Significant political reforms were made by the government.

____

More voices joined the call to economic action.

____

Exercise 56C: Diagramming

On your own paper, diagram every word of the following sentences.

The sneeze from the elephant echoed across his enclosure at the zoo and startled many of the visitors.

Mr. Williamson's amusement waned with the realization of Lucy's involvement in the prank.

The little boy stumbled on the rickety bridge and became fearful.

The unexpected knock at the door gave me a start and made me quite curious.

WEEK 15

Specialized Pronouns

— LESSON 57 —

Parts of Speech
Parts of the Sentence
Intensive and Reflexive Pronouns

Anita made herself a huge brownie sundae!

Reflexive pronouns refer back to the subject.
Usually, reflexive pronouns act like objects.

Part of speech is a term that explains what a word does.
Part of the sentence is a term that explains how a word functions in a sentence.

He adapted himself to their knowledge.
He gave himself a task.
He praises in himself what he blames in others.

myself, himself, herself, itself, yourself, yourselves, ourselves, themselves

Intensive pronouns emphasize a noun or another pronoun.

The Queen of England herself gave the speech.
The Queen of England gave the speech herself.

> The Queen of England gave herself. (DO: herself)
>
> The Queen of England gave herself the speech. (IO: herself)
>
> The Queen of England gave the speech to herself. (OP: herself)

Aristotle himself observed these variations.

He jumped into the sea and drowned himself.

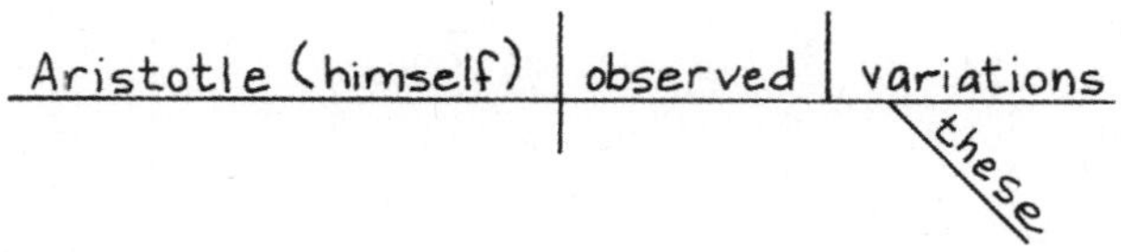

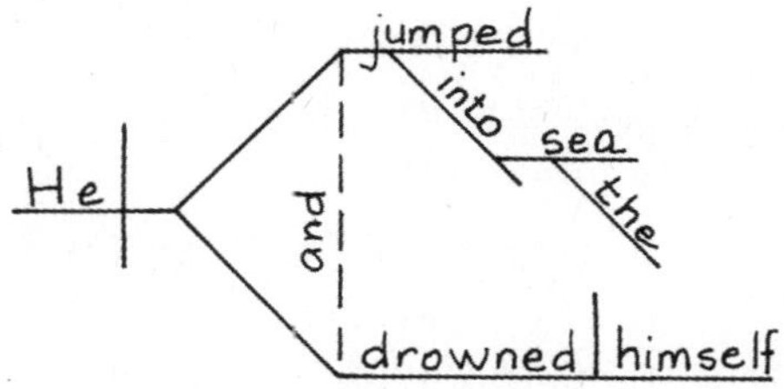

Do NOT use theirselves, hisself, or ourself.

Diana and myself cooked a casserole.
Diana and I cooked a casserole.
I myself cooked a casserole.
Take care of yourself.

Exercise 57A: Identifying Intensive and Reflexive Pronouns

Underline the intensive and reflexive pronouns in the following sentences. Above each pronoun, write *I* for intensive or *R* for reflexive. If the pronoun is reflexive, also mark it as *DO* (direct object), *IO* (indirect object), or *OP* (object of the preposition). The first is done for you.

These sentences are adapted from *Gulliver's Travels*, by Jonathan Swift.

I was struck with the utmost fear and astonishment, and hid myself (R DO) in the corn.

We brought the materials of diseases, folly, and vice, to spend among ourselves.

I myself heard him give directions that one of his pages should be whipped.

They are dressed by men till four years of age, and then must dress themselves.

The author gives some account of himself and family.

The farmer was glad enough to have his daughter preferred at court, and the poor girl herself was not able to hide her joy.

Whenever he begins to praise you to others or to yourself, you are from that day forlorn.

She behaved herself at our house as cheerfully as the rest.

But the danger is much greater when the ministers themselves are commanded to show their dexterity.

We therefore trusted ourselves to the mercy of the waves.

Exercise 57B: Using Intensive and Reflexive Pronouns Correctly

The following sentences may contain errors in the usage of intensive or reflexive pronouns. Cross out each incorrect word and write the correction in the blank. If a sentence has no errors, write "Correct" in the blank.

Silvia and myself will sing together in the talent show. ____________________

The commencement address was given by the president hisself. ____________________

Susan B. Anthony herself died before all women in the United States were granted suffrage. ____________________

We all reminded ourself about the prize we would get if our team won. ____________________

The basketball players got theirselves water after the game. ____________________

Take this to the office by yourself. ____________________

Please hand herself this note. ____________________

Exercise 57C: Diagramming Intensive and Reflexive Pronouns

Diagram every word in the following sentences.

The speaker carried himself to the podium with confidence.

The key itself is scribbled in a corner of the map.

After their explanation, I approved the plan myself.

The two adventurers must discover the treasure by themselves.

— LESSON 58 —

Demonstrative Pronouns
Demonstrative Adjectives

Questions	Punch lines
What did the teacher say to make the student eat his quiz?	That opens up a whole new can of worms.
What did the customer in the butcher shop hear that scared him?	This will be a piece of cake!
What did the fisherman say when he dropped his bucket of bait?	These cost an arm and a leg.

Demonstrative pronouns demonstrate or point out something. They can take the place of a single word or a group of words.

this, that, these, those

"Your cousin wrote this," said Aunt Alexandra. "He was a beautiful character."

"Didn't know it was this dark. Didn't look like it'd be this dark earlier in the evening."

Demonstrative adjectives modify nouns and answer the question *which one.*

That was the only time I ever heard Atticus say it was a sin to do something . . .

"I destroyed his last shred of credibility at that trial, if he had any to begin with."

It was times like these when I thought my father, who hated guns and had never been to any wars, was the bravest man who ever lived.

I was beginning to notice a subtle change in my father these days, that came out when he talked with Aunt Alexandra.

"Dill, those were his own witnesses."

Mrs. Merriweather was one of those childless adults who find it necessary to assume a different tone of voice when speaking to children.

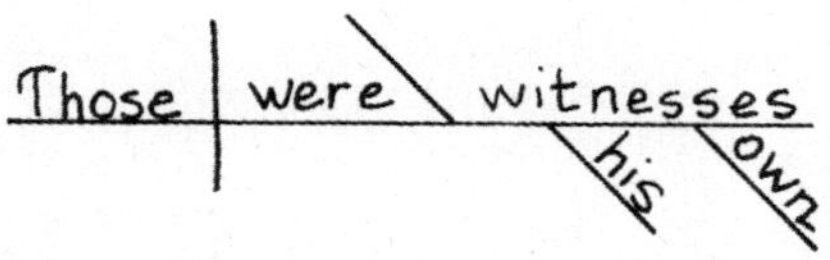

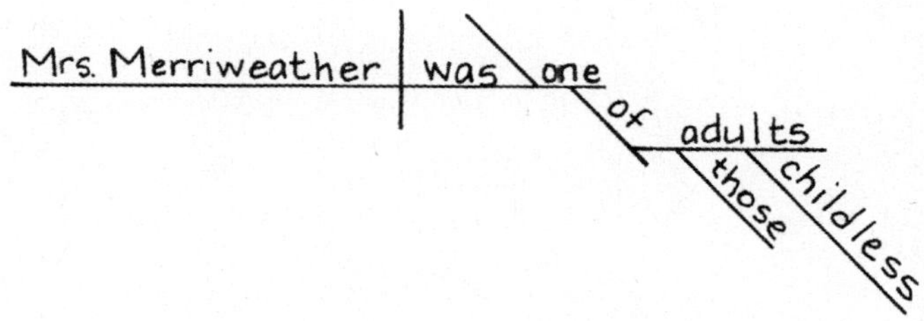

(The above sentences are from *To Kill a Mockingbird*, by Harper Lee.)

Did you see the coaster? That is one scary ride.

Raindrops on roses and whiskers on kittens, bright copper kettles and warm woolen mittens, brown paper packages tied up with strings–these are a few of my favorite things.

Exercise 58A: Demonstrative Pronouns and Demonstrative Adjectives

In the sentences below, label every occurrence of *this*, *that*, *these*, and *those* as either *DP* (for demonstrative pronoun) or *DA* (for demonstrative adjective). Draw an arrow from each demonstrative adjective to the noun it modifies. Label each demonstrative pronoun as *S* (subject), *DO* (direct object), *IO* (indirect object), or *OP* (object of the preposition).

The sentences below are from *The Merry Adventures of Robin Hood*, by Howard Pyle.

Now the Sheriff of Nottingham swore he himself would bring this knave, Robin Hood, to justice.

"Now, Reynold Greenleaf," quoth the Sheriff, "thou art the fairest hand at the long bow mine eyes ever beheld, next to that false knave, Robin Hood, from whose wiles Heaven forfend me!"

"I and these brethren were passing peacefully along the high-road with our packhorses, and a half score of men to guard them."

"Now yield thee," quoth the Tinker, "for thou art my captive." To this Robin Hood made no answer, but, clapping his horn to his lips, he blew three blasts, loud and clear.

But the Sheriff grew grave, for he did not like this so well.

So these also came to the church, and there Sir Stephen leaped from his horse, and, coming to the litter, handed fair Ellen out therefrom.

"Come, busk thee, Little John! Stir those lazy bones of thine."

At this Will Scarlet laughed again. "Be not too sure of that, good uncle," quoth he.

"Now, thou art a man after mine own heart!" cried the Cook right heartily; "and, as thou speakest of it, that is the very service for me."

Behind these were two of the higher brethren of Emmet.

Not far from the trysting tree was a great rock in which a chamber had been hewn. This was the treasure-house of the band.

"It used to gall me to hear him speak up so boldly to my father, who, thou knowest, was ever a patient man to those about him."

Then next they met a stout burgher and his wife and their two fair daughters. These Little John saluted gravely.

Some among them shouted, "Hey for Reynold Greenleaf!" for this was the name Little John had called himself that day.

Exercise 58B: Demonstrative Pronouns

In the blank beneath each sentence, write a possible description of the thing or person that the underlined demonstrative pronoun stands for. Make sure to choose the correct number. (And use your imagination.)

These are absolutely delicious!

____

This is not very sturdy.

____

That may be the most adorable thing in the world.

____

Those are quite ancient.

____

Exercise 58C: Diagramming

On your own paper, diagram every word in the following three sentences.

That object moves others, and is itself also moved by something from the outside.

Of this, I myself am certain and am fully resolved.

All of those, great and small, are problems, but can be resolved with fortitude and a certain determination.

— LESSON 59 —

Demonstrative Pronouns
Demonstrative Adjectives
Interrogative Pronouns
Interrogative Adjectives

Interrogative pronouns take the place of nouns in questions.

who, whom, whose, which, what

"Who started this?" said Uncle Jack.
"Talk like what in front of whom?" he asked.
Whose is that blanket?
Which is correct?

Whose blanket is missing?
What madness is this?
Which shoes are yours?

Interrogative adjectives modify nouns.

REMEMBER #1: Don't confuse *whose* and *who's.*

Whose orange flip-flops are those? — *Interrogative pronoun*
Who's cooking dinner? — *Contraction of who is*

I don't know whose/who's coming to dinner.

Whose/who's plate is still empty?

REMEMBER #2: Use *whom* as an object and *who* as a subject or predicate nominative.

CORRECT

Who started this?	*She started this. They started this. I started this. Jack started this.*
Talk like what in front of whom?	*In front of him? In front of her? In front of them? In front of Jack?*

Whom/Who is calling?

To whom/who did you speak?

REMEMBER #3: Diagram interrogative adjectives like any other adjective, and diagram interrogative pronouns like any other pronoun.

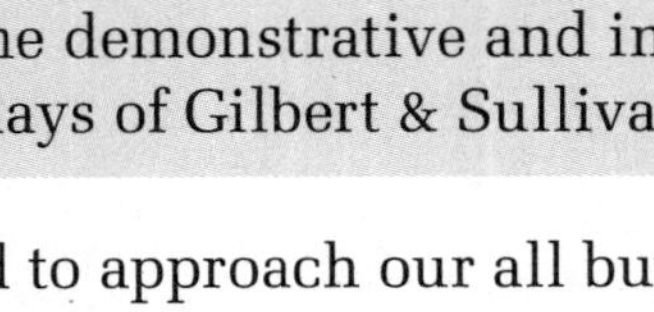

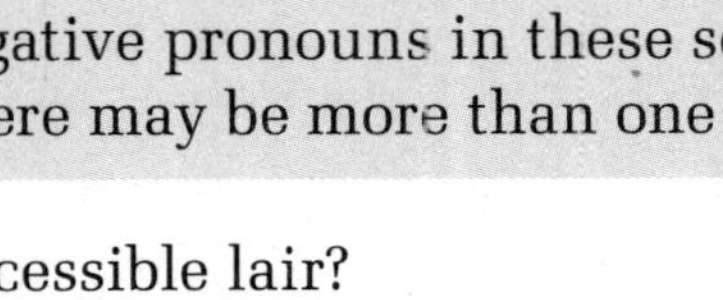

Exercise 59A: Identifying Demonstrative and Interrogative Pronouns

Underline all of the demonstrative and interrogative pronouns in these sentences, which are all from the plays of Gilbert & Sullivan. There may be more than one in each sentence.

Who has ventured to approach our all but inaccessible lair?

But who are you, sir? Speak!

Kind sir, you cannot have the heart
Our lives to part

From those to whom an hour ago
We were united!

Who knows whose husband you are?

But which is it? There are two of them!

Dear, dear, dear! this is very tiresome.

She has twice as much money, which may account for it.

But heaven ha' mercy, whom wouldst thou marry?

I didn't anticipate that,
When I first put this uniform on!

You see before you
The men to whom you're plighted!

Whom were you talking with just now?

Aye, she knows all about that.

Now what can that have been—
A shot so late at night,
Enough to cause a fright!

That's not true, but let it pass.

I say, which of us has married her?

Why, who is this whose evil eyes
Rain blight on our festivities?

Bless your heart, they've been staring at us through those windows for the last half-hour!

Those who would separate us woe betide!

But they're nothing at all, compared
With those of his daughter-in-law elect!

And this is the certificate of his death.

What shall I do? Before these gentle maidens
I dare not show in this alarming costume!

But which of you is married to which of us, and what's to become of the other?

These were my thoughts; I kept them to myself,
For at that age I had not learnt to speak.

Exercise 59B: Using Interrogative and Demonstrative Pronouns Correctly

Choose the correct word in parentheses. Cross out the incorrect word.

(Who/Whom) are you going to choose to play the clown?

(Who/ Whom) was shrieking so loudly last night?

(This/These) are the most comfortable pajamas I've ever worn.

For (who/whom) are the flowers in the graveyard?

(Who's/Whose) cousins are coming to visit?

(Who/Whom) did Aaron Burr challenge to a duel?

(This/That) is my calculator right here, so (this/that) one over there must be Nara's.

(Who's/Whose) is this clown makeup?

(This/These) is not very clean.

(Who/Whom) is the eccentric woman in the red and purple hat?

(Who/Whom) is the veterinarian in charge of delivering the new foal?

(Who's/Whose) delivering the cauliflower and caviar pizza?

Exercise 59C: Diagramming Interrogative and Demonstrative Pronouns

Diagram the following sentences.

Whose stomach is growling so loudly?

She ate what?

My sister ate all of that.

Who spilled this Smoking Bishop punch on the floor?

From whom did Charles Dickens get the recipe for Smoking Bishop punch?

Petra gave you which box of salt caramel truffle chocolates?

Do not forget this letter and that ring.

— LESSON 60 —

Pronoun Review

Sentences Beginning with Adverbs

A pronoun takes the place of a noun.
An antecedent is the noun that is replaced by the pronoun.

Personal Pronouns
I, me, my, mine,
you, your, yours
he, she, him, her, it
his, hers, its
we, us, our, ours,
they, them, their, theirs

Indefinite pronouns are pronouns without antecedents.

Singular

anybody	anyone	anything
everybody	everyone	everything
nobody	no one	nothing
somebody	someone	something
another	other	one
either	neither	each

Plural

both few many several

Singular or Plural

all any most none some

Reflexive pronouns refer back to the subject.
myself, himself, herself, itself, yourself, yourselves, ourselves, themselves

She tripped and hurt herself.
She herself tripped.

Intensive pronouns emphasize a noun or another pronoun.
Demonstrative pronouns demonstrate or point out something. They can take the place of a single word or a group of words.
this, that, these, those

Interrogative pronouns take the place of nouns in questions.
who, whom, whose, which, what

Interrogative adjectives modify nouns.

What are you doing? Don't you know what direction to go?

That is she.
What is that?
Which is yours?
Where are you?
There you are.
So it is.

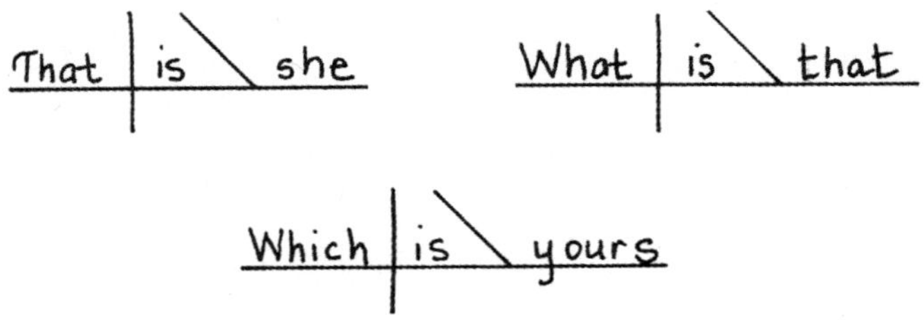

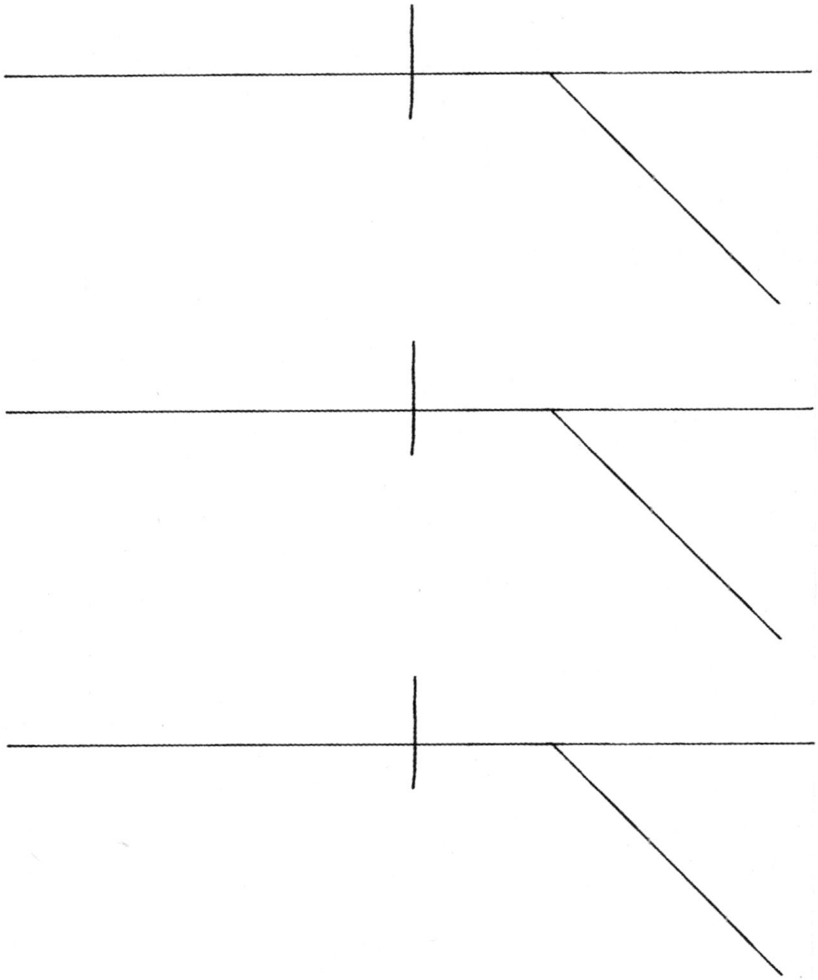

Exercise 60A: Singular/Plural Indefinite Pronouns

Cross out the incorrect verb in each sentence.

Each of the villains (laugh/laughs) evilly.

"No one (is/are) able to stop us!" they cry.

Some of the heroes (narrow/narrows) their eyes.

"All of us (is/are) prepared for whatever you have planned," they promise.

Most of the villains (look/looks) nervous, but one (is/are) undaunted by the heroes.

Exercise 60B: Interrogatives and Demonstratives

In each of the following sentences, underline the interrogatives and demonstratives. If they are acting as adjectives, draw a line from each to the noun it modifies. If they are acting as other parts of the sentence, label them (*S* for subject, *DO* for direct object, *IO* for indirect object, or *OP* for object of the preposition).

These sentences are from Elizabeth George Speare's *The Witch of Blackbird Pond.*

So this is the orphan from Barbados?

What difference does that make?

The next job is some new thatch for that roof.

What am I offered for it?

There's scarce a house in this town but has a sick child in it.

Even that could not disturb her, poor child.

What had poor Hannah ever done to them?

Read that for us, child, beginning right there.

From that moment in the meadow Kit ceased to plan at all.

Exercise 60C: Diagramming Practice

Diagram every word of the following sentences. These sentences are from Elizabeth George Speare's *The Witch of Blackbird Pond.*

This girl could have been the toast of a regiment!

You're not making that fuss about one old wolf?

There, without a thought, she left the pathway, plunged into a field, and fell on the grass.

Hannah accepted the miracle and the prospect of a journey like a docile child.

— REVIEW 5 —

Weeks 13-15

Topics
Pronouns and Antecedents
Possessive Pronouns
Subject and Object Pronouns
Indefinite Pronouns (and Subject-Verb Agreement)
Troublesome Verbs
Active and Passive Voice
Conjugating Passive Voice
Intensive and Reflexive Pronouns
Demonstrative and Interrogative Pronouns

Review 5A: Types of Pronouns

Put each pronoun from the word bank in the correct category. Some words may belong in more than one category.

her that he who
his myself them
we someone what ours
which it both
this yourself these many
herself

Personal Subject _______________ _______________ _______________

Personal Object _______________ _______________ _______________

Personal Possessive _______________ _______________ _______________

Indefinite _______________ _______________ _______________

Demonstrative _______________ _______________ _______________

Interrogative _______________ _______________ _______________

Intensive/Reflexive _______________ _______________ _______________

Review 5B: Using Correct Pronouns

Circle the correct word in parentheses.

The actress with the blue hat was (her / she).

(There / Their / They're) were several obstacles in (there / their / they're) way, but (they / them) still got (there / their / they're) in time.

Marina and (herself / her / she) climbed over the fence and hurt (theirselves / themselves) on the way down.

All the purple properties in the game belong to (him / he).

(Who's / Whose) carrying Mrs. Prior's bags for (her / she)?

Jason, Titus, and (myself / me / I) are deciding (who's / whose) science project is the best.

(Who / Whom) was repeating (himself / hisself)?

(Who / Whom) is (your / you're) mother scolding?

Simeon and (he / him) are tossing the ball to (who / whom)?

(Who's / Whose) locket is over (there / their / they're) on the table?

Review 5C: Pronouns and Antecedents

Circle the THIRTEEN personal pronouns (subject, object, and possessive) in the following excerpt from *Betsy-Tacy* by Maud Hart Lovelace. Draw arrows to each pronoun's antecedent.

Then, find the single reflexive pronoun. Underline it. Draw an arrow to its antecedent.

Julia had already taken Betsy to the door, and had said to Miss Dalton, the teacher: "This is my little sister Betsy."

Now Katie said, "This is my little sister Tacy." And she added, "She's very bashful."

"Never mind," said Miss Dalton, smiling brightly. "I'll take care of that. I'll put her right by me." And she placed a little chair beside her desk and put Tacy into that.

Tacy didn't like that. Betsy could tell from the way she scrunched down and hid herself beneath her curls. She was less happy than ever when Betsy was put far away at a regular desk in one of the rows of desks filling the room.

Review 5D: Agreement with Indefinite Pronouns

Choose the correct word in parentheses to agree with the indefinite pronouns. Cross out the incorrect word.

No one (has/have) closed the door.

Most of the birds (has/have) flown away, but one (is/are) still sitting on the fence.

Everyone with a ticket (is/are) lined up by the door.

(Has/Have) anyone forgotten (his or her/their) lunch?

(Has/Have) all the dancers picked up (his or her/their) shoes?

In the sun, most of the snow (has/have) melted already, but some (remains/remain) in the shade.

Few of the tables at the restaurant (is/are) occupied.

Neither of the wounds (requires/require) stitches.

If anyone (wants/want) fabric, (he or she/they) should take a number at the cutting counter.

(Is/Are) either of the Collins twins coming on the trip?

Review 5E: Distinguishing between Active and Passive Voice

Identify each sentence as *A* for active or *P* for passive. These sentences are from *The Pony Express: Hoofbeats in the Wilderness*, by Joseph J. DiCerto.

The settlement of the West was made possible by people of great character and foresight. ________

Senator Gwin of California enthusiastically described the idea of a central-route mail service. ________

These locations were called relay stations. ________

Management increased the mail run service to twice each week. ________

Thousands of emigrants on their way west climbed the sloped walls of Independence Rock to engrave their names and dates for future historians. ________

The records of many of these stations were lost. ________

In 1860, Mark Twain was making a trip across the country by stagecoach. ________

The two men were paralyzed by fear. ________

Bill Cody had ridden an amazing 384 miles without a regular sleeping break. ________

By August 1861, most of the transcontinental telegraph line was completed. ________

Review 5F: Troublesome Verbs

Circle the correct verb form in parentheses. These sentences are from *The Golden Fleece and the Heroes Who Lived before Achilles*, by Padraic Colum.

The blue sky was above him, the great trees stood away from him, and the little child (laid / lay) at his feet.

In a quiet place he (sat/set) down, and for a while he lost sight of Pandora.

The Argonauts shouted, but the rude Bebrycians (raised / rose) their clubs to rush upon them.

The master of the ship (let / left) the sail take the breeze of the evening.

No sooner did they (sit / set) their feet upon the shore than the hero went off into the forest, to pull up a tree that he might shape into an oar.

Medea went to her couch and (laid / lay) down upon it.

And then, even as Telamon said these angry words, a strange figure (raised / rose) up out of the waves of the sea.

Straightaway he gave orders to his guard to (lay / lie) hands upon the youth.

The Graces put necklaces around her neck and (sat / set) a golden crown upon her head.

Once it came into the mind of Zeus that he would destroy the fourth race and (leave / let) the earth to the nymphs and the satyrs.

WEEK 16

Imposters

— LESSON 61 —

Progressive Tenses
Principal Parts
Past Participles as Adjectives
Present Participles as Adjectives

One Sunday afternoon in 1917, cousins named Frances Griffiths and Elsie Wright, aged nine and fifteen, saw some fairies and took clear snapshots of them with their box camera . . . In 1983, sixty-six years later, Elsie Wright and Frances Griffiths decided that it was time to confess what people had suspected all along. The fairies were paper dolls . . . propped up on the grass with pins.

—Kathryn Ann Lindskoog, *Fakes, Frauds, & Other Malarkey*

	First Principal Part Present	Second Principal Part Past	Third Principal Part Past Participle
	plan	planned	planned
	burst	burst	burst
	catch	caught	caught
	fall	fell	fallen

The planned vacation did not go well.

The burst balloon fit inside the honey jar.

The caught fish wriggled on the hook.

I climbed over the fallen tree.

The past participle of a verb can act as a descriptive adjective.

The freshly picked peaches were full of flavor.

As the clock struck twelve, he heard a rustling noise in the air.

By the side of the road, he saw a fox sitting.

Her mother stirred the pot of boiling water.

The snoring guards lay at the doorstep, fast asleep.

A simple verb simply tells whether an action takes place in the past, present, or future.

I thought, I think, I will think.

A perfect verb describes an action which has been completed before another action takes place.

I had thought, I have thought, I will have thought.

A progressive verb describes an ongoing or continuous action.

I was thinking, I am thinking, I will be thinking.

First Principal Part Present	Second Principal Part Past	Third Principal Part Past Participle	Present Participle
rustle	rustled	rustled	rustling
sit	sat	sat	sitting
snore	snored	snored	snoring
am	was	been	being

The present participle of a verb can act as a descriptive adjective.

The burst balloon fit inside the honey jar.

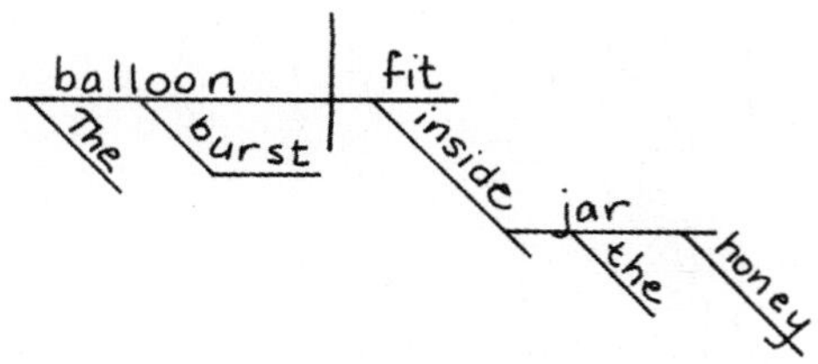

The snoring guards lay at the doorstep, fast asleep.

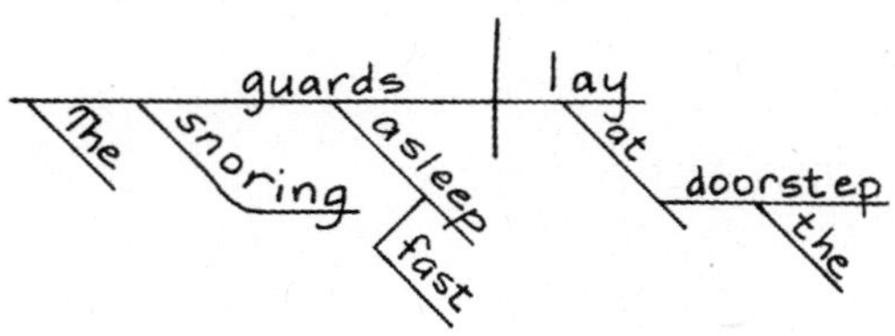

Sparkling stars shone.

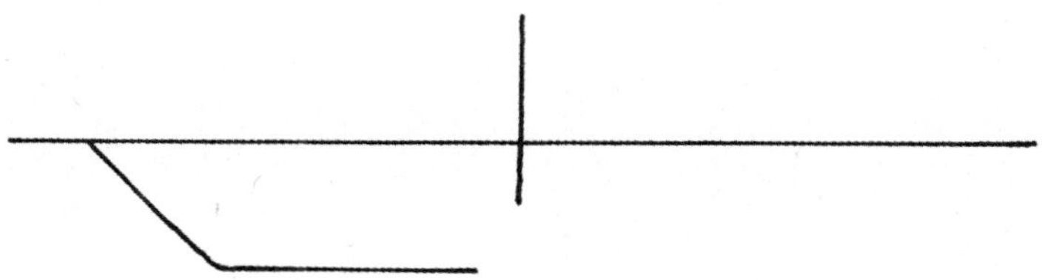

The forgotten cheese molded.

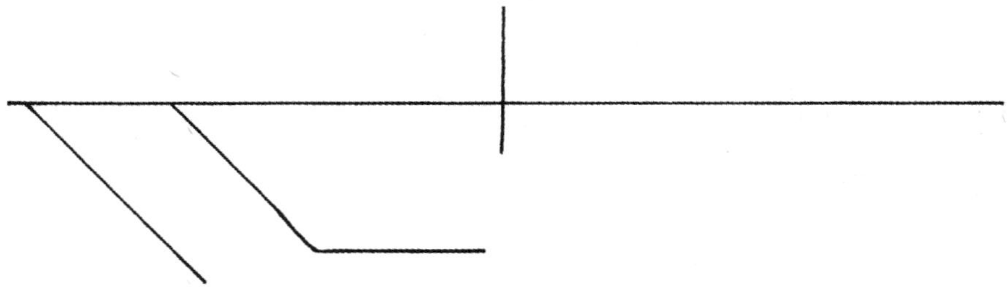

OPTIONAL:
The rustling leaves told us that the wind was rising.
The leaves, being rustled, signified the coming of fall.
Having rustled the leaves, the wind died down.
The leaves having been rustled, the wind died down.
The rustled leaves finally stilled.

Present (Active) Participle	Present (Passive) Participle	Perfect Present (Active) Participle	Perfect Present (Passive) Participle	Past Participle
add *-ing*	**being + past participle**	**having + past participle**	**having + been + past participle**	**add *-ed* (second principle part)**
rustling	being rustled	having rustled	having been rustled	rustled
eating				eaten
reading				read

Exercise 61A: Identifying Past Participles Used as Adjectives

Underline the past participles used as adjectives in the following sentences, adapted from *Vitamins and Minerals* by Alvin Silverstein, Virginia Silverstein, and Robert Silverstein. Draw a line to each word modified.

Our bodies need balanced amounts of minerals.

In some areas, people eat mostly refined rice, and their diet lacks key vitamins.

The best way to get vitamins is through a diet with varied foods at each meal.

Fresh or frozen foods, rather than canned foods, can help you get more nutrients.

Milled grains and peeled vegetables lose some of their nutrients.

Exercise 61B: Identifying Present Participles Used as Adjectives

Underline the present participles used as adjectives in the following sentences, taken from *The Moffats* by Eleanor Estes. Draw a line to each word modified.

This consisted of a slight rocking motion from heel to toe.

And the red steed sent sparks from his nostrils that disappeared like shooting stars into the still night air.

A few heavy jerks and a harsh grating noise made Rufus realize what was happening.

Way off on the other side of the harbor they could just make out the slumbering form of the Sleeping Giant.

"At your service," said he, and he gave Joe a meaning look.

Janey scuffled through the dry, crackling leaves in the gutter.

Her yellow eyes shone with a knowing gleam.

Exercise 61C: Diagramming Present & Past Participles Used as Adjectives

On your own paper, diagram the following sentences.

Flowering plants beautify gardens.
Menacing goblins brandished their curved swords.
Her drumming fingers sounded rhythmic.
Jim replaced his torn jacket.
A watched pot never boils.

— LESSON 62 —

Parts of Speech and Parts of Sentences
Present Participles as Nouns (Gerunds)

The cuckoo is one of the great con artists of the animal world. It can trick other birds into raising its children by laying their eggs in the stranger's nest. When the cuckoo chicks hatch, the youngsters continue their parents' strategy by killing any other birds in the nest before they reveal their identity. Scientists have found the imposter cuckoo even fools the foster parent into thinking its chicks are still alive by flapping yellow patches on its wings. This also creates the illusion there more mouths to feed and tricks the foster parents into delivering more food.

—Augustus Brown, *Why Pandas Do Handstands: And Other Curious Truths About Animals*

The running rabbit was darting towards the briar patch.

Part of speech is a term that explains what a word does.

A noun names a person, place, thing, or idea.

Part of the sentence is a term that explains how a word functions in a sentence.

subject direct object indirect object object of a preposition

A gerund is a present participle acting as a noun.

Careful sailing was the duty of the captain's mate.

This day was lost from pure whim, for the pleasure of going ashore.

Providence gives the deserving their due.

With the other hand, he repressed the beatings of his heart.

Running is my favorite exercise.

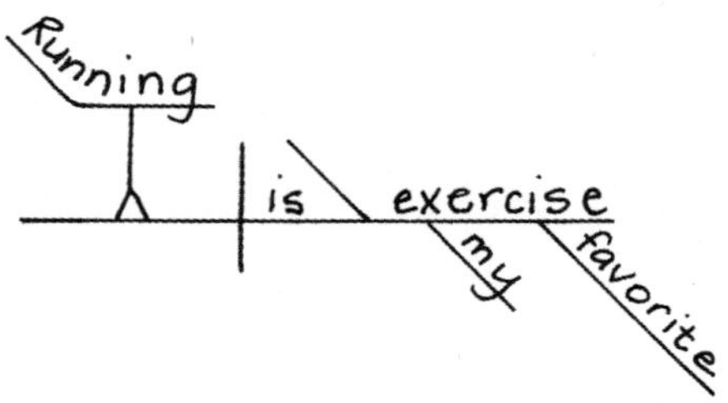

He feared falling.

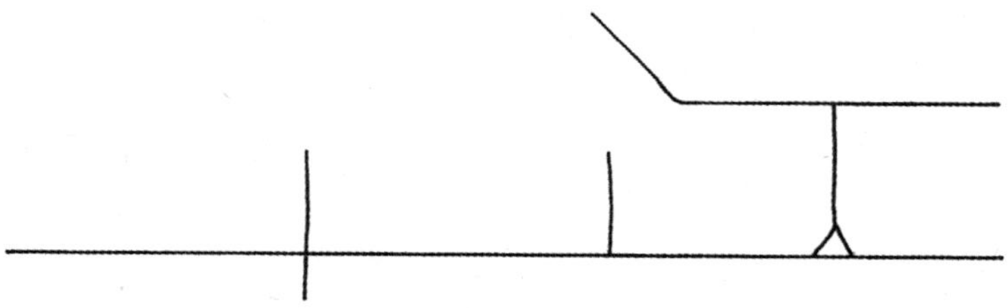

Exercise 62A: Identifying Gerunds

In the following sentences, slightly condensed from George B. Schaller's *The Year of the Gorilla*, circle each gerund. Underline each subject once and each predicate twice. Write *DO* above any direct objects, *IO* above any indirect objects, and *OP* above any objects of prepositions.

Gorillas require two hours of feeding in the morning, and each animal is intent on filling up.

Between nine and ten o'clock, the foraging generally comes slowly to a stop.

The crackling of the undergrowth revealed the presence of the gorillas about forty yards ahead.

I heard rustling at my approach.

Immediately after and sometimes during chest beating, the animal runs sideways for a few steps before dropping to all fours and dashing along.

I give the charging animal all benefit of the doubt.

Illegal hunting is a large industry.

Exercise 62B: Diagramming Gerunds

On your own paper, diagram every word in the following sentences.

Arguing will not solve your problems.
Tess earns extra money by coaching.
The suspect's confusing responses befuddled the detectives.
The owl is hunting mice.
Joe enjoys hunting.

— LESSON 63 —

Gerunds
Present and Past Participles as Adjectives
Infinitives
Infinitives as Nouns

The comings and goings of her acquaintances provided Mrs. Jennings great entertainment.

This circumstance was a growing attachment between her eldest girl and the brother of Mrs. John Dashwood.

The presence of the two Miss Steeles, lately arrived, gave Elinor pain.

An infinitive is formed by combining *to* and the first person singular present form of a verb.

	Present Tense		Infinitive
	Singular	**Plural**	
First person	I give	we give	
Second person	you give	you give	_______________
Third person	he, she, it gives	they give	

	Present Tense		Infinitive
	Singular	**Plural**	
First person	I think	we think	
Second person	you think	you think	__________
Third person	he, she, it thinks	they think	
First person	I have	we have	
Second person	you have	you have	__________
Third person	he, she, it has	they have	

To err is human.
To forgive is divine.
—Alexander Pope

To wish was to hope.

To hope was to expect.
—Jane Austen

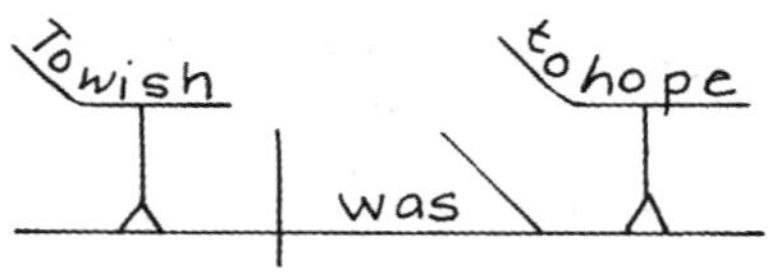

Exercise 63A: Identifying Gerunds and Infinitives

Underline the gerunds and infinitives in the following quotes. Identify the imposters as *G* for gerund or *I* for infinitive. Then, identify each gerund or infinitive as a subject (*S*), predicate nominative (*PN*), direct object (*DO*), or object of a preposition (*OP*).

The instinct of nearly all societies is to lock up anybody who is truly free.
—Jean Cocteau

Learning is what most adults will do for a living in the 21st century.
—Lewis Perelman

To exist is to change.
—Henri Bergson

I criticize by creation, not by finding fault.
—Cicero

Avoiding danger is no safer in the long run than outright exposure.
—Helen Keller

Living at risk is jumping off the cliff and building your wings on the way down.
—Ray Bradbury

One of the most important tasks of a manager is to eliminate his people's excuses for failure.
—Robert Townsend

He that is good for making excuses is seldom good for anything else.
—Benjamin Franklin

I don't mind lying, but I hate inaccuracy.
—Samuel Butler

Our whole life is solving puzzles.
—Ernő Rubik

Learning preserves the errors of the past, as well as its wisdom.
—Alfred North Whitehead

We must learn to live together as brothers or perish together as fools.
—Martin Luther King Jr.

Exercise 63B: Diagramming Gerunds and Infinitives

On your own paper, diagram the following sentences.

Creating is my criticism.
To exist is to change.
Learning preserves the errors of the past.
I don't mind lying, but I hate inaccuracy.
We must learn to live or to perish.
Living is jumping.

— LESSON 64 —

Gerunds
Present and Past Participles
Infinitives
Gerund, Participle, and Infinitive Phrases

I love eating.

I love eating

A phrase is a group of words serving a single grammatical function.
I love eating pancakes with maple syrup, yellow cake with chocolate frosting, and grilled ribeye steaks.

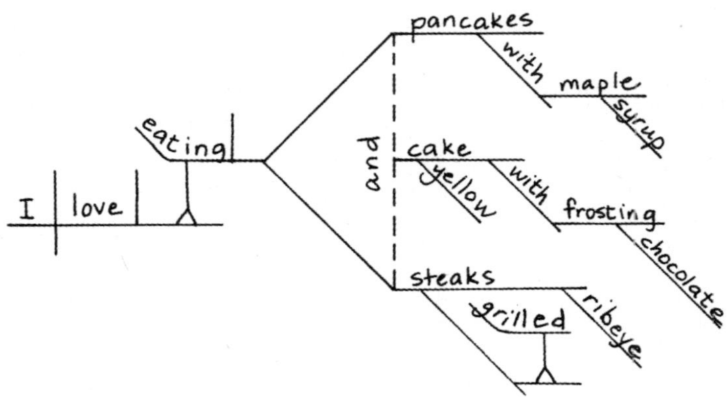

To give without expecting a reward is to receive an even greater gift.

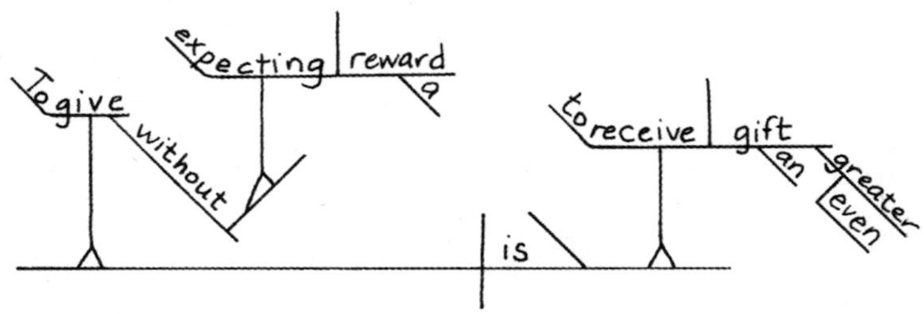

He saw the priceless antique vase shattered across the floor and scattered on the rug.

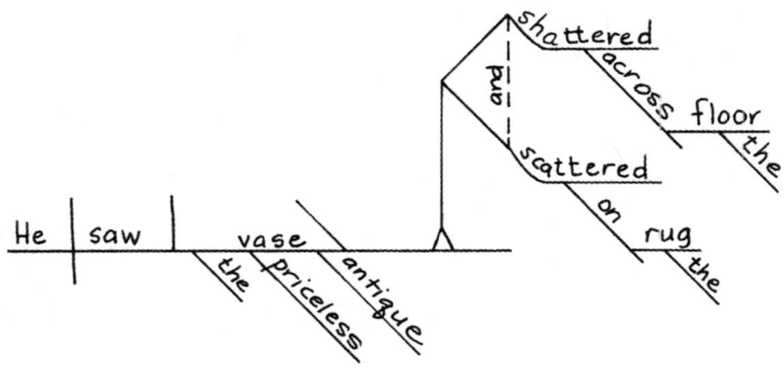

Exercise 64A: Identifying Phrases that Serve as Parts of the Sentence

In the following sentences, begin by underlining each prepositional phrase.

- Then, circle each group of words that contains a gerund, infinitive, or past participle. Each one serves as a part of the sentence. (Those circled phrases might include some of your prepositional phrases!)
- Label each circled phrase. Your options are: *ADJ* (adjective), *ADV* (adverb), *S* (subject), *IO* (indirect object), *DO* (direct object), *OC* (object complement), *OP* (object of the preposition), *PN* (predicate nominative), or *PA* (predicate adjective).
- You might find that a circled phrase with a gerund, infinitive, or past participle in it contains other phrases with gerunds, infinitives, or past participles!

These sentences are taken from *The Matchlock* Gun, by Walter D. Edmonds.

She had black hair braided round her head.

Now he seemed absorbed in examining his powder horn and filling it from the big horn beside the chimney.

They preferred to build their own house.

John Mynderse rode down after lunch, carrying his musket in his hands, balancing it on the withers of his bright bay horse.

Tell him not to worry about us.

Gertrude had no trouble in leading them up the knoll beyond the garden.

To stay seemed the best way to her.

Exercise 64B: Diagramming

On your own paper, diagram all of the sentences from Exercise 64A.

WEEK 17

Comparatives and Superlatives Subordinating Conjunctions

— LESSON 65 —

Adjectives
Comparative and Superlative Adjectives

An adjective modifies a noun or pronoun.
Adjectives tell what kind, which one, how many, and whose.

The positive degree of an adjective describes only one thing.
The comparative degree of an adjective compares two things.
The superlative degree of an adjective compares three or more things.

Most regular adjectives form the comparative by adding *-r* or *-er.*
Most regular adjectives form the superlative by adding *-st* or *-est.*

Positive	**Comparative**	**Superlative**
large	larger	largest
big	bigger	biggest
silly	sillier	silliest

Spelling Rules

If the adjective ends in *-e* already, add only *–r* or *–st.*

noble	nobler	noblest
pure	purer	purest
cute	________	________

If the adjective ends in a short vowel sound and a consonant, double the consonant and add *–er* or *–est.*

red	redder	reddest
thin	thinner	thinnest
flat	________	________

If the adjective ends in –*y*, change the *y* to *i* and add –*er* or –*est*.

hazy	hazier	haziest
lovely	lovelier	loveliest
lucky	________	________

Many adjectives form their comparative and superlative forms by adding the word *more* or *most* before the adjective instead of using –*er* or –*est*.

unusual	more unusual	most unusual
fascinating	more fascinating	most fascinating
fun	more fun	most fun

She is more lovely than the dawn.
She is lovelier than the dawn.

She is the most lovely of all women.
She is the loveliest of all women.

The taller boy glanced around uneasily.

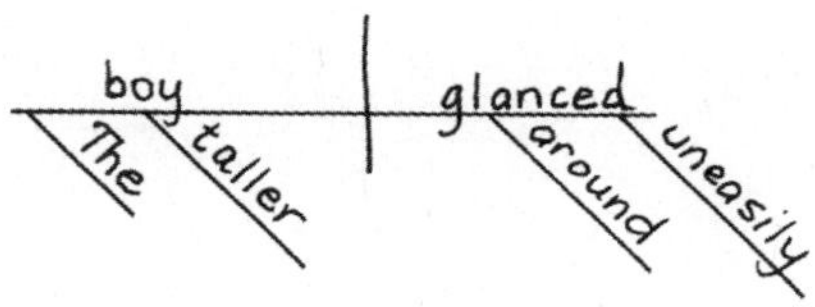

His more confident friend rang the doorbell.

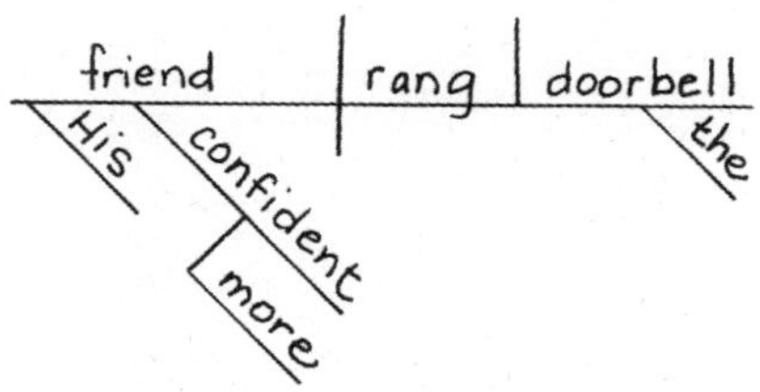

In comparative and superlative adjective forms, the words *more* and *most* are used as adverbs.

Exercise 65A: Identifying Positive, Comparative, and Superlative Adjectives

Identify the underlined adjective forms as *P* for positive, *C* for comparative, or *S* for superlative. These lines are from William Shakespeare's *A Midsummer Night's Dream*.

I am that merry wanderer of the night. ________

Or, rather, do I not in plainest truth ________
Tell you I do not, nor I cannot love you?

Effect it with some care, that he may prove
More fond on her than she upon her love. ________

The will of man is by his reason sway'd;
And reason says you are the worthier maid. __________
Things growing are not ripe until their season; __________
So I, being young, till now ripe not to reason. __________
[It] leads me to your eyes, where I o'erlook
Love's stories, written in love's richest book. __________

Injurious Hermia! most ungrateful maid! __________
Have you conspir'd, have you with these contriv'd
To bait me with this foul derision? __________

Exercise 65B: Forming Comparative and Superlative Adjectives

Fill in the blank with the correct form of the adjective in parentheses. Some of these adjectives use *more* or *most*, while others use *-er* or *-est* endings. You may consult a dictionary if you're not sure!

These sentences are taken from *The World's Great Explorers: Explorers of the Ancient World*, by Charnan Simon.

Egyptians found that they needed ________________, ________________, ________________ boats than those they initially built. (large, heavy, seaworthy)

The Cretans of four thousand years ago were ________________ than people living in the United States just two hundred years ago! (modern)

Timber from Phoenician cedar trees was always in great demand around the Mediterranean. But an even ________________ item was Phoenicia's exquisite purple dye. (desirable)

By 800 BC the Phoenician city of Carthage, located on the northern coast of Africa, was the ________________ and ________________ city in the western Mediterranean. (large, rich)

The ________________ Greek historian and geographer of them all was Herodotus. (famous)

In 330 BC, Massilia was a thriving center of trade. Its ________________ rival of all was the Phoenician port of Carthage. (great)

From the Yüeh-chih king, Chang Ch'ien learned of a rich country to the south and another to the southwest. And he learned of an even ________________ and ________________ country still farther to the west. (rich, powerful)

Exercise 65C: Diagramming Comparative and Superlative Adjectives

Diagram the following sentences.

A single tear revealed Commander Parrish's more tender side.

The shortest distance between two points is a straight line.

The leading actress appears more confident about tonight's performance.

The tallest mountain in Africa is a volcano in Tanzania.

Will voters be more apathetic in the next election?

— LESSON 66 —

Adverbs
Comparative and Superlative Adverbs
Coordinating Conjunctions
Subordinating Conjunctions

An adverb describes a verb, an adjective, or another adverb.
Adverbs tell how, when, where, how often, and to what extent.

The positive degree of an adverb describes only one verb, adjective, or adverb.
The comparative degree of an adverb compares two verbs, adjectives, or adverbs.
The superlative degree of an adverb compares three or more verbs, adjectives, or adverbs.

Most adverbs that end in –*ly* form their comparative and superlative forms by adding the word *more* or *most* before the adverb instead of using –*er* or –*est*.

thoughtfully	more thoughtfully	most thoughtfully
sadly	more sadly	most sadly
angrily	more angrily	most angrily

A few adverbs ending in -*y* change the -*y* to *i* and add –*er* or –*est*.

early	earlier	earliest

He worked more efficiently.

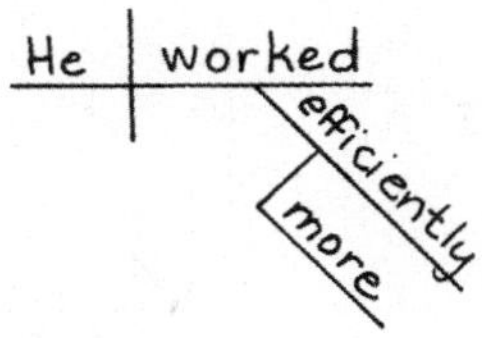

He worked more efficiently than his brother.

A conjunction joins two words or groups of words together.
and, or, nor, for, so, but, yet

A coordinating conjunction joins equal words or groups of words together.

The sun and the moon give us light.
The moon shines fitfully yet brightly.

A subordinating conjunction joins unequal words or groups of words together.

to subordinate: to place in a lower order or rank; to make secondary
    sub: from *Latin preposition sub,* beneath, under
    ordinate: from *Latin verb ordo,* to rank

He worked more efficiently than his brother.
He worked more efficiently than his brother [worked].

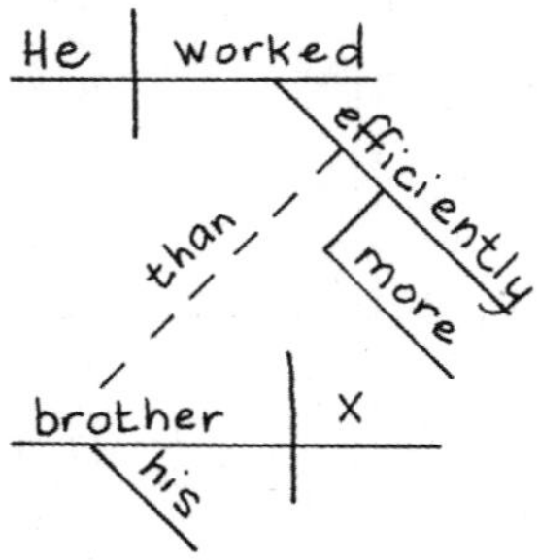

He is older than his brother.
He is older than his brother [is].

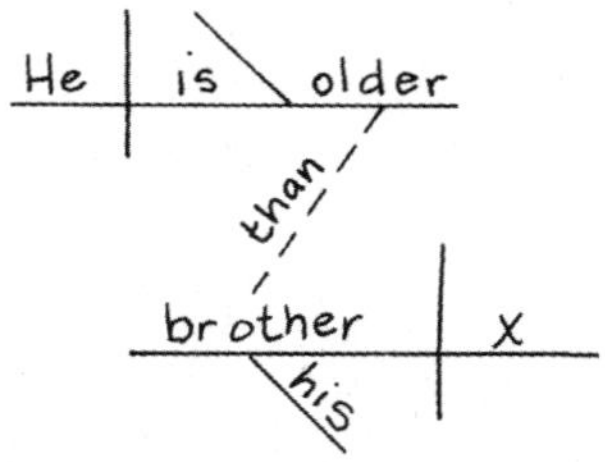

Exercise 66A: Diagramming Comparatives

Diagram the first two sentences on the frames provided. Diagram the remaining sentences on your own paper.

The light in the hall shines more dimly than the one in the kitchen.

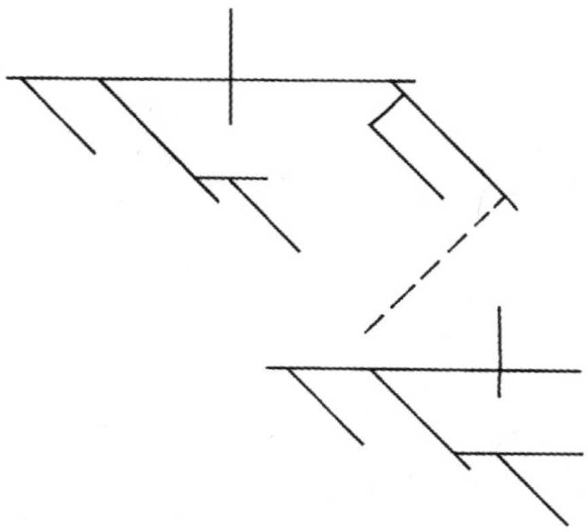

Greta reached the field more swiftly than her brother.

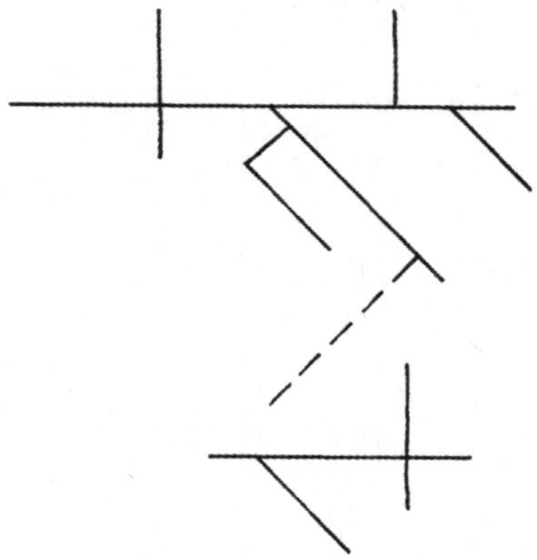

This story is even more bizarre than the last one was.

Jeffrey's comments during the debate were wittier than Sebastian's.

Sebastian has worked more diligently than Jeffrey.

Exercise 66B: Identifying Positive, Comparative, and Superlative Adverbs

In the blanks, identify the degree of each underlined adverb form as *P* for positive, *C* for comparative, or *S* for superlative. These sentences are from Jane Austen's *Pride and Prejudice*.

After a polite request that Elizabeth would lead the way, which the other as politely and more earnestly negatived, she seated herself. __________

Mrs. Bennet, who quarreled with no compliments, answered most readily. __________

Oh! yes—it would be much better to wait till Jane was well, and by that time most likely Captain Carter would be at Meryton again. __________

You will not find him more favorably spoken of by anyone. __________

Steady to his purpose, he scarcely spoke ten words to her through the whole of Saturday, and though they were at one time left by themselves for half-an-hour, he adhered most conscientiously to his book, and would not even look at her. __________ __________

They were of a respectable family in the north of England; a circumstance more deeply impressed on their memories than that their brother's fortune and their own had been acquired by trade. __________

Mrs. Bennet and her daughters apologized most civilly for Lydia's interruption, and promised that it should not occur again, if he would resume his book. __________

And when we got to the George, I do think we behaved very handsomely, for we treated the other three with the nicest cold luncheon in the world. __________

Your conjecture is totally wrong, I assure you. My mind was more agreeably engaged. __________

More than once did Elizabeth, in her ramble within the park, unexpectedly meet Mr. Darcy. __________

Exercise 66C: Forming Comparative and Superlative Adverbs

Fill in the blank with the correct form of the adverb in parentheses.

Who will finish the race the ____________________? (fast)

My sister usually wakes up ____________________ than I do. (early)

All three of my aunts have shipped me birthday gifts; I don't know which will arrive the ____________________. (soon)

Morgan presented her project ____________________ than Kira. (late)

Excuse me, but I believe I have been waiting in this line ____________________ than you have. (long)

The person who sits ____________________ to me in class is James. (close)

Mr. Gilbert stands ____________________ than anyone else I know! (tall)

— LESSON 67 —

Irregular Comparative and Superlative Adjectives and Adverbs

Exercise 67A: Best and Worst Jobs

Put the following jobs in the columns according to your opinion. (There are no correct answers—it all depends on you.)

ice cream taster
children's book illustrator
garbage collector
grass cutter
fashion designer
professional sky diver

good: ____________________ **bad:** ____________________

better: ____________________ **worse:** ____________________

best: ____________________ **worst:** ____________________

Irregular Comparative and Superlative Adjectives

Adjective	Comparative Form	Superlative Form
good	better	best
bad	worse	worst
little	less	least
much	more	most
many	more	most

I have more legs than a snake.
The octopus has the most legs of the three.

Irregular Comparative and Superlative Adverbs

Adverb	Comparative Form	Superlative Form
well	better	best
badly	worse	worst
little	less	least
much	more	most
far	farther	farthest

Do not use *more* with an adjective or adverb that is already in the comparative form. Do not use *most* with an adjective or adverb that is already in the superlative form.

Use an adjective form when an adjective is needed and an adverb form when an adverb is needed.

INCORRECT	CORRECT	S LV ADV PA
The team played good.	The team played well.	I am (not) well.
The tomato smells badly.	The tomato smells bad.	

Common Linking Verbs
am, is, are, was, were, be, being, been
taste, feel, smell, sound, look, prove, grow, remain, appear, stay, become, seem

The music sounds beautiful/beautifully.

Exercise 67B: Using Comparative and Superlative Adverbs Correctly

Choose the correct form in parentheses. Cross out the incorrect form.

The disc golf tournament will raise money for a local charity; people are donating (more generous/more generously) this year than they did last year.

Monique can toss a flying disc (farther/more far) than Landon.

Landon's throws are (more accurately/more accurate) than Monique's, because he focuses (more deliberately/more deliberate) on his target.

Judith believes Landon will do (better/more well) than Monique overall; she watches the tournament (most enthusiastically/most enthusiastic).

Augustin looks (more naturally/more natural) tossing the disc than standing still.

When the players take a break for a snack, Augustin eats (more hungrily/hungrier) than anyone else.

Exercise 67C: Using Correct Comparative Forms of Modifiers

Choose the correct form in parentheses. Cross out the incorrect form.

The first seven sentences are from *A Christmas Carol* and the last four from *Oliver Twist*, both by Charles Dickens.

"You couldn't have met in a (better/best) place," said old Joe.

He was obliged to sit close to the fire, and brood over it, before he could extract the (less/least) sensation of warmth from such a handful of fuel.

But soon the steeples called good people all to church and chapel, and away they came flocking through the streets in their (best/most good) clothes.

I fear you (more/the most) than any specter I have seen.

No eye at all is (better/best) than an evil eye, dark master!

If he could have helped it, he and his child would have been (farther/more far) apart, perhaps, than they were.

That shirt is the (better/best) he had, and a fine one too.

The (worse/worst) of these women is, that a very little thing serves to call up some long-forgotten feeling; and the (better/best) of them is, that it never lasts.

Don't be (harder/more hard) upon the poor fellows than is indispensably necessary.

The dog advanced, retreated, paused an instant, turned, and scoured away at his (most hard/hardest) speed.

I have (more little/less) hesitation in dealing with two people, when I find that there's only one will between them.

Exercise 67D: Using Correct Adverbs and Adjectives

Choose the correct word in parentheses. Cross out the incorrect word.

Rachel mended this shirt very (good/well). I can't even tell where the hole was!

The new attorney argued his case (bad/badly); he isn't very (good/well) at cross-examination.

I can juggle pretty (good/well). I always feel (good/well) about making an audience smile.

Your statements prove my point (good/well); your words support my argument.

The character proved (good/well) in the end; he had supported the hero secretly all along.

The painting looks (bad/badly) above the sofa.

My nose healed (bad/badly) and is still a little crooked.

— LESSON 68 —

Coordinating and Subordinating Conjunctions
Correlative Conjunctions

When my mother makes *tacos al pastor*, she uses ancho chilies and pasilla chilies and cumin seed and garlic and pork roast and fresh cilantro.

A coordinating conjunction joins equal words or groups of words together.
and, but, for, nor, or, so, and yet

For dessert, I will have *tres leches* cake with fresh raspberries or caramel sandwich cookies with ice cream.
In my opinion, pork without pineapple is much better than pork with pineapple.

A subordinating conjunction joins unequal words or groups of words together.

We are cooking either pork roasts or goat chops tonight.
The patient was neither worse nor better.

Correlative conjunctions work in pairs to join words or groups of words.
Coordinating correlative conjunctions join equal words or groups of words.
both . . . and
not only . . . but/but also
either . . . or
neither . . . nor
although/though . . . yet/still
if . . . then

In the beginning, both the Sun and the Moon were dark.

Not only the town itself, but also the ranches in the neighborhood are built on hilltops.

Although he did not remember the way, still he pressed on.

If we run faster, then we will escape.

Though weary, still he presses on.

If unseated, then he will be unable to continue jousting.

Subordinating correlative conjunctions join unequal words or groups of words.
although/though . . . yet/still
if . . . then

In the beginning, the Sun and the Moon were dark.
In the beginning, both the Sun and the Moon were dark.

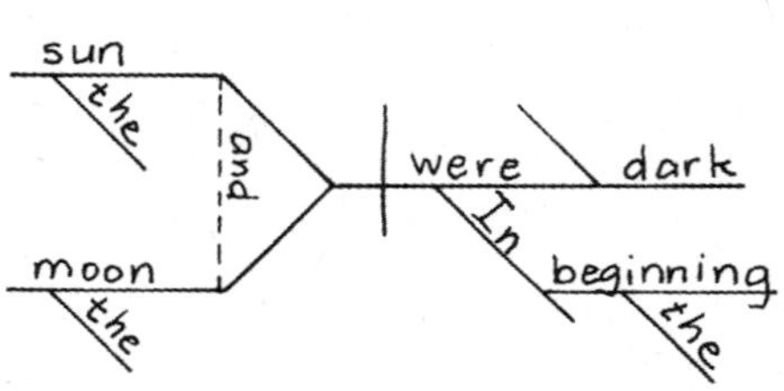

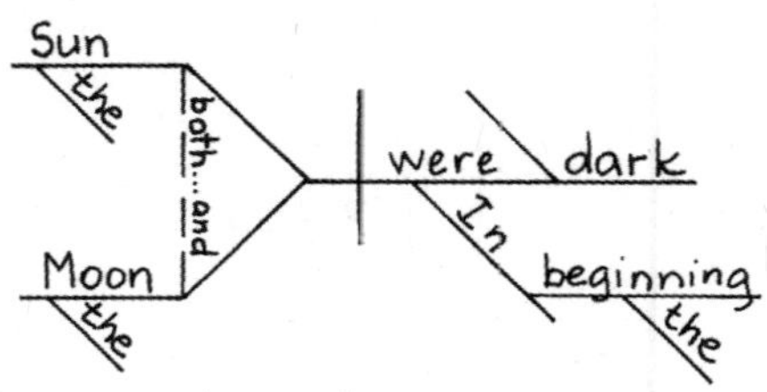

Although he did not remember, still he pressed on.

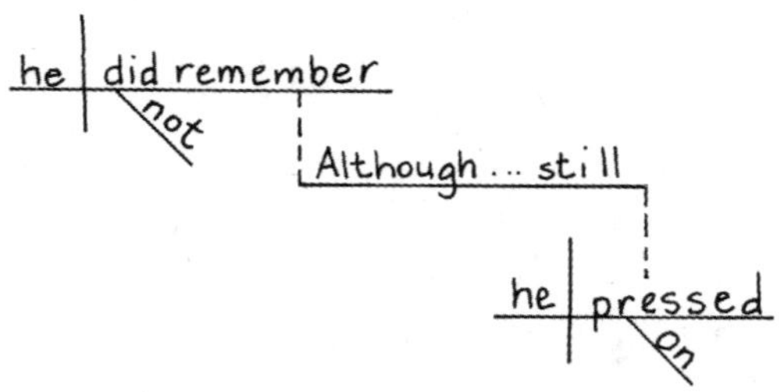

Both the grey foxes and the lion are watching for rabbits.

Not only the grey foxes but also the lion is watching for rabbits.
Either the mountain lion or the bears are growling.
Neither the butterflies nor the hummingbird was in the garden.

When compound subjects are connected by *not only . . . but/but also*, *either . . . or*, or *neither . . . nor*, the verb agrees with the subject that is closest to the verb.

Exercise 68A: Coordinating and Subordinating Correlative Conjunctions

In each of the following sentences, circle the correlative conjunctions. Underline the words or groups of words that the conjunctions connect. In the blank, write *C* for coordinating or *S* for subordinating.

These sentences are from *The Call of the Wild*, *White Fang*, and *The Cruise of the Snark*, all by Jack London.

Not only did they not know how to work dogs, but they did not know how to work themselves. ________

For two days and nights he neither ate nor drank. ________

Although not wishing to offend, yet it would be madness to take to the bay in such a craft. ________

Both Dave and Sol-leks flew at him and administered a sound trouncing. ________

Not only did he not pick fights, but he avoided them whenever possible. ________

Here was neither peace, nor rest, nor a moment's safety. ________

Though following her, still he was dubious. ________

If they could fast prodigiously, then they could feed prodigiously. ________

Between him and all domestic animals there must be no hostilities. If not amity, then neutrality must obtain. ________

He crawled to his feet, badly disheveled, hurt both in body and in spirit. ________

Though bearing the marks of her teeth, yet they never replied in kind, never defended themselves against her. ________

Exercise 68B: Subject-Verb Agreement

Cross out the incorrect word or words in each set of parentheses.

Neither the Big Dipper nor the Little Dipper (is a true constellation/are true constellations).

Not only the dippers but also Orion's Belt (is an asterism/are asterisms).

Not only Saturn but all the gas giants (has/have) rings.

Both Mercury and Venus (revolves/revolve) around the sun more quickly than Earth does.

Either mythology or Shakespeare's work (provides/provide) names for most moons in our solar system.

When NASA discovered bright spots on the minor planet Ceres early in 2015, a spokesperson said that either ice or salt (is/are) probably the cause.

Neither Pluto nor the other objects in the Kuiper belt (satisfies/satisfy) the International Astronomical Union's definition of a planet.

Both asteroids and comets (contains/contain) rocky materials, but their other components are different.

Exercise 68C: Diagramming

On your own paper, diagram every word of the following sentences. These sentences are adapted from *The Arabian Nights*, edited by Kate Douglas Wiggin and Nora A. Smith.

Aladdin not only commanded them to desist from their work, but ordered them to return all their jewels to the sultan.

The sultan will either laugh at me or be in a great rage.

Neither your discourse nor your remonstrances shall change my mind.

Both mother and son sat down and ate with relish.

WEEK 18

Clauses

— LESSON 69 —

Phrases
Sentences
Introduction to Clauses

A phrase is a group of words serving a single grammatical function.

A verb phrase is the main verb plus any helping verbs.

Four musketeers were waiting their turn.

A prepositional phrase begins with a preposition and ends with a noun or pronoun.

The center of the most animated group was a musketeer of great height.

A prepositional phrase that describes a noun or pronoun is called an adjective phrase.

He wore a long cloak of crimson velvet.

A prepositional phrase that describes a verb, adjective, or adverb is called an adverb phrase.

The young man advanced into the tumult and disorder.

(Sentences adapted from *The Three Musketeers* by Alexandre Dumas.)

A clause is a group of words that contains a subject and a predicate.

Behind the dusty wardrobe.
Lucy opened the door.
Leaping and bounding.
They did not believe her.
He tasted the delicious candy.
Because he wanted more.

An independent clause can stand by itself as a sentence.

A sentence is a group of words that usually contains a subject and a predicate. A sentence begins with a capital letter and ends with a punctuation mark. A sentence contains a complete thought.

> *Can we measure intelligence without understanding it?* Possibly so. *Physicists measured gravity and magnetism long before they understood them theoretically. Maybe psychologists can do the same with intelligence.*
>
> Or maybe not.
>
> —James W. Kalat, *Introduction to Psychology*

A dependent clause is a fragment that cannot stand by itself as a sentence.

Although Jamie didn't mean to eat the entire cake. ________

Whether they won or lost. ________

He picked up the pieces. ________

That milk is from Uncle Louie's cow. ________

Since she was already covered in mud. ________

Because my grandmother came to visit.
I cleaned up my room.

Because my grandmother came to visit, I cleaned up my room.

Dependent clauses begin with subordinating words.
Dependent clauses are also known as subordinate clauses.

Exercise 69A: Distinguishing Between Phrases and Clauses

Identify the following groups of words as *phrases* or *clauses.* The clauses may be independent or dependent, but you only need to identify them as *clauses.* In each clause, underline the subject once and the verb twice.

Past the juggling clown ________________

Orbiting the planet ________________

When I was riding my bicycle ________________

Since the earliest days ________________

Because of the late start ________________

Although the assembly started late ________________

Eating her curds and whey ________________

Since we began ____________________

Wrestling with a dinosaur ____________________

I ate too many pickles ____________________

Aboard the pirate ship ____________________

Danced and twirled ____________________

Exercise 69B: Distinguishing Between Independent and Dependent Clauses

Identify the following clauses as independent (*IND*) or dependent (*DEP*).

These clauses are taken from Edgar Allan Poe's "The Tell-Tale Heart." Some have been slightly adapted.

The disease had sharpened my senses ______________

Whenever the eye fell upon me ______________

I looked in upon him ______________

While he slept ______________

I kept quite still ______________

When I had waited a long time ______________

It was the beating of the old man's heart ______________

The sound would be heard by a neighbor ______________

When I describe my precautions ______________

As the bell sounded the hour ______________

While I answered cheerily ______________

The noise steadily increased ______________

Exercise 69C: Identifying Dependent Clauses in Complete Sentences

Circle the dependent clause in each sentence below. Within each dependent clause you circle, underline the subject once and the verb twice.

I will wait here until you are ready.

While the competitors dance, the judges will observe carefully.

Before it changes direction, the train will go to the East Hill station.

The moon appears larger when it is near the horizon.

My clock is wrong because its battery died.

As you watched the show, did you notice the leading actor's new haircut?

— LESSON 70 —

Adjective Clauses
Relative Pronouns

Intro 70: Introduction to Adjective Clauses

Match the dependent clause on the right with the correct independent clause on the left. The first one has been done for you.

1. George Orwell, _B_, worked as a teacher and as a bookstore assistant.	A. that has the ability to use tools
2. Elvis Presley, ____, won three Grammy Awards.	B. who wrote *Animal Farm* and *1984*
3. Augusta, Georgia, is known for hosting the Masters golf tournament,____.	C. whom people nicknamed "The Wizard of Menlo Park"
4. The honey badger is a carnivorous animal ____.	D. whose first single was "Heartbreak Hotel"
5. Thomas Edison, ____, was almost completely deaf.	E. which takes place during the first full week of April each year

Dependent clauses can act as adjectives, adverbs, or nouns.

An adjective clause is a dependent clause that acts as an adjective in a sentence, modifying a noun or pronoun in the independent clause.

They banded together in small groups that whispered and discussed and disputed.

A man who passed by spoke to them.

Relative pronouns introduce adjective clauses and refer back to an antecedent in the independent clause.
who, whom, whose, which, that

The men **who had been champions before Finn came** rallied the others against him.

Among the young princes was a boy **whom the High King preferred**.

The Chain of Silence was shaken by the servant **whose duty and honor it was.**

The thing **which was presented to us** is not true.

The people believed in gods **that the king did not accept**.

Use *who, whom,* and *whose* to refer to persons.
Use *which* to refer to animals, places, and things.
Use *that* and *whose* to refer to persons, animals, places, or things.

She saw him, and he saw her.

Use *P* for prepositions, *OP* for objects of prepositions, *ADJ* for adjectives, *ADV* for adverbs, *IO* for indirect objects, *DO* for direct objects, and *OC* for object complements.

I who speak to you have seen many evils.

At the door is a gentleman for whom no seat has been found.

He was the boy whom they called Little Fawn.

They are men whose happiness lies in ambition.

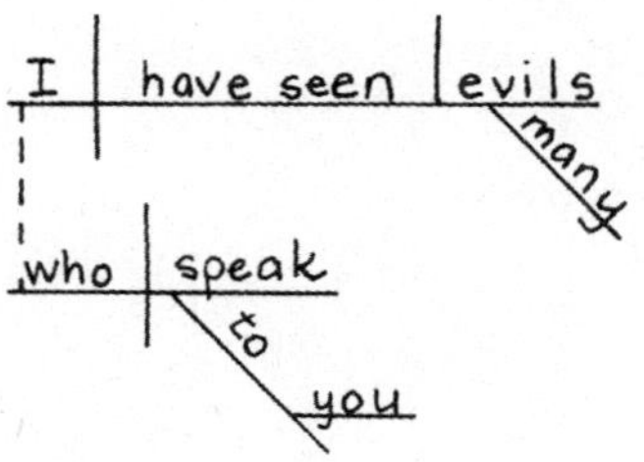

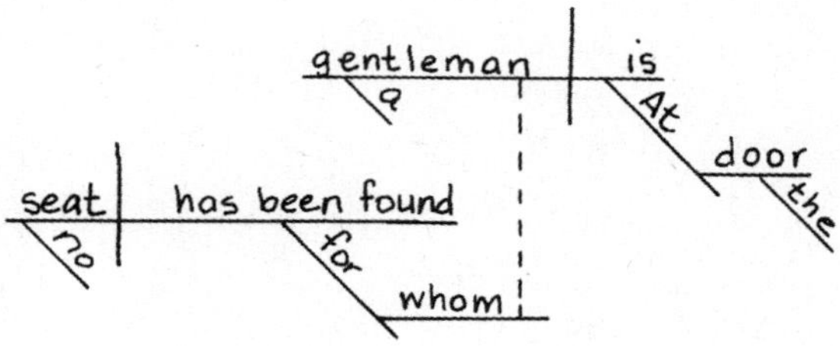

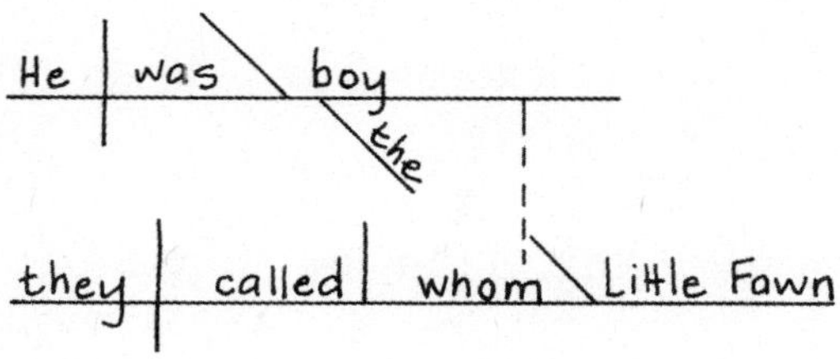

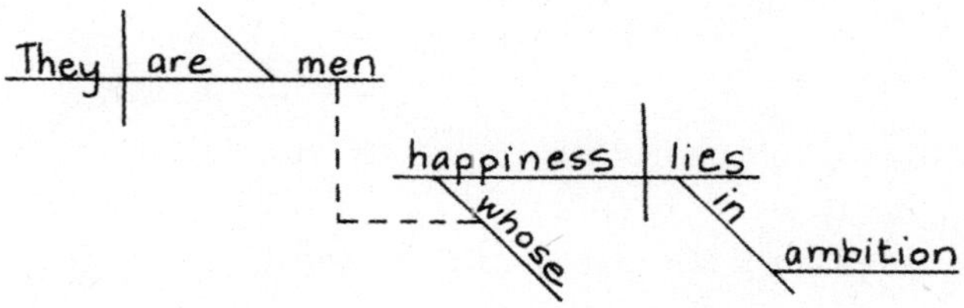

Exercise 70A: Identifying Adjective Clauses and Relative Pronouns

Underline the adjective clauses in the following sentences, and circle the relative pronouns. Draw an arrow from each relative pronoun to its antecedent.

John Dalton is the scientist whom we credit with the atomic theory of matter.

Dalton, who lived from 1766 to 1844, did not say anything about the internal structure of atoms.

"Atom" comes from a Greek word that means "uncuttable."

But atoms, which no one has ever seen, are actually made of even smaller particles.

Electrons, neutrons, and protons are the particles that comprise atoms.

Neutrons and protons, which are much heavier than electrons, are found in an atom's nucleus, or center.

Hydrogen, whose nucleus does not have any neutrons, is the element with the smallest atoms.

Exercise 70B: Choosing the Correct Relative Pronoun

In each sentence, cross out the incorrect relative pronoun. Above the correct pronoun, write *S* for subject, *OP* for object of the preposition, or *DO* for direct object to show how the relative pronoun is used within the dependent clause.

These sentences are adapted from the fairy tale "The Golden Goose," by the Brothers Grimm.

A man (who/whom) lived in the village had three sons.

He had two sons (who/whom) thought themselves wise.

His youngest son, (who/whom) they called Simpleton, was ridiculed by the others.

When the eldest and middle brothers, (who/whom) went into the forest to cut wood, were asked to share their food and drink with an old man, they refused.

The youngest brother, to (who/whom) the other brothers had given more meager food and drink, was willing to share with the old man.

In exchange for this kindness, the old man, (who/whom) knew of a goose with feathers of gold, told Simpleton where to find it.

Three sisters decided to take feathers from the goose, to (who/which) they became stuck.

The King of that kingdom had a daughter (who/whom) never laughed.

The King declared that his daughter should marry the man (who/whom) made her laugh.

When the princess saw Simpleton, the goose, and the people (who/whom) were stuck behind them, she burst out laughing.

Simpleton was able to marry the princess because of the old man in the forest, to (who/whom) he had shown kindness.

Exercise 70C: Diagramming Adjective Clauses

On your own paper, diagram every word of the following sentences.

The birthday cake that Sarah made for Fritz was absolutely delicious!

Alice, whose opinions we value, was sick and could not attend the meeting.

The ball bounced toward Jose, who was not paying attention.

My new shirt, which I bought yesterday, already has a hole in the sleeve.

We will soon visit our cousin, who lives in Maryland.

The young boy wanted the toy that made loud noises.

— LESSON 71 —

Adjective Clauses
Relative Adverbs
Adjective Clauses with Understood Relatives

A phrase is a group of words serving a single grammatical function.
A clause is a group of words that contains a subject and a predicate.

An independent clause can stand by itself as a sentence.
A dependent clause is a fragment that cannot stand by itself as a sentence.

Dependent clauses begin with subordinating words.
Dependent clauses are also known as subordinate clauses.

Adjective clauses are also known as relative clauses because they relate to another word in the independent clause.

Relative pronouns introduce adjective clauses and refer back to an antecedent in the independent clause.
who, whom, whose, which, that

This was the very spot **where** a proud tyrant raised an undying monument to his own vanity.

He was going back to serve his country at a time **when** death was the usual reward for such devotion.

The reasons **why** he vented his ill humor on the soldiers were many.
—Adapted from *The Scarlet Pimpernel* by Baroness Emmuska Orczy

Relative adverbs introduce adverb clauses and refer back to a place, time, or reason in the independent clause.
where, when, why

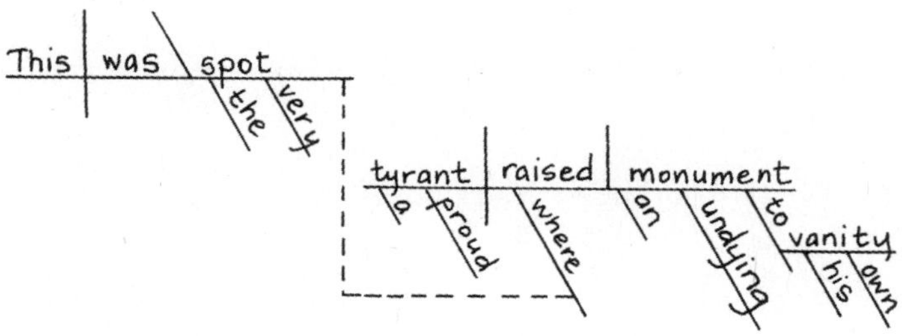

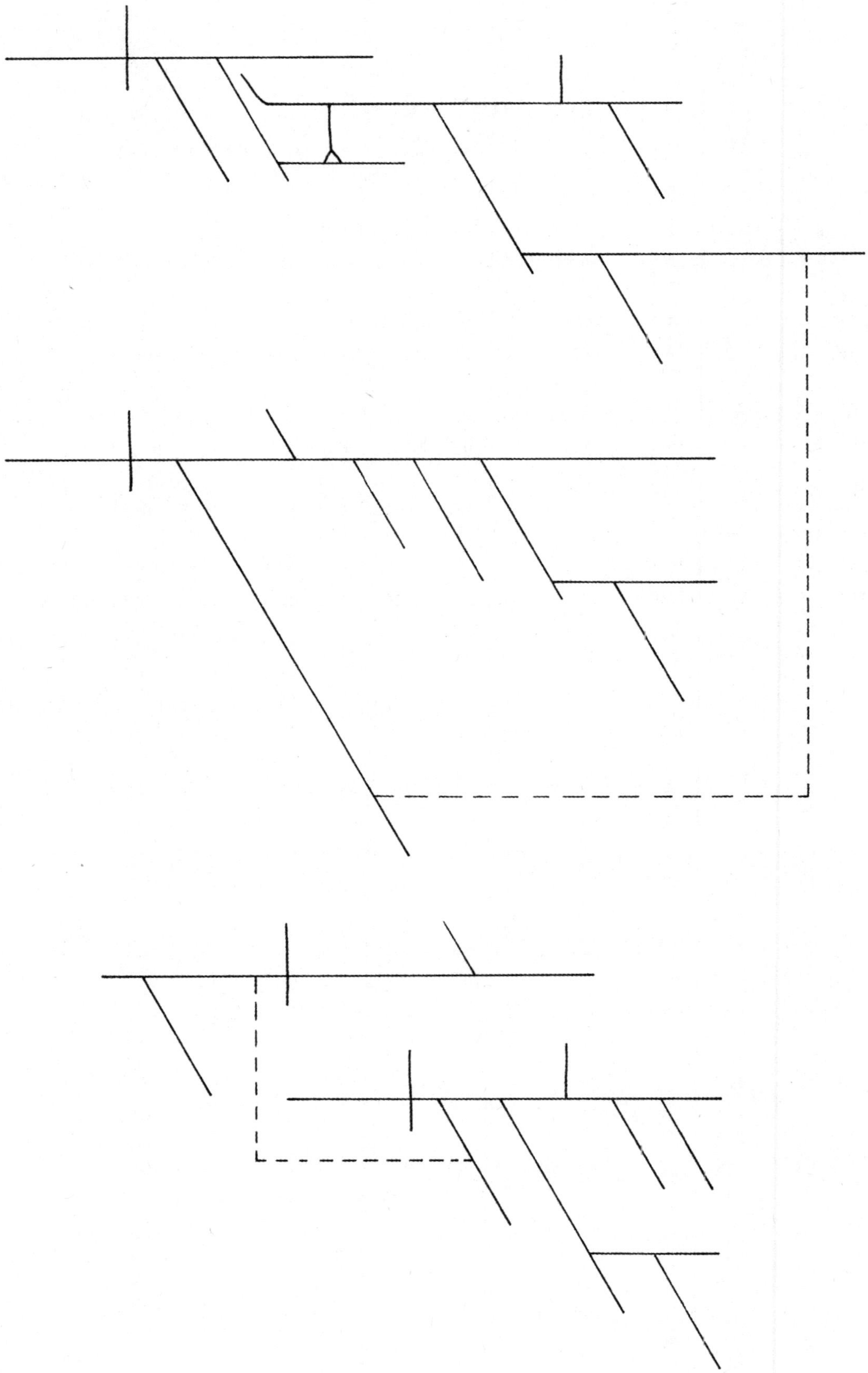

The evil men do lives after them.

I read the book you sent me.

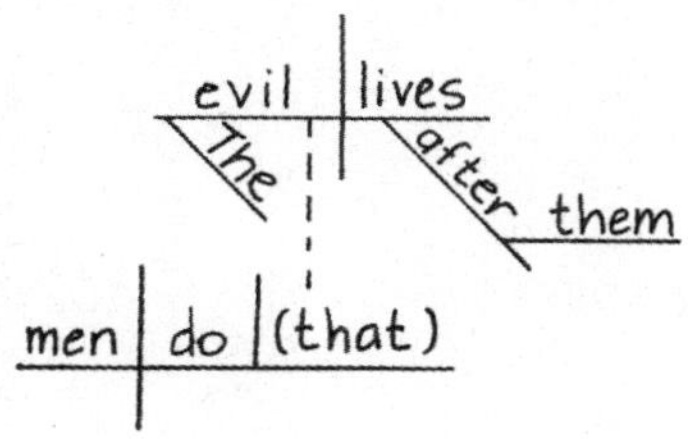

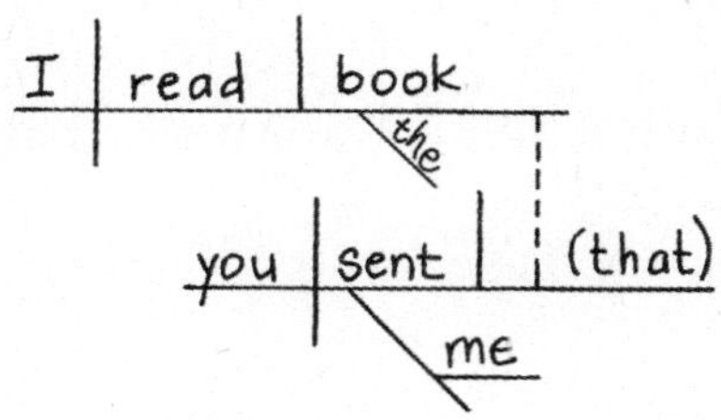

Exercise 71A: Relative Adverbs and Pronouns

In the following sentences, underline each adjective clause. Circle each relative word and label it as *RP* for relative pronoun or *RA* for relative adverb. Draw an arrow from each relative word back to its antecedent in the independent clause.

Be alert—one sentence has *two* adjective clauses in it!

Christopher Columbus was influenced by a book that was called *The Travels of Sir John Mandeville.*

Mandeville, who told of his travels around the world, was probably not a real person.

The book was written at a time when faraway lands were mysterious to many Europeans.

Many of the places where Mandeville went were real places, but his descriptions were more fantasy than reality.

He mentioned one island where the people had human bodies but dog heads.

He also told of trees whose fruit contains little beasts that are like lambs. (*You should find two adjective clauses in this sentence!*)

The fantastic stories are interwoven with real facts from travelers who actually visited different places.

Scholars have different ideas about the actual author or authors who wrote Mandeville's *Travels.*

One possible reason why the name "Mandeville" was used is an earlier story about an imaginary heroic traveler named Mandevie.

Exercise 71B: Missing Relative Words

Draw a caret in front of each adjective clause and insert the missing relative pronoun. (For the purposes of this exercise, *which* and *that* may be used interchangeably.)

The drink of water I had after the race was refreshing.

Jonathan introduced me to the librarian you had mentioned.

The sunrise we saw this morning was breathtaking.

The screen on the computer we just bought is smaller than the screen on our older computer.

Please put the bananas you got at the market on the counter.

The little orange kitten loves the toy Aiko selected.

The piano composition Bria played was written by the composer you met at the party.

Beside the volcano Annika made is my project.

Exercise 71C: Diagramming

On your own paper, diagram the following sentences from your first two exercises.

Christopher Columbus was influenced by a book that was called *The Travels of Sir John Mandeville.*

The book was written at a time when faraway lands were mysterious to many Europeans.

The fantastic stories are interwoven with real facts from travelers who actually visited different places.

He mentioned one island where the people had human bodies but dog heads.

Please put the bananas you got at the market on the counter.

Beside the volcano Annika made is my project.

— LESSON 72 —

Adverb Clauses

A clause is a group of words that contains a subject and a predicate.

A dependent clause is a fragment that cannot stand by itself as a sentence. Dependent clauses begin with subordinating words.

Dependent clauses are also known as subordinate clauses.

Dependent clauses can act as adjective clauses, adverb clauses, or noun clauses.

Adverb clauses modify verbs, adjectives, and other adverbs in the independent clause. They answer the questions where, when, how, how often, and to what extent.

When the supper was finished, the king expressed a wish.

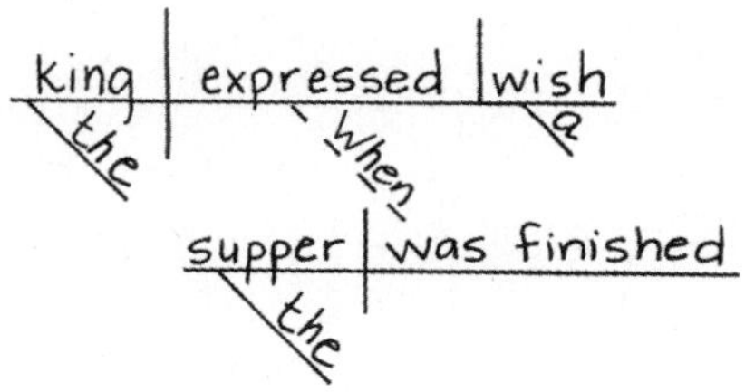

Adverb clauses can be introduced by adverbs.

Common Adverbs that Introduce Clauses
as (and its compounds: as if, as soon as, as though)
as if
how (and its compound: however)
when (and its compound: whenever)
whence
where (and its compounds: whereat, whereby, wherein, wherefore, whereon)
while
whither

A subordinating conjunction joins unequal words or groups of words together.

An honest enemy is better than an agreeable coward.

An honest enemy is better than an agreeable coward [is].

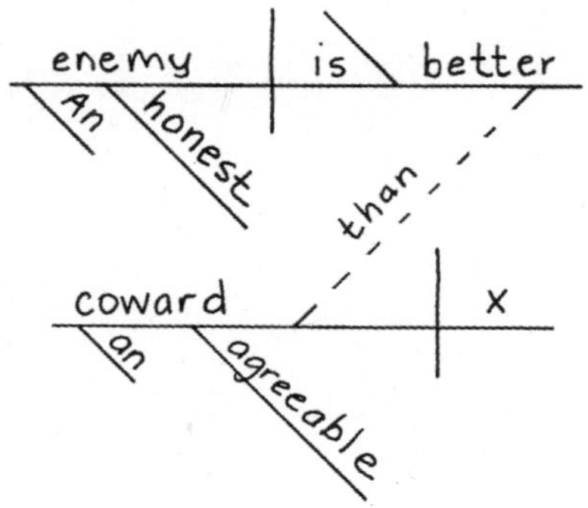

Subordinating conjunctions and subordinating correlative conjunctions often join an adverb clause to an independent clause.

Common Subordinating Conjunctions
after
although
as (as soon as)
because
before
if
in order that
lest
since
though
till
unless
until
although/though . . . yet/still
if . . . then

Because she loves Korean food, my aunt taught me to cook kimchi.

I will put six plates on the table unless our neighbors are also coming for dinner.

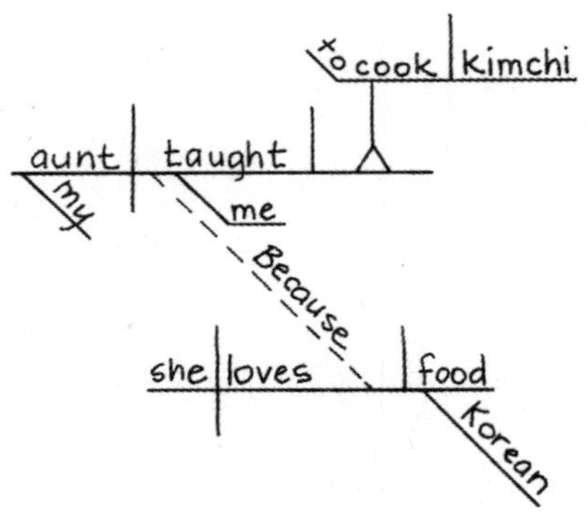

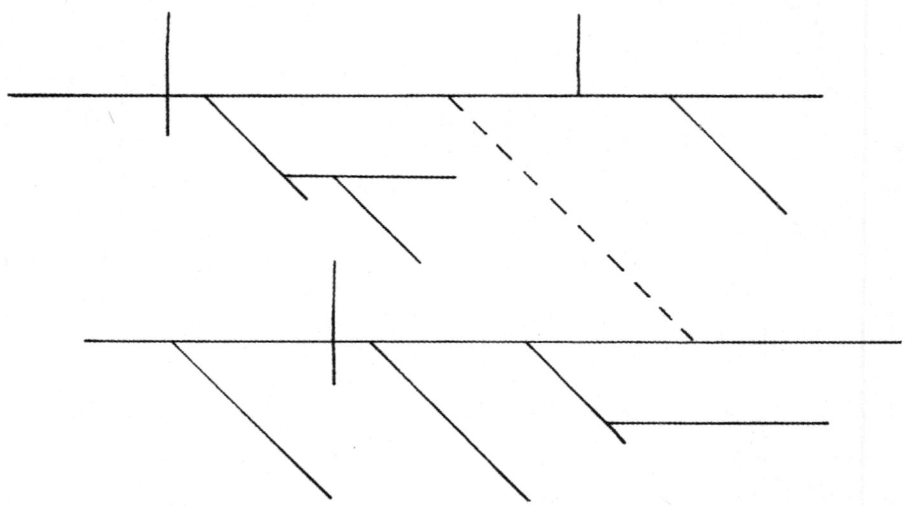

The task is difficult if you do not take care.

She was confident that she could reach the top of the mountain.

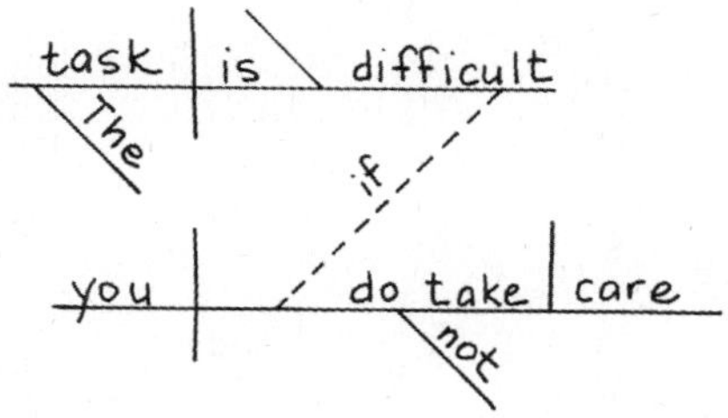

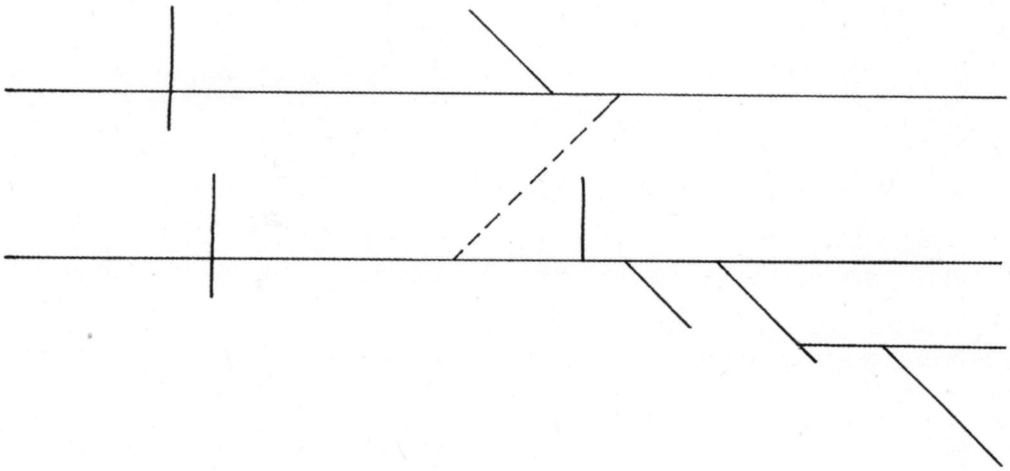

He sprinted quickly as though he were being chased by monsters.

The judge spoke severely because the attorney was not paying attention.

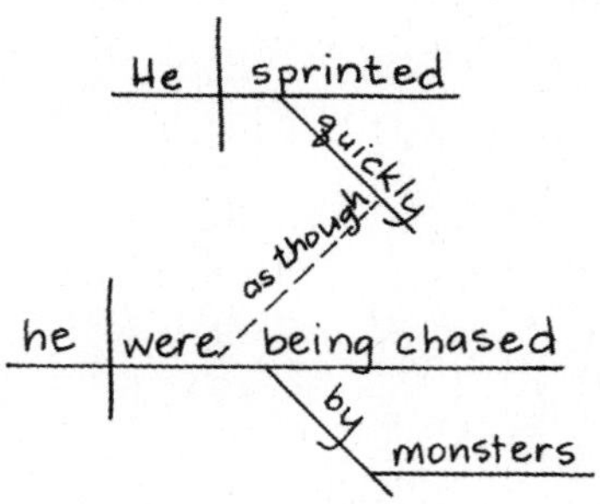

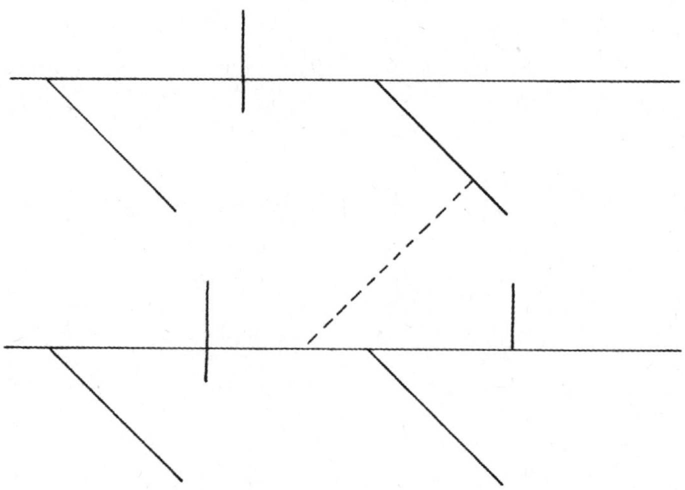

I will wait where I am.

I waited at the place where I had marked the ground.

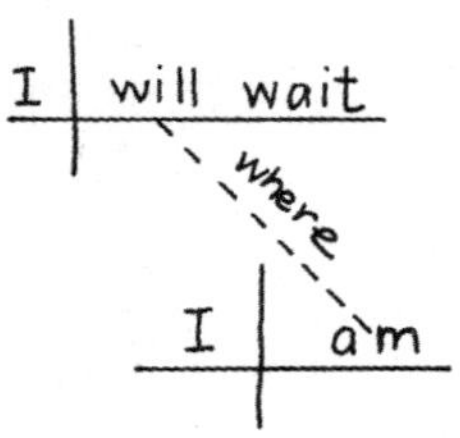

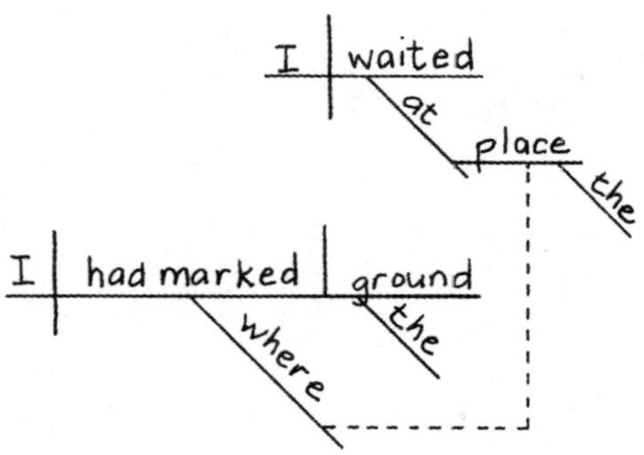

Exercise 72A: Adverb Clauses

In the following sentences, underline each adverb clause. Circle the subordinating word(s) at the beginning of each clause and label it *ADV* for adverb or *SC* for subordinating conjunction. Draw an arrow from the subordinating word back to the verb, adverb, or adjective that the clause modifies.

These sentences are taken from Sir Arthur Conan Doyle's *The Hound of the Baskervilles.* Some have been adapted or condensed.

If we take this as a working hypothesis we have a fresh basis from which to start our construction of this unknown visitor.

He could not have been on the staff of the hospital, since only a man well-established in a London practice could hold such a position.

I laughed incredulously as Sherlock Holmes leaned back in his settee and blew little wavering rings of smoke up to the ceiling.

I said, if I remember right, amiable, unambitious, and absent-minded.

The appearance of our visitor was a surprise to me, since I had expected a typical country practitioner.

A cast of your skull, sir, until the original is available, would be an ornament to any anthropological museum.

Because you are a practical man of affairs, you stand alone.

But the young maiden, being discreet and of good repute, would ever avoid him, because she feared his evil name.

And while the revellers stood aghast at the fury of the man, one more wicked than the rest cried out for the hounds. (*TWO adverb clauses*)

The man cried out, whence Hugo ran from the house.

Exercise 72B: Descriptive Clauses

Complete a dependent clause in each sentence using the subordinating word in bold print. After each sentence, circle *ADJC* or *ADVC* to show whether the clause is acting as an adjective or as an adverb.

While ____, Javier did thirty push-ups. ADJC or ADVC

Anna, **who** ____, encouraged her friends to tell the truth. ADJC or ADVC

For my birthday, I received a gift **that** ____. ADJC or ADVC

You will be late **if** ____. ADJC or ADVC

The bookshelves, **which** ____, looked somewhat unsteady. ADJC or ADVC

Ari began hesitantly **as though** ____. ADJC or ADVC

We will eat dinner **whenever** ____. ADJC or ADVC

Ginevra, **whom** ____, rushed into the room at the start of the meeting. ADJC or ADVC

Exercise 72C: Diagramming

On your own paper, diagram every word of the following sentences. These are adapted from Sir Arthur Conan Doyle's *The Hound of the Baskervilles.*

Down this walk is a gate which leads to the moor.

Since no practical good could result from it, I did not tell all that I knew.

I went to the spot where the animal had been.

After the tragedy occurred, I heard about several incidents which seem unusual.

Although he would walk in his own grounds, nothing would induce him to go out upon the moor at night.

— REVIEW 6 —

Weeks 16-18

Topics
Personal Pronouns: Subject, Object, Possessive, Reflexive
Verb Voice (Active and Passive)
Verb Tense
Adjectives
Gerunds and Participles
Phrases
Clauses (Independent and Dependent)

Review 6A: Pronouns

In the following passage, circle each pronoun. Label each as *S* (subject form of pronoun), *O* (object form), *P* (possessive form), *R* (reflexive), *I* (indefinite), *D* (demonstrative), or *RP* (relative pronoun).

This passage is from Carol Ryrie Brink's *Caddie Woodlawn*.

Eyes round with wonder and anticipation, the young Woodlawns did as they were told. To think of Father ever being small enough to wear those breeches and clogs, and dancing in them, too, in faraway England. How strange it was! They had heard so much of Boston, but nobody spoke of England where the strange little boy, who had grown to be Father, had danced in red breeches and clogs. Caddie thought of what Father had said about England on the night when the circuit rider had been with them. How often she had wondered about that since then!

"You have grown up in a free country, children," began Mr. Woodlawn. "I want you to think of yourselves as young Americans, and I want you to be proud of that. It is difficult to tell you about England, because there all men are not free to pursue their own lives in their own ways. Some men live like princes, while other men must beg for the very crusts that keep them alive."

"And your father's father was one of those who live like princes, children," cried Mrs. Woodlawn proudly.

Review 6B: Using Comparative and Superlative Modifiers Correctly

Choose the correct form in parentheses and cross out the incorrect form. These sentences are from *Call It Courage*, by Armstrong Sperry.

Into the (nearest/most near) canoe he flung half a dozen green drinking nuts, and his fish spear.

Mafatu found the cool liquid from the drinking nut (refreshinger/more refreshing) than spring water, cool on the (hottest/most hot) days, and as sustaining as food.

The island was high and peaked, its valleys blue-shadowed against the (paler/more pale) tone of the sky.

When he had bound on the leafy bandage with a twist of vine, it seemed that already his leg felt (better/more good).

He searched for a (smaller/more small) piece of the same wood, then propped the (larger/more large) piece against a rock.

It might be even (deeper/more deep) than he thought, for the clarity of the water confused all scale of distance.

There in submarine gloom a boy fought for his life with the (dreadedest/most dreaded) monster of the deep.

The measured booming grew (louder/more loud) with every inch that he advanced.

The warriors were a sight to quake the (stoutest/most stout) heart.

Review 6C: Verbs

Underline the main verb in each sentence. In the space above it, write the tense (*SIMP PAST, PRES, FUT; PROG PAST, PRES, FUT; PERF PAST, PRES, FUT*) and voice (*ACT* for active or *PASS* for passive) of the verb. If the verb is active, also note whether it is transitive (*TR*) or intransitive (*INTR*). The first is done for you.

These sentences are taken from *Save Our Forests*, by Ron Hirschi.

SIMP PRES, ACT, INTR

As winter approaches, grizzly bears search for a place to sleep through the coldest month.

Kids have already made a difference in helping wolves by adopting them as special animals for their school.

Tangles of berry vines and a large variety of trees and shrubs will make a healthier and more meaningful forest.

A disease called chestnut blight was introduced into our country from Asia in about 1900.

The disappearance of forests is happening right now in Oregon, California, Washington, Idaho, Montana, and Alaska.

No single animal in recent years has drawn our attention to the need for forest protection more than the northern spotted owl.

Trees grew on valley sides and on steep mountain slopes.

Under these regulations, erosion is allowed to continue, essentially unchecked.

The survival of many animals will take lots of work and the help of many more people.

Review 6D: Identifying Dependent Clauses

Underline each dependent clause in the following sentences. Circle the subordinating word. Label each clause as either adjective (*ADJ*) or adverb clause (*ADV*), and draw a line from each subordinating word to the word it modifies.

These sentences are from Laura Baskes Litwin's *Benjamin Banneker: Astronomer and Mathematician.*

The land that Benjamin Banneker was going to help map was still a marshy wilderness.

For Banneker, who had never visited a large city before, the bustling activity on the wharves of the Alexandria seaport was strange and thrilling.

When a cow kicked over the pail, Molly Welsh was accused of stealing the milk.

As soon as the land was legally his, Robert Banneky went to work.

Benjamin and his father also filled wheelbarrows with the rich, loamy marsh earth that ran along the river's edge.

Although the family was never prosperous, they were not hungry or wanting in any way.

An ephemeris is an astronomical table that tells the positions of the sun, moon, and planets for every day of the year.

There were many people at this time who doubted a black man's ability to figure an ephemeris.

While he contemplated his next steps, Banneker got word of his selection to accompany Major Ellicott on the survey of the Federal Territory.

Before he made any commitment he wanted to discuss it with his trusted friend George Ellicott.

In one corner of the room was suspended a clock of his own construction, which was a true herald of departing hours.

We must think well of that man, who uses his best endeavors to associate with none but virtuous friends.

Review 6E: Gerunds and Past Participles

Underline each gerund (present participle) and past participle in the following sentences. Indicate what part of the sentence each serves as with the labels *ADJ* for adjective, *ADV* for adverb, *S* for subject, *DO* and *IO* for direct and indirect object, and *OP* for object of the preposition. For adverbs and adjectives, draw an arrow back to the word modified.

These sentences are from *Microorganisms: The Unseen World*, by Edward R. Ricciuti.

Specialized structures within the single cell help with many of the vital functions accomplished by organs in multicellular organisms.

Protozoans eliminate their carbon dioxide waste by passing it through the cell membrane.

The volvox is a protozoan that lives in a colony composed of thousands of cells.

Despite their tiny size, microorganisms are much like all other living things on Earth.

The main functions of touch for protozoans seem to be to get food and to avoid becoming the food of something else.

This behavior may be related to feeding.

Getting food, storing it, and then converting it to energy involve chemical processes that keep organisms alive.

Trapped within the amoeba, this water droplet becomes an organelle called a food vacuole.

Lining the inside of a bacterium's cell wall is a flexible cell membrane.

In Holland, a self-taught scientist named Anton van Leeuwenhoek had become fascinated with making lenses for the simple microscopes in use at the time.

Review 6F: Diagramming

On your own paper, diagram every word of the following sentences from *A Treasury of Turkish Folktales for Children*, retold by Barbara K. Walker.

When he arrived, there was his uncle waiting by the path to greet him.

By poking his head way out, he could just see the doorstep.

Boldly Hasan began to whistle the tune the village watchman whistled as he came down the street.

Leaving him in the sorry state in which the rabbit had come upon him, they went on their way.

As Keloğlan finished speaking, the princess felt a strange prickling in her scalp.

On the next day he encountered several of his students on the street that ran past the public fountain.

WEEK 19

More Clauses

— LESSON 73 —

Adjective and Adverb Clauses
Introduction to Noun Clauses

A clause is a group of words that contains a subject and a predicate.

I know that a noun is the name of a person, place, thing, or idea.

I know an old lady who swallowed a fly while she was sitting on the front porch.

Dependent clauses can act as adjective clauses, adverb clauses, or noun clauses.

An adjective clause is a dependent clause that acts as an adjective in a sentence, modifying a noun or pronoun in the independent clause.
Relative pronouns introduce adjective clauses and refer back to an antecedent in the independent clause.

Adverb clauses modify verbs, adjectives, and other adverbs in the independent clause.
They answer the questions where, when, how, how often, and to what extent.
Adverb clauses can be introduced by adverbs.
Subordinating conjunctions and subordinating correlative conjunctions often join an adverb clause to an independent clause.

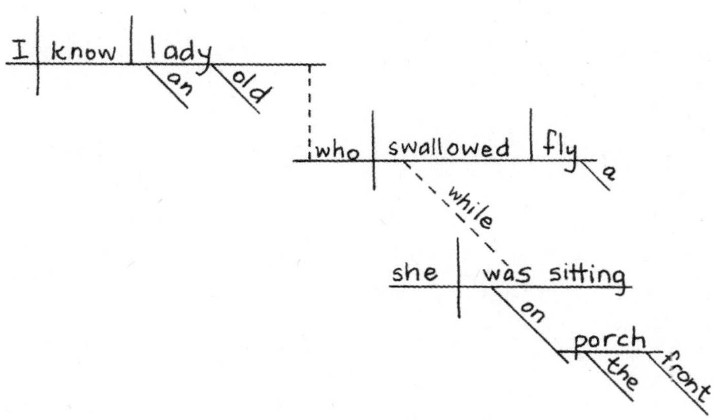

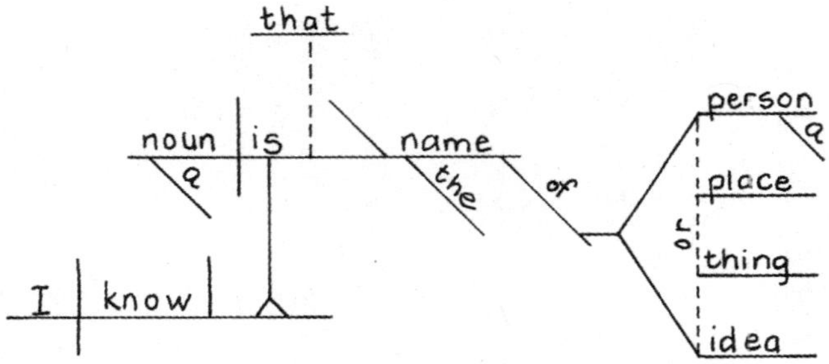

A noun clause takes the place of a noun.
Noun clauses can be introduced by relative pronouns, relative adverbs, subordinating conjunctions, or understood subordinating words.

I know where your lost keys are.

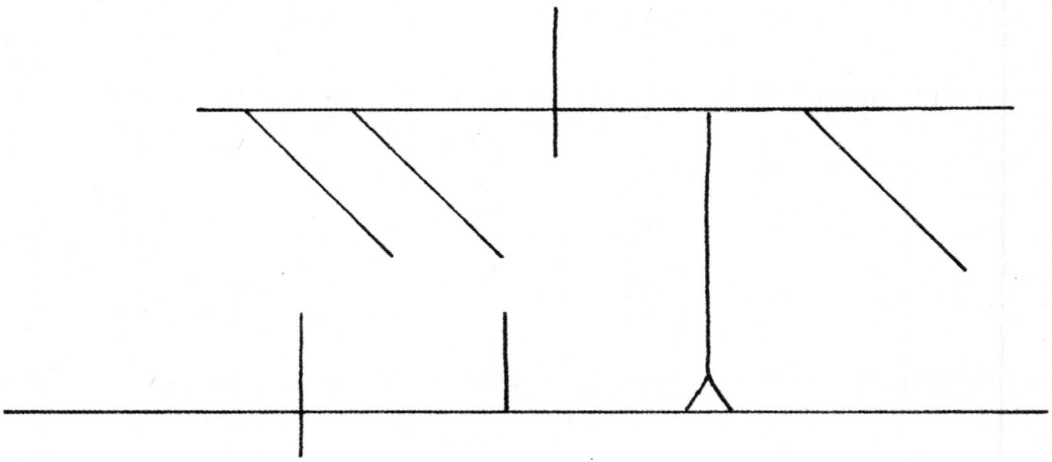

Whoever runs fastest will win the race.

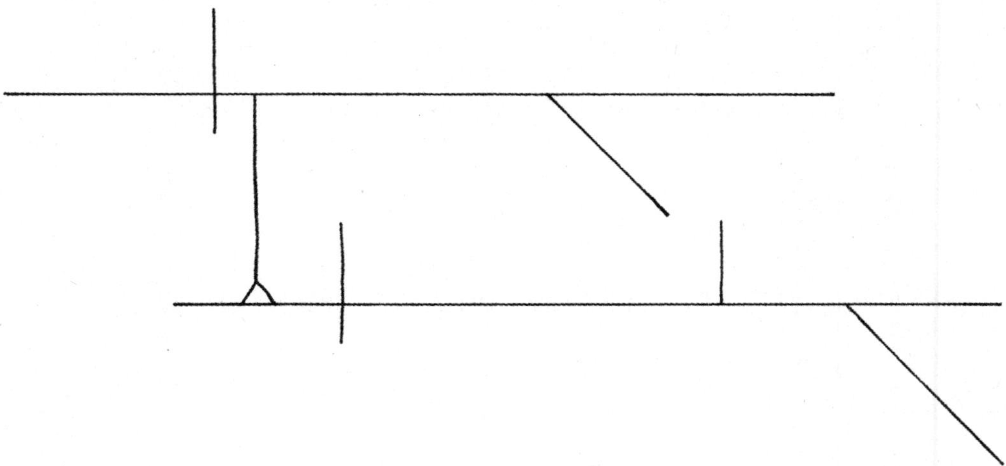

I really wish I had more chocolate.

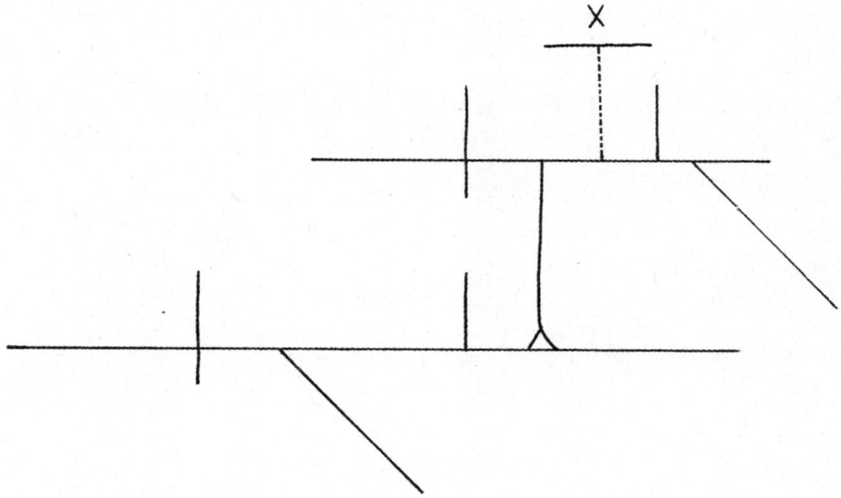

Nothing was as it should be.

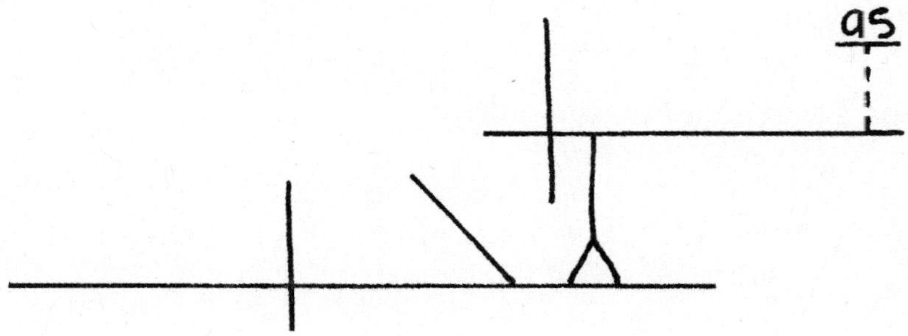

What matters most in this situation is how you feel about it.

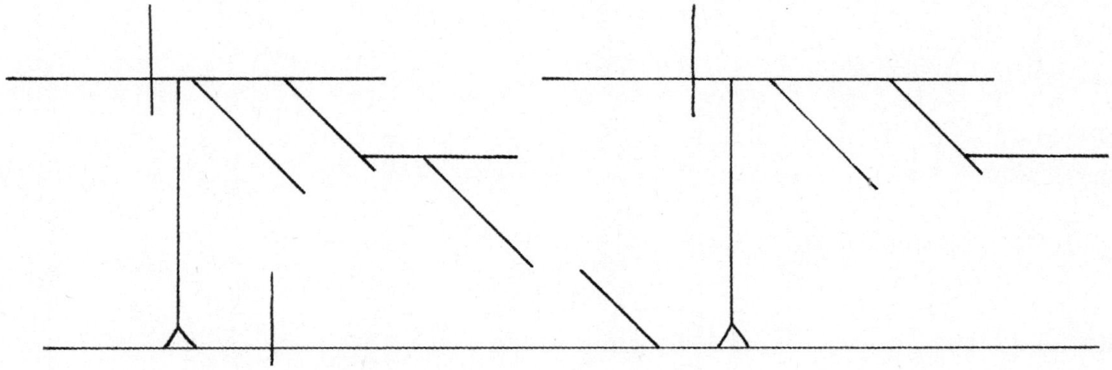

Exercise 73A: Identifying Clauses

In the following sentences, circle each dependent clause. Label each as *N* for noun, *ADJ* for adjective, or *ADV* for adverb.

- For noun clauses, indicate the part of the sentence that each noun clause fulfills (*S* for subject, *DO* for direct object, *IO* for indirect object, *PN* for predicate nominative, or *OP* for object of the preposition).
- For adjective and adverb clauses, draw a line from the subordinating word of each adjective and adverb clause back to the word it modifies. If the subordinating word is understood, draw a caret and insert the understood subordinating word in brackets.
- Dependent clauses may contain other dependent clauses! Do your best to find them all.

These sentences are from Laurence Yep's *Dragonwings*.

This figure does not even reflect the large number of Tang men who could not get into the country for the first time.

What's here belongs neither to us nor to the demons.

I remembered stories about how the hills were made by burrowing dragons.

I decided not to put my boots on, because the echoes might tell Father I was behind him.

When I finally finished looking around her kitchen, I realized I had gone through four more of the cookies.

That very evening I found out that there can be some bad demons too.

He unbound his queue until his hair hung down loose on his back.

That was a sign the Stove King had returned to his place above our stove.

At that moment there was a loud explosion that made us all duck.

I had my employer, who knows your landlord, call him and find out what was the matter.

Exercise 73B: Creating Noun Clauses

For each of the following sentences, write a noun clause that fits into the blank.

If you have trouble coming up with a dependent clause, try starting out with one of the following subordinating words: *that, how, why, what/whatever, who/whoever* (these are always subjects within the dependent clause); *whom/whomever* (these are always objects within the dependent clause); or *where, whether.* (This is not an exhaustive list of the possibilities—just a jumping-off place for you.)

I always love to see ______________________________.

______________________________ was a huge help to us.

Please remember ______________________________.

______________________________ is exceedingly difficult.

Do you understand ______________________________?

Exercise 73C: Diagramming

On your own paper, diagram every word of the following sentences, taken or adapted from Laurence Yep's *Dragonwings*.

I scooped up some of the sand and saw that it was really tiny sapphires that made noises like laughter when I rubbed some of them between my palms.

Anyone who could laugh and tell stories and jokes and sing while he was alone among the demons must know what he was doing.

Finally they admitted that I was who I claimed to be.

What was best about flying any of the kites was what it did for Mother.

— LESSON 74 —

Clauses Beginning With Prepositions

The sun itself, which makes time, is elder by a year now.

Any man's death diminishes me, because I am involved in mankind.

What we call fortune here has another name above.

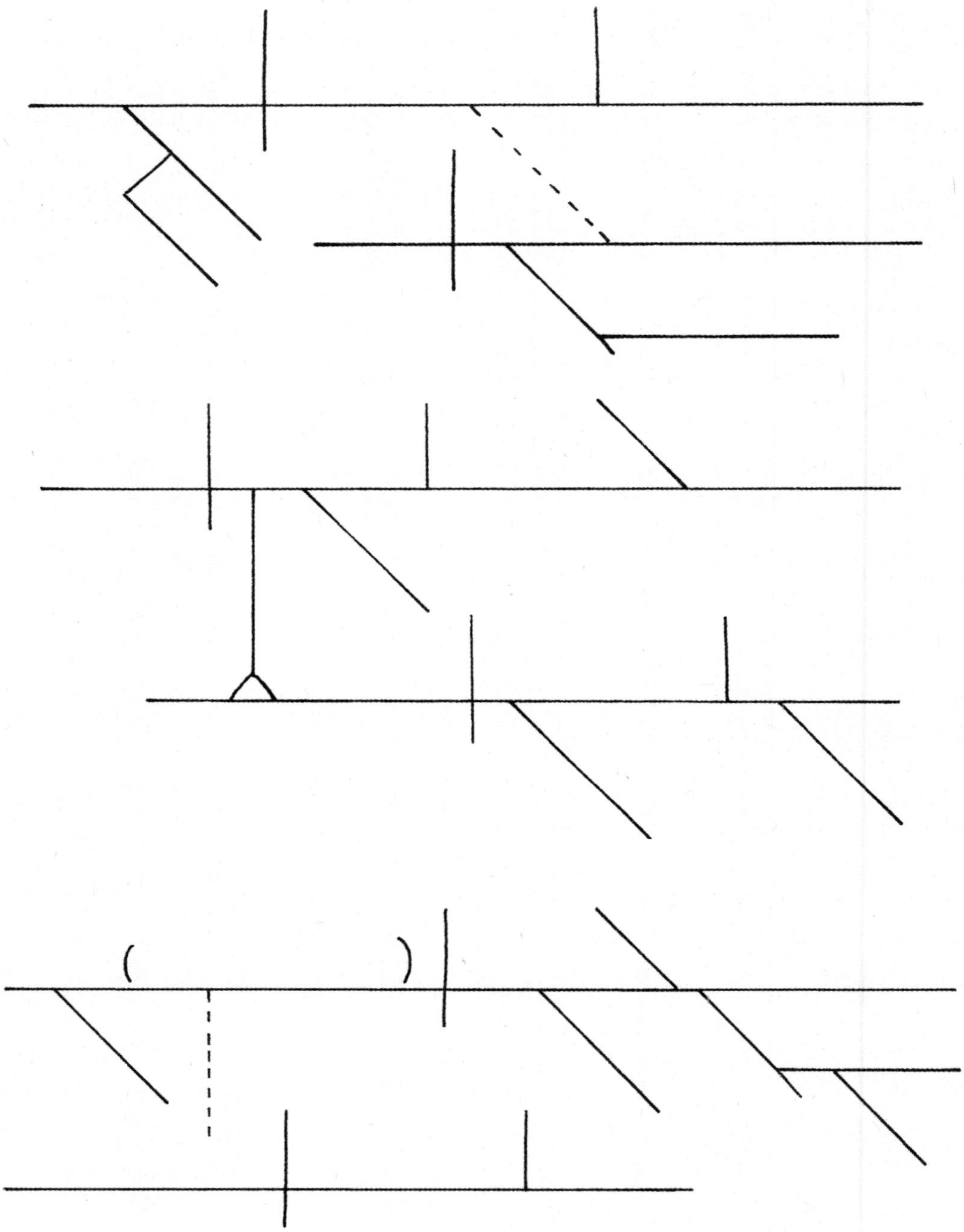

That carrack is the ship in which they are to sail.

He sent for his friends, of whom he took a solemn farewell.

Do not ask for whom the bell tolls.

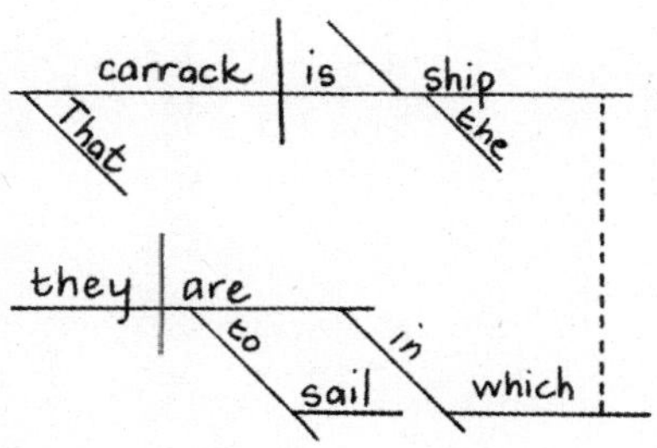

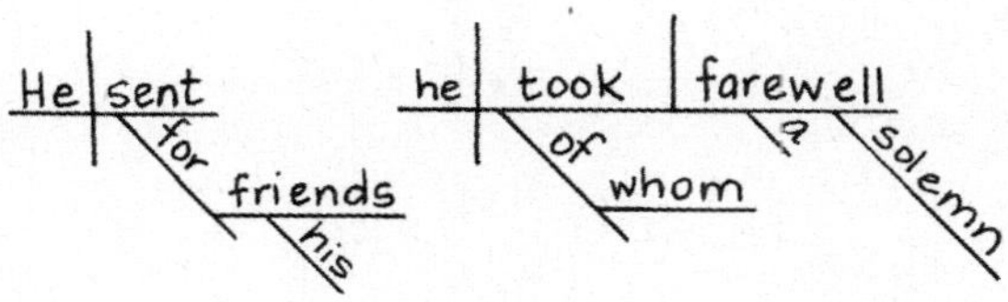

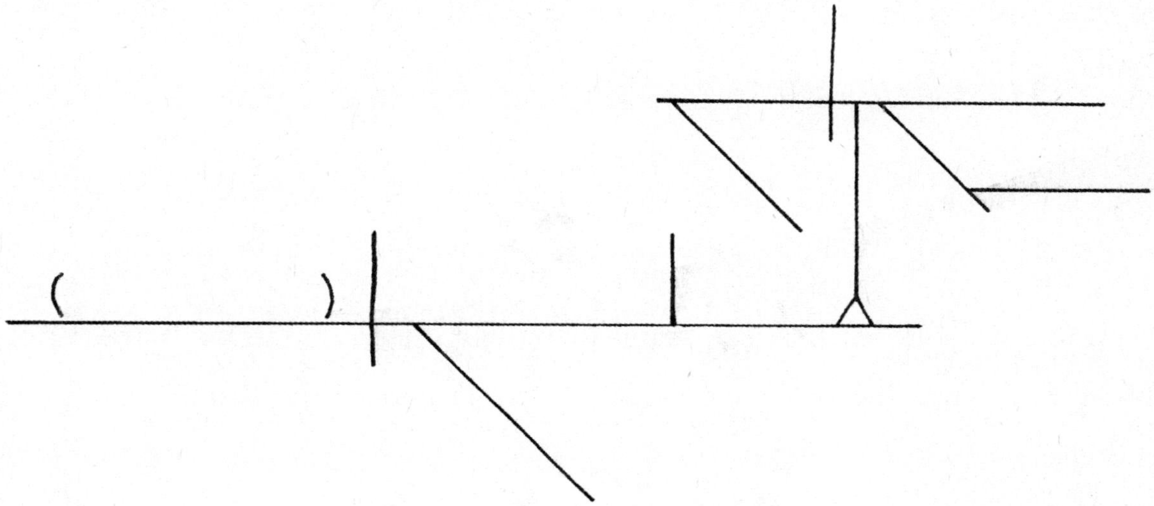

***Who* always acts as a subject or predicate nominative within a sentence. *Whom* always acts as an object.**

INCORRECT
He sent for his friends, of who he took a solemn farewell.
Do not ask for who the bell tolls.

ALSO INCORRECT (Informal)
He sent for his friends, who he took a solemn farewell of.
Do not ask who the bell tolls for.

CORRECT (Informal)
He sent for his friends, whom he took a solemn farewell of.
Do not ask whom the bell tolls for.

She is growing angry at the person who/whom she is arguing with.

____

Rude behavior is something I won't put up with!
Rude behavior is something up with which I will not put!

Exercise 74A: Adjective Clauses Beginning with Prepositions

In the following sentences, circle each adjective clause. Draw a line from the subordinating word back to the word the clause modifies. If the clause begins with a preposition, underline that preposition and label its object with *OP*.

The sentences below are taken or adapted from H. D. F. Kitto's *The Greeks*.

The Dorian Greeks were preceded, by at least two centuries, by Achaean Greeks, about whom we know something, though not enough.

It is interesting to note one of the inaccuracies of the tradition on which Homer worked later.

Greek is well stocked with little words whose sole function is to make the structure clear.

Such was one side of Mediterranean trade, not only in this Dark Age, but in every other age too in which there has been no government strong enough to police the coasts and control the seas.

The imprecision into which English occasionally deviates and from which German occasionally emerges, is quite foreign to Greek.

Homer does not forget those to whom another man's glory brings sorrow.

A very large number of these names go back to the period with which we are now concerned.

Just before the Peloponnesian War there were something like 125,000 slaves in Attica, of whom something like 65,000 were in domestic employment.

This is the way in which the earliest work of European literature opens.

Sparta was the only state which had a standing army.

But Philip's successor was not commonplace—he was Alexander the Great, one of the most astonishing men of whom we know.

From others he took hostages, and deposited them in one of the islands of which he had control.

It is hard to believe that the dramatists never, even by accident, portrayed the stunted creatures among whom they actually lived.

Exercise 74B: Correct Use of Who and Whom

Choose the correct pronoun within the parentheses; cross out the incorrect pronoun.

(Who/Whom) will deliver the pizza?

(Who/Whom) will the pizza be delivered to?

It's nice to spend time with those (who/whom) you love.

Looking carefully at the picture, I zoomed in on the girl for (who/whom) we'd been searching.

I will give these cookies to the person (who/whom) wants them badly enough to clean the kitchen!

(Who/Whom) did you guess would be the winner?

There's the man (who/whom) I bumped into earlier!

The client for (who/whom) we provided the samples would like to hire us for the whole project.

(Who/Whom) did you peel the apple for?

The referee (who/whom) blew the whistle is very upset.

Do you know (who/whom) they added to the list in the past week?

This letter is from my aunt, to (who/whom) we'll pay a visit next month.

There was only one child in the whole class (who/whom) remembered her pencil today.

Though their culture was different than mine, I became very fond of the people among (who/whom) I lived for three years.

Exercise 74C: Formal and Informal Diction

On your own paper, rewrite the following informal sentences in formal English, placing the preposition before its object. The first has been done for you.

Place a star by any sentence that sounds better in informal English.

Whom should I look for?

For whom should I look?

The rule everyone complained about has been changed.

Your sister is the one you should apologize to.

The city he's returning to is much larger than this village.

Whose account should I charge this to?

The guests whom we contained the dogs for are leaving now.

Someone has taken the space I normally park in!

Josh, Delia, and Abram are some of the friends whom I like to play with at the park.

Exercise 74D: Diagramming

On your own paper, diagram every word of the following two sentences from Exercise 74A.

Homer does not forget those to whom another man's glory brings sorrow.

From others he took hostages, and deposited them in one of the islands of which he had control.

— LESSON 75 —

Clauses and Phrases
Misplaced Adjective Phrases
Misplaced Adjective Clauses

In many East Asian countries, the day a baby is born is considered its first birthday.

The first birthday after a baby is born is considered its second birthday.

A phrase is a group of words serving a single grammatical function.

A clause is a group of words that contains a subject and a predicate.

Western birthdays are often celebrated with a cake made especially for the occasion.

The first reference to a "birthday cake" dates from 1785, when the Oxford Dictionary listed the phrase for the first time.

The young woman went to the awards ceremony with her father in a gorgeous ball gown.

She gave the cookie to the little girl made of gingerbread.

Paige gave a birthday cake to her cousin which she had baked herself.

Adjective clauses and phrases should usually go immediately before or after the noun or pronoun they modify.

Exercise 75A: Correcting Misplaced Modifiers

Circle the misplaced adjective clauses and phrases in the following sentences. Draw an arrow to the place where each modifier should be. In the blank, indicate whether the modifier is a phrase or a clause by writing *P* or *C*.

The orange juice slaked my thirst that I found in the refrigerator. __________

The clock is on the yellow wall made by the renowned clockmaker. __________

The dog wearing the pink swimsuit belongs to the girl. __________

Redwood trees provide homes for many animals, which can grow over 350 feet tall. __________

The trucks that were grown by farmers in my hometown are carrying the tomatoes. __________

My neighbor's son with a perfect shell searched high and low for a snail. __________

A few buttons make a perfect addition to the little girl's dress shaped like flowers. __________

The teacher's sneeze resulted in giggles from every student that echoed across the gymnasium. __________

Neville drew a picture for his teacher that resembled a monster. __________

Written with childish spellings, the mother smiled at her son's first story. __________

This opal ring will be a wonderful addition to the museum, which belonged to my great-great-grandmother. __________

Exercise 75B: Diagramming

Each of the following sentences has at least one misplaced clause or phrase. On your own paper, diagram each sentence correctly, and then read the corrected sentence out loud to your instructor.

The sentences below are adapted from L. M. Boston's *The Children of Green Knowe.*

He put his hand, which was real horsehair, on the rocking horse's mane.

There was a high garden wall that must once have been windows with arched slits in it.

With a soft purr, each domino, which startled the inquisitive chaffinch up into the air, in turn fell forward.

The horse nuzzled Toby's cheek, who had lowered his head to receive the bridle.

— LESSON 76 —

Noun, Adjective, and Adverb Clauses
Restrictive and Non-Restrictive Modifying Clauses

Type of clause	Function in the sentence	Introduced by . . .	Diagram by . . .	Also known as
Adjective clause	Modifies a noun or pronoun in the main clause. Answers the questions *Which one? What kind? How many? Whose?*	. . . a relative pronoun, relative adjective, or relative adverb that refers back to a noun or pronoun in the main clause. The most common are *who, whom, whose, that, which, where, when, why.*	. . . placing every word of the dependent clause on a separate diagram below the diagram of the main clause. Connect the relative pronoun, adjective, or adverb to the word it refers to in the main clause with a dotted line.	Relative clause, dependent clause, subordinate clause

Type of clause	Function in the sentence	Introduced by . . .	Diagram by . . .	Also known as
Adverb clause	Modifies a verb, adjective, or adverb in the main clause. Answers the questions *Where? When? How? How often? To what extent?*	. . . subordinating conjunctions, such as *when, until, before, after, as, while, where, although, unless, because, since, though, so that, even though.* (NOTE: There are many other subordinating conjunctions.)	. . . placing every word of the dependent clause EXCEPT for the subordinating word on a separate diagram below the diagram of the main clause. Draw a dotted line connecting the predicate of the dependent clause to the word modified in the independent clause, and write the subordinating word on the dotted line.	Subordinate clause, dependent clause
Noun clause	Stands in as any part of the sentence that a noun can fill: subject, direct object, indirect object, predicate nominative, object of the preposition, appositive [see Lesson 94], object complement.	. . . most commonly, *that.* Can also be introduced by *who, whom, which, what, whether, why, when, where, how,* or other subordinating words.	. . . drawing a tree in the appropriate "noun" space on the diagram and placing each word in the noun clause on a diagram that sits on top of the tree. If the subordinating word only connects the dependent clause to the rest of the sentence and doesn't have a grammatical function *within* the dependent clause, diagram it on a line that floats above the predicate of the clause and is attached to the predicate by a dotted line.	Nominal clause, subordinate clause, dependent clause

Exercise 76A: Clause Review

For each of the three sentences below, complete these steps:

1. Find and circle the dependent clause. Label each one as adjective, adverb, or noun.
2. Identify and underline the subordinating word.
3. For the adverb and adjective clauses, draw a line from the subordinating word to the word modified. For the noun clauses, identify the part of the sentence that the clause is serving as.
4. Diagram each sentence on your own paper.

These sentences are from *The Book of Three* by Lloyd Alexander.

Whatever had seized him made snorting noises.

At last he dropped the hammer and turned to Coll, who was watching him critically.

Those who fell into his clutches would be counted fortunate if they perished quickly.

A restrictive modifying clause defines the word that it modifies. Removing the clause changes the essential meaning of the sentence.

A non-restrictive modifying clause describes the word that it modifies. Removing the clause doesn't change the essential meaning of the sentence.

In much of Asia, the day that a baby is born is considered to be its first birthday.

Wei's second birthday, which would have been considered his first in North America, was celebrated with a feast of long noodles and red-dyed eggs.

The movie, which lasted far too long, was quite boring.
I get very angry at people who talk during a movie.
My sister, who enjoys ballet and *muay thai* fighting, has gone to climb Denali.
She ran faster because there was a mountain lion behind her.

Only non-restrictive clauses should be set off by commas.

CORRECT
Hammurabi, who spent much of his life at war, created one of the first law codes.
INCORRECT
Hammurabi who spent much of his life at war created one of the first law codes.

CORRECT
The bricks that formed their city walls were made of mud.
INCORRECT
The bricks, that formed their city walls, were made of mud.

The king had no firm foundation on which to build. ____________________

The king had no firm foundation, on which to build. ____________________

Exercise 76B: Non-Restrictive Clauses and Missing Commas

In the following sentences, taken from Sylvia Engdahl's *Enchantress from the Stars*, underline each dependent clause. If you find a dependent clause within another dependent clause, use a double underline for the inner one. Using proofreader's marks ^, , place commas around each non-restrictive clause. Leave sentences with restrictive clauses as they are.

Although there was seldom more than dry bread or thin gruel on their table they were not miserable.

While our main objective is to study the Younglings there are occasions on which we do take action.

The place where we had come down was an idyllic one.

When I stopped to think about it I realized that she was of a race very much like the Andrecians.

It's chancy, but not impossible in a culture like this one which is very favorably disposed toward it.

It wasn't till then that I really took in what it meant!

I'm supposed to make them feel that I want them to succeed.

The cup remained poised in the air where she had placed it.

If there were no problems to solve no one would get very far.

Then all at once his eye fell upon the Stone which he now saw had been bound to his belt.

Exercise 76C: Restrictive Clauses and Unnecessary Commas

In the following sentences, taken from Rod and Ken Preston-Mafham's *Butterflies of the World*, underline each dependent clause. If you find a dependent clause within another dependent clause, use a double underline for the inner one. Delete the incorrect commas that have been placed around restrictive clauses. Use the proofreader's mark for delete: ___ℓ . Leave sentences with non-restrictive clauses as they are.

The way, in which holdings are established and defended, has been closely studied in the European speckled wood butterfly, Pararge aegeria.

That the crushed and withered stems of certain plants can prove irresistible to male danaines, cannot be disputed.

In these instances, apparently, the surface of the soil or rock is first daubed with saliva, into which the salts dissolve, before it is re-imbibed.

Anyone, who feels, that such an event may occur too infrequently to be worth mimicking, should take a walk in a tropical rain forest at night during a bout of heavy rain.

In this position it mimics the kind of leaf decay, which is commonly found in the tropics.

Some tropical caterpillars positively bristle with an impenetrable thicket of interlocking spines, which probably serve to deter both vertebrate and invertebrate predators.

The mimetic concept was later expanded by the realization, that unrelated unpalatable butterflies bore similar color patterns.

The fields and copses had been completely wiped out and replaced by the urban desert of a light industrial estate, which even today is creeping irrevocably outwards.

Butterfly species, whose caterpillars are gregarious in their early stages, seem to be particularly vulnerable.

A prime example of this may be found in the African swallowtail, which is widespread throughout sub-Saharan Africa.

WEEK 20

Constructing Sentences

— LESSON 77 —

Constructing Sentences

Exercise 77A: Making Sentences out of Clauses and Phrases

The independent clauses below are listed in order and make up a story—but they're missing all their supporting pieces.

- On your own paper, rewrite the story by attaching the dependent clauses and phrases in Lists 2 and 3 to the independent clauses in List 1 to make complete sentences. You may insert dependent clauses that act as adjectives or adverbs into the beginning, middle, or end of independent clauses (usually by putting them right before or after the word they modify), and you may change any capitalization or punctuation necessary. But do not add or delete words.
- The first sentence has been constructed for you.
- Crossing out each clause or phrase as you use it will help you not to repeat yourself! (The phrase "at night" appears twice in the story, so it appears twice in your list.)

List 1. Independent Clauses

~~There once was a King.~~
They all slept.
The King locked and bolted the door.
He saw.
The King said.
He should have forfeited his life.
A poor soldier met an old woman.
She told him.
She also gave him a cloak.
The Princesses descended.
The soldier put on his cloak and went down last.
He followed the Princesses.
He took a twig.
The soldier reported.
They confessed all.

List 2. Dependent Clauses

where the Princesses danced their shoes
where the trees had leaves
that the Princesses danced
when he unlocked the door
~~who had twelve daughters~~
that were silver, gold, and diamond
that he was going to find out
if a man tried and failed to discover the secret
when the Princesses saw
while he pretended to sleep
when they were
how that had come to pass
where he was going
that falsehood would be
when the King asked
who had watched everything
when he said
in which their beds stood side by side
that someone should find out
that would make him invisible
whoever could discover
that startled the youngest Princess
who asked him
where the Princesses danced
that their shoes were worn out
that he must pretend to be sound asleep

List 3. Phrases

with twelve Princes
for his wife
in the morning
should choose a princess
with the youngest
into holes
in one chamber
in an underground castle
from each type
through a secret opening
to a place
making sounds
in their beds

of tree
for an answer
at night
at night
after three nights
of no avail
with dancing

FIRST SENTENCE

There once was a King who had twelve daughters.

— LESSON 78 —

Simple Sentences
Complex Sentences

A sentence is a group of words that usually contains a subject and a predicate.
A sentence begins with a capital letter and ends with a punctuation mark.
A sentence contains a complete thought.

(The following sentences are from *The Cricket in Times Square* by George Selden.)

A mouse was looking at Mario.

Gradually the dirt that had collected on the insect fell away.

A complex sentence contains at least one subordinate clause.
A simple sentence contains one independent clause and no subordinate clauses.

But in all his days, and on all his journeys through the greatest city in the world, Tucker had never heard a sound quite like this one.

No matter what else is in a simple sentence, it will only have *one* subject-predicate set in it.

Then he folded a sheet of Kleenex, tucked it in the box, and put the cricket in it.

The thrumming of the rubber tires of automobiles, and the hooting of their horns, and the howling of their brakes made a great din.

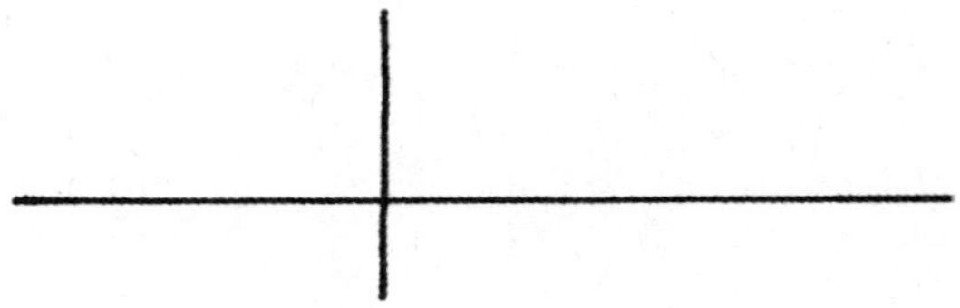

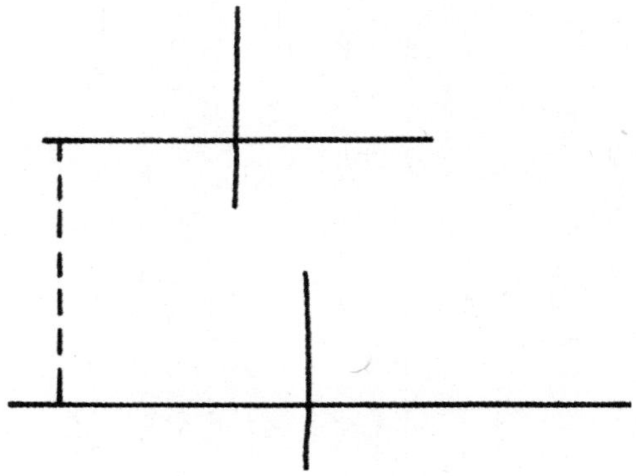

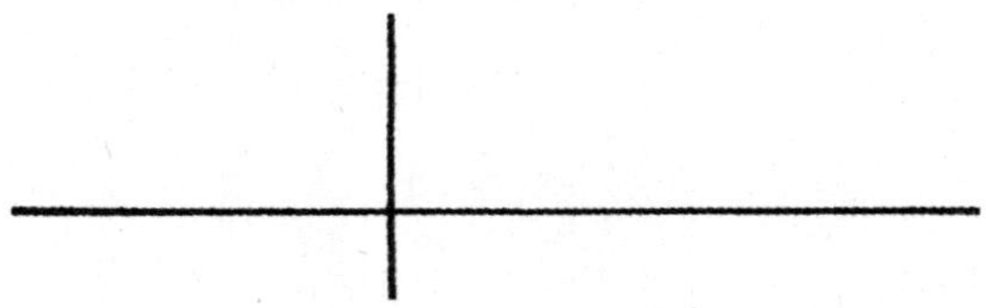

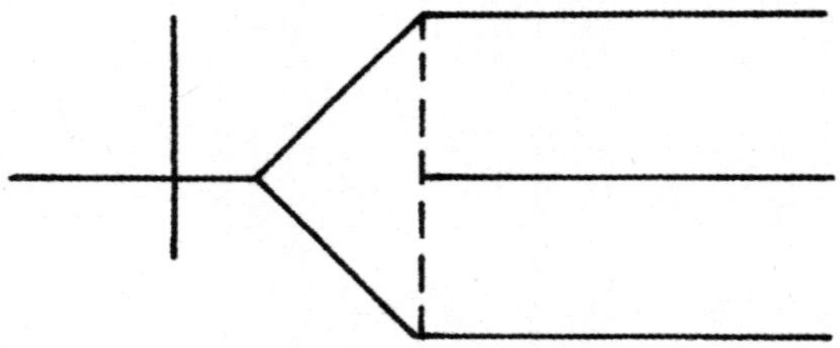

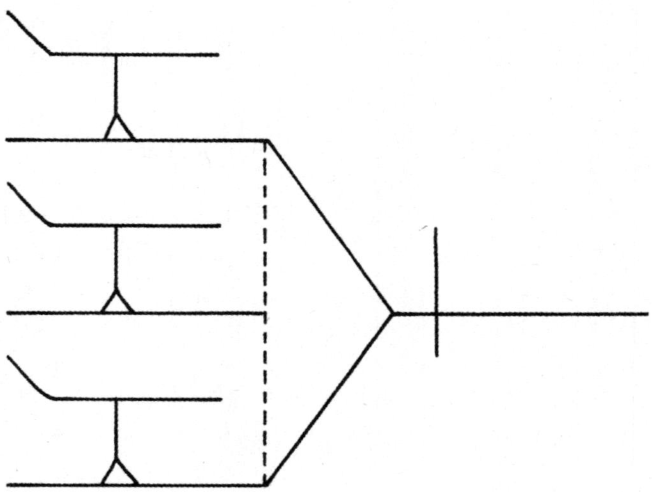

My closest friend and my greatest enemy met on the battlefield and fought bitterly.

Exercise 78A: Identifying Simple and Complex Sentences

In the sentences below, underline each subject once and each predicate twice. (Find the subjects and predicates in both independent and dependent clauses.) Write any understood subject in parentheses to the left of the sentence. In the blank at the end of each sentence, write *S* for simple or *C* for complex.

These sentences are adapted from *The King's Mirror*, translated from Old Norse by Laurence Marcellus Larson.

The man who is to be a trader will have to brave many perils. ______

Keep your table well provided and set with a white cloth, clean victuals, and good drinks. ______

After the meal you may either take a nap or stroll about a little while for pastime. ______

But although I have most to say about laws, I regard no man perfect in knowledge unless he has thoroughly learned and mastered the customs of the place where he is sojourning. ______

Soon the east wind is crowned with a golden glory and robed in all his raiments of joy. ______

Not long since, we mentioned a certain fact which must be thought exceedingly strange elsewhere. ______

The farmers raise cattle and sheep in large numbers and make butter and cheese in great quantities. ______

I gather from what you have said that the ocean is deep and also very salt and always in commotion. ______

Since every question looks toward a reply, I shall explain this to you in a few words, as it seems most reasonable to me. ______

His chief business, however, is to maintain an intelligent government and to seek good solutions for difficult problems and demands. ______

You also heard in the earlier account how the king and the city of Themar perished because the king, being friendly to one side and very hostile to the other, had distorted a just decision. ______

Exercise 78B: Forming Complex Sentences

On the blanks provided, rewrite each pair of simple sentences as a single complex sentence. The first is done for you. The sentences below are adapted from Washington Irving's *The Legend of Sleepy Hollow.*

There are peculiar quavers still to be heard in that church. They may even be heard half a mile off.

There are peculiar quavers still to be heard in that church, which may even be heard half a mile off.

She wore the ornaments of pure yellow gold. Her great-great-grandmother had brought the ornaments over from Saardam.

____

____

Ichabod laid his eyes upon these regions of delight. The peace of his mind was at an end.

____

____

Brom had a degree of rough chivalry in his nature. Brom would fain have carried matters to open warfare.

____

____

He approached the stream. His heart began to thump.

____

____

A thief might get in with perfect ease. The thief would find some embarrassment in getting out.

____

____

Exercise 78C: Diagramming

On your own paper, diagram the following four sentences. Beside each diagram, write the number of vertical lines dividing subjects from predicates, along with the label *S* for simple or *C* for complex.

Along came a spider, who sat down beside her, and frightened Miss Muffet away.
Little Bo-Peep has lost her sheep, and doesn't know where to find them.

Pat it, and prick it, and mark it with T, and put it in the oven for Tommy and me.

If Peter Piper picked a peck of pickled peppers, where's the peck of pickled peppers Peter Piper picked?

— LESSON 79 —

Compound Sentences
Run-on Sentences
Comma Splice

(The sentences in this lesson are taken from *Pride and Prejudice* by Jane Austen.)

Bingley had never met with more pleasant people or prettier girls in his life; everybody had been most kind and attentive to him; there had been no formality, no stiffness; he had soon felt acquainted with all the room.

A compound sentence is a sentence with two or more independent clauses.

Everybody was surprised.
Darcy, after looking at her for a moment, turned silently away.

Everybody was surprised, and Darcy, after looking at her for a moment, turned silently away.

A coordinating conjunction joins similar or equal words or groups of words together.
and, or, nor, for, so, but, yet

Run-on sentence

INCORRECT (run-on sentences)
I ran quickly down the road, it was a very long way to the end.
The rabbit leaped out of the bushes, the children watched with eager interest.

CORRECT
I ran quickly down the road, **but** it was a very long way to the end.
The rabbit leaped out of the bushes, **and** the children watched with eager interest.

Comma Splice

Mr. Bennet, you are wanted immediately.

We are all in an uproar.

Mr. Bennet, you are wanted immediately; we are all in an uproar.

colon :

semicolon ;

The envelope contained a sheet of elegant, little, hot-pressed paper, well covered with a lady's fair, flowing hand.

Elizabeth saw her sister's countenance change as she read it.

The envelope contained a sheet of elegant, little, hot-pressed paper, well covered with a lady's fair, flowing hand; and Elizabeth saw her sister's countenance change as she read it.

The independent clauses of a compound sentence must be joined by a comma and a coordinating conjunction, a semicolon, or a semicolon and a coordinating conjunction. They cannot be joined by a comma alone.

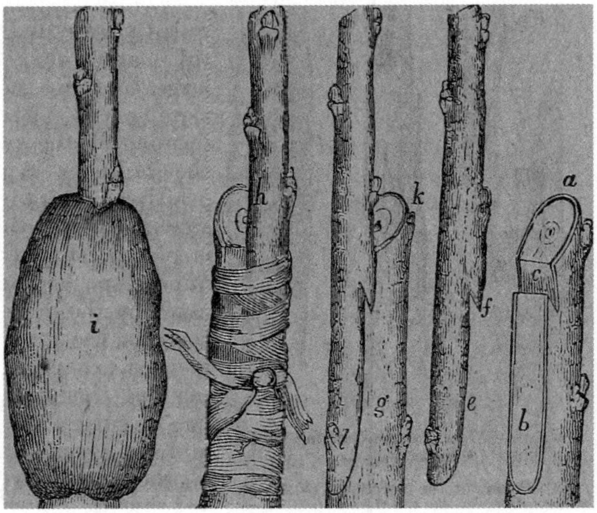

An illustration of splicing from A. J. Downing's 1889 manual *The Fruits and Fruit Trees of America*

Mr. Collins was not agreeable; his society was irksome, and his attachment to her must be imaginary.

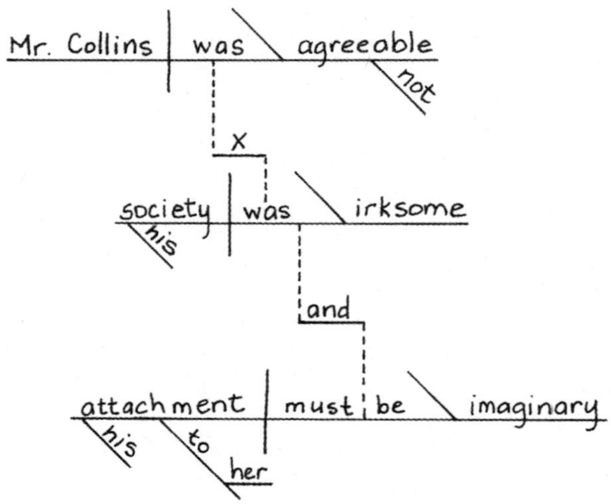

Mr. Collins is a conceited, pompous, narrow-minded, silly man; you know it, and you shall not defend Charlotte Lucas.

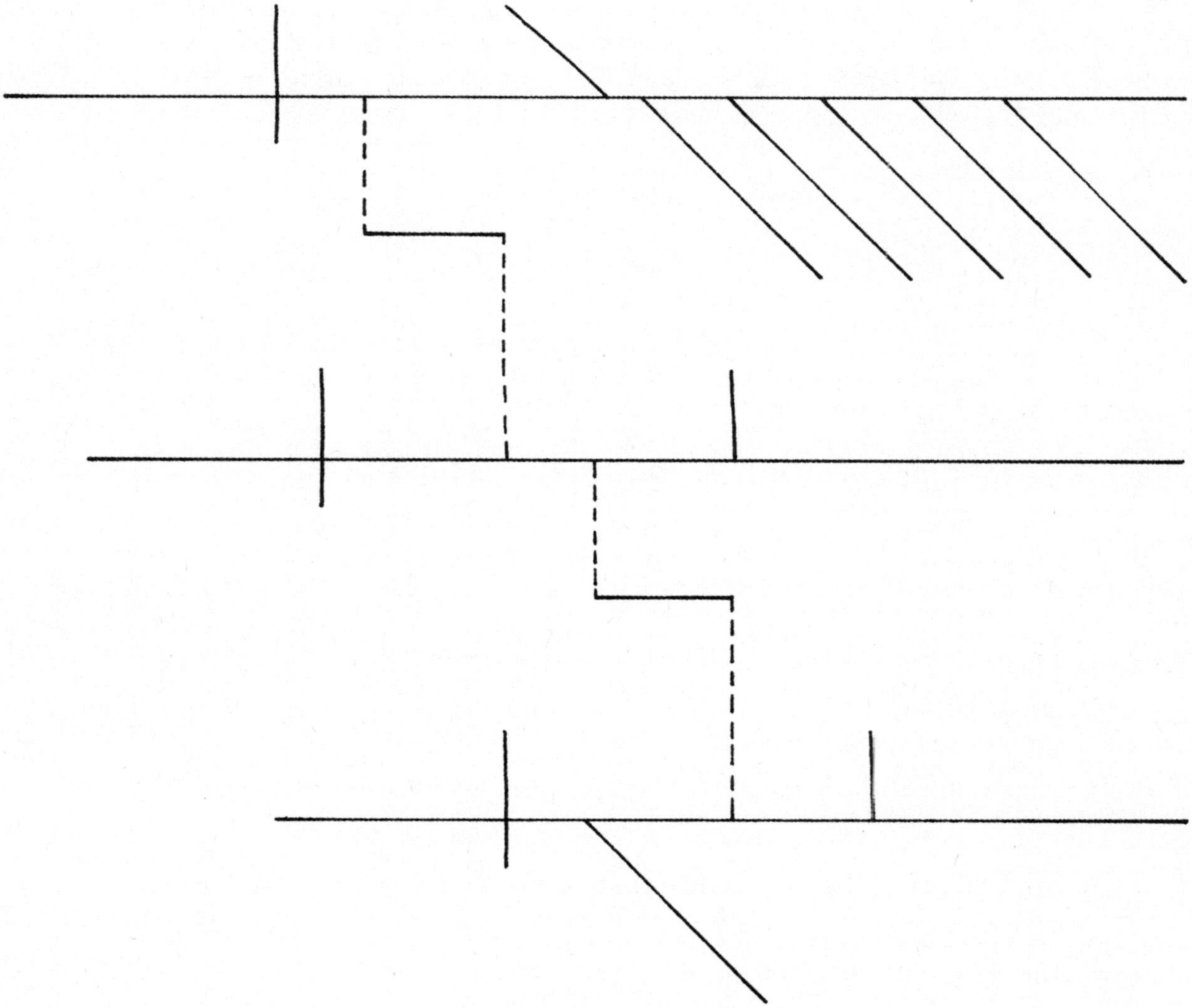

Coordinating Conjunction	Meaning/Function	Example
and	simply *in addition to*	I ran and he ran.
or	presents alternatives	He can teach or his assistant can teach.
nor	presents negative alternatives	He did not work, nor did he sleep.
for	*because*	I sang loudly, for I was happy.
so	showing results	He ate too much, so his stomach hurt.
but	*despite that*	I ran ten miles, but I wasn't tired.
yet	*nevertheless*	I had little money, yet I was content.

Exercise 79A: Forming Compound Sentences

Choose at least one independent clause from Column 1 and at least one independent clause from Column 2. Using correct punctuation and adding coordinating conjunctions as needed, combine the clauses into a compound sentence. (You may use more than two clauses, as long as your sentence makes sense!) Write your new compound sentences on your own paper. Use every clause at least once.

COLUMN 1	COLUMN 2
The dragon breathed fire.	They are the only marsupials in the United States.
The boy had never visited the town before.	Ducks were waddling by the pond.
The cat may pounce on the mouse.	You can buy six for five dollars.
Cows were grazing in the fields.	He felt his surroundings were familiar somehow.
Opossums carry their young in pouches.	She has a great interest in onomastics.
Eleanor knows the meanings of many names.	The hero avoided the flames.
She bought the item at this store.	The children may startle the cat.
Raffle tickets cost one dollar each.	She lost her receipt.

Exercise 79B: Correcting Run-On Sentences (Comma Splices)

Using proofreader's marks (∧ to insert a word, ∧, to insert a comma, ∧; to insert a semicolon), correct each of the run-on sentences below.

These sentences are from George Orwell's *Animal Farm.*

The animals settled down in the straw, the whole farm was asleep in a moment.

He was a brilliant talker he had a persuasive way of skipping from side to side and whisking his tail.

Their efforts were rewarded, the harvest was a big success.

The birds did not understand Snowball's long words they accepted his explanation.

The earth was like iron nothing could be done in the fields.

They were happy in their work they grudged no effort or sacrifice.

The Commandment had not been violated clearly there was good reason for killing the traitors.

Exercise 79C: Diagramming

On your own paper, diagram every word of the following sentences, adapted from Thomas Paine's *Common Sense.*

Society in every state is a blessing, but government even in its best state is a necessary evil; in its worst state it is an intolerable one.

Government is the badge of lost innocence; the palaces of kings are built on the ruins of the bowers of paradise.

Five men united would be able to raise a tolerable dwelling in the midst of a wilderness, but one man might labor out the common period of life without accomplishing anything.

Men of all ranks have embarked in the controversy, from different motives, with various designs; but all have been ineffectual, and the period of debate is closed.

— LESSON 80 —

Compound Sentences
Compound-Complex Sentences
Clauses with Understood Elements

The rabbit jumped, and the lion roared, and the giraffe ambled.

The boy **who had the tickets** boarded the train, but his brother decided to hail a taxi instead; their mother knew **that they would both arrive home by bedtime**.

A compound-complex sentence is made up of two or more independent clauses, at least one of which is a complex sentence.

He was the proudest, most disagreeable man in the world, and everybody hoped that he would never come there again.

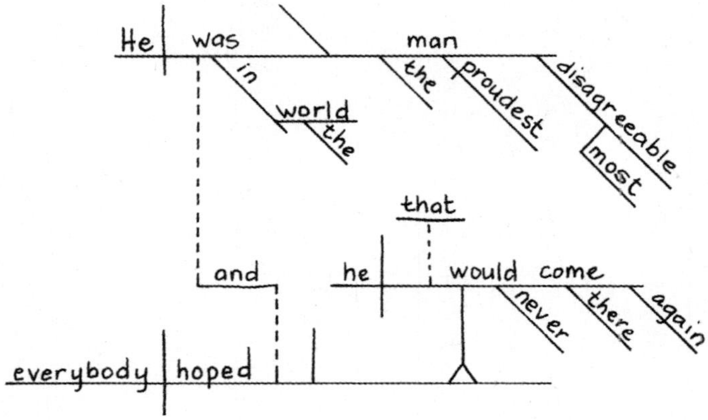

She could not recover from the surprise of what had happened; it was impossible to think of anything else; and, totally indisposed for employment, she resolved, soon after breakfast, to indulge herself in air and exercise.

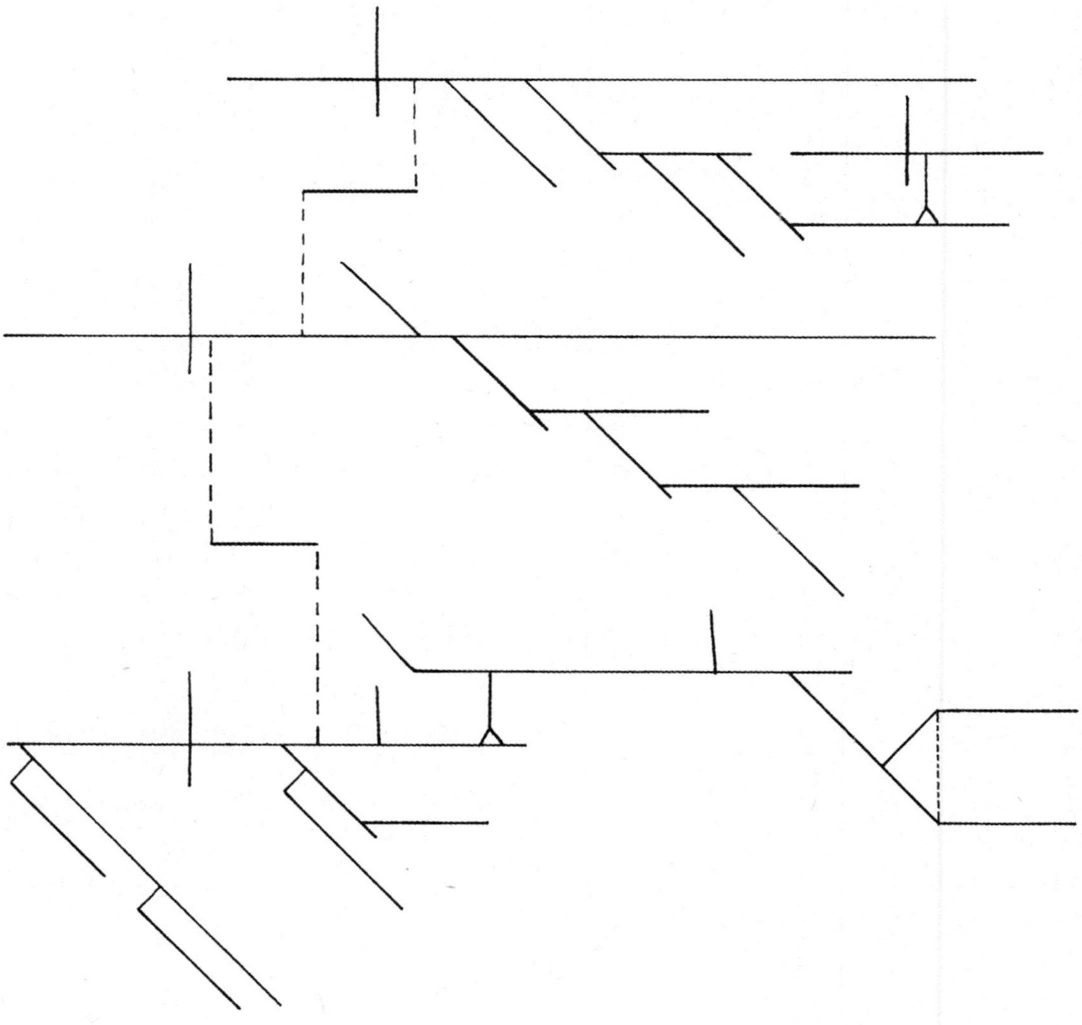

That was the weirdest thing I have ever seen.

The apples I bought yesterday had just been picked.

The speech he made was short and powerful.

He is vain, and you know he is not a sensible man.

He was at the same time haughty, reserved, and fastidious, and his manners, although well-bred, were not inviting.

The situation that troubled her remained the same, her peace equally disturbed by the circumstances.

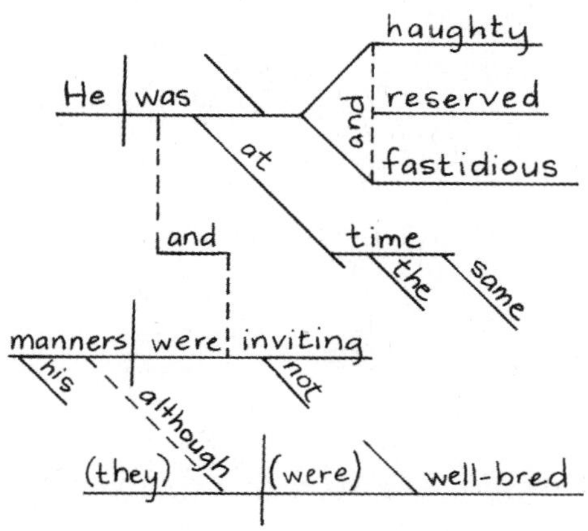

Exercise 80A: Analyzing Complex-Compound Sentences

The sentences below are all complex-compound sentences. For each sentence, carry out the following steps:

a. Cross out each prepositional phrase.
b. Circle any dependent clauses. Label them as *ADJ, ADV,* or *NOUN.* Draw a line from adjective and adverb clauses to the word modified. Label noun clauses with the part of the sentence that they function as.
c. Underline the subject of each independent clause once and the predicate twice.
d. Draw a vertical line between each simple and/or complex sentence.
e. Insert missing words (if any).

The first sentence has been done for you.

These sentences are adapted from *Cheaper by the Dozen*, by Frank B. Gilbreth Jr. and Ernestine Gilbreth Carey.

ADV

He hadn't remembered to count noses (when he came ~~down the gangplank~~), | and he didn't

ADV NOUN DO

notice, (~~until the gangplank was pulled in~~), (that Dan was missing).

What would work in the home would work in the factory, and what would work in the factory would work in the home.

Dad decided we were going to have to help them, and he wanted us to offer the help of our own accord.

He knows where the razor is, but first he must locate it with his eye.

Most photographers prefer sunlight for their pictures, but Dad liked it best when there was no sun.

We had better success with another guest whom we set out deliberately to discourage; she was a woman psychologist who came to Montclair from New York.

Exercise 80B: Constructing Complex-Compound Sentences

From each set of independent clauses, construct a single complex-compound sentence. You may turn any of the clauses into dependent clauses by adding subordinating words, insert any other words necessary, omit unnecessary words, and make any other needed changes, but try to keep the original meaning of each clause. You must use every clause in the set!

You may turn a clause into a prepositional phrase or another form, as long as your resulting sentence has at least two independent clauses and one dependent clause and contains all of the information in the listed clauses.

Write your sentences on your own paper. The first has been done for you. The other four sets of clauses are adapted from Patricia Lauber's *Fur, Feathers, and Flippers: How Animals Live Where They Do.*

We usually go out for ice cream.
We go to the little ice cream shop.
The little ice cream shop is next to the grocery store.
We usually go after the club meetings.
The club meetings are on Tuesday evenings.

On Tuesday evenings, we have our club meetings, and then we usually go out for ice cream at the little shop that is next to the grocery store.

Leopards attack their prey from hiding.
Leopards hunt at night.
Leopards may drag their catch up into a tree.
Leopards hunt alone.
Leopards may finish eating their catch later.

New England has cold winters.
The deeper soil does not freeze.
Tree roots can reach the deeper soil.
The New England region has forests and woods.
Forests are large areas.
Forests have thick growths of trees.
Woods are smaller areas of trees.

Many birds build their nests in the forest understory.
Birds in the understory are sheltered from storms.
Birds in the understory are out of reach of predators.
Young trees are in the forest understory.
Low-growing trees are in the forest understory.

Gila woodpeckers search for insects to eat in saguaros.
Saguaros are a type of giant cactus.
Gila woodpeckers make nest holes in saguaros.
Other birds use the same holes in subsequent years.
Some of these birds are sparrow hawks, screech owls, and flycatchers.

Exercise 80C: Diagramming

On your own paper, diagram the following sentences from Anne Frank's *The Diary of a Young Girl* (translated from the Dutch by B. M. Mooyaart).

I don't think I shall ever feel really at home in this house, but that does not mean that I loathe it here.

I have previously written about how much we are affected by atmospheres here, and I think that in my own case this trouble is getting much worse lately.

I know quite well that I'd be desperately jealous, but Margot only says that I needn't pity her.

I have one outstanding trait in my character, which must strike anyone who knows me for any length of time, and that is my knowledge of myself.

WEEK 21

Conditions

— LESSON 81 —

Helping Verbs
Tense and Voice
Modal Verbs

Helping Verbs
am, is, are, was, were
be, being, been
have, has, had
do, does, did
shall, will, should, would, may, might, must
can, could

In a sentence with an active verb, the subject performs the action.
In a sentence with a passive verb, the subject receives the action.

The progressive past tense uses the helping verbs *was* and *were*.
The progressive past passive voice uses the helping verbs *was/were being.*
The progressive present tense uses the helping verbs *am, is,* and *are*.
The progressive present passive voice uses the helping verbs *is/are being.*
The progressive future tense uses the helping verbs *will* and *be*.
The progressive future passive voice uses the helping verbs *will be being.*

Perfect past verbs describe an action that was finished in the past before another action began.
The active voice uses the helping verb *had.*
The passive voice uses the helping verbs *had been.*
Perfect present verbs describe an action that was completed before the present moment.
The active voice uses the helping verb *have.*
The passive voice uses the helping verbs *has/have been.*
Perfect future verbs describe an action that will be finished in the future before another action begins.
The active voice uses the helping verb *will have.*
The passive voice uses the helping verbs *will have been.*

NOTE: Shall and will are different forms of the same verb.

I do not believe in aliens.

He does not believe in aliens.

We did not believe in aliens (until they landed).

Do you believe in aliens?
Does he believe in aliens?
Did we believe in aliens (after they landed)?

I do too believe in aliens!
He does believe in aliens!
We did believe in aliens (once they had landed)!

Use the helping verbs *do, does,* and *did* to form negatives, ask questions, and provide emphasis.

	SIMPLE PRESENT		SIMPLE PRESENT EMPHATIC	
First person	I believe	we believe	I do believe	we do believe
Second person	you believe	you believe	you do believe	you do believe
Third person	he, she, it believes	they believe	he, she, it does believe	they do believe

	SIMPLE PAST		SIMPLE PAST EMPHATIC	
First person	I believed	we believed	I did believe	we did believe
Second person	you believed	you believed	you did believe	you did believe
Third person	he, she, it believed	they believed	he, she, it did believe	they did believe

We should be prepared for the arrival of alien spacecraft.
On earth, a Martian would weigh three times more than on Mars.
Strange creatures may visit Earth in our lifetime.
Alien invaders might want to conquer us.
The arrival of aliens must change our world.
We can scarcely imagine what that change will be.
We could find out that the aliens are friendly.

Modal verbs express situations that have not actually happened.
would, can, could, may, might: **possibility**
must, should: **obligation**
may: **permission**
can: **ability**

I would love to go eat a huge cheeseburger.
I can either sleep or eat.
I could probably finish my work by supper.
I may go down to the hamburger stand on the boardwalk.

I might get a burger with onions and Swiss cheese.

I must stop eating this cheeseburger!
I really should eat more vegetables.

Yes, you may eat that burger!

I can exercise self-control!

SIMPLE PRESENT MODAL		
First person	I could eat	We could eat
Second person	You could eat	You could eat
Third person	He could eat	They could eat

PERFECT PRESENT MODAL		
First person	I should have eaten	We should have eaten
Second person	You should have eaten	You should have eaten
Third person	She should have eaten	They should have eaten

I should've finished my work early; I could've finished it, if I'd had peace and quiet; I would've finished it, if everyone hadn't kept interrupting me.

Exercise 81A: Using Do, Does, and Did

On your own paper, rewrite each sentence, putting it into the form described in brackets. Use the appropriate form of the helping verb along with any interrogatives or negatives necessary. Don't forget that you may have to change the form of the verb! The first is done for you.

These sentences are adapted from Irene Hunt's *Across Five Aprils.*

His body had need of green food. [Provide emphasis.]
His body did have need of green food.

Bill, talk about it more. [Turn into a negative command.]

This makes you want to throw up your hat and say that it's all about over. [Change into a question.]

You have to be in such an all-fired hurry. [Turn into a negative statement.]

He knew how much he would tell about the ugly words of Guy Wortman and the others. [Turn into a negative statement.]

The tragedy of that summer impressed Jethro deeply. [Provide emphasis.]

Need I say that the men in the Army of the Potomac cheer General Burnside? [Turn the dependent clause into a negative statement.]

The President removed General Grant. [Turn into a negative statement.]

You see Mr. Lincoln. [Change into a question.]

You want to tell me more of the things on your mind. [Change into a question.]

Exercise 81B: Modal Verbs

Fill in the blanks below with an appropriate helping verb (*should, would, may, might, must, can, could*) to form a modal verb. There may be more than one correct answer for each sentence. Use each helping verb at least once.

These sentences are from Robert Newton Peck's *A Day No Pigs Would Die*. After you finish the exercises, be sure to read the original sentences in the key.

He even said I ____________________ feed her some new food, and to mix some meat scraps into her mash.

I ____________________ have turned Rutland upside down just trying to find some soap.

And because I ____________________ not read, I knew to listen with a full heart. It ____________________ be the last and only time I ____________________ learn its meaning.

I think I ____________________ need a new winter coat.

The only other thing I'd wanted was a bicycle, but I knew we ____________________ not afford it, so there was no sense in asking. Besides, both Mama and Papa ____________________ have looked at a bicycle as a work of the Devil.

Well, nobody ____________________ call Pinky a frill. Anybody who had half an eye ____________________ see she was a pig.

With Pinky next to me that night, I guess I ____________________ have been the luckiest boy in Learning.

Having a big hired man around like Ira ____________________ be sinful.

Care taking of a pig ____________________ keep a body as nervous as a longtail cat in a room full of rocking chairs.

And every man ____________________ face his own mission.

"So," she said, writing as fast as she talked, "I am going to write out a sentence, and you ____________________ diagram it."

Exercise 81C: Verb Tense and Voice

For each sentence below, underline each verb phrase (in both dependent and independent clauses) and identify the tense and voice of the verb. Do *not* mark gerunds, past participles, or infinitives. For state-of-being verbs, which are neither active nor passive in voice, identify the tense and write *state-of-being.* The first verb is done for you.

These sentences are from *The Journals of Lewis and Clark*.

simple past
passive

As I, being surrounded, was not permitted by them to return, I sent all the men except two interpreters to the boat.

The fleas are so troublesome that I have slept but little for two nights past.

If the boat had struck the submerged tree, her bow must have been knocked off, and in course she must have sunk in the deep water below.

Our men that had been sick for some time past recovered fast, and we are in hopes that they will be fully recovered by the time that we are ready to proceed on down the river.

It appears to be navigable for canoes and perogues at this time, and I have no doubt but that it might be navigated with boats of a considerable size in high water.

The chief drew me a kind of chart of the river, and informed me that a greater chief than himself was fishing at the river half a day's march from his village; that he was called The Twisted Hair; and that the river forked a little below his camp.

We intend to delay a few days for the laying in of some meat, by which time we calculate that the snows will have melted off the mountains.

The beaver have cut great quantities of timber; we saw a tree nearly three feet in diameter that had been felled by them.

The French inform us that lead ore has been found in different parts of this river.

— LESSON 82 —

Conditional Sentences
The Condition Clause
The Consequence Clause

(The following sentences are from *The Phantom Tollbooth* by Norton Juster.)

If you have any more questions, please ask the giant.

If one is right, then ten are ten times as right.

If you are not perfectly satisfied, your wasted time will be refunded.

A condition is a circumstance that restricts, limits, or modifies.

Snow only falls when three conditions are met: the temperature up high is freezing, the temperature at ground level is freezing, and there are water droplets in the air.

A condition clause describes a circumstance that has not yet happened.
A consequence clause describes the results that will take place if the condition clause happens.

Unless it gets warmer, I will stay inside.

I will not go for a walk if it remains this cold.

When the temperature reaches 70 degrees, I will go outside.

Should it rain, I will not come.

Had he been fired, he could have left immediately.

Refuse my conditions, and I will become your enemy!

A conditional sentence expresses the conditions under which an action may take place.
It contains a condition clause and a consequence clause.

CONDITION CONSEQUENCE
If you have any more questions, please ask the giant. ____________________

CONDITION CONSEQUENCE
If one is right, then ten are ten times as right. ____________________

CONDITION CONSEQUENCE
If you are not perfectly satisfied, your wasted time will be refunded. ____________________

First conditional sentences express circumstances that might actually happen.

The predicate of the condition clause is in a ________________________ tense.

The predicate of the consequence clause is an ________________________ or is in a

________________________ or ________________________ tense.

If only Rhyme and Reason were here, things would improve.

If you walked as fast as possible and looked at nothing but your shoes, you would arrive at your destination more quickly.

Second conditional sentences express circumstances that are contrary to reality.

The predicate of the condition clause is in a ________________________ tense.

The predicate of the consequence clause is in the ________________________ tense.

Modal verbs express situations that have not actually happened.

Simple Present

I would improve	We would improve
You would improve	You would improve
He would improve	They would improve

Perfect Past

I could have arrived	We could have arrived
You could have arrived	You could have arrived
She could have arrived	They could have arrived

If we had told you then, you might not have gone.

If the kingdom had been divided equally, both sons would now rule as kings.

Third conditional sentences express past circumstances that never happened.

The predicate of the condition clause is in the ______________________ tense.

The predicate of the consequence clause is in the ______________________ or ______________________ tense.

Exercise 82A: Identifying Conditional Sentences

Some of the sentences in this exercise are conditional sentences—and others are not! Identify each conditional sentence by writing a *C* in the margin. For each conditional sentence, label the clauses as *condition* or *consequence*.

After I finish my carrots, I will get some ice cream.

Mother will not be pleased if I do not clean my room.

Though Shirin wondered about the noise, she did not investigate.

If he practices diligently, Michael will perform well in the violin competition.

Don't answer the door unless you are expecting a visitor.

As the minutes ticked by, the girl's family awaited the surgeon's report.

"If we don't hear something soon, I'll go and ask someone."

"They will have news for us when the surgery is finished."

While it took a long time, the procedure was successful.

Exercise 82B: Tense in Conditional Sentences

Fill in each blank below with the correct tense and form of the verb in brackets. Some sentences may have more than one possible correct answer.

First Conditional Sentences

If you __________________ [remember] these guidelines, you __________________ [state-of-being verb] a good houseguest.

If your skin ____________________ [itch], ____________________ [use] this cream to help.

If the audience ____________________ [applaud] for a long time, ____________________ [take] another bow.

If you ____________________ [pedal] too quickly, you ____________________ [grow] tired.

If Aaron ____________________ [trade] his rare card for a chance to ride Benjamin's scooter, he ____________________ [regret] his decision tomorrow.

Second Conditional Sentences

If Maria ____________________ [taste] the bread, she ____________________ [want] to eat the whole loaf.

If the ball ____________________ [bounce] onto the balcony, it ________________________ [startle] Grandpa.

If I ____________________ [know] the correct tool for this job, I ________________________ [use] it.

If I ____________________ [marry] royalty, I ______________________ [state-of-being verb] rich and famous.

If the detective ____________________ [suspect] you, he ______________________ not ____________________ [tell] you anything about the case.

Third Conditional Sentences

If we ________________________ [press] the red button, something horrible _____________ ____________________ [happen].

If the nurse ____________________ [inject] you with this instead of with the correct medicine, you ____________________ [die].

If Melissa ________________________ [multiply] correctly in the first step, she __________ ______________________ [have] the right solution now.

If you ____________________ [delay] us any longer, we ____________________ not ____________________ [arrive] in time for the show.

I ____________________ [get] away with my crime, if those kids ____________________ ____________ not ____________________ [meddle]!

Exercise 82C: Diagramming

On your own paper, diagram these sentences from Sophocles's *Antigone* (translated by Dudley Fitts and Robert Fitzgerald). A conditional clause should be diagrammed like any other dependent clause.

All these men here would praise me were not their lips frozen shut with fear of you.

If I am young, and right, what does my age matter?

It is no City if it takes orders from one voice.

— LESSON 83 —

Conditional Sentences

The Subjunctive

First conditional sentences express circumstances that might actually happen.
The predicate of the condition clause is in a present tense.
The predicate of the consequence clause is an imperative, present or future tense.

If we surrender and I return with you, will you promise not to hurt this man?

So bow down to her if you want, bow to her.

If she is otherwise when I find her, I shall be very put out.

Unless I am wrong (and I am never wrong), they are headed dead into the fire swamp.

Second conditional sentences express circumstances that are contrary to reality.
The predicate of the condition clause is in a past tense.
The predicate of the consequence clause is in the simple present modal tense.

I would not say such things if I were you!

If I had a month to plan, maybe I could come up with something.

If we only had a wheelbarrow, that would be something.

Third conditional sentences express past circumstances that never happened.
The predicate of the condition clause is in the perfect past tense.
The predicate of the consequence clause is in the perfect present modal or simple present modal tense.

But they would have killed Westley, if I hadn't done it.

CONTRARY TO FACT	FACT
____________________	__________________
If we surrender	We surrender.
If you want	We want.
If she is	She is.
If I were	I was.
If we had	We had.

Subjunctive verbs express situations that are unreal, wished for, or uncertain.
Indicative verbs affirm or declare what actually is.

I eat gingerbread men.

If I eat too many gingerbread men, I will not want any dinner.

The three little pigs build houses.

If the three little pigs build straw houses, the wolf will blow them all down.

INDICATIVE SIMPLE PAST		
First person	I was	we were
Second person	you were	you were
Third person	he, she, it was	they were

SUBJUNCTIVE SIMPLE PAST		
First person	I were	we were
Second person	you were	you were
Third person	he, she, it were	they were

CORRECT	I would not say such things if I were you!
INCORRECT	I would not say such things if I was you!

CORRECT	I was cold.
CORRECT	If I were cold, I would put on a hat.
INCORRECT	If I was cold, I would put on a hat.

He was smart.

If he __________ smart, he would go immediately.

I insist <u>that she leave the door open.</u>

I recommend that he arrive early.

The professor asked that the student read out loud.

	INDICATIVE SIMPLE PRESENT		SUBJUNCTIVE SIMPLE PRESENT	
First person	I leave	we leave	I leave	we leave
Second person	you leave	you leave	you leave	you leave
Third person	he, she, it leaves	they leave	he, she, it leave	they leave

It is vital that a life guard ____________ the children swim. [subjunctive present of *watch*]

The life guard ____________________ the children swim. [indicative present of *watch*]

The woman demanded that the mechanic __________ her car. [subjunctive present of *fix*]

The mechanic ________________ her car. [indicative present of *fix*]

My mother suggested that my sister ____________ to bed early. [subjunctive present of *go*]

My sister ______________ to bed early. [indicative present of *go*]

Exercise 83A: Subjunctive Forms in Conditionals

Fill in the blanks with the correct verb forms to make the type of conditional indicated after each sentence. Circle each verb you write that is a different form because it is subjunctive.

The sentences below are from *What Katy Did Next*, by Susan Coolidge.

She ___________________ [state-of-being verb] lonely if she ___________________ [state-of-being verb] left to herself. [second conditional]

If I ___________________ [have] her with me, I _______________ not _______________ [state-of-being verb] afraid of anything. [first conditional]

If I ___________________ [state-of-being verb] going, I ___________________ simply ___________________ [stand] on my head every moment of the time! [second conditional]

If it ___________________ [state-of-being verb] for her to choose, she _________________ ____________________ [fly] back to the shore then and there. [third conditional]

Oh, if ever the happy day __________________ [come] when Deniston consents to move into town, I never __________________ [wish] to set my eyes on the country again. [first conditional]

I __________________ [consider] your second cousin a lucky man if he __________________ [persuade] her. [first conditional]

If this __________________ [state-of-being verb] English history, I never __________________ [mean] to learn any more of it. [first conditional]

If he __________________ [state-of-being verb] good, you __________________ not __________________ [mind] his being big, would you? [second conditional]

I __________________ [state-of-being verb] very lonely sometimes if it __________________ [state-of-being verb] not for my dear little fawn. [second conditional]

Polly's life __________________ [state-of-being verb] so lonely if Amy __________________ [state-of-being verb] to die. [second conditional]

You __________________ [state-of-being verb] perfectly right to go home if you __________________ [feel] so. [first conditional]

You have given me the loveliest six months' treat that ever was, and I __________________ [state-of-being verb] a greedy girl indeed if I __________________ [find] fault because it is cut off a little sooner than we expected. [second conditional]

Exercise 83B: Subjunctive Forms in Complex Sentences

Cross out the incorrect verb forms in parentheses.

It is essential that the buyer (signs/sign) these papers before five o'clock.

Walking through the park, Min-jae sang as if she (was/were) on stage.

Mr. Nettles demanded that the receptionist (interrupt/interrupts) the board meeting.

The manager recommended that she (arrive/arrives) a few minutes early.

The mother suggested that the young child (carries/carry) his cup with both hands.

If the man (was/were) awake, he would hear our warnings.

The director (was/were) determined that Tobias (play/plays) the lead in the musical.

It (seems/seem) important that the student (corrects/correct) his work in order to learn.

Catherine's parents insist that she (removes/remove) her shoes before entering the house.

The guest has requested that the front desk (alert/alerts) him when the pizza arrives.

— LESSON 84 —

Conditional Sentences
The Subjunctive
Moods of Verbs
Subjunctive Forms Using *Be*

Tense
A simple verb simply tells whether an action takes place in the past, present, or future.
A progressive verb describes an ongoing or continuous action.
A perfect verb describes an action which has been completed before another action takes place.

__________ __________

__________ __________

__________ __________

The air <u>was</u> bracing, yet with a cold edge which <u>made</u> the travelers grateful for the cloaks

____

____

____

Medwyn <u>had given</u> them.

Voice
In a sentence with an active verb, the subject performs the action.
In a sentence with a passive verb, the subject receives the action.

____

____

____

It <u>is</u> not <u>given</u> to men to know the ends of their journeys.

Mood
Indicative verbs express real actions.
Subjunctive verbs express unreal actions.
Imperative verbs express intended actions.
Modal verbs express possible actions.

"Drink," the stranger said again, while Taran took the flask dubiously. "You look as though I were trying to poison you."

There can be no victory over the Cauldron-Born, but with luck, we can hold.

First conditional sentences express circumstances that might actually happen.
The predicate of the condition clause is in a present tense.
The predicate of the consequence clause is an imperative, present or future tense.

Unless I am wrong (and I am never wrong), they are headed dead into the fire swamp.

Second conditional sentences express circumstances that are contrary to reality.
The predicate of the condition clause is in a past tense.
The predicate of the consequence clause is in the simple present modal tense.

If we only had a wheelbarrow, that would be something.

Third conditional sentences express past circumstances that never happened.
The predicate of the condition clause is in the perfect past tense.
The predicate of the consequence clause is in the perfect present modal or simple present modal tense.

But they would have killed Westley, if I hadn't done it.

SIMPLE PAST INDICATIVE
He left me behind.

SIMPLE PAST SUBJUNCTIVE SIMPLE PRESENT MODAL
If he left me behind, I would feel quite upset.

	INDICATIVE PRESENT (SIMPLE)		SUBJUNCTIVE PRESENT (SIMPLE)	
First person	I leave	we leave	I leave	we leave
Second person	you leave	you leave	you leave	you leave
Third person	he, she, it leaves	they leave	he, she, it **leave**	they leave

INDICATIVE He leaves at noon.
SUBJUNCTIVE It's important that he leave at noon.

	INDICATIVE PAST (SIMPLE)		SUBJUNCTIVE PAST (SIMPLE)	
First person	I was	we were	I were	we were
Second person	you were	you were	you were	you were
Third person	he, she, it was	they were	he, she, it were	they were

SIMPLE PRESENT MODAL PAST SUBJUNCTIVE
I would not say such things if I were you!

SIMPLE PRESENT INDICATIVE SIMPLE PAST SUBJUNCTIVE
CORRECT You look as though I were trying to poison you.

SIMPLE PRESENT INDICATIVE SIMPLE PAST INDICATIVE
INCORRECT You look as though I was trying to poison you.

I wish he were here.

A trace of a smile appeared on his face, as though he were savoring something pleasant.

	INDICATIVE PRESENT (SIMPLE)		SUBJUNCTIVE PRESENT (SIMPLE)	
First person	I am	we are	I be	we be
Second person	you are	you are	you be	you be
Third person	he, she, it is	they are	he, she, it be	they be

INDICATIVE I am well-organized.
SUBJUNCTIVE My job requires that I be well-organized.

INDICATIVE You are on time.
SUBJUNCTIVE I strongly suggest that you be on time.
SUBJUNCTIVE/MODAL Tomorrow, you should be on time.

He suggested that she be given a new task.

The captain ordered that the anchor be lifted.

It is vital that we all be properly prepared.

The present passive subjunctive is formed by pairing *be* with the *past participle* of a verb.

enjoy ______________________

juggle ______________________

plan ______________________

roast ______________________

Exercise 84A: Parsing Verbs

Underline each predicate, in both main clauses and dependent clauses. Above each, write the tense, voice, and mood of the verb.

These sentences are from Kenneth Grahame's "The Reluctant Dragon."

Tense: Simple past, present, future; progressive past, present, future; perfect past, present, future

Voice: Active, passive

Mood: Indicative, subjunctive, imperative, modal, subjunctive/modal

One evening the shepherd, who for some nights past had been disturbed and preoccupied, and off his usual mental balance, came home all of a tremble.

"Of course I was terrible frightened," the shepherd went on; "yet somehow I couldn't keep away."

He had his chin on his paws, and I should say he was meditating about things.

Rules always come right if you wait quietly. Now, please, just leave this all to me. And I'll stroll up tomorrow. Perhaps in the evening, if I'm quite free, I'll go up and have a talk to him.

Now I'm going to tell you something! You'd never guess it if you tried ever so!

I'm hoping the other neighbours will be equally agreeable.

They had always left that branch to him, and they took his word without a murmur.

This sort of thing couldn't be allowed to go on.

I'm not seeing anybody at present.

I've never fought in my life, and I'm not going to begin now.

And as soon as you'd really gone away, why, I'd come up again gaily, for I tell you frankly, I like this place, and I'm going to stay here!

"St. George," said the dragon, "just tell him, please—what will happen after I'm vanquished in the deadly combat?"

Exercise 84B: Forming Subjunctives

Fill in the blanks in the following sentences with the correct verb form indicated in brackets.

__________ I ______________________ [perfect past subjunctive of *know*] his position in the company, I ______________________ [perfect present modal of *choose*] my words more carefully.

The queen ______________________ [simple present indicative of *command*] that the prisoner ________________ [simple present passive subjunctive of *set*] free immediately.

If the piano ____________ [simple past subjunctive of *am*] in tune, it __________________ [simple present modal of *sound*] much better!

It __________________________ [simple present passive indicative of *recommend*] that the patient ____________________ [simple present subjunctive of *rest*] while recovering from this illness.

I __________ not __________ [simple present modal of *eat*] at that restaurant if I __________ [simple past subjunctive of *am*] you; the last time I __________ [simple past indicative of *am*] there, the chicken __________ not __________ [simple past passive indicative of *cook*] thoroughly.

Our teacher __________ [simple present indicative of *insist*] that our papers __________ [simple present passive subjunctive of *staple*] in this manner.

The event's director __________ [perfect present indicative of *request*] that traffic __________ [simple present subjunctive of *flow*] in this direction; please __________ [simple present imperative of *move*] out of the way.

If Alejandro __________ [simple past subjunctive of *am*] here, we __________ [simple present passive modal/subjunctive of *seat*] already.

Mother __________ [simple past indicative of *ask*] that Dayana __________ [simple present subjunctive of *put*] her toys away before going outside.

Exercise 84C: Diagramming

On your own paper, diagram the following sentences from Andrew Peterson's *The Monster in the Hollows.*

A boy swaggered into the doorway and leaned against it as if he didn't have a care in the world.

He wore a white shirt without sleeves, and his pants were held up with suspenders.

He tilted his head so the lock of his long black hair that wasn't slicked back didn't cover his eyes.

— REVIEW 7 —

Weeks 19-21

Topics
Phrases and Clauses
Adjective, Adverb, and Noun Clauses
Pronouns
Mood: Modal, Subjective, Imperative, Indicative
Conditional Sentences

Review 7A: Improving Sentences with Phrases

In the blanks below, supply phrases that meet the descriptions in brackets. You may supply more than one phrase in any blank, as long as at least one phrase fulfills the requirements (often, additional prepositional phrases may be needed). The first is done for you, with explanations provided.

The original sentences are taken from *A Tale of Two Cities*, by Charles Dickens. This is a challenging assignment—prepare to spend some time on it!

When you are finished, compare your sentences with the originals in the Answer Key.

[adverbial prepositional phrase answering the question *how* and describing *mashed*; preposition should have a compound object] [adverbial prepositional phrase answering the question *where*]

______________, the horses mashed their way ______________.

[adverbial prepositional phrase answering the question *how* and describing *mashed*; preposition should have a compound object] [adverbial prepositional phrase answering the question *where*]

With drooping heads and tremulous tails, the horses mashed their way through the thick mud.

EXPLANATION: The phrase modifies the verb *mashed* and tells *how* the horses mashed.

EXPLANATION: The phrase modifies the verb *mashed* and tells where the horses *mashed.*

[adjectival prepositional phrase describing *linen*]

His linen, though not ______________, was as white as

[adverbial prepositional phrase answering the question *where* and describing *broke*]

the tops of the waves that broke______________, or

[adverbial prepositional phrase answering the question *where* and describing *glinted*]

the specks of sail that glinted ______________.

[adverbial prepositional phrase answering the question *where* and describing *laid*] [adverbial prepositional phrase answering the question *how* and describing *tended*]

She softly laid the patient ______________, and tended her ______________.

[adjectival present participle phrase describing *Mr. Jarvis Lorry* and *Miss Manette*]

Mr. Jarvis Lorry and Miss Manette, ______________________________,

joined Monsieur Defarge in the doorway to which he had directed his other company just

[adverbial prepositional phrase answering the question *where* and describing *opened*]

before. It opened ______________________________, and was the

[adjectival past participle phrase describing *houses* and also including a prepositional phrase serving as the object of the past participle]

general public entrance to a great pile of houses, ______________________________.

[adverbial prepositional phrase answering the question *where* and describing *dropped*] [adverbial prepositional phrase answering the question *how* and describing *lay*]

He had gradually dropped ____________________, and lay there ____________________,

[adverbial past participle phrase answering the question *how* and describing *lay*]

______________________________.

[present participle phrase acting as a noun and serving as the object of the preposition *after*]

After ______________________________, you fell into

[adverbial prepositional phrase answering the question *where* and describing *came*]

Tellson's down two steps, and came to your senses ______________________________.

[adverbial prepositional phrase with a compound object, answering the question *how* and describing *was dressed*]

He was plainly dressed ______________________________, and his hair, which

[adverbial prepositional phrase answering the question *where* and describing *was gathered*]

was long and dark, was gathered ______________________________.

[infinitive phrase acting as a noun and serving as the direct object of *told*]

"Ten o'clock at night?" "Yes, sir. Your honour told me ______________________________."

[adjectival prepositional phrase describing *way*]

This man stood still on his way ______________________________, and saw for a

[adverbial present participle phrase answering the question *where* and describing *saw*]

moment, ______________________________, a mirage of honourable ambition, self-denial, and perseverance.

Review 7B: Improving Sentences with Clauses

Rewrite each sentence on your own paper, adding a dependent clause that meets the description in brackets.

The first is done for you, with explanations provided.

The original sentences are taken from *A Tale of Two Cities*, by Charles Dickens.

When you are finished, compare your sentences with the originals in the Answer Key.

[noun clause serving as the subject]

_______________ will never be read, but he had written something.

[noun clause serving as the subject]

What the unknown prisoner had written will never be read, but he had written something.

EXPLANATION: The entire clause "What the unknown prisoner had written" is the subject, which will never be read (*never* is an adverb modifying *will be read*).

Those venerable and feeble persons were always seen by the public in the act of bowing, and were popularly believed, [adverb clause telling *when*] _______________, still to keep on bowing in the empty office [adverb clause telling *when*] _______________.

He was not missed; for, nobody [adjective clause describing *nobody*] _______________ looked for him.

Defarge raised his head thoughtfully, [adverb clause telling *how*] _______________.

[adverb clause telling *when*] _______________, she had neither engaged herself in her usual work, nor had she read to him.

My dear Manette, I am anxious to have your opinion, in confidence, on a very curious case [adjective clause describing *case*] _______________.

Presently, the château began to make itself strangely visible by some light of its own, [adverb clause telling *how*] _______________.

Review 7C: Conditional Clauses

Label the following sentences as first, second, or third conditional by writing *1*, *2*, or *3* in the blank next to each one. Underline each conditional clause. Circle each consequence clause.

These sentences are taken or adapted from *The Warden and the Wolf King*, by Andrew Peterson.

If I fight, I fight for the Hollows, not for a monster. ________

If they hadn't acted so weirdly, Janner would have suspected that there was some true danger at hand. ________

Unless he found more wood the little fire would weaken again. ________

I want him to have it if that's all right. ________

Of course, if you don't show up at Ban Rona for a week or so, we'll send out a search party to bring you home. ________

The thing stank, it was from a race of brutes, and it would happily squeeze them all to death if it were awake. ________

I can't rest until I finally learn what that means. ________

If he hadn't been so serious, and if there hadn't been real danger outside, it would have been humorous. ________

If he bore southward he would eventually run into a road that led to Ban Rugan. ________

Review 7D: Pronoun Review

The following paragraphs are taken from Katherine Paterson's *Bridge to Terabithia*. Circle every pronoun. Label each as personal (*PER*), possessive (*POSS*), reflexive (*REF*), relative (REL), demonstrative (*DEM*), or indefinite (*IND*). Beside this label, add the abbreviation for the part of the sentence (or clause) that the pronoun serves as: adjective (*ADJ*), subject (*SUBJ*), direct object (*DO*), indirect object (*IO*), or object of the preposition (*OP*).

The first has been done for you.

POSS/ADJ

Jess pushed (his) damp hair out of his face and plunked down on the wooden bench. He dumped two spoonfuls of sugar into his cup and slurped to keep the hot coffee from scalding his mouth.

"Oooo, Momma, he stinks." Brenda pinched her nose with her pinky crooked delicately. "Make him wash."

"Get over here to the sink and wash yourself," his mother said without raising her eyes from the stove. "And step on it. These grits are scorching the bottom of the pot already."

"Momma! Not again," Brenda whined.

Lord, he was tired. There wasn't a muscle in his body that didn't ache.

"You heard what Momma said," Ellie yelled at his back.

Review 7E: Parsing

In the sentences below, underline every verb or verb phrase that acts as the predicate of a clause (dependent *or* independent). Label each verb with the correct tense, voice, and mood.

Tense: Simple past, present, future; progressive past, present, future; perfect past, present, future

Voice: Active, passive (or state-of-being)

Mood: Indicative, subjunctive, imperative, modal, subjunctive/modal

The first is done for you.

The following paragraphs are taken from Milton Meltzer's *The Amazing Potato: A Story in Which the Incas, Conquistadors, Marie Antoinette, Thomas Jefferson, Wars, Famines, Immigrants, and French Fries All Play a Part.*

simple past
active
indicative

What finally did make the potato more acceptable to everyone? The commands of a king were much less important than broad social changes. A French historian who studied the issue writes: "In all places and at all times the potato has always arrived in the baggage carts of distress. . . ." He then cites the many wars and cereal-crop failures that ravaged Europe in the eighteenth century. When such disasters brought about hunger, the potato could save the day.

The potato was planted in poor regions at first, and spread from there to meet food shortages. Government officials soon realized how effective the new crop was. Given an equal surface of land to grow on, the potato crop could feed five times as many people as wheat. So for the poor farmer who held only a small bit of land, potatoes had great appeal. And when the wheat or rye crops failed, less harm was done to the community if potatoes were on hand.

The following sentences are taken from *The History and Social Influence of the Potato*, by Redcliffe N. Salaman and William Glynn Burton.

It is obvious that in thirty-five years many more advances will have been made.

In the interests of the army in the field, the countryside had been denuded of labour and horses; steam-tackle had been demobilized; the accessory trades, even that of the blacksmith, were closed down or brought to a standstill; to which must be added an acute shortage of potash and phosphate fertilizers.

Review 7F: Diagramming

On your own paper, diagram every word of the following sentence from J. R. R. Tolkien's *The Return of the King*.

Had I done so, I could have sent this thing hither to your keeping and spared myself and others much anguish.

WEEK 22

Parenthetical Elements

— LESSON 85 —

Verb Review

INDICATIVE TENSES

SIMPLE		**Active**	**Passive**
	Past	he followed he was	he was followed
	Present	he follows he is	he is followed
	Future	he will follow he will be	he will be followed
PROGRESSIVE			
	Past	he was following he was being	he was being followed
	Present	he is following he is being	he is being followed
	Future	he will be following he will be being	he will be being followed
PERFECT			
	Past	he had followed he had been	he had been followed
	Present	he has followed he has been	he has been followed
	Future	he will have followed he will have been	he will have been followed

MODAL TENSES
(would OR should, may, might, must, can, could)

SIMPLE		Active	Passive
	Present	he would follow he would be	
PERFECT			
	Past	he would have followed he would have been	

SUBJUNCTIVE TENSES

SIMPLE		Active	Passive
	Past	he followed he were	
	Present	he follow he be	

Complete the following chart with the third person singular form of the verb indicated in the left-hand column. If you need help, ask your instructor.

INDICATIVE TENSES

		Active	Passive
SIMPLE			
hunt	Past	[he, she, it]	[he, she, it]
film	Present	[he, she, it]	[he, she, it]
bake	Future	[he, she, it]	[he, she, it]
PROGRESSIVE			
notice	Past	[he, she, it]	[he, she, it]
marry	Present	[he, she, it]	[he, she, it]
release	Future	[he, she, it]	[he, she, it]
PERFECT			
squash	Past	[he, she, it]	[he, she, it]
pop	Present	[he, she, it]	[he, she, it]
weigh	Future	[he, she, it]	[he, she, it]

MODAL TENSES
(would OR should, may, might, must, can, could)

		Active	Passive
SIMPLE			
grip	Present	[he, she, it]	
PERFECT			
claim	Past	[he, she, it]	

SUBJUNCTIVE TENSES

		Active	Passive
SIMPLE			
balance	Past	[he, she, it]	
chase	Present	[he, she, it]	

On your own paper, write sentences that use each of the forms above as the predicate of an independent or dependent clause. If you need help (or ideas), ask your instructor.

— LESSON 86 —

Restrictive and Non-Restrictive Modifying Clauses
Parenthetical Expressions

In after-years Piglet liked to think that he had been in Very Great Danger during the Terrible Flood, but the only danger he had really been in was in the last half-hour of his imprisonment, when Owl, who had just flown up, sat on a branch of his tree to comfort him, and told him a very long story about an aunt who had once laid a seagull's egg by mistake, and the story went on and on, rather like this sentence, until Piglet, who was listening out of his window without much hope, went to sleep quietly and naturally, slipping slowly out of the window towards the water until he was only hanging on by his toes, at which moment luckily a sudden loud squawk from Owl, which was really part of the story, woke Piglet up and just gave him time to jerk himself back into safety and say, "How interesting, and did she?" when—well, you can imagine his joy when at last he saw the good ship *The Brain of Pooh* (*Captain,* C. Robin; *1st Mate,* P. Bear) coming over the sea to rescue him.

—From *Winnie-the-Pooh* by A. A. Milne

A restrictive modifying clause defines the word that it modifies. Removing the clause changes the essential meaning of the sentence.

A non-restrictive modifying clause describes the word that it modifies. Removing the clause doesn't change the essential meaning of the sentence.

Only non-restrictive clauses should be set off by commas.

Parentheses ( ) can enclose words that are not essential to the sentence.

singular: parenthesis
plural: parentheses

when Owl who had just flown up sat on a branch of his tree to comfort him

until Piglet who was listening out of his window without much hope went to sleep quietly

a sudden loud squawk from Owl which was really part of the story woke Piglet up

Parenthetical expressions often interrupt or are irrelevant to the rest of the sentence.

Punctuation goes inside the parentheses if it applies to the parenthetical material; all other punctuation goes outside the parentheses.

Parenthetical material only begins with a capital letter if it is a complete sentence with ending punctuation.

As soon as he saw his companion fall, the other soldier, with a loud cry, jumped out of the boat on the far side, and he also floundered through the water (which was apparently just in his depth) and disappeared into the woods of the mainland.

If you can swim (as Jill could) a giant bath is a lovely thing.

He had only once been in a ship (and then only as far as the Isle of Wight) and had been horribly seasick.

The cabin was very tiny but bright with painted panels (all birds and beasts and crimson dragons and vines) and spotlessly clean.

From the waist upward he was like a man, but his legs were shaped like a goat's (the hair on them was glossy black) and instead of feet he had goat's hoofs.

Get me a score of men-at-arms, all well mounted, and a score of Talking Dogs, and ten Dwarfs (let them all be fell archers), and a Leopard or so, and Stonefoot the Giant.

Edmund had had no gift, because he was not with them at the time. (This was his own fault, and you can read about it in the other book.)

Because it was such an important occasion they took a candle each (Polly had a good store of these in her cave).

I read the *Chronicles of Narnia* (all seven of them!) in three days.
Did you know that C. S. Lewis wrote the *Chronicles of Narnia* (all seven of them)?
C. S. Lewis and J. R. R. Tolkien were good friends (amazing, isn't it?).

Exercise 86A: Restrictive and Non-Restrictive Modifying Clauses

In the following sentences, mark each bolded clause as either *ADV* for adverb or *ADJ* for adjective, and draw an arrow from the clause back to the word modified. Some sentences contain more than one modifying clause.

Then, identify each bolded modifying clause as either restrictive (*R*) or non-restrictive (*N*).

Finally, set off all of the non-restrictive clauses with commas. Use the proofreader's mark ^, for comma insertion. When you are finished, compare your punctuation with the original.

These sentences are from Richard Peck's *The Ghost Belonged to Me*. The original commas around the non-restrictive clauses have been removed.

There are several opinions **that people hold** regarding ghosts, and not one of them would clinch an argument.

But she was a secret **I could not keep**, and so other people were drawn in.

There's hardly a topic **you can raise** without reminding Cousin Elvera of a point of interest down at the fair.

In seasonable weather, they run the open-sided cars, and you can hear the people talking **as they glide behind the barn**.

She'll marry him **if she gets half a chance**.

Dad would have put him on the payroll at the business **which is house construction**.

When Gladys called me in to noon dinner I found Mother and Lucille making a whole batch of paper roses.

The chauffeur **who wore gaiters** hopped out and darted up the steps to Mother.

Gladys took a supper tray upstairs to Mother **who said she could not face anybody anymore that night or maybe ever**.

Here was a man **who would never believe anything told to him in a barnloft**.

But after a few steep yards we came to a path **that zigzagged down**.

The only voice **I could make out** was Dad's.

We could all go down the cellar and hide out in the coal bin **until he's gone**.

When I got down to the dining room Dad was trying to finish his breakfast in peace.

She seemed to be passing the time of day with the men **who were unloading the train**.

Exercise 86B: Identifying Parenthetical Expressions

Identify each parenthetical expression as a phrase, dependent clause, or sentence.

CHALLENGE EXERCISE

- Provide a fuller description of each expression. What kind of phrase, clause, or sentence is it? What does it do or modify?
- When you are finished, ask your instructor for the fuller explanations. Compare your descriptions to these explanations.

The sentences below are adapted from Esther Hautzig's *The Endless Steppe*.

At the state store, we lined up for bread, flour, millet (which tasted ghastly), and occasional treats.

The Russian movies (including some of the great ones) were all right, but nothing was as exciting as an American movie.

The light dimmed (there was electricity here, of course, the first I had seen since I left Vilna) and everyone quieted down and waited attentively.

So Svetlana told me that her father had gotten a large quantity of hospital gauze. (How and why I did not know or care to ask.)

This she did, warning me to watch the thirty-ruble note for dear life—scarcely an exaggeration—and begging me to count the change carefully (for me, two and two did not always readily add up to four).

I ripped the red sweater with ice-cold fingers and a cold heart, and when it was too cold to stay out of bed, I knitted in bed, wearing socks (old socks of Father's had replaced my outgrown ones), my sweater, and often a shawl over my head.

One of the directors of the tractor factory, Yosif Isayevich, would give us food (in addition to our own rations) and lodging in exchange for caring for him and his house while his wife and children were away.

Shurik came to help us pack (as if our belongings couldn't have been packed in an hour) and his mother sent some flour and half a dozen eggs for us to bake some cookies for the road.

Exercise 86C: Punctuating Sentences with Parenthetical Expressions

Correct each of the following sentences, using the proofreader's marks listed below.

delete:
insert comma:
insert period:
insert exclamation point:
insert question mark:
move punctuation mark:

If the sentence is correct, write *C* in the margin next to it.

These sentences are adapted from *Cannibal Animals: Animals That Eat Their Own Kind*, by Anthony D. Fredericks.

Tiny black widow spiderlings often eat one another. (until they can build their own webs)

As larvae, midges develop inside their mother's body (and feed on her from the inside out.)

Skeletons indicate that the Tyrannosaurus rex may have been a cannibal (but scientists aren't sure!)

In some groups of tiger salamanders (particularly those living in crowded conditions,) the young eat one another.

The Chinese giant salamander grows up to 5 feet long and weighs about 220 pounds (is it bigger than you are)?

When they are hungry, horned frogs jump at anything that moves (including other horned frogs).

The male damselfish guards the eggs laid by his mate (up to 300,000 of them)! but sometimes grows hungry and eats some of the eggs.

Did you know that a female gerbil may eat her own babies (when her diet is lacking in protein?)

Alaskan brown bear cubs (especially male cubs) are at risk of being eaten by adult male bears, who want to ensure their control of a specific area.

— LESSON 87 —

Parenthetical Expressions
Dashes

(The sentences in this lesson are from Lewis Carroll's novel *Through the Looking-glass.)*

A little provoked, she drew back, and after looking everywhere for the queen (whom she spied out at last, a long way off), she thought she would try the plan, this time, of walking in the opposite direction.

There was a Beetle sitting next to the Goat (it was a very queer carriage-full of passengers altogether).

Or—let me see—suppose each punishment was to be going without a dinner; then, when the miserable day came, I should have to go without fifty dinners at once!

I can see all of it when I get upon a chair—all but the bit behind the fireplace.
I can see all of it when I get upon a chair, all but the bit behind the fireplace.

But the beard seemed to melt away as she touched it, and she found herself sitting quietly under a tree—while the Gnat (for that was the insect she had been talking to) was balancing itself on a twig just over her head, and fanning her with its wings.

Parentheses ( ) can enclose words that are not essential to the sentence.
Parenthetical expressions often interrupt or are irrelevant to the rest of the sentence.
Punctuation goes inside the parentheses if it applies to the parenthetical material; all other punctuation goes outside the parentheses.
Parenthetical material only begins with a capital letter if it is a complete sentence with ending punctuation.

Dashes — — can enclose words that are not essential to the sentence.
Dashes can also be used singly to separate parts of a sentence.

I read Lewis Carroll's poem "Jabberwocky" which, I thought, was very weird.
I read Lewis Carroll's poem "Jabberwocky" which—I thought—was very weird.
I read Lewis Carroll's poem "Jabberwocky" which (I thought) was very weird.

Commas make a parenthetical element a part of the sentence.
Dashes emphasize a parenthetical element.
Parentheses minimize a parenthetical element.

1. You can set off parenthetical elements in three different ways.
2. You can turn a dependent clause into a parenthetical element just by putting it inside dashes or parentheses.
3. You can use a dash in place of a comma to emphasize the part of the sentence that follows.

The independent clauses of a compound sentence must be joined by a comma and a coordinating conjunction, a semicolon, or a semicolon and a coordinating conjunction. They cannot be joined by a comma alone.

CORRECT
Alice ventured to taste it, and finding it very nice (it had, in fact, a sort of mixed flavour of cherry tart, custard, pineapple, roast turkey, toffee, and hot buttered toast) she very soon finished it off.

INCORRECT
Alice ventured to taste it, and finding it very nice, it had, in fact, a sort of mixed flavour of cherry tart, custard, pineapple, roast turkey, toffee, and hot buttered toast, she very soon finished it off.

Exercise 87A: Types of Parenthetical Expressions

Identify each parenthetical expression as a phrase, dependent clause, or sentence.

CHALLENGE EXERCISE

- Provide a fuller description of each expression. What kind of phrase, clause, or sentence is it? What does it do or modify?
- When you are finished, ask your instructor for the fuller explanations. Compare your descriptions to these explanations.

These sentences are from James Hilton's *Goodbye, Mr. Chips.*

When you are getting on in years (but not ill, of course), you get very sleepy at times, and the hours seem to pass like lazy cattle moving across a landscape.

And years later, when Colley was an alderman of the City of London and a baronet and various other things, he sent his son (also red-haired) to Brookfield.

But he resaw the glorious hump of the Gable (he had never visited the Lake District since), and the mouse-gray depths of Wastwater under the Screes; he could resmell the washed air after heavy rain, and refollow the ribbon of the pass across to Sty Head.

About a quarter to four a ring came, and Chips, answering the front door himself (which he oughtn't to have done), encountered a rather small boy wearing a Brookfield cap and an expression of anxious timidity.

And then, in the shadows behind Merivale, he saw Cartwright, the new Head (he thought of him as "new," even though he had been at Brookfield since 1919), and old Buffles, commonly called "Roddy."

Exercise 87B: Punctuating Parenthetical Expressions

On either side of each bolded parenthetical expression, place parentheses, dashes, or commas. There are not necessarily "correct" answers for these, but compare them to the originals when you have finished.

These sentences are adapted from *A Dog on Barkham Street*, by M. S. Stolz.

It was getting so he couldn't be interested in anything for very long **not even dogs** because the problem of Martin was always in the way.

In this **as in so many matters concerning adults** Edward failed to see the reason but accepted the fact.

As quietly as they could **which was pretty noisily** the fifth grade made itself ready.

And then Connie climbed the stepladder **garlanded** on the outside of the box and the lid flew back.

The man nodded and moved forward **the young dog keeping at his side** and put out his hand.

What bothers me is that we **Edward and his father and I** have discussed this matter for . . . oh, for years.

When she'd driven off, the two boys turned to the man **their faces alight** and waited for him to say something, anything.

It gave them a splendid, unchecked, adventurous feeling **though they could not at the moment think of any forbidden thing they wished to do**, but in another way they didn't altogether care for it.

> **Note to Student:** The underlined phrase is a parenthetical expression within the longer parenthetical expression in bold print. Punctuate both expressions!

I was going to shout after him, but **as I say** he was kind of a big fellow with an ugly expression.

They asked Uncle Josh whether they could tie a rope around her neck so that Edward **who certainly wouldn't leave Argess behind** could accompany his friend.

They'd lasted till what they thought was three or four in the morning **it turned out to be just short of midnight**, and then had crept back in the house.

Exercise 87C: Using Dashes for Emphasis

On your own paper, rewrite the next four sentences, substituting dashes for the underlined punctuation marks and making any other capitalization or punctuation changes needed.

These sentences are taken from *Over Sea, Under Stone*, by Susan Cooper.

You stand in the doorway and look on both sides. The landing stops before it gets that far.

Would you like to go off swimming and come home for a late lunch (about one thirty)?

But they must have been behind it all, the ransacked books, the stolen maps, the attempt to look for a secret hiding-place under the floor.

It's like the way they searched the house, all at random, without any sort of plan.

— LESSON 88 —

Parenthetical Expressions

Dashes

Diagramming Parenthetical Expressions

We met the new neighbors today, who, we think, are very pleasant people.
It was a glorious morning—a cool, sunny, sweet-scented morning.
The chef decided to put liver, which was one of his favorites, on the dinner menu.
The liver (which most diners didn't order) was cooked with onions and red wine.

Recognizing Parenthetical Elements

Dashes and parentheses always turn a clause or phrase into a parenthetical element—even if there's actually a grammatical relationship between the clause or phrase and the rest of the sentence.

If a clause or phrase is set off by commas, but doesn't have a clear grammatical relationship to the rest of the sentence, it is parenthetical.

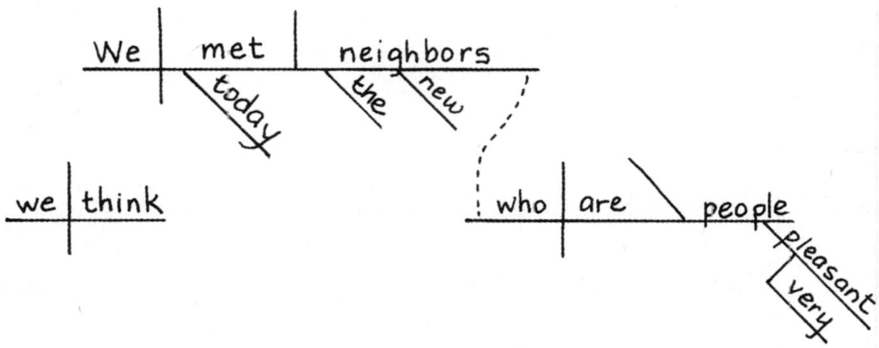

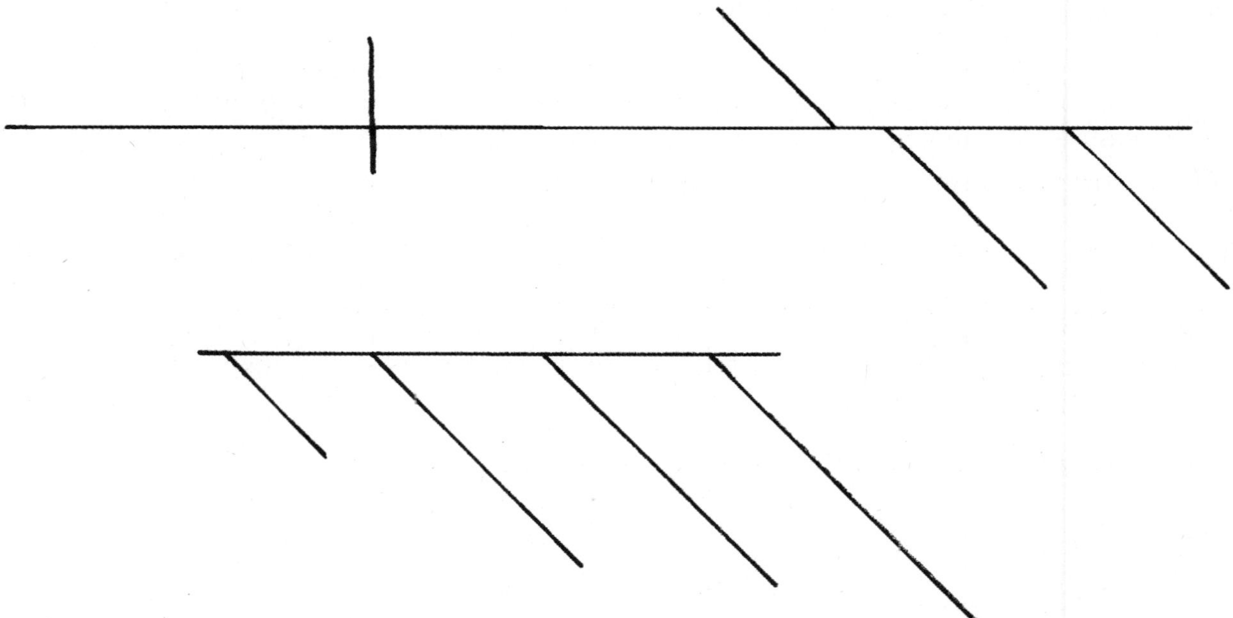

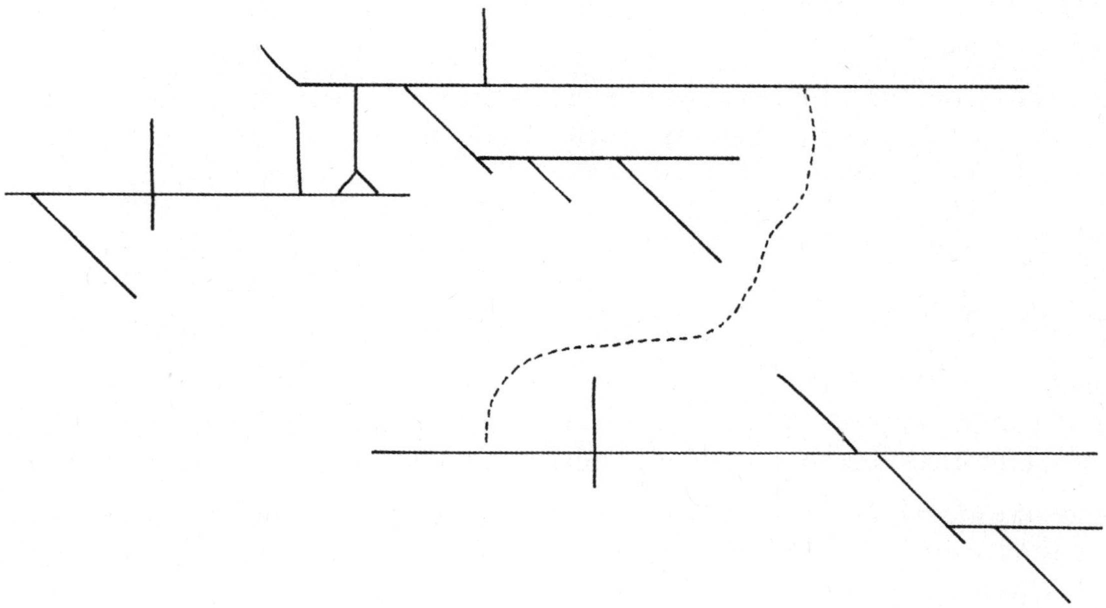

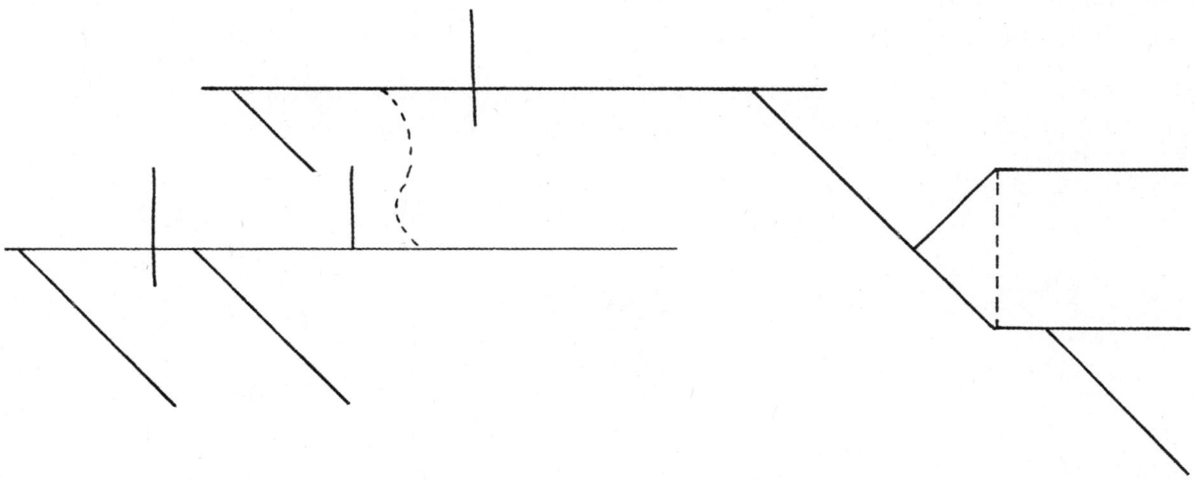

The train—can you believe it?—was on time (a rare and happy occurrence!).

Exercise 88A: Diagramming Parenthetical Expressions

On your own paper, diagram each of the following sentences (not including the citation in the grey box).

The next four sentences are drawn from Frederick Douglass's autobiography, *Narrative of the Life of Frederick Douglass.*

My mother and I were separated when I was an infant—before I knew her as my mother.

Aunt Hester went out once—where or for what I do not know—and happened to be absent when my master desired her presence.

During the summer months, people came from far and near—from Baltimore, Easton, and Annapolis—to see it.

A single word from the white men was enough—against our wishes, prayers, and entreaties—to sunder forever the dearest friends, dearest kindred, and strongest ties known to human beings.

The following sentences are slightly condensed from *David Copperfield*, by Charles Dickens.

When we got into the street (which was strange enough to me), and smelt the fish, and pitch, and oakum, and tar, and saw the sailors walking about, and the carts jingling over the stones, I felt that I had done so busy a place an injustice.

I listen to all they tell me with a vague feeling of solemnity and awe, which makes me glad that they are so near, and frightens me (though I feign to laugh) when Traddles pretends to see a ghost in the corner.

I passed the night at Peggotty's, in a little room in the roof (with the crocodile-book on a shelf by the bed's head) which was to be always mine, Peggotty said, and should always be kept for me in the same state.

When I dress (the occupation of two hours), for a great ball given at the Larkins's (the anticipation of three weeks), I indulge my fancy with pleasing images.

WEEK 23

Dialogue and Quotations

— LESSON 89 —

Dialogue

"I'm sorry, Ender," Valentine whispered. She was looking at the band-aid on his neck.

Ender touched the wall and the door closed behind him. "I don't care. I'm glad it's gone."

"What's gone?" Peter walked into the parlor, chewing on a mouthful of bread and peanut butter.

Ender did not see Peter as the beautiful ten-year-old boy that grown-ups saw, with dark, thick, tousled hair and a face that could have belonged to Alexander the Great. Ender looked at Peter only to detect anger or boredom, the dangerous moods that almost always led to pain. Now as Peter's eyes discovered the band-aid on his neck, the telltale flicker of anger appeared.

Valentine saw it too. "Now he's like us," she said, trying to soothe him before he had time to strike.

—From *Ender's Game* by Orson Scott Card

Dialogue: the actual words characters speak
Narrative: the rest of the story

Dialogue is set off by quotation marks.

A dialogue tag identifies the person making the speech.
When a dialogue tag comes after a speech, place a comma, exclamation point, or question mark inside the closing quotation marks.

"I ate the cookie," my brother said.

"I ate seventeen cookies!" my brother exclaimed.
"Do you think I'll be sick?" my brother asked.

INCORRECT:
"I ate the cookie." My brother said.

When a dialogue tag comes before a speech, place a comma after the tag. Put the dialogue's final punctuation mark inside the closing quotation marks.

My brother said, "I ate the cookie."

My brother exclaimed, "I ate seventeen cookies!"

My brother asked, "Do you think I'll be sick?"

Speeches do not need to be attached to a dialogue tag as long as the text clearly indicates the speaker.

"I've watched through his eyes, I've listened through his ears, and I tell you he's the one. Or at least as close as we're going to get."

"That's what you said about the brother."

"The brother tested out impossible. For other reasons. Nothing to do with his ability."

"Same with the sister. And there are doubts about him. He's too malleable. Too willing to submerge himself in someone else's will."

"Not if the other person is his enemy."

"So what do we do? Surround him with enemies all the time?"

"If we have to."

—From *Ender's Game* by Orson Scott Card

Usually, a new paragraph begins with each new speaker.

CORRECT:
"I'm not afraid to say what I think," George retorted. "I wish you could be honest too."
"I'm not afraid to say what I think," George retorted, "whether or not you like it."

INCORRECT: (Run-on sentence):
"I'm not afraid to say what I think," George retorted, "I wish you could be honest too."

INCORRECT: (Ends with a sentence fragment):
"I'm not afraid to say what I think," George retorted. "Whether or not you like it."

When a dialogue tag comes in the middle of a speech, follow it with a comma if the following dialogue is an incomplete sentence. Follow it with a period if the following dialogue is a complete sentence.

Exercise 89A: Punctuating Dialogue

The excerpt below is from Lois Lowry's *The Giver.* All of the dialogue is missing quotation marks, and some of it is missing ending punctuation as well. Do your best to supply the missing punctuation marks.

When you are finished, compare your versions with the originals.

I felt very angry this afternoon, Lily announced. My Childcare group was at the play area, and we had a visiting group of Sevens, and they didn't obey the rules at all. One of them—a male; I don't know his name—kept going right to the front of the line for the slide, even though the rest of us were all waiting. I felt so angry at him. I made my hand into a fist, like this. She held up a clenched fist and the rest of the family smiled at her small defiant gesture.

Why do you think the visitors didn't obey the rules? Mother asked.

Lily considered, and shook her head. I don't know. They acted like . . . like . . .

Animals? Jonas suggested. He laughed.

That's right, Lily said, laughing too. Like animals.

Where were the visitors from? Father asked.

Lily frowned, trying to remember. Our leader told us, when he made the welcome speech, but I can't remember. I guess I wasn't paying attention. It was from another community. They had to leave very early, and they had their midday meal on the bus.

Mother nodded. Do you think it's possible that their rules may be different? And so they simply didn't know what your play area rules were?

Lily shrugged, and nodded. I suppose.

You've visited other communities, haven't you? Jonas asked. My group has, often.

Exercise 89B: Writing Dialogue Correctly

On your own paper, rewrite the following sentences as dialogue, using the past tense for the dialogue tags. Use the notations in parentheses to help you.

You may choose to place dialogue tags before, in the middle of, or after dialogue, or to leave the tags out completely. But you must use at least three of those four options.

When you are finished, compare your answers with the original, which is from George MacDonald's *The Shadows.* Note that Ralph Rinkelmann is the king's name.

(The Shadow repeats, solemnly) We are the Shadows.

(The king says) Well?

(The Shadow says) We do not often appear to men.

(The king says) Ha!

(The Shadow says) We do not belong to the sunshine at all. We go through it unseen, and only by a passing chill do men recognise an unknown presence.

(The king says again) Ha!

(The Shadow says) It is only the twilight of the fire, or when one man or woman is alone with a single candle, or when any number of people are all feeling the same thing at once, making them one, that we show ourselves, and the truth of things.

(The king says) Can that be true that loves the night?

(The Shadow answers) The darkness is the nurse of light.

(The king says) Can that be true which mocks at forms?

(The Shadow answers) Truth rides abroad in shapeless storms.

(Ralph Rinkelmann thinks) Ha! ha! it rhymes. The Shadow caps my questions with his answers. Very strange! And he grew thoughtful again.

(The Shadow says, resuming the conversation) Please, your majesty, may we present our petition?

(The king replies) By all means. I am not well enough to receive it in proper state.

Exercise 89C: Proofreading

Using the following proofreading marks, correct these incorrect sentences. They are from the O. Henry short story "The Skylight Room."

Insert quotation marks: ∨
insert exclamation point: ↑!
insert comma: ^,
insert period: ⊙
delete: ℓ
move punctuation mark: ↷

"It's that star." explained Miss Leeson, pointing with a tiny finger. "Not the big one that twinkles—the steady blue one near it. I can see it every night through my skylight. I named it Billy Jackson.

"Well, really"! said Miss Longnecker. "I didn't know you were an astronomer, Miss Leeson."

"Oh, yes, said the small star gazer, I know as much as any of them about the style of sleeves they're going to wear next fall in Mars."

"Well, really" said Miss Longnecker! "The star you refer to is Gamma, of the constellation Cassiopeia. It is nearly of the second magnitude, and its meridian passage is—"

"Oh," said the very young Mr. Evans. "I think Billy Jackson is a much better name for it."

"Same here, said Mr. Hoover, loudly breathing defiance to Miss Longnecker, "I think Miss Leeson has just as much right to name stars as any of those old astrologers had."

"Well, really!" said Miss Longnecker!

— LESSON 90 —

Dialogue
Direct Quotations

The stranger said, "I have come far seeking Mali and have found great wealth here. But I must tell your king that great wealth that the world has not seen is worth less to your children's children than a rumor of water to a people dying of thirst."

The elders wondered silently about this stranger who presumed to lecture the king of Mali, but they were much too polite to say anything that might make a guest feel less than welcome.

"You will have to go to Niani, the capital city, to speak with the *mansa*—that is, the king—of Mali," said Musa Weree, with a smile that seemed to mask a secret.

But the stranger showed no interest in Niani. "The king has heard me!" he said.

—From *Mansa Musa: The Lion of Mali* by Khephra Burns

During the two months he remained in Mali, Ibn Battuta paid grudging respect to the safety and justice of the kingdom: "A traveler may proceed alone among them, without the least fear of a thief or robber," he noted.

In Sulayman's twenty-four years on the throne, Mali remained firmly under his authority. Sulayman surrounded himself with the trappings of an emperor: gold arms and armor; ranks of courtiers and Turkish mamluks, warrior slaves bought from Egypt, surrounding him. They were required to keep solemn and attentive in his presence: "Whoever sneezes while the king is holding court," al-'Umari explains, "is severely beaten."

—From *The History of the Renaissance World* by Susan Wise Bauer

Dialogue: the exact words of a speaker
Direct quotation: the exact words of a writer

Dialogue tags attach dialogue to a speaker.
Attribution tags attach direct quotations to a writer.

When an attribution tag comes after a direct quote, place a comma, exclamation point, or question mark inside the closing quotation marks.

"Many ships sank that day," the chronicler wrote.
"Seventeen ships sank that day!" the chronicler lamented.
"Who can say how many lives were lost?" the chronicler mourned.

INCORRECT:
"Many ships sank that day." The chronicler wrote.

When an attribution tag comes before a direct quote, place a comma after the tag. Put the dialogue's final punctuation mark inside the closing quotation marks.

According to the chronicler, "Many ships sank that day."
The chronicler tells us, "Seventeen ships sank that day!"
One witness asked, "Who can say how many lives were lost?"

When an attribution tag comes in the middle of a direct quotation, follow it with a comma if the remaining quote is an incomplete sentence. Follow it with a period if the remaining quote is a complete sentence.

"Many ships," the chronicler tells us, "sank that day."
"Seventeen ships sank that day," the chronicler tells us. "Who can say how many lives were lost?"

Speeches do not need to be attached to a dialogue tag as long as the text clearly indicates the speaker.

Every direct quote must have an attribution tag.

CORRECT:

The soldiers chased Yazdegerd north into the province of Kirman, but the Arab army was caught in a blizzard and froze. "The snow reached the height of a lance," al-Tabari says. Only the commander, one soldier, and a slave girl survived, the latter because her owner slit open the stomach of a camel and packed her inside it to keep her warm.

—*The History of the Medieval World* by Susan Wise Bauer

INCORRECT:

> The soldiers chased Yazdegerd north into the province of Kirman, but the Arab army was caught in a blizzard and froze. "The snow reached the height of a lance." Only the commander, one soldier, and a slave girl survived, the latter because her owner slit open the stomach of a camel and packed her inside it to keep her warm.

Exercise 90A: Punctuating Dialogue

The paragraphs below, from C. S. Lewis's *Prince Caspian*, are missing punctuation. Write in all of the missing punctuation marks (insert them directly rather than using proofreader's marks). When you are finished, compare your answers to the original sentences.

Look! Look! Look! cried Lucy

Where? What asked everyone

The Lion said Lucy Aslan himself. Didn't you see Her face had changed completely and her eyes shone.

Do you really mean— began Peter

Where did you think you saw him asked Susan

Don't talk like a grown-up said Lucy, stamping her foot I didn't think I saw him. I saw him

Where, Lu asked Peter

Right up there between those mountain ashes. No, this side of the gorge. And up, not down. Just the opposite of the way you want to go. And he wanted us to go where he was—up there

How do you know that was what he wanted asked Edmund

He—I—I just know said Lucy by his face

Exercise 90B: Punctuating Direct Quotations

Write in all of the missing punctuation marks (insert them directly rather than using proofreader's marks). When you are finished, compare your answers to the original sentences.

The following passages are from *The Fall of the Roman Empire*, by Don Nardo.

According to Rostovtzeff, the Roman Empire underwent a series of violent internal struggles between the lower classes and the upper classes, with the army increasingly taking the side of the peasants against the ruling aristocracy. The army fought the privileged classes he wrote and did not cease fighting until these classes had lost all their social prestige and lay powerless and prostrate under the feet of the half-barbarian soldiery.

Baynes finds little credence in the notion that the peasants and soldiers often found common cause in a struggle against the upper classes. Solomon Katz, formerly of the University of Washington, agrees. There is little evidence he contends that the army was made up of a class-conscious proletariat which hated the urban upper classes. On the contrary, in its greed the army plundered town and country alike.

According to Westermann, Egypt was a clear-cut example. All the land of Egypt belonged to the sovereign he wrote. The mass of the native subject population . . . were increasingly bound to their villages, to their agricultural duties, and certain villein [feudal] services due to the state.

Slavery grew comments Walbank and as it invaded the various branches of production it led inevitably to the damping down of scientific interest.

Thus classical civilization inevitably decayed from within, in a sense rotted at the very roots from which it had once grown strong; as Walbank says an absolutely low technique and, to compensate for this, the institution of slavery.

The following passages are taken from *The Celtic Empire: The First Millennium of Celtic History 1000 BC–AD 51*, by Peter Berresford Ellis.

Appian of Alexandria, writing AD c.160, disapprovingly comments: For this Didius was actually honoured with a triumph!

Sotion, who wrote accounts of the philosophers of different schools, became a main source of Diogenes Laertius (writing in the third century AD), who says the study of this philosophy had its beginning among the barbarians.

Caesar was proud of his troops. They did nothing unworthy of them he reported.

Exercise 90C: Attribution Tags

In the following paragraphs, find and underline the direct quotes that are missing their attribution tags. In the blank below each paragraph, write an attribution tag for each quote; the source of each one is noted in parentheses. Place a caret (∧) to show where you would insert the attribution tag. Do not worry about marking necessary punctuation changes for inserting the tag.

When an apple becomes ripe, it changes the starch inside of it into sugar. "The presence of sugar, plus the bright light of the sun, produces chemical reactions in the apple. These reactions cause the cells in the apple's skin to produce a red pigment called anthocyanin." (quote from *Apple Trees*, by Sylvia A. Johnson)

____

____

In Renaissance Europe, decisions to marry were not generally based on a couple's love for one another. "Fathers chose husbands and wives for their children based on political and financial considerations." (quote from *Life During the Renaissance*, by Patricia D. Netzley)

____

____

Mexican leaders in 1844 were apprehensive about the US presidential election. "The unpleasant reality was that if an annexationist won the 1844 election and Texas joined the Union, they would feel compelled to preserve Mexico's integrity by declaring war on the United States." Many of these leaders hoped this could be avoided. (quote from *The Mexican-American War*, by Don Nardo)

____

____

Apple growers must spend a long time caring for trees before they see the fruits of their labor. "A few varieties have been developed that bear apples when they are only 3 years old, but most other kinds of trees must be 7 to 10 years old before they reach their reproductive stage." (quote from *Apple Trees*, by Sylvia A. Johnson)

____

____

"Individual patrons were members of the middle class who wanted to gain prestige by offering economic support to artists." Renaissance artists could also receive support from a guild or from the Catholic Church. (quote from *Life During the Renaissance*, by Patricia D. Netzley)

____

____

Following the battle of Cerro Gordo, Americans were able to learn about the nature of their enemy, by the actions of people like the Mexican army surgeons. "What amazed the Americans was that these Mexican physicians, without being asked or coerced, also treated the American wounded, in one instance actually saving the life of an American officer who had sustained a serious head injury." (quote from *The Mexican-American War*, by Don Nardo)

____

____

— LESSON 91 —

Direct Quotations
Ellipses
Partial Quotations

A few clouds of dust moving to and fro signify that the army is encamping. Humble words and increased preparations are signs that the enemy is about to advance. Violent language and driving forward as if to the attack are signs that he will retreat. When the light chariots come out first and take up a position on the wings, it is a sign that the enemy is forming for battle. Peace proposals unaccompanied by a sworn covenant indicate a plot. When there is much running about and the soldiers fall into rank, it means that the critical moment has come. When some are seen advancing and some retreating, it is a lure.
—Sun Tzu, *The Art of War,* trans. Lionel Giles

The good general not only deceives the enemy himself, but assumes that his enemy is always deceiving him: "Humble words and increased preparations are signs that the enemy is about to advance," Sun Tzu explains. "Violent language and driving forward as if to the attack are signs that he will retreat . . . Peace proposals unaccompanied by a sworn covenant indicate a plot." Both Confucius and Sun-Tzu, roughly contemporary as they are, offer a philosophy of order, a way of dealing with a disunified country; stability through the proper performance of social duties, or stability through intimidation.
—Susan Wise Bauer, *The History of the Ancient World*

Ellipses show where something has been cut out of a sentence.

élleipsis Greek for "omission"
ellipsis (singular), ellipses (plural)

The Roman historian Varro mentions an early division of Rome's people into three "tribes" of some kind.

The attackers were thoroughly thrashed, since the army of debtors that came

charging out to meet them was, as Livy puts it, "spoiling for a fight."

The present participle of a verb can act as a descriptive adjective.

The city needed laws "which every individual citizen could feel that he had . . .

consented to accept."

Every direct quote must have an attribution tag.

A second or third quote from the same source does not need another attribution tag, as long as context makes the source of the quote clear.

A clause is a group of words that contains a subject and a predicate.
A dependent clause is a fragment that cannot stand by itself as a sentence.
Dependent clauses begin with subordinating words.
Dependent clauses are also known as subordinate clauses.

Adjective clauses are also known as relative clauses because they relate to another word in the independent clause.
Relative pronouns introduce adjective clauses and refer back to an antecedent in the independent clause.
A noun clause takes the place of a noun.

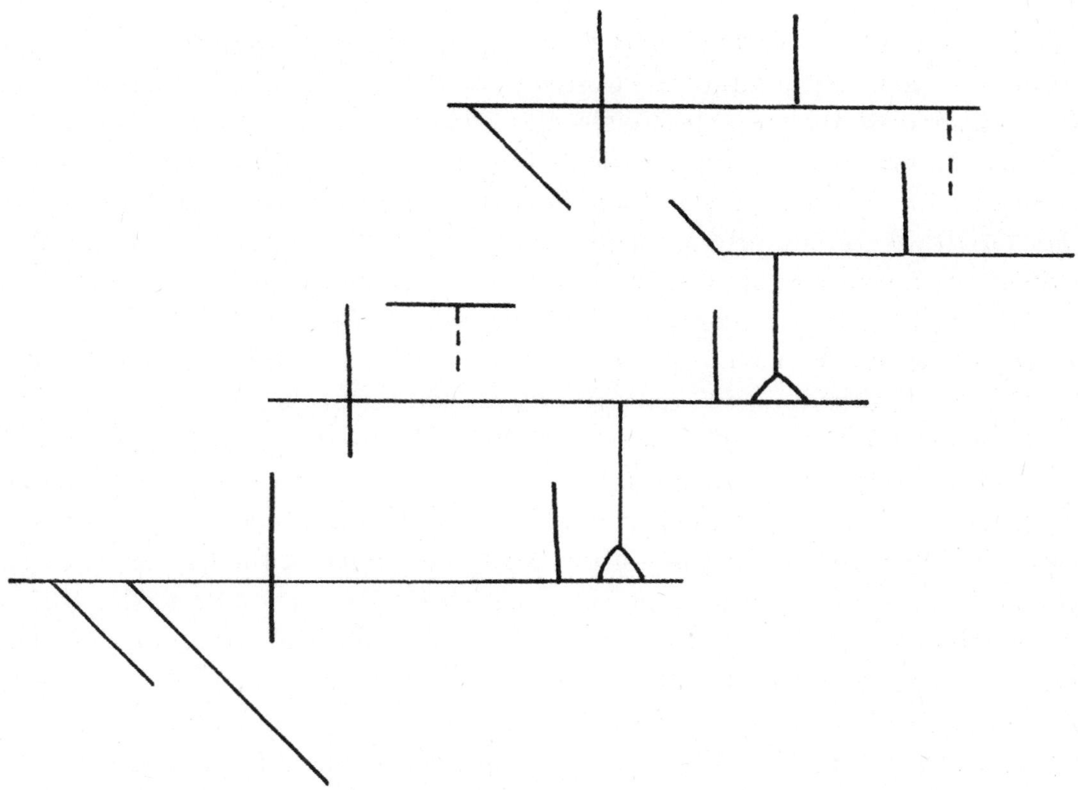

The city of Veii, Livy writes, had "inflicted worse losses than she suffered," which means that the siege had significantly weakened the Roman army.

Such was the fall of Veii, the wealthiest city of Etruria. Even her final destruction witnessed to her greatness, for after a siege of ten summers and ten winters, during which she inflicted worse losses than she suffered, even when her destined hour had come she fell by a stratagem and not by direct assault.

—Livy, *The Early History of Rome*

> He had heard, "in the silence of the night," an inhuman voice saying, "Tell the magistrates that the Gauls are coming."

Direct quotes can be words, phrases, clauses, or sentences, as long as they are set off by quotation marks and form part of a grammatically correct original sentence.

Exercise 91A: Using Ellipses

The following two paragraphs are taken from John Fiske's *The American Revolution*. This excerpt is 398 words long. On your own paper, rewrite it so that it has no more than 200 words. Use ellipses wherever you omit words. Do not cut the opening or closing words of any paragraph. Make sure that you don't end up with run-on sentences or fragments!

When you are finished, compare your version with the condensed version found in the key.

During the dreary winter at Valley Forge, Washington busied himself in improving the organization of his army. The fall of the Conway cabal removed many obstacles. Greene was persuaded, somewhat against his wishes, to serve as quartermaster-general, and forthwith the duties of that important office were discharged with zeal and promptness. Conway's resignation opened the way for a most auspicious change in the inspectorship of the army. Of all the foreign officers who served under Washington during the War for Independence, the Baron von Steuben was in many respects the most important. Member of a noble family which for five centuries had been distinguished in the local annals of Magdeburg, Steuben was one of the best educated and most experienced soldiers of Germany. His grandfather, an able theologian, was well known as the author of a critical treatise on the New Testament. His uncle, an eminent mathematician, had been the inventor of a new system of fortification. His father had seen half a century of honourable service in the corps of engineers. He had himself held the rank of first lieutenant at the beginning of the Seven Years' War, and after excellent service in the battles of Prague, Rossbach, and Kunersdorf he was raised to a position on the staff of Frederick the Great. At the end of the war, when the thrifty king reduced his army, and Blücher with other officers afterward famous left the service, Steuben retired to private life, with the honorary rank of General of the Circle of Swabia. For more than ten years he was grand marshal to the Prince of Hohenzollern-Hechingen. Then he went travelling about Europe, until in the spring of 1777 he arrived in Paris, and became acquainted with Franklin and Beaumarchais.

The American alliance was already secretly contemplated by the French ministry, and the astute Vergennes, knowing that the chief defect of our armies lay in their want of organization and discipline, saw in the scientific German soldier an efficient instrument for remedying the evil. After much hesitation Steuben was persuaded to undertake the task. That his arrival upon the scene might excite no heart-burning among the American officers, the honorary rank which he held in Germany was translated by Vergennes into the rank of lieutenant-general, which the Americans would at once recognize as more eminent than any position existing in their own army except that of the commander-in-chief.

Exercise 91B: Partial Quotations

On your own paper, rewrite the five statements below so that each one contains a partial quotation. Draw the partial quotation from the bolded sentences that follow each statement. The authors of the bolded sentences are provided for you—be sure to include an attribution tag for each direct quote!

You may change and adapt the statements freely.

One of your sentences should contain a very short one- to three-word quote; one should contain a preposition phrase, gerund phrase, participle phrase, or infinitive phrase; and one should quote a dependent clause.

If you need help, ask your instructor to show you sample answers.

Saint-Exupéry wrote the novella The Little Prince.

"As lost as Saint-Exupéry was, some of the best drawing rooms of Paris were open to him. His existence became a chaotic one of lavish dinners and low rents, skimpy meals and sumptuous lodgings, a habit to which he ultimately became accustomed. We have no record of how he dressed during these times, but he was neither the world's first nor last impoverished aristocrat, and was eccentric enough to have been allowed some latitude."

—Stacy Schiff, biographer

During the Middle Ages, women were not encouraged to form friendships with others outside their families.

"In his book of instruction the wealthy merchant of Paris . . . advised his bride against such ties. In fact, he demanded that she walk through town, on those rare occasions when she went out at all, without stopping to speak to any man or woman on the road. This would presumably keep her from harm while protecting his reputation."

—Marty Williams and Anne Echols, historians

Susan B. Anthony met with resistance from some women in her work for women's rights.

"Susan went from door to door during the cold blustery days of December and January 1854 to get signatures on her petitions for married women's property rights and woman suffrage. Some of the women signed, but more of them slammed the door in her face, declaring indignantly that they had all the rights they wanted."

—Alma Lutz, biographer

All animals brought to a wildlife clinic are in danger of death.

"When animals arrive at the KSTR wildlife clinic, they are all essentially dying—some more quickly than others. That means our job is to reverse the path to death and heal them so they can make it back to where they belong—in the jungle. The only reason a person is ever able to physically pick up a wild animal is because it is injured, orphaned, or in shock and can't run away and save itself."

—Sam Trull, conservationist

Paper mills in the eighteenth century were not large enterprises.

"Hundreds of paper mills were established in North America in the eighteenth century. Most were small operations, using only one vat. Sometimes paper was made in mills that also ground grain or that were used as sawmills. Papermaking was done during only part of the year, in accordance with agricultural needs and the demands of boat traffic and competition with other mills for use of the river."

—Mark Kurlansky, author

Exercise 91C: Diagramming

On your own paper, diagram every word of the following sentences. These are from *Glacier*, by Ronald H. Bailey.

These are difficult! Do your best, and then compare your answers with the key.

Meticulous ground surveys—ever more numerous and accurate with the passing of time—proved to be the key to understanding the complex processes of glacier movement.

A transverse crevasse—across the direction of the ice's flow—occurs where there is a sudden change in the slope of the underlying bedrock and the glacier speeds up on the steeper slope.

The problem is complicated by the fact that the bergs posing the gravest threat—the pinnacled, unstable ones—are also the most elusive.

An expedition member called him "the strongest combination of a strong mind in a strong body that I have ever known."

— LESSON 92 —

Partial Quotations
Ellipses
Block Quotes
Colons
Brackets

If a direct quotation is longer than three lines, indent the entire quote one inch from the margin in a separate block of text and omit quotation marks.

If you change or make additions to a direct quotation, use brackets.

> And I doubt not but posterity will find many things, that are now but Rumors, verified into practical Realities. It may be some ages hence, a voyage to the Southern unknown Tracts, yea possibly the Moon, will not be more strange than one to America. To them, that come after us, it may be as ordinary to buy a pair of wings to fly into remotest Regions; as now a pair of Boots to

ride a Journey. And to confer at the distance of the Indies by Sympathetick conveyances, may be as usual to future times, as to us in a litterary correspondence. The restauration of gray hairs to Juvenility, and renewing the exhausted marrow, may at length be effected without a miracle: And the turning of the now comparative desert world into a Paradise, may not improbably be expected from late Agriculture.

Now those, that judge by the narrowness of former Principles, will smile at these Paradoxical expectations: But questionless those great Inventions, that have in these later Ages altered the face of all things; in their naked proposals, and meer suppositions, were to former times as *ridiculous.* To have talk'd of a *new Earth* to have been discovered, had been a Romance to Antiquity. And to sayl without sight of Stars or shoars by the guidance of a Mineral, a story more absurd, than the flight of Daedalus.

—Joseph Glanvill, *Scepsis Scientifica: Or, Confest Ignorance, The Way to Science; In an Essay of the Vanity of Dogmatizing and Confident Opinion*

In 1661, the English philosopher Joseph Glanvill predicted the invention of "many things, that are now but Rumors." Among them were space travel, airplanes, and conversation over long distances. In his essay *Scepsis Scientifica,* Glanvill admits that these inventions seem farfetched, but he argues that the discovery of a new continent must have seemed just as unlikely:

> It may be some ages hence, a voyage to the Southern unknown Tracts, yea possibly the Moon, will not be more strange than one to America. To them, that come after us, it may be as ordinary to buy a pair of wings to fly into remotest Regions; as now a pair of Boots to ride a Journey. And to confer at the distance of the Indies by Sympathetick conveyances, may be as usual to future times, as to us in a litterary correspondence . . . [T]hose great Inventions, that have in these later Ages altered the face of all things . . . were to former times as *ridiculous.* To have talk'd of a *new Earth* [the North and South American continents] to have been discovered, had been a Romance [Glanvill means a "fairy tale"] to Antiquity.

Glanvill goes on to point out that navigating a ship by compass ("the guidance of a Mineral," as he puts it) instead of by the stars must have seemed just as impossible to ancient sailors as moon travel does to people of his own day.

When using a word processing program, leave an additional line space before and after a block quote.

Block quotes should be introduced by a colon (if preceded by a complete sentence) or a comma (if preceded by a partial sentence).

As the English philosopher Joseph Glanvill predicted in 1661,

> It may be some ages hence, a voyage to the Southern unknown Tracts, yea possibly the Moon, will not be more strange than one to America. To them, that come after us, it may be as ordinary to buy a pair of wings to fly into remotest Regions; as now a pair of Boots to ride a Journey.

If you change or make additions to a direct quotation, use brackets.

Exercise 92A:Writing Dialogue Correctly

The following speeches, from *Matilda* by Roald Dahl, are listed in the correct order, but are missing the dialogue tags. On your own paper, rewrite the speeches as dialogue, making use of the dialogue tags below. You must place at least one dialogue tag before a speech, one in the middle of a speech, and one following a speech.

A list of the rules governing dialogue follows, for your reference.

When you are finished, compare your dialogue to the original passage in the Key.

A. DIALOGUE (IN CORRECT ORDER)

Can you really turn the mileage back with an electric drill?

I'm telling you trade secrets. So don't you go talking about this to anyone else. You don't want me put in jug, do you?

I won't tell a soul. Do you do this to many cars, dad?

Every single car that comes through my hands gets the treatment. They all have their mileage cut to under ten thou before they're offered for sale.

And to think I invented that all by myself. It's made me a mint.

But daddy, that's even more dishonest than the sawdust. It's disgusting. You're cheating people who trust you.

If you don't like it then don't eat the food in this house. It's bought with the profits.

It's dirty money. I hate it.

B. DIALOGUE TAGS (NOT IN CORRECT ORDER)

Matilda said
Matilda, who had been listening closely, said
young Michael asked
the boy said
the father said

the father said
he added proudly
the father said

C. FOR REFERENCE: RULES FOR WRITING DIALOGUE

A dialogue tag identifies the person making the speech.

When a dialogue tag comes after a speech, place a comma, exclamation point, or question mark inside the closing quotation marks.

When a dialogue tag comes before a speech, place a comma after the tag. Put the dialogue's final punctuation mark inside the closing quotation marks.

Speeches do not need to be attached to a dialogue tag as long as the text clearly indicates the speaker.

Usually, a new paragraph begins with each new speaker.

When a dialogue tag comes in the middle of a speech, follow it with a comma if the following dialogue is an incomplete sentence. Follow it with a period if the following dialogue is a complete sentence.

Exercise 92B: Using Direct Quotations Correctly

On your own paper, rewrite the following three paragraphs, inserting at least one quote from each of the following three sources into the paragraph. Use the following guidelines:

- At least one quote must be a block quote.
- At least one quote must be a complete sentence.
- At least one quote must be a partial sentence incorporated into your own sentence.

In addition:

- Each quote must have an attribution tag.
- At least one quote must be condensed, using an ellipsis.
- You must make at least one change or addition that needs to be put in brackets.

A list of the rules governing direct quotations follows, for your reference.

When you are finished, compare your paragraphs to the sample answer in the Key.

A. PARAGRAPHS

The year 1860 saw national tensions grow even stronger, culminating with the secession of South Carolina in December. The pivotal point in the year was in early November, when the ballots were cast and Abraham Lincoln was selected as the country's next president. At the start of the year, however, Lincoln's selection as the Republican party's candidate was not at all certain.

Lincoln had been working for quite some time to lay the groundwork for his candidacy before the Republican nominating convention in May. He took every opportunity to make appearances and speeches around the nation in order to build his reputation. In line with the Republican party's position, he worked to stop slavery from expanding, but not to abolish it altogether.

At the start of the nominating convention, Republicans knew that their candidate was likely to win the election, particularly since the Democratic party had just split into different factions. The frontrunner for the Republican nomination was William H. Seward, but Seward proved to have some opinions that the Republicans worried might cause division among the electorate. Between Seward's perceived weaknesses and some deals made on Lincoln's behalf by those representing him at the convention, the delegates ultimately selected Lincoln as their candidate, leading to his election in November as President of the United States.

B. SOURCES

> **Note:** Two of the selections below include words that are themselves quoted from elsewhere. Because each full selection is in quotation marks, the smaller quotations are enclosed in single quotation marks. If you choose to use a block quote that includes a smaller quotation, you should change the single quotation marks back to double, since the block quote is not enclosed in quotation marks.

"On the first ballot, Lincoln had little more than half Seward's numbers but more than anyone else. On the second he was only a few short of Seward. After the third, the country discovered that the three-term state legislator and one-term moderate antislavery congressman, who had held no other office, who had no executive experience, who was resented for his opposition to the Mexican War, and whom many considered a clumsy Western primitive without formal education or drawing-room manners, was almost certain to be elected president."

—Fred Kaplan, biographer

"Certainly Lincoln occupied a surprisingly strong position as 1860 unfolded. His stature as a politician was noticeable, but not so noticeable as to appear threatening to Seward and the other front-runners. His 1858 Senate race and the Cooper Union speech had put him on the national stage—just. He had the support of those who knew him well—Illinois Republicans were solid for him—and competitors who did not yet know him well did not pay enough attention to him. He had devoted his energies to slavery expansion, the issue that defined his party—the 'question about which all true men do care,' he had called it at Cooper Union—without blotting his record with inconvenient positions on other issues."

—Richard Brookhiser, historian

"For many Republicans, Seward was entitled to the nomination by virtue of his clear, consistent, forceful argument against the extension of slavery. Almost every American knew that Seward believed that a 'higher law' dedicated the territories to freedom. But others opposed him for precisely this reason; they believed he was a radical who could not win moderate or conservative votes."

—Walter Stahr, author

C. FOR REFERENCE: RULES FOR USING DIRECT QUOTATIONS

When an attribution tag comes after a direct quote, place a comma, exclamation point, or question mark inside the closing quotation marks.

When an attribution tag comes before a direct quote, place a comma after the tag. Put the dialogue's final punctuation mark inside the closing quotation marks.

When an attribution tag comes in the middle of a direct quotation, follow it with a comma if the remaining quote is an incomplete sentence. Follow it with a period if the remaining quote is a complete sentence.

Direct quotes can be words, phrases, clauses, or sentences, as long as they are set off by quotation marks and form part of a grammatically correct original sentence.

An ellipsis shows where something has been cut out of a sentence.

Every direct quote must have an attribution tag.

If a direct quotation is longer than three lines, indent the entire quote one inch from the margin in a separate block of text and omit quotation marks.

If you change or make additions to a direct quotation, use brackets.

WEEK 24

Floating Elements

— LESSON 93 —

Interjections
Nouns of Direct Address
Parenthetical Expressions

Oh dear, I've dropped my keys.
Oops! The keys fell through the grate into the sewer.
Alas, I will not be able to unlock my door.
Whew! That was a close one.
Whoa, let's just slow down here for a minute.
Hush, I'm on the phone.

inter between
jacere to throw

Interjections express sudden feeling or emotion. They are set off with commas or stand alone with a closing punctuation mark.

Friends, Romans, countrymen, lend me your ears!
Stars, hide your fire!
I am afraid, my dear, that you are too late.
Run, baby, run.
Get down, dog!

Nouns of direct address name a person or thing who is being spoken to. They are set off with commas. They are capitalized only if they are proper names or titles.

Parentheses ( ) can enclose words that are not essential to the sentence.
Parenthetical expressions often interrupt or are irrelevant to the rest of the sentence.
Punctuation goes inside the parentheses if it applies to the parenthetical material; all other punctuation goes outside the parentheses.
Parenthetical material only begins with a capital letter if it is a complete sentence with ending punctuation.
Parenthetical expressions can also be set off by commas.

The doctor was so late, in fact, that the baby was born before he arrived.

To be sure, she will tell a very plausible story.

When Marco Polo travelled to China he crossed, as it were, the horizon of European knowledge.

Fear was, no doubt, the greatest enemy the army had.

In a word, he supported the other candidate.

These things are always difficult, you know.

Short parenthetical expressions such as the following are usually set off by commas: *in short, in fact, in reality, as it were, as it happens, no doubt, in a word, to be sure, to be brief, after all, you know, of course.*

Whew! That was a close one.

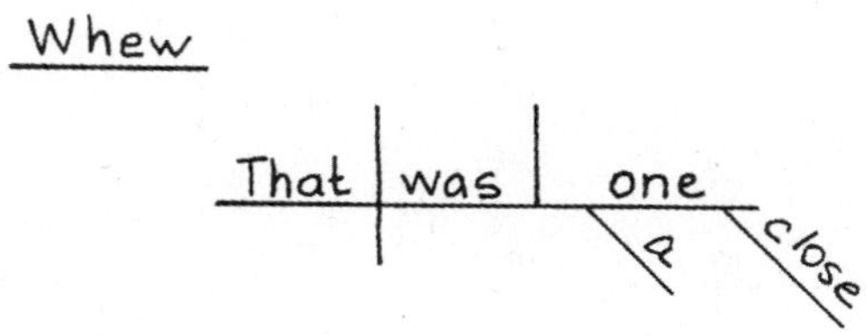

Friends, Romans, countrymen, lend me your ears!

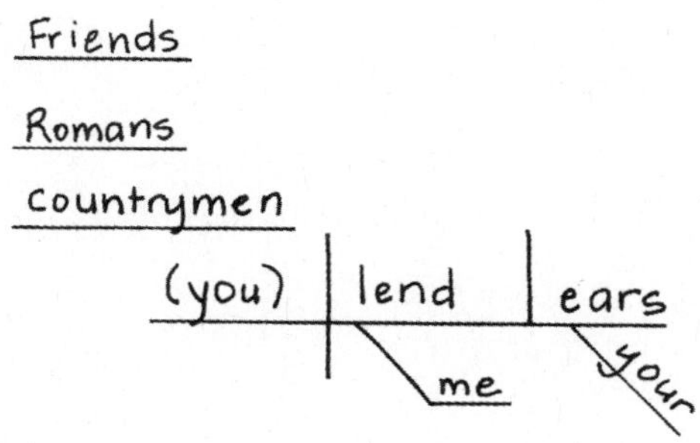

In a word, he supported the other candidate.

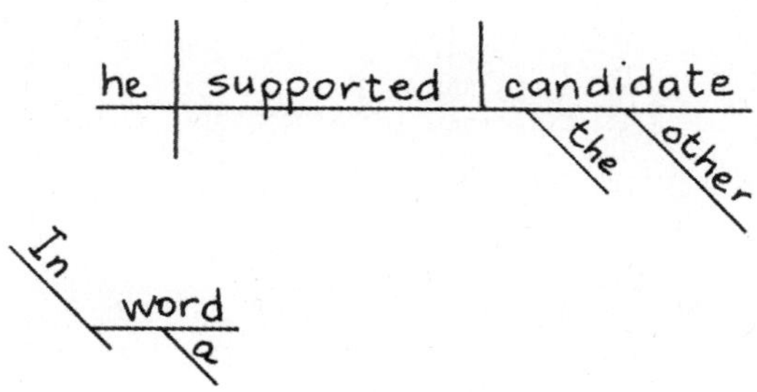

The following sentences are taken from *The Scarlet Pimpernel* by Baroness Emmuska Orczy.

Your heroism, your devotion, which I, alas, so little deserved, have atoned for that unfortunate episode of the ball.

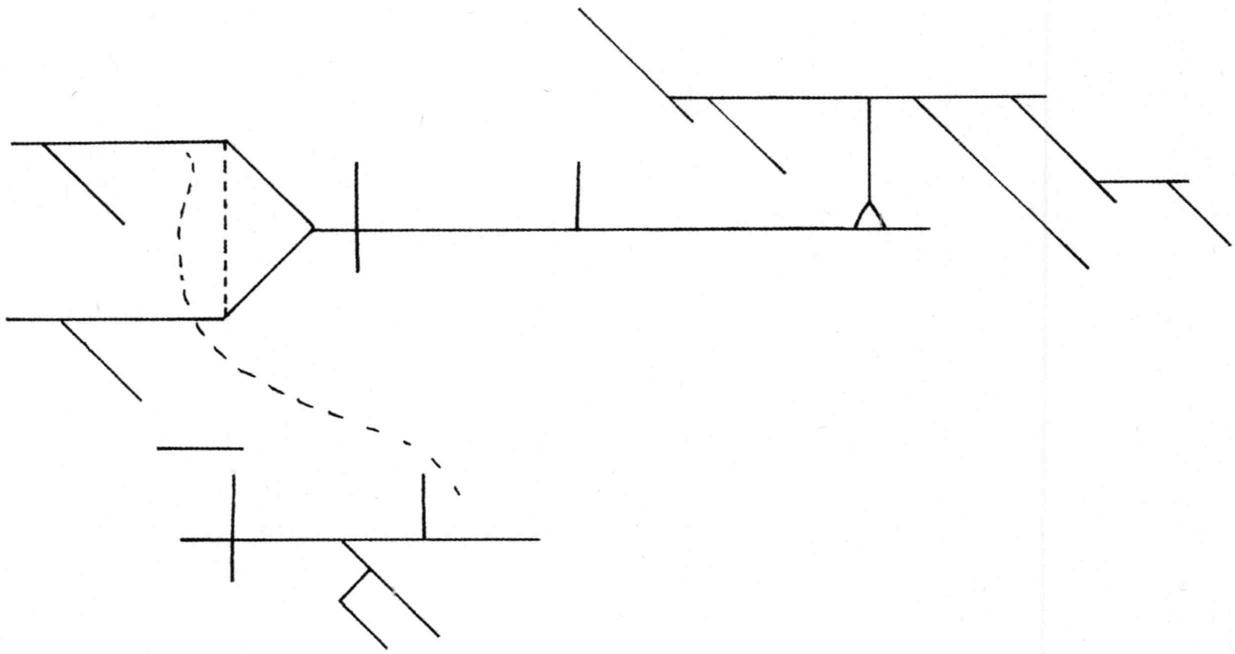

Do you impugn my bravery, Madame?

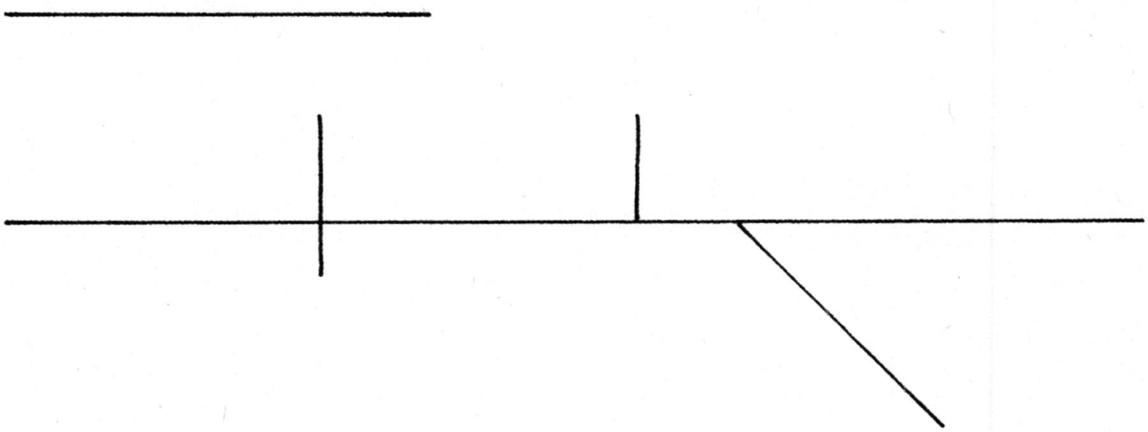

This restriction, of course, did not apply to her, and Frank would, of course, not dare to oppose her.

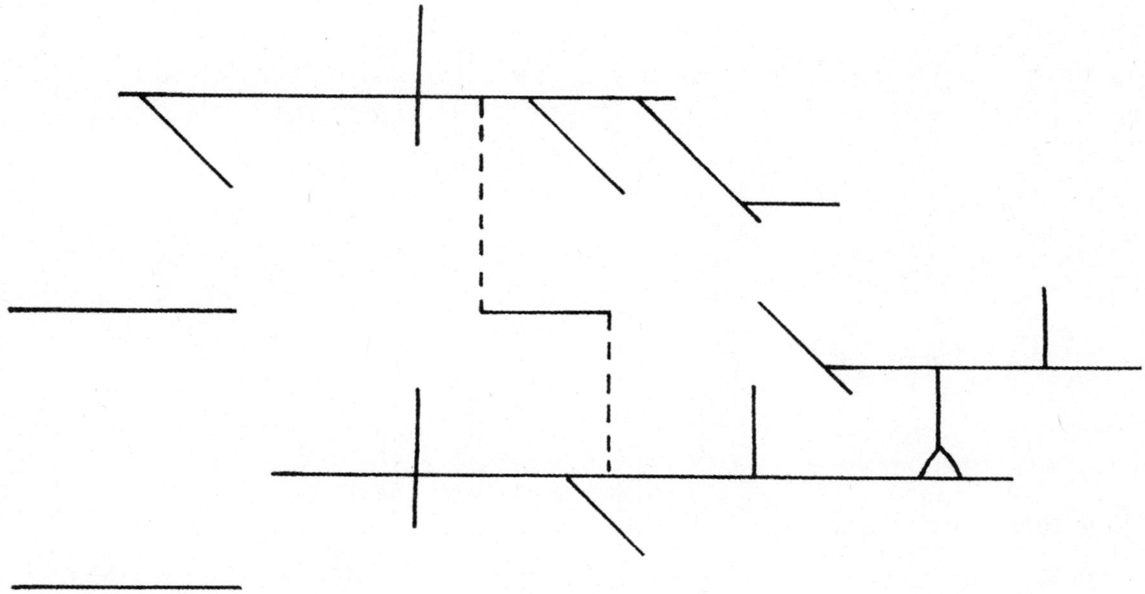

The storm will, no doubt, snarl the traffic.

There is no doubt that the storm is coming.

We aren't ready yet, you know.

You know that we aren't ready yet.

The snow caused school to be cancelled, of course.

In case of snow, school is cancelled as a matter of course.

Exercise 93A: Using Floating Elements Correctly

On your own paper, rewrite the following sentences in List 1, inserting interjections, nouns of direct address, and parenthetical expressions from List 2. You must use every item in List 2 at least once. Every sentence in List 1 must have at least one insertion.

Interjections may either come before or after sentences on their own, or may be incorporated directly into the sentence.

List 1. Sentences

The pig got dirty.
This little girl was found walking along the street with a balloon in her hand.
The fundraiser will happen on Saturday.
Please eat these leftovers for lunch tomorrow.
We're going to the zoo today!
You are in favor of the proposed amendment.

We'll finish this project on time.

List 2. Interjections, Nouns of Direct Address, Parenthetical Expressions

no doubt
of course
Mr. Smith
in fact
come what may
everyone
hooray
Robert
rain or shine
Katherine
dear

Exercise 93B: Parenthetical Expressions

In the following pairs of sentences, underline each subject once and each predicate twice. In each pair, cross out the parenthetical expression that is not essential to the sentences. If the expression is used as an essential part of the sentence, circle it and label it with the correct part of the sentence. If it acts as a modifier, draw an arrow back to the word it modifies.

The train, in reality, is hardly ever on time.

The train was present in reality, not just in my imagination.

This isn't my first time speaking in front of an audience, you know.

You know this isn't my first time speaking in front of an audience.

After all we've done, we deserve a break.

After all, tomorrow is another day!

I believe, in short, that our candidate will win this election.

The votes will be counted in short order.

We promise to be brief in our explanation.

To be brief, we need to borrow your car.

Exercise 93C: Diagramming

On your own paper, diagram every word of the following sentences. They come from Rudyard Kipling's *The Jungle Book*.

Rann had never seen Mowgli before, though of course he had heard of him.

Because he had been appointed a servant of the village, as it were, he went off to a circle that met on a masonry platform under a great fig-tree.

Hm, tide's running strong tonight.

Well, if I am a man, a man I must become.

Mowgli, hast thou anything to say?

— LESSON 94 —

Appositives

Rome, the Eternal City, is built on seven hills that lie on both sides of the Tiber River.

Dubrovnik, the Pearl of the Adriatic, is a walled seaside fortress in Croatia.

Helsinki, the White City of the North, gets no sunshine at all for about fifty days every winter.

In Mumbai, the City of Dreams, almost seven million people ride the trains every day.

Chinese tin miners founded the Malaysian city Kuala Lumpur, the Golden Triangle, in 1857.

The people of Sydney, the Harbour City, celebrate Harbour Day, a commemoration of the first convict ships landing in Sydney Cove, on January 26.

An appositive is a noun, pronoun, or noun phrase that usually follows another noun and renames or explains it.

Rome's first ruler, Romulus, killed his brother and seized power.
In the Middle Ages, many Spanish Jews, *Conversos*, migrated to Dubrovnik.
A 1981 movie about the USSR, *Reds,* was actually filmed in Helsinki.

Rome is built on seven hills that lie on both sides of the Tiber River.
Dubrovnik is a walled seaside fortress in Croatia.
Helsinki gets no sunshine at all for about fifty days every winter.

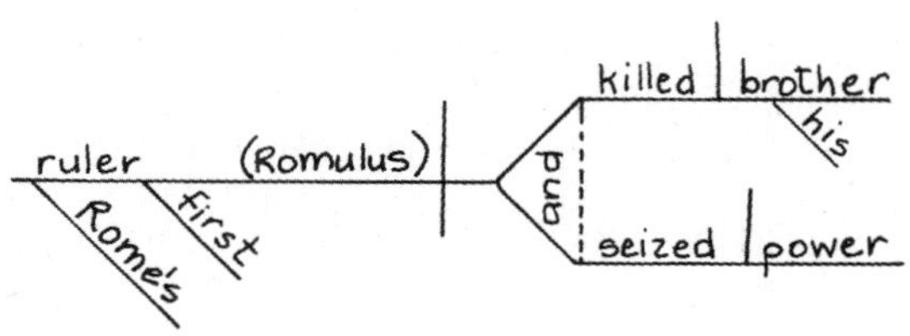

In Mumbai, the City of Dreams, almost seven million people ride the trains every day.

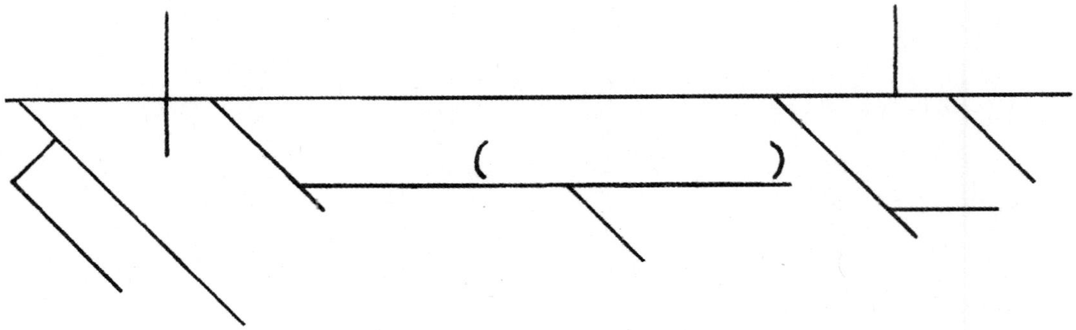

Chinese tin miners founded the Malaysian city Kuala Lumpur, the Golden Triangle, in 1857.

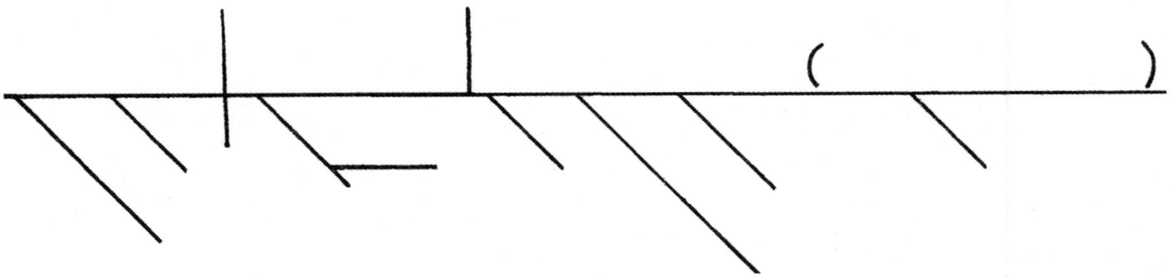

An appositive is a noun, pronoun, or noun phrase that usually follows another noun and renames or explains it.

The wisest philosopher of the ancients, Socrates wrote nothing.

A better-known destination, Marseilles is less picturesque than the surrounding villages.

An ancient breed, the Kuvasz protects helpless livestock.

Appositives are set off by commas.

The wisest philosopher of the ancients, Socrates, wrote nothing.

A better-known destination, Marseilles, is less picturesque than the surrounding villages.

An ancient breed, the Kuvasz, protects helpless livestock.

An appositive that occurs within a sentence has commas both before and after it. An appositive at the beginning of a sentence has one comma that follows it. An appositive at the end of a sentence has one comma that precedes it.

My grandfather, Aquilino Ramos, makes the best pork adobo I've ever eaten.

The best supper ever, pineapple chicken adobo waited for us on the table.

My grandfather prepared a fantastic meal, squid adobo with tomatoes.

An appositive is a noun, pronoun, or noun phrase that usually follows another noun and renames or explains it. Appositives are set off by commas.

Exercise 94A: Using Appositives

On your own paper, rewrite each group of sentences below as a single sentence using one or more appositives.

The moon takes a little over 27 days to orbit the earth.
The moon is Earth's natural satellite.

Franklin Delano Roosevelt served as the governor of New York before becoming president.
Franklin Delano Roosevelt was the thirty-second president of the United States.
New York is nicknamed the Empire State.

Labor Day has been observed nationally in the United States since 1894.
Labor Day is the first Monday in September.

The eardrum allows sound to pass through to the ossicles.
The eardrum is the tympanic membrane.
Ossicles are bones in the middle ear.

Other than February 29, the days in the year when the smallest number of people have birthdays are December 25 and January 1.
December 25 is Christmas.
January 1 is New Year's Day.

Star Wars: Episode IV—A New Hope was released in US theaters in 1977.
Star Wars: Episode IV—A New Hope was the first movie in the original *Star Wars* trilogy.

Exercise 94B: Identifying Appositives

In each of the following sentences, underline the subject once and the predicate twice. You do not need to mark subjects and predicates in dependent clauses, but watch for compound sentences! Circle each appositive or appositive phrase. Draw an arrow from each circled word or phrase back to the noun or pronoun it renames.

These sentences are slightly condensed from Rudyard Kipling's *The Jungle Book*.

It is I, Shere Khan, who speak!

And it is I, Raksha, who answer.

Akela, the great gray Lone Wolf, who led all the Pack by strength and cunning, lay out at full length on his rock.

It was Bagheera, the black Panther, inky black all over, but with the panther markings showing up in certain lights like the pattern of watered silk.

Perhaps Ikki, the Porcupine, had told him.

I am sleepy, Bagheera, and Shere Khan is all long tail and loud talk, like Mao, the Peacock.

He is a man—a man's child, and from the marrow of my bones I hate him!

But for the sake of the Honor of the Pack—a little matter that, by being without a leader, ye have forgotten—I promise that if ye let the man-cub go to his own place, I will not, when my time comes to die, bare one tooth against ye.

More I cannot do; but, if ye will, I can save ye the shame that comes of killing a brother against whom there is no fault—a brother bought into the Pack according to the Law of the Jungle.

I, the man, have brought here a little of the Red Flower.

Akela, the grim old wolf who had never asked for mercy in his life, gave one piteous look at Mowgli.

The boy could climb almost as well as he could swim, and swim almost as well as he could run; so Baloo, the Teacher of the Law, taught him the Wood and Water laws.

Exercise 94C: Diagramming

On your own paper, diagram every word of these sentences from Exercise 94B.

It is I, Shere Khan, who speak!

I, the man, have brought here a little of the Red Flower.

He is a man—a man's child, and from the marrow of my bones I hate him!

Akela, the grim old wolf who had never asked for mercy in his life, gave one piteous look at Mowgli.

More I cannot do; but, if ye will, I can save ye the shame that comes of killing a brother against whom there is no fault—a brother bought into the Pack according to the Law of the Jungle.

— LESSON 95 —

Appositives
Intensive and Reflexive Pronouns
Noun Clauses in Apposition
Object Complements

myself, himself, herself, itself, yourself, yourselves, ourselves, themselves

Reflexive pronouns refer back to the subject.
Intensive pronouns emphasize a noun or another pronoun.

I may have expressed myself badly.

I myself was never top in anything!

An appositive is a noun, pronoun, or noun phrase that usually follows another noun and renames or explains it. Appositives are set off by commas.

I may have expressed myself badly.

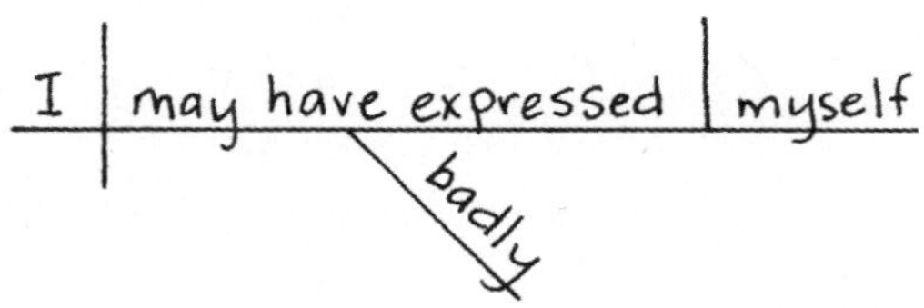

I myself was never top in anything!

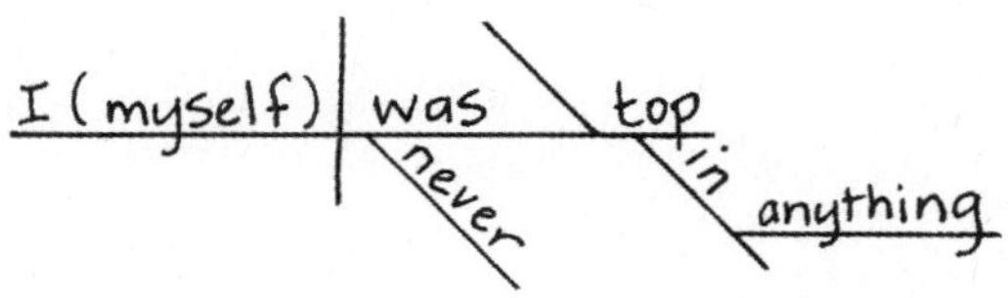

The author, Fyodor Dostoyevsky, was born in Moscow in 1821.

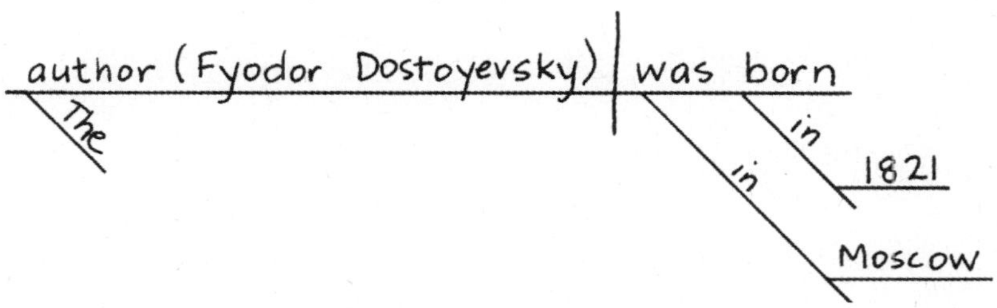

Exercise 95A: Reflexive and Intensive Pronoun Review

In the following sentences, slightly condensed from Oscar Wilde's *The Picture of Dorian Gray*, underline each reflexive or intensive pronoun. Put parentheses around each intensive pronoun. Label each reflexive pronoun with the correct part of the sentence (*DO*, *IO*, or *OP*).

Sin is a thing that writes itself across a man's face.

"Perhaps, after all, America never has been discovered," said Mr. Erskine; "I myself would say that it had merely been detected."

You know yourself, Harry, how independent I am by nature.

In front of it, some little distance away, was sitting the artist himself, Basil Hallward.

But the bravest man amongst us is afraid of himself.

She consoled herself by telling Sibyl how desolate she felt her life would be, now that she had only one child to look after.

And, certainly, to him Life itself was the first, the greatest, of the arts, and for it all the other arts seemed to be but a preparation.

Don't flatter yourself, Basil: you are not in the least like him.

You know we poor artists have to show ourselves in society from time to time, just to remind the public that we are not savages.

The praise of folly, as he went on, soared into a philosophy, and Philosophy herself became young.

I thought I would do myself the honour of coming round in person.

And what sort of lives do these people, who pose as being moral, lead themselves?

A dependent clause can act as an appositive if it renames the noun that it follows.

The article's argument, that studying grammar is good for your brain, didn't convince me.

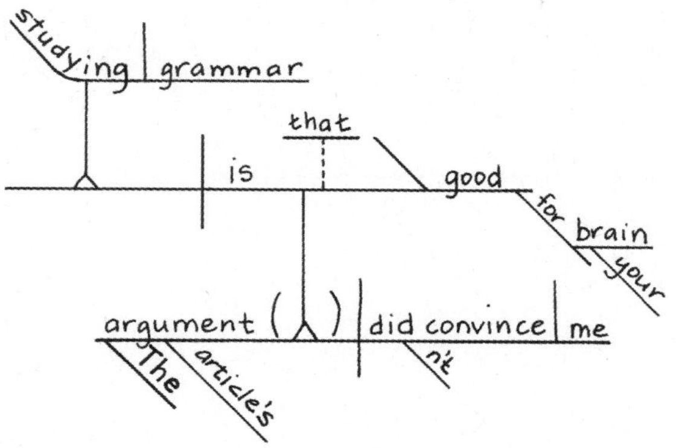

Don't forget our story, that we left early and didn't stop on the way.

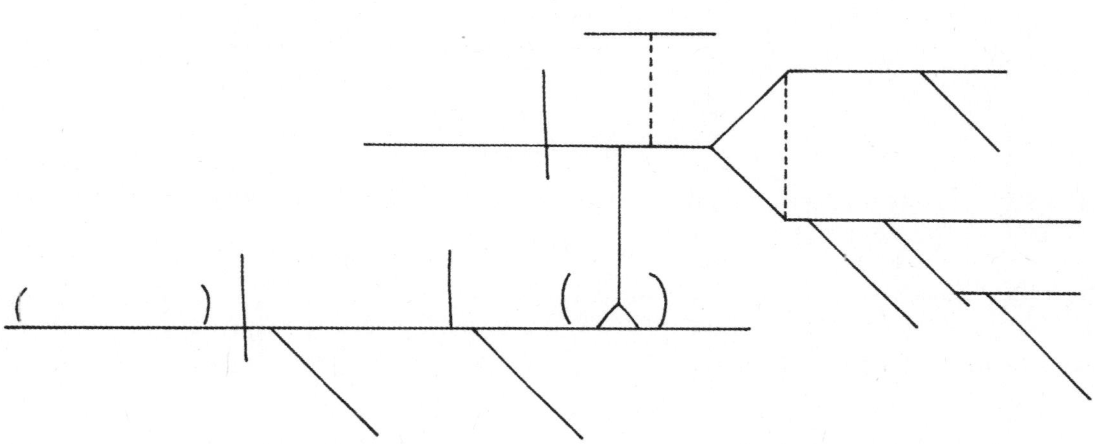

Dependent clauses can act as adjective clauses, adverb clauses, or noun clauses.

An adjective clause is a dependent clause that acts as an adjective in a sentence, modifying a noun or pronoun in the independent clause. Relative pronouns introduce adjective clauses and refer back to an antecedent in the independent clause.

A noun clause takes the place of a noun. Noun clauses can be introduced by relative pronouns, relative adverbs, or subordinating conjunctions.

Reread the story that made you happy.

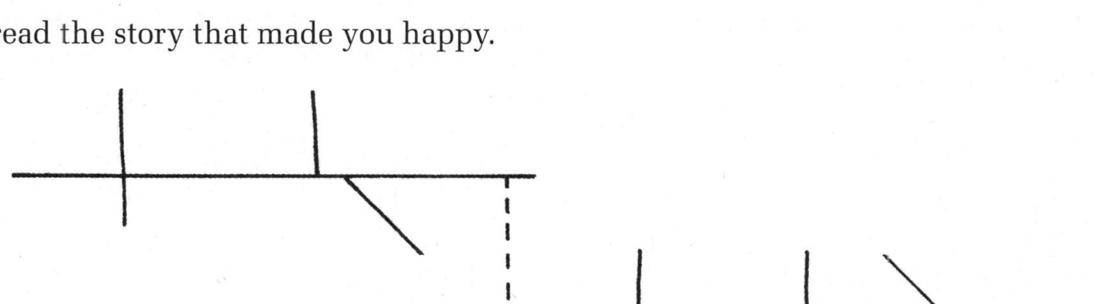

An object complement follows the direct object and renames or describes it.

The story, a long boring tale that seemed to go on forever, took up most of the evening.

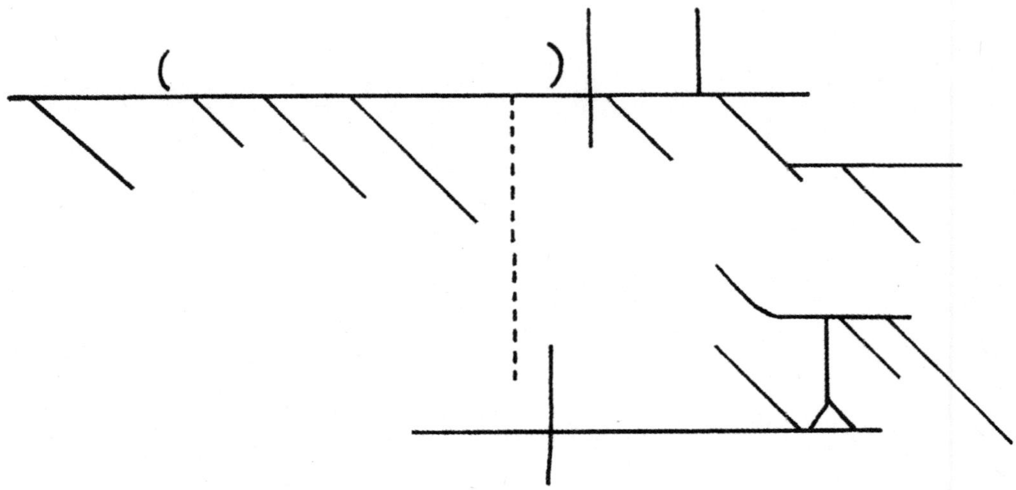

Exercise 95B: Distinguishing Noun Clauses in Apposition from Adjective Clauses

In the following sentences, identify each noun, noun phrase, or noun clause acting as an appositive by underlining it and writing the abbreviation *APP* above it. Draw an arrow from each appositive back to the noun it renames or explains. Circle each adjective clause and draw an arrow from each circle back to the noun that the adjective clause modifies.

The intricate doily, the only one of my grandmother's handmade projects that I owned, was missing.

My alibi—what I needed the detective to accept as truth—was my presence at the concert.

The problem, how they were going to escape the locked cellar, was causing a bit of panic at that moment.

Oh, no! We've forgotten Morgan's stuffed bear that he needs for bedtime!

Natalie's advice, that Soren skip the chicken at the roadside café, proved wise; three other people became ill from it.

I could never reveal the truth, that I was actually taking a pottery class.

Miss Kim gave me a suggestion, that we should ask local businesses to donate items for the auction.

Peregrine wished that he could find the book which Opal had loaned him.

Mother was much relieved by the result of the lab test, that Shelley did not have the flu.

Could you pick up the dress that is at the drycleaner?

The question, which competition I should enter, had been on my mind all week.

She stroked the cat, a purring ball of fur that had been her companion since childhood, and considered the problem that her friend had mentioned.

Jensen's, the store at the end of Main Street, sells mailboxes that come in all sorts of animal shapes.

The prince knew his beloved had but one flaw, that she was not a princess.

Exercise 95C: Diagramming

On your own paper, diagram every word of these two sentences from G. K. Chesterton's *A Short History of England*. Do your best to place each word on the diagram, but ask your instructor if you need help.

This truth, that there was something which can only vaguely be called Tory about the Yorkists, has at least one interest, that it lends a justifiable romance to the last and most remarkable figure of the fighting House of York, with whose fall the Wars of the Roses ended.

Henry of Anjou, who brought fresh French blood into the monarchy, brought also a refreshment of the idea for which the French have always stood: the idea in the Roman Law of something impersonal and omnipresent.

— LESSON 96 —

Appositives
Noun Clauses in Apposition
Absolute Constructions

I am absolutely serious, my friend.

The whole story is absolutely untrue.

There is absolutely no question as to the alibi!

He appeared to be in an absolute frenzy.

Her face and voice were absolutely cold and expressionless.

Having no near relations or friends, I was trying to make up my mind what to do, when I ran across John Cavendish. (Adjective)

Our efforts having been in vain, we had abandoned the matter. **(Absolute construction)**

Semantic: having to do with meaning

(Greek *sēmantikós*, "having meaning")

An absolute construction has a strong semantic relationship but no grammatical connection to the rest of the sentence.

To tell the truth, an idea, wild and extravagant in itself, had once or twice that morning flashed through my brain.

Dr. Bauerstein remained in the background, his grave bearded face unchanged.

He has lived by his wits, as the saying goes.

> To tell the truth, an idea, wild and extravagant in itself, had once or twice that morning flashed through my brain.

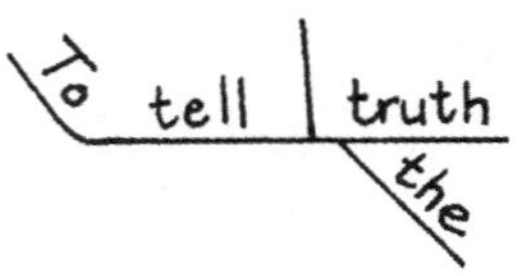

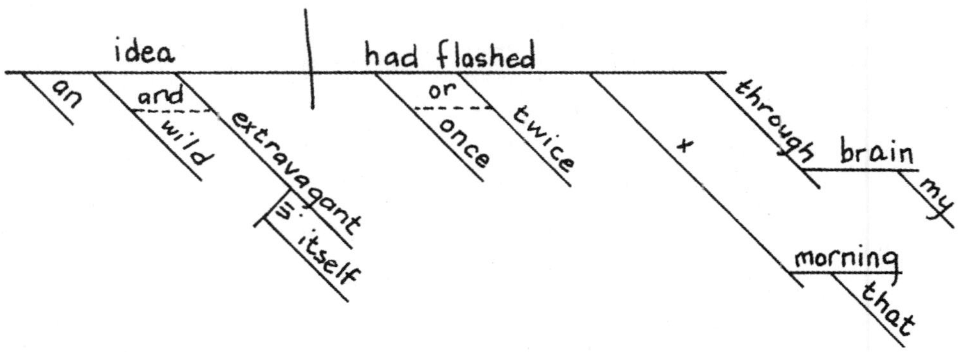

Dr. Bauerstein remained in the background, his grave bearded face unchanged.

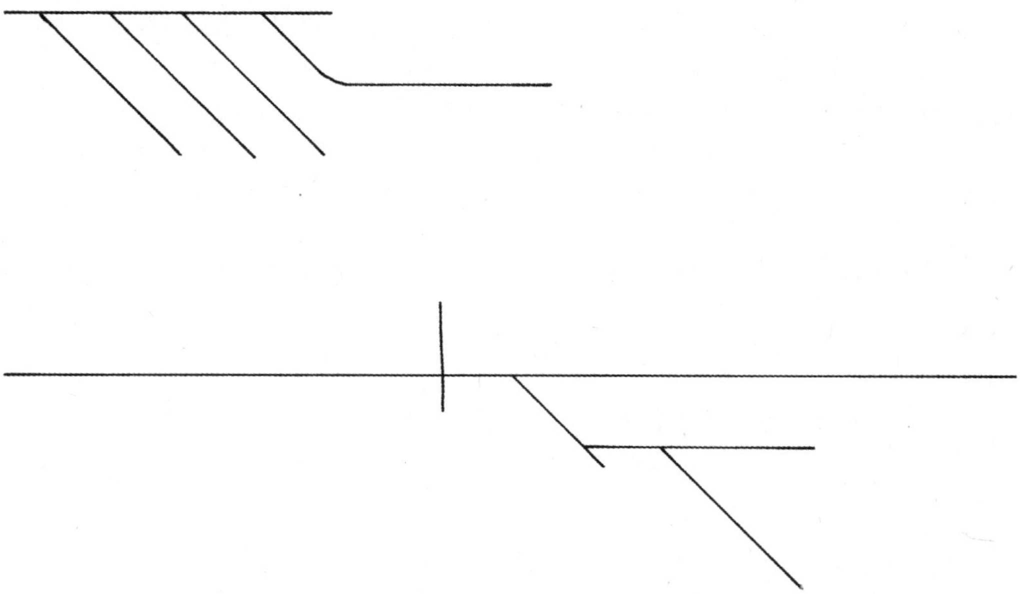

He has lived by his wits, as the saying goes.

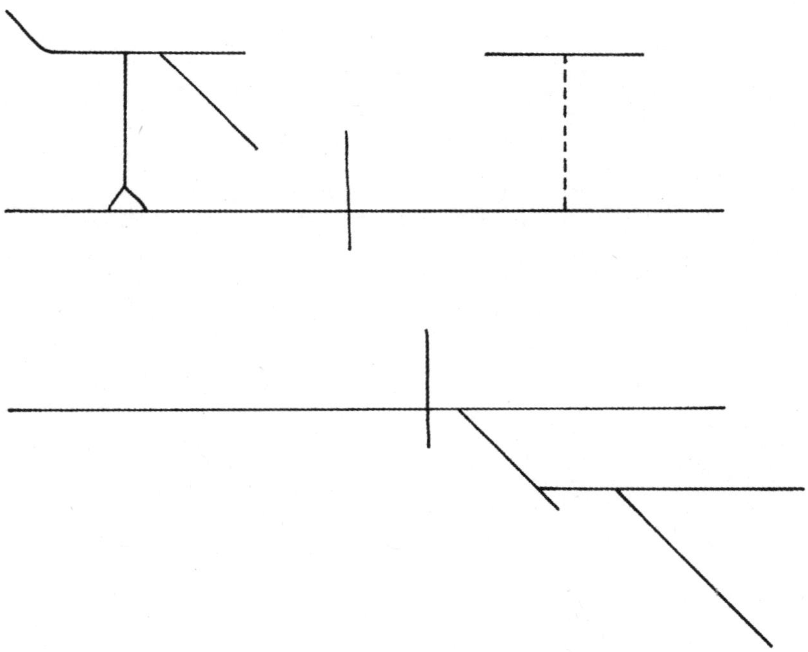

Exercise 96A: Identifying Absolute Constructions

Circle the absolute construction in each sentence. Label each absolute construction as *CL* for clause or *PHR* for phrase. For clauses, underline the subject of each clause once and the predicate twice.

The geese having safely crossed the road, we continued our drive to the hospital.

Her brow furrowed in concentration, Zoe knelt to examine the antique chair.

He left the room hurriedly, his hat and glasses askew, and ran to his car.

Tours of the facility must be rescheduled, the educational director being sick today.

Travis answered with clipped sentences, his eyes on the sidewalk.

They proceeded with the unpleasant task, Nora whistling absentmindedly and John mumbling about his plans for the weekend.

Marilyn, her heart racing as she gasped for breath, thought that perhaps she wasn't quite ready to run a marathon after all.

Its midafternoon nap complete, the cat stretched and searched for a place to begin its late-afternoon nap.

The British athletes, as we should have mentioned, arrived too late to join the competition.

Exercise 96B: Appositives, Modifiers, and Absolute Constructions

The sentences below, taken from *And Then There Were None* by Agatha Christie, each contain phrases or clauses set off by dashes. Some are appositives, some are modifiers, and some are absolute constructions. Identify them by writing *APP*, *MOD*, or *AC* above each one. For appositives and modifiers, draw an arrow back to the word being renamed or modified.

An accurate diagnosis, a couple of grateful women patients—women with money and position—and word had got about.

This island place ought to be rather good fun—if the weather lasted.

One of them must wait till the slow train from Exeter gets in—a matter of five minutes.

That bluff cheery gent—he wasn't a real gentleman.

Over it, in a gleaming chromium frame, was a big square of parchment—a poem.

On the table was a gramophone—an old-fashioned type with a large trumpet attached.

We got orders—by letter again—to prepare the rooms for a houseparty and then yesterday by the afternoon post I got another letter from Mr. Owen.

I've no doubt in my own mind that we have been invited here by a madman—probably a dangerous homicidal lunatic.

Lombard laughed—a sudden ringing laugh.

If there's a lunatic hiding on this island, he's probably got a young arsenal on him—to say nothing of a knife or dagger or two.

Murder—and I've always been such a law-abiding man!

It came again—someone moving softly, furtively, overhead.

There is plenty of food, sir—of a tinned variety.

Our main preoccupation is this—to save our lives.

We all went into the next room with the exception of Miss Brent who remained in this room—alone with the unconscious woman.

Exercise 96C: Diagramming

On your own paper, diagram every word of the following sentences, taken from G. K. Chesterton's *The Man Who Knew Too Much*.

I believe Hoggs—I mean my cousin Howard—was coming down specially to meet him.

March followed him to the bar parlor with some wonder, and his dim sense of repugnance was not dismissed by the first sight of the innkeeper, who was widely different from the genial innkeepers of romance, a bony man, very silent behind a black mustache, but with black, restless eyes.

Morton had just placed himself in front of the nearest window, his broad shoulders blocking the aperture.

— REVIEW 8 —

Weeks 22-24

Topics
Parenthetical Expressions
Dashes, Colons, and Brackets
Dialogue and Dialogue Tags
Direct Quotations and Attribution Tags
Ellipses and Partial Quotations
Block Quotes
Interjections
Nouns of Direct Address
Appositives
Noun Clauses in Apposition
Absolute Constructions

Review 8A: Definition Review

You've learned many definitions in the past three weeks! Look at each statement below and write *TRUE* or *FALSE* in the box to the right. If a statement is false, cross out and add words as necessary to make it true.

A nonrestrictive modifying clause defines the word that it modifies. Removing the clause changes the essential meaning of the sentence.	
A nonrestrictive modifying clause describes the word that it modifies. Removing the clause changes the essential meaning of the sentence.	
Only a nonrestrictive modifying clause should be set off by commas.	
Parentheses can enclose words that are not essential to the sentence.	
A parenthetical expression is always very important to the rest of the sentence.	
Punctuation goes inside the parentheses if it applies to the parenthetical expression; all other punctuation goes outside the parentheses.	

A parenthetical expression only begins with a capital letter if it is a complete sentence with ending punctuation.	
A parenthetical expression can also be set off by commas.	
Short parenthetical expressions such as the following are never set off by commas: in short, in fact, in reality, as it were, as it happens, no doubt, in a word, to be sure, to be brief, after all, you know, of course.	
Dashes can enclose words that are not essential to the sentence.	
Dashes can also be used singly to separate parts of a sentence.	
Commas cannot make a parenthetical element a part of the sentence.	
Dashes minimize a parenthetical element.	
Parentheses emphasize a parenthetical element.	
The independent clauses of a compound sentence must be joined by a comma and a coordinating conjunction, a semicolon, or a semicolon and a coordinating conjunction. They can also be joined by a comma alone.	
When a dialogue tag comes before a speech, place a comma after the tag. Put the dialogue's final punctuation mark inside the closing quotation marks.	
Speeches do not need to be attached to a dialogue tag as long as the text clearly indicates the speaker.	
Usually, a new paragraph begins with each new speaker.	

When a dialogue tag comes in the middle of a speech, follow it with a period if the following dialogue is an incomplete sentence. Follow it with a comma if the following dialogue is a complete sentence.	
When an attribution tag comes after a direct quote, place a comma, exclamation point, or question mark outside the closing quotation marks.	
When an attribution tag comes before a direct quote, place a comma after the tag. Put the dialogue's final punctuation mark inside the closing quotation marks.	
When an attribution tag comes in the middle of a direct quotation, follow it with a comma if the remaining quote is an incomplete sentence. Follow it with a period if the remaining quote is a complete sentence.	
Every direct quote must have an attribution tag.	
An ellipsis shows where something has been added to a sentence.	
A second or third quote from the same source does not need another attribution tag, as long as context makes the source of the quote clear.	
Direct quotes can be words, phrases, clauses, or sentences, as long as they are set off by commas and form part of a grammatically correct original sentence.	
If a direct quotation is longer than two lines, indent the entire quote one inch from the margin in a separate block of text and omit quotation marks.	
If you change or make additions to a direct quotation, use brackets.	
When using a word processing program, leave no additional line spaces before and after a block quote.	
Block quotes should be introduced by a semicolon (if preceded by a complete sentence) or a comma (if preceded by a partial sentence).	

Conjunctions express sudden feeling or emotion. They are set off with commas or stand alone with a closing punctuation mark.	
Nouns of direct address name a person or thing who is being spoken to. They are set off with commas. They are capitalized only if they are proper names or titles.	
An appositive is a noun or noun phrase that usually follows another noun and renames or explains it.	
A dependent clause can act as an appositive if it modifies the noun that it follows.	
An absolute construction has a strong semantic relationship but no grammatical connection to the rest of the sentence.	

Review 8B: Punctuating Restrictive and Non-Restrictive Clauses, Compound Sentences, Interjections, and Nouns of Direct Address

The sentences below contain restrictive clauses, non-restrictive clauses, interjections, and nouns of direct address. Some are compound sentences. But all of them have lost their punctuation! Insert all necessary punctuation directly into the sentences (use the actual punctuation marks rather than proofreader's marks).

These sentences are from *The Mystery of Drear House*, by Virginia Hamilton.

On weekends they often helped his father and old Pluto in the great cavern where they polished the priceless glass

Macky was a huge bear that came straight at him lumbering right over him like a grizzly over a log

They crossed the old covered bridge and the stream that was so like a moat protecting the house

Well Thomas you came back

Thomas it's a grand old house she said finally as they took her by the arms and gently helped her from the car

From within the sound of the night's blizzard that had awakened Thomas was faint

After that he would have time for lunch at home his mama would pick him up in the car

When can I meet her Pesty asked

Move on out Mr Thomas she told him

Grandmother Rhetty I'm sorry but we have to be going

Well Martha this is so sweet of you she said

Billy covered his mouth to keep in the giggle that was bubbling up inside him

He was going down the hall to the parlor room which had become his study

Well I know Grandmother Rhetty when she makes up her mind about something his papa said

Review 8C: Dialogue

In the following passage of dialogue, taken from Louisa May Alcott's *Little Women*, all of the punctuation around, before, and after the lines of dialogue is missing. Insert all necessary punctuation directly into the sentences (use the actual punctuation marks rather than proofreader's marks).

As they gathered about the table, Mrs. March said, with a particularly happy face I've got a treat for you after supper.

A quick, bright smile went round like a streak of sunshine. Beth clapped her hands, regardless of the biscuit she held, and Jo tossed up her napkin, crying A letter! a letter! Three cheers for father!

Yes, a nice long letter. He is well, and thinks he shall get through the cold season better than we feared. He sends all sorts of loving wishes for Christmas, and an especial message to you girls said Mrs. March, patting her pocket as if she had got a treasure there.

Hurry and get done! Don't stop to quirk your little finger, and simper over your plate, Amy cried Jo, choking in her tea, and dropping her bread, butter side down, on the carpet, in her haste to get at the treat.

Beth ate no more, but crept away, to sit in her shadowy corner and brood over the delight to come, till the others were ready.

I think it was so splendid in father to go as a chaplain when he was too old to be drafted, and not strong enough for a soldier said Meg warmly.

Don't I wish I could go as a drummer, a vivan—what's its name? or a nurse, so I could be near him and help him exclaimed Jo, with a groan.

It must be very disagreeable to sleep in a tent, and eat all sorts of bad-tasting things, and drink out of a tin mug sighed Amy.

When will he come home, Marmee asked Beth, with a little quiver in her voice.

Not for many months, dear, unless he is sick. He will stay and do his work faithfully as long as he can, and we won't ask for him back a minute sooner than he can be spared. Now come and hear the letter.

They all drew to the fire, mother in the big chair with Beth at her feet, Meg and Amy perched on either arm of the chair, and Jo leaning on the back, where no one would see any sign of emotion if the letter should happen to be touching.

Review 8D: Parenthetical Expressions, Appositives, Absolute Constructions

Each one of the sentences below (taken or adapted from David Lindley's *Uncertainty: Einstein, Heisenberg, Bohr, and the Struggle for the Soul of Science*) contains an element not closely connected to the rest of the sentence: parenthetical, appositive, or absolute.

- In each sentence, find and circle the unconnected element (word, phrase, or clause).
- Above it, write *PAR* for parenthetical, *APP* for appositive, or *AB* for absolute.
- In the blank at the end of the sentence, note whether the element is set apart with commas (*C*), parentheses (*P*), or dashes (*D*).

Rising early, he taught himself German (nouns and their declensions before breakfast, his diary records, conjugation of auxiliary verbs afterward) so that he could master the considerable German literature on botany, his chosen subject. ________

An admirer of Boltzmann's dense and, frankly, long-winded monographs, Einstein had become fascinated by statistical questions in physics and by the attendant controversy over the existence of atoms. ________

Physicists, it turned out, had been making X-rays for years without knowing it. ________

Some years before, working with his young colleague Hans Geiger (of Geiger counter fame), he had finally pinned down the identity of radioactive alpha emanations. ________

These two processes, in other words—the radioactive decay of a nucleus and the hopping of an electron from one orbit to another—were not only both spontaneous, but spontaneous in the same way. ________

It was now August 1914, a fateful month. ________

The mechanics of the orbits followed entirely from old physics—the electrons obeying Newtonian rules (with occasional modifications from Einstein), controlled by an inverse square law of attraction between electrons and nucleus. ________

Finishing *Gymnasium* just as the war was ending, Werner had to serve in the local militia, a ragtag collection of teenagers charged with keeping order in the strife-torn city. ________

Sommerfeld having come back from Madison in the spring of 1923, Heisenberg returned to Munich from Göttingen to finish his doctorate. ________

Review 8E: Direct Quotations

The following excerpt from *The Narnian*, a biography of C. S. Lewis by Alan Jacobs, contains two different direct quotations. Those quotations are bolded, but they are not properly punctuated. Rewrite the paragraph on your own paper, spacing and punctuating both quotations correctly.

- When you are finished, circle any places where words have been left out of the direct quotations.
- Underline any places where words have been added to the direct quotations.

Compare your paragraph with the original in the Key.

A knowledge of Lewis's miseries in school reveals that some scenes in the Narnia books are more important than they might appear. In *The Lion, the Witch, and the Wardrobe*, when Edmund is being nasty to his younger sister, Lucy, their older brother, Peter, tells him **You've always liked being beastly to anyone smaller than yourself; we've seen that at school before now.** But after Edmund has met Aslan and fought on Aslan's behalf, we have this scene **When at last [Lucy] was free to come back to Edmund she found him . . . looking better than she had seen him look—oh, for ages; in fact ever since his first term at that horrid school which was where he began to go wrong. He had become his real old self again and could look you in the face**. Edmund, then . . . is a "product of the system" as much as George Orwell was.

Review 8F: Diagramming

On your own paper, diagram every word of the following sentences from historical letters (as they appear in *Letters of a Nation*, edited by Andrew Carroll).

I have sat and watched the cornfields of Iowa darken, seen the homesteads pass by—a white house, a red barn and a brave cluster of green trees in the midst of oceans of flat fields—like an oasis in a desert.

—From a letter from Anne Morrow Lindbergh to Charles Lindbergh (1944)

The prisoners lived in rows of one-story, green wooden barracks—the men being segregated from the women.

—Joseph Fogg, describing a Nazi concentration camp in a letter to his parents (1945)

Tell Mildred I got a beautiful Dutch doll for little Emma Jones—one of those crying babies that can open and shut their eyes and turn their head.

—From a letter from Robert E. Lee to his wife, Mary (1856)

WEEK 25

Complex Verb Tenses

— LESSON 97 —

Verb Tense, Voice, and Mood
Tense Review (Indicative)
Progressive Perfect Tenses (Indicative)

Moods
- Indicative
- Subjunctive
- Imperative
- Modal

(The following sentences are from Beverly Cleary's novel *Fifteen*.)

He spoke rapidly, as if he were anxious to get the words out of the way.

Mood: ______________________

And be home by ten thirty.

Mood: ______________________

To hide her discomfort she took small bites of ice cream.

Mood: ______________________

Should they talk awhile, or should she suggest that they leave, or should she wait for him to suggest it?

Mood: ______________________

Indicative verbs express real actions.
Subjunctive verbs express unreal actions.
Imperative verbs express intended actions.
Modal verbs express possible actions.

Here everything looked brand-new, as if the furniture had been delivered only the day before.

Mood: ____________________

Voice: ____________________

Now the fat pug dog rose and shook himself, scattering his hair over the carpet.

Mood: ____________________

Voice: ____________________

Voice
In a sentence with an active verb, the subject performs the action.
In a sentence with a passive verb, the subject receives the action.

Tense
A simple verb simply tells whether an action takes place in the past, present, or future.
A progressive verb describes an ongoing or continuous action.
A perfect verb describes an action which has been completed before another action takes place.

Exercise 97A: Review of Indicative Tenses

The following partially completed chart shows the active and passive tenses of the regular verb *scold* (in the third-person singular), the irregular verb *choose* (in the third-person plural), and the irregular verb *lead* (in the first-person singular). Review your indicative tenses by completing the chart now.

		Active	Passive
SIMPLE TENSES			
	Past	he scolded they I	he they were I
	Present	he they I lead	he is they I
	Future	he they will choose I	he will be they I

		Active	Passive
PROGRESSIVE TENSES			
	Past	he they I was	he was being scolded they I
	Present	he they I am leading	he is they I
	Future	he they will be I	he they I will be being led
PERFECT TENSES			
	Past	he they had chosen I	he had been they I
	Present	he has they I	he they I have been led
	Future	he they I will have led	he they I

A progressive perfect verb describes an ongoing or continuous action that has a definite end.

progressive perfect past
I had been running for half an hour before I decided to stop.
progressive perfect present
I have been running all morning.
progressive perfect future
I will have been running for an hour by the time you arrive.

PAST

Simple	I rejoiced over my grammar!
Progressive	I was rejoicing over my grammar.
Perfect	I had rejoiced over my grammar.
Progressive Perfect	I had been rejoicing over my grammar, until I realized I had done the wrong exercises.

PRESENT

Simple	I enjoy this schoolwork!
Progressive	I am enjoying this schoolwork.
Perfect	I have enjoyed this schoolwork.
Progressive Perfect	I have been enjoying this schoolwork, but unfortunately I have to stop now and go play Minecraft.

FUTURE

Simple	I will expect to receive a prize!
Progressive	All afternoon, I will be expecting to receive a prize.
Perfect	By dinner time, I will have expected to receive my prize.
Progressive Perfect	By dinner time, I will have been expecting to receive a prize for at least four hours.

PROGRESSIVE PERFECT PAST

Active The house had been showing signs of wear.

Passive The house had been being shown to prospective buyers for months.

PROGRESSIVE PERFECT PRESENT

Active I have been sending letters out every day.

Passive I have been being sent to the post office by my mother every day.

PROGRESSIVE PERFECT FUTURE

Active Come June, the professors will have been teaching Latin for two years.

Passive Come June, the students will have been being taught Latin for two years.

PROGRESSIVE PERFECT TENSES

Past	**Active**	**Passive**
Active: helping verb had + *helping verb* been + *present participle* *Passive: helping verb* had + *helping verb phrase* been being + *past participle*	I had been amusing you had been amusing he, she, it had been amusing we had been amusing you had been amusing they had been amusing	I had been being amused you had been being amused he, she, it had been being amused we had been being amused you had been being amused they had been being amused
Present	**Active**	**Passive**
Active: helping verb have *or* has + *helping verb* been + *present participle* *Passive: helping verb* have *or* has + *helping verb phrase* been being + *past participle*	I have been amusing you have been amusing he, she, it has been amusing we have been amusing you have been amusing they have been amusing	I have been being amused you have been being amused he, she, it has been being amused we have been being amused you have been being amused they have been being amused

PROGRESSIVE PERFECT TENSES

Future	Active	Passive
Active: helping verb phrase will have been *+ present participle*	I will have been amusing you will have been amusing he, she, it will have been amusing	I will have been being amused you will have been being amused he, she, it will have been being amused
Passive: helping verb phrase will have been being *+ past participle*	we will have been amusing you will have been amusing they will have been amusing	we will have been being amused you will have been being amused they will have been being amused

Perfect Future Passive	The students will have been taught Latin very thoroughly.
Progressive Perfect Future Passive	Come June, the students will have been being taught Latin for two years.
Progressive Perfect Future Passive (Understood)	Come June, the students will have been taught Latin for two years

Exercise 97B: Parsing Verbs

In the following sentences, underline the main verb of every clause (both independent and dependent). Above each verb, write the tense and voice. (All verbs are in the indicative mood.)

You may abbreviate: *PROG, PERF, SIMP, PAST, PRES, FUT, ACT, PASS, ST-OF-BE.*

As she was cleaning the empty theater, she reflected on how well the cast had been prepared for the performance.

After seven to ten days have elapsed, the seeds will sprout.

Mr. Quinn will have been working at the library for ten years this October.

The baby has been sleeping wonderfully, but only when her parents are awake!

I have been being asked for a contribution to your organization six times a year since I moved to this city, and I am unhappy about it!

I see that the girl who was wearing your hat has returned it.

We expect that by the end of Tuesday, this amusement park will have been being enjoyed by over a million people.

The old man had whistled on his way to work every day since the factory opened.

Sam pretended that he was unfamiliar with the game, but he'd been playing it since he was four.

The scarf that I found while I was shopping with my best friend will go perfectly with the dress I've chosen for Saturday.

Exercise 97C: Completing Sentences

Complete the following sentences by providing an appropriate verb in the tense and voice indicated beneath each blank. (All verbs are in the indicative mood.)

Paula ______________________ waffles for breakfast every day for a month.
progressive perfect present, active

Since last Tuesday, I ______________________ a puppy.
progressive perfect present, active

Several of the young children ______________________ by Tristan's costume.
progressive perfect past, passive

Some of the flowers ______________________ before the family ______________.
progressive perfect past, active — simple past, active

Certain facts ______________________ from the county's reports before they ______________________ to the press.
progressive perfect past, passive — simple past, passive

Ana ______________________ that pencil for two full minutes soon!
progressive perfect future, active

In August, the game show ______________________ by the same celebrity for forty years.
progressive perfect future, passive

Your phone ____________ (progressive perfect present, active) nonstop since you ____________ (simple past, active) away from your desk.

Millions of people ____________ (progressive perfect future, active) the election results all night, while

just as many ____________ (progressive perfect future, active) them.

The singer ____________ (progressive perfect past, active) for his recital for three months.

— LESSON 98 —

Simple Present and Perfect Present Modal Verbs

Progressive Present and Progressive Perfect Present Modal Verbs

Modal verbs express situations that have not actually happened.

Should, would, may, might, must, can, could

Would, may, might, can, could: **possibility**

He was afraid that, in a little while, death ____________ meet him.

I fear that we ____________ never see him in this life again.

Oh, that I ____________ strike a blow for him before I die!

Only a knight of true valor ____________ hope to win.

Madam, how then ____________ I help you?

Must, should: **obligation**

I ____________ find a man whom I can truly love.

You ____________ do homage to King Arthur for your kingdom.

May: **permission**

____________ I go to Camelot, to see the jousting?

Can: **ability**

Nothing ____________ heal his wound on this side of the water.

Simple Present Modal (Active)

First person	I could help	we could help
Second person	you could help	you could help
Third person	he, she, it could help	they could help

Perfect Present Modal (Active)

First person	I should have helped	we should have helped
Second person	you should have helped	you should have helped
Third person	he, she, it should have helped	they should have helped

MODAL TENSES

	Simple Present	**Simple Past**	**Simple Future**
Active	I should help	none	none
Passive	I should be helped	none	none
	Progressive Present	**Progressive Past**	**Progressive Future**
Active	I could be helping	none	none
Passive	I could be being helped	none	none
	Perfect Present	**Perfect Past**	**Perfect Future**
Active	I would have helped	none	none
Passive	I would have been helped	none	none
	Progressive Perfect Present	**Prog Perfect Past**	**Prog Perfect Future**
Active	I might have been helping	none	none
Passive	I might have been being helped	none	none

Use the simple present or progressive present when the situation isn't happening in the present.

Since I slept badly last night, I might go take a nap.

mood	indicative	modal
tense	______	______
voice	______	______

People are being left in the hospital when they could be being nursed at home.

mood	indicative	______
tense	______	______
voice	______	______

Use the perfect present or the progressive perfect present when the situation didn't happen in the past.

I was eating cheese and crackers when I could have been sitting down to a big juicy steak.

mood	indicative	______
tense	progressive past	______
voice	active	______

While the floors were being scrubbed, I could have vacuumed the rugs.

mood	indicative	______
tense	progressive past	______
voice	passive	______

Modal Present: Simple or Progressive
Modal Past: Perfect or Progressive Perfect

MODAL TENSE FORMATION

Simple Present

Active	I can help	modal helping verb + first person singular
Passive	I should be helped	modal helping verb + be + past participle

Progressive Present

Active	I might be helping	modal helping verb + be + present participle
Passive	I could be being helped	modal helping verb + be + being + past participle

Perfect Present

Active	I would have helped	modal helping verb + have + past participle
Passive	I may have been helped	modal helping verb + have + been + past participle

Progressive Perfect Present

Active	I must have been helping	modal helping verb + have + been + present participle
Passive	I could have been being	modal helping verb + have + been + being + past participle

Exercise 98A: Parsing Verbs

Write the tense, mood, and voice of each underlined verb above it. The first is done for you. These sentences are from *Pippi Longstocking*, by Astrid Lindgren.

simple present, modal, active
Why, she could lift a whole horse if she wanted to!

I wonder what you would have said if I had come along walking on my hands the way they do in Farthest India.

"Now you must be lying," said Tommy.

He should have been left at home to pick fleas off the horse. That would have served him right.

No doubt they would have liked a little pie too.

His ears were so big that he could use them for a cape.

Annika sighed with relief and hoped that the meeting would last a long time.

Tommy let out a terrified shriek that could be heard all through the woods.

"Oh, Pippi, I could have died of fright," said Annika.

He said that no new food should be prepared for Peter until he had eaten a swallow's nest for Daddy.

Tommy and Annika looked around cautiously, just in case the king of the Cannibal Isles might be sitting in a corner somewhere.

"Oh, I can answer all right," said Pippi.

Exercise 98B: Forming Modal Verbs

Fill in the blanks with the missing modal verbs. Using the helping verbs indicated, put each action verb provided into the correct modal tense.

The customer ______________________________ about the small number of employees in the store today, but her ranting was so incoherent that we're not completely sure.

helping verb: may
progressive perfect present active of *complain*

I did not think his ravenous appetite ______________________________ by such a meager meal, but I was wrong.

helping verb: would
perfect present passive of *satisfy*

Our grandparents ______________________________ on tomorrow's earliest flight from Atlanta.

helping verb: should
progressive present active of *arrive*

Last year, Mrs. Hannachi ______________________________ me to get away with shoddy work, but her expectations have increased.

helping verb: would
perfect present active of *allow*

The remaining cookies ______________________________ by your brother and his friends.

helping verb: might
perfect present passive of *eat*

The birds ______________________________ to a warmer place within the next few weeks.

helping verb: should
simple present active of *migrate*

My flower ______________________________ last night while I was asleep.

helping verb: must
perfect present active of *open*

Kwame's favorite book ______________________________ on the bottom shelf.

helping verb: can
simple present passive of *find*

— LESSON 99 —

Modal Verb Tenses
The Imperative Mood
The Subjunctive Mood
More Subjunctive Tenses

Indicative verbs express real actions.
Subjunctive verbs express unreal actions.
Imperative verbs express intended actions.
Modal verbs express possible actions.

Turn to the end of your book.
Eat more vegetables!
Go away.

Be checked by a doctor before you come back to work.

The present passive imperative is formed by adding the helping verb *be* to the past participle of the verb.

Subjunctive verbs express situations that are unreal, wished for, or uncertain.

If we kept our ponies up in the winter time, we gave them fodder to eat.

We kept our ponies up in the winter time, and we gave them fodder to eat.

	Simple Present Subjunctive State-of-Being Verb		**Simple Past Subjunctive State-of-Being Verb**	
First person	I be	we be	I were	we were
Second person	you be	you be	you were	you were
Third person	he, she, it be	they be	he, she, it were	they were

Should you be in town, come by and see me.

If I were a bird, I would fly across the water.

	Simple Present Subjunctive Action Verb: Active		Simple Present Subjunctive Action Verb: Passive	
First person	I leave	we leave	I be left	we be left
Second person	you leave	you leave	you be left	you be left
Third person	he, she, it leave	they leave	he, she, it be left	they be left

He leaves early to avoid traffic.

I suggest that he leave early to avoid traffic.

The present passive subjunctive is formed by pairing *be* with the past participle of a verb.

The tent was left behind.
The guide recommended that the tent be left behind.

	Simple Past Subjunctive Action Verb: Active		Simple Present Subjunctive Action Verb: Passive	
First person	I left	we left	I were left	we were left
Second person	you left	you left	you were left	you were left
Third person	he, she, it left	they left	he, she, it were left	they were left

If I left early, I might be able to pick up the milk.
I left early to pick up the milk.

If I were left behind, I would be upset.
I was left behind, which made me very upset.

Simple Future Subjunctive Action Verb: Active	Simple Future Subjunctive Action Verb: Passive
None	None

Use the simple past subjunctive state-of-being verb, plus an infinitive, to express a future unreal action.

If I were to die tomorrow, I would have no regrets.

PROGRESSIVE TENSES

	Progressive Present Subjunctive Action Verb: Active	
First person	I am leaving	we are leaving
Second person	you are leaving	you are leaving
Third person	he, she, it is leaving	they are leaving

	Progressive Present Subjunctive Action Verb: Passive	
First person	I am being left	we are being left
Second person	you are being left	you are being left
Third person	he, she, it is being left	they are being left

If I be running late, I must throw myself upon your kind mercies.

If I am running late, I will call you.

It is unlikely that I am being penalized.

	Progressive Past Subjunctive Action Verb: Active	
First person	I **were** leaving	we were leaving
Second person	you were leaving	you were leaving
Third person	he, she, it **were** leaving	they were leaving

	Progressive Past Subjunctive Action Verb: Passive	
First person	I **were** being left	we were being left
Second person	you were being left	you were being left
Third person	he, she, it **were** being left	they were being left

If I were running in the race, I would certainly win.

I was running in the race.

If I were being left behind, I would make a huge fuss.

I was being left behind.

Progressive Future Subjunctive
Action Verb: Active

None

Progressive Future Subjunctive
Action Verb: Passive

None

PERFECT TENSES

	Perfect Present Subjunctive Action Verb: Active	
First person	I have left	we have left
Second person	you have left	you have left
Third person	he, she, it has left	they have left

	Perfect Present Subjunctive **Action Verb: Passive**	
First person	I have been left	we have been left
Second person	you have been left	you have been left
Third person	he/she/it has been left	they have been left

	Perfect Present Subjunctive **Action Verb: Active**	
First person	I had left	we had left
Second person	you had left	you had left
Third person	he, she, it had left	they had left

	Perfect Past Subjunctive **Action Verb: Passive**	
First person	I had been left	we had been left
Second person	you had been left	you had been left
Third person	he, she, it had been left	they had been left

Perfect Future Subjunctive
Action Verb: Active

None

Perfect Future Subjunctive
Action Verb: Passive

None

PROGRESSIVE PERFECT TENSES

	Progressive Perfect Present Subjunctive **Action Verb: Active**	
First person	I have been leaving	we have been leaving
Second person	you have been leaving	you have been leaving
Third person	he, she, it has been leaving	they have been leaving

	Progressive Perfect Present Subjunctive Action Verb: Passive	
First person	I have been being left	we have been being left
Second person	you have been being left	you have been being left
Third person	he, she, it has been being left	they have been being left

	Progressive Perfect Present Subjunctive Action Verb: Passive	
First person	I have been being left	we have been being left
Second person	you have been being left	you have been being left
Third person	he, she, it has been being left	they have been being left

	Progressive Perfect Past Subjunctive Action Verb: Active	
First person	I had been leaving	we had been leaving
Second person	you had been leaving	you had been leaving
Third person	he, she, it had been leaving	they had been leaving

	Progressive Perfect Past Subjunctive Action Verb: Passive	
First person	I had been being left	we had been being left
Second person	you had been being left	you had been being left
Third person	he, she, it had been being left	they had been being left

Progressive Perfect Future Subjunctive
Action Verb: Active

None

Progressive Perfect Future Subjunctive
Action Verb: Passive

None

Exercise 99A: Complete the Chart

Fill in the missing forms on the following chart. Use the verbs indicated above each chart, in order. The first form on each chart is done for you.

INDICATIVE

(establish, delight, ignore, spot, compare, borrow, report, roll, attack, need, question, obey)

Indicative Tense	Active Formation	Examples	Passive Formation	Examples
Simple present	Add *-s* in third- person singular	I establish he, she, it ______	am/is/are + past participle	I am established you ______ he, she, it ______
Simple past	Add *-d* or *-ed*, or change form	I ______	was/were + past participle	I ______ you ______
Simple future	+ will OR shall	they ______	will be + past participle	it ______
Progressive present	am/is/are + present participle	I ______ you ______ he, she, it ______	am/is/are being + past participle	I ______ you ______ he, she, it ______
Progressive past	was/were + present participle	I ______ you ______ he, she, it ______	was/were being + past participle	I ______ you ______ he, she, it ______
Progressive future	will be + present participle	I ______	will be being + past participle	it ______

Indicative Tense	Active Formation	Examples	Passive Formation	Examples
Perfect present	has/have + past participle	I ____________ you ____________ he, she, it ____________	has/have been + past participle	I ____________ you ____________ he, she, it ____________
Perfect past	had + past participle	they ____________	had been + past participle	you ____________
Perfect future	will have + past participle	we ____________	will have been + past participle	they ____________
Progressive perfect present	have/has been + present participle	I ____________ he, she, it ____________	have/has been being + past participle	I ____________ he, she, it ____________
Progressive perfect past	had been + present participle	you ____________	had been being + past participle	you ____________
Progressive perfect future	will have been + present participle	you ____________	will have been being + past participle	they ____________

MODAL

(request, carry, complete, store)

Modal Tense	Active Formation	Examples	Passive Formation	Examples
Simple present	modal helping verb + simple present main verb	I could request you ____________ he, she, it ____________	modal helping verb + be + past participle	I ____________ they ____________

Modal Tense	Active Formation	Examples	Passive Formation	Examples
Progressive present	modal helping verb + be + present participle	I ______________	modal helping verb + be + being + past participle	it ______________
Perfect present	modal helping verb + have + past participle	you ______________	modal helping verb + have + been + past participle	it ______________
Progressive perfect present	modal helping verb + have been + present participle	I ______________	modal helping verb + have been being + past participle	we ______________

IMPERATIVE

(worry, change)

Imperative Tense	Active Formation	Examples	Passive Formation	Examples
Present	Simple present form without subject	Worry ! ______________!	be + past participle	______________! ______________!

SUBJUNCTIVE
(support, supply, include, notice, provide, rule, stretch, spare)

Subjunctive Tense	Active Formation	Examples	Passive Formation	Examples
Simple present	No change in any person	I support you ____ he, she, it ____ we ____ you ____ they ____	be + past participle	I ____ they ____
Simple past	**Same as indicative:** Add *-d* or *-ed*, or change form	I ____ you ____ he, she, it ____	were + past participle	he ____ you ____
Progressive present	**Same as indicative:** am/is/are + present participle	I ____ you ____ he, she, it ____	**Same as indicative:** am/is/are being + past participle	I ____ you ____ he, she, it ____
Progressive past	were + present participle	I ____ you ____ he, she, it ____	were being + past participle	I ____ you ____ he, she, it ____

Subjunctive Tense	Active Formation	Examples	Passive Formation	Examples
Perfect present	**Same as indicative:** has/have + past participle	I ____________ he, she, it ____________ they ____________	**Same as indicative:** has/have been + past participle	I ____________ he, she, it ____________ they ____________
Perfect past	Same as indicative: had + past participle	we ____________	Same as indicative: had been + past participle	we ____________
Progressive perfect present	**Same as indicative:** have/has been + present participle	I ____________ you ____________ he, she, it ____________	**Same as indicative:** have/has been being + past participle	I ____________ you ____________ he, she, it ____________
Progressive perfect past	**Same as indicative:** had been + present participle	you ____________	**Same as indicative:** had been being + past participle	you ____________

Exercise 99B: Parsing

Write the mood, tense, and voice of each underlined verb above it. These sentences are taken from Laura Ingalls Wilder's *Little House on the Prairie*.

The first one is done for you.

indicative, simple past active

He said to Ma: "Take your time, Caroline. We won't move the wagon till we want to."

When the sun rose, they were driving on across the prairie.

If we hadn't come by, there's no telling when they would have been found.

Pet and Patty are good swimmers, but I guess they wouldn't have made it if I hadn't helped them.

If we are going this year, we must go now. We can't get across the Mississippi after the ice breaks.

A shadow came over the prairie just then because the sun had gone down, and Pa said, "I'll tell you about it later."

He wore fringed leather leggings, and his moccasins were covered with beads.

That big fellow trotted by my stirrup as if he were there to stay.

I guess they had just eaten all they could hold.

At milking-time Ma was putting on her bonnet, when suddenly all Jack's hair stood up stiff on his neck and back, and he rushed out of the house. They heard a yell and a scramble and a shout: "Call off your dog! Call off your dog!"

—LESSON 100—

Review of Moods and Tenses
Conditional Sentences

First conditional sentences express circumstances that might actually happen.

The predicate of the condition clause is in a present tense.
The predicate of the consequence clause is an imperative or is in a present or future tense.

If we surrender and I return with you, will you promise not to hurt this man?
So bow down to her if you want, bow to her.
If she is otherwise when I find her, I shall be very put out.
Unless I am wrong (and I am never wrong), they are headed dead into the fire swamp.

Second conditional sentences express circumstances that are contrary to reality.
The predicate of the condition clause is in a past tense.
The predicate of the consequence clause is in the simple present modal tense.

I would not say such things if I were you!
If I had a month to plan, maybe I could come up with something.
If we only had a wheelbarrow, that would be something.

Third conditional sentences express past circumstances that never happened.
The predicate of the condition clause is in the perfect past tense.
The predicate of the consequence clause is in the perfect present modal or simple present modal tense.

But they would have killed Westley, if I hadn't done it.

If I were you, I would go home.

If I were you, I would be dancing with joy.

If I had been wrong, I would say so now.

If I had been wrong, I would be apologizing with sincerity.

If I had been wrong, I would have said so.

If I had been wrong, I would have been running for my life.

(The examples below are adapted from Mary Shelley's *Frankenstein*.)

First conditional sentences express circumstances that might actually happen.
The predicate of the condition clause is in a present tense.
The predicate of the consequence clause is an imperative or is in a present or future tense.

If I <u>fail</u>, you <u>will see</u> me again soon, or never.

If you <u>believe</u> that she is innocent, <u>rely</u> on the justice of our laws.

If I could bestow animation upon lifeless matter, I might renew life.

Second conditional sentences express circumstances that are contrary to reality.
The predicate of the condition clause is in a past tense.
The predicate of the consequence clause is in the simple or progressive present modal tense.

Unless such symptoms had been shown early, a sister or brother could never suspect the other of fraud.

If you cherished a desire of revenge against me, you would be rejoicing in my destruction.

Third conditional sentences express past circumstances that never happened.
The predicate of the condition clause is in the perfect past tense.
The predicate of the consequence clause is in any modal tense.

If she had earnestly desired it, I should have willingly given it to her,

If you had known me as I once was, you would not recognize me in this state of degradation.

If the voice of conscience had been heeded, Frankenstein would yet have lived.

Exercise 100A: Conditional Sentences

Identify the following sentences from George Selden's *The Cricket in Times Square* as first, second, or third conditional by writing *1*, *2*, or *3* in the blank to the right.

If a leaf in a green forest far from New York had fallen at midnight through the darkness into a thicket, it might have sounded like that. ________

If we come down with peculiar diseases—out he goes! ________

He saw the cardboard shells that open up into beautiful paper flowers if you put them in a glass of water. ________

He was afraid that if he moved, he would be buried under an avalanche of Chinese novelties. ________

She would certainly have known if he had two dollars to leave anybody. ________

They might have gone on bowing all night if Sai Fong hadn't said something in Chinese to his friend. ________

If the Bellinis find me gone, they'll think I set the fire and ran. ________

What good is it to be famous if it only makes you unhappy? ________

If Mario couldn't find him in a few minutes, Chester would give a quick chirp as a hint. ________

If a thief had taken it, he would have taken the money from the cash register too. ________

Exercise 100B: Parsing

Write the correct mood, tense, and voice above each underlined verb. These sentences are taken or adapted from *South American Jungle Tales*, by Horacio Quiroga.

The first is done for you.

indicative simple past active

The panther understood that the rays were packed close in along the shore; and he figured that if he could jump away out into the stream he would get beyond them and their stingers.

"If you don't get out of the way, we will eat every ray, and every son of a ray, and every grandson of a ray, not counting the women and children!" said the panthers.

Though many more of the rays were being trampled on, and scratched and bitten, they held their ground.

Sometimes when a ray had been tossed into the air by a panther's paw, he would return to the fight after he had fallen back into the water.

One day when the cubs had grown to be quite large sized raccoons, their mother took them up all together to the top of an orange tree—you must know that in South America orange trees, which came originally from Spain, now grow wild in the forest—and spoke to them.

Cublets, there is one thing more you must all be afraid of: dogs! dogs! Never go near a dog! Once I had a fight with a dog. Do you see this broken tooth? Well, I broke it in a fight with a dog! And so I know what I am talking about! . . . Whenever you hear a dog, or a man, or a gun, jump for your lives no matter how high the tree is, and run, run, run!

Exercise 100C: Diagramming

On your own paper, diagram every word of the following sentences adapted from *South American Jungle Tales*, by Horacio Quiroga.

I should not have gotten into that trouble if I had worked, like the other bees.

The snake understood that if his trick of spinning the top with his tail was extraordinary, this trick of the bee was almost miraculous.

He fell ill, and the doctors told him he would never get well unless he left town and went to live in the country where there was good air and a warm climate.

WEEK 26

More Modifiers

—LESSON 101—

Adjective Review
Adjectives in the Appositive Position
Correct Comma Usage

> It was a dark and stormy night; the rain fell in torrents, except at occasional intervals, when it was checked by a violent gust of wind which swept up the streets (for it is in London that our scene lies), rattling along the house-tops, and fiercely agitating the scanty flame of the lamps that struggled against the darkness.
>
> —From *Paul Clifford* by Edward Bulwer-Lytton

An adjective modifies a noun or pronoun.
Adjectives tell what kind, which one, how many, and whose.
Descriptive adjectives tell what kind.
A descriptive adjective becomes an abstract noun when you add *-ness* to it.
Possessive adjectives tell whose.

Hastings kissed the duke's hand in silence.

Nouns become adjectives when they are made possessive.
Form the possessive of a singular noun by adding an apostrophe and the letter *s*.

duchess ____________________

Form the possessive of a plural noun ending in *-s* by adding an apostrophe only.

emperors ____________________

Form the possessive of a plural noun that does not end in *-s* as if it were a singular noun.

noblemen ____________________

Since choice was mine, I chose the man love could not choose, and took this sad comfort to my heart.

—From *The Last of the Barons,* by Edward Bulwer-Lytton

An adjective that comes right before the noun it modifies is in the attributive position.
An adjective that follows the noun it modifies is in the predicative position.

On the floor is the image of a dog in mosaic, with the well-known motto "Cave canem" upon it.

My name is well known, methinks, in Pompeii.
—From *The Last Days of Pompeii,* by Edward Bulwer-Lytton

Possessive Pronouns (Adjectives)

Attributive	**Predicative**
my	mine
your	yours
his, her, its	his, hers, its
our	ours
your	yours
their	theirs

The eyes were soft, dark, and brilliant, but dreamlike and vague; the features in youth must have been regular and beautiful, but their contour was now sharpened by the hollowness of the cheeks and temples.

His face was far less handsome than Marmaduke Nevile's, but infinitely more expressive, both of intelligence and command,—the features straight and sharp, the complexion clear and pale, and under the bright grey eyes a dark shade spoke either of dissipation or of thought.
— From *The Last of the Barons,* by Edward Bulwer-Lytton.

Appositive adjectives directly follow the word they modify.

The sea, blue and tranquil, bounded the view.

To add to the attractions of his house, his wife, simple and good-tempered, could talk with anybody, take off the bores, and leave people to be comfortable in their own way.

It was a spot remote, sequestered, cloistered from the business and pleasures of the world.

The latter was a fine dark-eyed girl, tall, self-possessed, and dressed plainly indeed, but after the approved fashion.
—From *Alice: or, The Mysteries,* by Edward Bulwer-Lytton

When three or more nouns, adjectives, verbs, or adverbs appear in a series, they should be separated by commas.

"Wrinkles" in the comma rule:

1. **When three or more items are in a list, a coordinating conjunction before the last term is usual but not necessary.**

   The horse spun, bucked, kicked with abandon.
   The horse spun, bucked, and kicked with abandon.

Chickens, roosters, ducks filled the yard.
Chickens, roosters, and ducks filled the yard.

I ran quickly, efficiently, easily.
I ran quickly, efficiently, and easily.

It was a spot remote, sequestered, cloistered.
It was a spot remote, sequestered, and cloistered.

It was a dark, stormy, frightening night.
It was a dark, stormy, and frightening night.

2. When three or more items are in a list and a coordinating conjunction is used, a comma should still follow the next-to-last item in the list.

The fourteen-year-old loved her sisters, Taylor Swift, and Jennifer Lawrence.
The fourteen-year-old loved her sisters, Taylor Swift and Jennifer Lawrence.

Oranges, apples, and plums filled the fruit bowl.
Oranges, apples and plums filled the fruit bowl.

3. When two or more adjectives are in the attributive position, they are only separated by commas if they are equally important in meaning.

Monday was a tiring, difficult day.
Monday was a tiring and difficult day.
Monday was a difficult, tiring day.

The old man was wearing a grey wool overcoat.
The old man was wearing a grey and wool overcoat.
The old man was wearing a wool grey overcoat.

INCORRECT: Monday was a tiring difficult day.
INCORRECT: The old man was wearing a grey, wool overcoat.

Exercise 101A: Identifying Adjectives

Underline every adjective (including verb forms used as adjectives) in the following sentences. Above each adjective, write *DESC* for descriptive or *POSS* for possessive. Then, label each as in the attributive (*ATT*), appositive (*APP*), or predicative (*PRED*) position. Finally, draw an arrow from each adjective to the word it modifies. Do not underline articles.

These sentences are from Edith Wharton's *Ethan Frome*.

I had been sent up by my employers on a job connected with the big power-house at Corbury Junction, and a long-drawn carpenters' strike had so delayed the work that I found myself anchored at Starkfield—the nearest habitable spot—for the best part of the winter.

I simply felt that he lived in a depth of moral isolation too remote for casual access, and I had the sense that his loneliness was not merely the result of his personal plight, tragic as I guessed that to be, but had in it, as Harmon Gow had hinted, the profound accumulated cold of Starkfield winters.

His unfinished studies had given form to his sensibility and even in his unhappiest moments field and sky spoke to him with a deep and powerful persuasion.

And there were sensations, less definable but more exquisite, which drew them together with a shock of silent joy; the cold red of sunset behind winter hills, the flight of cloud-flocks over slopes of golden stubble, or the intensely blue shadows of hemlocks on sunlit snow.

The sunrise burned red in a pure sky, the shadows on the rim of the wood-lot were darkly blue, and beyond the white and scintillating fields patches of far-off forest hung like smoke.

The cat, unnoticed, had crept up on muffled paws from Zeena's seat to the table, and was stealthily elongating its body in the direction of the milk-jug, which stood between Ethan and Mattie.

Exercise 101B: Punctuation Practice

The sentences below are missing all of their punctuation marks! Using everything you have learned about punctuation, insert correct punctuation. You may simply write the punctuation marks in, rather than using proofreader's marks.

These sentences are taken or adapted from Frances Hodgson Burnett's *A Little Princess.*

Her short black locks tumbled about her ears and she sat still

She was a pretty little curly headed creature and her round eyes were like wet forget-me-nots

When she spoke it was in a quiet steady voice she held her head up and everybody listened to her

Her show pupil had melted into nothingness leaving only a friendless beggared little girl.

The fact was that Miss Minchins pupils were a set of dull matter of fact young people

And at last evidently in response to it a gray whiskered bright eyed head peeped out of the hole

I am sure the Large Family have fat comfortable armchairs and sofas and I can see that their red flowery wallpaper is exactly like them.

It was the picturesque white swathed form and dark faced gleaming eyed white turbaned head of a native Indian man-servant a Lascar Sara said to herself quickly

I only spare you because I am a princess and you are a poor stupid unkind vulgar old thing and don't know any better

And it was a bakers shop and a cheerful stout motherly woman with rosy cheeks was putting into the window a tray of delicious newly baked hot buns fresh from the oven large plump and shiny with currants in them

Yesterday when she was out he said I entered bringing with me small sharp nails which can be pressed into the wall without blows from a hammer

You insolent unmanageable child she cried

Exercise 101C: Diagramming

On your own paper, diagram the following sentences from *Ethan Frome*, by Edith Wharton.

His unfinished studies had given form to his sensibility and even in his unhappiest moments field and sky spoke to him with a deep and powerful persuasion.

The sunrise burned red in a pure sky, the shadows on the rim of the wood-lot were darkly blue, and beyond the white and scintillating fields patches of far-off forest hung like smoke.

The cat, unnoticed, had crept up on muffled paws from Zeena's seat to the table, and was stealthily elongating its body in the direction of the milk-jug, which stood between Ethan and Mattie.

—LESSON 102—

Adjective Review
Pronoun Review
Limiting Adjectives

(All sentences in this lesson are taken from *The Two Towers* by J. R. R. Tolkien.)

They had come to the desolation that lay before Mordor: the lasting monument to the dark labour of its slaves that should endure when all their purposes were made void; a land defiled, diseased beyond all healing—unless the Great Sea should enter in and wash it with oblivion.

brown curling hair	old tired horse
long black hair	white horse
snowy hair	running horse
his hair	king's horse

Descriptive adjectives *describe* by giving additional details.
Limiting adjectives *define* by setting limits.

Descriptive Adjectives	**Limiting Adjectives**
Regular	Possessives
Present participles	Articles
Past participles	Demonstratives
	Indefinites
	Interrogatives
	Numbers

The articles are *a, an,* and *the.*

Demonstrative pronouns demonstrate or point out something. They take the place of a single word or a group of words.

this, that, these, those

Demonstrative adjectives modify nouns and answer the question *which one.*

If those unhappy hobbits are astray in the woods, it might draw them hither.

The prisoners are NOT to be searched or plundered; those are my orders.

Indefinite pronouns are pronouns without antecedents.

Singular

anybody	anyone	anything
everybody	everyone	everything
nobody	no one	nothing
somebody	someone	something
another	other	one
either	neither	each

Plural
both few many several

Singular or Plural
all any most none some

I do not understand all that goes on myself, so I cannot explain it to you. Some of us are still true Ents, and lively enough in our fashion, but many are growing sleepy, going tree-ish, as you might say.

Indefinite adjectives modify nouns and answer the questions *which one* and *how many.*

We will ride for a few hours, gently, until we come to the end of the valley.

The cord hurts us, yes it does, it hurts us, and we've done nothing.

Some are quite wide awake, and a few are, well, ah, well, getting Entish.

Each Palantir replied to each, but all those in Gondor were ever open to the view of Osgiliath.

Interrogative pronouns take the place of nouns in questions.
who, whom, whose, what, which

Interrogative adjectives modify nouns.

Then if not yours, whose is the wizardry?

At whose command do you hunt Orcs in our land?

Which way do we go from here?

How far back his treachery goes, who can guess?

Cardinal numbers represent quantities (one, two, three, four . . .).
Ordinal numbers represent order (first, second, third, fourth . . .).

Treebeard was at their head, and some fifty followers were behind him.

Fifteen of my men I lost, and twelve horses, alas!

"Not Elves," said the fourth, the tallest, and as it appeared, the chief among them.

Gollum was the first to get up.

It was his turn to sleep first, and he was soon deep in a dream.

Exercise 102A: Identifying Adjectives

The following paragraph is slightly condensed from *Moby Dick*, by Herman Melville. Underline every word that acts as an adjective.

Do not include phrases or clauses acting as adjectives. Also, do not include articles. (There are just too many!)

Label each one using the following abbreviations:

Descriptive Adjectives		**Limiting Adjectives**	
Regular	*DA-R*	Possessives	*LA-P*
Present participles	*DA-PresP*	~~Articles~~	~~*LA-A*~~
Past participles	*DA-PastP*	Demonstratives	*LA-D*
		Indefinites	*LA-IND*
		Interrogatives	*LA-INT*
		Numbers	*LA-N*

For some time past, though at intervals only, the unaccompanied, secluded White Whale had haunted those uncivilised seas mostly frequented by the Sperm Whale fishermen. But not all of them knew of his existence; only a few of them had knowingly seen him; while the number who as yet had actually and knowingly given battle to him, was small indeed. For, owing to the large number of whale-cruisers; the disorderly way they were sprinkled over the entire watery circumference, many of them adventurously pushing their quest along solitary latitudes, so as seldom or never for a whole twelvemonth or more on a stretch, to encounter a single news-telling sail of any sort; the inordinate length of each separate voyage; the irregularity of the times of sailing from home; all these, with other circumstances, direct and indirect, long obstructed the spread through the whole world-wide whaling-fleet of the special individualizing tidings concerning Moby Dick. It was hardly to be doubted, that several vessels reported to have encountered, at such or such a time, or on such or such a meridian, a sperm whale of uncommon magnitude and malignity, which whale, after doing great mischief to his assailants, had completely escaped them; to some minds it was not an unfair presumption, I say, that the whale in question must have been no other than Moby Dick. Yet as of late the Sperm Whale fishery had been marked by various and not unfrequent instances of great ferocity, cunning, and malice in the monster attacked; therefore it was, that those who by accident ignorantly gave battle to Moby Dick; such hunters, perhaps, for the most part, were content to ascribe the peculiar terror he bred, more, as it were, to the perils of the Sperm Whale fishery at large, than to the individual cause. In that way, mostly, the disastrous encounter between Ahab and the whale had hitherto been popularly regarded.

Exercise 102B: Analysis

The passage above shows you how a good writer uses adjectives: a mix of colorful descriptive adjectives and sparer, simpler limiting adjectives.

The total word count of the excerpt is 317 words. Now count each type of adjective and fill out the chart below. For the purpose of our calculations, hyphenated words (e.g., news-telling) should be counted as single words, while compound adjectives that are not hyphenated (e.g., Sperm Whale) should be counted as separate words.

Descriptive Adjectives		**Limiting Adjectives**	
Regular	________	Possessives	________
Present participles	________	~~Articles~~	________
Past participles	________	Demonstratives	________
		Indefinites	________
		Interrogatives	________
		Numbers	________

Total Descriptive Adjectives ________ Total Limiting Adjectives ________

Total Adjectives Used ________

Good prose can't be reduced to *just* formulas—but formulas can give you some extra help in writing well. The total word count of the excerpt is 317 words. You can figure out what fraction of the total word count is taken up by adjectives by dividing the total word count by the total number of adjectives used. Determine that quotient now, and ask your instructor for help if necessary.

317

The sum above tells you that 1 out of every _____________ [insert answer to division problem!] words in this passage is an adjective. In other words, adjectives do not make up more than about 1/______ of this descriptive writing.

Now let's look at the relationship between limiting and descriptive adjectives. Complete the following division problem:

[number of limiting adjectives] _________ | ___________ [number of descriptive adjectives]

The quotient above tells you that 1 out of every _____________ [insert answer to second division problem!] adjectives used is a limiting adjective. In other words, limiting adjectives do not make up more than about _______________ of this descriptive writing.

Ask your instructor to share the last part of this exercise with you.

Exercise 102C: Using Adjectives

On your own paper, rewrite the passage below. It is taken from Herman Melville's short story "The Apple Tree Table"—but all of the adjectives (except for articles) have been removed.

Where adjectives could be removed without making the sentence ungrammatical, they have simply been deleted without a trace. Where removing an adjective made the sentence unreasonable, a blank has been inserted instead. So you know that adjectives go in the blanks—but you'll have to find a lot of other places to put them as well!

You can also insert adverbs, additional articles, and conjunctions as necessary to make your insertions work.

Use the same proportions as the passage in Exercise 102B. This excerpt originally had 326 words, so use:

47–54 total adjectives, not including articles.
- Use between 15 and 27 limiting adjectives:
  - Use at least three different kinds of limiting adjectives (your choice!).
- The remainder should be descriptive adjectives:
  - Use at least three participles (present or past) as adjectives.

When you are finished, compare your work with the original passage in the Key.

Under the apex of the roof was a step-ladder, something like a pulpit-stairway, leading to a platform, from which a still _______________ ladder—a sort of ladder—led somewhat higher to the scuttle. The slide of _______________ scuttle was about _______________ feet _______________, all in _______________ piece, furnishing a frame for a pane of glass, inserted into it like a bull's-eye. The light of the garret came from _______________ source, filtrated through a curtain of cobwebs. Indeed, the stairs, and platform, and ladder, were festooned, and carpeted, and canopied with cobwebs; which, in accumulations, hung, too, from the ceiling, like the moss in the forest. In _______________ cobwebs, swung, as in catacombs, myriads of tribes of insects. . . .

Wishing to shed a light through the place, I sought to withdraw the scuttle-slide. But ______________ sign of latch or hasp was ______________. Only after peering, did I discover a padlock, ______________, like an oyster at the bottom of the sea, amid masses of webs, chrysalides, and eggs. Brushing these away, I found it ______________. With a nail, I tried to pick the lock, when scores of ants and flies, ______________, crawled forth from the keyhole. . . . As if ______________ at ______________ invasion of ______________ retreat, bands darted up from below, beating about ______________ head, like hornets. At last, with a jerk, I burst open the scuttle. And ah! what a change. As from the gloom of the grave and the companionship of worms, men shall at last rapturously rise into the greenness and glory, so, from ______________ garret, I thrust forth my head into the air, and found myself ______________ by the tops of trees, growing in the garden below—trees, ______________ leaves soared high above ______________ slate.

—LESSON 103—

Misplaced Modifiers
Squinting Modifiers
Dangling Modifiers

The party organizer passed around stuffed mushrooms to the guests on tiny bamboo mats.

Churning inexorably towards the coast, we breathlessly watched the weather reports about the hurricane.

Miranda spotted a blue heron on the way home.

The movie star rode through the crowds of fans in a limousine.

The inconsiderate child was kicking the back of the airplane seat.
The child was kicking the inconsiderate back of the airplane seat.

Mari upset almost every colleague she worked with.
Mari almost upset every colleague she worked with.

I slept for barely an hour.
I barely slept for an hour.

A misplaced modifier is an adjective, adjective phrase, adverb, or adverb phrase in the wrong place.

The chocolate fudge cake that I baked recently fell off the table onto the dirty floor.

Doing fifty chin-ups quickly strengthens your biceps.

My friend said on Monday we would go camping.

A squinting modifier can belong either to the sentence element preceding or the element following.

After reading more on the subject, the article turned out to be incorrect.
The experiment failed, not having procured the correct ingredients.
Exhausted by long days at work, the secretary's joy was unbounded when the office closed because of snow.

A dangling modifier has no noun or verb to modify.

How to Fix a Dangling Modifier

1. Provide the missing word in the main clause.

   After reading more on the subject, I discovered that the article was incorrect.

2. Turn the dangling phrase into a clause by putting the missing word(s) into the phrase itself.

   After I read more on the subject, the article turned out to be incorrect.

INCORRECT: Having been delayed by traffic, the bride's frustration was easily understood.

1. Provide the missing noun or verb in the main clause.

   ____

   ____

2. Turn the dangling phrase into a clause by putting the missing noun or verb into the phrase itself.

   ____

   ____

Exercise 103A: Correcting Misplaced Modifiers

Circle each misplaced modifier and draw an arrow to the place in the sentence that it should occupy.

The gold belonged to the queen in the treasure chest.

The giraffe ate lettuce from my hand that I saw at the zoo.

After wrapping the present, the table was beautifully decorated by my mother.

The couple strolled in the center of the park past the ornate fountain.

Sitting in the top row of the bleachers, the football game was hard for us to see.

The arcade game required three quarters, on which I had the high score.

Molly ate the dinner her father had prepared with a voracious appetite.

Shane had promised to perform in the New Year's Day concert in October.

Packed with souvenirs, we couldn't fit our suitcases into the car.

I learned how to knit with great difficulty.

Exercise 103B: Clarifying Squinting Modifiers

Circle each squinting modifier. On your own paper, rewrite each sentence twice, eliminating the ambiguity by moving the squinting modifier to produce sentences with two different meanings. Insert commas and change capitalization/punctuation as needed.

The first is done for you.

Zoe sang the second song (at least) as loudly as the soloist.

Zoe sang at least the second song as loudly as the soloist.
Zoe sang the second song as loudly, at least, as the soloist.

Jasper wished immediately to disappear.
The governor vowed earnestly to defend the proposal against criticism.
Tell Micah if he has the book I will read to him.
The director instructed us poorly to redo the scene.
The red sweater I bought yesterday got a snag.
The smell of the bread she baked slowly filled the air.
The athlete who had been training intensely stared at his opponent.
My cousin realized eventually the toy would be worth a lot of money.
Morgan decided during the class to work more diligently.

Exercise 103C: Rewriting Dangling Modifiers

On your own paper, rewrite each of these sentences twice, using each of the strategies described in the lesson.

Reading the instructions, the bookshelf appeared simple enough to put together.
Flying above the clouds, the town grew smaller and smaller.
Left without supervision, a baseball went through the window.
Terrified out of their wits, the knocks at the door continued.
The bus pulled away from the curb, having hugged our parents.

—LESSON 104—

Degrees of Adjectives

Comparisons Using *More, Fewer,* and *Less*

Good, better, best,
Never let it rest,
Till your good is better,
And your better, best.
—Julia Richman, *School Work 3,* No. 2 (June, 1904)

And summer days were sad and long,
And sad the uncompanioned eyes,
And sadder sunset-tinted leaves.
Of all sad words of tongue or pen,
The saddest are these: "It might have been!"
—John Greenleaf Whittier

The positive degree of an adjective describes only one thing.
The comparative degree of an adjective compares two things.
The superlative degree of an adjective compares three or more things.

Most regular adjectives form the comparative by adding *-r* or *-er.*
Most regular adjectives form the superlative by adding *-st* or *-est.*

positive	comparative	superlative
______________	______________	______________

Irregular adjectives may change form completely.

positive	comparative	superlative
______________	______________	______________

For a moment the general did not reply; he was smiling his curious red-lipped smile. Then he said slowly, "No. You are wrong, sir. The Cape buffalo is not the most dangerous game." He sipped his wine. "Here in my preserve on this island," he said in the same slow tone, "I hunt more dangerous game."
—Richard Connell, "The Most Dangerous Game" (1924)

Many adjectives form their comparative and superlative forms by adding the word *more* or *most* before the adjective instead of using *–er* or *–est.* In comparative and superlative adjective forms, the words *more* and *most* are used as adverbs.

positive	comparative	superlative
______________	______________	______________

So long as people will drink, drink will be made; and so long as drink is made, there will be those to sell it. Well, the more the restrictions, the fewer to sell; the fewer to sell, the less sold; the less sold, the less made; the less made, the less drunk; the less drunk, the fewer the inebriates—and that's what the temperance people are after.

—*The Grip,* Vol. 20, 1882

The more thoroughly we searched, the fewer treasures we found.
The more love I offered, the less enthusiasm he showed.

Use *fewer* for concrete items and *less* for abstractions.

He would do very well if he had fewer cakes and sweetmeats sent him from home.
I wanted to tease you a little to make you less sad.

—Charlotte Bronte, *Jane Eyre*

In comparisons using *more . . . fewer* and *more . . . less, more* and *less* can act as either adverbs or adjectives and *the* can act as an adverb.

We searched (the) more thoroughly. We found (the) fewer treasures.
I offered (the) more love. He showed (the) less enthusiasm.

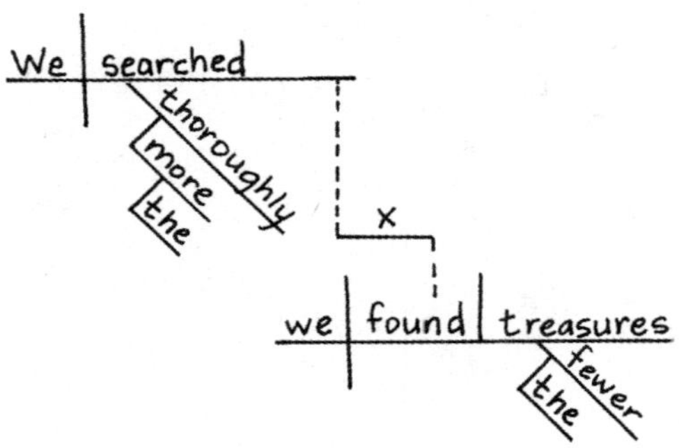

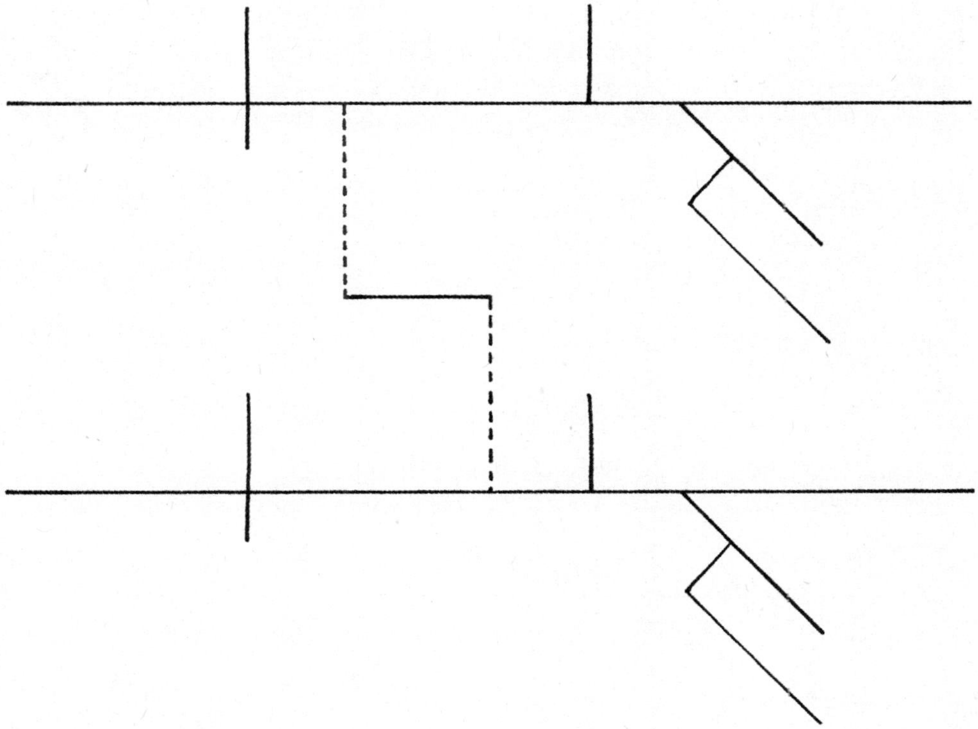

The more the building shook, the less he wanted to be there.

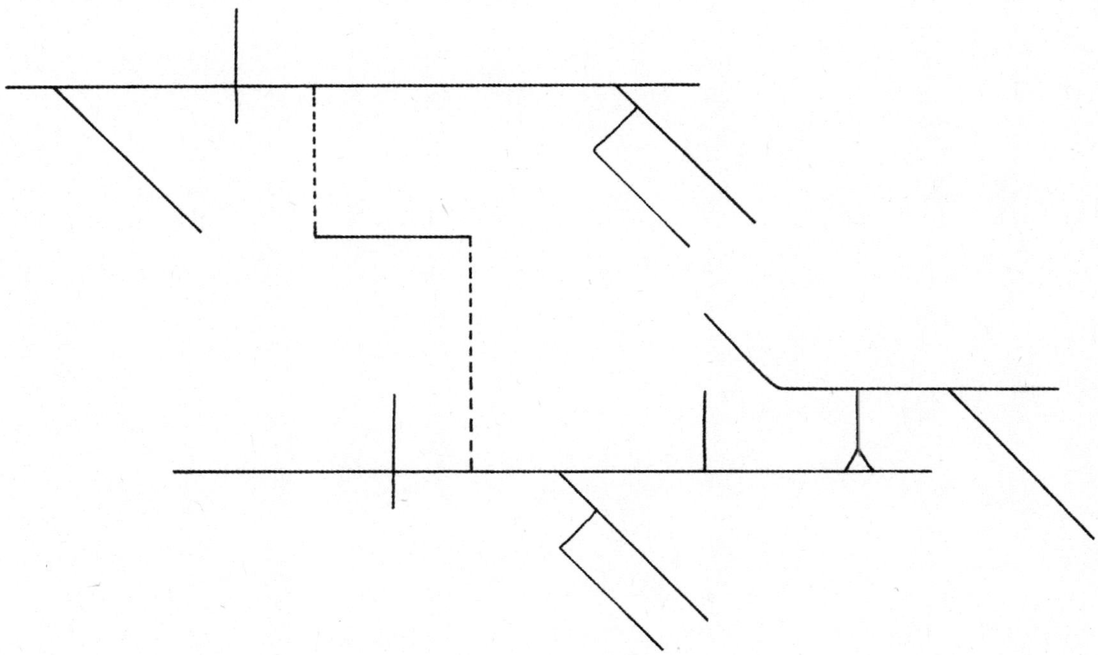

The more the building shook, the more we held on.
The less we saw, the less we knew.

The more the wave rose, the faster we ran.
The less we worried, the better we felt.
The happier we were, the more we rejoiced.
The louder the wind, the fewer words we were able to exchange.

The better we felt, the longer we stayed.
The longer the tail grew, the better the horse could swat flies.

The better we felt, the longer we stayed.

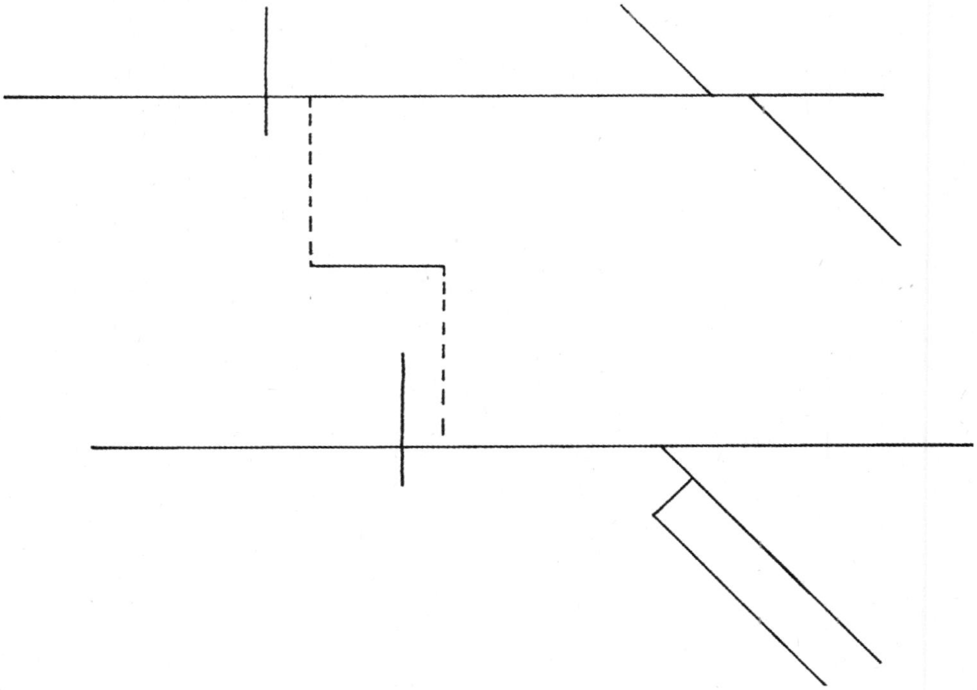

The longer the tail grew, the better the horse could swat flies.

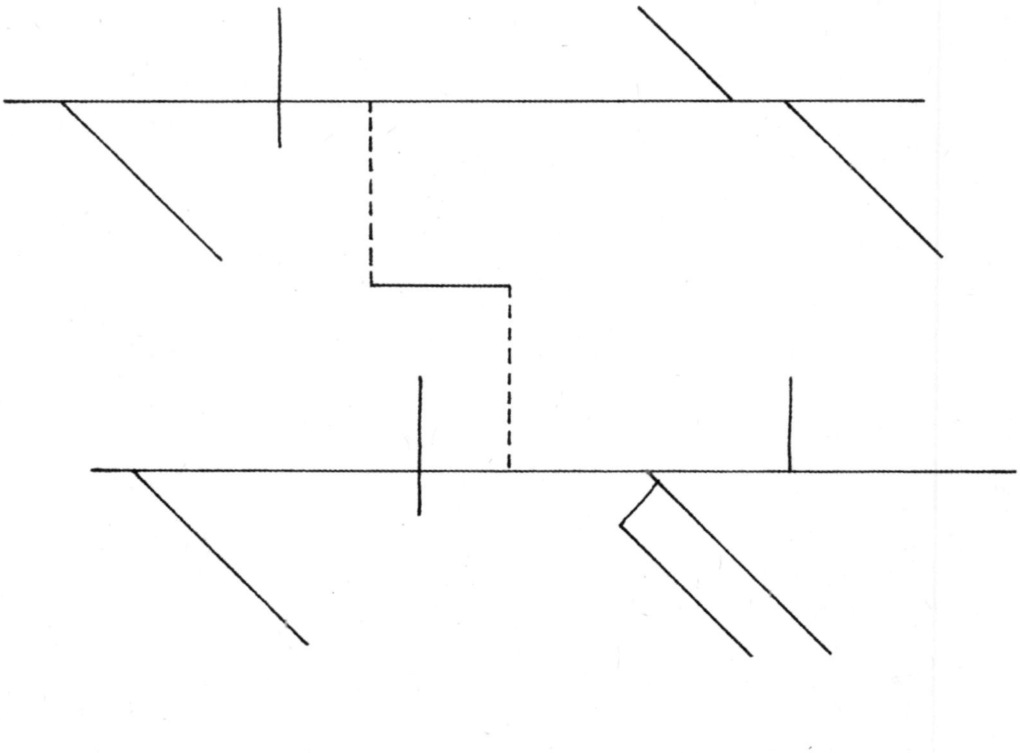

Use *fewer* for concrete items and *less* for abstractions.

Comparisons can be formed using a combination of *more* and *fewer* or *less;* a combination of *more* and *more* or *fewer/less* and *fewer/less*; a combination of *more* or *fewer/less* with a comparative form; or simply two comparative forms.

In comparisons using *more, fewer,* and *less, more* and *less* can act as either adverbs or adjectives, and *the* can act as an adverb.

In comparisons using two comparative forms, the forms may act as either adverbs or adjectives, and *the* can act as an adverb.

Exercise 104A: Positive, Comparative, and Superlative Adjectives

Using the following chart to review spelling rules for forming degrees of adjectives. Then, fill in the blank in each sentence with each adjective indicated in brackets (properly spelled!).

These sentences are all drawn from Charlotte Bronte's classic novel *Jane Eyre.*

Spelling Rules:

If the adjective ends in e already, add only –*r* or –*st.*

noble	nobler	noblest
pure	purer	purest
cute	________	________

If the adjective ends in a short vowel sound and a consonant, double the consonant and add –*er* or –*est.*

red	redder	reddest
thin	thinner	thinnest
flat	________	________

If the adjective ends in –*y*, change the *y* to *i* and add –*er* or –*est.*

hazy	hazier	haziest
lovely	lovelier	loveliest

When thus gentle, Bessie seemed to me the ________________, ________________, ________________ being in the world. [in order, the superlatives of good, pretty, and kind]

But I believed in the existence of other and ______________________ kinds of goodness, and what I believed in I wished to behold. [comparative of vivid]

Could not even self-interest make you ______________________ ? [comparative of wise]

Then she ought to look ______________________. [comparative of cheerful]

Take your palette, mix your ________________, ________________, ________________ tints; choose your ____________________ camel-hair pencils; delineate carefully the ________________ face you can imagine; paint it in your ____________________ shades and ____________________ hues, according to the description given by Mrs. Fairfax of Blanche Ingram. [in order, the superlatives of fresh, fine, clear, delicate, lovely, soft, and sweet]

The one who went with me appeared some years ______________. [comparative of young]

I would fain exercise some ____________________ faculty than that of fierce speaking. [comparative of good]

It was Mr. Brocklehurst, buttoned up in a surtout, and looking ____________________, ____________________, and ____________________ than ever. [comparatives of long, narrow, and rigid]

Until she heard from Bessie and could discover by her own observation that I was endeavoring in good earnest to acquire a ____________________ and child-like disposition, a ____________________ and sprightly manner—something ____________________, ____________________, ____________________, as it were—she really must exclude me from privileges intended only for contented, happy little children. [in order, the comparatives of sociable, attractive, light, frank, and natural]

Miss Miller was ____________________. [comparative of ordinary]

I felt physically weak and broken down: but my ____________________ ailment was an unutterable wretchedness of mind. [superlative of bad]

But the three ____________________ —partly, perhaps, because the ______________ figures of the band—were the Dowager Lady Ingram and her daughters, Blanche and Mary. They were all three of the ____________________ stature of women. [in order, the superlatives of distinguished, tall, and lofty]

I believed he was naturally a man of ____________________ tendencies, ____________________ principles, and ____________________ tastes than such as circumstances had developed, education instilled, or destiny encouraged. [in order, the comparatives of good, high, and pure]

Exercise 104B: Forming Comparisons

Rewrite each set of independent clauses so that they form a comparative sentence making use of *more*, *less*, *fewer*, and/or comparative forms of the adjectives indicated. The first is done for you.

When you are finished, ask your instructor to show you the original sentences, which are taken from Carl von Clausewitz's nineteenth-century classic *On War*, a guide to military strategy.

Our political object is small.
We shall set less value upon it.

The smaller our political object, the less value shall we set upon it.

We ascend higher.
The difficulties increase.

____

____

We demand a small sacrifice from our opponent.
Our opponent employs a smaller means of resistance.

____

____

The motives of a War are great and powerful.
A war affects the whole existence of a people.

____

____

We go back farther.
Military history becomes less useful.
It gets much more meagre and barren of detail.

____

____

This victory is sought for near our own frontiers.
It is easier.

____

____

Exercise 104C: Using "Fewer" and "Less"

Complete the sentences by filling in each blank with either "fewer" or "less."

The original sentences are taken from Carl von Clausewitz's nineteenth-century classic *On War*, a guide to military strategy.

While the number of cavalry and guns is the same, there are ____________ horses, and therefore, there is ____________ forage required.

It is certainly always of advantage to strengthen the flanks in this manner, as ____________ troops are then required at those points.

He who uses force unsparingly, without reference to the bloodshed involved, must obtain a superiority if his adversary uses ____________ vigour in its application.

The ____________ favourable circumstances exist, the more will all depend on superior skill in combination, and promptitude and precision in the execution.

Napoleon always showed great foresight in the provision he made in this manner in the rear of his Army; and in that way, even in his boldest operations, he incurred ____________ risk than might be imagined at first sight.

Exercise 104D: Diagramming

On your own paper, diagram every word of the following sentences from various stories in Andrew Lang's *The Blue Fairy Book*.

The more she hunted for it the more frightened she got, and at last she began to cry.
—from "The Yellow Dwarf"

The slower he went, the more time had everyone to stare and look at him; and they used it too, and no one can imagine how tired out and ragged he looked after his dance with the calf.
—from "The Master-Maid"

The more difficult it became to obtain the fruit, the more the Queen was determined that have it she would.
—from "The White Cat"

WEEK 27

Double Identities

—LESSON 105—

Clauses with Understood Elements
Than as Conjunction, Preposition, and Adverb
Quasi-Coordinators

I like chocolate better than vanilla.
Other than pistachio, I'll eat any flavor of ice cream.
I am more than satisfied with chocolate, but less than happy with pistachio.

I will starve rather than eat pistachio.

A coordinating conjunction joins equal words or groups of words together.
A subordinating conjunction joins unequal words or groups of words together.

He worked more efficiently than his brother.
He worked more efficiently than his brother [worked].

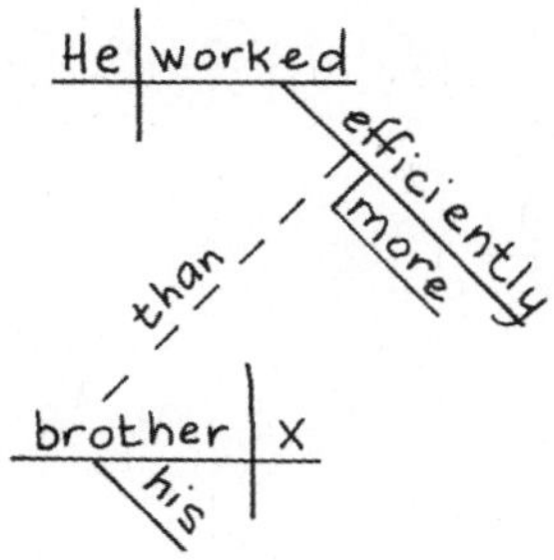

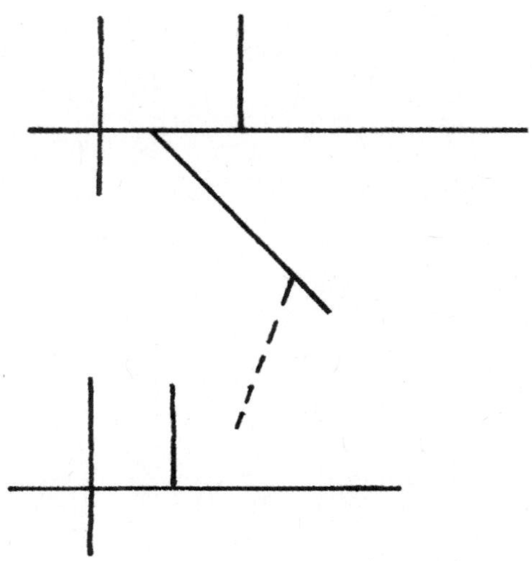

Tomorrow should be sunnier than today.
A new broom sweeps better than an old one.
The cook added more salt than he should have.

I love him more than you.

He is stronger than I.
    INCORRECT: He is stronger than me.

He is stronger than I am.
    not He is stronger than me.

When *than* is used in a comparison and introduces a clause with understood elements, it is acting as a subordinating conjunction.

Other than pistachio, I'll eat any flavor of ice cream.

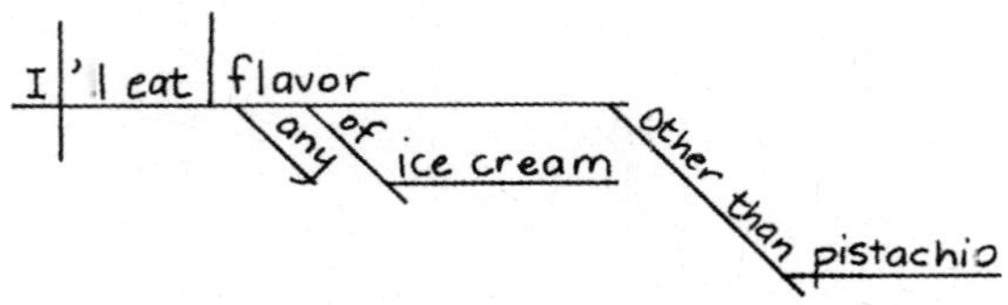

***Other than* is a compound preposition that means "besides" or "except."**

I am more than satisfied with chocolate, but less than happy with pistachio.

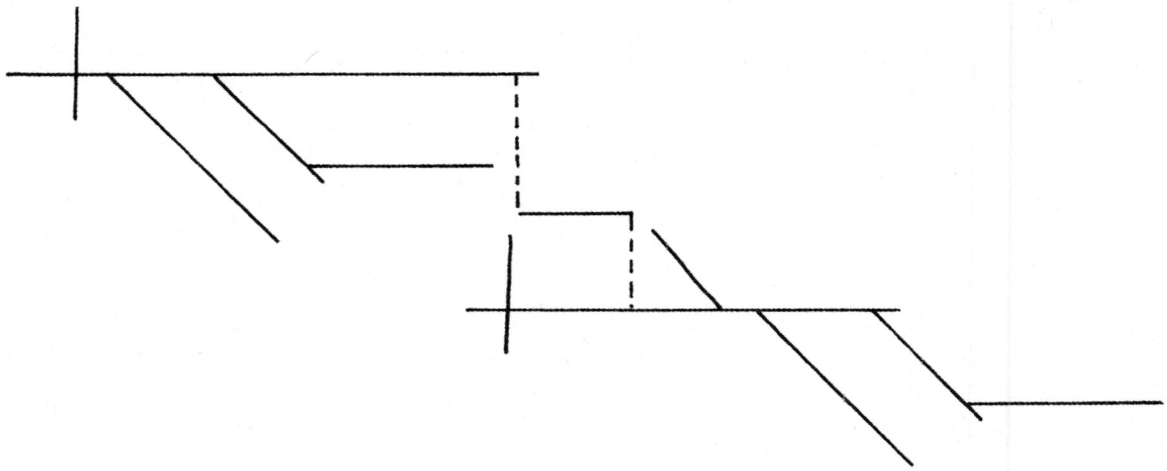

***More than* and *less than* are compound modifiers.**

I will starve rather than eat pistachio.

I will starve *and* eat pistachio.

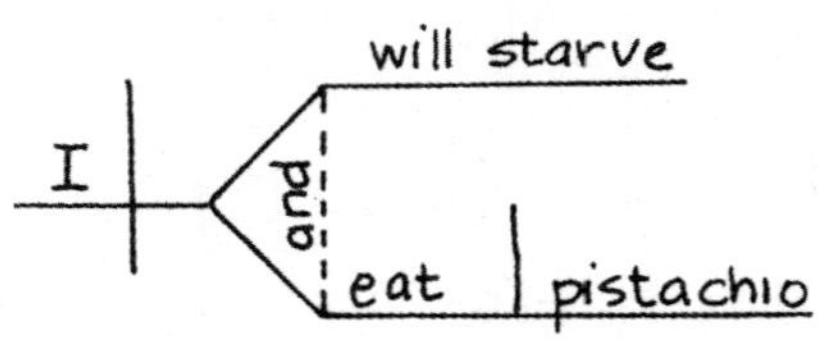

Quasi-coordinators link compound parts of a sentence that are unequal. Quasi-coordinators include *rather than, sooner than, let alone,* and *not to mention.*

I will starve rather than eat pistachio.

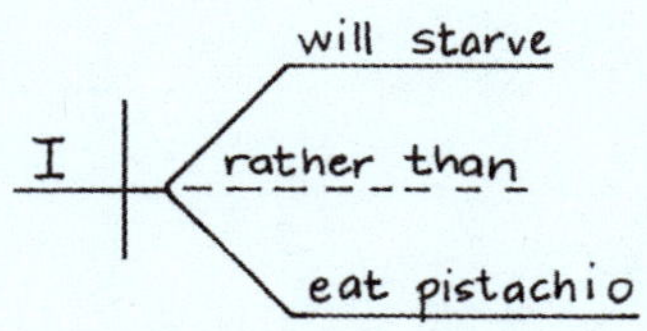

Rather than going home, she drove back up to the lake.

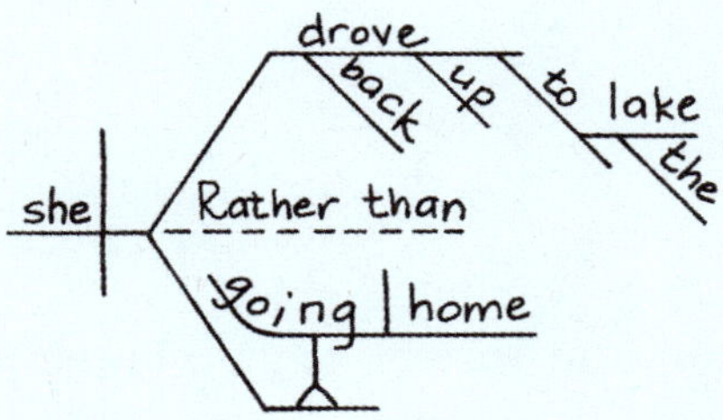

He could not keep up with Patel, let alone Krishna.

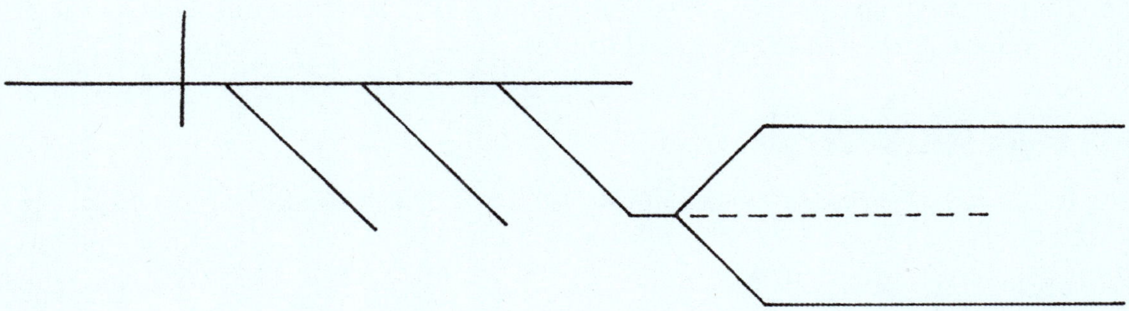

The expense, not to mention the risk, was simply too great.

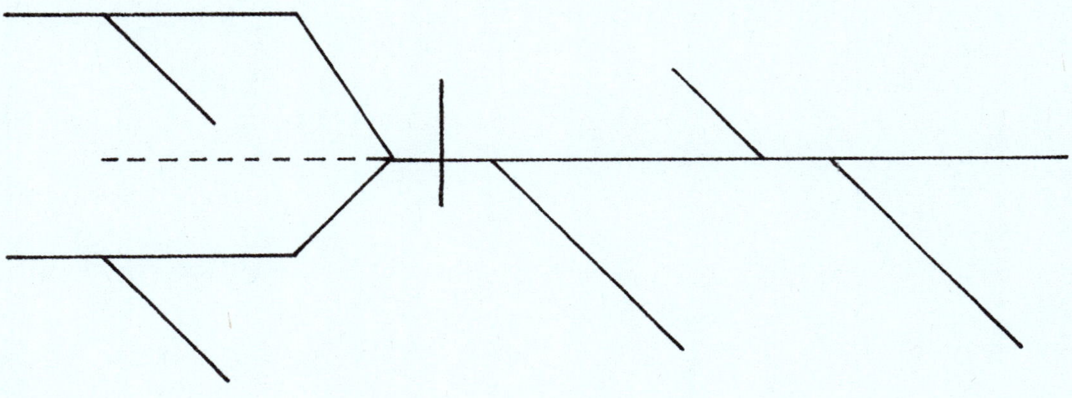

He would walk in a hailstorm sooner than pay ten dollars for a cab.

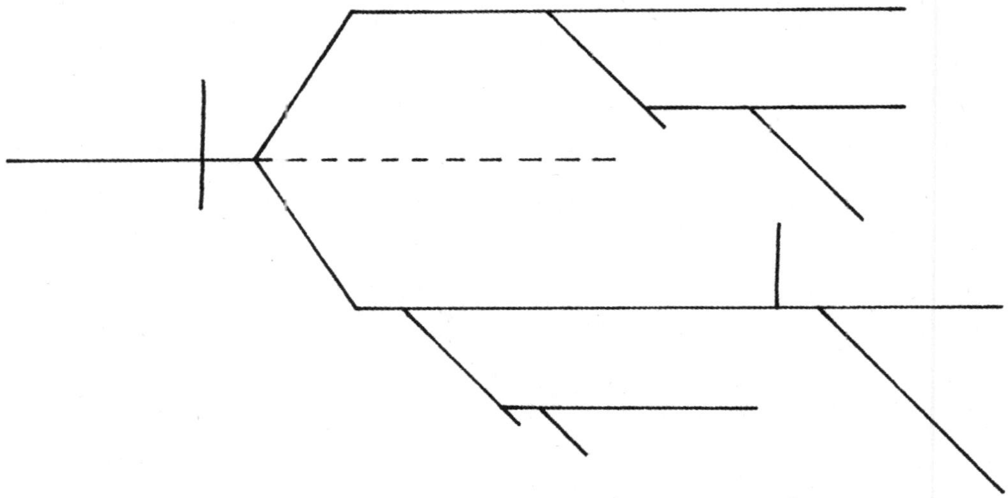

When *than* is used in a comparison and introduces a clause with understood elements, it is acting as a subordinating conjunction.
***Other than* is a compound preposition that means *besides* or *except*.**
***More than* and *less than* are compound modifiers.**

Quasi-coordinators link compound parts of a sentence that are unequal. Quasi-coordinators include *rather than, sooner than, let alone,* and *not to mention.*

Exercise 105A: Comparisons Using *Than*

Each of the following sentences, taken from Robert B. Kebric's *Greek People*, contains a comparison clause introduced by *than* and missing some of its words. Using carets, do your best to insert the missing words.

Since [the hoplite soldier] fought in a formation called the "phalanx," which was several ranks deep, he was less vulnerable than an individual warrior fighting by himself.

Soldiers, not the state, provided their own equipment, and although hoplite armor was far more expensive than what they had previously worn as support troops, their improved status as first-line heavy infantry made most members of the newly wealthy families willing to absorb the cost.

This one passage probably did more to disturb aristocrats of [Archilochus's] own generation—and later—than any other he wrote.

No athlete in antiquity enjoyed greater celebrity than Milo of Croton, whose wrestling prowess endeared him to fans of his own generation and those that followed.

No painter blended war, art, and politics better than the most famous Greek muralist, Polygnotus of Thasos.

Even worse than the death of a loved one was the knowledge that he had died a dishonorable death, an embarrassment with which his family had to live.

Exercise 105B: Identifying Parts of the Sentence

In the following sentences, drawn from Andrew Lang's *The Blue Fairy Book*, identify each bolded word or phrase as *SC* for subordinating conjunction, *QC* for quasi-coordinator, *PREP* for preposition, or *ADV* for adverb.

They said that the yellow water-lily could be none **other than** their sister, who was not dead, but transformed by the magic ball.

Not to mention the richness of the furniture, which was inestimable, there was such profuseness throughout that the Prince, instead of ever having seen anything like it, owned that he could not have imagined that there was anything in the world that could come up to it.

It is calculated that eleven hundred persons have at different times suffered death **rather than** break their eggs at the smaller end.

You will find the effect of it in **less than** an hour's time.

Now this man was no other **than** the father of the boy's mother.

She has carried off **more than** one Prince like this, and she will certainly have anything she takes a fancy to.

"O admirable potion!" she said: "it has wrought its cure much sooner **than** you told me it would."

A lovely princess like you must surely prefer to die **rather than** be the wife of a poor little dwarf like myself.

In **less than** three hours I was raised and slung into the engine, and there tied fast.

"I ask for no more **than** I am able to carry with me," said the prince.

Exercise 105C: Diagramming

On your own paper, diagram every word of the following sentences from Exercise 105B.

They said that the yellow water-lily could be none other than their sister, who was not dead, but transformed by the magic ball.

It is calculated that eleven hundred persons have at different times suffered death rather than break their eggs at the smaller end.

A lovely princess like you must surely prefer to die rather than be the wife of a poor little dwarf like myself.

In less than three hours I was raised and slung into the engine, and there tied fast.

—LESSON 106—

The Word *As*

Quasi-Coordinators

Middle English *alswa* "similarly" *as*

> The twenty-fourth object would be as big as a sugar cube, the twenty-seventh would be about the size of a large mammal, the fifty-fourth would be the size of the planet Jupiter and the fifty-seventh would be about as big as the Sun, where even atoms are destroyed by gravity, leaving a mixture of nuclei and free electrons called a plasma.
>
> — John R. Gribbin, *The Scientists: A History of Science Told Through the Lives of its Greatest Inventors*

The twenty-fourth object would be as big as a sugar cube ^. [is big]

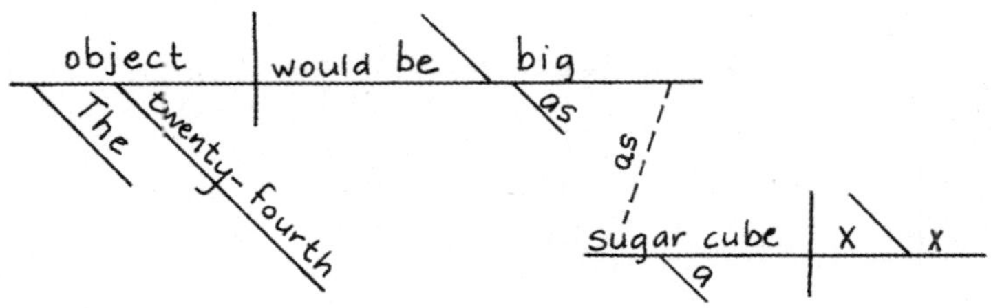

(The following sentences are all from Gribbin's *The Scientists* as well.)

. . . [A]n equally important factor, as many people have argued, was the depopulation of Europe by the Black Death . . .

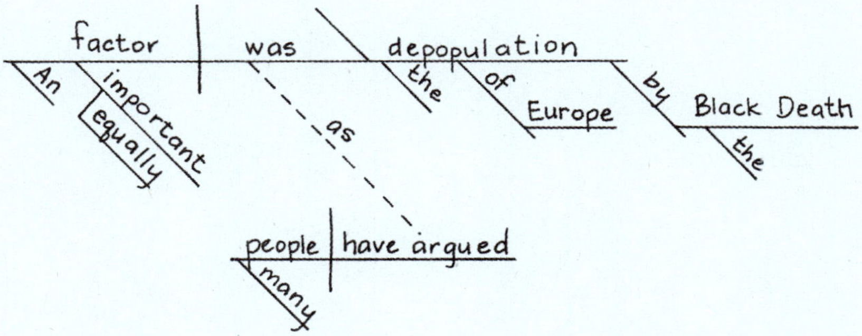

As long as Frederick remained on the throne, Tycho was able to enjoy an unprecedented amount of freedom to run his observatory just as he liked.

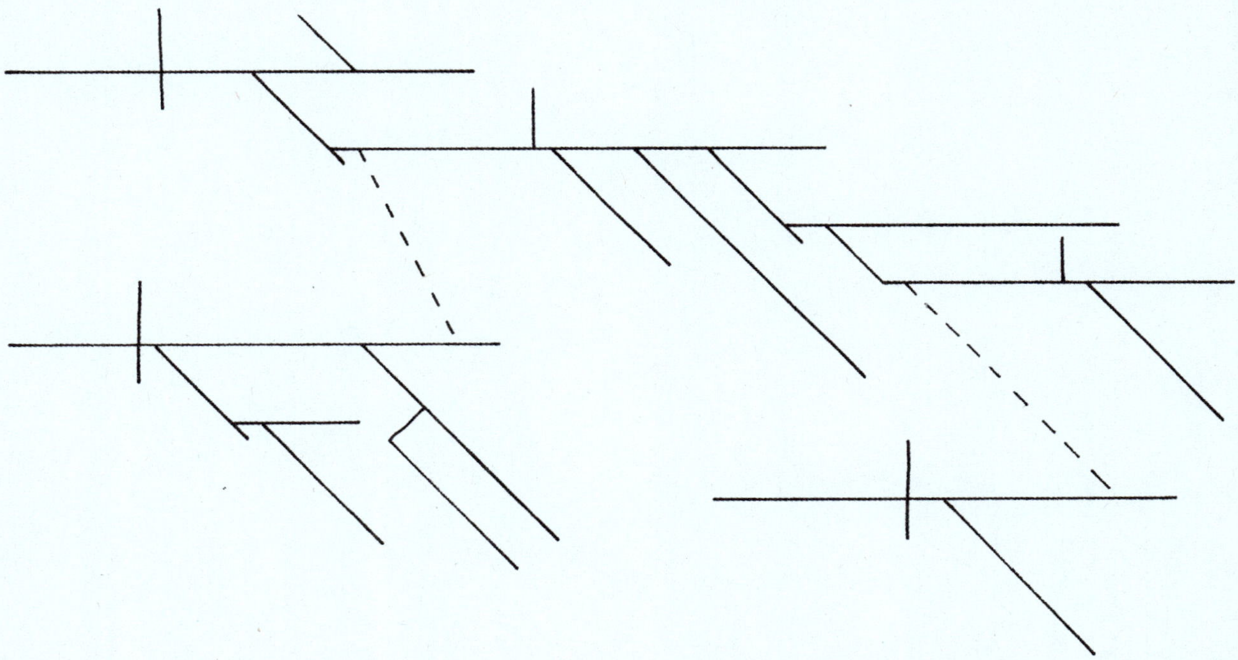

There were many translations and new editions of the book, which laid the foundations for chemistry as a genuinely scientific discipline.

Lavoisier . . . played a full part in the activities of the Academy, and during his time as a member worked on very many reports covering topics as diverse as . . . meteorites, cultivation of cabbages, the mineralogy of the Pyrenees and the nature of the gas arising from cesspools.

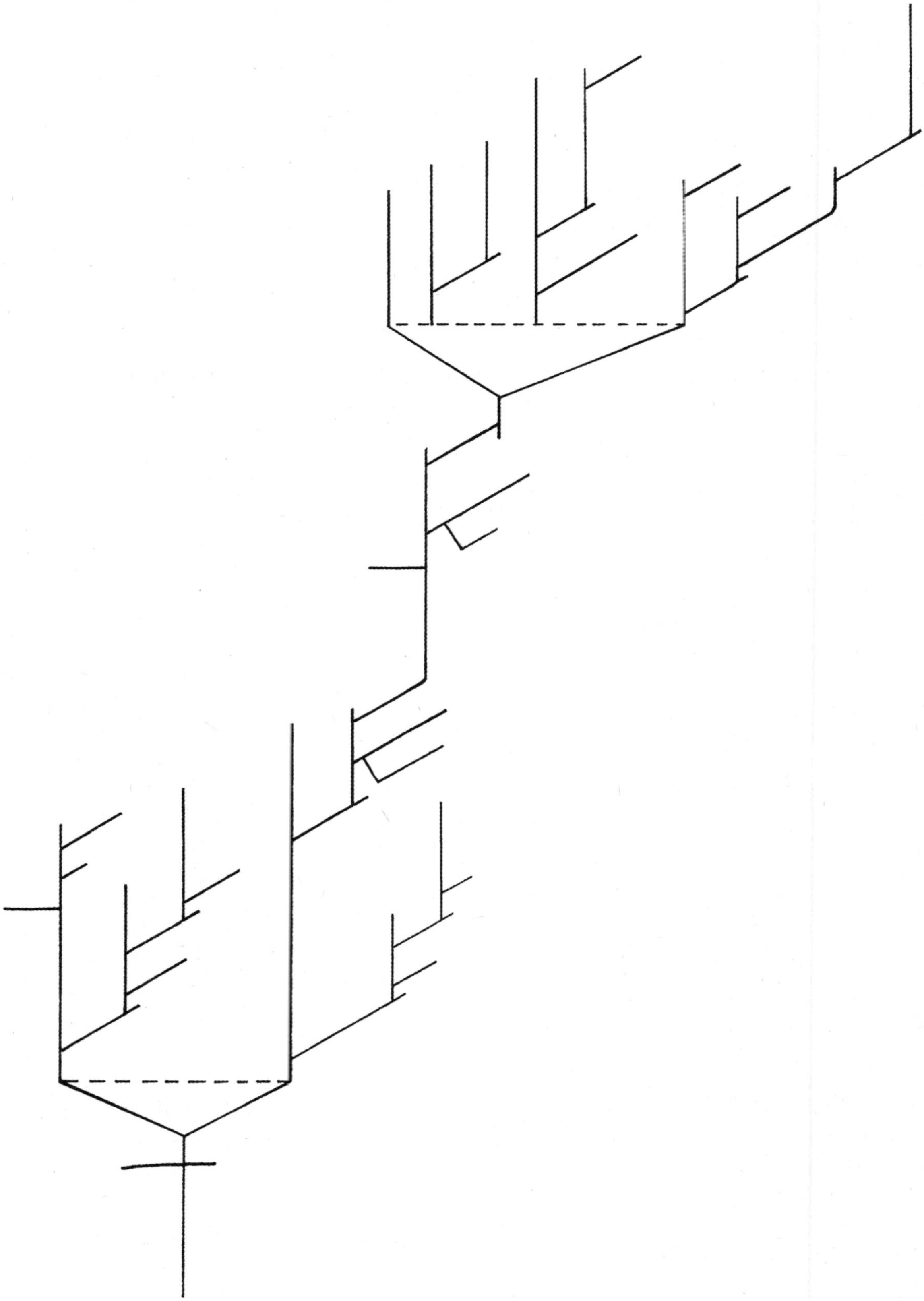

At the time of his marriage, as well as considerable property, Charles Cavendish had a disposable annual income of at least £2000, which grew as time passed.

Quasi-coordinators link compound parts of a sentence that are unequal. Quasi-coordinators include *rather than, sooner than, let alone, as well as,* and *not to mention.*

As well as his fame as a geologist, Darwin also received acclaim as a writer, in the mould of Lyell.

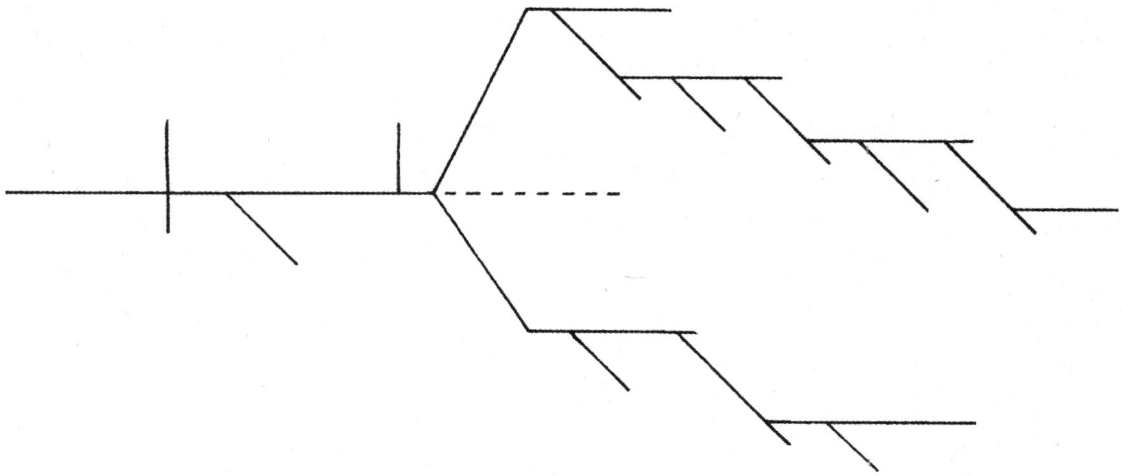

Exercise 106A: Identifying Parts of the Sentence

In the following sentences, find and underline every adverb, preposition, conjunction, and quasi-coordinator. Then label each as *ADV* for adverb, *PREP* for preposition, *CC* for coordinating conjunction, *SC* for subordinating conjunction, and *QC* for quasi-coordinator. Remember that a quasi-coordinator can be a short phrase as well as a single word.

These sentences are adapted from Robert Louis Stevenson's *The Strange Case of Dr. Jekyll and Mr. Hyde.*

I was never more disappointed in any man than Lanyon.

And then he condemned the fear as a disloyalty, and broke the seal.

He was the usual cut and dry apothecary, of no particular age and colour, with a strong Edinburgh accent, and about as emotional as a bagpipe.

But he had an approved tolerance for others, sometimes wondering, almost with envy, at the high pressure of spirits involved in their misdeeds; and in any extremity inclined to help rather than to reprove.

The lawyer liked this letter well enough; it put a better colour on the intimacy than he had looked for.

He could have wished it otherwise; never in his life had he been conscious of so sharp a wish to see and touch his fellow-creatures; for struggle as he might, there was borne in upon his mind a crushing anticipation of calamity.

"I see you feel as I do," said Mr. Enfield.

He must know his own state and that his days are counted; and the knowledge is more than he can bear.

There he opened his safe, took from the most private part of it a document endorsed on the envelope as Dr. Jekyll's Will, and sat down with a clouded brow to study its contents.

This was brought to the lawyer on the next morning, before he was out of bed; and he had no sooner seen it, and been told the circumstances, than he shot out a solemn lip.

But I have been pedantically exact, as you call it.

But it is more than ten years since Henry Jekyll became too fanciful for me.

The tradesmen came while we were yet speaking, and we moved in a body to old Dr. Denman's surgical theatre, from which (as you are doubtless aware) Jekyll's private cabinet is most conveniently entered.

Exercise 106B: Diagramming

On your own paper, diagram every word of the following sentences from Exercise 106A.

He was the usual cut and dry apothecary, of no particular age and colour, with a strong Edinburgh accent, and about as emotional as a bagpipe.

He could have wished it otherwise; never in his life had he been conscious of so sharp a wish to see and touch his fellow-creatures; for struggle as he might, there was borne in upon his mind a crushing anticipation of calamity.

There he opened his safe, took from the most private part of it a document endorsed on the envelope as Dr. Jekyll's Will, and sat down with a clouded brow to study its contents.

The tradesmen came while we were yet speaking, and we moved in a body to old Dr. Denman's surgical theatre, from which (as you are doubtless aware) Jekyll's private cabinet is most conveniently entered.

—LESSON 107—

Words That Can Be Multiple Parts of Speech

(The sentences from this lesson have been slightly adapted and condensed from *Bleak House* by Charles Dickens.)

But ______________________________ ______________________________

I had an illness, but it was not a long one.

He has never hurt anybody but himself.

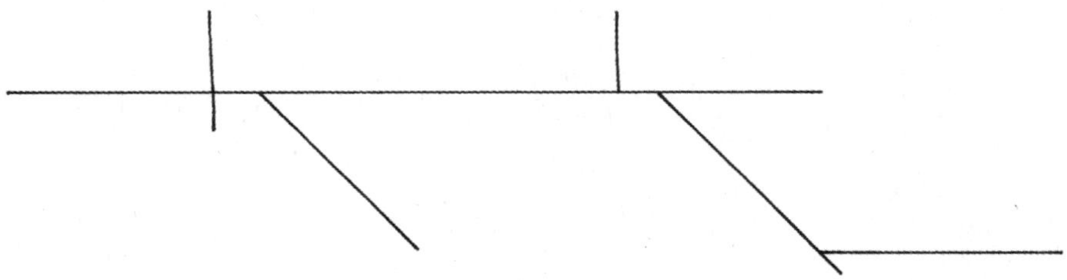

For ______________________________ ______________________________

I can answer for him as little as for you.

I should have been ashamed to come here to-day, for I know what a figure I must seem to you two.

About ______________________________ ______________________________

You could hear the horses being rubbed down outside the stable and being told to "Hold up!" and "Get over," as they slipped about very much on the uneven stones.

What with making notes on a slate about jams, and pickles, and preserves, and bottles, and glass, and china, and a great many other things; and what with being generally a methodical, old-maidish sort of foolish little person, I was so busy that I could not believe it was breakfast-time when I heard the bell ring.

Yet ______________________ ______________________

Is he here yet?
At this time, Jo has not yet died.
It is good, yet it could be improved.

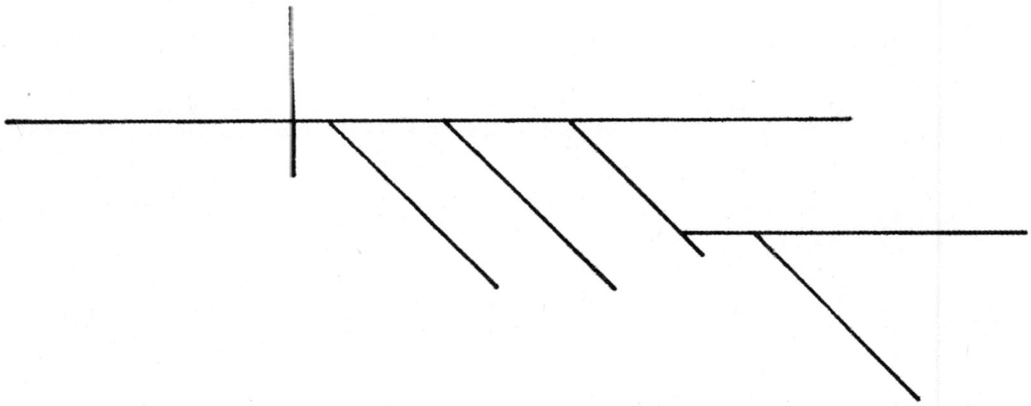

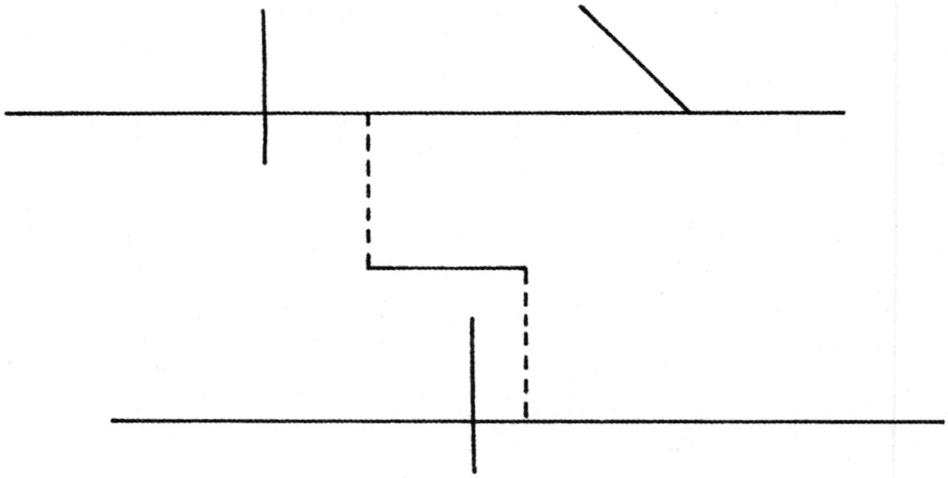

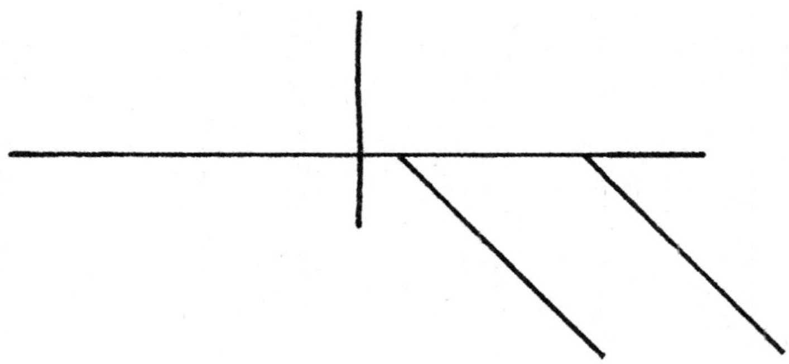

Any pronoun adjective adverb

I could not reproach myself any less.

It would be an insult to the discernment of any man with half an eye to tell him so.

I wonder whether any of the gentlemen remembered him.

I then asked Richard whether he had thought of any more congenial pursuit.

I thought it was impossible that you could have loved me any better.

Before _____________ _____________ _____________

Weariness of soul lies before her, as it lies behind.

It was past twelve before he took his candle and his radiant face out of the room.

He seemed to have been completely exhausted long before.

Above preposition _____________ _____________

The flame of gas was burning so sullenly above the iron gate.

His eyes were fixed high above.

But it is all blank, blank as the darkness above.

After preposition adverb _____________

In half an hour after our arrival, Mrs. Jellyby appeared.

I once more saw him looking at me after he had passed the door.

He presented himself soon after.

Otherwise _____________ _____________ _____________

We are not so prejudiced as to suppose that in private life you are otherwise than a very estimable man.

How could you do otherwise?

Love her and all will go well; otherwise, all will go ill.

Still

It is quite still and silent. _____________

She remained perfectly still until the carriage turned into the drive. _____________

The cause was hopeless; still, they fought. _____________

Still yourself, my dear, and wait in patience. _____________

In the still, the woods seemed massively hushed in sleep. _____________

Exercise 107A: Identifying Parts of Speech

Identify the part of speech of each underlined word by writing the correct abbreviation above it: *N* (noun), *PRO* (pronoun), *V* (verb), *ADJ* (adjective), *ADV* (adverb), *PREP* (preposition), *CC* (coordinating conjunction), or *SC* (subordinating conjunction).

The following sentences are from Charles Dickens's *A Tale of Two Cities.*

The nose, beautifully formed otherwise, was very slightly pinched at the top of each nostril.

He added the last words after there had been a vivid flash which had shown him lounging in the window.

It is fifteen years since we—since I—came last from France.

After this odd description of his daily routine of employment, Mr. Lorry flattened his waxen wig upon his head with both hands (which was most unnecessary, for nothing could be flatter than its shining surface was before), and resumed his former attitude.

This time a pair of haggard eyes had looked at the questioner before the face had dropped again.

Take that message back, and they will know that I received this.

The banker would not have gone so far in his expression of opinion on any less solid ground than moral certainty.

He had a wild, lost manner of occasionally clasping his head in his hands, that had not been seen in him before; yet he had some pleasure in the mere sound of his daughter's voice, and invariably turned to it when she spoke.

At last the top of the staircase was gained, and they stopped for the third time.

His linen, though not of a fineness in accordance with his stockings, was as white as the tops of the waves that broke upon the neighboring beach, or the specks of sail that glinted in the sunlight far at sea.

A gentleman of sixty, formally dressed in a brown suit of clothes, pretty well worn, but very well kept, with large square cuffs and large flaps to the pockets, passed along on his way to breakfast.

"You do me too much honour," said the Marquis; "still, I prefer that supposition."

I think a messenger was sent after him to beg the favour of his waiting for me here.

The Lord above knows what the compromising consequences would be to numbers of people if some of our documents were seized or destroyed.

With the same intention he drew the key across it, three or four times before he put it clumsily into the lock, and turned it as heavily as he could.

"True," said he, "and fearful to reflect upon."

You are a pretty fellow to object and advise!

He had no good-humour left in his face, nor any openness of aspect left, but had become a secret, angry, dangerous man.

But the time was not come yet.

I should be so much more at my ease about your state of mind.

The coachman was sure of nothing but the horses.

Many leaves of burning red and golden yellow still remained upon the trees.

A few passers turned their heads, and a few shook their fingers at him as an aristocrat; otherwise, that a man in good clothes should be going to prison was no more remarkable than that a labourer in working clothes should be going to work.

The plane tree whispered to them in its own way above their heads.

Her knitting was before her, but she had laid it down to pick her teeth with a toothpick.

There was a character about Madame Defarge, from which one might have predicted that she did not often make mistakes against herself in any of the reckonings over which she presided.

Darnay, unable to restrain himself any longer, touched Mr. Stryver on the shoulder, and said: "I know the fellow."

No one heard them as they went about with muffled tread.

Mr. Lorry got his arm securely round the daughter's waist and held her; for he felt that she was sinking.

He found them safe, and strong, and sound, and still, just as he had last seen them.

The majesty of the law fired blunderbusses in among them, loaded with rounds of shot and ball.

He stopped there, and faced round.

A supper-table was laid for two, in the third of the rooms; a round room, in one of the chateau's four extinguisher-topped towers.

Exercise 107B: Diagramming

On your own paper, diagram every word of the following sentences from *A Tale of Two Cities.*

His judges sat upon the bench in feathered hats; but the rough red cap and tricoloured cockade was the headdress otherwise prevailing.

I don't suppose anything about it but what Ladybird tells me.

His hurried right hand parcelled out the herbs before him into imaginary beds of flowers in a garden; and his efforts to control and steady his breathing shook the lips from which the colour rushed to his heart.

For some minutes after he had emerged into the outer presence of Saint Antoine, the husband and wife remained as he had left them, lest he should come back.

Little Lucie sat by her grandfather with her hands clasped through his arm; and he, in a tone not rising much above a whisper, began to tell her a story of a great and powerful fairy who had opened a prison-wall and let out a captive who had once done the fairy a service.

—LESSON 108—

Nouns Acting as Other Parts of Speech
Adverbial Noun Phrases

Exercise 108A: Nouns

In the five sentences below, identify the part of the sentence or clause that each underlined noun plays by labeling it as *S* for subject, *DO* for direct object, or *OP* for object of the preposition.

Please select chicken, beef, fish, or none of the above.

I watched through the window as a glorious morning dawned.

Charlotte opted to rest for a little while before the evening's festivities.

Once you have finished your work, you may choose how to spend the rest of the afternoon.

The pillow filled with down belongs in the other bedroom.

Exercise 108B: Nouns as Other Parts of Speech

Each of the following sets of sentences is missing one of the nouns from the exercise above. Your task: figure out which noun can fill every blank in one set of sentences. Each set must use the *same* noun in each blank!

In the ______________________________ I will begin my journey. (noun)

The sound of the ______________________________ bells awakened me. (adj)

We will continue to ______________________________ on this problem until we reach a solution agreeable to everyone. (verb)

I need to do laundry this evening; all of my ____________________ clothes are dirty. (adj)

Dr. Klein has done important _________________________ in the field of linguistics. (noun)

I watered each plant carefully; Mr. Minton stared at me all the ________________. (noun)

Sigourney liked to _____________________ away the rainy afternoons with her cousin, playing charades, hide-and-seek, and dress-up. (verb)

____________________ you clean the kitchen, I will wrap Joel's birthday presents. (subordinating conjunction)

As we walked into the room, something flew at us from ____________________. (noun)

Miguel watched the birds soaring ____________________. (adv)

The clouds ____________________ formed curious shapes; one of them, I was certain, was a monkey holding a fish. (adj)

The hat you're looking for is on the shelf ____________________ you. (prep)

The baby bird, covered in soft, fluffy ____________________, captured the children's attention immediately. (noun)

Gary can ____________________ the rest of his soda in one long gulp. (verb)

Hearing their grandmother's voice, the children ran excitedly ____________________ the stairs. (prep)

"____________________, Rover!" said the man to the overly enthusiastic dog. (interjection)

Our usual teacher is ____________________ with the flu, so we have a substitute today. (adj)

A solitary leaf floated ____________________ as I sat beneath the chestnut tree. (adv)

Mary and her lamb went into the school.

Mary and her lamb went home.

He followed her to school on Monday.

He followed her to school one day.

An adverbial noun tells the time or place of an action, or explains how long, how far, how deep, how thick, or how much. It can modify a verb, adjective, or adverb. An adverbial noun plus its modifiers is an adverbial noun phrase.

Before the lamb had travelled a mile, Mary turned around.

The road to school was two miles long.

The mud puddle in the road was three inches deep.

The lamb splashed in the puddle until he was covered with inch-thick mud.

The lamb splashed in the puddle until he was covered with mud an inch thick.

The storm continued all night.

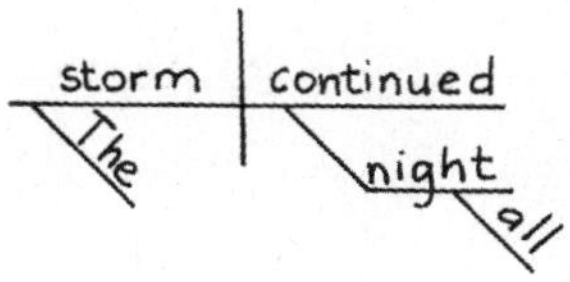

The earth's mantle is roughly 1,800 miles thick.

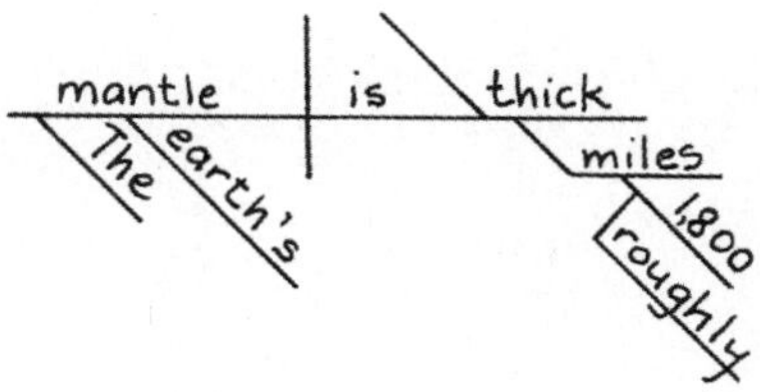

He slept eight hours and then woke up early the next morning.

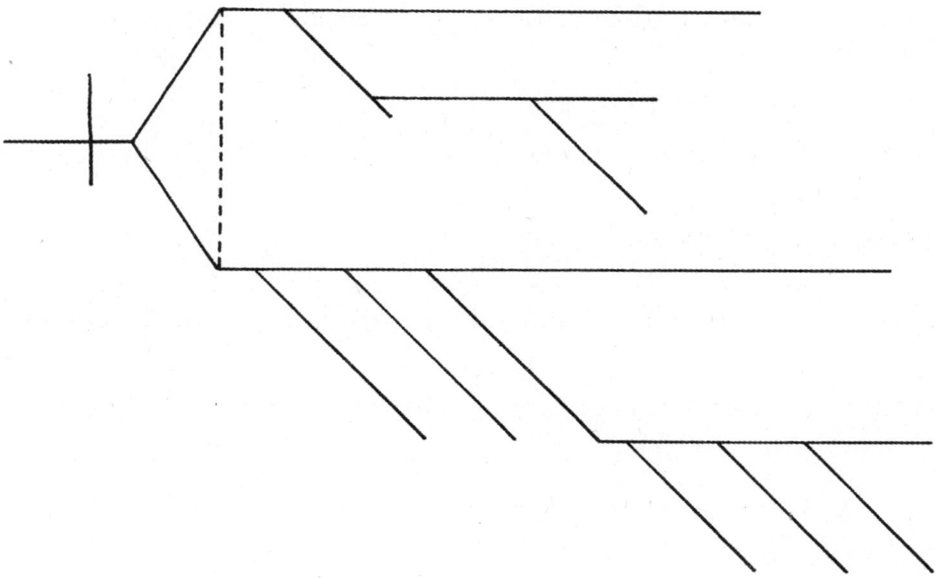

After our delicious picnic lunch, we walked the two miles to the battlefield.

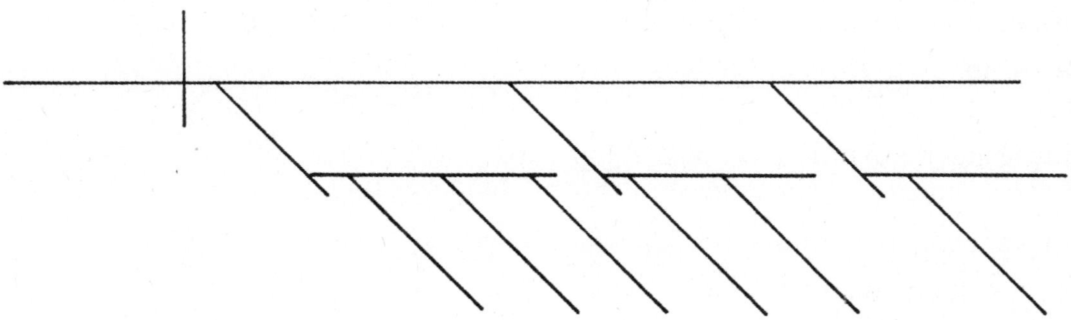

Exercise 108C: Identifying Parts of Speech

Identify the part of speech of each underlined word by writing the correct abbreviation above it: *N* (noun), *ADV-N* (adverbial noun), *PRO* (pronoun), *V* (verb), *ADJ* (adjective), *ADV* (adverb), *PREP* (preposition), *CC* (coordinating conjunction), *SC* (subordinating conjunction), or *QC* (quasi-coordinator).

These sentences are taken from Oscar Wilde's *The Importance of Being Earnest.*

The happiness of more than one life depends on your answer.

As far as the piano is concerned, sentiment is my forte.

Nothing annoys people so much as not receiving invitations.

Oh! it is absurd to have a hard-and-fast rule about what one should read and what one shouldn't.

I haven't quite finished my tea yet! and there is still one muffin left.

Tell it to come round next week, at the same hour.

I don't really know what a Gorgon is like, but I am quite sure that Lady Bracknell is one.

Surely such a utilitarian occupation as the watering of flowers is rather Moulton's duty than yours?

I forgave you before the week was out.

Memory, my dear Cecily, is the diary that we all carry about with us.

The gentleman whose arm is at present round your waist is my dear guardian, Mr. John Worthing.

I have never loved anyone in the world but you.

Miss Fairfax, ever since I met you I have admired you more than any girl . . . I have ever met since . . . I met you.

I have introduced you to everyone as Ernest.

I'll reveal to you the meaning of that incomparable expression as soon as you are kind enough to inform me why you are Ernest in town and Jack in the country.

I have never met any really wicked person before.

I have a country house with some land, of course, attached to it, about fifteen hundred acres, I believe; but I don't depend on that for my real income.

While I am making these inquiries, you, Gwendolen, will wait for me below in the carriage.

Exercise 108D: Adverbial Noun Phrases

Circle each adverbial noun or noun phrase, and draw an arrow from the circle to the word modified. Be careful—in one sentence, an understood element is being modified! You should insert it with a caret and then draw the arrow.

These sentences are adapted from *The Autobiography of Benjamin Franklin.*

In this manner we lay all night, with very little rest; but the wind abating the next day, we made a shift to reach Amboy before night, having been thirty hours on the water, without victuals, or any drink but a bottle of filthy rum, the water we sailed on being salt.

In walking through the Strand and Fleet Street one morning at seven o'clock, I observed there was not one shop open, though it had been daylight and the sun up above three hours.

I had been absent seven months, and my friends had heard nothing of me; for my brother Holmes was not yet returned, and had not written about me.

He told me that, when he had been detained a month, he acquainted his lordship that his ship was grown foul to a degree that must necessarily hinder her fast sailing.

Each pine made three palisades eighteen feet long, pointed at one end.

In this journey I spent the summer, traveled about sixteen hundred miles, and did not get home till the beginning of November.

Philadelphia was a hundred miles farther; I set out, however, in a boat for Amboy, leaving my chest and other things to follow me round by sea.

Exercise 108E: Diagramming

On your own paper, diagram every word of these sentences from Exercise 108D.

In this manner we lay all night, with very little rest; but the wind abating the next day, we made a shift to reach Amboy before night, having been thirty hours on the water, without victuals, or any drink but a bottle of filthy rum, the water we sailed on being salt.

In walking through the Strand and Fleet Street one morning at seven o'clock, I observed there was not one shop open, though it had been daylight and the sun up above three hours.

I had been absent seven months, and my friends had heard nothing of me; for my brother Holmes was not yet returned, and had not written about me.

In this journey I spent the summer, traveled about sixteen hundred miles, and did not get home till the beginning of November.

WEEK 28

— REVIEW 9 —

Weeks 25-27

Topics
Progressive Perfect Indicative Tenses
Progressive Present and Progressive Perfect Present Modal Verbs
Conditional Sentences
Adjectives in the Appositive Position
Correct Comma Usage
Limiting Adjectives
Misplaced, Squinting, and Dangling Modifier Comparisons
Using "More," "Fewer," and "Less" Quasi-Coordinators
Words That Can Be Multiple Parts of Speech
Nouns Acting as Other Parts of Speech
Adverbial Nouns

Review 9A: Definition Fill-in-the-Blank

In the last three weeks, you learned (and reviewed) even more definitions than in Weeks 22, 23, and 24! Fill in the blanks in the definitions below with one of the terms from the list. Many of the terms will be used more than once.

abstract noun	active	adjective
adjectives	adverb	adverbial noun
adverbs	apostrophe	appositive
attributive	cardinal numbers	clause
comma	commas	compound modifiers
compound preposition	comparative	coordinating conjunction
dangling modifier	demonstrative adjectives	demonstrative pronouns
descriptive adjective	fewer	First Conditional
imperative	indefinite adjectives	indefinite pronouns
indicative	interrogative adjectives	interrogative pronouns
less	misplaced modifier	present
modal	noun	ordinal numbers
passive	past	past participle
perfect	perfect past	perfect present
plural	positive	possessive adjective
predicative	progressive	progressive perfect
progressive present	quasi-coordinators	Second Conditional
simple	simple present	singular
squinting modifier	state of being	subjunctive
subordinating conjunction	superlative	Third Conditional
		future

____________________ verbs express real actions.

____________________ verbs express situations that are unreal, wished for, or uncertain.

____________________ verbs express intended actions.

____________________ verbs express possible actions and situations that have not actually happened.

In a sentence with an ____________________ verb, the subject performs the action.

In a sentence with a ____________________ verb, the subject receives the action.

A ____________________ verb simply tells whether an action takes place in the past, present, or future.

A ____________________ verb describes an ongoing or continuous action.

A ____________________ verb describes an action which has been completed before another action takes place.

A ________________________ verb describes an ongoing or continuous action that has a definite end.

The present passive imperative is formed by adding the helping verb *be* to the ____________________ of the verb.

The present passive subjunctive is formed by pairing *be* with the ____________________ of a verb.

Use the simple past subjunctive ____________________ verb, plus an infinitive, to express a future unreal action.

____________________ sentences express circumstances that might actually happen. The predicate of the condition clause is in a ____________________ tense. The predicate of the consequence clause is an ____________________ or is in a ____________________ or ____________________ tense.

____________________ sentences express circumstances that are contrary to reality. The predicate of the condition clause is in a ____________________ tense. The predicate of the consequence clause is in the ____________________ or ____________________ modal tense.

____________________ sentences express past circumstances that never happened. The predicate of the condition clause is in the ____________________ tense. The predicate of the consequence clause is in the ____________________ modal or ____________________ modal tense.

A ____________________ tells what kind.

A ____________________ becomes an ____________________ when you add *-ness* to it.

A ____________________ tells whose.

A ____________________ becomes an ____________________ when it is made possessive.

Form the possessive of a ____________________ noun by adding an ____________________ and the letter *s*.

Form the possessive of a ____________________ noun ending in *-s* by adding an ____________________ only.

Form the possessive of a ____________________ noun that does not end in *-s* as if it were a ____________________ noun.

An ____________________ that comes right before the noun it modifies is in the ____________________ position.

An ____________________ that follows the noun it modifies is in the ____________________ position.

____________________ adjectives directly follow the word they modify.

When three or more nouns, adjectives, verbs, or adverbs appear in a series, they should be separated by____________________.

When three or more items are in a list, a ____________________ before the last term is usual but not necessary.

When three or more items are in a list and a ______________________________ is used, a ________________ should still follow the next-to-last item in the list.

When two or more adjectives are in the _________________________ position, they are only separated by ________________ if they are equally important in meaning.

______________________________ demonstrate or point out something. They take the place of a single word or a group of words.

______________________________ modify nouns and answer the question "which one."

______________________________ are pronouns without antecedents.

______________________________ modify nouns and answer the questions "which one" and "how many."

______________________________ take the place of nouns in questions.

______________________________ modify nouns.

______________________________ represent quantities (one, two, three, four . . .).

______________________________ represent order (first, second, third, fourth . . .).

A ____________________________ is an adjective, adjective phrase, adverb, or adverb phrase in the wrong place.

A ____________________________ can belong either to the sentence element preceding or the element following.

A ____________________________ has no noun or verb to modify.

The ____________________ degree of an adjective describes only one thing.

The ____________________ degree of an adjective compares two things.

The ____________________ degree of an adjective compares three or more things.

Most regular adjectives form the ____________________ by adding *-r* or *-er*.

Most regular adjectives form the ______________________ by adding *-st* or *-est.*

Many adjectives form their ______________________ and ______________________ forms by adding the word *more* or *most* before the adjective instead of using *–er* or *–est.* In ____________________ and ____________________ adjective forms, the words *more* and *most* are used as ______________________.

Use "______________________" for concrete items and "______________________" for abstractions.

In comparisons using *more . . . fewer* and *more . . . less, more* and *less* can act as either ______________________ or ______________________ and *the* can act as an ______________________.

In comparisons using two comparative forms, the forms may act as either ______________ or ______________________, and *the* can act as an adverb.

A ______________________ joins equal words or groups of words together.

A ______________________ joins unequal words or groups of words together.

When *than* is used in a comparison and introduces a ______________________ with understood elements, it is acting as a ______________________.

Other than is a ______________________ that means "besides" or "except."

More than and *less than* are ______________________.

______________________ link compound parts of a sentence that are unequal. ______________________ include *rather than, sooner than, let alone, as well as,* and *not to mention.*

An ______________________ tells the time or place of an action, or explains how long, how far, how deep, how thick, or how much. It can modify a verb, ______________________, or ______________________.

An ______________________ plus its modifiers is an ______________________ phrase.

Review 9B: Parsing

Above each underlined verb, write the complete tense, the voice, and the mood. These sentences are adapted from *Jane Goodall: 40 Years at Gombe*, by Jennifer Lindsey.

The first is done for you.

simple present
active indicative

Yahaya Almasi bows his head; his weathered, brown face is wrinkled up in deep concentration.

I pointed out that the little creatures would find it altogether too hot and stuffy beneath the feathers.

This insatiable curiosity about life, its origins and complexities, its mysteries and failures, has never left her.

By observing Flo, Fifi and her offspring, the other community members, and the relationships among them, Jane learned that young chimpanzees stay with their mothers until they are at least seven years old, that adult chimpanzees form strong bonds, and, to her dismay, that rival communities can engage in brutal and bloody warfare.

Each chimpanzee builds a new nest for itself each night, although infants will sleep with their mothers until the age of five, or until the next infant is born.

Leaves are used to make sponges, which the chimpanzees use to sop up moisture in the hollow of a tree trunk.

He was resting peacefully when Fifi hurled herself onto him. He indulgently pushed her to and fro with one hand.

A mother will touch her child when she is about to move away, and may tap on a tree trunk when she wants the youngster to come down.

The researchers at Gombe had observed a phenomenon rarely recorded in field studies.

If he <u>had</u> not <u>been rescued</u>, young Kipara <u>would have met</u> with a cruel fate.

<u>Refuse</u> to buy products from companies, corporations, that <u>do</u> not <u>conform</u> to new environmental standards.

Review 9C: Provide the Verb

Complete each line below by providing an appropriate verb in the tense indicated. You may want to use the chart in Lesson 99 for reference. The original lines are from William Shakespeare's *Julius Caesar*; when you are finished, compare your answers to the original.

If you can't think of a verb, ask your instructor for help.

Caesar:	
The valiant never ________________ of death but once.	*simple present, active, indicative*
Of all the wonders that I yet ________________,	*perfect present, active, indicative*
It ________________ to me most strange that men ________________,	*1: simple present, active, indicative;* *2: simple present, active, modal*
Seeing that death, a necessary end,	
________________ when it ________________.	*1: simple future, active, indicative;* *2: simple future, active, indicative*

Brutus:	
Those that ________________ me speak, ________________ 'em stay here;	*1: simple future, active, indicative;* *2: simple present, active, imperative*
Those that ________________ Cassius, ________________ with him;	*1: simple future, active, indicative;* *2: simple present, active, imperative*
And public reasons ________________	*simple future, passive, indicative*
Of Caesar's death.	

Antony	
Friends, Romans, countrymen, ____________ me your ears;	*simple present, active, imperative*
I ____________ to bury Caesar, not to praise him.	*simple present, active, indicative*
The evil that men ____________ ____________ after them;	*1: simple present, active, indicative;* *2: simple present, active, indicative*
The good ____________ oft ____________ with their bones;	*simple present, passive, indicative (oft is an adverb)*
So let it be with Caesar. The noble Brutus	
____________ you Caesar ____________ ambitious:	*1: perfect present, active, indicative;* *2: simple present, active, indicative (state of being)*
If it ____________ so, it ____________ a grievous fault;	*1: simple present, active, subjunctive (state of being);* *2: simple past, active, indicative (state of being)*
And grievously ____________ Caesar ____________ it.	*perfect present, active, indicative (Caesar is the subject)*
Here, under leave of Brutus and the rest,—	
For Brutus ____________ an honourable man;	*simple present, active, indicative (state of being)*
So ____________ they all, all honourable men,—	*simple present, active, indicative (state of being)*
____________ I to speak in Caesar's funeral.	*simple present, active, indicative*

Lucilius:	
When you ________________ him, or alive or dead,	*simple present, active, indicative, with do for emphasis*
He ________________ like Brutus, like himself.	*simple future, passive, indicative*

Review 9D: Identifying Adjectives and Punctuating Items in a Series

In the following lines (from the poem "Rain in Summer," by Henry Wadsworth Longfellow), do the following:

a) Underline once and label all adjectives (except for articles), using the following abbreviations:

Descriptive Adjectives		Limiting Adjectives	
Regular	DA-R	Possessives	LA-P
Present participles	DA-PresP	~~Articles~~	~~LA-A~~
Past participles	DA-PastP	Demonstratives	LA-D
		Indefinites	LA-IND
		Interrogatives	LA-INT
		Numbers	LA-N

b) Circle all adjectives that are in the predicate or in the predicative position and draw an arrow from each to the noun it modifies.

How beautiful is the rain!

After the dust and heat,

In the broad and fiery street,

In the narrow lane,

How beautiful is the rain!

How it clatters along the roofs,

Like the tramp of hoofs

How it gushes and struggles out

From the throat of the overflowing spout!

Across the window-pane
It pours and pours;
And swift and wide,
With a muddy tide,
Like a river down the gutter roars
The rain, the welcome rain!

The sick man from his chamber looks
At the twisted brooks;
He can feel the cool
Breath of each little pool;
His fevered brain
Grows calm again,
And he breathes a blessing on the rain.

From the neighboring school
Come the boys,
With more than their wonted noise
And commotion;
And down the wet streets
Sail their mimic fleets,
Till the treacherous pool
Ingulfs them in its whirling
And turbulent ocean.

In the country, on every side,

Where far and wide,

Like a leopard's tawny and spotted hide,

Stretches the plain,

To the dry grass and the drier grain

How welcome is the rain!

In the furrowed land

The toilsome and patient oxen stand;

Lifting the yoke encumbered head,

With their dilated nostrils spread,

They silently inhale

The clover-scented gale,

And the vapors that arise

From the well-watered and smoking soil.

For this rest in the furrow after toil

Their large and lustrous eyes

Seem to thank the Lord,

More than man's spoken word.

Review 9E: Correcting Modifiers

The following sentences all have modifier problems! Correct each sentence, using proofreader's marks, and be ready to explain the problems to your instructor. The first one is done for you.

The man chased the monkey in the yellow hat.

Joy believed spring was the wonderfullest time of the year.

Sleeping soundly, the tent protected us from the rain outside.

Wednesday's soccer game will be played on the more large field.

Sucking contentedly on her thumb, the mother placed the baby gently into the crib.

The worm startled the little boy wriggling on the ground.

The whistle sounded loudly in my ears that signaled the end of the game.

Our annual fundraising walk attracted over three hundred walkers organized by Marcia Trostle.

My uncle, who had just broken the school record for home runs, clapped enthusiastically for the player.

He's sleeping peacefully now, but that panther can be one of the most fierce animals in the zoo.

My sister is a diligenter student than I am.

Gloria instructed us quickly to tidy the room.

The money is for spending at the circus in my wallet.

Our area gets less earthquakes than the area where my cousins live.

The city hosts a famous golf tournament in which I grew up.

Review 9F: Identifying Adverbs

In the following sentences, taken from Frances Hodgson Burnett's *The Secret Garden*, carry out the following three steps:

a) Underline each word, phrase, or clause that is acting as an adverb.
b) Draw a line from the word/phrase/clause to the verb, adjective, or adverb modified.
c) Above the word or phrase, note whether it is a regular adverb (*ADV*), an adverbial noun (*AN*), a prepositional phrase (*PrepP*), an infinitive phrase (*INF*), a present participle phrase (*PresP*), a past participle phrase (*PastP*), or an adverbial clause (*C*).

Remember: within a phrase or clause acting as an adverb, there might also be an adverb modifying an adjective or verb form within the phrase or clause. Underline these adverbs a second time.

The guard lighted the lamps in the carriage, and Mrs. Medlock cheered up very much over her tea and chicken and beef.

She had never thought much about her looks, but she wondered if she was as unattractive as Ben Weatherstaff and she also wondered if she looked as sour as he had looked before the robin came.

She looked at the key quite a long time.

She liked the name, and she liked still more the feeling that when its beautiful old walls shut her in no one knew where she was.

Her hair was ruffled on her forehead and her cheeks were bright pink.

No one believes I shall live to grow up.

After another week of rain the high arch of blue sky appeared again and the sun which poured down was quite hot.

The fox was lying on the grass close by him, looking up to ask for a pat now and then, and Dickon bent down and rubbed his neck softly and thought a few minutes in silence.

He had lifted his head and whinnied softly the moment he saw Dickon and he had trotted up to him and put his head across his shoulder and then Dickon had talked into his ear and Jump had talked back in odd little whinnies and puffs and snorts.

Ben Weatherstaff had not quite got over his emotion, but he had recovered a little and answered almost in his usual way.

Review 9G: Comma Use

The following sentences have lost all of their commas. Insert commas directly into the text (no need to use proofreader's marks) wherever needed.

The first ten sentences are adapted from *Owls Aren't Wise and Bats Aren't Blind*, by Warner Shedd; the remaining sentences are adapted from *Fifty Animals that Changed the Course of History*, by Eric Chaline.

Given the near ubiquity of beavers today most people shouldn't find it difficult to locate a beaver dam that they can scrutinize at leisure.

These "dispossessed" beavers must now seek new territory find mates and begin new colonies.

While the beaver's tail is rounded and relatively short very wide and flattened top to bottom the muskrat's is long quite slender and flattened from side to side.

Such behavior though it might seem unjust probably results in something like a fair exchange in most cases.

However it most certainly was given great credence by that famous Roman Pliny the Elder who died in the cataclysmic eruption of Vesuvius that buried Pompeii and Herculaneum in AD 79.

The bat's fifth finger or "thumb" incidentally far from being elongated in the manner of its other digits is a small hook used for climbing or walking.

Possums aren't to use a current expression the brightest bears in the woods and they don't think in terms of playing dead to deceive an enemy.

On dark rainy days however efts emerge in daylight hours to forage and wander about.

Based on two personal experiences I would say that owls regard mice and voles in about the same light as we might view lobster steak or a rich chocolate dessert.

Suburban sprawl timber cutting wetland drainage development and other human disturbances are slowly but surely nibbling away at this critical nesting habitat which rarely has any legal protection.

The English word "mosquito" is derived from a diminutive of the Spanish word for "fly" mosca and translates as "little fly."

At first this consisted of the hunting of smaller species that came into inshore coastal waters.

The crusaders whose ostensible aim was the liberation of the Holy Land conquered the Christian Byzantine Empire.

After the war silk was not able to regain its earlier preeminence.

Although the camel has now been supplanted by the truck and motorcar it remains an important source of milk wool and meat in the Arab world.

In Europe where the horse and oxen did the heavy lifting the traditional roles of the dog have been in hunting and in animal husbandry.

Horse-drawn chariots were important weapons in Bronze Age ancient Egypt Minoan Crete and Mycenaean Greece.

Even after it became a protected species the eagle like the falcon and other birds of prey fell victim to pesticides that almost caused its extinction from across much of the continental US.

Squanto was a member of the Patuxet tribe a tributary of the Wampanoag who had been kidnapped and forcefully taken to Europe by British sailors in 1614.

As we have seen in earlier entries fiber can be obtained from a variety of animals including goats rabbits and camels but with selective breeding the sheep has become the animal that produces the largest quantities of white wool.

Review 9H: Conjunctions

In the following sentences from L. Frank Baum's *The Marvelous Land of Oz*, find and circle every conjunction. Label each as coordinating (*C*), subordinating (*SUB*), coordinating correlative (*CC*), subordinating correlative (*SC*), or quasi-coordinator (*QC*).

He ran up beside her and tried to keep pace with her swift footsteps—a very difficult feat, for she was much taller than he, and evidently in a hurry.

He is a proud man, as he has every reason to be, and it pleases him to be termed Emperor rather than King.

Mombi had no sooner arrived at the royal palace than she discovered, by means of her secret magic, that the adventurers were starting upon their journey to the Emerald City.

It is nearly dark, and unless we wait until morning to make our flight we may get into more trouble.

The throne of the Emerald City belongs neither to you nor to Jinjur, but to this Pastoria from whom the Wizard usurped it.

I ought to know by heart every step of this journey, and yet I fear we have already lost our way.

Although I am of tin, I own a heart altogether the warmest and most admirable in the whole world.

Tip also noticed that Jack's pumpkin head had twisted around until it faced his back; but this was easily remedied.

Review 9I: Identifying Independent Elements

The following sentences, taken from *The Secret Garden*, all contain independent elements: absolutes (*ABS*), parenthetical expressions (*PE*), interjections (*INT*), nouns of direct address (*NDA*), appositives (*APP*), and/or noun clauses in apposition (*NCA*). Locate, underline, and label each one.

Some elements may legitimately be labeled in more than one way. The difference between an absolute and a parenthetical expression is particularly tricky; generally, a parenthetical element can be removed without changing the meaning of the sentence, while an absolute construction cannot.

Be ready to explain your answers.

She did not miss her at all, in fact, and as she was a self-absorbed child she gave her entire thought to herself, as she had always done.

And there's nothing likely to improve children at Misselthwaite—if you ask me!

I don't know anythin' about anythin'—just like you said. I beg your pardon, Miss.

He turned about to the orchard side of his garden and began to whistle—a low soft whistle.

Eh! there does seem a lot of us then.

The sun was shining and a little wind was blowing—not a rough wind, but one which came in delightful little gusts and brought a fresh scent of newly turned earth with it.

I never did many things in India, but there were more people to look at—natives and soldiers marching by—and sometimes bands playing, and my Ayah told me stories.

You could not do any harm, a child like you!

For one thing, he's afraid he'll look at him some day and find he's growed hunchback.

The nurse, Mrs. Medlock and Martha had been standing huddled together staring at her, their mouths half open.

Well, sir, you'll scarcely believe your eyes when you see him.

And this, if you please, this is what Ben Weatherstaff beheld and which made his jaw drop.

The robin used to secrete himself in a bush and watch this anxiously, his head tilted first on one side and then on the other.

Review 9J: Words with Multiple Identities

In the following sentences, taken from *Ozma of Oz* by L. Frank Baum, identify each underlined word as an adverb (*ADV*), adjective (*ADJ*), noun (*N*), pronoun (*PRO*), preposition (*PREP*), subordinating conjunction (*SC*), coordinating conjunction (*CC*), or quasi-coordinator (*QC*).

He accomplished the feat without breaking <u>any</u> bones.

Their battle-axes were poised <u>as if</u> to strike <u>down</u> their foes; <u>yet</u> they remained motionless <u>as</u> statues, awaiting the word of command.

I make <u>but</u> one condition.

So she sat <u>down</u> in a corner of the coop, leaned her <u>back</u> against the slats, nodded at the friendly stars <u>before</u> she closed her eyes, and was asleep in <u>half</u> a <u>minute</u>.

It would not be <u>enough</u> to fill one of my <u>back</u> teeth.

Then the bell above the throne, which sounded whenever an enchantment was broken, began to ring.

This the private managed to do, waiting until a time when he was nearest the ground and then letting himself drop upon the Scarecrow.

If none of the eleven objects you touch proves to be the transformation of any of the royal family of Ev, then you will yourself become enchanted.

They walked slowly down the path between the rocks, Tiktok going first, Dorothy following him, and the yellow hen trotting along last of all.

You'll be sorry for treating me in this way.

He gave a sort of gurgle and stopped short, waving his hands frantically until suddenly he became motionless, with one arm in the air and the other held stiffly before him with all the copper fingers of the hand spread out like a fan.

They turned and fled madly into the cavern, and refused to go back again.

Ozma of Oz and her people, as well as Dorothy, Tiktok and Billina, were splendidly entertained by the Queen mother.

So she retraced her steps until she found the entrance to the palace.

But the little Prince was shy, and shrank away from the painted Scarecrow because he did not yet know his many excellent qualities.

Oh, no; you are mistaken about that.

He won't need to be wound up any more, for he has now become a very neat ornament.

"There is no rea-son to be a-fraid of the Wheel-ers," said Tiktok, the words coming more slowly than before.

But as the yellow hen tried to enter after them, the little maid cried "Shoo!" and flapped her apron in Billina's face.

Review 9K: Verb Forms Functioning in Other Ways

The following sentences are from *Sophie's Diary*, by Dora Musielak. The book gives a fictionalized account of the life of mathematician Sophie Germain, who was a young teen living in Paris during the French Revolution.

In these sentences, present participles, past participles, and infinitives are used as nouns and modifiers. Circle each of these verb forms and label each one as noun (*N*), adjective (*ADJ*), or adverb (*ADV*).

For adjectives and adverbs, draw a line to the word modified. For nouns, add a label describing the part of the sentence it fulfills: subject (*S*), direct object (*DO*), indirect object (*IO*), predicate nominative (*PN*), or object of the preposition (*OP*).

The first is done for you.

ADJ

Father says the privileged aristocrats are fiercely opposed, and they will do anything

ADV N DO

to avoid losing their wealth and property.

Armed with pitchforks, the women walked for six hours to Versailles.

Thus, I also must know the amount of water displaced by a certain amount of gold and a certain amount of silver.

Even after moving to the Tuileries Palace in Paris, the king cannot resolve the social conflicts and the financial crisis of the nation.

Now I just imagine the huge numbers on the squares of the fourth row and the remaining squares on the chessboard.

My sister was enchanted and was more interested in learning to play.

My dream is to devote my life to seeking out answers to difficult questions.

At home we try to preserve a sense of normality.

Actors waved banners inscribed with the names of Voltaire's plays.

Review 9L: Diagramming

On your own paper, diagram every word of the following sentences, adapted from Charlotte Bronte's *Jane Eyre*.

Had I attended to the suggestions of pride and ire, I should immediately have left him: but something worked within me more strongly than those feelings could.

He was never married, and had no near kindred but ourselves, and one other person, not more closely related than we.

Tell me now, fairy as you are—can't you give me a charm, or a philter, or something of that sort, to make me a handsome man?

I burned for the more active life of the world—for the more exciting toils of a literary career—for the destiny of an artist, author, anything rather than that of a priest.

Of course (as St. John once said) I must seek another interest in life to replace the one lost: is not the occupation he now offers me truly the most glorious man can adopt or God assign?

She had no great talents, no marked traits of character, no peculiar development of feeling or taste which raised her one inch above the ordinary level of childhood; but neither had she any deficiency or vice which sunk her below it.

You are not to suppose, reader, that Adèle has all this time been sitting motionless on the stool at my feet.

A ridge of lighted heath, alive, glancing, devouring, would have been a meet emblem of my mind when I accused and menaced Mrs. Reed: the same ridge, black and blasted after the flames are dead, would have represented as neatly my subsequent condition, when half an hour's silence and reflection had shown me the madness of my conduct, and the dreariness of my hated and hating position.

WEEK 29

Still More Verbs

—LESSON 109—

Hortative Verbs
Subjunctive Verbs

A hortative verb encourages or recommends an action.

Latin *hortari*: to encourage or urge

English derivatives:
to exhort (verb): to urge, or to give urgent recommendations
I exhorted him to keep running despite his weariness.
hortative (adjective): encouraging or urging on
Patience, Charity, and Praise-God are all hortative names.

Let's be more careful next time.

Let's run faster.

Let's be finished now.

In first person plural hortative verbs, the helping verb *let* is used.
The state-of-being verb takes the form *be*.
The active verb is the same form as the present active indicative.
The passive verb combines *be* with the past participle.

May you be happy.

May you walk in joy.

May you be saved from your own foolishness.

In second person hortative verbs, the helping verb *may* is used.
The state-of-being verb takes the form *be*.
The active verb is the same form as the present active indicative.
The passive verb combines *be* with the past participle.

Let the trumpets be sounded.

May no creature on earth be silent.

Let the Lord of the Black Lands come forth.

Third person hortative verbs use the helping verbs *let* or *may*.
The state-of-being verb takes the form *be*.
The active verb is the same form as the present active subjunctive.

The passive verb combines *be* with the past participle.

Active indicative, first person — We **sing** with happiness.
second person — You **sing** with happiness.

Active hortative, first person — Let us **sing** with happiness.
second person — May you **sing** with happiness.

Active indicative, third person — He **sings** with happiness.
Active subjunctive, third person — Should he **sing**, he will be happy.
Active hortative, third person — Let him **sing** with happiness.

May you travel safely.
Let us travel safely.

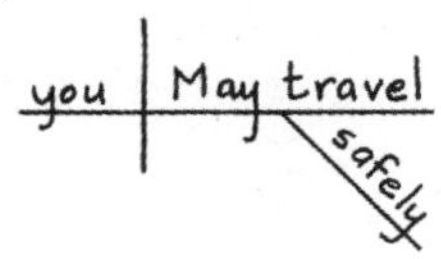

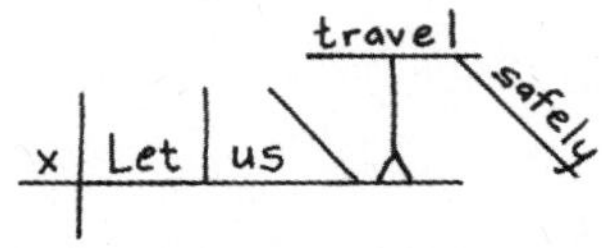

An object complement follows the direct object and renames or describes it.

DO OC
We elected Marissa leader.

May the evildoers come forth.
Let the Lord of the Black Lands come forth.

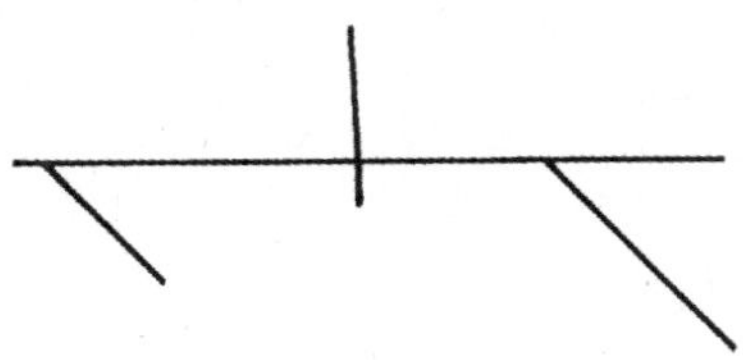

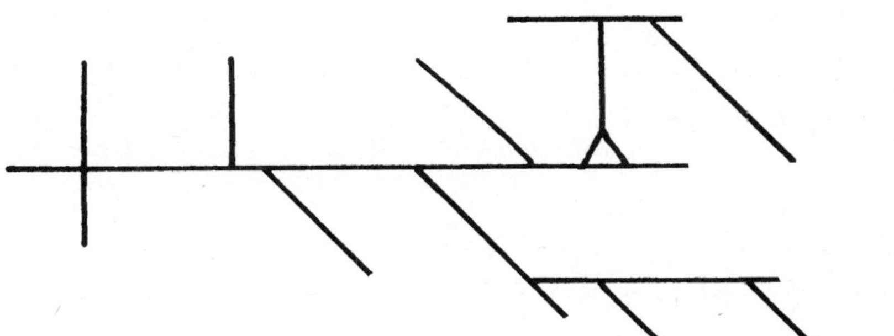

Exercise 109A: Identifying Hortative Verbs

Sacred and religious texts are often exhorting their readers—so they tend to use many hortative verbs! In the following sentences, underline twice every element of each hortative verb (*let* or *may*, any other helping verbs, and the main verb). Above the verb, identify it as state-of-being, active, or passive. If the person or thing being exhorted is present in the sentence, circle the noun or pronoun that identifies him/her/it, and identify it as *S* for subject or *O* for object.

Be careful—some sentences may not include any hortative verbs!

The first is done for you.

passive
S
So may we be acquainted with thine innermost benevolence:
Neglect us not, come hitherward.
—*Rig Veda*

Though one may conquer a thousand times a thousand men in battle, yet he is indeed the noblest victor who conquers himself.
—The *Dhammapada*

Come, let me speak with you.
—The *Analects* of Confucius

Let us arm ourselves with the armor of righteousness, and let us teach ourselves first to walk in the commandment of the Lord.
—Polycarp 4:1

So let them answer Me, and have faith in Me, that they may be rightly guided.
—Qur'an 186

Let not a mortal's evil will obstruct us.
—Rig Veda

Indeed, angry speech hurts, and retaliation may overtake you.
—The *Dhammapada*

And God said, Let there be lights in the firmament of the heaven to divide the day from the night; and let them be for signs, and for seasons, and for days, and years.

—Genesis 1:14 (King James Version)

May He grant unto you a lot and portion among His saints.

—Polycarp 12:2

The Guru has given me this one understanding: there is only the One, the Giver of all souls. May I never forget Him!

—Guru Granth Sahib

May the swift Wanderer, Lord of refreshments, listen to our songs, who speeds through cloudy heaven:

And may the Waters, bright like castles, hear us, as they flow onward from the cloven mountain.

—*Rig Veda*

The Master having visited Nan-tsze, Tsze-lu was displeased, on which the Master swore, saying, "Wherein I have done improperly, may Heaven reject me, may Heaven reject me!"

—The *Analects* of Confucius

But let all those that put their trust in thee rejoice: let them ever shout for joy, because thou defendest them: let them also that love thy name be joyful in thee.

—Psalm 5:11 (King James Version)

Only let thy heart be with God, and doubt not in thy mind about that which thou seest.

—*Shepherd of Hermas*

Abandoning the dark way, let the wise man cultivate the bright path. Having gone from home to homelessness, let him yearn for that delight in detachment, so difficult to enjoy.

—The *Dhammapada*

The Master said, "Let the will be set on the path of duty. Let every attainment in what is good be firmly grasped. Let perfect virtue be accorded with. Let relaxation and enjoyment be found in the polite arts."

—The *Analects* of Confucius

Let all the earth fear the Lord: let all the inhabitants of the world stand in awe of him.

—Psalm 33:8 (King James Version)

And let there be witnesses whenever you conclude a contract, and let no harm be done to either scribe or witness.

—Qur'an 282

Exercise 109B: Rewriting Indicative Verbs as Hortative Verbs

Hortative verbs are also common in speeches. In the excerpts from famous speeches below, the statements and commands in bold type originally contained hortative verbs. On your own paper, rewrite each bolded clause so that the main verbs are hortative. Then, compare your answers with the original.

If you need help, ask your instructor.

But if anyone has a better proposal to make, **he should make it, and give us his advice.**

Tyrants ought to fear; I have always so behaved myself that, under God, I have placed my chiefest strength and safeguard in the loyal hearts and good will of my subjects.

He should make up his mind to do his duty in politics without regard to holding office at all, and he should know that often the men in this country who have done the best work for our public life have not been the men in office.

I will hope this movement will spread throughout all branches of applied science and industry and that women may come to share with men the joy of doing.

We will begin, then, with Grammar.

Exercise 109C: Diagramming

On your own paper, diagram every word of the following sentences.

The war is inevitable—and let it come!

Patrick Henry, "Liberty or Death" (1775)

Sir, well may you start at the suggestion that such a series of wrongs, so clearly proved by various testimony, so openly confessed by the wrong-doers, and so widely recognized throughout the country, should find apologies.
Charles Sumner, "The Crime Against Kansas" (1856)

My fellow citizens: let no one doubt that this is a difficult and dangerous effort on which we have set out.
John F. Kennedy, "On the Cuban Missile Crisis" (1962)

—LESSON 110—

Transitive Verbs
Intransitive Verbs
Sit/Set, Lie/Lay, Rise/Raise
Ambitransitive Verbs

The reindeer broke the first house apart.

The ice between the two floes broke apart.

Transitive verbs express action that is received by some person or thing.
Intransitive verbs express action that is not received by any person or thing.

ambi- from the Latin: prefix meaning "both"

ambidextrous ______________________________

ambiguous ______________________________

ambitransitive both transitive and intransitive

When I hear my voice on a record I absolutely loathe my voice. I cannot stand my voice.
—Roger Daltrey

Music in the soul can be heard by the universe.
—Laozi

Transitive verbs can be active or passive.
Intransitive verbs can only be active.

I hate thunderstorms.
The goat bleated.

***Sit*, *lie*, and *rise* are intransitive.**
***Set*, *lay*, and *raise* are transitive.**

(simple present)	Strong women ____________ above adverse circumstances.
(simple present)	The waiter ____________ the coffee carefully on the table.
(progressive past)	The hen ____________ four or five eggs every week.
(simple present)	She ____________ primly on the elaborate throne.
(simple past)	The farmer ____________ corn, wheat, and rye.
(progressive present)	The horse ____________ peacefully on its side in the pasture.

The cook tied on his apron and set to work.
The travelers set off first thing in the morning.
As we reached the ocean, the sun was setting.

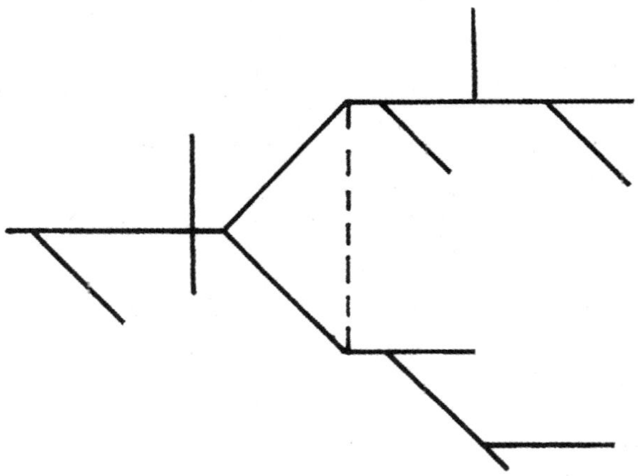

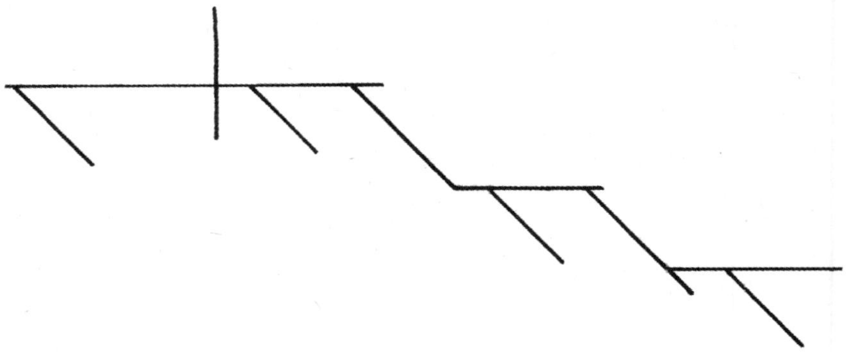

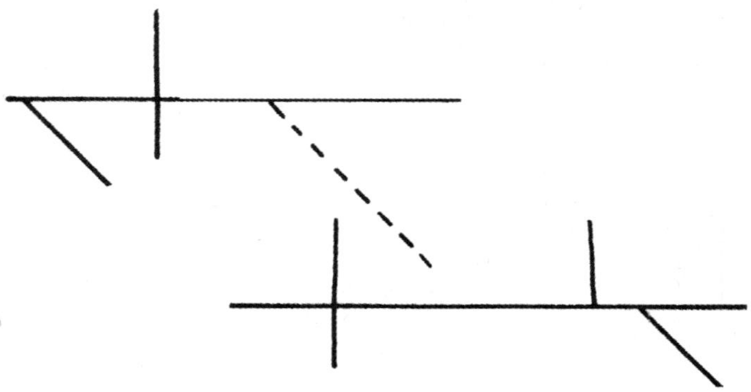

Transitive verbs can be active or passive.
Intransitive verbs can only be active.
Ambitransitive verbs can be either transitive or intransitive.
Transitive verbs express action that is received by some person or thing.
Intransitive verbs express action that is not received by any person or thing.

Exercise 110A: Ambitransitive Verbs

The sentences below have been adapted from traditional Peruvian folktales. For each sentence, carry out the following steps:

a) Underline the verbs that are acting as predicates (of both subordinate AND independent clauses), and label each one as *TR* for transitive or *INT* for intransitive.

b) Label each transitive verb as *A* for active or *P* for passive.

c) Circle the direct object of each active transitive verb and label it as *DO (TR)*. Circle the subject of each passive transitive verb and label it as *S (TR)*.

d) Choose two sentences with passive transitive verbs. On your own paper, rewrite them so that the verb becomes active. You may need to invent your own subject!

Ayar Cachi, the strongest of all, threw rocks with his slingshot and knocked down mountains.

I will throw out of this world anyone who throws me out of my house.

The first pomegranate was grown in Lima.

The skirmish grew in intensity, and the onlookers whispered worriedly.

Ahar Acu grew wings, and flew away to Pampa del Sol.

They whispered foul gossip through the streets.

The creature El Tunche whistles; if you listen, you will give away your place in the rainforest.

You there! Give these scoundrels a good beating!

You can only recognize El Tunche by looking at his goat-like hooves.

Her authority was recognized by the royal tribunal.

Sink this stick into the ground. Where it sinks, build your kingdom there.

The flagship blazed up and then sank.

They hid the letter, and then ate a second melon, that delicious fruit which acts gold in the morning, silver at noon, and death in the evening.

They were eating in holy peace, when suddenly the dog growled, and the cat arched its back.

A dry throat can neither growl nor sing.

The minions of the law fell upon him, and took him to jail.

They were felled by the sickness and growled their pain to the skies.

Exercise 110B: The Prefix *Ambi-*

Find two more words using the prefix *ambi-*, where the prefix carries the meaning of "both." On your own paper, write the words and their definitions, and then use each correctly in a sentence. If the word is too technical for you to write an original sentence, you may locate a sentence using an Internet search and write it down.

Exercise 110C: Diagramming

On your own paper, diagram every word of the following quotations.

When you are finished, label each action verb occupying a predicate space with *T* for transitive or *INT* for intransitive.

When the sword is once drawn, the passions of men observe no bounds of moderation.
—Alexander Hamilton

She who succeeds in gaining the mastery of the bicycle will gain the mastery of life.
—Susan B. Anthony

The freedom which we enjoy in our government extends also to our ordinary life.
—Pericles

I agree to this Constitution with all its faults, if they are such; because I think a general Government necessary for us.
—Benjamin Franklin

Without peace, all other dreams vanish and are reduced to ashes.
—Jawaharlal Nehru

— LESSON 111 —

Ambitransitive Verbs
Gerunds and Infinitives
Infinitive Phrases as Direct Objects
Infinitive Phrases With Understood *To*

I may not succeed, but I will try.

Try the chocolate cake.

The concert-goers tried arriving early.

Every night, he tries to go to bed by ten.

A gerund is a present participle acting as a noun.
An infinitive is formed by combining *to* and the first person singular present form of a verb.

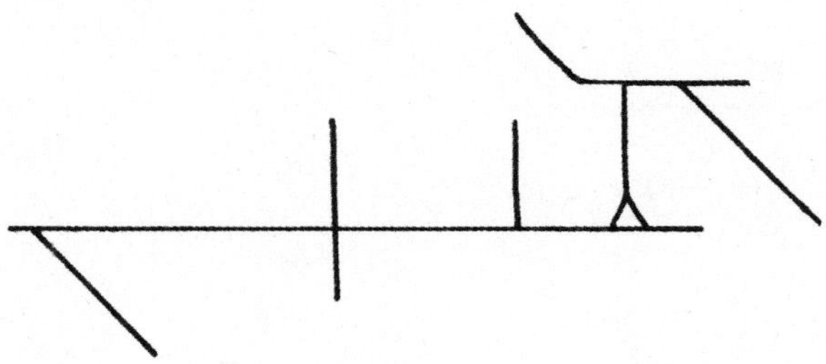

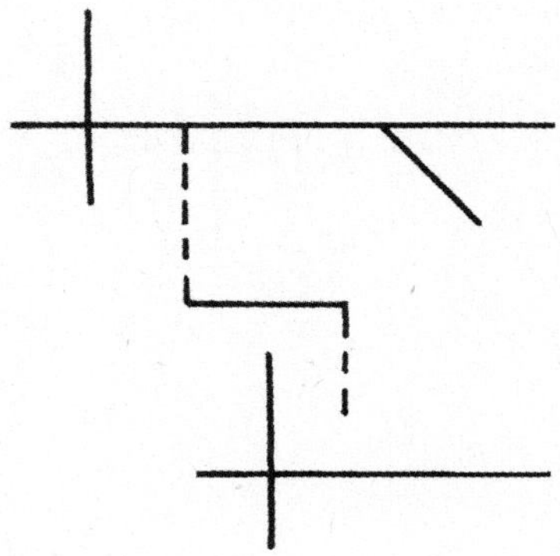

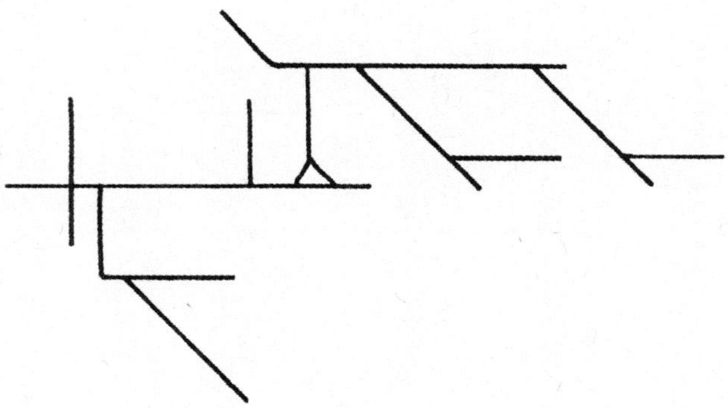

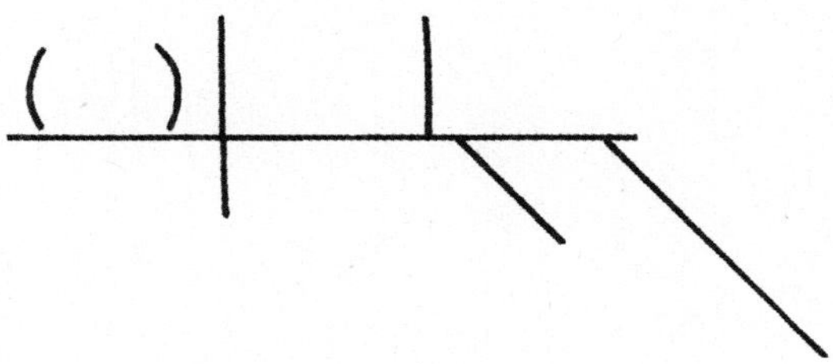

Mother told me to clean my room.

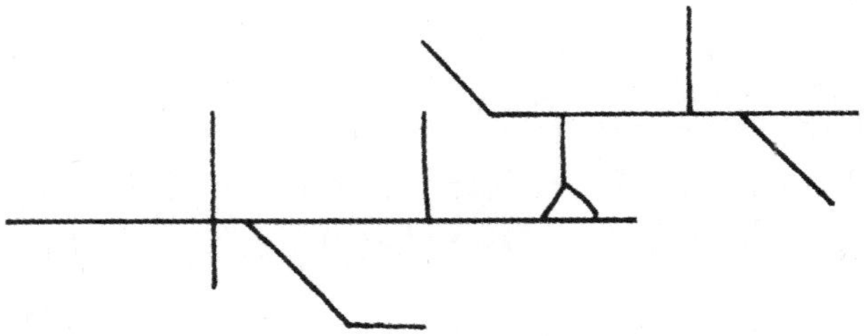

The duchess ordered the maid to arrange the flowers.

His mistake made me lose money.

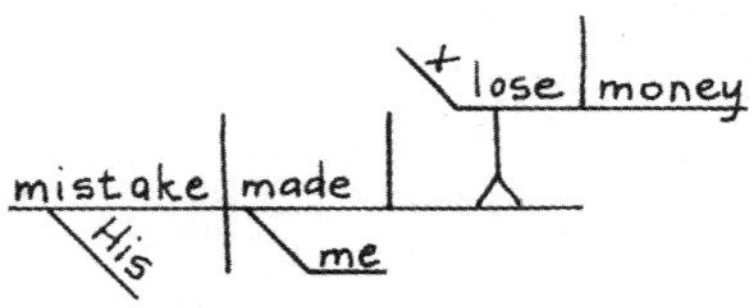

You must come and make Lizzy marry Mr. Collins, for she vows she will not have him.
—*Pride and Prejudice*

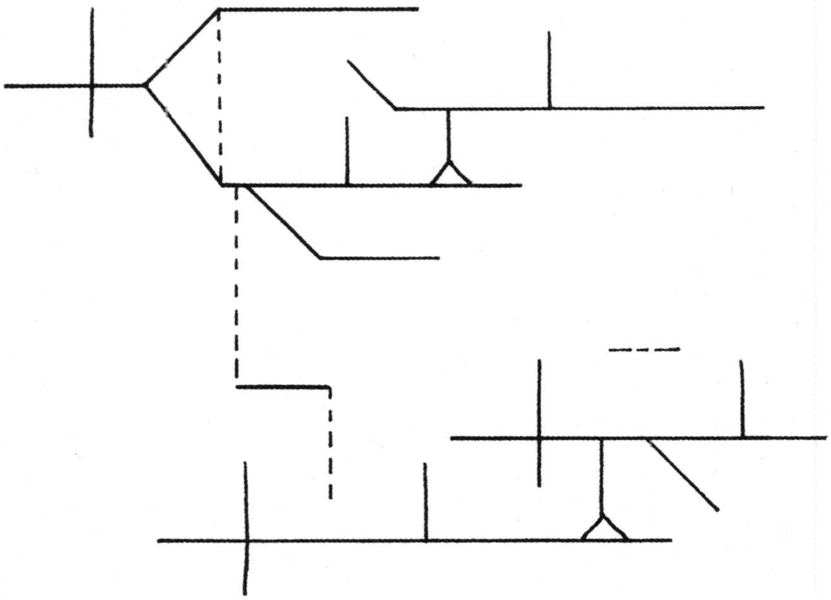

I was made to love you.

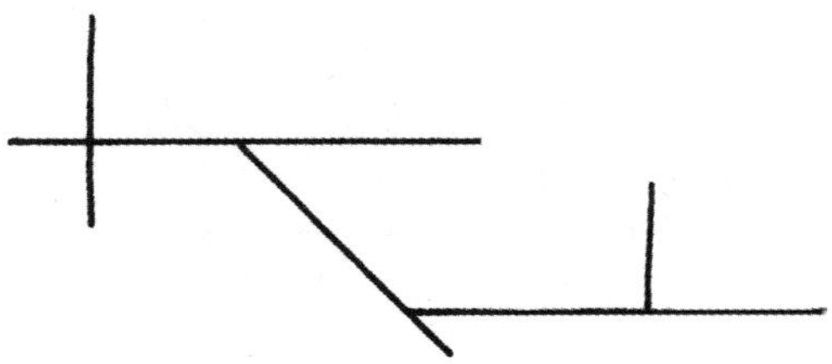

He was good enough to sing.

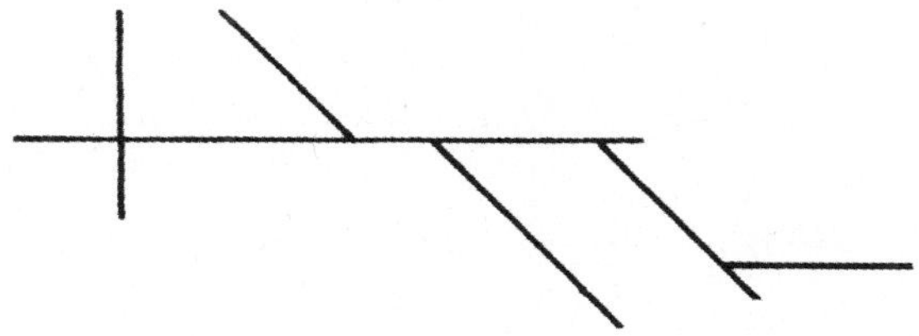

You ought to go home.

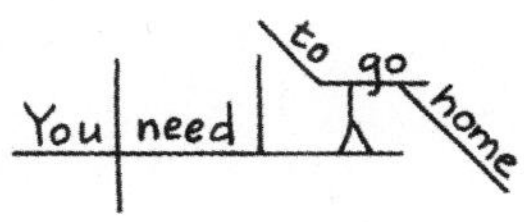

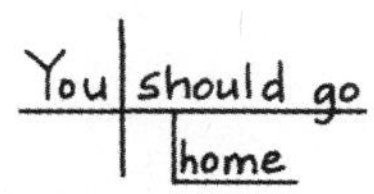

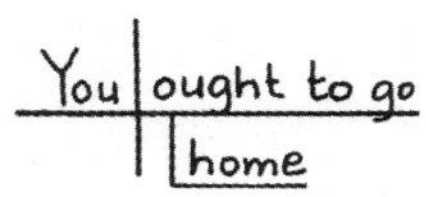

The politician ought to have been thrown in jail.

The politician should have been thrown in jail.

Exercise 111A: Infinitives and Other Uses of "To"

In the following sentences from Johann David Wyss's *The Swiss Family Robinson*, underline every phrase that incorporates the word *to*. For infinitives, underline just the infinitive itself; for prepositional phrases and verbs, underline the entire phrase.

- Label each phrase as *INF* for infinitive, *PREP* for prepositional, or *V* for verb.
- For prepositional phrases, also label the object of the preposition as *OP*.
- Further identify each entire phrase as *S* for subject, *DO* for direct object, *PA* for predicate adjective, *PN* for predicate nominative, *ADJ* for adjective, or *ADV* for adverb.
- For adjective and adverb phrases, draw an arrow to the word modified.
- For verbs, parse the verb.

The first is done for you.

PREP ADV
OP

Fritz completed a dish and some plates, to his great satisfaction, but we considered that, being so frail, we could not carry them with us.

We therefore filled them with sand, that the sun might not warp them, and left them to dry, till we returned.

We began to consider how we should come at the contents of the hogshead without exposing the perishable matter to the heat of the sun.

I then tied the flamingo to a stake, near the river, by a cord long enough to allow him to fish at his pleasure, and in fact, in a few days, he learned to know us, and was quite domesticated.

This reconciled them a little to their lot, and they left us.

I proceeded to suspend this infernal machine against the side of the ship near our work.

It could not be worse than the buffalo they had assisted me to subdue.

Especially I warned them against the *manchineel*, which ought to grow in this part of the world.

To accustom them to come to this shelter of themselves, we took care to fill their racks with the food they liked best, mingled with salt.

Our first care, when we stepped in safety on land, was to kneel down and thank God, to whom we owed our lives, and to resign ourselves wholly to his fatherly kindness.

Exercise 111B: Diagramming

On your own paper, diagram every word of the following sentences, adapted from *The Swiss Family Robinson.*

I had neglected to take my cloak and boots, and my dear little fellow had volunteered to bring them to Tent House.

I am impatient to learn if Fritz has any tidings of Captain Johnson, for it was on the shore near Tent House that he and Jack passed the night.

I agreed to this reasonable request, and only begged to know how they would procure water for their fountains.

I saw that my presence was necessary to restrain and aid him; and I decided, with a heavy heart, to leave Ernest alone to protect the vessel.

Exhausted by fatigue, we were glad to take a good night's rest in the captain's cabin, on an elastic mattress, of which our hammocks had made us forget the comfort.

— LESSON 112 —

Principal Parts

Yet More Troublesome Verbs

Exercise 112A: Verb Definitions

For each definition, choose the best term from the word bank. Write it into the blank next to the definition.

ambitransitive verb	first principal part	gerund
hortative	imperative	indicative
infinitive	intransitive verb	modal
perfect verb	present participle	progressive verb
second principal part	simple verb	subjunctive
third principal part	transitive verb	

Expresses action that is not received by any person or thing	
The simple past	
Describes an action which has been completed before	
Expresses situations that are unreal, wished for, or uncertain	
A verb form ending in -ing	
Formed by combining *to* and the first-person singular present form of a verb	
Expresses action that is received by some person or thing	
Can be either transitive or intransitive	
The perfect past, minus helping verbs	
Describes an ongoing or continuous action	

Affirms or declares what actually is	
Expresses possible actions	
The simple present (first-person singular)	
Expresses intended actions	
Simply tells whether an action takes place in the past, present, or future	
Present participle acting as a noun	
Encourages or recommends an action	

English verbs have three principal parts.

First principal part: The Simple Present (Present)
(I) pontificate (I) sing (I) cut (I) become

Second principal part: The Simple Past (Past)
(I) pontificated (I) sang (I have) cut (I) became

Third principal part: The Perfect Past, Minus Helping Verbs (Past Participle)
(I have) pontificated (I have) sung (I have) cut (I have) become

pontificate, pontificated, pontificated
sing, sang, sung
cut, cut, cut
become, became, become

***Sit*, *lie*, and *rise* are intransitive.**
***Set*, *lay*, and *raise* are transitive.**

lie		**lay**		**lay**	
Simple Past		**Simple Present**		**Simple Past**	
I lay	we lay	I lay	we lay	I laid	we laid
you lay	you lay	you lay	you lay	you laid	you laid
he, she, it lay	they lay	he, she, it lays	they lay	he, she, it laid	they laid

(simple past) The child ____________ out her clothes for the birthday party the night before.

(simple past) She got sunburned because she ______________ out in the sun too long.

(simple present) ______________ down and go to sleep now.

(simple present) ______________ your head down and close your eyes.

	First Principal Part Present	Second Principal Part Past	Third Principal Part Past Participle
I	lie	lay	lain
	lay	laid	laid
	sit	sat	sat
	set	set	set
	rise	rose	risen
	raise	raised	raised

Exercise 112B: Using Troublesome Verbs Correctly

In the following sentences from *Turkish Fairy Tales and Folk Tales* (collected by Dr. Ignácz Kúnos, translated by R. Nisbet Bain), fill in the blanks. The first blank (above the sentence) should be filled in with the first principal part of the correct verb: *lie* or *lay* in the first set of sentences, *sit* or *set* in the second set, and *rise* or *raise* in the third set. You will be able to tell from the context of the sentence whether you should use the transitive verbs *lay, set,* and *raise* (the verb is passive, or has a direct object) or the intransitive verbs *lie, sit,* and *rise* (the action of the verb is not passed on to any other word in the sentence).

The second blank in the sentence itself should be filled in with the correct form of that verb.

The first sentence in each section is done for you.

(simple past active indicative of lie)

There in the rippling water in front of the prince, like a dream-shape, lay a large garden.

(simple past active indicative of ______________)

They ______________ down together, and together they rose up.

(perfect past active indicative of ______________)

One day she put her ring upon her sewing-table, but scarcely ____________ she ____________ it down when there came a little dove and took up the ring and flew away with it.

(perfect present active modal of ______________)

Then, auguring some evil, he beat in the door, and lo! the place where the damsel ________ was cold.

(infinitive of ______________)

They were just going ______________ down to sleep when all at once such a roaring, such a bellowing arose that the very mountains fell down from their places.

(simple present active imperative of _______________)

Moisten these three wooden tablets with water, _______________ them on the face of the damsel, and I will come out of her, and a rich reward will be thine.

(simple present active hortative of _______________)

"Come now!" said some of them, "__________ us steal a march upon Mehmed one day and _______________ hands upon his table, and then there will be an end to the fool's glory."

(simple past active indicative of _______________)

Now his mother knew that thou wert my destined bride, so she _____________ the curse of her spells upon me.

(simple past active indicative of _______________)

He sent to the cemetery, had the tomb opened, and there in her coffin _____________ the Rose-beauty of his dreams.

(simple present active indicative of _______________)

The wise men and the leeches cannot help the damsel; the only medicine that can cure her _______________ hidden elsewhere.

(simple past active indicative of set)

She put the room tidy, cooked the meal, set everything in order, and then leaped back upon the rafter and became a feather again.

(simple past passive indicative of _____________)

Then rich meats on rare and precious dishes _______________ before him, and then the dancers and the jugglers diverted him till the evening.

(progressive passive infinitive of _______________)

His wife chanced just then _________________ at the window, and when she saw her husband she leaped clean out of the window to him.

(simple past active indicative of _____________)

The crow begged and prayed till at last he let her go free, and again he _____________ the

(simple past active indicative of _____________)

snare in the tree and _____________ down at the foot of it to wait.

(simple past active indicative of _______________)

Here they _____________ down to rest a while, and as they were looking about them to the right hand and to the left, the valley was suddenly shaken as if by an earthquake.

(perfect past active indicative of ______________)

In the evening the lion came home sure enough, and when they ____________ down together and begun to talk, the girl asked him what he would do if any of her brothers should chance to come there.

(simple past active indicative of ______________)

But the young man brought out his table, ____________ it in the midst, and cried: "Little table, give me to eat!"

(simple past active indicative of raise)

When Aleodor heard these words, and how the ant called him by his name, he raised his foot again and let the ant go where it would.

(simple past active indicative of ______________)

On the morning of the reception of guests she ____________ up early and commanded that on the

(simple present active modal of ______________)

spot where the little hut stood a palace ______________, the like of which eye hath never seen nor ear heard.

(simple past active indicative of ______________)

She ____________ from her bed and promised the youth a great treasure if he would bring her to that tower.

(simple active infinitive of ______________)

His eyelids were so heavy that he had ____________ them on high with his hands.

(simple present active imperative of ______________)

"______________ up, poor man, and fear not," said the ghost.

(simple past active indicative of ______________)

But the good steed ____________ into the air like a dart, and Boy Beautiful shot an arrow which struck off one of the witch's three heads.

(simple past active indicative of ______________)

They lay down together, and together they ____________ up.

	First Principal Part Present	Second Principal Part Past	Third Principal Part Past Participle
I	give	gave	given
	come	came	come
	write	wrote	written
	go	went	gone
	eat	ate	eaten

She had gave her outgrown shoes to her sister.

Has she came home from the movies yet?

The policeman had wrote her a speeding ticket.

When Mom got home, I had already went to bed.

He has ate his dinner too fast.

Exercise 112C: More Irregular Principal Parts

Fill in the chart below with the missing principal parts of each verb. (You may use a dictionary if necessary.) Then, in the sentences below (from *The Wind in the Willows* by Kenneth Grahame), fill in the blanks with the correct verb, in the tense, mood, and voice indicated in brackets at the end of each sentence. Each verb is used one time.

	First Principal Part **Present**	Second Principal Part **Past**	Third Principal Part **Past Participle**
I	forbid		
	burst		
	shrink		
	bind		
	overtake		
	beset		

	First Principal Part **Present**	Second Principal Part **Past**	Third Principal Part **Past Participle**
	cling		
	ride		
	drive		

The rapid nightfall of mid-December ______________ quite ______________ the little village as they approached it on soft feet over a first thin fall of powdery snow. [perfect past active indicative]

"Seize him!" they cried, "seize the Toad, the wicked animal who stole our motor-car! __________________ him, chain him, drag him to the nearest police-station!" [simple present active imperative]

Then out of the tunnel ________________ the pursuing engine, roaring and whistling, her motley crew waving their various weapons and shouting, "Stop! stop! stop!" [simple past active indicative]

Though it was past ten o'clock at night, the sky still ________________ to and retained some lingering skirts of light from the departed day. [simple past active indicative]

Who persuaded them into letting him see if he __________________? [simple present active modal]

The Mole recollected that animal-etiquette __________________ any sort of comment on the sudden disappearance of one's friends at any moment, for any reason or no reason whatever. [simple past active indicative]

You ______________ easily __________________ me on the road, for you are young. [simple present active modal]

As the sun rose royally behind us, we ______________ into Venice down a path of gold. [simple past active indicative]

But the constant chorus of the orchards and hedges __________________ to a casual evensong from a few yet unwearied performers. [perfect past active indicative]

WEEK 30

Still More About Clauses

—LESSON 113—

Clauses and Phrases

The sentences in this lesson are taken from *Redwall* by Brian Jacques.

> All eyes were on the Father Abbot. He took a dainty fork loaded precariously with steaming fish. Carefully he transferred it from plate to mouth. Chewing delicately, he turned his eyes upwards then closed them, whiskers atwitch, jaws working steadily, munching away, his tail curled up holding a napkin which neatly wiped his mouth.
>
> —Brian Jacques, *Redwall*

A clause is a group of words that contains a subject and a predicate.

An independent clause can stand by itself as a sentence.

A sentence is a group of words that usually contains a subject and a predicate. A sentence begins with a capital letter and ends with a punctuation mark. A sentence contains a complete thought.

A phrase is a group of words serving a single grammatical function.

A dependent clause is a fragment that cannot stand by itself as a sentence.

Dependent clauses can act as adjective clauses, adverb clauses, or noun clauses.

An adjective clause is a dependent clause that acts as an adjective in a sentence, modifying a noun or pronoun in the independent clause.

Relative pronouns (who, whom, whose, which, that) introduce adjective clauses and refer back to an antecedent in the independent clause.

Relative adverbs (where, when, why) introduce adjective clauses when they refer back to a place, time, or reason in the independent clause.

Matthias started to slide down the rope on the Mossflower side of the wall, where the woods came close up to the Abbey.

The Father Abbot halted in front of the wall on which hung a long tapestry.

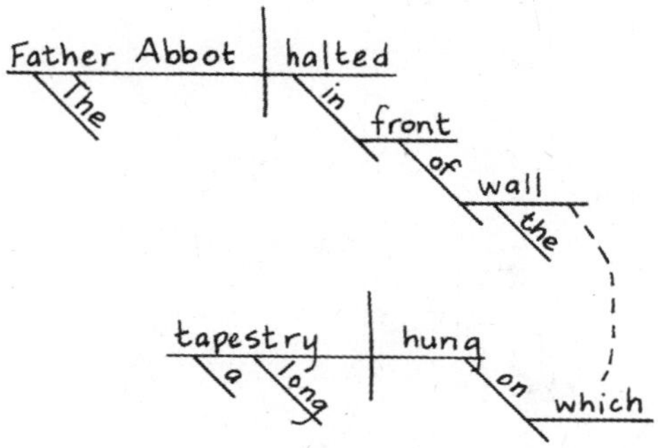

He arrived here in the deep winter when the Founders were under attack from many foxes, vermin, and a great wildcat.

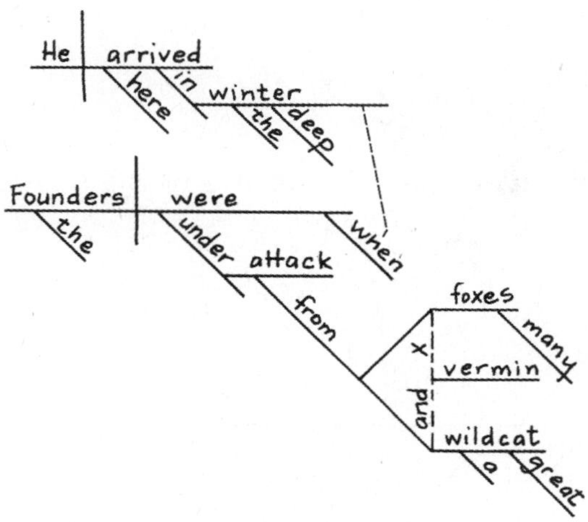

Adverb clauses can be introduced by adverbs.

Common adverbs that introduce adverbial clauses are:

as and its compounds (as if, as soon as, as though)
how and its compound (however)
when and its compound (whenever)
whence
where and its compounds (whereat, whereby, wherein, wherefore, whereon)
while
whither

Her blunt claws churned the roadside soil as she propelled the cart through a gap in the hawthorn hedge, down to the slope of the ditch where she dug her paws in, holding the cart still and secure while John Churchmouse and Cornflower's father jumped out and wedged the wheels firmly with stones.

A subordinating conjunction joins unequal words or groups of words together.

Subordinating conjunctions and subordinating correlative conjunctions often join an adverb clause to an independent clause.

Common subordinating conjunctions are:

after
although
as (as soon as)
because
before
if
in order that
lest
since
though
till
unless
until
although/though . . . yet/still
if . . . then

All the mice took a solemn vow never to harm another living creature, unless it was an enemy that sought to harm our Order by violence.

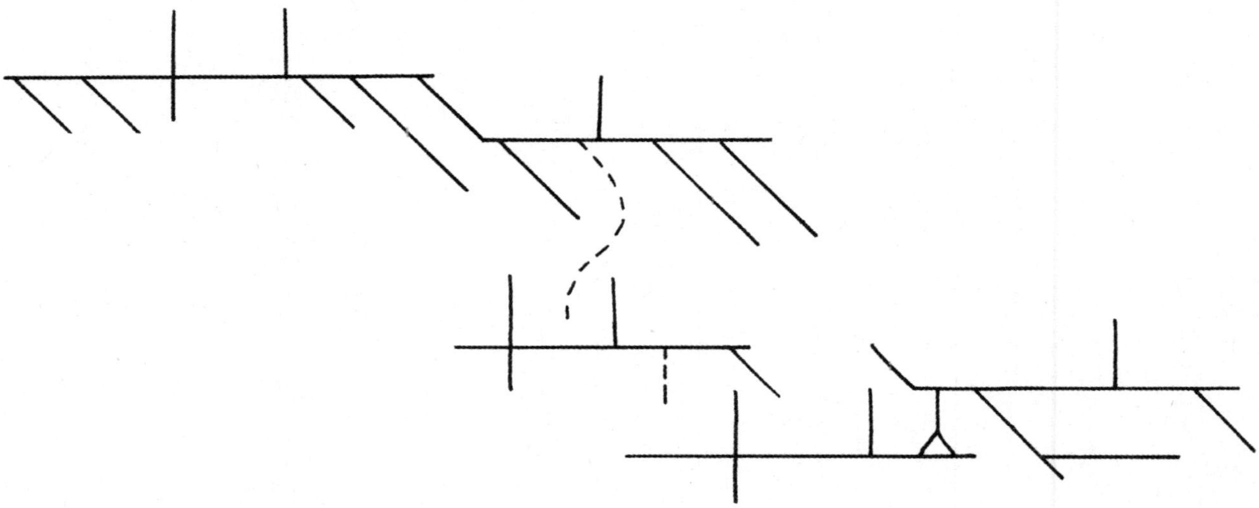

A noun clause takes the place of a noun. Noun clauses can be introduced by relative pronouns, relative adverbs, or subordinating conjunctions.

Somewhere there had to be a clue, a single lead that might tell him where the resting place of Martin the Warrior could be found, or where he could regain possession of the ancient sword for his Abbey.

The defenders stood and cheered in the depression above what had once been Killconey's tunnel.

It is because you are kind and good.

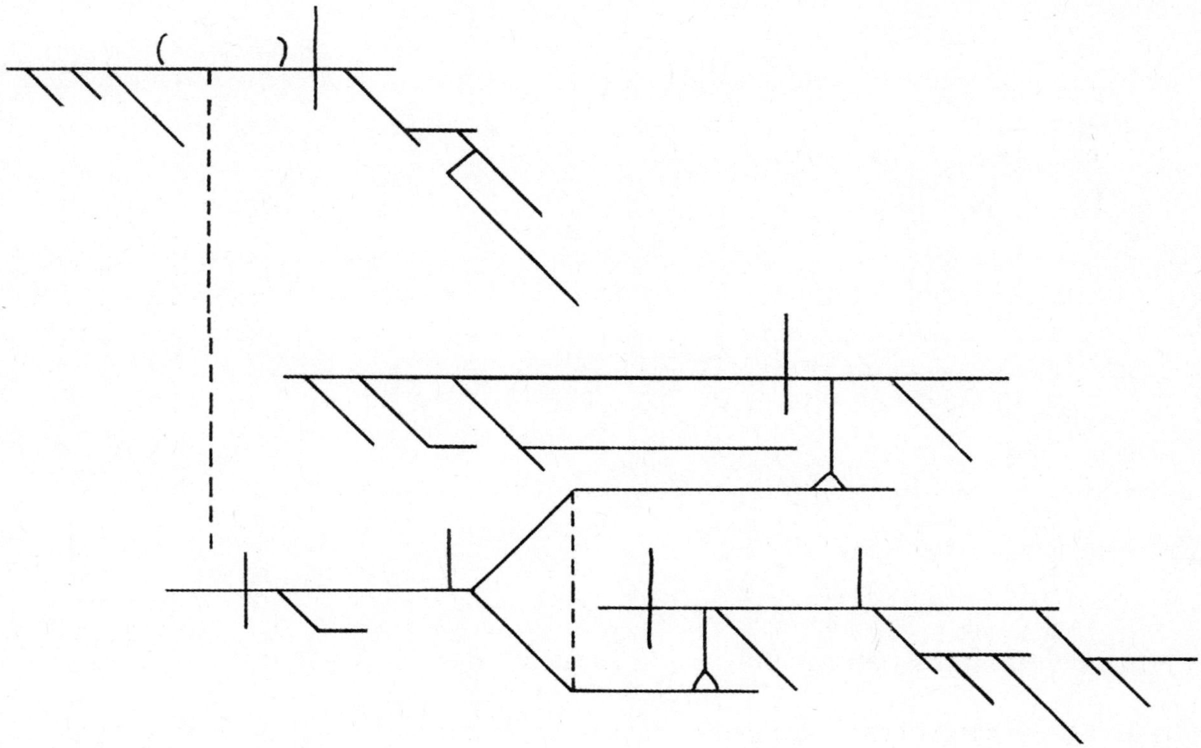

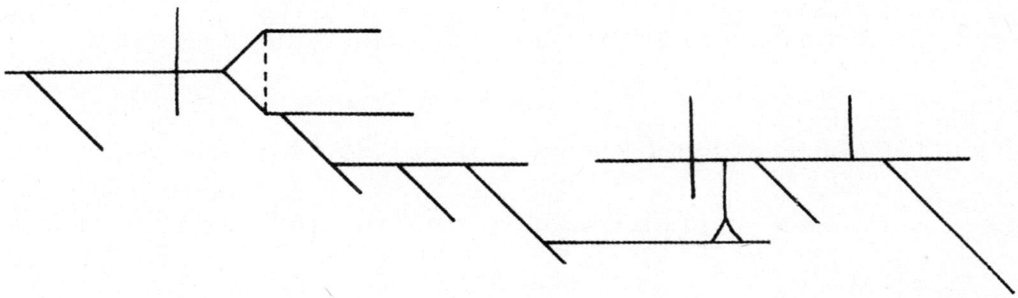

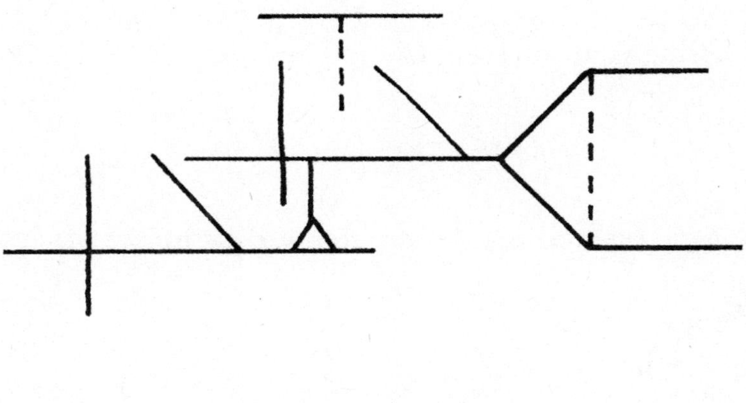

Exercise 113A: Phrases and Clauses

In the sentences below from Johnny Gruelle's *Raggedy Ann Stories*, identify each bolded set of words as *PH* for phrase or *CL* for clause.

- Then, identify the part of the sentence (*S, DO, IO, OP, PN, PA, ADV, ADJ*) that each set of words functions as.
- For adjective and adverb phrases and clauses, draw an arrow to the word modified.
- For phrases, further identify the phrase as *PREP, INF* (infinitive), *PRESP* (present participle) or *PASTP* (past participle).
- For clauses, underline the subject of the clause once and the predicate twice.

The first is done for you. Notice that it contains two separate sets of bolded words—*to be nice children* is one set of words (a phrase), and *while she was away* is a second set of words (a clause). If a phrase contains a clause, mark both the phrase and the clause. If a clause or phrase contains additional phrases, there is no need to mark each phrase separately—just label the overall clause or phrase.

PH DO INF

Their little mistress had placed them all around the room and told them **to be nice**
CL ADV
children while she was away.

They swarmed **upon the pantry shelves** and **in their eagerness** spilled a pitcher of cream **which ran all over the French dolly's dress**.

Raggedy Ann knew just **how it all happened** and her remaining shoe-button eye twinkled.

When a tail had been fastened to the kite and a large ball of heavy twine tied to the front, one of the boys held the kite up **in the air** and another boy walked off, **unwinding the ball of twine.**

But I had no way **of telling your mistress where Fido was**, for she cannot understand dog language!

The dolls lost no time in **scrambling into bed and pulling up the covers**, for they were very sleepy.

Well, I know you will not tell anyone **who would not be glad to know about it**, so I will tell you the secret and **why I am wearing my smile a trifle broader**!

The puppy dog ran up to Raggedy Ann and twisted his head about **as he looked at her**.

I did not notice **how pleasant her face looked** last night!

"Play something lively!" said the French doll, **as she giggled behind her hand**, so Uncle Clem began **hammering the eight keys** upon the piano **with all his might** until a noise was heard upon the stairs.

As Raggedy watched, her candy heart went pitty-pat **against her cotton stuffing**, for she saw a tiny pink foot **sticking out of the bundle of light**.

So we can hardly tell **when it is day** and **when it is night**.

I was so interested **in looking out of the window** I did not pay any attention to **what they said**, for we were on a train and the scenery was just flying by!

Exercise 113B: Diagramming

On your own paper, diagram every word of the following sentences, taken from *Raggedy Ann Stories* by Johnny Gruelle.

When Mistress had me out playing with me this morning, she carried me by a door near the back of the house and I smelled something which smelled as if it would taste delicious!

I think it would be a good plan to elect Raggedy Ann as our leader on this expedition!

They swarmed upon the pantry shelves and in their eagerness spilled a pitcher of cream which ran all over the French dolly's dress.

Once a strange dog ran out at them, but Peterkins told him to mind his own business and the strange dog returned to his own yard.

She kicked and twisted as much as she could, but the puppy dog thought Raggedy was playing.

Both new dolls were silent for a while, thinking deeply.

— LESSON 114 —

Restrictive and Non-Restrictive Modifying Clauses
Punctuating Modifying Clauses
Which and *That*

Why does the mechanism of the p-value, which seems so reasonable, work so very badly in this setting?

If the first throw is tails and the second is heads, an event which happens 1/4 of the time, Paul gets two ducats.

—From *How Not to Be Wrong: The Power of Mathematical Thinking* by Jordan Ellenberg

A non-restrictive modifying clause describes the word that it modifies. Removing the clause doesn't change the essential meaning of the sentence. Only non-restrictive clauses should be set off by commas.

A restrictive modifying clause defines the word that it modifies. Removing the clause changes the essential meaning of the sentence.

I especially like the "Methods" section, which starts "One mature Atlantic Salmon (*Salmo salar*) participated in the fMRI study."

I especially like the "Methods" section which starts "One mature Atlantic Salmon (*Salmo salar*) participated in the fMRI study."

A noun clause takes the place of a noun. Noun clauses can be introduced by relative pronouns, relative adverbs, or subordinating conjunctions.

In principle, if you carry out a powerful enough study, you can find out, which it is.

The reason the 0.999 . . . problem is difficult is, that it brings our intuitions into conflict.

An appositive is a noun, noun phrase, or noun clause that usually follows another noun and renames or explains it. Appositives are set off by commas.

The Goldbach conjecture, that every even number greater than 2 is the sum of two primes, is another one that would have to be true if primes behaved like random numbers.

The chocolate brownies that
The chocolate brownies which

The chocolate brownies that were on the counter are gone now.

The chocolate brownies, which were made with olive oil instead of butter, have been sitting on the counter since lunch time.

When the relative pronoun introducing a modifying clause refers to a thing rather than a person, *which* introduces non-restrictive clauses and *that* introduces restrictive clauses.

"These are but shadows of the things that have been," said the Ghost.

It was shrouded in a deep black garment, which concealed its head, its face, its form, and left nothing of it visible save one outstretched hand.

He lived in chambers which had once belonged to his deceased partner.

At last she said, and in a steady, cheerful voice, that only faltered once, "I have known him walk with—I have known him walk with Tiny Tim upon his shoulder, very fast indeed."

—From *A Christmas Carol* by Charles Dickens

That's certainly an impressive figure, but one which clearly indicates that the percentage doesn't mean quite what you're used to it meaning.

—From *How Not to Be Wrong* by Jordan Ellenberg

He lived in chambers that had once belonged to his deceased partner.
At last she said, and in a steady, cheerful voice, which only faltered once, "I have known him walk with—I have known him walk with Tiny Tim upon his shoulder, very fast indeed."

That's certainly an impressive figure, but one that clearly indicates that the percentage doesn't mean quite what you're used to it meaning.

Exercise 114A: Restrictive and Non-Restrictive Adjective Clauses

Find every adjective clause in the following sentences, taken from *Symbolic Logic* by John Venn, and then follow these steps:

1) Underline each adjective clause.
2) Circle the relative pronoun that introduces each clause.
3) Draw an arrow from the pronoun back to the word modified.
4) Label each clause as *R* for restrictive or *NR* for non-restrictive.
5) Draw an asterisk or star next to each sentence that does *not* follow the *which/that* rule.

What we here have to do is to conceive, and invent a notation for, all the possible combinations which any number of class terms can yield.

I may heap up one such term upon another, provided I put in some expression at the end which shall neutralize the surplus.

When it is asked, What are the limits of not-x? the symbolic answer is invariably the same, "all that is excluded from x is taken up by not-x."

On this plan of notation *xy* stands for the compartment, or class, of things which are both *x* and *y*.

To one point, which has already been noticed, attention must be very persistently directed, as any vagueness of apprehension here will be fatal to the proper understanding of symbolic reasoning.

The assertion that Dr. Boole's system is in any way founded on the doctrine of the Quantification of the Predicate—is, in fact, not directly hostile to that doctrine—is so astonishing that one is inclined to suspect some lurking confusion of meaning.

The vanishing of every term is an indication that no information whatever is obtainable.

The accurate language of symbols requires us to insert a final term which common language had rejected for the sake of brevity.

The disproval of this fact, which would be equivalent to showing that the subject had no existence, would at most show that I had been hasty.

The only complication that is thus produced is that the final elements or subdivisions of such an ill-expressed fractional form may possess other numerical factors, positive or negative, besides the true typical four.

Exercise 114B: Dependent Clauses within Dependent Clauses

The following sentences, adapted from George Boole's *An Investigation of the Laws of Thought,* all contain dependent clauses that have other dependent clauses within them.

Underline the entire dependent clause, including additional dependent clauses that act as nouns or modifiers within it. Place a box around the subject of the main dependent clause and underline its predicate twice. In the right-hand margin, write the abbreviation for the part of the sentence that the main dependent clause is fulfilling: *N-SUB* for a noun clause acting as subject, *N-PN* for predicate nominative, *N-DO* for direct object, *N-OP* for object of the preposition, and then *ADJ* for adjective and *ADV* for adverb. For *ADJ* and *ADV* clauses, also write the word that the clause modifies.

Then, circle any additional clauses that fall within the main dependent clause. Label each clause, above the circle, as *N* for noun, *ADJ* for adjective, or *ADV* for adverb. Then, also label noun clauses as *S, PN, DO,* or *OP.* For these additional *ADJ* and *ADV* clauses, draw a line from the circle to the word in the main dependent clause modified.

The first sentence is done for you.

ADJ

But if the general truths of Logic are of a nature that at once commands the mind's assent, ADV consists
wherein consists the difficulty of constructing the Science of Logic?

The reader may be curious to inquire what effect would be produced if we literally translated this expression.

A little consideration will here show that the class represented by 1 must be "the Universe," since this is the only class in which are found *all* the individuals that exist in *any* class.

Now the above system of processes would conduct us to no intelligible result, unless the final equations resulting therefrom were in a form which should render their interpretation, after we have restored to the symbols their logical significance, possible.

It is necessary that the reader should apprehend what are the specific ends of the investigation upon which we are entering, as well as the principles which are to guide us to the attainment of them.

It now remains to show that those constituent parts of ordinary language which have not been considered in the previous sections of this chapter are either resolvable into the same elements as those which have been considered, or are subsidiary to those elements by contributing to their more precise definition.

I apprehend therefore that the solution indicates, that when a particular condition has prevailed through the whole of our *recorded experience*, it assumes the above character with reference to the class of phaenomena over which that experience has extended.

Such knowledge is, indeed, unnecessary for the ends of science, which properly concerns itself with what is, and seeks not for grounds of preference or reasons of appointment.

I do not here speak of that perfection only which consists in power, but of that also which is founded in the conception of what is fit and beautiful.

Exercise 114C: Diagramming

On your own paper, diagram every word of the following sentences from Mary Everest Boole's *The Preparation of the Child for Science*. If you need help, ask your instructor.

Some readers may be tempted to think that in mathematics there are no tolerated and mutually corrective errors.

The efficient and intelligent teacher learns all he or she can of principles of psychology and general tendencies, and then carries them out by methods which, in detail, are his or her own.

The first thing we must do is to resolve seriously that a good deal of time before the age of ten, and of the vacations afterwards, shall be resolutely dedicated to the training of the unconscious mind.

Many parents seem to think that all the time is wasted for their children which is not spent in taking in consciously some special idea which some adult already understands.

There are some conceptions in physical science which present no difficulty to one who, years before he hears any discussion about matter and force, has made a long series of experiments with the same object rotating under varied conditions.

— LESSON 115 —

Conditional Sentences

Conditional Sentences as Dependent Clauses
Conditional Sentences with Missing Words
Formal *If* Clauses

The sentences in this lesson are from *Pride & Prejudice & Zombies*, by Jane Austen and Seth Grahame-Smith.

simple past, active, subjunctive

I have nothing to say against him; he has felled many a zombie; and if he had the fortune he

simple present, active modal

ought to have, I should think you could not do better. SECOND

Active verbs are active or passive in voice.
State-of-being verbs do not have voice.
Subjunctive verbs express situations that are unreal, wished for, or uncertain.

If my children are silly, I must hope to be always sensible of it. ________________

If I had known as much this morning I certainly would not have called him. ____________

If I were not afraid of judging harshly, I should be almost tempted to demand satisfaction.

____

First conditional sentences express circumstances that might actually happen.
The predicate of the condition clause is in a present tense.
The predicate of the consequence clause is an imperative or is in a present or future tense.

Second conditional sentences express circumstances that are contrary to reality.
The predicate of the condition clause is in a past tense.
The predicate of the consequence clause is in the simple or progressive present modal tense.

Third conditional sentences express past circumstances that never happened.
The predicate of the condition clause is in the perfect past tense.

The predicate of the consequence clause is in any modal tense.

In her postscript it was added that if Mr. Bingley and his sister pressed them to stay longer, she could spare them.

However, I recollected afterwards that if he had been prevented going, the wedding need not be put off.

If he fears me, why come hither?

If he no longer cares for me, why silent?

Should you wish to, meet me in the drawing room.

Formal conditional sentences drop *if* from the condition clause and reverse the order of the subject and helping verb.

Were you not otherwise agreeable, I should be forced to remove your tongue with my saber.

If he fears me, why come hither?

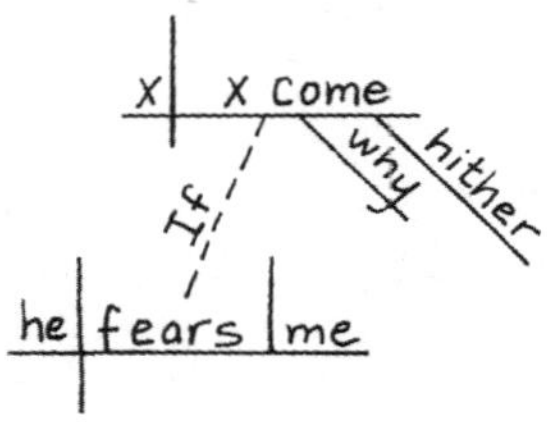

If he no longer cares for me, why silent?

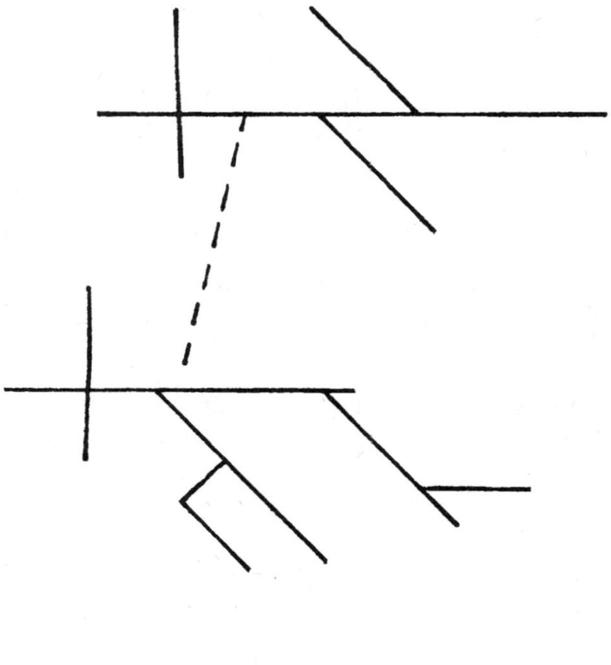

Should you wish, meet me in the drawing room.

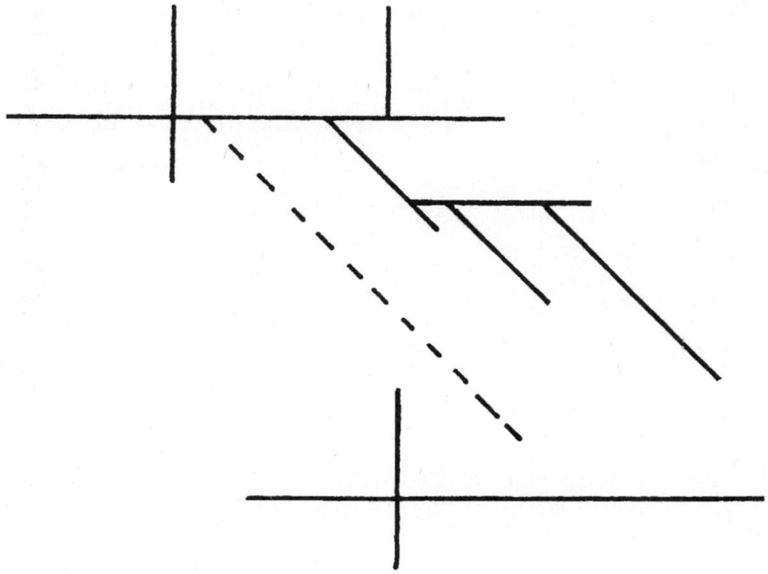

Were you not otherwise agreeable, I should be forced to remove your tongue with my saber.

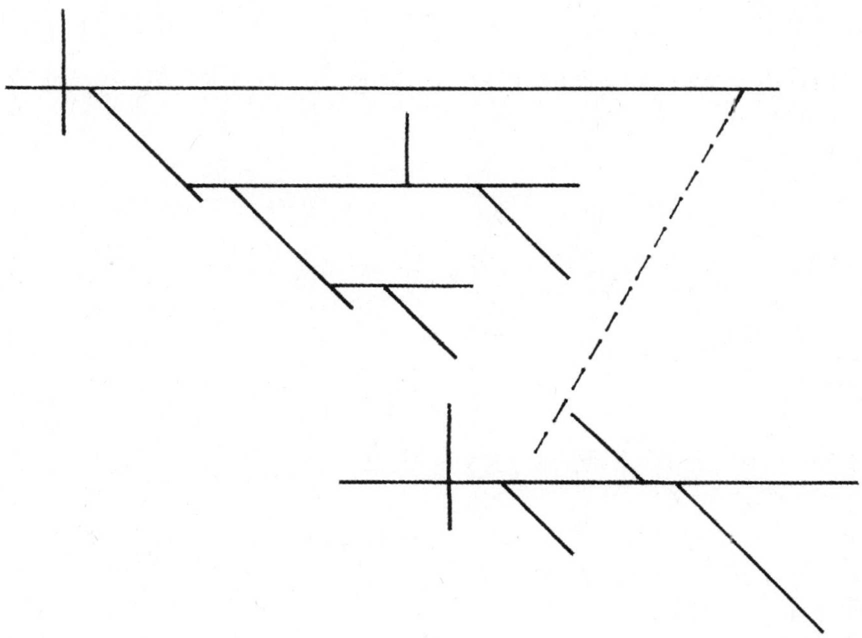

Exercise 115A: Conditional Clauses

In the following sentences, from *World War Z: An Oral History of the Zombie War* by Max Brooks, circle every conditional sentence. This may mean circling the entire sentence, or circling simply the part of it that makes up the conditional-consequence clause set, or circling the conditional and consequence clauses separately if they are divided by other words.

After you have circled the conditional sentences, underline twice and then parse the predicate in each conditional and consequence clause.

Finally, write a *1*, *2*, or *3* in the blank to indicate *First*, *Second*, or *Third Conditional*.

The first is done for you.

simple past, active, subjunctive — simple present, active, modal

If you showed any signs of advanced infection, they wouldn't go near you. ___2___

Zombies don't really smell that bad, not individually and not if they're fresh. ________

He thought that if we abandoned our tribal homeland and relocated to a city, there would be a brand-new house and high-paying jobs just sitting there waiting for us. ________

If you didn't know the true story, if you didn't know it from my end, you'd think it was an efficient crackdown. ________

If you had a loved one, a family member, a child, who was infected, and you thought there was a shred of hope in some other country, wouldn't you do everything in your power to get there? ________

At least if we had gone north, we might have had a chance. ________

If we blew it now, not only would we be sending dozens of people hurtling to their deaths, but we would be trapping thousands on the other side. ________

If we could provide them with the necessary equipment, they might be able to start raising enough food to stretch our existing provisions for years. ________

I know that if we had the resources to clear them all we would. ________

The only risk might be if Zack were clinging to you during the ascent. ________

Exercise 115B: Diagramming

On your own paper, diagram every word of the following sentences from Exercise 115A.

He thought that if we abandoned our tribal homeland and relocated to a city, there would be a brand-new house and high-paying jobs just sitting there waiting for us.

If you didn't know the true story, if you didn't know it from my end, you'd think it was an efficient crackdown.

I know that if we had the resources to clear them all we would.

—LESSON 116—

Words That Can Be Multiple Parts of Speech
Interrogatives
Demonstratives
Relative Adverbs and Subordinating Conjunctions

Exercise 116A: Words Acting as Multiple Parts of Speech

Use these sentences to identify the parts of speech that the bolded words can serve as. Fill in the blanks with the correct labels from the following list:

adjective	adverb
coordinating conjunction	noun
preposition	subordinating conjunction

The following sentences are from *The Moffats* by Eleanor Estes.

Down ____________________ ____________________

She looked up the street and down the street.

Here she refreshed herself with a deep drink from a sparkling spring and sank down into the moss to await the White Prince.

Until ____________________ ____________________

So we will just forget about that old sign until Dr. Witty actually does sell the house to someone.

Hurrah! School was all over until next September.

Before ____________________ ____________________ ____________________

But this little nod did not come naturally to Jane and required some practice before the mirror.

Rufus had never been in school before except for one day last year when Jane brought him to her class for Visiting Day.

He had seen now where the hatch was and he meant to escape before that ghost could catch up with him.

Still ____________________ ____________________ ____________________

However, she still walked on tiptoe when she passed his house, in order not to disturb him should he be napping.

And the red steed sent sparks from his nostrils that disappeared like shooting stars into the still night air.

Why, he knew nothing of that, of course, and although he was inclined to toss the matter lightly aside, still he blanched visibly when again from some mysterious dark recess of the house came the same wild howl.

About ____________________ ____________________

Mama did not like this business about the yards.

Everybody on the street stopped to stare and wave their arms about in excitement.

The following sentences are from *Ginger Pye* by Eleanor Estes.

After ____________________ ____________________

"That is all book stuff," Jerry had reasoned ruefully after it was all over and Rachel had skipped off with Addie Egan.

After the singing there was quiet for a time, with only an occasional sharp command from the one in charge of all these goings-on.

Around ____________________ ____________________

This time, however, there weren't any other people around and it was a splendid opportunity.

When Uncle Bennie got tired of the new game, Rachel and Jerry tied the dusters around their own waists and slid back and forth across the pews themselves.

Since ____________________ ____________________

After all she had been up since dawn with bee-bite.

Since they were already hungry they ate these.

Below ____________________ ____________________

Of course he dropped Jerry's pencil but fortunately it dropped on the windowsill and not down below.

Early in the morning Rachel and Jerry set out to explore the great field below the railroad station for wild strawberries which usually grew there in abundance and which they were very fond of, crushed up with milk and sugar.

Past ________________ ________________ ________________ ________________

The trains went streaking past, running back and forth from Boston to New York, from New York to Boston.

Concealing his impatience, since the leash was still handy, Ginger looked up at Mrs. Pye with what, in the past, he had found to be a winning pose, head to side, tongue dangling out.

Now Ginger was going past the Carruthers' driveway.

When Rachel recovered from the surprise she said to herself, "That man is more interested in sudden perils than in past ones."

who, whom, whose, what, which

Interrogative pronouns take the place of nouns in questions.
Interrogative adjectives modify nouns.

Interrogative Pronouns	**Interrogative Adjectives**
Who was Dragging Canoe?	Whose side was Dragging Canoe on?
With whom did Dragging Canoe fight?	What war did he fight?
What did Dragging Canoe do?	Which tribe did Dragging Canoe belong to?
Which of his countrymen followed him?	

In the American Revolution, Dragging Canoe fought against the colonists who were rebelling against the British.

Dragging Canoe and his brother chiefs, whom he had known for many years, joined together and allied with the British.

Dragging Canoe told his tribesmen to consider the case of the Delaware, whose land had been swallowed by the American colonies.

At first, the American colonists did not know what Dragging Canoe was planning.

Dragging Canoe led attacks on the settlements which were in southeast North America.

The interrogative words *who, whom, whose, what,* and *which* can also serve as relative pronouns in adjective clauses or introductory words in noun clauses.

What was the name of Dragging Canoe's father? ______________________

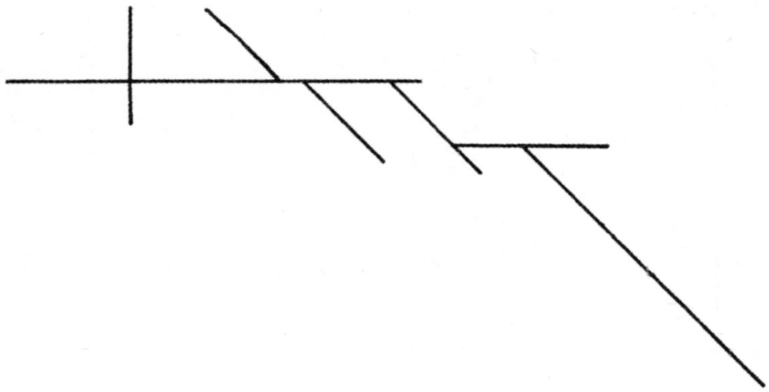

What five towns did Dragging Canoe build? ______________________

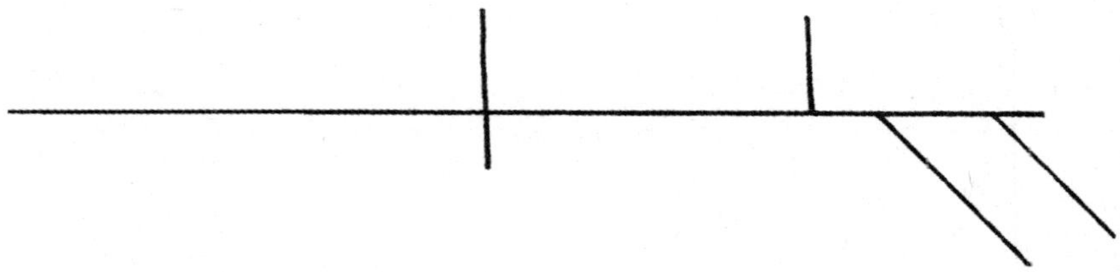

Dragging Canoe did not believe what the governor of North Carolina told him. ______________________

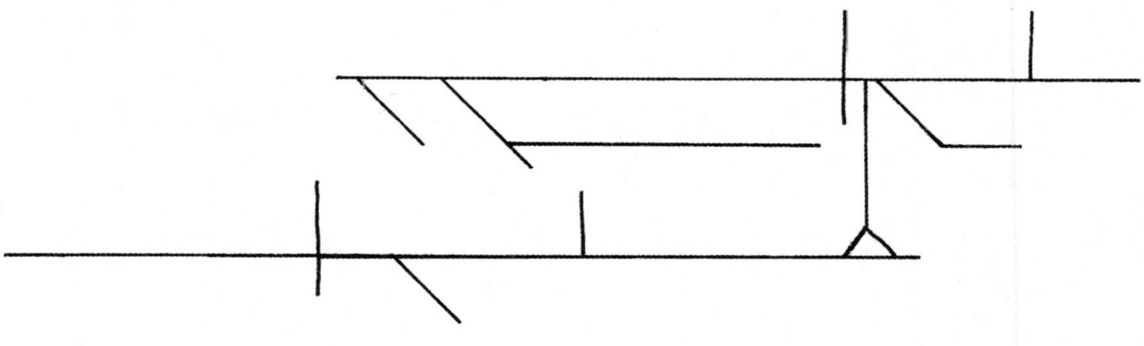

Dragging Canoe led the Cherokees who refused to stay neutral. ____________________

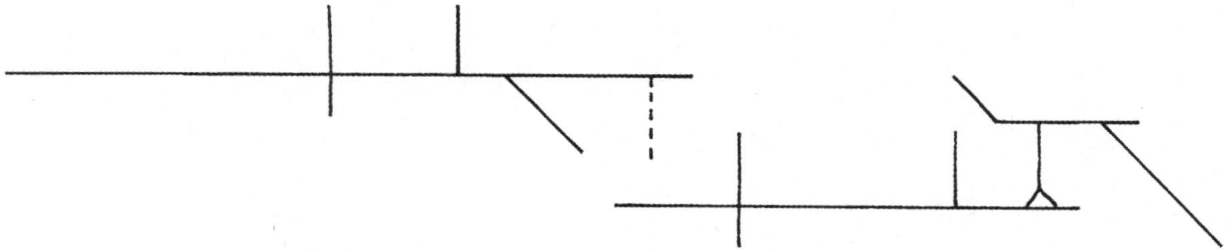

this, that, these, those

Demonstrative pronouns demonstrate or point out something. They take the place of a single word or a group of words.

Demonstrative adjectives modify nouns and answer the question *which one*.

Those were the first Spanish ships to touch American shores.

While a young boy, this future chief wanted to accompany his father, Attakullakulla, and a Cherokee war party going to battle the Shawnee.

During one of these council sessions, a young chief named Dragging Canoe exploded into prominence.

Now that hope is gone.

This was the first invasion of the Middle Towns by an enemy force on record.
—From Pat Alderman, *Nancy Ward: Cherokee Chieftainess, Dragging Canoe: Cherokee-Chickamauga War Chief*

He had come to the council because of his admiration for that great chief.

They set off at a rapid pace, little guessing that a silent scout followed them.

That would be a catastrophe for the Cherokee and their allies.

An adverb describes a verb, an adjective, or another adverb.
Adverbs tell how, when, where, how often, and to what extent.

Relative adverbs introduce adverb clauses and refer back to a place, time, or reason in the independent clause.

where, when, why

(The remaining sentences in the lesson are slightly adapted from *Trail of Tears: The Rise and Fall of the Cherokee Nation* by John Ehle.)

It was the orderly village to which he was heir, and where his mother was the pivot of the world.

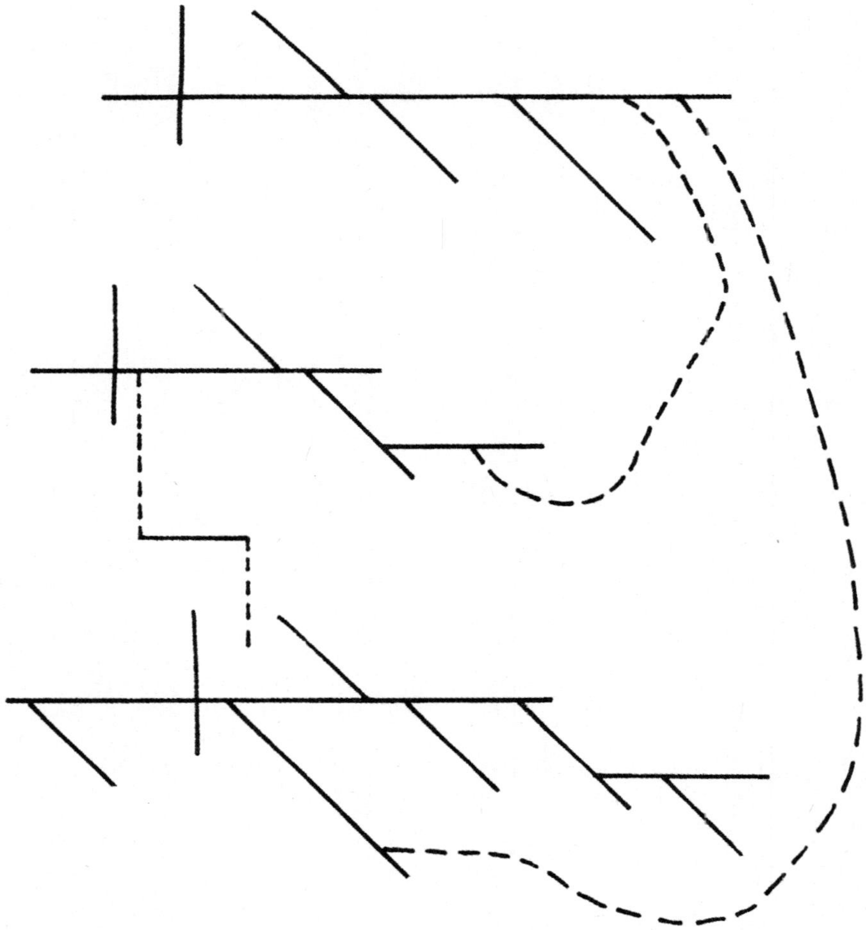

My heart rejoices when I look upon you.

Adverbs can act as subordinating conjunctions when they connect adverb clauses to a verb, adjective, or adverb in the main clause.

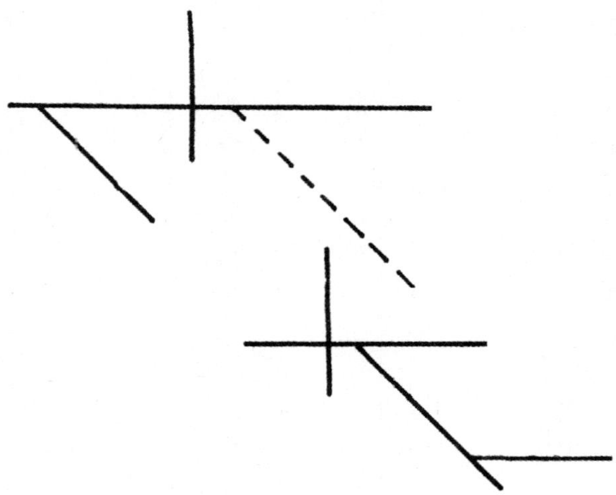

Their land was taken away because they fought for the British.

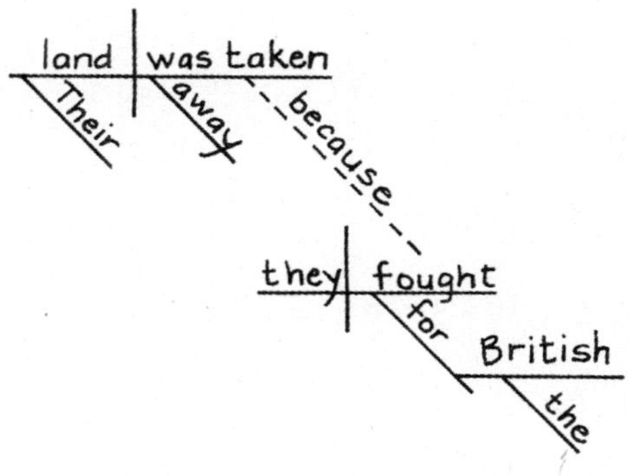

Exercise 116B: Words Introducing Clauses

In the following sentences, taken from *Around the World in Eighty Days* by Jules Verne, circle each subordinate clause. Then, carry out the following steps:

1) Underline the introductory word of the clause. (Note: When the introductory word is the object of a preposition, underline the word itself, not the preposition that precedes it. See the first sentence below.)
2) Label the entire clause as noun, *ADJ* (for adjective), or *ADV* (for adverb).
3) For noun clauses, further identify them as subject or object.
4) For adjective or adverb clauses, draw an arrow from the circle to the word modified.
5) Finally, label the introductory word as one of the following: *RP* for relative pronoun, *RAdj* for relative adjective (a relative pronoun functioning as an adjective and introducing an adjective clause), *RAdv* for relative adverb, *SC* for subordinating conjunction, or *A-SC* for adverb functioning as a subordinating conjunction.

He was pleased, on the day after leaving Suez, to find on deck the obliging person with whom he had walked and chatted on the quays.

Aouda seized a moment when Mr. Fogg was asleep to tell Fix and Passepartout whom she had seen.

It was Phineas Fogg, whose head now emerged from behind his newspapers, who made this remark.

But could he even wait till they reached Hong Kong?

This was Fix, one of the detectives who had been despatched from England in search of the bank robber; it was his task to narrowly watch every passenger who arrived at Suez, and to follow up all who seemed to be suspicious characters, or bore a resemblance to the description of the criminal, which he had received two days before from the police head-quarters at London.

Who dares to say the contrary?

The other was a small, slight-built personage, with a nervous, intelligent face, and bright eyes peering out from under eyebrows which he was incessantly twitching.

A true Englishman doesn't joke when he is talking about so serious a thing as a wager.

But how could Passepartout have discovered that he was a detective?

Fix looked intently at his companion, whose countenance was as serene as possible, and laughed with him.

Half an hour later several members of the Reform came in and drew up to the fireplace, where a coal fire was steadily burning.

He gazed with wonder upon the fortifications which make this place the Gibraltar of the Indian Ocean, and the vast cisterns where the English engineers were still at work, two thousand years after the engineers of Solomon.

You must know that I shall lose twenty thousand pounds, unless I arrive in London by a quarter before nine on the evening of the 21st of December.

They chatted about the journey, and Passepartout was especially merry at the idea that Fix was going to continue it with them.

Mudge was not afraid of being stopped by the Platte River, because it was frozen.

Exercise 116C: Diagramming

On your own paper, diagram every word of the following sentences from Jules Verne's *The Clipper of the Clouds.*

Aeronef is an archaic word for airplane (derived from the French).

Here Frycollin gave vent to a long groan, which might have been taken for his last had he not followed it up with several more.

Who was this Robur, of whom up to the present we know nothing but the name?

The prisoners, although they did not understand how the help had come to them, broke their bonds, while the soldiers were firing at the aeronef.

Rewards were offered to whoever would give news of the three absentees, and even to those who would find some clue to put the police on the track.

When she reached Port Famine the *Albatross* resumed her course to the south.

WEEK 31

Filling Up the Corners

After the feast (more or less) came the Speech. Most of the company were, however, now in a tolerant mood, at that delightful stage which they called "filling up the corners." They were sipping their favourite drinks, and nibbling at their favourite dainties, and their fears were forgotten. They were prepared to listen to anything, and to cheer at every full stop.

—J. R. R. Tolkien, *The Fellowship of the Ring*

— LESSON 117 —

Interrogative Adverbs
Noun Clauses
Forming Questions
Affirmations and Negations
Double Negatives

An adverb describes a verb, an adjective, or another adverb.
Adverbs tell how, when, where, how often, and to what extent.

Relative adverbs introduce adverb clauses and refer back to a place, time, or reason in the independent clause.

where, when, why

I found a shop where I could buy cheese and chocolate.

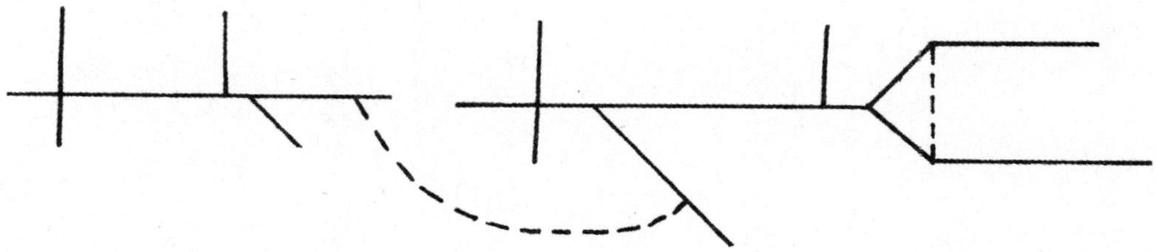

Where did you get the cheese and chocolate?

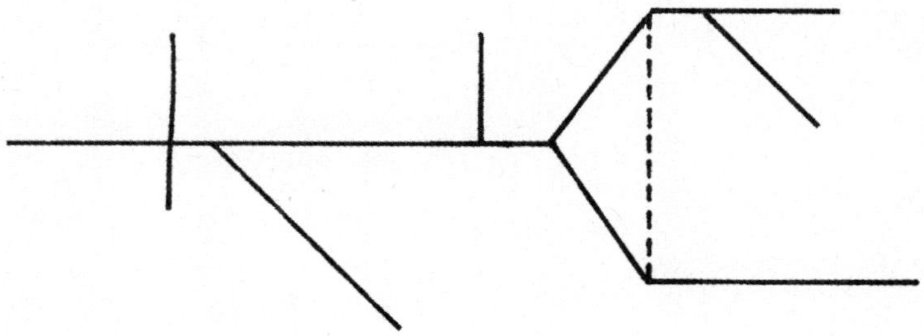

He asked me where I got the cheese and chocolate.

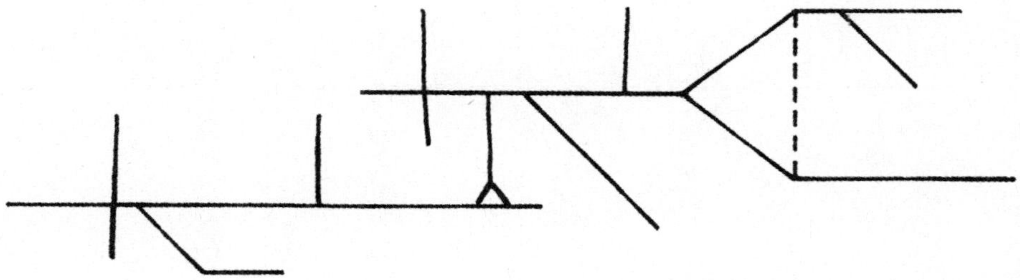

An interrogative adverb asks a question.

where, when, why, how

The interrogative adverbs can also introduce noun clauses.

I desired to know how this thing came to Gollum, and how long he had possessed it.

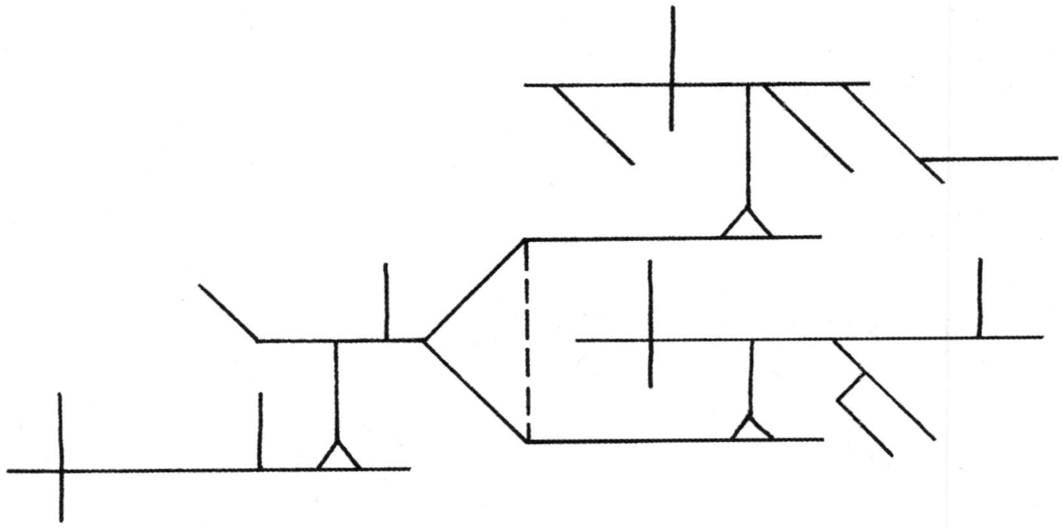

How do the Wise know that this ring is his?

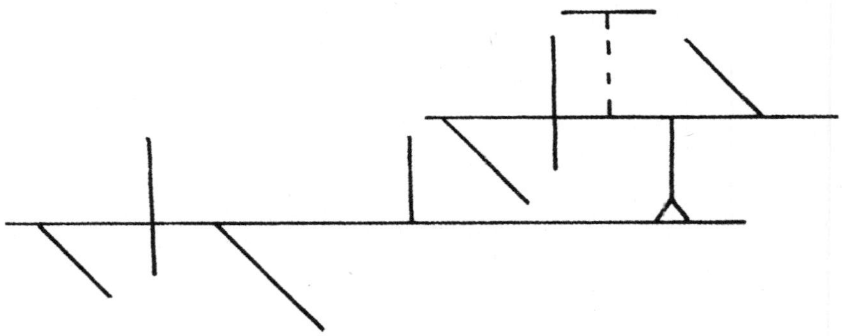

You are hungry.
Are you hungry?

You would like a big bowl of pozole.
Would you like a big bowl of pozole?

Use the helping verbs *do, does,* and *did* to form negatives, ask questions, and provide emphasis.

He fixed green pozole with sliced avocados.
Did he fix green pozole with sliced avocados?

Simple Present

I do	we do
you do	you do
he, she it, does	they do

Simple Past

I did	we did
you did	you did
he, she it did	they did

They love to nibble on chalupas.

Do they love to nibble on chalupas?

Who is bringing the bread pudding with flaming brandy?

What kind of frosting are you using for the cake?

When will the mangos be ripe enough to make mango cake?

Which limes did you use in the lime pudding?

Whom have you invited to the party?

How many loaves of challah did you bake?

Whose presents are those?

An affirmation states what is true or what exists.
A negation states what is not true or does not exist.

Adverbs of affirmation
yes, surely, definitely, certainly, absolutely, very

Did he invite her in?
And he invited her in; yes, he did.

Were they merry?
Surely they were very merry.

Was the roast chicken ready?
The roast chicken was definitely ready to eat.

Were the mushrooms good?
The mushrooms were absolutely delicious.

Adverbs of negation	**Adjective of negation**
no, not, never	no

Did anyone go hungry?
No man, woman or child went hungry.

When did they stop feasting?
They did not stop feasting until well after sundown.

How much merriment was there?
Never was there so much merriment.

There is not no doubt.

I haven't heard no good of such folk.

I don't know nothing about jewels.

Do not use two adverbs or adjectives of negation together.

Exercise 117A: Identifying Adverbs, Interrogative and Demonstrative Pronouns and Adjectives, and Relatives

In the following sentences from Roald Dahl's *James and the Giant Peach*, follow these steps:

a) Label each bolded word as one of the following:

ADV for adverb.
Draw an arrow from the adverb to the word modified.
If the adverb also introduces a clause, underline the clause.

PRO for pronoun.
If the pronoun has an antecedent, label the antecedent as *ANT*.
If the pronoun introduces a clause, underline the clause.
Label each pronoun as *S* for subject, *PN* for predicate nominative, *DO* for direct object, *IO* for indirect object, or *OP* for object of the preposition.

ADJ for adjective.
Draw an arrow from the adjective to the word modified.
If the adjective introduces a clause, underline the clause.

N for noun.
Label the noun as *S*, *PN*, *DO*, *IO*, or *OP*.

b) Label each underlined clause as *ADV-C* for adverb clause, *ADJ-C* for adjective clause, or *N-C* for noun clause.

c) Draw an arrow from each *ADV-C* and *ADJ-C* clause to the word modified. Label each *N-C* noun clause as *S* for subject, *DO* for direct object, *IO* for indirect object, or *OP* for object of the preposition.

The first is done for you.

PRO S
But **who's** telling this story anyway?

And don't whisper a word of **this** to **those** two horrible aunts of yours!

Then at last, **when** it had become nearly as tall as the tree **that** it was growing on, as tall and wide, in fact, as a small house, the bottom part of it gently touched the ground—and **there** it rested.

And meanwhile I wish you'd come over **here** and give me a hand with **these** boots.

He can't see **how** splendid I look.

That is **why** people **who** travel in airplanes never see anything.

"And **who** knows **where** it will end," muttered the Earthworm, "if *you* have anything to do with it."

He stopped **when** he was about three yards away, and he stood **there** leaning on his stick and staring hard at James.

Then **why** did we start sinking?

Where, for example, do you think that I keep my ears?

Exercise 117B: Forming Questions

On your own paper, rewrite the following statements as questions.

Use each of the three methods for forming questions (adding an interrogative pronoun, reversing the subject and helping verb, adding the helping verb *do, does,* or *did* in front of the subject and adjusting the tense of the main verb) at least once. You may change tenses, add or subtract words, or alter the statements in any other necessary ways, as long as the meaning remains the same.

These statements are all adapted from famous questions in books and movies. When you have transformed your statements into questions, compare them with the originals.

You solve a problem like Maria in some way.
It is secret. It is safe. [two questions]
She even has that lever.
You are crying.
There is somebody else in this house.
You have considered piracy.
Your dog is wearing glasses.
When you got a hundred voices singing, someone can hear a lousy whistle blow.
You are telling me that you built a time machine out of a DeLorean.
You would do something with a brain if you had one.
The name of his other leg is something.

Exercise 117C: Affirmations and Negations

On your own paper, rewrite each of the following statements.

- Change affirmative statements into negations, using one adverb or adjective of negation. You may add or subtract words or change tenses as necessary.
- Change negative statements into affirmatives, using at least one adverb of affirmation.
- Change double negations into affirmatives, also using at least one adverb of affirmation.

When you are finished, compare your answers with the original sentences, adapted from *Beeton's Book of Poultry and Domestic Animals*.

Small stones or pebbles are not essential to the existence of fowls.

A person dared venture within the line of devastation.

The turtle dove will not take advantage of the door of its cage or aviary being left open to escape.

They're not quick in none of their movements.

A well-behaved bird may tumble.

Handle the pups during the first week more than is necessary.

The impatience which prompted the purchase will not manifest itself now that the longed-for treasure is obtained.

There seems to be something of use or value in these unusual characteristics.

—LESSON 118—

Diagramming Affirmations and Negations
Yet More Words That Can Be Multiple Parts of Speech
Comparisons Using *Than*
Comparisons Using *As*

Are you ready for your lesson?
Absolutely.
Do you remember the definition of a noun?
Definitely.
How sure are you?
Very.
Have you forgotten it?
No.
Will you ever forget it?
Never.

Affirmative and negative adverbs can also act as interjections.

Never
Absolutely

I can be **very** deaf when I need.

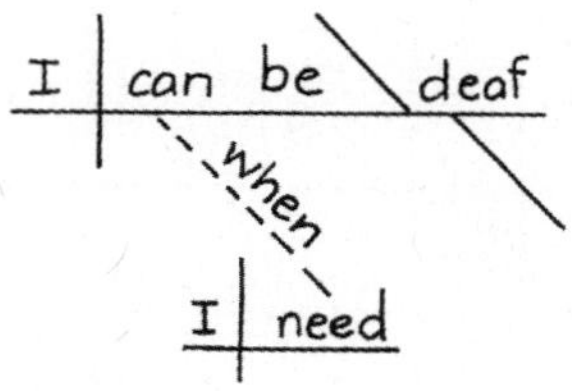

Yes, I will paint you, Juanico.

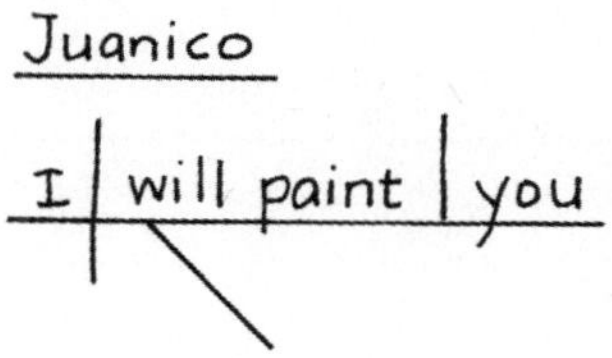

You will **never** be beaten again.

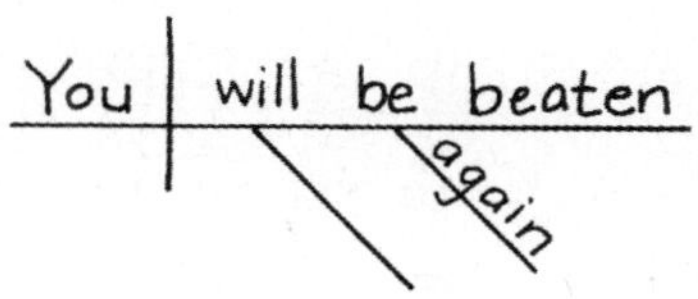

I am **no** longer a slave.

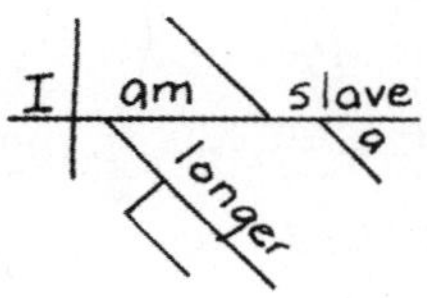

(From *I, Juan de Pareja* by Elizabeth Borton de Treviño)

Yes, I said.

He's unbeatable and drops the dehuller with a fat Yes.

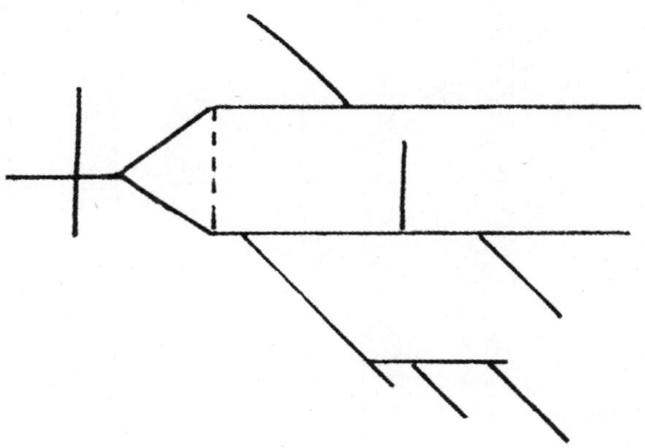

(From *Drown* by Junot Diaz)

Father might say no.

It has no shoestrings.

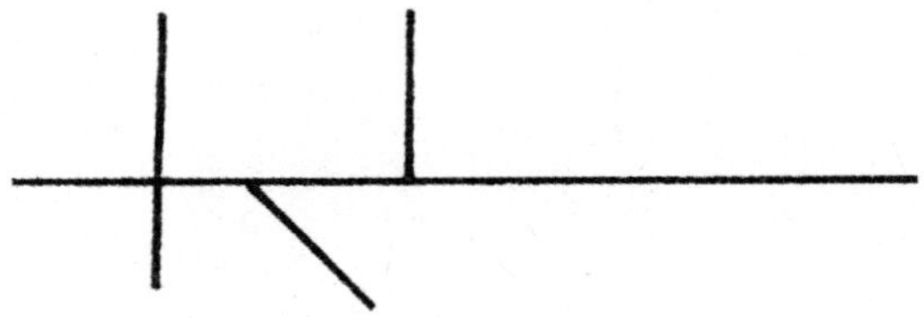

(From *The Dreamer* by Pam Muñoz Ryan)

QC: quasi-coordinator PREP: preposition ADV: adverb SC: subordinating conjunction

The stone was black and shiny, so you could see your reflection as well as the blooming trees and the clouds in the sky.
—From *Return to Sender* by Julia Alvarez

Mamadre nodded and smiled as she left the room.

As my partner, how do you think we should proceed?
—From *The Dreamer* by Pam Muñoz Ryan

When we arrived, nothing was as promised.
—From *Esperanza Rising* by Pam Muñoz Ryan

His affections became poems, as warm and supple as the wool of a well-loved sheep.
—From *The Dreamer* by Pam Muñoz Ryan

When *than* is used in a comparison and introduces a clause with understood elements, it is acting as a subordinating conjunction.

That wool is warmer than my wool.

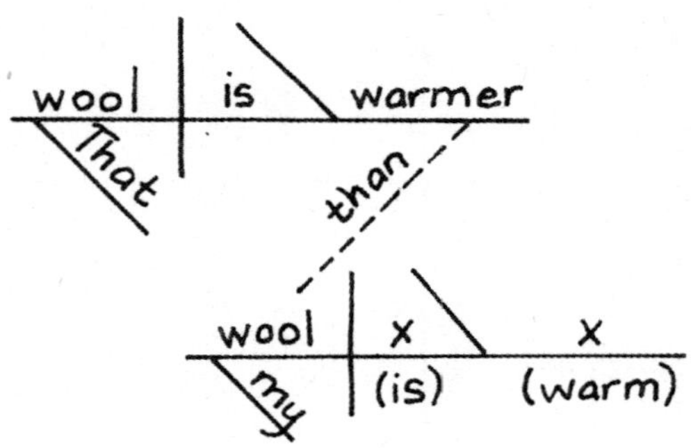

His affections became poems, as warm and supple as the wool of a well-loved sheep.
—From *The Dreamer* by Pam Muñoz Ryan

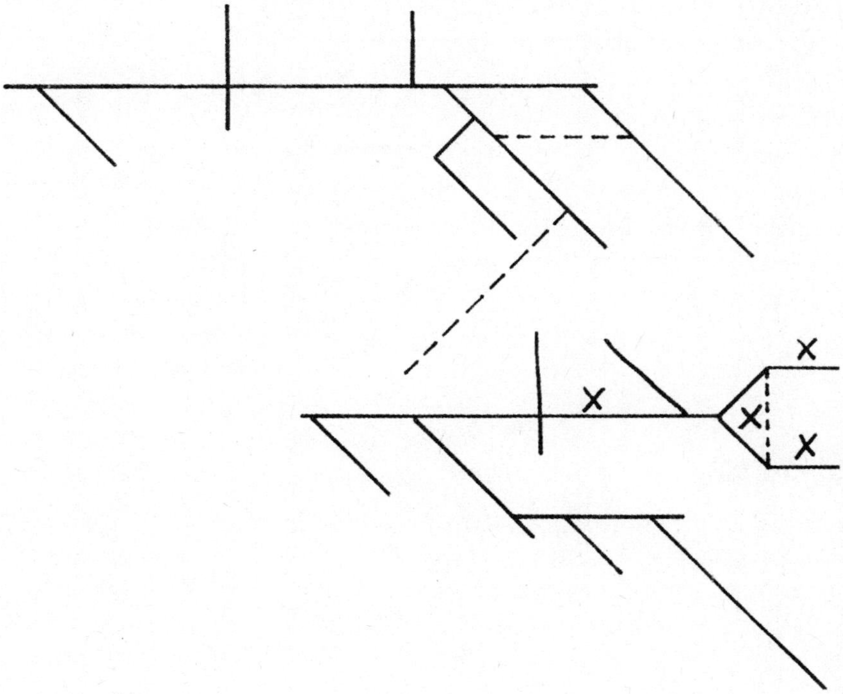

I did as he asked.

He had the same concerns as you have had.

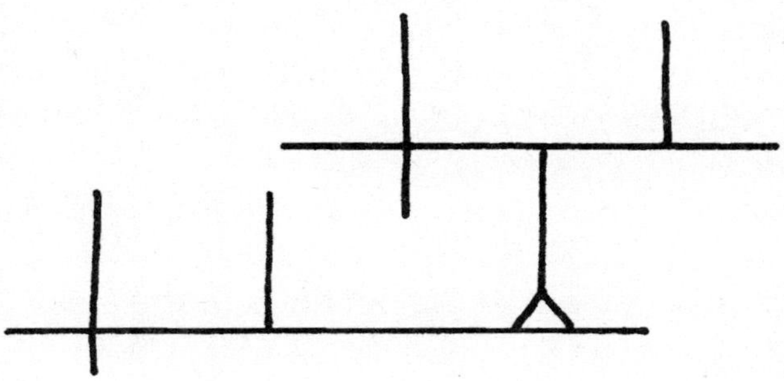

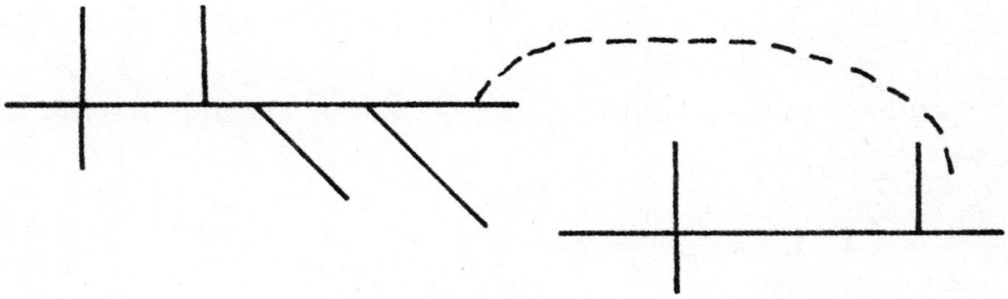

The farmer struggled with the same difficulties as you.

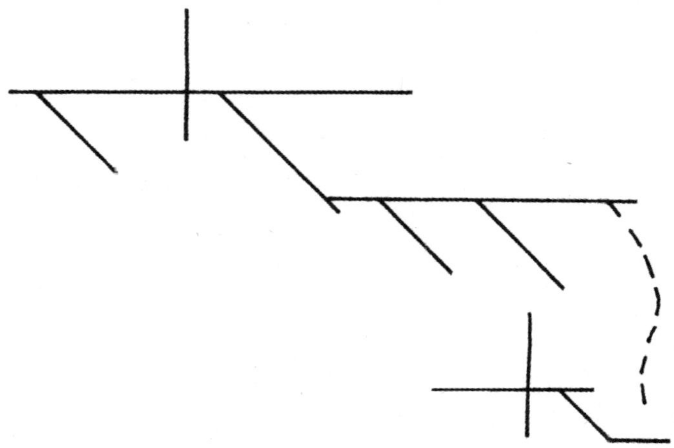

Exercise 118A: Identifying Parts of Speech

Label each of the bolded words in these sentences (from A. A. Milne's *The Red House Mystery*) with one of the following abbreviations.

ADJ: adjective
ADV: adverb
ADV-N: adverb of negation
ADV-A: adverb of affirmation
ADV-R: relative adverb
SC: subordinating conjunction
PREP: preposition
RP: relative pronoun
DP: demonstrative pronoun
P: plain ol' pronoun
N: noun

Where a subordinating conjunction introduces a comparison clause with missing words, draw a caret and insert the missing words.

But, as soon as Antony suggested trying the windows, Cayley saw **that that** was the obvious thing to do.

"Well," he said eagerly, **as** he sat **down** to the business of the meal, "what are we going to do this morning?"

If he **never** went into the office at all, then **where** is he **now**?

Bill was silent, wondering **how** to put into words thoughts **which** had **never** formed themselves **very definitely** in his own mind.

I was never the **one** to pretend to be **what** I wasn't.

You asked me to be **quite** frank, you know, and tell you **what** I thought.

He was supposed, by his patron and **any** others **who** inquired, to be "writing"; but **what** he wrote, other than letters asking for more time to pay, has **never** been discovered.

Audrey threaded a needle, held her hand **out** and looked **at** her nails critically for a moment, and **then** began to sew.

Why did Mark need to change from brown to blue, or **whatever** it was, **when** Cayley was the only person **who** saw him in brown?

As he came **down** the drive and approached the old red-brick front of the house, **there** was a lazy murmur of bees in the flower-borders, a gentle cooing of pigeons in the tops of the elms, and from distant lawns the whir of a mowing-machine.

He had a sponge in **one** hand, a handkerchief in the **other**.

Miss Norris was hurried away **because** she knew **about** the secret passage.

The window was open, and he felt **very** sorry for the owner of it all, **who** was **now** mixed **up** in **so** grim a business.

Anyway, biographies are just **as** interesting **as** most novels, so **why** linger?

Exercise 118B: Diagramming

On your own paper, diagram every word of the following sentences from A. A. Milne's *The Sunny Side*. Ask your instructor for help if you need it.

Yes, dear reader, you are right.

And if the young dramatist answers callously, "Yes," it simply shows that he has no feeling for the stage whatever.

No, I have had enough of writing in the Army and I never want to sign my own name again.

What you want to do is to write a really long letter to Mrs. Cardew, acquainting her with all the facts.

When we arrive you will introduce us as your friends, Mr. and Mrs. Mannering.

For we cannot listen always for that FLOP, and hear it always; nothing in this world is as inevitable as that.

Yes, he was to be a writer; there could be no doubt about that.

—LESSON 119—

Idioms

I'm confused because I don't know what you are **driving at**.

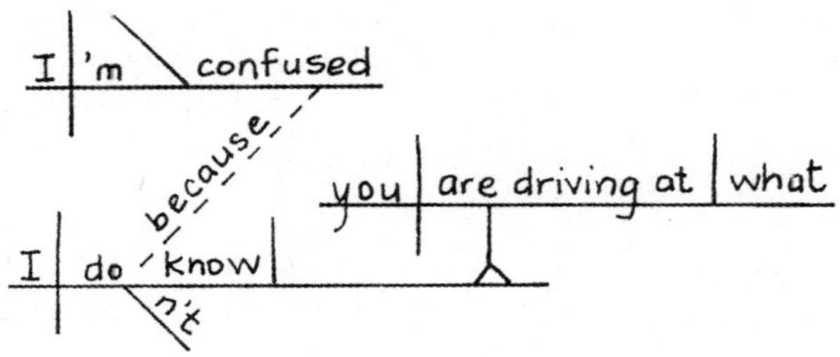

We did our best, but we failed, and now it is **back to the drawing board**.

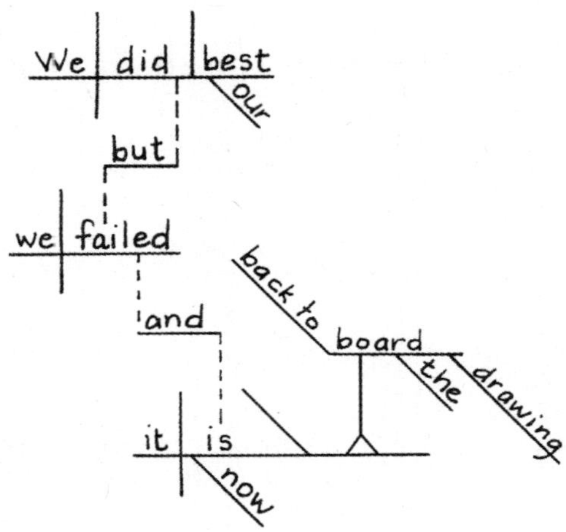

Kerensa found the dress quite ugly but decided **to hold her tongue**.

I decided to eat my vegetables.

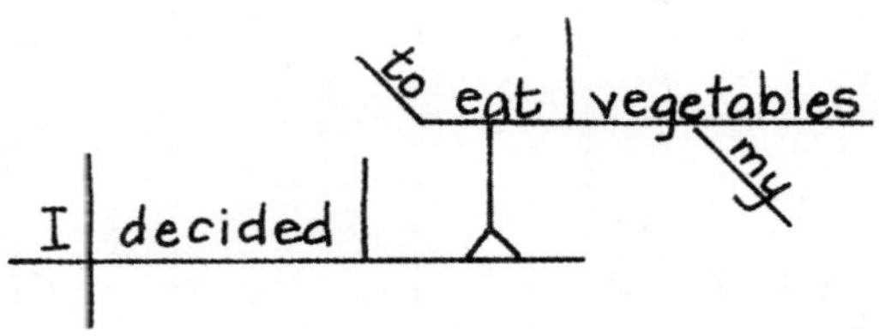

Kerensa decided to hold her tongue.

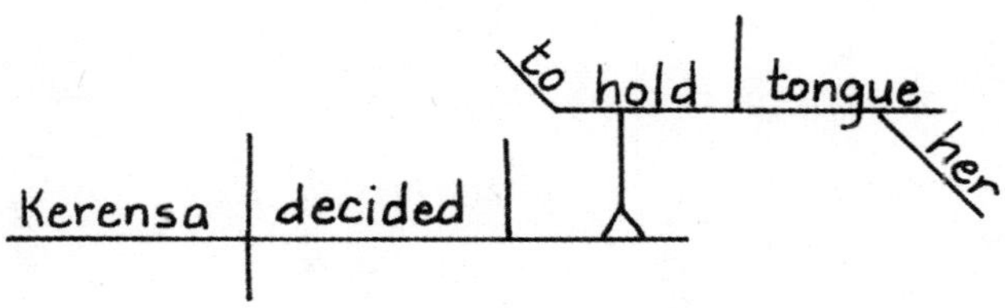

For Diana's surprise party, we'll have a big cake, party hats, **the whole nine yards**.

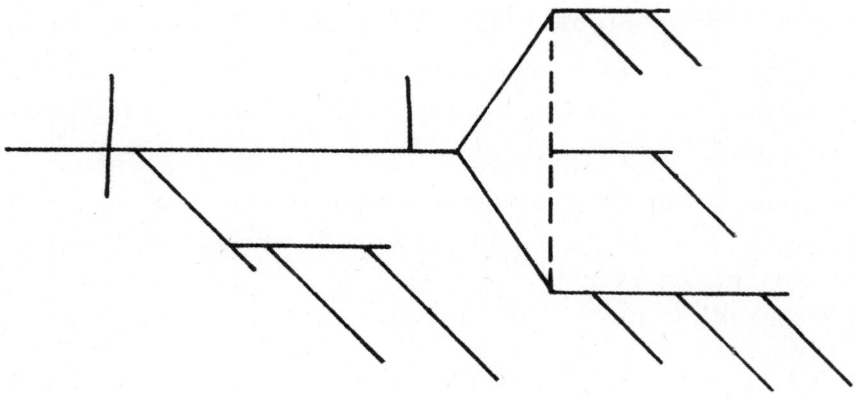

Did I just say that **out loud**?

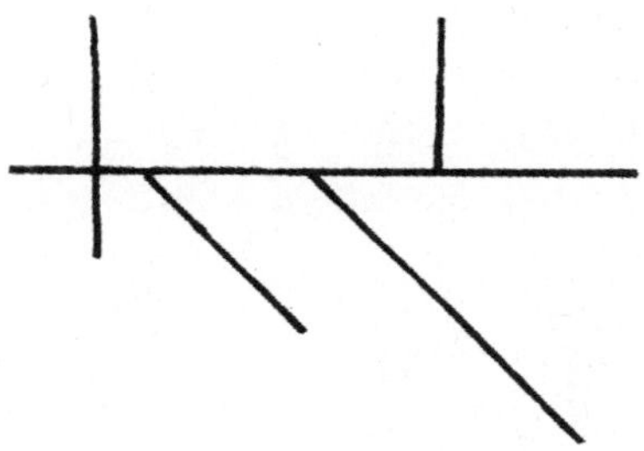

I would like to **make sure** we're **on the same page**.

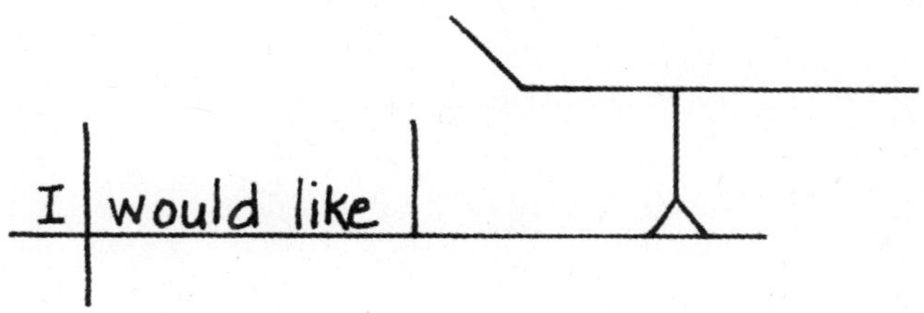

As a rule of thumb, the pH of an aquarium should be between 6.5 and 8 for fresh water.
—Terry Fairfield, *A Common Sense Guide to Fish*

I had an ugly dream, which I can't remember. I went to pieces. I don't know what came over me.
—J. R. R. Tolkien, *The Fellowship of the Ring*

We've got you dead to rights, so no monkey business.
—George Barr, *Anderson Crow, Detective*

Exercise 119A: Identifying Idioms

Circle each complete idiom in the following sets of sentences. (Sometimes, more than one sentence has been provided for context.) There is one obvious idiom in each set, but you may find others.

Write the meaning of each idiom above it in your own words. (You can use more than one word!) The first is done for you.

You will notice that the last set of sentences is from a play. Instead of having traditional dialogue tags such as "he said" or "she answered," the sentences are preceded by the name of the speaker in all capitals, followed by a period. Play dialogue can also be written so that the speaker's name is bolded or italicized and is followed by a colon, like this:

If you plant a couple of turnips and let nature take its course, you'll have turnips all over the place.

With good things it were always thus.

There is always a fly in the custard.

In spite of his sarcasm, and in the face of all criticism, I insist that I was beginning to learn.

—From *That House I Bought: A Little Leaf From Life*,
by Henry Edward Warner

She was the youngest of the two daughters of a most affectionate, indulgent father; and had, in consequence of her sister's marriage, been mistress of his house from a very early period.

Her visit to Abbey-Mill, this summer, seems to have done his business. He is desperately in love and means to marry her.

Ah! there I am—thinking of him directly. Always the first person to be thought of! How I catch myself out!

The evening is closing in, and grandmama will be looking for us.

Her character depends upon those she is with; but in good hands she will turn out a valuable woman.

I am sure if Jane is tired, you will be so kind as to give her your arm.

I shall do very well again after a little while—and then, it will be a good thing over; for they say everybody is in love once in their lives, and I shall have been let off easily.

It was adventuring too far, assuming too much, making light of what ought to be serious, a trick of what ought to be simple.

No, indeed, I shall grant you nothing. I always take the part of my own sex.

—From *Emma*, by Jane Austen

THE MOTHER. Yes, and what of it? You are always asking all sorts of questions, and in that way you spoil the better part of your life—There is Lena, now.

MASTER OF Q. Yes, it comes hard. But here every one must stop who hails from plague-stricken places.

THE OFFICER. But she will come—She will come! [*Walks up and down*] But come to think of it, perhaps I had better call off the dinner after all—as it is late?

MASTER OF Q. I wish often that I could forget—especially myself. That is why I go in for masquerades and carnivals and amateur theatricals.

—From *The Dream Play*, by August Strindberg

Exercise 119B: Diagramming

On your own paper, diagram every word of the following sentences.

These sentences are taken from Marie Brennan's novel *A Natural History of Dragons: A Memoir by Lady Kent.*

Whether he dined at our house, or we at his, we talked of little else, and the earl made good on his promise (or perhaps threat) to pick my brain about my readings.

The astute among you will have noticed that almost all of my expeditions have been to the warmer regions of the world: Akhia, the Broken Sea, and so forth.

Come to that, Astimir had "found" the first print, behind our house; he'd even been the one to cry out the monster's name, setting everyone's thoughts in the proper direction.

Crawling in a dress, for those gentlemen who have never had occasion to try it, is an exercise in frustration, all but guaranteed to produce feelings of homicidal annoyance in the crawler.

—LESSON 120—

Troublesome Sentences

Grammar is the art of speaking or writing a language correctly.
—William Greatheed Lewis, *A Grammar of the English Language* (1821)

Perfect grammar—persistent, continuous, sustained—is the fourth dimension, so to speak: many have sought it, but none has found it.
—Mark Twain, *Autobiography* (posthumous edition, 1925)

Grammar is to literary composition what a linch-pin is to a waggon. It is a poor pitiful thing in itself; it bears no part of the weight; communicates nothing to the force; adds not in the least to the celerity; but, still the waggon cannot very well and safely go on without it; she is constantly liable to reel and be compelled to stop, which, at the least, exposes the driver to be laughed at, and that, too, by those who are wholly unable to drive themselves.
—William Cobbett, *Grammar of the English Language* (1818)

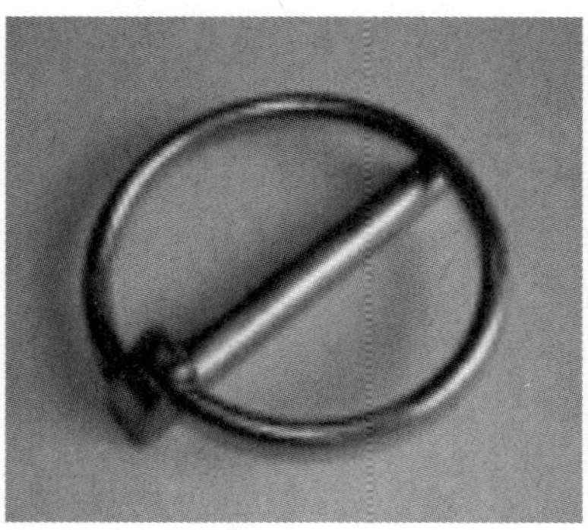

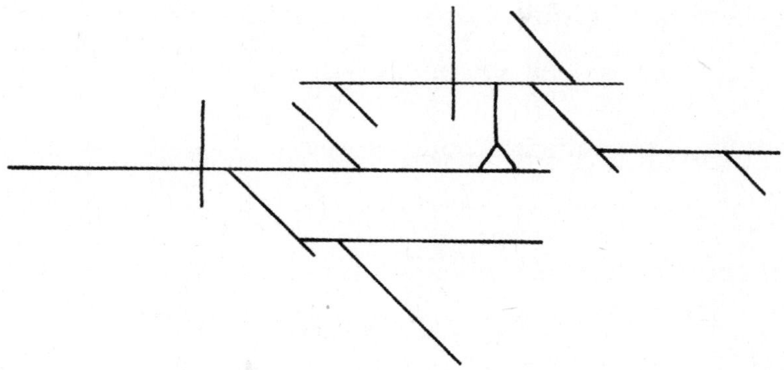

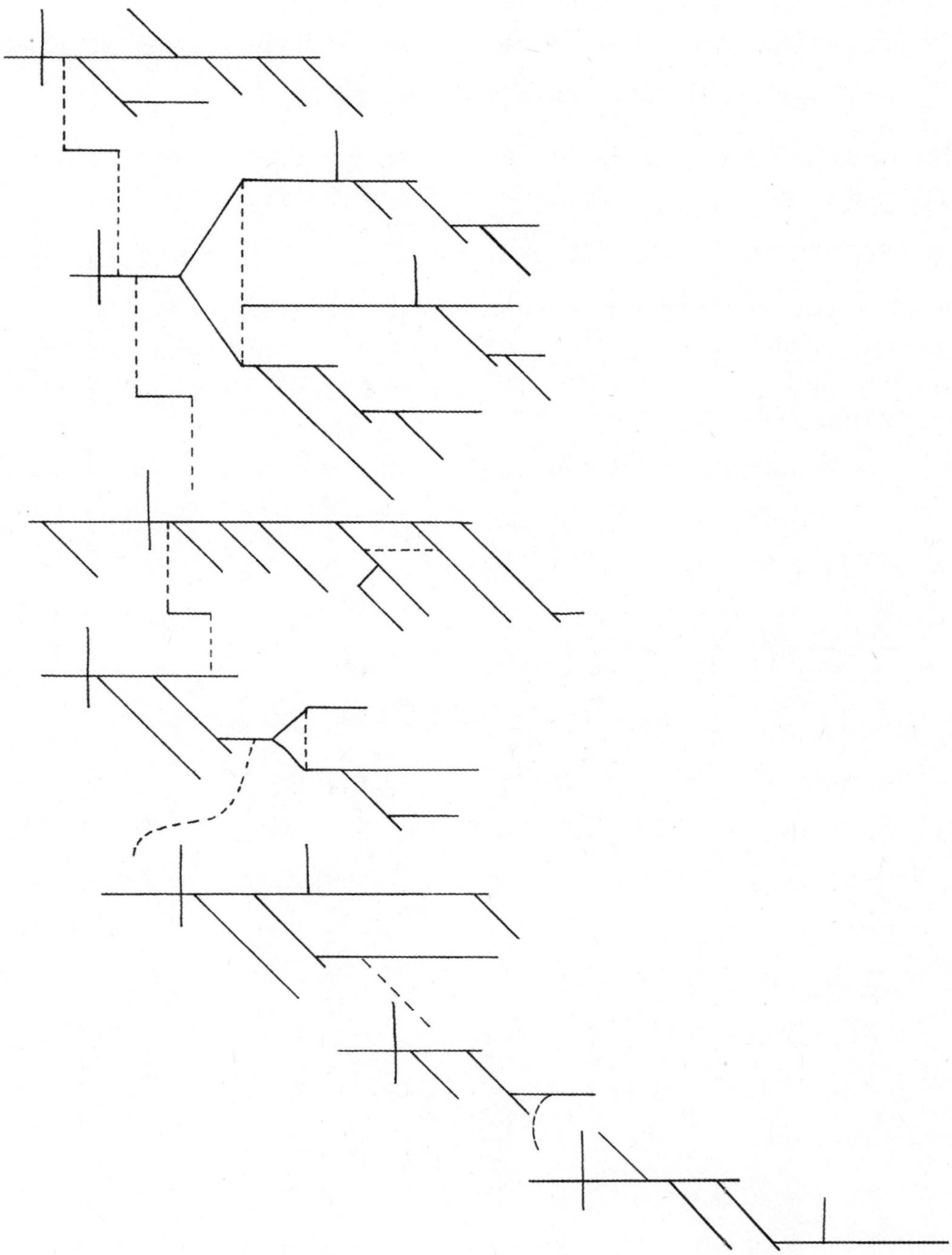

Exercise 120A: A Selection of Oddly Constructed Sentences

After your instructor discusses each sentence with you, diagram it on your own paper.

Freedom now appeared, to disappear no more forever.

—Frederick Douglass, *Narrative of the Life of Frederick Douglass* (1845)

Let this enlightened country take precedence in this noble cause, and we shall soon find that France is not backward to follow, nay, perhaps to accompany our steps.

—William Wilberforce, "Abolition" (1789)

Hence he had made himself out of whole cloth a life full of complications and drama.

—Albert Camus, *The Fall* (1956)

It is a debt we owe to the purity of our religion to show that it is at variance with that law which warrants slavery.

—Patrick Henry, "The Slave Trade" (personal letter, 1773)

In such a society, also, our private economies will depend less and less upon the private ownership of real, usable property, and more and more upon property that is institutional and abstract, beyond individual control, such as money, insurance policies, certificates of deposit, stocks, and shares.

—Wendell Berry, *The Art of the Commonplace: The Agrarian Essays* (2002)

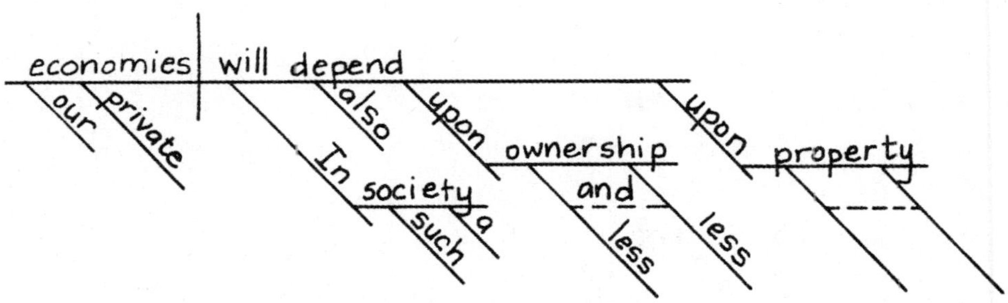

WEEK 32

—REVIEW 10—

Weeks 29-31

Topics
Hortative Verbs
Ambitransitive Verbs
Infinitive Phrases as Objects
Infinitive Phrases With Understood "To"
Principal Parts of Irregular Verbs
Noun Clauses as Appositives
Which/That in Restrictive and Non-Restrictive Clauses
Formal Conditionals
Words Acting as Multiple Parts of Speech
Affirmations and Negations
Idioms

All of the sentences in this exercise are taken from (or slightly adapted from) the 19th-century magazine called *Prairie Farmer: A Weekly Journal for the Farm, Orchard and Fireside.* It first appeared in 1841 and continued to be published from the city of Chicago for the next half-century.

Review 10A: The Missing Words Game

Fill in each blank below with the exact form described—but choose your own words!

Read each word to your instructor, who will insert them into the matching blanks in the short essay in the Key.

Your instructor will then show you the original essay—and your version.

(Verbs are indicative unless another mood is specified.)

present active participle of transitive verb ____________________

adjective ____________________

present passive participle ____________________

present perfect passive verb, third-person singular ____________________

active infinitive of intransitive verb ____________________

singular concrete noun ____________________
ordinal number ____________________
present active participle of transitive verb ____________________
idiom functioning as a noun and meaning "remnants" ____________________
adjective ____________________
adverb ____________________
plural concrete noun ____________________
plural concrete noun ____________________
regular adverb ____________________
regular adverb ____________________
adjective formed with un- ____________________
past participle of transitive verb ____________________
compound plural concrete noun ____________________
active infinitive of transitive verb ____________________
active imperative verb ____________________
simple present passive modal verb, third-person singular ____________________
plural concrete noun ____________________
plural concrete noun ____________________
active infinitive of transitive verb ____________________
active imperative, negative form, of transitive verb ____________________
adjective ____________________
active imperative of transitive verb ____________________
possessive noun acting as an adjective ____________________
subordinating conjunction introducing an adverb clause ____________________
singular abstract noun ____________________
simple present modal passive verb, third-person singular ____________________
adjective ____________________
present participle of intransitive verb ____________________
adjective ____________________

cardinal number ________________

singular concrete noun ________________

simple present modal active verb, first-person plural, negative form ________________

active infinitive of transitive verb ________________

adverb of negation ________________

adjective ________________

progressive present, active, third-person singular of transitive verb ________________

adjective ________________

singular demonstrative pronoun ________________

adjective in the comparative form ________________

past passive participle ________________

concrete noun acting as an adjective ________________

same concrete noun as in previous blank ________________

present active participle of transitive verb ________________

adverb ________________

passive infinitive ________________

adjective ________________

plural concrete noun ________________

singular concrete hyphenated compound noun ________________

compound adjective ________________

adverb introducing a subordinate adverb clause ________________

plural compound noun ________________

adjective ________________

active infinitive of transitive verb ________________

singular indefinite adjective ________________

singular indefinite pronoun ________________

plural compound concrete noun ________________

simple present modal state of being verb, third-person singular ________________

present participle of intransitive verb ________________

coordinating conjunction ______________________

adjective ______________________

present perfect passive verb, third-person singular ______________________

singular demonstrative adjective ______________________

abstract singular noun ______________________

abstract singular noun ______________________

perfect present active indicative transitive verb, third-person plural ______________________

plural concrete noun ______________________

compound adjective ______________________

relative pronoun ______________________

active infinitive of transitive verb ______________________

concrete noun that is acting as an adjective modifying another noun ______________________

same concrete noun as in previous blank ______________________

passive infinitive ______________________

perfect present passive participle ______________________

adjective of negation ______________________

plural subject pronoun ______________________

concrete plural compound noun ______________________

present active participle of transitive verb ______________________

present passive participle ______________________

past participle acting as adjective ______________________

singular demonstrative pronoun ______________________

present progressive of transitive verb, second-person singular ______________________

possessive personal pronoun ______________________

adjective ______________________

subordinating conjunction introducing a noun clause ______________________

singular concrete noun ______________________

simple present modal verb, second-person singular ______________________

indefinite pronoun that can be either singular or plural ______________________ active infinitive of transitive verb ____________________

adjective ____________________

adjective in the superlative form ____________________

simple present intransitive verb, third-person singular ____________________

abstract singular noun ____________________

abstract singular noun ____________________

adverb ____________________

Review 10B: Identifying Infinitive Phrases, Noun Clauses, and Modifying Clauses

In the following excerpt, follow these four steps:

a) Identify every set of underlined words as *INF* for infinitive phrase, *PREP* for prepositional phrase, or *CL* for clause.
b) Infinitive phrases, prepositional phrases, or clauses may occur within other phrases or clauses. If words are double-underlined (or even triple underlined!), identify them as a separate element within the single-underlined phrase or clause.
c) Label each phrase or clause as *ADV* for adverb, *ADJ* for adjective, or *N* for noun.
d) For adjective and adverb phrases and clauses, draw an arrow from the label to the word modified.
e) For noun phrases and clauses, add the appropriate part of the sentence label: *S* for subject, *DO* for direct object, *IO* for indirect object, *PN* for predicate nominative, *OP* for object of the preposition, *APP* for appositive.

The first is done for you.

This is taken from a book called *Thrilling Stories of the Great War: On Land and Sea, In the Air, Under the Water*, by Logan Marshall. It was written in 1915, during the second year of World War I. (World War I was known simply as the Great War until World War II.) Here, Mr. Marshall tells the story of the sinking of the RMS *Lusitania*, a British passenger ship that was torpedoed by a German submarine on May 7, 1915.

Because the *Lusitania* was a civilian ship, not a military vessel, the German attack was against internationally recognized rules of warfare. Over a thousand passengers died, and anger over the sinking was one of the factors that eventually led the United States to enter the war—although this did not happen for two more years.

CL ADV

One of the passengers, Dr. Daniel Moore, of Yankton, S. D., declared that before he

CL N DO

went downstairs to luncheon shortly after one o'clock he and others with him noticed

PREP ADV

through a pair of marine glasses, a curious object in the sea, possibly two miles or more away. What it was he could not determine, but he jokingly referred to it later at luncheon as a submarine.

While the first cabin passengers were chatting over their coffee cups they felt the ship give a great leap forward. Full speed ahead had suddenly been signaled from the bridge . . .

The *Lusitania* began to swerve to starboard, heading for the submarine, but before she could really answer her helm a torpedo was flashing through the water toward her at express speed. Myers and his companions, like many others of the passengers, saw the white wake of the torpedo and its metal casing gleaming in the bright sunlight . . .

In far less time than it takes to tell, the torpedo had crashed into the *Lusitania's* starboard side, just abaft the first funnel, and exploded with a dull boom in the forward stoke-hole.

Captain Turner at once ordered the helm put over and the prow of the ship headed for land, in the hope that she might strike shallow water while still under way. The boats were ordered out, and the signals calling the boat crews to their stations were flashed everywhere through the vessel. . . .

Down in the dining saloon the passengers felt the ship reel from the shock of the explosion and many were hurled from their chairs. Before they could recover themselves, another explosion occurred. There is a difference of opinion as to the number of torpedoes fired. Some say there were two; others say only one torpedo struck the vessel, and that the second explosion was internal.

In any event, the passengers now realized their danger. The ship, torn almost apart, was filled with fumes and smoke, the decks were covered with débris that fell from the sky, and the great *Lusitania* began to list quickly to starboard. Before the passengers below decks could make their way above, the decks were beginning to slant ominously, and the air was filled with the cries of terrified men and women, some of them already injured by being hurled against the sides of the saloons. Many passengers were stricken unconscious by the smoke and fumes from the exploding torpedoes.

The stewards and stewardesses, recognizing the too evident signs of a sinking ship, rushed about urging and helping the passengers to put on life-belts, of which more than 3,000 were aboard. . . .

The first life-boat that struck the water capsized with some sixty women and children aboard her, and all of these must have been drowned almost instantly. Ten more boats were lowered, the desperate expedient of cutting away the ropes being resorted to to prevent them from being dragged along by the now halting steamer.

The great ship was sinking by the bow, foot by foot, and in ten minutes after the first explosion she was already preparing to founder. Her stern rose high in the air, so that those in the boats that got away could see the whirring propellers, and even the boat deck was awash.

Captain Turner urged the men to be calm, to take care of the women and children, and megaphoned the passengers to seize life-belts, chairs—anything they could lay hands on to save themselves from drowning. There was never any question in the captain's mind that the ship was about to sink, and if, as reported, some of the stewards ran about advising the passengers not to take to the boats, that there was no danger of the vessel going down till she reached shore, it was done without his orders. But many of the survivors have denied this, and declared that all the crew, officers, stewards and sailors, even the stokers, who dashed up from their flaming quarters below, showed the utmost bravery and calmness in the face of the disaster, and sought in every way to aid the panic-stricken passengers to get off the ship.

Review 10C: Parsing

Parse every bolded verb in the following.

This was written by the British politician David Lloyd George, who was prime minister during World War I. In this excerpt, Lloyd George, writing twenty years after the fact, reflects back on 1914, when Great Britain first joined the Allied fight against the Central Powers.

Provide the following information:

Person:	First, second, or third
Number:	Sing. or pl.
Tense:	Simple past, present, or future; perfect past, present, or future; progressive past, present, or future; or progressive perfect present
Voice:	Active, passive, or state-of-being
Mood:	Indicative, subjunctive, imperative, hortatory, or modal If the verb is also emphatic, add this label to the mood.

The first is done for you.

"Boom!"

third pl, simple past, active, indicative

The deep notes of Big Ben **rang** out into the night, the first strokes in Britain's most fateful hour since she arose out of the deep. A shuddering silence **fell** upon the room. Every face **was** suddenly **contracted** in a painful intensity.

"Doom!" "Doom!" "Doom!" to the last stroke. The big clock **echoed** in our ears like the hammer of destiny. What destiny? Who **could tell**? We **had challenged** the most powerful military empire the world **has** yet **brought** forth. France **was** too weak alone to challenge its might and Russia was ill-organised, ill-equipped, corrupt. We knew what brunt Britain **would have** to bear. **Could** she **stand** it? There was no doubt or hesitation in any breast.

But **let** it **be admitted** without shame that a thrill of horror quickened every pulse.

Did we know that before peace **would be restored** to Europe we **should have** to wade through four years of the most concentrated slaughter, mutilation, suffering, devastation and savagery which mankind **has** ever **witnessed**?

That 12 millions of the gallant youth of the nations **would be slain**, that another 20 millions would be mutilated? That Europe **would be crushed** under the weight of a colossal war debt? That only one empire **would stand** the shock? That the three other glittering empires of the world **would have been flung** to the dust, and shattered beyond repair? That revolution, famine and anarchy would sweep over half of Europe, and that their menace would scorch the rest of this hapless continent?

Has the full tale yet **been told**? Who can tell? But **had** we **foreseen** it all on the fourth of August, we **could have done** no other.

Twenty minutes after the hour, Mr. Winston Churchill came in and informed us the wires **had** already **been sent** to the British ships of war in every sea, announcing that war had been declared and that they were to act accordingly. Soon afterward we dispersed. There was nothing more to say that night. Tomorrow **would bring** us novel tasks and new bearings. As I left, I felt like a man standing on a planet that **had been** suddenly **wrenched** from its orbit by a demoniacal hand, and that **was spinning** wildly into the unknown.

—From *The War Memoirs of David Lloyd George* (Nicholson & Watson, 1933–38)

Review 10D: Which and That Clauses

In the following sentences, taken from the 1919 book *History of the World War: An Authentic Narrative of the World's Greatest War* by Francis March and Richard Beamish, underline each clause introduced by *which* or *that.*

- If *that* is understood, underline the clause and use a caret to insert the missing *that.*
- If a *which* or *that* clause falls within another clause, underline the entire larger clause once, and the clause-within-a-clause a second time.
- Label each underlined clause as *ADJ* for adjective, *ADV* for adverb, or *N* for noun.
- For adjective and adverb clauses, draw an arrow back to the word modified.
- For noun clauses, label the part of the sentence that the clause fulfills (*S, PN, DO, IO, APP*).
- Finally, label each adjective clause as R for restrictive or NON-R for nonrestrictive.

The first clause is done for you.

ADJ R

Germany's military machine was ready. A gray-green uniform that at a distance would fade into misty obscurity had been devised after exhaustive experiments by optical, dye and cloth experts co-operating with the military high command . . . German soldiers had received instructions which enabled each man at a signal to go to an appointed place where he found everything in readiness for his long forced marches into the territory of Germany's neighbors.

Messages which might help any of the belligerents in any way were barred.

German cruisers that had raided sea-going commerce were destroyed.

There had been no time to intrench the position properly, but the troops showed a magnificent front to the terrible fire which confronted them.

The Allies found they had a formidable army to aid them, and the enemy learned finally that he had one to reckon with.

An examination of exploded shells indicated that the new German gun was less than nine inches in caliber, and that the projectiles, which weighed about two hundred pounds, contained two charges, in two chambers connected by a fuse, which often exploded more than a minute apart.

The Air Service, the Tank Corps, the development of heavy mobile artillery, the proper organization of divisions, corps, and armies, all will be set forth in the scheme which will be submitted to you with the recommendation that it be transmitted for the consideration of Congress.

We made steady headway in the almost impenetrable and strongly held Argonne Forest, for, despite this reinforcement, it was our army that was doing the driving.

The role of the French army, which was operating to the right of the British army, was threefold. It had to support the British attacking on its left. It had on its right to support the center, which, from September 7th, had been subjected to a German attack of great violence. Finally, its mission was to throw back the three active army corps and the reserve corps which faced it.

To give this victory all its meaning it is necessary to add that it was gained by troops which for two weeks had been retreating, and which, when the order for the offensive was given, were found to be as ardent as on the first day. It has also to be said that these troops had to meet the whole German army.

Knowing that the war was over for other American soldiers, the morale of the troops declined throughout the winter.

Our Third Corps crossed the Meuse on the 5th and the other corps, in the full confidence that the day was theirs, eagerly cleared the way of machine guns as they swept northward. . . . The strategical goal which was our highest hope was gained.

Review 10E: Words Acting as Multiple Parts of Speech

In the sentences below, identify the part of speech of each underlined word. Label them as *N* for noun, *V* for verb, *PRO* for pronoun, *ADV* for adverb, *ADJ* for adjective, *PREP* for preposition, *CC* for coordinating conjunction, or *SC* for subordinating conjunction.

When you are finished, write each word (once) in the left-hand column. In the right-hand column, list the parts of speech that it fulfills.

The first is done for you.

These sentences are all taken from poems written by Wilfred Owen, an English poet who fought in World War I. Owen was killed in action in November 1918, just a week before the end of the war, at the age of 25.

PREP
And by his smile, I knew that sullen hall;
With a thousand fears that vision's face was grained;
Yet no blood reached there from the upper ground,
And no guns thumped, or down the flues made moan.

And He, picking a manner of worm, which half had hid
Its bruises in the earth, but crawled no further,
Showed me its feet . . .

Rain, guttering down in waterfalls of slime
Kept slush waist high, that rising hour by hour,
Choked up the steps too thick with clay to climb.

A few, a few, too few for drums and yells,
May creep back, silent, to still village wells
Up half-known roads.

But many there stood still
To face the stark, blank sky beyond the ridge,
Knowing their feet had come to the end of the world.

Now, he will spend a few sick years in Institutes . . .

Also, they read of Cheap Homes, not yet planned;
For, said the paper, "When this war is done
The men's first instinct will be making homes."

And there's no light to see the voices by—
No time to dream, and ask—he knows not what.

Let us lie down and dig ourselves in thought.

Smiling they wrote his lie; aged nineteen years.

Courage leaked, as sand
From the best sandbags after years of rain.

About this time Town used to swing so gay
When glow-lamps budded in the light-blue trees
And girls glanced lovelier as the air grew dim,
—In the old times, before he threw away his knees.

Dullness best solves
The tease and doubt of shelling . . .

. . . Where once an hour a bullet missed its aim
And misses teased the hunger of his brain.

Move him into the sun—
Gently its touch awoke him once,
At home, whispering of fields unsown.

Hour after hour they ponder the warm field—
And the far valley behind, where the buttercups
Had blessed with gold their slow boots coming up . . .

We two will stay behind and keep our troth.

I forgot him there
In posting next for duty, and sending a scout . . .
To beg a stretcher somewhere, and floundering about
To other posts under the shrieking air.

Why speak they not of comrades that went under?

In all my dreams before my helpless sight

He plunges at me, guttering, choking, drowning.

Northward incessantly, the flickering gunnery rumbles,

Far off, like a dull rumour of some other war.

Nurse looks so far away. And everywhere

Music and roses burnt through crimson slaughter.

. . . shell on frantic shell

Hammered on top, but never quite burst through.

I, too, have dropped off fear—

Behind the barrage . . .

I'd ask no night off when the bustle's over . . .

So, soon they topped the hill, and raced together

Over an open stretch of herb and heather

Exposed.

How cold steel is, and keen with hunger of blood;

Blue with all malice, like a madman's flash . . .

by	preposition		

Review 10F: Idioms

Circle each idiom in the following sentences. Above each one, write its meaning within the sentence. These sentences are taken from *The Untold Story of the First World War*, by Anna Revell.

World War I turned the world on its head, and prepared the way for the coming of our own world.

These wars were generally viewed as proof that the Great Powers had the sense to compromise when they could see they were on the edge of the precipice.

In July 1914 Europe was a powder keg waiting to go off.

Franz Ferdinand decided to change his plans for the rest of the day in favour of visiting the wounded in hospital.

China was forced to concede all but the most savage of the demands.

Now all eyes looked to Great Britain.

When the smoke had cleared the British had lost fourteen warships and almost seven thousand men, to the Germans' eleven ships and three thousand men.

The Tsar and his wife seemed blind to these things.

He hoped that he might save his crown by personally leading the troops back from the front.

Review 10G: Transitive, Intransitive, and State-of-Being Verbs

The following poem, "In Flanders Fields," is probably the most famous piece of literature from World War I. It was written by the Canadian doctor John McCrae in 1915, right after McCrae conducted the funeral of his friend and fellow officer Alexis Helmer. Helmer was killed in battle on May 2, 1915.

Flanders Fields is the name for an area of World War I battlefields that now lie in Belgium and France.

Poppies grew on the battlefields because they flourish where the ground has been disturbed. Because of this poem, the red poppy became an international symbol for the memory of those who have died in battle.

Underline each predicate in the poem (in both independent and subordinate clauses).

- Mark each as *T* for transitive, *IT* for intransitive or *SB* for state-of-being.
- For transitive verbs, circle the word that receives the action of the verb and draw a line from the circled word to the appropriate transitive verb.

In Flanders fields the poppies blow

Between the crosses, row on row,

That mark our place; and in the sky

The larks, still bravely singing, fly

Scarce heard amid the guns below.

We are the Dead. Short days ago

We lived, felt dawn, saw sunset glow,

Loved and were loved, and now we lie

In Flanders fields.

Take up our quarrel with the foe:

To you from failing hands we throw

The torch; be yours to hold it high.

If ye break faith with us who die

We shall not sleep, though poppies grow

In Flanders fields.

Review 10H: Hunt and Find

In the following excerpt, from the first chapter of the classic World War I adventure novel *The Thirty-Nine Steps* by John Buchan, find, underline, and label one example of each of the following:

Restrictive adjective clause	Compound Modifier
Nonrestrictive adjective clause	Infinitive phrase acting as a noun
Infinitive phrase with an understood *to*	Comparison
Ordinal number acting as a noun	Superlative adjective
Appositive	Adverbial noun
Present participle acting as direct object of verb	Present participle phrase acting as object of preposition
Past participle phrase acting as an adverb	Predicate nominative
Adverb clause	Clause introduced by a relative adverb
Third conditional sentence	Infinitive phrase acting as an adjective
Indirect object	Infinitive phrase acting as an adverb
Clause with an understood *that*	*That* acting as a demonstrative pronoun
To as a preposition	Reflexive pronoun acting as direct object
Idiom (be ready to explain it)	Adjective clause modifying an idiom
Noun clause acting as a direct object	

CHAPTER ONE

The Man Who Died

I returned from the City about three o'clock on that May afternoon pretty well disgusted with life. I had been three months in the Old Country, and was fed up with it. If anyone had told me a year ago that I would have been feeling like that I should have laughed at him; but there was the fact . . . I couldn't get enough exercise, and the amusements of London seemed as flat as soda-water that has been standing in the sun. "Richard Hannay," I kept telling myself, "you have got into the wrong ditch, my friend, and you had better climb out."

. . . I had got my pile—not one of the big ones, but good enough for me; and I had figured out all kinds of ways of enjoying myself. My father had brought me out from Scotland at the age of six, and I had never been home since; so England was a sort of Arabian Nights to me, and I counted on stopping there for the rest of my days.

But from the first I was disappointed with it. In about a week I was tired of seeing sights, and in less than a month I had had enough of restaurants and theatres and race-meetings. I had no real pal to go about with, which probably explains things. Plenty of people invited me to their houses, but they didn't seem much interested in me. They would fling me a question or two about South Africa, and then get on their own affairs. A lot of Imperialist ladies asked me to tea to meet schoolmasters from New Zealand and editors from Vancouver, and that was the dismalest business of all. Here was I, thirty-seven years old, sound in wind and limb, with enough money to have a good time, yawning my head off all day. I had just about settled to clear out and get back to the veld, for I was the best bored man in the United Kingdom.

That afternoon I had been worrying my brokers about investments to give my mind something to work on, and on my way home I turned into my club—rather a pot-house, which took in Colonial members. I had a long drink, and read the evening papers. They were full of the row in the Near East, and there was an article about Karolides, the Greek Premier. I rather fancied the chap. From all accounts he seemed the one big man in the show; and he played a straight game too, which was more than could be said for most of them. I gathered that they hated him pretty blackly in Berlin and Vienna, but that we were going to stick by him, and one paper said that he was the only barrier between Europe and Armageddon. I remember wondering if I could get a job in those parts. . . About six o'clock I went home, dressed, dined at the Cafe Royal, and turned into a music-hall. It was a silly show . . . and I did not stay long. The night was fine and clear as I walked back to the flat

I had hired near Portland Place. The crowd surged past me on the pavements, busy and chattering, and I envied the people for having something to do. These shop-girls and clerks and dandies and policemen had some interest in life that kept them going. I gave half-a-crown to a beggar because I saw him yawn; he was a fellow-sufferer. At Oxford Circus I looked up into the spring sky and I made a vow. I would give the Old Country another day . . . if nothing happened, I would take the next boat for the Cape.

My flat was the first floor in a new block behind Langham Place…I was just fitting my key into the door when I noticed a man at my elbow. . . . He was a slim man, with a short brown beard and small, gimlety blue eyes. I recognized him as the occupant of a flat on the top floor, with whom I had passed the time of day on the stairs.

"Can I speak to you?" he said. "May I come in for a minute?" He was steadying his voice with an effort, and his hand was pawing my arm.

I got my door open and motioned him in. No sooner was he over the threshold than he made a dash for my back room, where I used to smoke and write my letters. Then he bolted back.

"Is the door locked?" he asked feverishly, and he fastened the chain with his own hand.

"I'm very sorry," he said humbly. "It's a mighty liberty, but you looked the kind of man who would understand. I've had you in my mind all this week when things got troublesome. Say, will you do me a good turn?"

"I'll listen to you," I said. "That's all I'll promise." I was getting worried by the antics of this nervous little chap.

There was a tray of drinks on a table beside him, from which he filled himself a stiff whisky-and-soda. He drank it off in three gulps, and cracked the glass as he set it down.

"Pardon," he said, "I'm a bit rattled tonight. You see, I happen at this moment to be dead."

Review 10I: Conditionals and Formal Conditionals

In each of the following conditional sentences, parse the underlined verbs, giving tense, voice (active, passive, or state-of-being), and mood. Then, classify the sentences as first, second, or third conditional by placing a *1*, *2*, or *3* in the blank at the end.

If the sentence is a formal conditional, write *FC* next to the blank.

The first is done for you.

These sentences are taken from *Tales of War*, a short story collection about World War I published in 1918. The author, Lord Dunsany (Edward Plunkett, the 18th Baron of Dunsany), was best known for his fantasy novels, such as *The King of Elfland's Daughter* and *The Book of Wonder*, but he also wrote plays, poems, poetry, and stories.

simple past, active, subjunctive (emphatic) — simple present, active, modal

And even if it did end, that would not bring their four sons home now. 2

If we do not see in them the saga and epic, how shall we tell of them? ______

Had he not done it we might have had ruins and German orders everywhere. ______

It is curious, after such a colossal event as this explosion must be in the life of a bar of steel, that anything should remain at all of the old bell-like voice of the metal, but it appears to, if you listen attentively. ______

If you went to them after great suffering they might speak to you; after nights and nights of shelling over in France, they might speak to you and you might hear them clearly. ______

Had it not been for him the crafty Belgians would have attacked the Fatherland, but they were struck down before they could do it. ______

If they fought among themselves, which is quite unthinkable, the police would run them in. ______

Probably had it not been for this the two men would have died among those desolate craters. ______

One's horse, if one is riding, does not very much like it. ________

If shells had come, or the Germans, or anything at all, you would know how to take it; but that quiet mist over huge valleys, and stillness! ________

If a part of the moon were to fall off in the sky and come tumbling to earth, the comment on the lips of the imperturbable British watchers that have seen so much would be, "Hullo, what is Jerry up to now?" ________

Review 10J: Affirmations and Negations

The following sentences, from the standard one-volume history *World War I* by S. L. A. Marshall, all contain adverbs of affirmation and negation. Circle each one, and label them as *AFF* or *NEG*.

Then, choose three sentences and rewrite them on your own paper, turning affirmatives into negatives and vice versa. Show your sentences to your instructor.

The first is done for you.

AFF

From the first go, both sides remained (absolutely) committed.

From the first go, both sides remained uncommitted. OR
From the first go, both sides were not committed.

Turning to Count Godard, Wilhelm said: "And now I must have a cup of good, hot, strong English tea, yes, make it English."

Wilhelm had reached the end of his emotional reserves, which were never abundant.

A large, mysterious object shipped around the country under canvas would surely whet public curiosity.

So while trenches had been carried, the line, in effect, was not broken.

No worthwhile subordinate could abide him for very long.

He had never commanded in combat in his life.

Here is a general definitely not commanding.

Every word of it was positively true—and absolutely deceptive.

The German cruisers Goeben and Breslau were then steaming around in mid-Mediterranean, possibly in anticipation of this very contingency, and certainly too far from home base to risk returning.

Review 10K: Diagramming

On your own paper, diagram every word of the following sentences, taken from Lucy Maud Montgomery's *Rilla of Ingleside* (the final novel in the Anne of Green Gables series, set during the final years of World War I).

No, we have lost—let us face the fact as other peoples in the past have had to face it.

It did not say where the wound was, which is unusual, and we all feel worried.

Lloyd George began to heckle the Allies regarding equipment and guns and Susan said you would hear more of Lloyd George yet.

In the big living-room at Ingleside Susan Baker sat down with a certain grim satisfaction hovering about her like an aura; it was four o'clock and Susan, who had been working incessantly since six that morning, felt that she had fairly earned an hour of repose and gossip.

For the first time since the blow had fallen Rilla felt—a different thing from tremulous hope and faith—that Walter, of the glorious gift and the splendid ideals, still lived, with just the same gift and just the same ideals.

Review 10L: Explaining Sentences

Tell your instructor every possible piece of grammatical information about the following sentences. Follow these steps:

a) Underline each clause. Describe the identity and function of each clause and give any other useful information (introductory word, relationship to the rest of the sentence, etc.)
b) Circle each phrase. Describe the identity and function of each phrase and give any other useful information.
c) Parse all verbs acting as predicates.
d) Describe the identity and function of each individual remaining word.

If you need help, ask your instructor.

All was to stay well for a time at least, for the war suddenly moved away from us that spring.

He told me how in the same action in which Captain Nicholls had been killed, his horse had been shot down from beneath him, and how only a few weeks before he had been an apprentice blacksmith with his father.

—Michael Morpurgo, *War Horse*

In March of the year of grace 1918 there was one week into which must have crowded more of searing human agony than any seven days had ever held before in the history of the world.

—L. M. Montgomery, *Rilla of Ingleside*

WEEK 33

Mechanics

—LESSON 121—

Capitalization Review
Additional Capitalization Rules
Formal and Informal Letter Format
Ending Punctuation

what an amazing place london was to me when i saw it in the distance and how i believed all the adventures of all my favourite heroes to be constantly enacting and re-enacting there and how i vaguely made it out in my own mind to be fuller of wonders and wickedness than all the cities of the earth i need not stop here to relate

What an amazing place London was to me when I saw it in the distance, and how I believed all the adventures of all my favourite heroes to be constantly enacting and re-enacting there, and how I vaguely made it out in my own mind to be fuller of wonders and wickedness than all the cities of the earth, I need not stop here to relate.
—Charles Dickens, *David Copperfield*

A proper noun is the special, particular name for a person, place, thing, or idea. Proper nouns always begin with capital letters.

1. Capitalize the proper names of persons, places, things, and animals.

boy	manuel
store	macy's
car	ford
horse	secretariat

2. Capitalize the names of holidays.

lent

ramadan

new year's day

3. Capitalize the names of deities.

zeus

buddha

holy spirit

god

4. Capitalize the days of the week and the months of the year, but not the seasons.

wednesday	february	spring
thursday	april	fall
saturday	september	winter

5. Capitalize the first, last, and other important words in titles of books, magazines, newspapers, stories, poems, and songs.

book	*green eggs and ham*
magazine	*the new yorker*
newspaper	*the philadelphia inquirer*
movie	*the hunger games: catching fire*
television show	*agents of s.h.i.e.l.d.*
story	"the lottery"
poem	"stopping by woods on a snowy evening"
song	"happy birthday to you"
chapter in a book	"an unexpected party"

6. Capitalize and italicize the names of ships, trains, and planes.

ship	*santa maria*
train	*hogwarts express*
plane	*air force one*

The titles mister, madame, and miss are capitalized and abbreviated Mr., Mrs., and Miss when placed in front of a proper name.

Miss Snevellicci made a graceful obeisance, and hoped Mrs. Curdle was well, as also Mr. Curdle, who at the same time appeared.
—Charles Dickens, *The Life and Adventures of Nicholas Nickleby*

A proper adjective is formed from a proper name. Proper adjectives are capitalized. Words that are not usually capitalized remain lower-case even when they are attached to a proper adjective.

	Proper Noun	**Proper Adjective**
Person	shakespeare	the shakespearean play
	kafka	a kafkaesque dilemna
Place	italy	an italian city
	korea	a non-korean tradition
Holiday	labor day	the labor day picnic
	christmas	an anti-christmas sentiment
Month	september	september storms
	december	the post-december blues

Capitalize the personal pronoun I.

Interjections express sudden feeling or emotion. They are set off with commas or stand alone with a closing punctuation mark.

I have prayed over them, oh, I have prayed so much.
Ahem! That is my name.
Ha, ha! The liars that these traders are!
—Charles Dickens, *David Copperfield*

Capitalize the interjection *O*. It is usually preceded by, but not followed by, a comma.

For a few weeks it was all well enough, but afterwards, O the weary length of the nights!

But, O dear, O dear, this is a hard world!
—Kenneth Grahame, *The Wind in the Willows*

After an interjection followed by an exclamation point, the next word may be lower-case.

Oh! let me see it once again before I die!
Alas! how often and how long may those patient angels hover above us!
—Charles Dickens, *The Life and Adventures of Nicholas Nickleby*

Capitalize the date, address, greeting, closing, and signature of a letter.

Your Street Address
Your City, State, and ZIP Code

June 14, 2018

Well-Trained Mind Press
18021 The Glebe Lane
Charles City, Virginia 23030

Dear Editors:

Thank you for *Grammar for the Well-Trained Mind.* It is the most exciting grammar book I have ever read. I only wish I could spend more time doing grammar.

Please publish more grammar books immediately.

Sincerely,

SIGNATURE

Your Greatest Fan

Your Street Address
Your City, State, and ZIP Code

June 14, 2018

Well-Trained Mind Press
18021 The Glebe Lane
Charles City, Virginia 23030

Dear Editors:

Thank you for *Grammar for the Well-Trained Mind.* It is the most exciting grammar book I have ever read. I only wish I could spend more time doing grammar.

Please publish more grammar books immediately.

Sincerely,

SIGNATURE

Your Greatest Fan

Abbreviations are typically capitalized when each letter stands for something.

The WHO has expressed concern about the Zika virus and its rapid spread.
Why did NASA cancel the lunar exploration program?
OPEC was founded in 1960 in Baghdad.

Capitalize the first word in every line of traditional poetry.

> "The Elephant"
> by Hilaire Belloc
>
> When people call this beast to mind,
> They marvel more and more
> At such a little tail behind,
> So large a trunk before.

A sentence is a group of words that contains a subject and a predicate. A sentence begins with a capital letter and ends with a punctuation mark.

A statement gives information. A statement always ends with a period.
An exclamation shows sudden or strong feeling. An exclamation always ends with an exclamation point.
A command gives an order or makes a request. A command ends with either a period or an exclamation point.
A question asks something. A question always ends with a question mark.

Look ahead, Rat

Hooray, this is splendid

I wonder which of us had better pack the luncheon-basket

Presently they all sat down to luncheon together

Exercise 121A: Proofreading

Use proofreader's marks to insert the missing capital letters and punctuation marks into the following sentences.

capitalize letter: ≡	make letter lowercase: /
insert period: ⊙	insert exclamation point: ↑!
insert comma: ^,	insert question mark: ^?
insert apostrophe: ∨'	

If a word or phrase should be italicized, indicate this by underlining.

bruce fuoco drifted downward through the frigid water, suspended by a harness connected to a ship on the surface, and protected from the icy cold by a diving suit that looked as if it had been made for star wars

the fitzgerald, often called the titanic of the great lakes, was not only the most famous freshwater shipwreck; it was also the biggest mystery in great lakes history

that same year, canadian folksinger gordon lightfoot recorded the wreck of the edmund fitzgerald, a ballad recalling the ships last voyage and the perils of sailing on the great lakes in november

a hotly disputed coast guard report, released after an extensive investigation into the accident, added to the fitzgeralds growing legend

dr joseph macinnis, an underwater explorer who had visited the wreckage of the titanic in the north atlantic in 1991, studied the fitzgerald in 1994 as part of a government-sponsored project examining the great lakes and the st lawrence river

both shannon and the shipwreck society had substantial monetary investments in their respective projects, shannon in paying for his dive to the wreck, the shipwreck society, along with the national geographic society and the canadian navy, in assembling the recovery team

down below, on the spar deck of the edmund fitzgerald, first mate jack mccarthy supervised the removal of the ship's hatch covers

Fortunately, dr e w davis of the university of minnesota, working with other researchers and scientists, developed a way of separating the iron ore from taconite.

on september 22 1958 the edmund fitzgerald skippered by captain bert lambert left rouge river bound for silver bay minnesota where it was scheduled to pick up a load of taconite pellets to be delivered to toledo

—michael schumacher, mighty fitz: the sinking of the edmund fitzgerald

in 1914, sir ernest shackleton set sail for antarctica on the ship endurance.

he planned to walk from the weddell sea on one side of antarctica to the ross sea on the other also on board endurance were 69 sled dogs and mrs chippy the carpenter's cat temperatures on the ice dipped to -30º fahrenheit (-34º celsius)

—alfred lansing, endurance: shipwreck and survival on a sea of ice

local knowledge of sandbanks, reefs, and rocks is simply negated at night british lights in the western approaches, for example, were as important to british fishermen from the isles of scilly, bred in those waters, as they were to german u-boat captains from wilhelmshaven who had never before ventured out of the north sea

jack binns radio operator of the republic sent the first cqd message — the precursor of the sos

in august 1914 that war arrived, and not long after the declaration, the lusitania was briefly commandeered by the admiralty, but soon returned to the cunard line when it was discovered how much coal she used.

although she was carefully searched by the special "neutrality squad" before she left new york, which certified that she carried no armament, her previous associations with the admiralty had ensured that her silhouette—the means by which a ship was identified from the periscope of a u-boat—had appeared in jane's fighting ships for 1914, and both the lusitania and the mauretania were categorized as "armed merchantmen" in the british naval pocket book of the same year

—sam willis, shipwreck: a history of disasters at sea

Exercise 121B: Correct Letter Mechanics

The following text is a rejection letter sent to the comic book artist Jim Lee. Lee is now the copublisher at DC Comics and is the author of *X-Men #1*, which the *Guinness Book of World Records* lists as the best-selling comic book of all time. But at the beginning of his career, Lee's work was rejected repeatedly. This letter came from Marvel Comics.

On your own paper (or with your own word processor), rewrite or retype the text so that it is properly formatted, punctuated, and capitalized. You may choose either letter format from this lesson.

The text of the letter is a single paragraph. The closing is "Best," which is an acceptable way to end a letter. There is no date in the letter. The sender chose to spell out the states rather than abbreviating them, which is also acceptable. The salutation ("Dear Mr. Lee") is followed by a comma (a colon is more common in a business letter, but a comma is also correct).

When you are finished, compare your letter with the two versions in the Answer Key.

marvel comics group 135 west 50th street, 7th Floor new york new york 10020 jim lee 12848 topping meadows st louis missouri 63131 dear mr lee your work looks as if it were done by four different people. your best pencils are on page 7, panel with agents (lower left corner) and close up of face. the rest of the pencils are of much weaker quality. the same can be said for your inking. resubmit when your work is consistent and when you have learned to draw hands. best
eliot r brown Submissions Editor

—LESSON 122—

Commas
Semicolons
Additional Semicolon Rules
Colons
Additional Colon Rules

1. **A comma and coordinating conjunction join compound sentences.**
2. **Commas separate three or more items in a series.**
3. **Commas separate two or more adjectives that come before a noun (as long as the adjectives can exchange position).**
4. **A comma precedes the *and* before the last item in a series of three or more (the "Oxford comma").**
5. **Commas set off terms of direct address.**
6. **Commas set off non-restrictive adjective clauses.**

7. Commas set off parenthetical expressions that are closely related to the sentence.

8. Commas set off most appositives (unless the appositive is only one word and very closely related to the word it renames).

9. Commas may surround or follow interjections.

10. Commas may surround or follow introductory adverbs of affirmation and negation.

11. Commas may set off introductory adverb and adjective phrases.

12. In dates, commas separate the day of the week from the day of the month and the day of the month from the year.

13. In addresses, commas separate the city from the state.

14. Commas follow the greeting and closing of a friendly letter, and the closing of a formal letter.

15. Commas divide large numbers into sets of thousands.

16. A comma follows a dialogue tag or attribution tag that precedes a speech or quote.

17. A comma comes after a speech or quote if a dialogue tag or attribution tag follows.

18. A comma may divide a partial sentence from the block quote it introduces.

19. Commas may be used at any time to prevent misunderstanding and simplify reading.

Exercise 122A: Comma Use

In the blank at the end of each sentence, write the number from the list above that describes the comma use. If more than one number seems to fit equally well, write all suitable numbers.

"My dear friends," said Doctor Heidegger, motioning them to be seated, "I am desirous of your assistance in one of those little experiments with which I amuse myself here in my study." ________

They looked as if they had never known what youth or pleasure was, but had been the offspring of nature's dotage, and always the gray, decrepit, sapless, miserable creatures, who now sat stooping round the doctor's table, without life enough in their souls or bodies to be animated even by the prospect of growing young again. ________

There, in fact, stood the four glasses, brimful of this wonderful water, the delicate spray of which, as it effervesced from the surface, resembled the tremulous glitter of diamonds. ________

The Widow Wycherley adjusted her cap, for she felt almost like a woman again. ________

"Dance with me, Clara!" cried Colonel Killigrew. ________

Had the changes of a lifetime been crowded into so brief a space, and were they now four aged people, sitting with their old friend, Doctor Heidegger? ________

Yes, they were old again! ________

With a shuddering impulse, that showed her a woman still, the widow clasped her skinny hands over her face, and wished that the coffin lid were over it, since it could be no longer beautiful. ________

—Nathaniel Hawthorne, "Dr. Heidegger's Experiment"

As a historical figure, Ponce de Leon left little evidence, and some basic facts, such as the exact year of his birth, remain uncertain. ________

By the 19th century, the story was a popular subject of painters, who often portrayed an aged Ponce de Leon in a long, flowing white beard. ________

Recent archaeological evidence combined with linguistic and DNA analysis suggests that the first migration to Australia and New Guinea was over a land bridge just before the last ice age, around 40,000 years ago, and a second migration occurred over water around 4,000 years ago. ________

Gilgamesh was told, however, that there was a fountain of healing waters on another island, and beside it grew a magical plant of immortality. ________

Over the course of two centuries, Robert de Boron's story was retold by a dozen other writers, and the story became deeply connected with the Fisher King, King Arthur, worthiness, and the right to rule over Britain. ________

Yet, the idea of a sacred, nonearthly object providing healing and rejuvenation for those very select few who could obtain it is constant. ________

The oldest recorded human life span is a French woman, Jeanne Louise Calment, who smoked until she was 117 years old and ate a typical French diet that included heavy sauces, olive oil, red wine, and chocolate. ________

Jeanne Calment was born in Arles, France, on February 21, 1875—the same year that Leo Tolstoy published *Anna Karenina* and a year before Alexander Graham Bell filed for a patent on his new telephone. ________

—Aharon W. Zorea, *Finding the Fountain of Youth: The Science and Controversy behind Extending Life and Cheating Death*

The independent clauses of a compound sentence must be joined by a comma and a coordinating conjunction, a semicolon, or a semicolon and a coordinating conjunction. They cannot be joined by a comma alone.

He knew—as the Athenians and Persians did not—exactly when the flooding of the Nile was about to occur, and he managed to hold the combined invasion force off until the waters began to rise rapidly around him.

Thousands of years ago, groups of hunters and gatherers roamed across Asia and Europe, following mammoth herds that fed on the wild grasses. Slowly the ice began to retreat; the patterns of the grass growth changed; the herds wandered north and diminished.

They eat and drink, and thank him for his generosity; but Atrahasis himself, knowing that the feast is a death meal, paces back and forth, ill with grief and guilt.

—Susan Wise Bauer, *The History of the Ancient World*

Block quotes should be introduced by a colon (if preceded by a complete sentence) or a comma (if preceded by a partial sentence).

Piankhe did not try to wipe out his enemies. Instead, he chose to see Egypt as a set of kingdoms, with himself as High King over them:

> Amun of Napata has appointed me governor of this land,

he wrote in another inscription,

> as I might say to someone: "Be king," and he is it, or: "You will not be king," and he is not.

—Susan Wise Bauer, *The History of the Ancient World*

Use a colon after the salutation of a business letter.

The White House
1600 Pennsylvania Ave NW
Washington, DC 20500

Dear Mr. President:

Use a colon to separate the hour from minutes in a time.

I went to bed at 11 59 on December 31.

Use a colon to separate the chapter from verse in a Biblical reference.

According to Ecclesiastes 12 12, "much study wearies the body."

If items in a series contain commas within the items, semicolons may separate two or more items in a series.

If semicolons separate items in a series, a colon may set off the series.

> Around the tomb complex, buildings recreated in stone the materials of traditional Egyptian houses: walls of stone, carved to look like reed matting; stone columns shaped into bundles of reeds; even a wooden fence with a partly open gate, chiseled from stone.
>
> Like the Great Pyramid, the Sphinx has attracted its share of nutty theories: it dates from 10,000 B.C. and was built by a disappeared advanced civilization; it was built by Atlanteans (or aliens); it represents a zodiacal sign, or a center of global energy.
>
> Between 4000 and 3000 B.C. is known as the Naqada Period, and was once divided into three phases: the Amratian, which runs from 4000 to 3500 B.C.; the Gerzean, from 3500 to 3200 B.C.; and the Final Predynastic, from 3200 to 3000 B.C.
>
> —Susan Wise Bauer, *The History of the Ancient World*

A colon may introduce a list.

> Stripped of personality, prehistoric peoples too often appear as blocks of shifting color on a map: moving north, moving west, generating a field of cultivated grain, or corralling a herd of newly domesticated animals.
>
> Many thousands of years ago, the Sumerian king Alulim ruled over Eridu: a walled city, a safe space carved out of the unpredictable and harsh river valley that the Romans would later name Mesopotamia.
>
> Plague, drought, and war: these were enough to upset the balance of a civilization that had been built in rocky dry places, close to the edge of survival.
>
> —Susan Wise Bauer, *The History of the Ancient World*

For emphasis, a colon may introduce an item that follows a complete sentence, when that item is closely related to the sentence.

> But the historian's task is different: to look for particular human lives that give flesh and spirit to abstract assertions about human behavior.
>
> *But the historian's task, to look for particular human lives that give flesh and spirit to abstract assertions about human behavior, is different.*

Exercise 122B: Capitalization and Punctuation

Insert all missing punctuation and correct all capitalization in the text that follows. Use these proofreader's marks:

capitalize letter: ≡	make letter lowercase: /
insert period: ⊙	insert exclamation point: ^!
insert comma: ^,	insert question mark: ^?
insert colon: ^:	insert semicolon: ^;
insert dash: (—)	insert quotation marks: ^“
insert hyphen: ^=	

If a word or phrase should be italicized, indicate this by underlining.

122B.1: Sentences

millions of tons of ice pressed inexorably upon the little ship that had dared the challenge of the antarctic. the endurance was now leaking badly, and at 9 p m i gave the order to lower boats gear provisions and sledges to the floe, and move them to the flat ice a little way from the ship

Then came a fateful day wednesday october 27

we are now 346 miles from paulet island the nearest point where there is any possibility of finding food and shelter.

it was a sickening sensation to feel the decks breaking up under ones feet the great beams bending and then snapping with a noise like heavy gunfire

nothing more could be done at that moment, and the men turned in again but there was little sleep

the cook got the blubber-stove going, and a little while later, when i was sitting round the corner of the stove, i heard one man say cook i like my tea strong

the ridges or hedgerows marking the pressure-lines that border the fast diminishing pieces of smooth floe-ice are enormous.

the ice moves majestically irresistibly

We are twenty eight men with forty nine dogs, including sues and sallies five grown up pups.

I tore the fly-leaf out of the bible that queen alexandra had given to the ship, with her own writing in it, and also the wonderful page of job containing the verse:

> out of whose womb came the ice?
> and the hoary frost of Heaven, who hath gendered it
> the waters are hid as with a stone,
> and the face of the deep is frozen

we also possessed a few books on antarctic exploration a copy of browning and a copy of the ancient mariner

The ship left south georgia just a year and a week ago, and reached this latitude four or five miles to the eastward of our present position on january 3 1915 crossing the circle on new years eve

—Ernest Shackleton, *The Heart of the Antarctic* and *South*

122B.2: Letter Format

The following letters are adapted from the book *Letters of Note*, compiled by Shaun Usher.

january 24 1960

buckingham palace

dear mr president

seeing a picture of you in todays newspaper standing in front of a barbecue grilling quail reminded me that I had never sent you the recipe of the drop scones which I promised you at balmoral

i now hasten to do so, and i do hope you will find them successful. though the quantities are for 16 people, when there are fewer, i generally put in less flour and milk, but use the other ingredients as stated

yours sincerely

elizabeth R.

10 downing street whitehall

june 27 1940

my darling

i hope you will forgive me if i tell you something that i feel you ought to know

one of the men in your entourage a devoted friend has told me that there is a danger of your being generally disliked by your colleagues and subordinates because of your rough sarcastic and overbearing manner My darling winston i must confess that i have noticed a deterioration in your manner, and you are not so kind as you used to be

your loving devoted and watchful

clemmie

122B.3: Quotes

These excerpts are taken from the biography *Winston Churchill*, by John Keegan.

I felt my spine stiffen. then the voice changed tempo, from rallentando to recitative

> A tremendous battle is raging in france and flanders. The germans . . . by a remarkable combination of air bombing and heavily armoured tanks . . . have broken through the french defences north of the Maginot Line, and strong columns of their armoured vehicles are ravaging the open country, which for the first day or two was without defenders.

churchill, however, rejected capitulation in absolute terms. "we shall not flag or fail he insisted. "we shall go on to the end. . . . We shall fight on the beaches, we shall fight on the landing-grounds, we shall fight in the fields and in the streets, we shall fight in the hills. We shall never surrender Those who heard those words it is said never forgot anything about them the rhythm of his sentences the timbre of his voice, above all the magnificently defiant "never" of "We shall never surrender" on may 9 1945 the day five years later when victory was finally proclaimed in europe he spoke from a balcony in whitehall to salute the crowds below “god bless you all! This is your victory”

—LESSON 123—

Colons
Dashes
Hyphens
Parentheses
Brackets

> But the historian’s task is different: to look for particular human lives that give flesh and spirit to abstract assertions about human behavior.

> But the historian’s task is different—to look for particular human lives that give flesh and spirit to abstract assertions about human behavior.
>
> —Susan Wise Bauer, *The History of the Ancient World*

A colon may introduce an item that follows a complete sentence, when that item is closely related to the sentence.

Dashes — — can enclose words that are not essential to the sentence.
Dashes can also be used singly to separate parts of a sentence.

A dash is twice as long as a hyphen.
When you write a dash, make it a little longer than a hyphen.
When you type a dash, use two hyphens for each dash.

well-educated (hyphen)
Well—that was a mistake. (dash)

Hyphens connect some compound nouns.
self-confidence
wallpaper
air conditioning

Hyphens connect compound adjectives in the attributive position.
self-confident woman
the woman was self confident

Hyphens connect spelled-out numbers between twenty-one and ninety-nine.
seventy-one balloons
he turned seventy-one on Friday

Hyphens divide words between syllables at the end of lines in justified text.

> . . . worth inhabiting by reason of its barrenness; and indeed, both for-
> saking it because of the prodigious number of tigers, lions, leopards,
> and others of the furious creatures which harbour there; so that the . . .

> . . . worth inhabiting by reason of its barrenness; and indeed, both
> forsaking it because of the prodigious number of tigers, lions, leo-
> pards, and others of the furious creatures which harbour there;
> so that the . . .

Parentheses ( ) can enclose words that are not essential to the sentence.
Parenthetical expressions often interrupt or are irrelevant to the rest of the sentence.
Punctuation goes inside the parentheses if it applies to the parenthetical material; all other punctuation goes outside the parentheses.
Parenthetical material only begins with a capital letter if it is a complete sentence with ending punctuation.

> I had no sooner said so, but I perceived the creature (whatever it was) within two oars' length.

Commas make a parenthetical element a part of the sentence.
Dashes emphasize a parenthetical element.
Parentheses minimize a parenthetical element.

> "Particularly," said I, aloud (though to myself), "what should I have done without a gun, without ammunition, without any tools to make anything, or to work with, without clothes, bedding, a tent, or any manner of covering?"

> Accordingly, having spent three days in this journey, I came home (so I must now call my tent and my cave); but before I got thither the grapes were spoiled; the richness of the fruit and the weight of the juice having broken them and bruised them, they were good for little or nothing; as to the limes, they were good, but I could bring but a few.

> Well, to take away this discouragement, I resolved to dig into the surface of the earth, and so make a declivity; this I began, and it cost me a prodigious deal of pains (but who grudge pains who have their deliverance in view?); but when this was worked through, and this difficulty managed, it was still much the same, for I could no more stir the canoe than I could the other boat.

> I first laid all the planks or boards upon it that I could get, and having considered well what I most wanted, I got three of the seamen's chests, which I had broken open, and emptied, and lowered them down upon my raft; the first of these I filled with provisions—bread, rice, three Dutch cheeses, five pieces of dried goat's flesh (which we lived much upon), and a little remainder of European corn, which had been laid by for some fowls which we brought to sea with us, but the fowls were killed.
>
> —Daniel Defoe, *Robinson Crusoe*

Exercise 123A: Hyphens

Some (but not all) of the following sentences contain words that should be hyphenated. Insert a hyphen into each word that needs one.

These sentences are adapted from *Of Six Medieval Women*, by Alice Kemp-Welch.

The abbess was generally a high born and influential woman.

The legends are mainly based on well known themes.

It has been maintained that the classic theatre decayed and disappeared as Christianity became all powerful in Europe.

The first was taken from a Latin translation of a fourth century Greek legend.

On went the easy going company, singing by the way, and with horns blowing.

The fresh petals were sprinkled over the surface of the water in the bath, and were distilled to make the rose water with which the knights and ladies washed their hands and faces when they left their much curtained beds.

Around Marie de France there must always remain an atmosphere of doubt and mystery, since she is only mentioned by an anonymous thirteenth century poet, and by an Anglo Saxon poet, Denys Pyramus.

Marie was born in Normandy, about the middle of the twelfth century.

These Courts of Love formed one of the semi serious pastimes of the Middle Ages.

If I were to speak one little word of the choirs of heaven, it would be no more than the honey that a bee can carry away on its feet from a full blown flower.

Odilio was Queen Adelheid's friend and one time confessor.

This dialogue takes place between the sorrow stricken nuns.

Serpents are often credited with a knowledge of life giving plants.

French was established by then as the language of those who were high born.

Christine de Pisan was possessed of profound common sense, and of a generous hearted nature.

She argued for the importance to France of a strong middle class.

She saw the thirst for knowledge as an ever present want of the soul.

The king's infamous and all powerful favorite was suddenly dismissed.

But the misery of France was ever increasing.

Exercise 123B: Parenthetical Elements

The following sentences are all from *A Journal of the Plague Year* by Daniel Defoe. Defoe liked to write very long sentences filled with parenthetical elements! Set off each bolded set of words with commas, dashes, or parentheses. Choose the punctuation marks that seem to fit best. Then, compare your answers with the original punctuation in the Answer Key.

NOTE: Depending on what punctuation marks you choose, you may have to add an additional comma, colon, or semicolon following some of the parenthetical elements. Be sure to look at the entire sentence to decide whether additional punctuation should be added. Keep in mind that, in contemporary English punctuation, a parenthesis can be followed by another punctuation mark, but a dash almost never is.

Another man **I heard him** adds to his words, "'Tis all wonderful; 'tis all a dream."

This was a very terrible and melancholy thing to see, and as it was a sight which I could not but look on from morning to night **for indeed there was nothing else of moment to be seen** it filled me with very serious thoughts of the misery that was coming upon the city, and the unhappy condition of those that would be left in it.

Business led me out sometimes to the other end of the town, even when the sickness was chiefly there; and as the thing was new to me **as well as to everybody else** it was a most surprising thing to see those streets which were usually so thronged now grown desolate, and so few people to be seen in them, that if I had been a stranger and at a loss for my way, I might sometimes have gone the length of a whole street **I mean of the by-streets** and seen nobody to direct me except watchmen set at the doors of such houses as were shut up, of which I shall speak presently.

But I mention it here on this account **namely** that it was a rule with those who had thus two houses in their keeping or care, that if anybody was taken sick in a family, before the master of the family let the examiners or any other officer know of it, he immediately would send all the rest of his family, whether children or servants **as it fell out to be** to such other house which he had so in charge, and then giving notice of the sick person to the examiner, have a nurse or nurses appointed, and have another person to be shut up in the house with them **which many for money would do** so to take charge of the house in case the person should die.

That abundance of them died is certain **many of them came within the reach of my own knowledge** but that all of them were swept off I much question.

One thing, however, must be observed: that as to ships coming in from abroad **as many you may be sure did** some who were out in all parts of the world a considerable while before, and some who when they went out knew nothing of an infection, or at least of one so terrible—these came up the river boldly, and delivered their cargoes as they were obliged to do, except just in the two months of August and September, when the weight of the infection lying **as I may say** all below Bridge, nobody durst appear in business for a while.

But even those wholesome reflections **which, rightly managed, would have most happily led the people to fall upon their knees, make confession of their sins, and look up to their merciful Saviour for pardon, imploring His compassion on them in such a time of their distress, by which we might have been as a second Nineveh** had a quite contrary extreme in the common people, who, ignorant and stupid in their reflections as they were brutishly wicked and thoughtless before, were now led by their fright to extremes of folly; and **as I have said before** that they ran to conjurers and witches, and all sorts of deceivers, to know what should become of them **who fed their fears, and kept them always alarmed and awake on purpose to delude them and pick their pockets** so they were as mad upon their running after quacks and mountebanks, and every practicing old woman, for medicines and remedies; storing themselves with such multitudes of pills, potions, and preservatives **as they were called** that they not only spent their money but even poisoned themselves beforehand for fear of the poison of the infection; and prepared their bodies for the plague, instead of preserving them against it.

—LESSON 124—

Italics
Quotation Marks
Ellipses
Single Quotation Marks
Apostrophes

In *Around the World in Eighty Days,* Jules Verne describes the arrival of the steamer *Mongolia* at the port of Suez.

Capitalize and italicize the names of ships, trains, and planes.

Italicize the titles of lengthy or major works such as books, newspapers, magazines, major works of art, and long musical compositions.

Use quotation marks for minor or brief works of art and writing or portions of longer works such as short stories, newspaper articles, songs, chapters, and poems.

Watership Down	"The Chief Rabbit"
The Hobbit	"An Unexpected Party"
The New York Times	"In Julia Child's Provençal Kitchen"
National Geographic	
The *Mona Lisa* of Da Vinci	"Saint Jerome in Penitence" by Dürer
The *David* of Michelangelo	
1812 Overture by Tchaikovsky	
The opera *Carmen* by Bizet	"Toreador Song"
	"Scarborough Fair"
	"The Lottery"
The *Odyssey*	"Stopping by Woods on a Snowy Evening"
	"The Raven"

Italicize letters, numbers, and words if they are the subject of discussion. In plural versions, do not italicize the *s*.

The letter *A* begins the alphabet, and a *Z* concludes it.

Most Americans hate the word *moist.*

*A*s and *F*s are hard to write in calligraphy.

Italicize foreign words not adopted into English.

What we call "rapid-eye-movement sleep" the French call *sommeil paradoxal* (paradoxical sleep) because the body is still but the mind is extremely active.
—Pamela Druckerman, *Bringing Up Bébé*

Mark Twain was the nom de plume of Samuel Langhorne Clemens.

English doesn't borrow from other languages. English follows other languages down dark alleys, knocks them over and goes through their pockets for loose grammar.

—Sir Terry Pratchett

Use quotation marks for minor or brief works of art and writing or portions of longer works such as short stories, newspaper articles, songs, chapters, and poems.

Then there crawled from the bushes a dozen more great purple spiders, which saluted the first one and said, "The web is finished, O King, and the strangers are our prisoners."

Dorothy did not like the looks of these spiders at all. They had big heads, sharp claws, small eyes and fuzzy hair all over their purple bodies.

—L. Frank Baum, *Glinda of Oz*

Direct quotations are set off by quotation marks.

Fear of spiders might come in part from children's stories, which often portray spiders as hostile predators. In *Glinda of Oz,* L. Frank Baum writes about a Spider King and his army of "great purple spiders, which . . . said, 'The web is finished, O King, and the strangers are our prisoners.'"

A quote within a quote is surrounded by single quotation marks.

An apostrophe is a punctuation mark that shows possession. It turns a noun into an adjective that tells whose.

Form the possessive of a singular noun by adding an apostrophe and the letter *s*.

spider wand

web sorceress

Form the possessive of a plural noun ending in -*s* by adding an apostrophe only.

spiders troubles

fields lakes

Form the possessive of a plural noun that does not end in -*s* as if it were a singular noun.

sheep hangmen

geese teeth

A contraction is a combination of two words with some of the letters dropped out. An apostrophe shows where the letters have been omitted.

they are ____________________

was not ____________________

were not ____________________

I am ____________________

Exercise 124A: Proofreading Practice

The sentences below have lost most punctuation and capitalization. Insert all missing punctuation marks, and correct all capitalization errors. When you are finished, compare your sentences with the originals.

Use these proofreader's marks:

capitalize letter: ≡	make letter lowercase: /
insert period: ⊙	insert exclamation point: !
insert comma: ^,	insert question mark: ?
insert colon: ^:	insert semicolon: ^;
insert apostrophe: ˇ'	insert quotation marks: ˇ"
insert dash: (—)	insert hyphen: ≑

If a word or phrase should be italicized, indicate this by underlining.

the following sentences are taken from the book a history of the vietnamese by k w taylor it has thirteen chapters including the ly dynasty the french conquest and franco vietnamese colonial relations

the plain of the red river along with the smaller plains of the ma and ca rivers immediately to the south make up the scene in which vietnamese history was lived until the fifteenth century

yue had been the name of a state on the south central coast of china the modern province of zhejiang during the sixth to fourth centuries bce.

thereafter king an duong lost the magic crossbow and was defeated

an imperial census was taken in the year 2 ce it recorded 143643 households and 981755 people in the three prefectures of giao chi cuu chan and nhat nam

another month passed and after the annual blood oath was administered le quy ly met with tran phu who is reported to have said you and i are of the same family

trinh tung then raised le duy bangs fifth son le duy dam to the throne

they laid the basis for what became in the independent vietnam of recent decades the academic fields of anthropology ethnology archaeology art geography history linguistics music philology religion and sociology

at the same time french security agents were busy with a clandestine struggle to thwart japanese cultivation of anti french vietnamese nationalists

phan khoi 1887-1959 had participated in the reformist movement led by phan chu trinh in the 1900s

in 1932 he published a poem entitled old love which criticized the practice of arranged marriage

this man had chosen his revolutionary name to celebrate the long March (truong chinh in Vietnamese) that had been a defining event in the history of the Chinese Communist Party during the 1930s.

Exercise 124B: Foreign Phrases That Are Now English Words

The following phrases and words are now part of English and are usually not italicized. Using a dictionary, look up each one. In the blank, write the original language that the word belongs to, the meaning in English, and the meaning in the original language. The first is done for you.

cul-de-sac French, a dead-end street, "bottom of the sack"

ad nauseam ______________________

prima donna ______________________

faux pas ______________________

mano a mano ______________________

per capita ______________________________

double entendre ______________________________

per se ______________________________

et al. ______________________________

hoi polloi ______________________________

WEEK 34

Advanced Quotations & Dialogue

—LESSON 125—

Dialogue
Additional Rules for Writing Dialogue
Direct Quotations
Additional Rules for Using Direct Quotations

Use dialogue in fiction and to bring other voices into memoir, profiles, and reporting.

> A man was thought to be the painter of "Portrait of an Unknown Lady" when it went on sale in 2014 at an auction in the southern English city of Salisbury. It was bought by Bendor Grosvenor, an art dealer and historian who recognized the work as Carlile's.
>
> In an interview with *The Telegraph*, Mr. Grosvenor said that the artist's style "is quite recognizable if you know what it looks like."
>
> —Roslyn Sulcas, "A 17th-Century Portrait Will Be the Earliest Painting by a Woman at the Tate." The *New York Times,* Sept. 21, 2016

A dialogue tag identifies the person making the speech.

When a dialogue tag comes after a speech, place a comma, exclamation point, or question mark inside the closing quotation marks before the tag.

When a dialogue tag comes before a speech, place a comma after the tag. Put the dialogue's final punctuation mark inside the closing quotation marks.

> "There goes Tommaso the painter," the people would say, watching the big awkward figure passing through the streets on his way to work.

> Diamante said to Filippo, "You have learned well, and it is time now to turn your work to some account."

Speeches do not need to be attached to a dialogue tag as long as the text clearly indicates the speaker.

> The father gave a hopeless sigh and turned away. "So, you will be a painter."

Usually, a new paragraph begins with each new speaker.

Michelangelo said nothing, but he mounted the scaffolding and pretended to chip away at the nose with his chisel. Meanwhile he let drop some marble chips and dust upon the head of the critic beneath. Then he came down.

"Is that better?" he asked gravely.

"Admirable!" answered the artist. "You have given it life."

"I am growing too old to help you," Leonardo said, but Raphael shook his head. "I will go with you to the ends of the earth," he said.

When a dialogue tag comes in the middle of a speech, follow it with a comma if the following dialogue is an incomplete sentence. Follow it with a period if the following dialogue is a complete sentence.

"The boy!" said one brother, nudging the other, "has found his brains at last."

The painter's quick eyes examined the work with deep interest. "Send him to me at once," he said. "This is indeed marvellous talent."

—Amy Steedman, *Knights of Art: Stories of the Italian Painters*

RULES FOR USING DIRECT QUOTATIONS

Direct quotations are set off by quotation marks.

Every direct quote must have an attribution tag.

When an attribution tag comes after a direct quote, place a comma, exclamation point, or question mark inside the closing quotation marks.

"Frederick, is God dead?" asked Sojourner Truth.

When an attribution tag comes before a direct quote, place a comma after the tag. Put the quote's final punctuation mark inside the closing quotation marks.

The orator paused impressively, and then thundered in a voice that thrilled his audience with prophetic intimations, "No, God is not dead; and therefore it is that slavery must end in blood!"

When an attribution tag comes in the middle of a direct quotation, follow it with a comma if the remaining quote is an incomplete sentence. Follow it with a period if the remaining quote is a complete sentence.

"A new world had opened up to me," Douglass wrote. "I lived more in one day than in a year of my slave life."

"It was my good fortune," he writes, "to get out of slavery at the right time, to be speedily brought in contact with that circle of highly cultivated men and women, banded together for the overthrow of slavery, of which William Lloyd Garrison was the acknowledged leader."

Direct quotes can be words, phrases, clauses, or sentences, as long as they are set off by quotation marks and form part of a grammatically correct original sentence.

In his autobiography Douglass commends Mr. Johnson for his "noble-hearted hospitality and manly character."

Ellipses show where something has been cut out of a sentence.

If a direct quotation is longer than three lines, indent the entire quote one inch from the margin in a separate block of text and omit quotation marks.

In a footnote to the *Life and Times of Garrison* it is stated:

> This enterprise was not regarded with favor by the leading abolitionists, who knew only too well the precarious support which a fifth anti-slavery paper . . . must have . . . As anticipated, it nearly proved the ruin of its projector; but by extraordinary exertions it was kept alive.

If you change or make additions to a direct quotation, use brackets.

Parker Pillsbury reported that "though it was late in the evening when the young man closed his remarks, none seemed to know or care for the hour. . . . The crowded congregation had been wrought up almost to enchantment during the whole long evening, particularly by some of the utterances of the last speaker [Douglass], as he turned over the terrible apocalypse of his experience in slavery."

A quote within a quote is surrounded by single quotation marks.

ADDITIONAL RULES FOR DIRECT QUOTATIONS

Use direct quotations to provide examples, cite authorities, and emphasize your own points.

An attribution tag may be indirect.

In the wild songs of the slaves he read, beneath their senseless jargon or their fulsome praise of "old master," the often unconscious note of grief and despair.

A colon may introduce a direct quote.

Douglass spent a year under Covey's ministrations, and his life there may be summed up in his own words: "The overwork and the brutal chastisements of which I was the victim, combined with that ever-gnawing and soul-destroying thought, 'I am a slave—a slave for life,' rendered me a living embodiment of mental and physical wretchedness."

—Charles W. Chesnutt, *Frederick Douglass*

To quote three or fewer lines of poetry, indicate line breaks by using a slanted line and retain all original punctuation and capitalization.

Likewise, Paul Laurence Dunbar's 1895 poem "We Wear the Mask" anticipates the "two-ness" of African-American existence expressed most poignantly and poetically by Du Bois nearly a decade later. Dunbar most famously writes: "We wear the mask that grins and lies,/It hides our cheeks and shades our eyes,—/This debt we pay to human guile".

—Rebecka Rutledge Fisher, *Habitations of the Veil*

Four or more lines of poetry should be treated as a block quote.

In his poem, "We Wear the Mask," Dunbar speaks of a double-consciousness that had been forced on African-Americans:

> We wear the mask that grins and lies,
> It hides our cheeks and shades our eyes,—
> This debt we pay to human guile;
> With torn and bleeding hearts we smile,
> And mouth with myriad subtleties.

Dunbar's biographer, Benjamin Brawley, wrote that Dunbar's poetry "soared above race and touched the heart universal."

—Joseph Nazel, *Langston Hughes*

Any poetic citation longer than one line may be treated as a block quote.

Direct quotes should be properly documented.

—LESSON 126—

(Optional)
Documentation

In *101 Gourmet Cookies for Everyone*, author Wendy Paul claims that her Chocolate Chip Pudding Cookies are "by far the softest chocolate chip cookies" that can be found.[1]

[1]Wendy Paul, *101 Gourmet Cookies for Everyone* (Bonneville Books, 2010), p. 18.

A sentence containing a direct quote should be followed by a citation.

A superscript number may lead to a citation at the bottom of the page (a footnote) or the end of the paper (an endnote).

1. Footnotes and endnotes should follow this format:

   Author name, *Title of Book* (Publisher, year of publication), p. #.

   If there are two authors, list them like this:

   Author name and author name, *Title of Book* (Publisher, year of publication), p. #.

   If your quote comes from more than one page of the book you're quoting, use "pp." to mean "pages" and put a hyphen between the page numbers.

   Author name, *Title of Book* (Publisher, date of publication), pp. #-#.

   If a book is a second (or third, or fourth, etc.) edition, put that information right after the title.

Author name, *Title of Book*, 2nd ed. (Publisher, date of publication), p. #.

If no author is listed, simply use the title of the book.

Title of book (Publisher, date of publication), p. #.

All of this information can be found on the copyright page of the book.

2. Footnotes should be placed beneath a dividing line at the bottom of the page. If you are using a word processing program, the font size of the footnotes should be about 2 points smaller than the font size of the main text.

3. Endnotes should be placed at the end of the paper, under a centered heading, like this:

ENDNOTES

[1] Wendy Paul, *101 Gourmet Cookies for Everyone* (Bonneville Books, 2010), p. 18.

[2] Author, *Title of book* (Publisher, year of publication), page number.

For a short paper (three pages or less), the endnotes can be placed on the last page of the paper itself. A paper that is four or more pages in length should have an entirely separate page for endnotes.

4. The second time you cite a book, your footnote or endnote only needs to contain the following information:

[2] Author last name, p. #.

5. If a paragraph contains several quotes from the same source, a single citation at the end of the entire paragraph can cover all quotations.

Every work mentioned in a footnote or endnote must also appear on a final Works Cited page.

WORKS CITED

Paul, Wendy. *101 Gourmet Cookies for Everyone.* Springville, UT: Bonneville Books, 2010.

1. List sources alphabetically by the author's last name.
2. The format should be: Last name, first name. *Title of Book.* City of publication: Publisher, year of publication.
3. If the work has no author, list it by the first word of the title (but ignore the articles *a*, *an*, and *the*).
4. If the city of publication is not a major city (New York, Los Angeles, London, Beijing, New Delhi, Tokyo), include the state (for a U.S. publisher) or country (for an international publisher).
5. For a short paper (three pages or less), the Works Cited section may be at the bottom of the last page. For a paper of four or more pages, attach a separate Works Cited page.

Additional Rules for Citing Sources (Turabian)

1. Magazine articles

In a footnote or endnote, use the following style:

[1] Author name, "Name of article." *Name of Magazine*, Date of publication, page number.

[2] Jacqueline Harp, "A Breed for Every Yard: Black Welsh Mountain Sheep Break New Ground." *Sheep!*, September/October 2013, p. 27.

In Works Cited, use the following style:

Author last name, first name. "Name of article." *Name of Magazine* volume number: issue number (Date of publication), total number of pages article takes up in magazine.

Harp, Jacqueline. "A Breed for Every Yard: Black Welsh Mountain Sheep Break New Ground." *Sheep!* 34:5 (September/October 2013), pp. 26–28.

2. Websites

In a footnote or endnote, use the following style:

[3] Author/editor/sponsoring organization of website, "Name of article," URL (date accessed).

[4] Mallory Daughtery, "Baa Baa Black and White Sheep Treats," http://www.southernliving.com/home-garden/holidays-occasions/spring-table-settings-centerpieces-00400000041389/page8.html (accessed Sept. 12, 2013).

In Works Cited, use the following style:

Author/editor/sponsoring organization of website. "Name of article." URL (date accessed).

Daughtery, Mallory. "Baa Baa Black and White Sheep Treats." http://www.southernliving.com/home-garden/holidays-occasions/spring-table-settings-centerpieces-00400000041389/page8.html (accessed Sept. 12, 2013).

3. Ebooks with flowing text (no traditional page numbers)

In a footnote or endnote, use the following style:

[5] Author name, *Name of book* (Publisher, date), Name of ebook format: Chapter number, any other information given by ebook platform.

[6] Paul de Kruif, *Microbe Hunters* (Harvest, 1996), Kindle: Ch. 7, Loc. 2134.

In Works Cited, use the following style:

Author last name, author first name. *Title of book.* City of publication: Publisher, date. Name of ebook format.

de Kruif, Paul. *Microbe Hunters.* Fort Washington, PA: Harvest, 1996. Kindle.

In-text citations may be used in scientific or technical writing.

The chemical reactions that take place within Chocolate Chip Pudding Cookies make them "by far the softest chocolate chip cookies" (Paul 2010, 18) that can be found.[1]

About Turabian

The style described in this lesson is the most common one for student papers. It is known as "Turabian," after Kate Turabian, the head secretary for the graduate department at the University of Chicago from 1930 until 1958.

Kate Turabian had to approve the format of every doctoral dissertation and master's thesis submitted to the University of Chicago. These papers were supposed to follow the format of the *University of Chicago Manual of Style*, but the *Manual of Style* is huge and complicated and many students couldn't figure out exactly how to use it. So Kate Turabian wrote a simplified version of the *Manual of Style*, intended just for the use of students writing papers. It was called *A Manual for Writers of Research Papers, Theses, and Dissertations*, and her book has sold over eight million copies.

Alternative Styles for Citation

A. **Turabian** (most common for students)

FOOTNOTE/ENDNOTE

[1] Susan Cooper, *Silver on the Tree* (Atheneum, 1977), p. 52.

IN-TEXT CITATION

(Cooper 1977, 52)

WORKS CITED

Cooper, Susan. *Silver on the Tree*. New York: Atheneum, 1977.

B. **Chicago Manual of Style**

FOOTNOTE/ENDNOTE

[1] Susan Cooper, *Silver on the Tree* (New York: Atheneum 1977), p. 52.

IN-TEXT CITATION

(Cooper 1977, 52)

WORKS CITED

Cooper, Susan. 1977. *Silver on the Tree*. New York: Atheneum, 1977.

C. **APA** (American Psychological Association, the standard for science writing)

FOOTNOTE/ENDNOTE

APA does not recommend the use of footnotes or endnotes.

IN-TEXT CITATION

(Cooper, 1977, p. 52)

WORKS CITED

Cooper, S. (1977). *Silver on the tree.* New York: Atheneum.

D. **MLA** (Modern Language Association, more often used in the arts and humanities)

FOOTNOTE/ENDNOTE

MLA does not recommend the use of footnotes or endnotes for citations. They should only be used to direct the reader to additional books or resources that should be consulted.

IN-TEXT CITATION

(Cooper 52)

WORKS CITED

Cooper, Susan. *Silver on the Tree.* New York, NY, United States: Atheneum, 1977. Print.

—LESSON 127—

Practicing Direct Quotations and Correct Documentation

Your assignment: Write a short essay called "Four Extraordinary Animals." It should be at least 250 words, although it will probably need to be longer.

You must quote directly from all four of the sources listed below, footnote each direct quote, and put all four on your Works Cited page.

Your essay must include the following:

a) A brief quote that comes before its attribution tag.
b) A brief quote that comes after its attribution tag.
c) A brief quote divided by its attribution tag.
d) A block quote.
e) A quote that is incorporated into a complete sentence and serves a grammatical function within that sentence.
f) A quote that has been altered with either brackets or ellipses.
g) A second quote from the same source.

One quote can fulfill more than one of these requirements.

If you need help, ask your instructor.

Author: C. William Beebe
Title of Book: The Pangolin or Scaly Anteater
City of Publication: New York
Publisher: New York Zoological Society
Date: 1914

Page 41

Hidden deep below the surface of the ground beneath the dry plains of central and southern Africa and the humid jungles of India, Burma and the great East Indian Islands, are thousands of great reptile-like creatures, some a full six feet in length, covered from nose to tail-tip with a complete armature of scales; lizards in appearance; mammals in truth; orphans in classification. The Malays call them Tanjiling, which English tongues have twisted to Pangolin.

Under his armor of scales, the Pangolin, or Scaly Anteater, conceals a bodily structure as confusing to the scientist as is his general appearance to the layman. In common with other toothless or nearly toothless devourers of ants, the Pangolin has usually been classed with armadillos and hairy anteaters. But his structure is so peculiarly Pangolin, his resemblances to other living creatures so slight, and the absence of fossil relatives so complete, that he has finally been assigned to an order of his own, Pholidota.

Throughout the days of violent sunshine or of tropical downpours, not one of the hosts of Pangolins ever shows himself; but in the dusk of evening the round, shingled ball stirs in its underground chamber, unrolls, stretches, and comes forth timidly, hesitating long at the entrance of the burrow before daring to shuffle forth on its quest for food.

In the embryo Pangolin, the scales are little more than a mass of felted hairs, which harden after birth. This armor is for defense alone, his muscles impel no offensive blows, his powerful claws are sheathed. With such perfect defense, flight is useless, so his fastest gait is a man's slow walk. And his normal position on the march is very unlike that conceived and executed by the average museum taxidermist. His tail drags, his head is held low and his back is steeply arched,

Page 42

reminding one of the old Stegosaurus of Jurassic days. Indeed flight is as impossible as it would be for an average man to attempt to run with armor of fifty pounds weight.

The Pangolin is made for ants, and ants alone: without them, he would starve at once. The mouth is tiny, as only ants pass in; the tongue is very long, serpent-like in its mobility and covered with glutinous saliva. Twenty very strong claws, backed by muscles of immense power, allow them to tear through the anthills, hard almost as concrete. I have counted five hundred fire ants in the gizzard of a Pangolin, their bites and stings powerless against the sticky, merciless tongue. Lacking teeth, the creature swallows tiny pebbles which, as in a chicken, aid in crushing the hard bodies of the ants.

Author: L. Hussakof
Title of Article: The Newly Discovered Goblin Shark of Japan
Magazine: Scientific American
Date: February 26, 1910
Volume and Issue Number: Vol. CII, No. 9
Page range of article: 186–187

Page 186

Japanese fishermen occasionally take on their lines a shark whose grotesqueness has won him among natives the name of "goblin shark." One of these "goblins" came into the hands of President David Starr Jordan of Leland Stanford University a dozen years ago and was at once recognized as an interesting archaic type whose close relatives had long since become extinct. President Jordan described it under the name of *Mitsukurina owstoni*—the name being given to honor at the same time the late Prof. Kakichi Mitsukuri, who for a quarter of a century was the leading light of Japanese zoology, and Mr. Alan Owston, a natural history dealer of Yokohama, who was instrumental in securing the specimen.

This name, by the way, does not stand at the present day, but must be replaced by *Scapanorhynchus*—a name which had previously been applied to the teeth of the extinct species of this type of shark found in the rocks of the Chalk period, in different parts of the world. In accordance with scientific usage, therefore, the Japanese shark described by President Jordan must now be known as *Scapanorhynchus owstoni.*

It is now to be recorded that a second species of goblin shark has turned up in a most unexpected way. It happened thus: All of the sharks caught in Japan in the past years and sent to the various museums—about twenty in all—were looked upon as belonging to the same species, *S. owstoni*. No one had ever thought of comparing several specimens; in fact, these sharks are so rare in museums that comparison is generally quite out of the question. It was therefore a pleasure for the writer to have had the opportunity of comparing several specimens in the collections at Columbia University, and the American Museum of Natural History, and to find among them a new species of the goblin shark. This has recently been described in the Bulletin of the American Museum of Natural History as *Scapanorhynchus jordani*—the specific name being given in honor of President Jordan, our greatest authority on the fish of Japan.

Now to come to the fish himself: The new shark is certainly grotesque, well deserving his sobriquet "goblin." The largest specimen in this country is one in the National Museum at Washington, measuring over eleven feet; and the species probably attains a length of fifteen. Fortunately it is not given to frequenting the bathing beach, but keeps to deeper waters—usually about fifty fathoms. As is generally the case with fish from deeper water, this shark is soft and pliable. Even after hardening in a preservative for several months, it can be rolled into a ball. The most remarkable feature is the curiously elongated "nose." It is this, together with its protruding jaw and small beady eyes, that gives the shark that ugly appearance. The teeth are sharp and slender, each like the pointed end of an awl. They constitute a most effective weapon, which must be fingered with discretion even on the laboratory table.

Page 187

As to the differences between the new species and the one already known, the new form is distinguished by a much less protruding jaw, by a very much smaller spiracle (the minute accessory gill-pore seen at some distance back of the eye), and by the fact that the eye is situated opposite the middle of the jaw instead of back of it. These features are quite sufficient, in the opinion of experts, for separating our goblin as a distinct "kind."

Author/Editor/Sponsoring Organization: Green Global Travel
Name of Web Article: 60 Weird Animals around the World
URL: https://greenglobaltravel.com/weird-animals-around-the-world/#WEIRD%20MAMMALS
Date of Access: Use the date on which you are writing your essay

Chinese Water Deer: More similar to a Musk Deer than a true Deer, Water Deer are proficient swimmers who live along the rivers and islands of China and Korea. But the Chinese subspecies is particularly unusual, with no antlers and prominent tusks (which are actually elongated canine teeth) that led to its English nickname, the Vampire Deer. Able to swim for several miles, the Chinese Water Deer can also pull their canine tusks back by using their facial muscles.

Author: George Brown Goode
Title of Book: *The Fisheries and Fishery Industries of the United States*
City of Publication: Washington, D. C.
Publisher: Government Printing Office
Date: 1884

Page 19

The Narwhal, *Monodon monoceros Linn.,* whose long spiral tusk has always been an object of curiosity, and gave rise to the stories of the imaginary creature known as the unicorn, is now found in only one part of the United States—along the northern shores of Alaska. It is still abundant in the Arctic Ocean. It has long since ceased to appear on the coasts of Great Britain, the last having been seen off Lincolnshire in 1800. There is a record of one having been seen in the Elbe at Hamburg in 1736.

The Narwhal is ten to fourteen feet long, somewhat resembling the white whale in form, is black, and in old age mottled or nearly white. The tusk, a modified tooth, grows out of the left side of the upper jaw, to the length of eight or ten feet. All its teeth, except its tusks, are early lost, and it is said to feed on fish and soft sea-animals.

WEEK 35

Introduction to Sentence Style

The definitions in this lesson use the categories laid out by Thomas Kane in *The New Oxford Guide to Writing.*

—LESSON 128—

Sentence Style: Equal and Subordinating
Sentences with Equal Elements: Segregating, Freight-Train, and Balanced

But, in a larger sense, we cannot dedicate—we cannot consecrate—we cannot hallow this ground.
—Abraham Lincoln, "The Gettysburg Address"

We shall defend our island, whatever the cost may be; we shall fight on the beaches, we shall fight on the landing grounds, we shall fight in the fields and in the streets, we shall fight in the hills; we shall never surrender.
—Winston Churchill, "We Shall Fight on the Beaches"

An equal sentence is made up of a series of independent grammatical elements.

Years and years ago, when I was a boy, when there were wolves in Wales, and birds the color of red-flannel petticoats whisked past the harp-shaped hills, when we sang and wallowed all night and day in caves that smelt like Sunday afternoons in damp front farmhouse parlors, and we chased, with the jawbones of deacons, the English and the bears, before the motor car, before the wheel, before the duchess-faced horse, when we rode the daft and happy hills bareback, it snowed and it snowed.
— Dylan Thomas, *A Child's Christmas in Wales*

Even when pressed by the demands of inner truth, men do not easily assume the task of opposing their government's policy, especially in time of war.
—Martin Luther King, "Beyond Vietnam—A Time to Break Silence"

A subordinating sentence is made up of both independent and dependent elements.

Equal sentences can be segregating, freight train, or balanced.

Segregating sentences express a single idea each, and occur in a series.

The barn was still dark. The sheep lay motionless. Even the goose was quiet.
—E. B. White, *Charlotte's Web*

He hadn't found any doweling that day. He hadn't checked the generator. He hadn't cleaned up the pieces of mirror. He hadn't eaten supper; he'd lost his appetite. That wasn't hard. He lost it most of the time.
—Richard Matheson, *I Am Legend*

They disappear among the poplars. The meadow is empty. The river, the meadow, the cliff and cloud. The princess calls, but there is no one, now, to hear her.
—John Fowles, *The Ebony Tower*

Freight-train sentences link independent clauses together to express a combined idea.

He was energetic and devout; he was polite and handsome; his fame grew in the diocese.
—Lytton Strachey, *Eminent Victorians*

There was much game hanging outside the shops, and the snow powdered in the fur of the foxes and the wind blew their tails.
—Ernest Hemingway, "In Another Country"

I'm very young, I have no real friend here in the barn, it's going to rain all morning and all afternoon, and Fern won't come in such bad weather.
—E. B. White, *Charlotte's Web*

Balanced sentences are made up of two equal parts, separated by a pause.

Darkness is cheap, and Scrooge liked it.
—Charles Dickens, *A Christmas Carol*

It is a far, far better thing that I do, than I have ever done; it is a far, far better rest that I go to than I have ever known.
—Charles Dickens, *A Tale of Two Cities*

But there is something that I must say to my people, who stand on the warm threshold which leads into the palace of justice: In the process of gaining our rightful place, we must not be guilty of wrongful deeds.
—Martin Luther King, "I Have a Dream"

Exercise 128A: Identifying Sentence Types

In the blank that follows each sentence or set of sentences, write *S* for segregating, *FT* for freight-train, or *B* for balanced.

There was no ship in sight, and the sea-gulls were motionless upon its even greyness. The sky was dark with lowering clouds, but there was no wind.
—W. Somerset Maugham, *The Explorer* ________

He must wish her good night; he was going; he should get home as fast as he could.
—Jane Austen, *Persuasion* ________

To me, she was in the place of a parent. Do not mistake me, however. I am not saying that she did not err in her advice.

—Jane Austen, *Persuasion* _________

Is this a costume? Does this say anything? It barely covers one man's nakedness!

—Robert Bolt, *A Man for All Seasons* _________

Let him die without an heir and we'll have them back again.

—Robert Bolt, *A Man for All Seasons* _________

Let them all be gathered together, let them stand up; yet they shall fear, and they shall be ashamed together.

—Isaiah 44:11 (KJV) _________

It is cold, and we have no blankets; the little children are freezing to death.

—Chief Joseph, "Surrender Speech" _________

I am tired of fighting. Our Chiefs are killed; Looking Glass is dead. Shute is dead. The old men are all dead.

—Chief Joseph, "Surrender Speech" _________

I know you're scared. That's okay. I think there may be things in there and we have to take a look. There's no place else to go. This is it. I want you to help me.

—Cormac McCarthy, *The Road* _________

To be given dominion over another is a hard thing; to wrest dominion over another is a wrong thing; to give dominion of yourself to another is a wicked thing.

—Toni Morrison, *A Mercy* _________

Agitation, in the interval, certainly had held me and driven me, for I must, in circling about the place, have walked three miles; but I was to be, later on, so much more overwhelmed that this mere dawn of alarm was a comparatively human chill.

—Henry James, *The Turn of the Screw* _________

The bay-sheltered islands and the great sea beyond stretched away to the far horizon southward and eastward; the little procession in the foreground looked futile and helpless on the edge of the rocky shore.

—Sarah Orne Jewett, *The Country of the Pointed Firs* _________

Time was growing short. His time was growing short. It had to be enough. He had to make it enough.

—Robert Jordan, *The Dragon Reborn* _________

And if you continue to give orders, they will continue to obey, for you will be the one who saved them, and who better to lead?

—Robert Jordan, *The Dragon Reborn* _________

—LESSON 129—

Subordinating Sentences:
Loose, Periodic, Cumulative, Convoluted, and Centered

In a loose sentence, subordinate constructions follow the main clause.

People always think that happiness is a far away thing, something complicated and hard to get.
—Betty Smith, *A Tree Grows in Brooklyn*

He was pacing the room swiftly, eagerly, with his head sunk upon his chest and his hands clasped behind him.
—A. Conan Doyle, "A Scandal in Bohemia"

The spotlight has often been focused on me because I was a late bloomer who turned out to be a prodigy, and perhaps, more than that, because I am a black woman excelling in a white world.
—Misty Copeland, *Life in Motion: An Unlikely Ballerina*

In a periodic sentence, subordinate constructions precede the main clause.

To be, or not to be: that is the question.
—William Shakespeare, *Hamlet*

When Galileo and Newton looked at nature, they saw simplicity.
—Edward Dolnick, *The Clockwork Universe: Isaac Newton, the Royal Society, and the Birth of the Modern World*

Some years ago—never mind how long precisely—having little or no money in my purse, and nothing particular to interest me on shore, I thought I would sail about a little and see the watery part of the world.
—Herman Melville, *Moby Dick*

A cumulative sentence puts multiple subordinate constructions before or after the main clause.

Beyond the obvious facts that he has at some time done manual labour, that he takes snuff, that he is a Freemason, that he has been in China, and that he has done a considerable amount of writing lately, I can deduce nothing else.
—A. Conan Doyle, "The Red-Headed League"

Lastly, she pictured to herself how this same little sister of hers would, in the after-time, be herself a grown woman; and how she would keep, through all her riper years, the simple and loving heart of her childhood; and how she would gather about her other little children, and make their eyes bright and eager with many a strange tale, perhaps even with the dream of Wonderland of long ago; and how she would feel with all their simple sorrows, and find a pleasure in all their simple joys, remembering her own child-life, and the happy summer days.

—Lewis Carroll, *Alice's Adventures in Wonderland*

In a convoluted sentence, subordinate constructions divide the main clause.

The dorm, with two narrow beds to a room, didn't just house dancers studying with ABT.

—Misty Copeland, *Life in Motion: An Unlikely Ballerina*

We, the people of the United States, in order to form a more perfect union, establish justice, insure domestic tranquility, provide for the common defense, promote the general welfare, and secure the blessings of liberty to ourselves and our posterity, do ordain and establish this Constitution for the United States of America.

—The Constitution of the United States

They knew, without my needing to spell it out, every setback or curve in the road: that I had fought for ten years to be recognized, to show that I had the talent and ability to dance in classical ballets.

—Misty Copeland, *Life in Motion: An Unlikely Ballerina*

In a centered sentence, subordinate constructions come on both sides of the main clause.

With an apology for my intrusion, I was about to withdraw when Holmes pulled me abruptly into the room and closed the door behind me.

—A. Conan Doyle, "The Red-Headed League"

And having got rid of this young man who did not know how to behave, she resumed her duties as hostess and continued to listen and watch, ready to help at any point where the conversation might happen to flag.

—Leo Tolstoy, *War and Peace*

Exercise 129A: Identifying Subordinating Sentences

In each sentence, underline the subject(s) of the main clause once and the predicate twice.

Label each sentence in the blank that follows it as *L* for loose, *P* for periodic, *CUMUL* for cumulative, *CONV* for convoluted, or *CENT* for centered.

For the purposes of this exercise, any sentence with four or more phrases and dependent clauses before or after the main clause should be considered cumulative. If two or three phrases or dependent clauses come before or after the main clause, the sentence should be classified as loose or periodic.

A single modifying phrase before or after the main clause does not turn it into a periodic or loose sentence.

If phrases or clauses come before and after the main clause, the sentence is centered, no matter how many phrases or clauses there are.

If any phrases or clauses come between the subject, predicate, or any essential parts of the main clause (objects, predicate nominatives, or predicate adjectives), the sentence is convoluted.

A phrase serving as an object or predicate nominative should be considered a single part of speech, not a subordinate phrase.

In the documentary, a man afflicted with cerebral palsy, his movements jerky and his speech low and drawled, detailed his life and his tribulations. _________

I still see the image of him clearly, sitting in a small courtyard with a knife in his hand, whittling ever so slowly, his forearms moving like two gears in mesh—a short burst of motion, then a pause, his eyes wide open behind wide-rimmed glasses, his mouth constantly open, not closing even as he tried to speak. _________

—Henry Jay Przybylo, MD, *Counting Backwards: A Doctor's Notes on Anesthesia*

King tides are driven by a particular alignment of the sun and moon and Earth that maximizes the gravitational tug on the oceans, as well as changes in the Gulf Stream current and the way the heat of a long summer causes the ocean to expand. _________

When the king tides arrived in 2014 it was clear that the mayor's political gamble had paid off. _________

—Jeff Goodell, *The Water Will Come: Rising Seas, Sinking Cities, and the Remaking of the Civilized World*

While the advantages of going to an elite college aren't questioned as often as they should be, the disadvantages are even less frequently broached, perhaps because a great many people can't imagine that there'd be any. ________

And he contended that the homogeneous group of overachievers who make it to Princeton or Yale have, to that point, known only one triumph after another, largely because they've been given extensive preparation to master precisely those tasks that the elite educational track values. ________

—Frank Bruni, *Where You Go Is Not Who You'll Be: An Antidote to the College Admissions Mania*

And if I have the gift of prophecy, and know all mysteries and all knowledge; and if I have all faith, so as to remove mountains, but have not love, I am nothing. ________

—1 Corinthians 13:2, NASB

The rest of us, bathed and changed into a required green velvet dress for evenings, sat in descending order of age and class until the youngest and most recently arrived sat at the distant foot of the table. ________

Telling myself that I would get her through one set of changes at a time, I temporized about my departure. ________

These I ate at favorite spots: in the middle of a deserted pear orchard alive with bees, or on the roadside at the brow of a hill where the patterns of agriculture—green, brown, gold, and red—could be looked at with half-closed eyes to produce an instant impressionist painting. ________

—Jill Ker Conway, *The Road from Coorain*

But I must confess, we're drawn here by other things as well: by the feeling of history in this city, more than 500 years older than our own nation; by the beauty of the Grunewald and the Tiergarten; most of all, by your courage and determination. ________

Standing before the Brandenburg Gate, every man is a German, separated from his fellow men. ________

—Ronald Reagan, "Tear Down This Wall"

Out of the bosom of the Air,
    Out of the cloud-folds of her garments shaken,
Over the woodlands brown and bare,
    Over the harvest-fields forsaken,
        Silent, and soft, and slow
        Descends the snow. __________

This is the secret of despair,
    Long in its cloudy bosom hoarded,
        Now whispered and revealed
        To wood and field. __________

—Henry Wadsworth Longfellow, "Snow-flakes"

Five or six wild duck flew overhead in a swiftly moving V, intent on some far-off destination. __________

Note to Student: *duck* is an unusual, but acceptable, plural version of *duck*.

As a bull, with a slight but irresistible movement, tosses its head from the grasp of a man who is leaning over the stall and idly holding its horn, so the sun entered the world in smooth, gigantic power. __________

Fiver stayed with him, keeping the wounds clean and watching his recovery. __________

If ever great danger arose, he would come back to fight for those who honored his name. __________

—Richard Adams, *Watership Down*

The Good Friday Agreement, overwhelmingly endorsed by the people on both sides of the Border, holds out the prospect of a peaceful long-term future for Northern Ireland, and the whole island of Ireland. __________

Those urges to belong, divergent as they are, can live together more easily if we, Britain and the Irish Republic, can live closer together too. __________

—Tony Blair, "Address to the Irish Parliament"

Unprovided with original learning, unformed in the habits of thinking, unskilled in the arts of composition, I resolved to write a book. _________

The various modes of worship, which prevailed in the Roman world, were all considered by the people as equally true, by the philosopher as equally false, and by the magistrate as equally useful. _________

It has always been my practice to cast a long paragraph in a single mould, to try it by my ear, to deposit it in my memory, but to suspend the action of the pen till I had given the last polish to my work. _________

—Edward Gibbon, *The History of the Decline and Fall of the Roman Empire*

She was listening to the third woman, a stout, pleasant-faced, elderly woman who was talking in a slow clear monotone which showed no signs of pausing for breath or coming to a stop. _________

Gathering up her despised money, the American lady followed suit, followed by the lady like a sheep. _________

This crime, we have reason to believe, took place at a quarter past one last night. _________

—Agatha Christie, *Murder on the Orient Express*

And then there were apple pies, and peach pies, and pumpkin pies; besides slices of ham and smoked beef; and moreover delectable dishes of preserved plums, and peaches, and pears, and quinces; not to mention broiled shad and roasted chickens; together with bowls of milk and cream, all mingled higgledy-piggledy, pretty much as I have enumerated them, with the motherly teapot sending up its clouds of vapor from the midst—Heaven bless the mark! _________

All the stories of ghosts and goblins that he had heard in the afternoon now came crowding upon his recollection. _________

About two hundred yards from the tree, a small brook crossed the road, and ran into a marshy and thickly-wooded glen, known by the name of Wiley's Swamp. _________

All these tales, told in that drowsy undertone with which men talk in the dark, the countenances of the listeners only now and then receiving a casual gleam from the glare of a pipe, sank deep in the mind of Ichabod. __________

—Washington Irving, "The Legend of Sleepy Hollow"

Like the waters of the river, like the motorists on the highway, and like the yellow trains streaking down the Santa Fe tracks, drama, in the shape of exceptional happenings, had never stopped there. __________

—Truman Capote, *In Cold Blood*

Is it not astonishing that, while we are plowing, planting, and reaping, using all kinds of mechanical tools, erecting houses, constructing bridges, building ships, working in metals of brass, iron, copper, silver, and gold; that while we are reading, writing, and ciphering, acting as clerks, merchants, and secretaries, having among us lawyers, doctors, ministers, poets, authors, editors, orators, and teachers; that we are engaged in all the enterprises common to other men—digging gold in California, capturing the whale in the Pacific, feeding sheep and cattle on the hillside, living, moving, acting, thinking, planning, living in families as husbands, wives, and children, and above all, confessing and worshipping the Christian God, and looking hopefully for life and immortality beyond the grave—we are called upon to prove that we are men? __________

—Frederick Douglass, "The Hypocrisy of American Slavery"

—LESSON 130—

Practicing Sentence Style

Choose one of the following assignments:

Exercise 130A: Rewriting

The following list of events, from the traditional Japanese fable "The Sagacious Monkey and the Boar," needs to be rewritten as a story.

This story must have at least one of each of the following types of sentences:

Segregating (at least three sentences in a row)
Freight-Train
Balanced

Loose
Periodic
Cumulative (with four or more subordinate phrases/clauses; main clause can come either first or last)
Convoluted
Centered

You may add, change, and subtract, as long as the finished story is at least 400 words long and makes good sense.

a traveling monkey-man had a monkey
he took it around and showed off its tricks
he came home angry
he told his wife to send for the butcher
the monkey kept forgetting his tricks
the monkey-man wanted to sell the monkey for meat
the wife pleaded for the monkey
the man was determined to sell him to the butcher
the monkey heard the conversation
the monkey knew there was a wise boar in the forest
he went to see the boar
he told the boar his problem
the boar asked if the monkey-man and his wife had a baby
the monkey said yes
the boar said that he had seen the baby playing by the door in the mornings
the monkey agreed
the boar offered to grab the baby and run away
he told the monkey to follow him
the monkey would rescue the baby
then the man and his wife would keep the monkey
the monkey went home
he did not sleep much
the next morning the wife put the baby on the floor
she started to do her morning chores
the baby gave a cry
she saw the boar carrying off the baby
she woke her husband up
they saw the monkey
the monkey was running after the boar

the monkey brought the baby back
the wife praised the monkey
they sent the butcher away
the monkey was petted
the monkey lived out his days in peace

Exercise 130B: Original Composition

Write an original composition of at least 400 words, with at least one of each of the following types of sentences:

Segregating (at least three sentences in a row)
Freight-Train
Balanced
Loose
Periodic
Cumulative (with four or more subordinate phrases/clauses; main clause can come either first or last)
Convoluted
Centered

This composition may be one of the following:

a) A plot summary of one of your favorite books or movies.

b) A narrative of some event, happening, trip, or great memory from your past.

c) A scene from a story that you create yourself.

d) Any other topic you choose.

WEEK 36

—REVIEW 11—

Final Review

Review 11A: Explaining Sentences

Tell your instructor every possible piece of grammatical information about the following sentences. Follow these steps (notice that these are slightly different than the instructions in your previous "explaining" exercise):

1) Identify the sentence type and write it in the left-hand margin.
2) Underline each subordinate clause. Describe the identity and function of each clause and give any other useful information (introductory word, relationship to the rest of the sentence, etc.)
3) Label each preposition as *P* and each object of the preposition as *OP*. Describe the identity and function of each prepositional phrase.
4) Parse, out loud, all verbs acting as predicates.
5) Describe the identity and function of each individual remaining word. Don't worry about the articles and coordinating conjunctions, though.
6) Provide any other useful information that you might be able to think of.

Among the most common residents of Alaska's forests (and northern cousins of the gray squirrels that inhabit most of the United States), red squirrels remain active year-round.

I had simply assumed the birds to be either tree swallows or violet-green swallows, the kinds most commonly seen in and around Anchorage.

—Bill Sherwonit, *Animal Stories: Encounters with Alaska's Wildlife*

There was just one very small improvement—after swearing that he wouldn't use her to send letters to any of his friends, Harry had been allowed to let his owl, Hedwig, out at night.

—J. K. Rowling, *Harry Potter and the Prisoner of Azkaban*

From a long habit of listening admiringly to everything that was said in her presence, and looking at the speakers as if she were mentally engaged in taking off impressions of their images upon her soul, never to part with the same but with life, her head had quite settled on one side.

—Charles Dickens, *Dombey and Son*

Throughout his papacy, the whole family of Rodrigo Borgia, who ascended the papal throne as Alexander VI, was surrounded by a buzz of scandal.

But if the whole is unsatisfactory, the *David*, taken part by part, is a work of overwhelming power and magnificence, and it is Michelangelo's first great assertion of the quality that is so often in our minds when we think of him — the heroic.

—J. H. Plumb, *The Italian Renaissance*

Review 11B: Correcting Errors

Rewrite the following sets of sentences on your own paper (or with a word-processing program), inserting all necessary punctuation and capitalization.

Include the citations in your corrections!

i feel like a salt crystal he often said in a mountain stream being washed away we dont belong here were earth people this is mars it was meant for martians for heavens sake cora lets buy tickets for home

but the american built town of cottages peach trees and theatres was silent

ray bradbury, dark they were, and golden eyed [short story]

the account of michelangelos career begins with his auspicious birth and early training and it chronicles his early works including the bacchus 1496-7 and the st peters pietà 1497-9 in rome before coming to the colossal and extraordinary statue of the david 1501-4 in florence and his unexecuted scheme for the enormous painting battle of cascina 1504-5

giorgio vasari, the life of michelangelo

michelangelo chafed at any restrictions placed on his freedom if your holiness wishes me to accomplish anything he wrote to pope clement viii i beg you not to have authorities set over me in my own trade but to have faith in me and give me a free hand

in 1475 about 50000 people lived within the tuscan capitals high walls at least an equal number lived in the contado the surrounding countryside where for thousands of years a large number of peasants and a smaller number of gentleman farmers had cultivated wine grain and olives in the rocky hillsides

michelangelo will employ the same complex twisting pose suggestive of struggle and internal contradictions in mature works like the famous night from the medici tombs

miles j unger, michelangelo a life in six masterpieces

worms can not only survive in faux martian soil they can start a new generation thats the conclusion from biologist wieger wamelink who recently discovered two baby worms in his simulated mars soil experiment

since 2013 scientists from wageningen university & research have been growing crops in mars and moon soil simulants designed by nasa

lauren sigfusson, good news worms make babies in martian soil. in discover science for the curious december 4 2017

Review 11C: Fill in the Blank

Each of the following sentences is missing one of the elements listed. Provide the correct required form of a word that seems appropriate to you. When you are finished, compare your sentences with the originals.

In ________ (singular abstract noun), the German infantry ________ (past participle) in the crossing ______ absolutely __________ (simple past, passive, indicative action verb), having had ____________ (adjective of negation) sleep to speak of ______ (preposition) 10 May and ______________ (perfect present passive participle, action verb) in heavy fighting the ______________ (adjective) day.

_______ (adverb) after, he spoke to General Georges, who __________ (linking verb, simple past) to have ________ (adverb) recovered from the previous __________ (possessive adjective) breakdown. Georges admitted __________ (subordinating word) there had been a ________ (adverb) breach of more than ten miles, but assured Churchill ______________________ (noun clause acting as object of *assured*). In this, _________ (short parenthetical expression), Georges was ________ (adverb) misinformed. _______ (short parenthetical expression), the French Ninth Army _________ (perfect past, active, indicative action verb) apart at the seams and a gap of ________ (adverb) fifty miles ____________________ (perfect past, passive, indicative action verb) in the line up to sixty miles deep.

—James Holland, *The Battle of Britain: Five Months That Changed History: May-October, 1940*

In the days ________ the Cheyennes ________ in the thousands, they had more ________
relative adverb — past participle — plural concrete noun

than any of the Plains tribes. They ________ the Beautiful People, but fate ________
simple past, passive, indicative action verb — perfect past, active, indicative action verb

against them both in the south and in the north. ________ twenty years of ________
preposition — abstract noun

they were ________ to ________ than the buffalo.
comparative adjective — abstract noun

The treaty commissioners ________ Captain Jack and the ________ head men that
simple past, active, indicative action verb — adjective

if they ________ ________ to a reservation in Oregon ________ family ________
simple present, active, modal action verb — adverbial noun — adjective — simple present, active, modal action verb

________ own land, teams of horses, ________, ________ implements,
possessive adjective (pronoun) — plural concrete noun — present participle

tools, clothing, and food—all ________ ________ the government.
past participle — preposition

—Dee Brown, *Bury My Heart at Wounded Knee: An Indian History of the American West*

Sometimes it is not ________ for people ________ clearly what ________. It
predicate adjective — active infinitive — simple past, passive, indicative action verb

is storytelling ________ people tend ________ ________.
relative pronoun — active infinitive — adverb

Fox ________ his home village of Fenny Drayton in Leicestershire four ________
perfect past, active, indicative action verb — adverbial noun, plural

earlier and ________ across England for ________ who ________ him
progressive perfect past, active, indicative action verb — indefinite pronoun — simple present, active, modal action verb

with his religious quest. He ________ a year with a ________ uncle in London
perfect past, active, indicative action verb — proper adjective

and ________ the army camps of the English Civil War ________
perfect past, active, indicative action verb — relative adverb

the ________ ________ religious ideas ________.
adverb — adjective — progressive past, active, indicative action verb

—Stephen W. Angell and Ben Pink Dandelion, eds., *The Cambridge Companion to Quakerism*

________ four days of ________ out of food, he'll barely be able ________ ________,
preposition — present participle — active infinitive — adverb

let alone control a rover. Plus, ________ ________ faculties ________ rapidly ________.
possessive pronoun — adjective — simple future, active, indicative action verb

He'________ a hard time even ________ ________.
simple present, active, modal action verb, condensed — present participle — adverb

It __________ my call from the __________, but you two __________ in and __________ me.
perfect present, state-of-being, active, modal verb — abstract noun — simple past, active, indicative action verb — simple past, indicative action verb

__________ all that, we agreed we'__________ them __________ there was __________.
present participle — simple present, active, modal action verb, condensed — relative adverb — abstract noun

—Andy Weir, *The Martian*

They __________ an orientation program __________ they came to Mars
perfect past, active, modal action verb — preposition

__________ them __________.
infinitive — noun clause acting as the object of the infinitive

__________ six legs fell upon the __________ highway with the __________ of a __________ rain
possessive pronoun — adjective — plural concrete noun — adjective

which __________ away, and from the back of the __________ a Martian with __________
simple past, active, indicative action verb — singular concrete noun — past participle

gold for eyes __________ down at Tomás as if he __________ into a __________.
simple past, active, indicative action verb — progressive past, active, subjunctive action verb — singular concrete noun

—Ray Bradbury, *The Martian Chronicles*

Review 11D: Diagramming

On your own paper, diagram every word of the following sentences.

According to more than one astronaut memoir, one of the most beautiful sights in space is that of a sun-illumined flurry of flash-frozen waste-water droplets.

The astronaut's job is stressful for all the same reasons yours or mine is—overwork, lack of sleep, anxiety, other people—but two things compound the usual stresses: the deprivations of the environment and one's inability to escape it.

—Mary Roach, *Packing for Mars: The Curious Science of Life in the Void*

Since Liddell first became public property—always walking in the arc light of fame—wherever he went and whatever he did or had once done was brightly illuminated.

The images, the music, the man, and what he achieved in the Olympics in 1924 are familiar to us because cinema made them so.

—Duncan Hamilton, *For the Glory: The Untold and Inspiring Story of Eric Liddell, Hero of Chariots of Fire*

The master and thirty sailors escaped in the boat; but they were dragged in chains to the Porte: the chief was impaled; his companions were beheaded; and the historian Ducas beheld, at Demotica, their bodies exposed to the wild beasts.

—Edward Gibbon, *History of the Decline and Fall of the Roman Empire*

There remained two growing girls; a shy midget of eight; John, tall, awkward, and eighteen; Jim, younger, quicker, and better looking; and two babies of indefinite age.

The function of the university is not simply to teach bread-winning, or to furnish teachers for the public schools or to be a center of polite society; it is, above all, to be the organ of that fine adjustment between real life and the growing knowledge of life, an adjustment which forms the secret of civilization.

—W. E. B. Du Bois, *The Souls of Black Folk*

I thought of my dead godmother, of the night when I read to her, of her frowning so fixedly and sternly in her bed, of the strange place I was going to, of the people I should find there, and what they would be like, and what they would say to me, when a voice in the coach gave me a terrible start.

—Charles Dickens, *Bleak House*